The Moral Vision of Proverbs

A VIRTUE-ORIENTED APPROACH TO WISDOM

Timothy J. Sandoval

Baker Academic
a division of Baker Publishing Group
Grand Rapids, Michigan

© 2024 by Timothy J. Sandoval

Published by Baker Academic
a division of Baker Publishing Group
Grand Rapids, Michigan
BakerAcademic.com

All rights reserved. No part of this publication may be reproduced, stored in a retrieval system, or transmitted in any form or by any means—for example, electronic, photocopy, recording—without the prior written permission of the publisher. The only exception is brief quotations in printed reviews.

Library of Congress Cataloging-in-Publication Data
Names: Sandoval, Timothy J., author.
Title: The moral vision of Proverbs : a virtue-oriented approach to wisdom / Timothy J. Sandoval.
Description: Grand Rapids, Michigan : Baker Academic, a division of Baker Publishing Group, [2024] | Includes bibliographical references and index.
Identifiers: LCCN 2023040039 | ISBN 9781540967206 (paperback) | ISBN 9781540967350 (casebound) | ISBN 9781493444649 (ebook) | ISBN 9781493444656 (pdf)
Subjects: LCSH: Bible. Proverbs—Criticism, interpretation, etc. | Virtue. | Ethics.
Classification: LCC BS1465.52 .S25 2024 | DDC 223/.706—dc23/eng/20231122
LC record available at https://lccn.loc.gov/2023040039

Unless otherwise indicated, Scripture quotations are from the New Revised Standard Version of the Bible, copyright © 1989 National Council of the Churches of Christ in the United States of America. Used by permission. All rights reserved.

Scripture quotations labeled NJPS are from the New Jewish Publication Society Version © 1985 by The Jewish Publication Society. All rights reserved.

24 25 26 27 28 29 30   7 6 5 4 3 2 1

"Sandoval presents Proverbs as a profoundly theological statement about the cultivation of moral character through the practice of the complex moral and intellectual activity that the sages call 'wisdom.' Eschewing conventional moralistic and utilitarian treatments, he brings to his reading a philosophical, cultural, and literary sophistication that encourages critical and self-critical engagement. This study will be essential for serious students of biblical wisdom traditions, in the academy and also in the church."

—**Ellen F. Davis**, Duke Divinity School

"The book of Proverbs finally receives its full ethical due from the able hands of Sandoval, who offers the most robust and nuanced moral treatment to date of this often-overlooked book. Sandoval's study is both sophisticated and engaging, philosophical and dialogical, offering its share of exegetical surprises, all to highlight Proverbs' overarching goal to impart the 'craft of living well.'"

—**William P. Brown**, Columbia Theological Seminary

"In a rich and incisive contribution to a burgeoning debate on Proverbs as a book of virtue ethics, Sandoval claims, by engaging with Aristotle and other classical writers on virtue ethics, that it is indeed an ancient, virtue-oriented moral discourse. Picking up on Proverbs' concern with character ethics, Sandoval discovers more profound aspects of its moral rhetoric and wider moral vision, including natural law, social virtues, and practical wisdom that together embody a coherent model for promoting human flourishing."

—**Katharine J. Dell**, University of Cambridge

"In this substantial and engaging study, Sandoval sheds light on why biblical scholarship has largely relegated Proverbs to second-tier status as a source of theological and ethical insight. Delivering his scholarly erudition in clear prose, Sandoval redresses this balance and reveals Proverbs' merits as such an intellectual resource by examining its moral perspective in light of ancient virtue ethics. As I have with Sandoval's other books on Proverbs, I have learned much from this book and recommend it to others."

—**Gilberto A. Ruiz**, Saint Anselm College

"In *The Moral Vision of Proverbs*, Sandoval helps dispel the all-too-common biases that Proverbs lacks moral complexity, displays simplistic act-consequence behavioral schemas, and promotes restrictive natural theologies. With precision, care, and wisdom, Sandoval demonstrates how Proverbs' engagement with premodern, virtue-oriented moral discourse yields instruction that is ethically and theologically relevant for the contemporary world. This is a must-have for any serious reader of Proverbs."

—**Patricia Vesely**, Memphis Theological Seminary

For Tony

Contents

Preface   ix
Abbreviations   xiii

Introduction   1

PART 1   The Case for Proverbs as Virtue-Oriented Moral Discourse   21

1. The Undervaluing of Proverbs' Moral Worth: The Role of Biblical Studies and Modern Ethics   23

2. The Prologue as Hermeneutical Key: Categories of Virtues and Figurative Language   53

3. The Anthropology of Proverbs: The Nature and Happiness of Human Beings   68

4. Proverbs' Way of Life: The Priority of Moral Agents over Right Acts   84

5. The Training of Desire for a Life of Flourishing in Proverbs   109

6. Desire, Knowledge, and Goodness: Beyond Wise and Just, Foolish and Wicked   147

7. The Centrality of Social Virtues for Flourishing   160

8. Practical Wisdom in Proverbs   175

9. The Efficacy and Limitations of Practical Wisdom in Proverbs   203

PART 2   The Implications of Proverbs as Virtue-Oriented Moral Discourse   217

    10. Proverbs' Virtue Ethics beyond Proverbs? The Shared Moral Discourse of Proverbs and Amos   219

    11. A Virtue-Ethics Approach to Cosmogony in Proverbs (Part 1): Reconsidering the Interpretive History of Natural Law, the Orders of Creation, and Empiricism in Proverbs   246

    12. A Virtue-Ethics Approach to Cosmogony in Proverbs (Part 2): Reading Proverbs 8:22–31 as a Test Case   270

    13. Wisdom as Practice (Part 1): Overview of Biblical Concepts and MacIntyrian Terms   310

    14. Wisdom as Practice (Part 2): How MacIntyrian Practice Informs an Understanding of Proverbs' Virtue Ethics   328

    Conclusion: Worthy Wisdom, Who Can Find?   349
    Works Cited   381
    Author Index   400
    Scripture and Ancient Sources Index   404
    Subject Index   411

Preface

In my classes at Brite Divinity School, when we talk about the wisdom literature I always begin with this question: What is biblical wisdom literature? Or, what are the biblical wisdom books? Inevitably students respond by naming texts such as Proverbs, Job, and Ecclesiastes. Others, often a bit more tentatively, will add the Psalms and Song of Songs to the list and perhaps even the deuterocanonical, or for Protestants "Apocryphal," books of Sirach (Wisdom of Ben Sira) and the Wisdom of Solomon. I then usually note both that the biblical wisdom tradition extends to a host of other texts, including some found among the Dead Sea Scrolls, and that "wisdom" works were quite common throughout the scribal cultures of ancient West Asia and Egypt, from which emerges a work like Instruction of Amenemope, which seems clearly at points to have impacted the composition of Proverbs 22:17—23:11.

I then ask students another question: How do you *know* that these texts are "wisdom" books? After someone boldly or sheepishly states what many others surely are thinking—"Because the textbook says so," which really isn't a bad answer (it shows, at least, they've done the day's reading!)—we slowly are able to uncover a series of criteria or family resemblances for identifying what "counts" as biblical wisdom literature. We also try to account for the arguments of those who call into question the category of "wisdom" itself.[1] But having identified a cluster of features that suggest the traditional wisdom texts stand in an important discursive relationship with one another, I also try to convince students that biblical wisdom literature offers us a kind of

---

1. See, e.g., Kynes, *Obituary for "Wisdom Literature."*

ancient theological ethics—though it is a theological ethic that is often not fully appreciated today.

Persuading students of the moral worth of Proverbs is sometimes a tough sell. The book's rhetoric and moral vision must compete with the compelling narratives and divine precepts of the Pentateuch, the soaring rhetoric of the prophetic books and the Psalter, and the engaging tales of Ruth and Esther. It also must compete with the other wisdom books: Job, which wrestles with the perennial issues of theodicy and the suffering of the just, and Qohelet, which rings uniquely modern in its pessimistic outlook and bold embrace of pleasure.

There have, however, long been scholars who have tried to appreciate Proverbs' theological and ethical orientation and to suggest that the constructive payoff for close study of this book might rival that of other "more central" biblical texts. In an effort to contribute to this endeavor, this study first strives hermeneutically to read Proverbs through the lens of virtue ethics. At the same time, it also suggests that, historically speaking, the text may best be understood as a species of ancient virtue-oriented discourse. Offered by a Christian scholar, this work is concerned both with (re)describing the historical-literary aspects of Proverbs' moral rhetoric and with constructively interpreting the book.

This project's origins trace most broadly to my initial scholarly work, in which I studied how wealth and poverty function in the book of Proverbs.[2] What follows is an extension of that work, or at least part of it. In earlier studies I emphasized how Proverbs' rhetoric of material reward and punishment for right and wrong conduct can and ought to be understood figuratively. It promises not merely or simply real, material goods to the book's hearers and readers who find wisdom; more fundamentally, it promises the incomparably valuable life of virtue itself. As I see now, this was an incomplete description of how Proverbs understands the relation between real material and social goods—for example, honor and wealth—and the attainment of wisdom. The key is recognizing Proverbs more fully as a virtue-oriented moral discourse. Like other such discourses (e.g., in the Aristotelian and Thomistic traditions), it has a clear and legitimate place for the human pursuit of happiness (eudaemonia) that involves, indeed must include, a desire and need for the sorts of real material and social goods that I understood more figuratively in my earlier work. This figurative dimension of wealth and poverty rhetoric in particular *is* at play in Proverbs, but it is only one aspect of what ought to be a fuller description of Proverbs' moral discourse.

2. Sandoval, *Discourse of Wealth and Poverty*.

The more immediate origins of this project, however, lie elsewhere. Having thought I had said all I wanted to say about Proverbs and happily having moved on to more focused study on books like Tobit, I was fortunate enough to be accepted into the "Human Distinctiveness Summer Seminar: A Program to Engage Theologians with the Dynamism of Anthropological and Evolutionary Approaches to the Human" at the University of Notre Dame. Participating in this project, led by Professors Celia Deane-Drummond and Agustín Fuentes, reinvigorated my interest in understanding biblical wisdom literature, especially Proverbs, in terms of premodern virtue-oriented moral discourses—for in striving to understand how humans might attain well-being, such moral discourses pay significant attention to the sorts of beings humans naturally are. To Dr. Deane-Drummond and Dr. Fuentes, as well as to all the contributors and participants in the seminar, I am grateful. Besides Dr. Deane-Drummond and Dr. Fuentes, several members of this group deserve special mention. Dr. Adam M. Willows, Dr. John Berkman, Dr. Joel Hodge, and Dr. Philip A. Rolnick on different occasions generously and patiently helped me grasp better the ins and outs of Aristotle, Thomas, and virtue ethics. Dr. Arthur Walker-Jones has continued to encourage me to think more fully about how a text like Proverbs understands the relation between humans and their wisdom and the lives and wisdom of nonhuman animals with whom we share our world. Others have prodded my thinking through their writings, in conversation on conference panels and in other contexts. These are too many to name and so I mention only William P. Brown, Michael V. Fox, and Bernd U. Schipper. I am continually surprised by how many times I have started out contesting one or another point that these scholars have made about Proverbs, only to find my own views, in the end, lining up very closely to theirs.

A brief but serendipitous meeting with Jim Kinney of Baker Academic at a gathering of the Catholic Biblical Association, which revealed a mutual interest in the work of Alasdair MacIntyre, led me to consider Baker as a publication venue for this book. I am grateful to the various editors at Baker for their work on the manuscript, especially to Brandy Scritchfield, who showed keen interest in my work early on, and to Eric Salo, who made many suggestions to improve my prose. The suggestions, and at points the words of both, have only improved the manuscript.

Although the following pages would not have come to see the light if not for my engagement with all these colleagues, any shortcomings belong to me alone.

Finally, I dedicate this book to my son Antonio James Sandoval Yax, the deepest joy of my life. My hope for him is only that, with God's help, he will grow to become a good, wise, and just person.

Abbreviations

[ ]	Alternative versification used by some English translations is included in brackets
AB	Anchor Bible
ABD	*Anchor Bible Dictionary*. Edited by David Noel Freedman. 6 vols. New York: Doubleday, 1992
AIL	Ancient Israel and Its Literature
BIS	Biblical Interpretation Series
BKAT	Biblischer Kommentar, Altes Testament
BLS	Bible and Literature Series
BZAW	Beihefte zur Zeitschrift für die alttestamentliche Wissenschaft
CBQMS	Catholic Biblical Quarterly Monograph Series
DCH	*Dictionary of Classical Hebrew*. Edited by David J. A. Clines. 9 vols. Sheffield: Sheffield Phoenix Press, 1993–2014
HALOT	Ludwig Koehler, Walter Baumgartner, and Johann J. Stamm. *The Hebrew and Aramaic Lexicon of the Old Testament*. Translated and edited under the supervision of Mervyn E. J. Richardson. 4 vols. Leiden: Brill, 1994–1999
HS	*Hebrew Studies*
JBL	*Journal of Biblical Literature*
JNES	*Journal of Near Eastern Studies*
JSOT	*Journal for the Study of the Old Testament*
JSOTSup	Journal for the Study of the Old Testament Supplement Series
LHBOTS	The Library of Hebrew Bible/Old Testament Studies
LQ	*Lutheran Quarterly*
LXX	Septuagint
MT	Masoretic Text
NE	Aristotle, *Nicomachean Ethics*. In *The Complete Works of Aristotle*. Edited by Jonathan Barnes. 2 vols. Princeton: Princeton University Press, 1984
NETS	*A New English Translation of the Septuagint*. Edited by Albert Pietersma and Benjamin G. Wright. New York: Oxford University Press, 2007
NIB	*The New Interpreter's Bible*. Edited by Leander E. Keck et al. 12 vols. Nashville: Abingdon, 1994–2004

NIV	New International Version
NJPS	New Jewish Publication Society Version
NRSV	New Revised Standard Version
RBS	Resources for Biblical Study
SJT	*Scottish Journal of Theology*
TDOT	*Theological Dictionary of the Old Testament*. Edited by G. Johannes Botterweck, Helmer Ringgren, and Heinz-Josef Fabry. Translated by John T. Willis et al. 17 vols. Grand Rapids: Eerdmans, 1974–2021
VT	*Vetus Testamentum*
VTSup	Supplements to Vetus Testamentum
ZAW	*Zeitschrift für die alttestamentliche Wissenschaft*
ZTK	*Zeitschrift für Theologie und Kirche*

Introduction

An interest in biblical ethics—whether the ethics *of* the Bible or the role and function of the Bible *in* ethics—is hardly a new concern of biblical scholars or of ethicists.[1] Yet the last decade or two has seen increased attention to the study of character ethics and the Bible, including a keen interest in how aspects of the Hebrew Bible might reflect a virtue-oriented moral discourse, or at least how the witness of the Scriptures might be appropriated into a normative "character ethics" framework. The ongoing interest in virtue ethics and the Bible among biblical scholars is evident from books with titles such as *Character Ethics and the Old Testament: Moral Dimensions of Scripture*; *The Good Life in the Old Testament*; *God and the Art of Happiness*; and *The Bible and the Pursuit of Happiness:*

---

1. See, e.g., the exhaustive Green et al., *Dictionary of Scripture and Ethics*. Two standard Christian handbooks on biblical ethics in English are Birch and Rasmussen, *Bible and Ethics*; and Spohn, *What Are They Saying about Scripture and Ethics?* See further the work of ethicists in Curran and McCormick, *Use of Scripture in Moral Theology*; and Ogletree, *Use of the Bible in Christian Ethics*. Each of these texts distinguishes between the ethics of the Bible and the use of the Bible in ethics, and is primarily concerned with the latter. A number of other studies more concerned with the former aspect of "biblical ethics" include Janzen, *Old Testament Ethics*, and Barton, *Understanding Old Testament Ethics*, both of which treat a range of issues in biblical ethics. See also Levinson, Otto, and Dietrich, *Recht und Ethik im Alten Testament*; Rogerson, *Theory and Practice in Old Testament Ethics*; and Brown, *Character and Scripture*. Mills considers the ethics of biblical narratives in *Biblical Morality*. On the wisdom literature and Proverbs in particular, see the works noted in the discussion below, as well as Delkurt, *Ethische Einsichten*. Newsom maps the contours of the moral self as this emerges in texts of the biblical tradition in "Models of the Moral Self." Cf. the responses to Newsom's work in *JSOT* 40, no.1 (2015), especially Camp, "Proverbs and the Problems of the Moral Self," 25–42; and Stewart, "Wisdom's Imagination," 351–72.

What the Old and New Testaments Teach Us about the Good Life.[2] As the "Old Testament" terminology intimates, this development in biblical studies is largely a Christian one, but not only so. Hava Tirosh-Samuelson argues that a range of biblical literature and subsequent Jewish texts can well be understood in light of an Aristotelian-oriented conception of virtue ethics.[3] In any case, the interest in considering the Bible's moral discourse in light of character ethics is a welcome development since, in the words of Walter Brueggemann, it "works against a caricature of the ... Old Testament ... as a set of commandments that are too familiarly labeled as 'legalism.'"[4] It is welcome, too, because it provides a hermeneutic through which to analyze biblical texts that is structured differently than those critical approaches most familiar to many biblical scholars.

Proverbs and Character Ethics

The wisdom literature of the Hebrew Bible, and especially the book of Proverbs with its educational ethos, presents ideal texts to analyze in terms of the concerns and questions of virtue ethics.[5] In 1996 William Brown did just that in a book-length study called *Character in Crisis: A Fresh Approach to the Wisdom Literature of the Old Testament.*[6] Brown's "fresh approach" was precisely to scrutinize wisdom texts in terms of character ethics. *Character in Crisis* thus fired what for some biblical scholars was the starting gun that precipitated a concern for thinking about the Bible, especially wisdom literature, in light of character ethics. Brown himself has reprised this earlier work under the title *Wisdom's Wonder: Character, Creation, and Crisis in the Bible's Wisdom Literature.*[7] Far from a simple "revised edition" of *Character in Crisis*, *Wisdom's Wonder* is a substantive rethinking and expansion of the earlier work. Most distinctively, Brown supplements his earlier study by

---

2. Carroll R. and Lapsley, *Character Ethics and the Old Testament*; Whybray, *Good Life in the Old Testament*; Charry, *God and the Art of Happiness*; and Strawn, *Bible and the Pursuit of Happiness.*
3. Tirosh-Samuelson, "Virtue and Happiness." Compare Tirosh-Samuelson, *Happiness in Premodern Judaism.*
4. Brueggemann, foreword to *Character Ethics and the Old Testament*, viii.
5. The category of biblical "wisdom literature," which regularly includes the books of Proverbs, Job, Ecclesiastes, and certain psalms, is one that scholars have long been somewhat uneasy about. See, e.g., Kynes, *Obituary for "Wisdom Literature."* Works such as Sirach (Ben Sira) and Wisdom of Solomon in the Old Testament canons of certain Christian traditions are also regularly regarded as wisdom books, and the category usually extends to other early Jewish texts, such as 4QInstruction from Qumran and certain ancient West Asian and Egyptian works.
6. Brown, *Character in Crisis.*
7. Brown, *Wisdom's Wonder.*

recasting it through a hermeneutic of wonder or "fear seeking understanding."[8] This hermeneutic, says Brown, permits him to integrate better what he, like Katharine Dell, regards as the two primary thematic axes of wisdom literature: its concern with ethics or right living and a robust theological interest in creation.[9]

As with Brown's earlier work, *Wisdom's Wonder* begins with a helpful sketch of the main elements of character that inform his study. He explains that moral character is "the tendency to act, feel, and think in certain describable ways" and "refers to the sum and range of specifically ethical qualities or traits the individual or community possesses."[10] Following Bruce Birch and Larry Rasmussen's handbook on biblical ethics, he underscores the importance of perception, intention, and virtue for understanding a person's character.[11] Importantly, Brown also acknowledges that narrative (as that which gives shape to a life over time so that long-term dispositions and excellencies of character can be discerned) is an important category for virtue ethics. As Alasdair MacIntyre puts it, for virtue-oriented moral systems, "I can only answer the question 'What am I to do?' if I can answer the prior question 'Of what story or stories do I find myself a part?'"[12] Of course, Proverbs consists primarily of instructional poems and short sayings. It has no clear "story" that it tells—an issue Brown resolves by identifying a metanarrative shape to Proverbs, whereby the silent youth that the book initially addresses "moves out from the household to the Grand Central Stations of urban life" and ends up in Proverbs 31 as "an adult male who has successfully fulfilled these responsibilities by marrying well and finding his place among the elders."[13]

Yet if Brown's *Character in Crisis* fired the starting shot for considering the Bible and especially wisdom literature in light of character or virtue ethics, the field of runners considering the book of Proverbs in this light was for some time rather small. Despite Brown's seminal work and the ongoing interest in character ethics in/and the Bible generally, Proverbs did not initially receive as much sustained attention as one might have expected given

---

8. Brown, *Wisdom's Wonder*, 24.
9. Brown, *Wisdom's Wonder*, 4. Brown cites Dell, *Book of Proverbs in Social and Theological Context*, 11, 91, 178–79.
10. Brown, *Wisdom's Wonder*, 8.
11. Brown, *Wisdom's Wonder*, 9–14; cf. Birch and Rasmussen, *Bible and Ethics*, esp. 35–65.
12. MacIntyre, *After Virtue*, 216.
13. Brown, *Wisdom's Wonder*, 64–65. Brown is not sanguine about all this, however. He recognizes the patriarchal nature of the text and its vision of the developing male and so subsequently the need for critical feminist and cultural critique of the book. On the adequacy of the "story" Brown finds in Proverbs for a virtue-ethics reading of the book, see chap. 9 below. For a more direct, critical engagement with the hierarchical and exclusionary facets of Proverbs' moral discourse, see the conclusion below.

the book's clear moral rhetoric and instructional goals. Most scholars of Proverbs, both before and after Brown's *Character in Crisis*, have instead been primarily concerned with other important issues: understanding the book's act-consequence rhetoric or the sages' supposed empirical methodology; exploring Proverbs' relation to "international" wisdom works from Egypt and Mesopotamia; attempting to discern the social location of the book's authors or editors; or considering the relationship of Proverbs' short sayings to the folk proverbs of different peoples throughout history—to name just a few lines of investigation.[14] Even the collection of essays published by the Society of Biblical Literature's "Character Ethics and Biblical Interpretation Group"—*Character Ethics and the Old Testament*—contains only two essays that treat wisdom texts in any significant way; one of these essays is also by Brown, and neither treats Proverbs directly.[15]

Despite such limited efforts to understand Proverbs in terms of character ethics after Brown's *Character in Crisis*, some studies of the book have begun to talk about virtues and vices, the formation of character, the role of moral exemplars in character formation, the ethics of being over the ethics of duty, and so forth—all concerns that belong to the discourse of character ethics. The present study builds on many of these efforts.

Michael Fox in his magisterial two-volume commentary on Proverbs, for instance, contends that the proverbial ethical program is most akin to the character ethics of Socrates. In particular, Fox finds in Proverbs an affinity with the Socratic dictums that "virtue is knowledge," "no one does wrong willingly," and "all virtues are one," as well as with the premium Socrates puts on the power of the intellect in controlling character.[16] Fox is no doubt correct that aspects of the Socratic vision resonate with Proverbs. However, other scholars look to Aristotle—and the ethical tradition that stems from him—as a better analogue for understanding Proverbs' moral discourse. In response to Fox's work, Christopher Ansberry, for instance, argues that Aristotle's *Nicomachean Ethics*, with its understanding of matters such as knowledge, virtue, and flourishing, "serves as a more useful heuristic model for understanding the moral vision of the book of Proverbs than Socrates' ethical theory."[17] As noted, Tirosh-Samuelson studies a range of Jewish lit-

---

14. As we shall see at different points in the following chapters, all these concerns bear on a reading of Proverbs as a virtue-oriented text.

15. See Brown, "Moral Cosmologies of Creation"; and Smith-Christopher, "Quiet Words of the Wise." If Song of Songs is considered a wisdom text, then one could also add Pleins, "Wine, Women, and Song (of Songs)."

16. Fox, *Proverbs 10–31*, 934–45.

17. Ansberry, "What Does Jerusalem Have to Do with Athens?," 161.

erature, including Proverbs, in light of Aristotelian perspectives on ethics. As she says, the Bible, especially the wisdom tradition, "shared the assumption of Greek philosophy that to act rightly the moral agent must acquire virtues through training that conditions the moral agent to live wisely."[18]

Ellen Davis, too, largely understands Proverbs in terms of a character ethics that seems ultimately to derive from Aristotle. She points to the importance of the virtues in Proverbs and highlights especially the central place of "prudence" in the book, while also noting ways Proverbs' creation theology is related to virtue—all matters with which the following pages are also concerned.[19] In a wide-ranging study, Zoltán Schwáb sees Proverbs' moral discourse in terms of a virtue-oriented tradition—that of Thomistic moral theology, itself profoundly indebted to Aristotle. He does so, in part, to demonstrate that Proverbs' concern with "interested piety" (my term)—people's quest for certain external goods such as wealth in the context of moral action—can be regarded as an important aspect of a *legitimate* ethical perspective that is of a piece with the social interdependence and just communal relations the book also values, something that has been difficult for Proverbs scholars in the modern epoch to understand.[20] Christine Roy Yoder's commentary on Proverbs is also broadly concerned with relating categories of character ethics to the text, while her work on the formation of "fearers of Yahweh" studies one "profile of virtue" in the book.[21] Yoder also considers the role that "natural" human emotions play in Proverbs, drawing on the Aristotelian tradition of virtue ethics that Martha Nussbaum elaborates.[22] Elsewhere Yoder attempts to sketch Proverbs' vision of the "good life."[23] L. Juliana Claassens also draws on Nussbaum to consider whether the Woman of Valor in Proverbs 31:10–31 might be reckoned as one who is fully flourishing or not.[24]

Anne Whitaker Stewart's study of the poetic ethics of Proverbs is another work that considers how Proverbs might be regarded as a text of virtue ethics, as her keen engagement with the likes of MacIntyre, Nussbaum, and Stanley Hauerwas suggests. Stewart recognizes the important role the training of

---

18. Tirosh-Samuelson, "Virtue and Happiness," 711. On the foundational role of Aristotle, cf. 701–11.

19. Davis, "Preserving Virtues." The "prudence" she speaks of appears to be closely related to the notion of *phronēsis* in the Greek tradition and what in Proverbs I will call "Practical Wisdom" (cf. chap. 8 below).

20. Schwáb, *Toward an Interpretation of the Book of Proverbs*.

21. See C. Yoder, *Proverbs* and "Forming 'Fearers of Yahweh.'" Cf. Fox, *Proverbs 10–31*, 934–45.

22. C. Yoder, "Objects of Our Affections." Cf. Nussbaum, *Upheavals of Thought*, 129–37.

23. C. Yoder, "Path and Possession in Proverbs 1–9."

24. Claassens, "Woman of Substance."

desire and emotion plays in virtue ethics and contends that Proverbs' poetic literary forms are indispensable for the virtue-oriented moral work that the text seeks to carry out.[25] Like Brown, Stewart also recognizes the fundamental place of narrative in much contemporary discourse of character ethics. However, she is not convinced Proverbs reveals the sort of narrative arc Brown discovers in the text. Rather, following the likes of Galen Strawson and Dan Zahavi, she proposes that character formation need not depend on narrative as strongly as the writings of MacIntyre, Hauerwas, and others suggest.[26] For her and her theoretical-ethical interlocutors, character and virtue can be recognized, even formed, episodically without "story." Indeed, for Stewart it almost seems that the mere existence of the nonnarrative book of Proverbs, with its concern for virtue and character, is proof of this.

Arthur Jan Keefer also studies Proverbs thoroughly in light of premodern virtue-oriented moral traditions—especially those of Aristotle and Thomas. To demonstrate that Proverbs itself constitutes a distinct moral tradition, Keefer identifies the central virtues and vices the book articulates and closely compares them with the range and conception of virtues and vices in Aristotle and Thomas. He "definitively" concludes "that many of the moral concepts in Proverbs constitute virtues in the Aristotelian and Thomistic senses, with the book itself emerging as a moral tradition in its own right."[27]

Others, though less explicitly turning to Aristotle and his interpreters, also broadly consider aspects of Proverbs' moral discourse in terms of character ethics. Sun Myung Lyu studies the book's notion of righteousness in this light, and I explore how the book's discourse of wealth and poverty relates to particular virtues that the book values.[28] Carol Newsom proposes an important way to map constructions of the moral self throughout the Hebrew Bible and in early Judaism, including Proverbs; the moral terms and categories she deploys resonate with a turn toward analyzing biblical texts in terms of character ethics. Newsom contends that "three elements form the fundamental grammar of the moral self in the Hebrew Bible: desire, knowledge, and the discipline of submission to external authority"—elements that are also common to ancient virtue-oriented traditions, though she does not invoke that tradition explicitly.[29]

25. Stewart, *Poetic Ethics in Proverbs*.
26. Stewart, *Poetic Ethics in Proverbs*, 203–7; cf. Strawson, "Against Narrativity"; Zahavi, "Self and Other."
27. Keefer, *Book of Proverbs and Virtue Ethics*, 203.
28. Lyu, *Righteousness in the Book of Proverbs*; Sandoval, *Discourse of Wealth and Poverty*.
29. Newsom, "Models of the Moral Self," 12. In a direct response to Newsom's contention that Proverbs presumes a coherent moral self, Camp ("Proverbs and the Problems of the Moral Self") questions the coherency of the moral subject in Proverbs. Focusing on minority

Beyond the relatively recent works just mentioned, other studies of Proverbs—including some older works published well before the last two decades—also implicitly analyze Proverbs, *at least in part*, via the idiom and categories of character ethics. A consideration of this phenomenon is instructive since it points to an important feature of many Proverbs studies in especially the late twentieth and early twenty-first centuries: namely, a significant ambiguity in descriptions of the nature of Proverbs' moral discourse. The ambiguity is one that seems to arise from efforts to interpret the book, consciously or unconsciously, primarily through modern moral orientations—especially utilitarian and deontological schemes—without fully recognizing how aspects of the text itself may represent a premodern moral discourse like the virtue-ethics traditions of ancient Greece. This ambiguity has at times meant that aspects of Proverbs' moral perspectives have not been clearly understood, and subsequently the book's moral worth has sometimes been only ambivalently appreciated.

The work here differs from other valuable studies in several ways. First, in part 1, I focus on several matters somewhat more than they do: the question of why Proverbs has not often been read, until recently, as a species of virtue ethics; the nature of human beings and how it relates to their quest for happiness or eudaemonia; the necessity of training a person's natural desires for goods that contribute to happiness; and the centrality of two particular virtues in traditions of character ethics—sociability and Practical Wisdom. In part 2, I explore several topics or questions that relate to and build on an understanding of Proverbs as a book of character ethics, which others—because of the focus and scope of their own work—do not much consider or approach from a somewhat different angle than I do. These concern how Proverbs' conception of wisdom and virtue might relate to similar notions elsewhere in the Hebrew Bible, how Proverbs' cosmogony might "fit" in a virtue-ethics reading of the book, and how Proverbs' moral tradition might be understood as a "practice" to be constructively engaged today (see "The Plan of This Book" below).

The primary task of this book is thus to describe and account for some of the ambiguity in portrayals of Proverbs' theological ethics, while also, more fundamentally, advancing descriptions of Proverbs as an ancient virtue-oriented moral discourse—an undertaking others have already ably begun.[30]

---

perspectives and contradictions in the text, Camp suggests that the moral self in the book ought to be regarded as more fragmented than Newsom's model and analysis suggest.

30. Throughout the volume I use expressions such as "theological ethics," "theological-ethical," or "moral-theological," which collapse two sorts of discourses that sometimes are analytically best kept separate—the theological and the ethical. These expressions, which signal the close link between the theological and ethical, are appropriate vis-à-vis Proverbs because the book's ethical concerns are inextricably bound up with its theology, most obviously evident through claims that associate creation and the fear of the divine (Adonai) with knowledge and

I hope the efforts here will also point to ways Proverbs offers a coherent and legitimate moral vision that may still, or again, prove valuable for the constructive moral-theological work of individuals and communities for whom the Bible remains an important ethical-theological resource.

Proverbs and Character Ethics?

Given the relatively recent turn to character ethics as a heuristic lens through which to understand Proverbs, it is not surprising that some question whether virtue ethics is the most useful conversation partner when studying the "Old Testament ethics" of Proverbs. John Barton, for example, once contended that although aspects of Proverbs' moral discourse might appear akin to that of character ethics, "on closer inspection" this proves to be only a superficial resemblance. As he suggested, "the gulf between" Proverbs and "a modern virtue ethic may be wider than first appears."[31] Barton has revised his views on Proverbs and now concedes that the book has more in common with character ethics than he once thought.[32] Nonetheless, it is worth rehearsing some of the earlier views of this leading interpreter of scriptural ethics, since many of these claims will surely still resonate with other students of Proverbs.

In his earlier work, Barton understood the human characters of Proverbs as static figures. "Everyone is either good or bad, wise or foolish," so that "living the good life appears to be an absolute, with no gradations or variations." For Barton this meant that "Proverbs eschews most ideas of moral progress," while the possibility for training and advancement in virtue is a key element of virtue ethics. Barton averred that a book like Proverbs seems "to inhabit a cruder world of thought, where character is indeed all important but is seen as fixed and unchanging, almost at times as predetermined."[33]

---

wisdom (e.g., 1:7; 3:19–20; 8:22–31; 15:33). As Quinn explains, "Any ethical doctrine that makes theistic assumption is theological. The ethical theories characteristic of the traditions of Judaism, Christianity, and ISLAM are thus theological." See "Theological Ethics" (capitalization original).

31. Barton, *Understanding Old Testament Ethics*, 67.
32. For Barton's recent perspectives, see "Ethics and Character Formation."
33. Barton, *Understanding Old Testament Ethics*, 67. Cf. Stewart's response to Barton in *Poetic Ethics in Proverbs*, 13–15. The two places Barton has room for character ethics in understanding biblical ethics are (1) in the analysis of (some) biblical narratives where distinct characters might serve as moral exemplars; and (2) as a normative conversation partner for those concerned with bringing biblical interpretation to bear on contemporary theological and ethical concerns (*Understanding Old Testament Ethics*, 65–74).

It is clear, however, from Proverbs itself that at least the book's simpletons and young addressees (and probably the כְּסִיל ["dolt"][34] and other moral types) can progress in wisdom and righteousness, though other figures, such as the אֱוִיל ("fool"), do seem incapable of moral progress (cf. 1:7; 15:5; 24:7; 27:22).[35] Indeed, the book's concern with instruction, discipline, and reproof assumes that at least some people who are not wise or just can become both, while others through discipline or punishment can at least be made not to act foolishly or wickedly. What is more, the prologue's (1:2–7) identification of the book's audience as not only simple youth (1:4) but also advanced sages (1:5) implies that study of the text can continue to shape the character of even those excelling in wisdom.[36] Proverbs, however, does not presume that a person's moral development is always in a positive direction. Bad human character is not necessarily static. As Newsom succinctly puts it, even the "inveterate fool in Proverbs is 'made' rather than 'born.'"[37] Finally, as we shall see further below, the entailments of the fundamental moral metaphor of the two ways, upon one of which a person must travel through life, also suggests that one can advance in wisdom. The path of a wise or just person heads somewhere;[38] it has a goal or end of flourishing or well-being (not mere success) toward which one moves via the continued cultivation and right exercise of wisdom's virtues.[39] As Stewart aptly summarizes matters (also in response to Barton), character for the ancient sages "can and must be cultivated, and this is why the character ethics approach is such a helpful resource for reading the book of Proverbs."[40]

Barton's earlier work, however, was largely concerned to characterize the ethics of the Old Testament as a whole. Subsequently, one might surmise he may have unduly assimilated the distinct moral discourse of Proverbs to

---

34. Whenever the NRSV renders כְּסִיל as "fool," I change this to "dolt" to distinguish it from אֱוִיל, which the NRSV also renders as "fool."

35. Cf. Fox, *Proverbs 1–9*, 38–43.

36. Most contemporary scholars recognize in the prologue a double addressee—the simple youth and the advanced sage. Cf. Brown, *Character in Crisis*, 23–30; Sandoval, "Revisiting the Prologue." For a somewhat distinct perspective, see Keefer, "Shift in Perspective."

37. Newsom, "Models of the Moral Self," 13.

38. Because no two lives are the same, moreover, how any particular wise or just person, or any wicked or foolish person, travels or progresses on their life's path will be distinct; the precise range of virtues (or vices) different people will more or less cultivate and how they will exhibit them may thus also be somewhat different.

39. This formulation of the relation between the possibility of human flourishing and the metaphor of the way in Proverbs is slightly distinct from the perspective C. Yoder offers in "Path and Possession in Proverbs 1–9." For her, it appears, following the way of wisdom is flourishing. As will be explained further, I understand following the way of wisdom in Proverbs more precisely as an indispensable prerequisite for flourishing.

40. Stewart, *Poetic Ethics in Proverbs*, 15.

the broader understanding of Old Testament ethics he seeks to promote. In this normative Christian endeavor he draws liberally on the New Testament and Protestant theological tradition to claim that the Old Testament's moral perspective in general is "far from the idea of moral good as the distillation of the way good people actually live"—a succinct articulation (and rejection) of a central dictum of virtue ethics that goes back to Aristotle.[41] Indeed, for Barton, not just in Proverbs but in the broader Old Testament, "the characteristic features of a virtue ethic are lacking" since "the emphasis" in that collection of texts "lies on the divine lawgiver rather than on human moral character."[42]

Yet if for the earlier Barton Proverbs was no virtue-oriented work, neither was it plainly a command-oriented, or deontological, moral discourse. Instead, Barton concluded that Proverbs is concerned to help readers attain "success." Its discourse is "more of a eudaemonism that we should have to call, in our terms, teleological, or consequentialist."[43] Such a view is redolent of the conclusions that scholars like C. H. Toy (and others) articulated a century earlier.[44] It is also one (as we shall shortly see) that in some shape or fashion has not been uncommon among Proverbs scholars up through the early twenty-first century.

Barton's earlier work is thus important, not only because it illustrates how few scholars have understood Proverbs as an ancient virtue-ethics discourse until recently. It is also significant because Barton explicitly names the two primary modern ethical discourses by which Proverbs has typically been (mis)understood (i.e., consequentialism and, particularly, utilitarian thought) and by which it has typically been evaluated or judged (i.e., deontological thought)—or so I will suggest.

---

41. Barton, *Understanding Old Testament Ethics*, 69. Among others, Barton invokes St. Paul and Luther, as well as the concept of "justification by faith" (67–68). Although it may be that Barton was at points led astray in his earlier analysis of Proverbs by what appear to be strong normative Protestant views, I do not wish to suggest that such normative interpretive projects and appeals to particular traditions, whether Christian, Jewish, or otherwise, are somehow illegitimate merely because they are normative projects. My own analysis of Proverbs' moral discourse has normative concerns and makes appeals to a largely Christian—both Protestant and Catholic—moral tradition. On some of these issues, see Levenson, *Hebrew Bible, the Old Testament, and Historical Criticism*.

42. Barton, *Understanding Old Testament Ethics*, 69.

43. Barton, *Understanding Old Testament Ethics*, 70. Although virtue-oriented traditions are regularly concerned with the telos of human life and so can be described as teleological, the term "teleological" as Barton uses it here (with "consequentialist") regularly refers to those modern ethical systems that judge the worth of a moral action in terms of the end or consequence the action produces (e.g., utilitarianism, for which an act is valued if it is of use for attaining some subjectively, if also rationally, determined good end—e.g., a person's pleasure, the most happiness for the most people). For more on how this is distinct from virtue-oriented moral systems, see chap. 1 below.

44. Toy, *Proverbs*, xiv.

Barton may be correct that much of the Old Testament canon is best viewed as "deontological rather than a virtue-based ethic."[45] However, this hardly means that all parts of the Bible are. What is more, the sort of virtue-oriented moral vision Proverbs offers may have significantly more in common with other biblical texts, such as the pronouncements of the great prophet of social justice Amos, than is usually thought. In any case, Tirosh-Samuelson's words about how the Bible's ethics are regularly reckoned is an apt characterization of Barton's earlier position: "The Bible . . . is usually adduced as an example of deontological ethics, whose major modern exponent was Immanuel Kant."[46] This is so even if one adds that the sort of theistic but still command-oriented perspective Barton presents can be distinguished from Kant's project (see below).

Funlola Olojede, writing out of an African context and critical hermeneutic, also questions the appropriateness of a virtue- or character-ethics approach to the study of Proverbs, but on grounds quite distinct from those of Barton.[47] She rightly notes that it is Western scholars who have regularly investigated Proverbs' ethics and they have done so with Western ethical and philosophical presuppositions. Hermeneutically, then, biblical scholarship has largely presented only one possible kind of reading of Proverbs' morality, and it is one that is skewed toward the normative ethical programs of Europe. For Olojede, the results of such scholarship are suspect because of their complicity with the modern European–North American projects of colonialism and imperialism.[48] Olojede's indictment of unhelpful approaches to Proverbs, however, includes more than modern, post-Enlightenment scholarship; it also includes work that draws on premodern virtue-oriented reflection as well, specifically that associated with Socrates and Aristotle. Olojede contends that an African lens applied to Proverbs better demonstrates the nature and extent of the book's emphasis on matters such as communal well-being. Such matters resonate deeply with the ethical orientations of traditional African social-moral visions.

Olojede is quite correct about the mostly unarticulated (European) modernist moral presuppositions brought to bear on Proverbs by many biblical scholars, as will be discussed in chapter 1. However, although Socrates and Aristotle do stand at the beginning of what becomes the European philosophical

---

45. Barton, *Understanding Old Testament Ethics*, 70.
46. Tirosh-Samuelson, "Virtue and Happiness," 711.
47. Olojede, "Woman Wisdom."
48. For a robust account of aspects of the complicity of biblical studies with European and North American colonial and imperial projects, see Cuéllar, *Empire, the British Museum, and the Making of the Biblical Scholar*.

tradition, her critique of the appropriateness of bringing these ancient discourses to bear on Proverbs may not be as apt. As premodern works, the classical tradition of virtue ethics emerged in a broader ancient Mediterranean context that included parts of the African continent and long before the emergence of a "Europe" or of European colonial-imperial hegemony. It is thus not surprising that some of the moral emphases of ancient virtue ethics—for instance, the high value placed on virtues that promote human sociality—resonate deeply with features of the traditional communitarian moralities of the African world that Olojede sketches.

Kwame Gyekye in fact offers a sketch of "African Ethics" that in many respects corresponds with aspects of the classical traditions of virtue ethics. He highlights the central place of "character" and character formation in the establishment of moral personhood in many African cultures.[49] In traditional African ethics, humans are not born virtuous but have the capacity to progress in virtue, to choose "to pursue good" but also to "pursue evil."[50] What is more, the sociality of human beings and a concern for their flourishing are taken for granted: "The ethical values of compassion, solidarity, reciprocity, cooperation, interdependence, and social well-being" are central.[51] Social or communitarian virtues are highly prized in order to establish a "common good" reckoned as a "good for human beings" that embraces "the needs that are *basic* to the enjoyment and fulfillment of the life of each individual."[52] All these features of African moral perspectives, as we shall see more fully in the following pages, resonate with key aspects of traditions of virtue ethics.

In light of Gyekye's work, one might think that differences between the classical tradition of ethics and African moral orientations may not be as sharp as Olojede intimates. Whatever the case, Olojede herself is ultimately not concerned to "pitch a Socratic-Aristotelian approach" to studying Proverbs against an African-centric approach; nor does she simply reject the insights of Western scholars who look to Aristotle or Socrates as heuristic guides to understanding Proverbs. Instead, she is most concerned "to show the need for an African approach to biblical ethics in the African context."[53] In her efforts to do so, Olojede clearly senses how the moral vision of Proverbs resonates deeply with traditional African morality. To the extent that this book strives to revise interpretations of Proverbs predicated on modernist European

---

49. Gyekye, "African Ethics."
50. Gyekye, "African Ethics," 14.
51. Gyekye, "African Ethics," 35.
52. Gyekye, "African Ethics," 27 (emphasis original).
53. Olojede, "Woman Wisdom," 3.

thought—by suggesting that an ethical perspective emerging from the ancient Mediterranean world is a more apt dialogue partner for studying the text—it is allied with Olojede's work.

Olojede's work and Barton's earlier studies suggest Proverbs might *not* best be read in light of character ethics. Though perhaps not fully compelling, they nonetheless serve as important cautions for any attempt to do so. As I noted, descriptions of the nature of Proverbs' moral discourse are often ambiguous, and despite some significant efforts to study Proverbs in light of character ethics, certainly not all is settled when it comes to describing the book's moral vision. Not all scholars have considered the possibility that Proverbs may in part be a book of virtue ethics; among those who have, not all are equally or fully persuaded of the ways in which it is. One can continue to ask: How and to what extent can or ought Proverbs be understood as a book of character ethics? What features of the text indicate that its moral discourse—its vision of wisdom—ought to be understood as a kind of virtue-oriented moral discourse? And one can still query about the interpretive implications of understanding Proverbs as a book of character ethics.

Reading the Book of Proverbs: Preliminary Matters

Israel's legendary wise king, Solomon, is traditionally considered the author of Proverbs. The text, however, is rather obviously an anthology of wisdom poems and collections of sayings. Several sections are ascribed to other individuals—sometimes anonymous, sometimes named. Some are derivative of other ancient and non-Israelite "wisdom" works. Proverbs 22:17–24:22 (or at least 22:17–23:11), for instance, is regularly regarded as dependent in some way on the Egyptian Instruction of Amenemope and perhaps began with the phrase "words of the wise."[54] Similarly, Proverbs 24:23 introduces the instruction that follows with the words, "These also are sayings of the wise" (גַּם־אֵלֶּה לַחֲכָמִים). Proverbs 30:1 speaks of "the words of Agur," and Proverbs 31:1 presents the short instruction that follows as "the words of King Lemuel . . . that his mother taught him."[55] Other sections of the book (Prov. 1–9; 10:1–22:16; 25–29), however, are directly

---

54. The reading of the superscription "words of the wise" in 22:17 is based on a well-known emendation of the line first proposed by Gressman, "Die neugefundene Lehre des Amen-emope," 274. Instead of MT's *haṭ ʾoznəkā ûšəmaʿ dibrê ḥăkāmîm*, read *dibrê ḥăkāmîm haṭ ʾoznəkā ûšəmaʿ dəbāray*; cf. LXX Prov. 22:17; Fox, *Proverbs 10–31*, 707.

55. For difficulties and questions surrounding both Prov. 30:1 and 31:1, see Fox, *Proverbs 10–31*, 852–54, 884.

associated with Solomon via superscriptions; Proverbs 25:1 also mentions the eighth-century-BCE Judahite king Hezekiah. However, allusions to Solomon are typically understood as traditional ascriptions and not claims of authorship. Critical scholarship thus rejects Solomonic authorship of the "book" of Proverbs.[56]

If it is clear that Solomon did not write Proverbs, how and when the different sections of the book were composed and brought together into a literary whole remains a complicated question. Most assume that the collections of proverbial sayings in 10:1–22:16 and 25–29 constitute the earliest, preexilic sections of Proverbs. To them were added the poems of Proverbs 1–9 sometime after the monarchy ended. Still later, chapters 30 and 31, and finally the book's prologue (1:2–7), were appended to a Proverbs scroll. When exactly the final form of the Hebrew (MT) version of Proverbs took shape may be as late as the Hellenistic era. Indeed, the placement and ordering of certain sections of Proverbs appear not to have been fixed across textual traditions even as late as the writing of the Greek version (LXX Proverbs), which differs not insignificantly from the Hebrew (MT), most notably in its moralizing rhetoric and especially its ordering of certain sections of the text.[57]

As interesting as arguments concerning the literary and textual development of Proverbs may be, for my purposes here it is not necessary to take a strong position on any of it. In the following pages, I strive to discern and analyze the nature of the ethical discourse and moral vision of Proverbs as they emerge in the final form of the book; my study is what biblical scholars call a synchronous one. But I hope my synchronous analysis is undertaken with a strong diachronic sensibility that recognizes that sections of the Proverbs anthology emerged from teachers and scribes in different historical periods and probably in distinct social-economic contexts. This is especially true of Proverbs 30 and 31, which likely date later than much of the book. But it can also be true for the relationship between the instructional poems of Proverbs 1–9 and the

---

56. Besides the obvious collections of material in Proverbs signaled by superscriptions, scholars have long suggested that Prov. 10–15, characterized by antithetically parallel sayings, constitutes a separate section within the broader block of material that makes up 10:1–22:16. Likewise, Prov. 30, though initially associated with Agur, seems to be a composite text, with the proverbs of "ascending numerical parallelism" in the second half of that chapter presenting a quite different literary feel than the chapter's initial eleven or fourteen verses. So too the acrostic poem praising the Woman of Valor at the end of Proverbs (31:10–31; cf. conclusion below) was likely an independent literary work adapted or composed to be juxtaposed to Lemuel's mother's words and to bring the book to a fitting close. Finally, Proverbs' opening verses (1:1–7) are thought to constitute a separate literary introduction or "prologue" to the book once it reached something near its final form.

57. E.g., in the LXX, the material of MT chaps. 24–31 is arranged as follows: 24:1–22; 30:1–14; 24:23–34; 30:15–33; 31:1–9; 25:1–29:27; 31:10–31. Fox alludes to the "moralizing additions" to LXX Proverbs in *Proverbs 1–9*, 361.

short sayings of Proverbs 10–29, the latter surely related in some complex way to the folk wisdom of the broader populations of ancient Israel and Judah.[58]

There is thus no specific historical reason to insist that the moral rhetoric and impulses of Proverbs' diverse sections will *precisely* correspond. Still, my own sense is that most of the book ultimately emerges from scribal and educational contexts, which may have been temporally distant from one another but are sufficiently analogous in sociological terms for them to have a high degree of consistency of moral vision and emphasis. In this regard, the Russian literary critic Mikhail Bakhtin and his close collaborator Pavel Medvedev offer helpful insights about how the distinct generic parts of a composite work might function. The distinguishable parts of such composite works, they contend, may well be "separate and finished [whole] utterances independently oriented in reality."[59] Yet such utterances also have become constitutive parts of some larger utterance. As parts of the larger utterance, they can mean more than they would as independent utterances because they "contribute to the whole utterance's meaning."[60] Just so, the different sections of Proverbs with their distinct literary genres can be regarded as independent utterances that entail somewhat unique ways of comprehending the world. Yet this diverse material now belongs to a single utterance that is the book of Proverbs and so informs the meaning of that larger work.[61] It is with the meaning(s) of the "whole utterance" of the book of Proverbs that I am most concerned.

The Plan of This Book

The task of part 1 of this book is to suggest how and to what extent Proverbs is an ancient, virtue-oriented, moral discourse. Part 2 considers several key texts and interpretive questions in light of part 1's claims. A central feature of the exegetical and constructive interpretive task of this book is thus to draw out

---

58. On this question see chap. 8 below and the literature cited there.
59. Medvedev, *Formal Method in Literary Scholarship*, 132, cited in Morson and Emerson, *Mikhail Bakhtin*, 274. The short sayings of Prov. 10–29 (and certainly the oral folk sayings they evoke), when read in isolation, can thus be said to "see the world" somewhat differently than the instructional poems of Prov. 1–9.
60. Morson and Emerson, *Mikhail Bakhtin*, 274. For Bakhtin, an utterance is a unit of "speech communication" that involves extralinguistic or pragmatic elements. It may be "as short as a grunt and long as War and Peace." What is key is that it must be addressed to someone, "respond to something and anticipate a response," and it "must be accomplishing something by the saying of it" (Morson and Emerson, *Mikhail Bakhtin*, 125–26).
61. For a lucid explanation of Bakhtin's understanding of genre, see Morson and Emerson, *Mikhail Bakhtin*, esp. 271–309.

and describe the moral-philosophical presuppositions and logic of Proverbs' moral rhetoric against which the book's explicit teachings might best make sense and be analyzed. For this task, premodern moral and philosophical thought and terminology—especially those of Aristotle and his contemporary interpreters—will be an apt guide, providing useful concepts and vocabulary for understanding Proverbs' teachings. This is so even though one might legitimately be suspicious of understanding a discourse from one time and place (the book of Proverbs) in light of another discourse from another time and place (classical traditions of virtue ethics). One must always remember that the conceptual links between Proverbs and other moral discourses are heuristic and not exact. The Hebrew book is no *Nicomachean Ethics*, presenting philosophical arguments or logical proofs for the presuppositions of its moral instruction and rhetoric.[62] Yet as Tirosh-Samuelson claims, although the Bible "was not a philosophical text and it did not propose a systematic account of any topic, including virtue and happiness," the "theologico-ethical outlook" of much of Scripture, "especially as expressed in the Wisdom stratum," shares similarities with virtue traditions and can be theorized or "expressed in propositional terms."[63]

My primary guides in this book's task include Aristotle himself and some of the most prominent contemporary interpreters of the Aristotelian moral tradition—Alasdair MacIntyre and Martha Nussbaum—as well as the eminent scholar of ancient Greek ethics, Julia Annas. My intention is not to explicate fully the work of these prominent thinkers. It is rather to argue that if Proverbs shows concerns sufficiently analogous to those highlighted by virtue-oriented moral traditions and thinkers, we can be more confident *that* Proverbs is a book of character ethics and *how* it is so. My ultimate thesis is simple: because Proverbs reveals genuine concern with matters of character ethics, one is warranted in studying the book's wisdom—its moral vision—and analyzing its discourse features in light of and in terms of virtue-oriented moral discourse.

In chapter 1, I suggest that biblical scholarship has not understood Proverbs clearly or sufficiently as an ancient virtue-ethics text. Instead, it has often ambiguously described the nature of the book's moral discourse. Consequently, Proverbs' moral worth has often been only ambivalently appreciated. I begin to account for this situation by considering certain trends within biblical studies, and wisdom studies in particular. On the one hand, such tendencies marginalize the theology and ethics of Proverbs within and in relation to the

---

62. Cf. Keefer, *Book of Proverbs and Virtue Ethics*.
63. Tirosh-Samuelson, "Virtue and Happiness," 711.

theology and ethics of the rest of the Bible. On the other hand, Proverbs scholarship has also tended to interpret and evaluate the book's moral discourse—whether consciously or unconsciously, explicitly or implicitly—through the lenses of modern ethical theory above all utilitarian schemes and deontological sensibilities. (Scholarship has also often applied to Proverbs literal-minded historical reading strategies likewise largely developed in modernity.) Much in this situation, I suggest, is due to what MacIntyre has identified as a kind of historical amnesia—an incomplete remembering—in the modern epoch of premodern modes of moral reflection.

Chapter 2 considers Proverbs' prologue (1:2–7) to underscore two key points about the book's moral discourse. First, Proverbs' opening lines reveal that—like character ethics—the book is concerned with virtue, whether intellectual and practical dispositions or moral-social virtue. Second, the prologue also makes clear that its readers should attend to the text's literal or plain-sense teachings, as well as to its figurative and symbolic dimensions. The final section of chapter 2 analyzes how these dual emphases inform our understanding of Proverbs' cause-and-effect rhetoric. Both features of the prologue are important for understanding the logic of the book's act-consequence rhetoric in light of premodern notions of causality or means-end relations, which MacIntyre also describes. The analysis points to subtle and symbolic ways the sages have imagined the exercise of the virtues to result not so much in various external goods but in a different internal relation to a broader conception of a flourishing life, which itself entails some enjoyment of external goods. This last section of chapter 2 also alludes to aspects of Proverbs' virtue-oriented discourse that subsequent chapters will elaborate and build on.

Chapter 3 explains the necessity of character-ethics traditions, of knowing what sort of being humans are and what constitutes their happiness or flourishing. The anthropology of Proverbs reveals that the ancient sages—not unlike traditions of character ethics—reckoned people as material, spiritual, intellectual, and social creatures with a range of needs and desires. Humans for Proverbs are also typically corrigible, able to learn virtue and advance in wisdom—at least up until adulthood—in ways that enable the proper understanding of how various goods contribute to human thriving and how such goods are appropriately pursued. For the sages, humans are quite like MacIntyre's description of the species as dependent rational animals.[64]

Chapter 4 considers how character-ethics traditions prioritize "moral agents" over "right acts." These traditions focus on the virtues and vices

---

64. McIntyre, *Dependent Rational Animals*.

that make up people's character rather than on other ethical matters, such as deontological rule following or utilitarian pleasure/happiness seeking. The chapter highlights the emphasis in virtue-oriented traditions on people's "way of life"—whether it be a good and virtuous path or a vicious and wicked path—and how this emphasis is abundantly evident in Proverbs too.

Chapter 5 takes up the importance of virtue ethics to rightly train a person's emotions and desires for goods that humans naturally pursue. Drawing on chapter 2's insistence that Proverbs itself signals the reader to attend to the figurative or symbolic dimensions of its moral discourse, chapter 5 describes how the book seeks to train the natural longings of its presumed young male audience—especially longings for things such as material wealth and sexual satisfaction. The sages reckon wisdom, or the acquisition of virtue, as more valuable and desirable than anything else because wisdom enables an understanding of both the place goods like sex and riches have in the quest for happiness and the appropriate ways to pursue such goods.

Chapter 6 briefly explores the relationship between ethical and intellectual virtue in Proverbs and how both relate to the desires of the individuals discussed in chapter 5. Here the focus is on a few moral types in the book who are not described as wise and just or foolish and wicked. These moral agents can helpfully be analyzed in terms of Aristotle's distinctions between virtuous or vicious people whose characters are fully settled and those he describes as enkratic or akratic—those whose desires are not fully trained, yet whose moral knowledge and rational wills make them able to do good (enkratic) or not (akratic).

The next three chapters (7–9) highlight the central place of two key virtues in traditions of character ethics and in Proverbs: sociability and Practical Wisdom. Proverbs considers the exercise of these to be essential for human flourishing (cf. chap. 3). Chapter 7 recalls dimensions of virtue-oriented ethical discourses—first mentioned in chapter 1—that are sometimes not well recognized or acknowledged. The chapter then describes the central place social virtue (e.g., justice or being just) holds in Proverbs' moral rhetoric. Chapters 8 and 9 turn to the more complex and implicit ways Proverbs construes a full understanding of "wisdom" as Practical Wisdom, analogous to the notion of *phronēsis* in classical traditions. Chapter 8 highlights especially the distinction Proverbs implicitly makes between *practical virtue* and *Practical Wisdom*. Chapter 9 considers the limits of both practical virtue and Practical Wisdom for Proverbs. It also considers the important role that narrative and moral exemplars—stories and lives in which a full Practical Wisdom is glimpsed—play in virtue ethics, describing how Proverbs both does and does not point its readers to moral agents who can serve as moral models.

After establishing in part 1 the manner in which Proverbs can be said to constitute an ancient virtue-ethics discourse, I consider in part 2 how Proverbs' rhetoric and long-standing interpretive questions might be analyzed afresh. In chapter 10, I revisit the question of the influence Proverbs' "wisdom" discourse might have had on the book of Amos. After discussing the history of this topic, I use a Bakhtinian conception of intertextuality to suggest not that Proverbs overtly drew on Amos or vice versa, but that the two texts reveal a significant relationship to one another in terms of their moral rhetoric. This fact might be explained by the place an early Proverbs scroll held in Israelite and Judahite education.

Chapters 11 and 12 are complementary chapters. Together they consider how Proverbs 8:22–31—the famous description of Woman Wisdom's activities at or before the creation of the cosmos—might be understood as consonant with a virtue-ethics reading of the book. I reconsider whether and how Proverbs' teaching might constitute or promote a kind of natural law. Chapter 11 sketches the way such a question has typically been formulated in Proverbs studies and contends that the matter might be better recast in terms of ancient conceptions of virtue ethics. Instead of suggesting that in Proverbs Wisdom's relation to the cosmos means that humans can discover objective moral orders of creation and thereby discern divinely ordained rules or "natural law" for individuals and society, I suggest that Wisdom's infusion of the primordial "stuff" out of which Adonai creates the cosmos means that humans (and other creatures) are created with a wisdom appropriate to the kind of being we are. Full and genuine wisdom is not discovered "out there" in the laws of the created world, but it can and should be developed from our own human nature—as material, intellectual, spiritual, and social beings whose happiness and well-being typically depend on the attainment of certain natural goods (cf. chap. 3). Because these sorts of conclusions about Woman Wisdom in Proverbs 8 are not common, chapter 12 offers a detailed exegetical discussion of Proverbs 8:22–31 in light of especially ancient Egyptian comparative material. In the end, I suggest it is warranted to consider Proverbs' moral discourse as related to conceptions of natural law, but only in a limited sense and not in ways that such a connection is usually construed.

Chapter 13 takes up the question of how different conceptions of wisdom in the Bible might be considered a "practice" in MacIntyre's sense of the term—that is, as a complex form of human activity that results in human excellencies and by which "conceptions of the ends of goods" are extended.[65] I contend that the notion of wisdom in some biblical texts, and certainly the (Practical)

---

65. MacIntyre, *After Virtue*, 187.

Wisdom of Proverbs, can be well regarded as a kind of moral practice. Chapter 14 points further to how MacIntyre's conception of a practice can inform an understanding of Proverbs as promoting the practice of wisdom. As with MacIntyre's "practice," the ancient sages believed that to be fully wise, one had to submit to a tradition of wisdom and its expert practitioners, while also coming to value the internal goods of that practice over any external goods that might be associated with it. What is more, advancing sufficiently in the practice of wisdom puts a person in the position to critically engage, modify, and advance that practice.

The conclusion of this book concerns itself with the possibility of adequately revising and extending a moral tradition like that of Proverbs. The chapter forthrightly faces the ethical limits and problems of ancient virtue-oriented ethical thought in general, and the contingent and provisional aspects of Proverbs' moral discourse in particular. I suggest that those who wish to stand in the tradition of the book's ancient wisdom must become the sort of expert practitioners of its wisdom who can and should modify and extend the book's insights and concerns to enable more well-being for more people. All of this must be done in light of changing social circumstances, new knowledge of the nature of humans, and the insights of diverse communities of wisdom. I offer an analysis of the final pericope of Proverbs—the poem to the Eshet Chayil—to point to ways the book itself starts to deconstruct the limits of its own moral vision and hence how this portion of Scripture warrants the ongoing work of critically engaging, revising, and extending Proverbs' moral perspectives and traditions.

PART 1

The Case for Proverbs as Virtue-Oriented Moral Discourse

1

The Undervaluing of Proverbs' Moral Worth

The Role of Biblical Studies and Modern Ethics

If the predominately Christian students I have taught over the years are a reliable barometer, many readers of Scripture are fascinated with aspects of the Bible's wisdom literature—especially Job's wrestling with questions of theodicy or "unjust suffering" and the skepticism and/or bold embrace of pleasure in Qohelet.[1] However, although some readers of Proverbs may be enamored with the wit and wisdom the book offers, most do not relish the long lists of everyday advice they encounter in the book. Others may come to appreciate the book, even if only as a text one needs to be familiar with to understand Job's and Ecclesiastes's more profound and engaging theological and ethical views. Whatever the case, few think the theological and moral weight of Proverbs matches that of these other two wisdom books. For many Bible readers, Proverbs is not the go-to text for understanding ancient Israelite or biblical religion and theology, or for theological meditation and ethical reflection on key moral issues facing the world today.

In this chapter I explain why the theological ethics of Proverbs has sometimes been underappreciated. On the one hand, tendencies in twentieth-century

---

1. Christianity is the religious tradition I know best and out of which my engagement with Proverbs' ethics emerges.

biblical studies led to a minimizing of Proverbs' theological-ethical value within the biblical canon. On the other hand, the generally unacknowledged modern moral contexts and presuppositions of the book's interpreters sometimes resulted in negative or, more often, ambiguous accounts of the nature of the book's moral discourse; and this likely also contributed to an ambivalent appreciation of its ethics, especially compared to the value ascribed to the theological-moral visions of other parts of the Hebrew Bible.

Getting No Proverbial Respect

One reason interest in Proverbs has not always been robust may have to do with the limited place it enjoys in the liturgy and life of faith communities. Various Christian denominations appear to share my students' evaluation of the theological-ethical worth of the wisdom literature, and Proverbs in particular. For example, the Revised Common Lectionary, used by a range of Protestant denominations, has only two readings in Ecclesiastes. The significantly longer "literary classic," the book of Job, supplies only seven readings to the lectionary. Readings from Proverbs also number only seven, and four or five of these focus on the image of personified Woman Wisdom (especially in Prov. 8), a historically significant figure in christological discussions and, more recently, a powerful resource for constructive feminist theological work—for example, in imagining nonmale images of the divine.[2]

The relative lack of appreciation for the theological-ethical value of Proverbs is also evident in the history of modern scholarly interpretation of wisdom literature, at least until a few decades ago.[3] Much of the twentieth century's lack of interest in wisdom literature was due to the approach of the so-called biblical theology movement. Especially prevalent in the mid-1900s, biblical theology sought and defined the theological center of the Hebrew Scriptures in terms of key events and notions—such as the exodus, covenant, and historical credos, none of which is particularly evident in Proverbs.[4] The fact that the biblical theology movement was largely carried out in Protestant

---

2. See, e.g., the few readings from Proverbs noted in https://lectionary.library.vanderbilt.edu. The liturgical reading of Proverbs likewise appears sparse in Roman Catholic and Jewish liturgical practice. See "Roman Catholic Lectionary," Word to Worship, https://wordtoworship.com/lectionary/catholic?year=2023; and "Calendar of Torah and Haftarah Readings," Movement for Reform Judaism, 2015, http://www.wimshul.org/wp-content/uploads/2015/03/Version-2-Calendar-of-Torah-and-Haftarah-Readings-5776-5778-.pdf.

3. For a similar but more extensive look at how Proverbs was marginalized, see Hatton, *Contradiction in the Book of Proverbs*, 17–45.

4. Cf. the influential (and at points controversially critical) account of the biblical theology movement and its practitioners offered by Barr in *The Concept of Biblical Theology*.

circles, as opposed to Roman Catholic theological contexts where emphasis on human virtue is more prominent, may also have contributed to earlier failures to recognize the virtue-oriented character of Proverbs' rhetoric.[5]

Yet wisdom studies were never completely marginalized. Various monographs continued to make claims about the nature of Proverbs' instruction, and major commentaries continued to be written. Much of this work touched on the book's theology and ethics.[6] Nonetheless, it was only after Gerhard von Rad devoted significant attention to wisdom texts, both in his *Old Testament Theology* and especially in a 1970 study of the Bible's wisdom texts,[7] that critical academic study of the wisdom literature started to gain steam. Von Rad's creative and robust effort in *Wisdom in Israel* to come to terms hermeneutically and theologically with biblical wisdom literature, including Proverbs, has rarely been matched by other studies.[8]

Despite the waning of the biblical theology movement and the influence of von Rad's book, critical studies of Proverbs after *Weisheit in Israel* (1970)— though increasingly abundant—still only sought in part to robustly appreciate the theological ethics of the book.[9]

The reasons for this are again complex. First, it remained clear that Proverbs does not speak much of significant religious and theological themes central to other parts of the canon—whether the exodus liberation, God's faithfulness (*chesed*) to the ancestors and Israel, the divine giving of Torah and establishment of covenants, or the grand prophetic demands for justice.[10] Additionally, the fact that Proverbs was deemed both universal in its

---

5. Roman Catholics who did participate in the biblical theology movement did so on the terms laid out in the contributions of the major Protestant biblical theologians. Jewish interest in the entire project of biblical theology has been ambivalent, as Levenson explains; see the chapter "Why Jews Are Not Interested in Biblical Theology" (33–61) in *Hebrew Bible, the Old Testament, and Historical Criticism*. More recently, however, some Jewish scholars have demonstrated a keen interest in revised conceptions of biblical theology. See, e.g., Kamili, *Jewish Bible Theology*.

6. See, e.g., Zimmerli's influential work: "Ort und Grenze der Weisheit," reprinted and translated as "The Place and Limit of the Wisdom." Cf. further the mostly German works mentioned in Plöger, *Sprüche Salomos*, xxx–xxxi.

7. Von Rad, *Old Testament Theology*, esp. 1:383–459; von Rad, *Weisheit in Israel* (1972 English translation *Wisdom in Israel*).

8. See, e.g., the critical judgments of various authors in Sandoval and Schipper, *Gerhard von Rad and the Study of Wisdom Literature*.

9. Studies that have treated seriously the ethics and theology of Proverbs after von Rad's *Wisdom in Israel* and prior to Brown's *Character in Crisis* include, but are not limited to, Perdue, *Wisdom and Creation*; and Delkurt, *Ethische Einsichten*.

10. Though, of course, a virtue like loyalty or *chesed* in the wisdom literature is an important trait that wise humans ought to cultivate and practice with others. See, e.g., Prov. 3:3; 11:17; 16:6; 19:22; 20:6, 28; 21:21; 31:26. Proverbs also deeply values justice and social virtue (cf. chap.

moral-theological perspectives and not centrally focused on Israel's particular deity—Adonai (YHWH)—likely also contributed to a limited appreciation of the book's theological ethics. In an influential commentary published the same year that von Rad's *Weisheit in Israel* appeared, William McKane contended that much of Proverbs is originally and fundamentally secular wisdom. Only subsequent redaction of the text resulted in this teaching being overlaid with Yahwistic material that brought it closer to the center of Israelite religion and theology.[11] Proverbs was even at times reckoned as a "foreign" body of literature in the Bible.[12] And the book is clearly related to the instructional material of non-Israelite texts from other ancient West Asian cultures and especially Egypt. A version of the Egyptian Instruction of Amenemope, for example, almost certainly affected the composition of Proverbs 22:17–23:11,[13] while the short sayings of the rest of the second half of Proverbs also resonate deeply with ancient West Asian and Egyptian proverb collections and instructions.[14] The instructional poems of Proverbs 1–9 are likewise influenced by Egyptian prototypes.[15] Proverbs also associates parts of its instruction with named, wise, non-Israelite teachers. Both Agur in Proverbs 30 and the mother of King Lemuel in Proverbs 31 are perhaps "of Massa."[16]

Finally, besides its lack of focus on key Israelite traditions and its supposed universalizing, secular, or foreign character, a further reason Proverbs' moral

---

7 below), though it articulates this concern with a rhetoric that is both similar to and somewhat distinct from that of the great prophets of social justice, such as Amos (cf. chap. 10 below).

11. McKane, *Proverbs*. McKane classified the sayings in Proverbs as "A" material (sayings directed toward individuals designed to help them achieve success); "B" material (proverbs concerned with the community and that censure antisocial behavior); and "C" material (sayings addressed to individuals but that have undergone a Yahwistic redaction).

12. Regularly cited in this regard is Preuss, "Erwägungen zum theologischen Ort alttestamentlicher Weisheitsliteratur"; cf. Steiert, *Die Weisheit Israels—Ein fremdkörper im Alten Testament?*, who argues against the view that wisdom is a foreign body in Israel's Scripture. Cf. the brief discussion in Fox, *Proverbs 10–31*, 948.

13. Cf. Fox, *Proverbs 10–31*, 705–33. Important early studies of Amenemope include Budge, *Facsimiles of Egyptian Hieratic Papyri*; Erman, "Eine ägyptische Quelle der 'Sprüche Salomos'"; Gressman, "Die neugefundene Lehre des Amen-em-ope"; more recently, cf. Bryce, *Legacy of Wisdom*; Römheld, *Wege der Weisheit*; and Washington, *Wealth and Poverty*.

14. Cf. the overview of Proverbs' relationship to "die altorientalischen Weisheit" in Schipper, *Proverbs 1–15*, 11–24. For translations of the ancient West Asian texts that have been compared to Proverbs, see Lambert, *Babylonian Wisdom Literature*. For the Egyptian instructions (and related literature), see Lichtheim, *Ancient Egyptian Literature*.

15. See Whybray, *Wisdom in Proverbs*; cf. Fox, *Proverbs 1–9*, 45–47.

16. The appropriate understanding of מַשָּׂא in Prov. 30:1 and 31:1 is debated. Is it a proper noun referring to "a northern Arabian tribe (Gen 25:14; 1 Chr 1:30; also mentioned in Assyrian sources)"? Or does it refer to an oracle or "pronouncement" (Fox, *Proverbs 10–31*, 852)? Cf. Sandoval, "Texts and Intertexts."

worth has been undervalued over the years surely has to do with the book's perceived naive ethics—what Anne Stewart calls the "simplicity thesis."[17] In particular, Proverbs' cause-and-effect rhetoric has proven a stumbling block to many readers who have understood this language quite literally as a reflection of the ancient writers' underlying view of reality, their straightforward moral-theological recipe for "success." That is, the sages of Proverbs, it has sometimes been thought, understood there to be an "act-consequence nexus" (or *Tun-Ergehen Zusammenhang*) at work in the cosmos whereby good or evil consequences follow almost mechanistically from good or evil deeds.[18] For many interpreters of the book—whether scholars or others—this Tun-Ergehen Zusammenhang becomes particularly problematic morally speaking when Proverbs' offers teaching on things like economic matters. For example, it sometimes appears that the book "blames the poor" for their poverty, understanding in reductionistic fashion a poor person's destitute condition to be caused by that person's failure to follow wisdom; at the same time, it appears to congratulate the rich for their virtue.[19] Proverbs 10:4, for instance, states,

> A slack hand causes poverty,
> but the hand of the diligent makes rich.[20]

And 13:22 says,

> The good leave an inheritance to their children's children,
> but the sinner's wealth is laid up for the righteous.

By contrast to those who see a problematic simplicity in Proverbs' ethics, other interpreters seem to presume that those who compiled Proverbs were not necessarily, or merely, morally naive—unaware of the structural, political, and social "causes" of poverty and wealth. Instead, these interpreters suggest that the sages—who likely formed a part of ancient Israel's political

---

17. Stewart, *Poetic Ethics in Proverbs*, 71 and passim.

18. The classic statement of the act-consequence nexus in the Bible (including Proverbs) is Koch, "Is There a Doctrine of Retribution," 57–87. This is a somewhat abridged translation of Koch's "Gibt es ein Vergeltungsdogma," 1–42. Koch distinguishes between consequences that inhered in certain acts and the retribution for good or wicked deeds that an agent, such as the deity, might enact, suggesting the former is prevalent in the Hebrew Bible. For criticism of Koch's position and articulations of other views that nuance Koch's claims, see, e.g., Adams, *Wisdom in Transition*; Freuling, "Wer eine Grube gräbt . . ."; Janowski, "Die Tat kehrt zum Täter zurück"; and Gese, *Lehre und Wirklichkeit*.

19. Washington, *Wealth and Poverty*, 1; cf. R. Murphy, *Proverbs*, 261; and Van Leeuwen, "Wealth and Poverty."

20. Cf. Prov. 8:18; 12:3, 14, 24; 13:4, 25; 14:14, 19, 23; 18:9; 19:15; 28:25.

and economic elite (or were ideologically beholden to them)—peddled an act-consequence view of reality to their own (and their overlords') benefit. For instance, Dianne Bergant, although she also finds liberative elements in the book, recognizes that "the instruction of Proverbs is a powerful political tool in the hands of the established institutions, whether these institutions are based on kinship, such as the family, clan, or tribe, or on political organization, such as court or scribal schools."[21] J. David Pleins similarly and more forthrightly relates "the values and practices advocated in the wisdom tradition" with "the political and economic leanings of the ruling classes."[22] In other words, some of Proverbs' rhetoric might be heard to suggest that if the wise and just receive real, good rewards, those who enjoy wealth and status must be wise! Once the book's moral discourse is characterized in this way, it is easy to understand why someone would not want to grapple seriously with such (self-serving) moral and theological perspectives.

All these ways of characterizing the "wisdom" of Proverbs—its distance from Scripture's central theological themes, its universalist or secular orientation and close relation to non-Israelite literature, and its simplistic or even ideologically suspect ethics—are somewhat understandable. It is not the case that "all" of this is "all wrong"; aspects are certainly defensible. Erudite and insightful scholars have adopted and promoted some of these typical characterizations of Proverbs, and compelling arguments have been made to support this picture of Proverbs' rhetoric and theological ethics. Indeed, a simple, straightforward, plain-sense reading of the book (in a post-Enlightenment world) will almost "naturally" result in such conventional views and evaluations of Proverbs' wisdom. Such portrayals of Proverbs may sound "kind of right." This view of Proverbs, however, is not so much wrong as it is not exactly right. It is like a portrait hanging crookedly on a wall. One can appreciate the art in its skewed position, but it would be better to straighten it and take another look. Our picture of Proverbs—especially its moral discourse—needs to be adjusted a bit.

Some understandings of Proverbs' moral vision that have left the portrait of the book askew have already been remedied to a significant extent. For example, the idea that wisdom literature was marginal to ancient Israel's particular religious and moral-theological imagination is now often regarded as incorrect. Such a formulation does not fully appreciate the centrality of creation theology in Proverbs or the manner in which the book's moral rhetoric relates

---

21. Bergant, *Israel's Wisdom Literature*, 93.
22. Pleins, *Social Visions of the Hebrew Bible*, 457, cf. 452–83; see also Pleins, "Poverty and the Social World of the Wise," 69; and Pleins, "Poor, Poverty."

to other ethical discourses in the Bible. The importance of God's creation of the cosmos in the wisdom corpus (e.g., Job 28; 38–41; Eccles. 1) rivals the centrality of creation themes in a range of other biblical traditions—whether in Genesis 1–3, Psalms 104 and 148, or the prophet Isaiah's soaring rhetoric of 40:12, 21–26; 43:1–7; 44:24–45:25; and 65:17–25. Indeed, a full reckoning with the role of creation theology in wisdom literature helps make clear that Proverbs, with its insistence on wisdom's place in God's construction of the cosmos (Prov. 3:19–20; 8:22–31), is not the theological outlier in the biblical canon that some have thought it to be.[23] Moreover, renewed efforts to understand the possible relationships between Proverbs' instruction and the Torah, of texts such as Deuteronomy, also indicate Proverbs may have been more central in the moral-theological discussions of ancient Israel than suggested by the paradigms constructed by the largely Protestant Christian efforts at biblical theology.[24]

The view that much of Proverbs is secular or foreign instruction and not fundamentally Yahwistic has likewise long been regarded as not quite right, misconstruing the book's Adonai-centric perspective. For instance, McKane's erudite effort to distinguish between early, secular, or non-Yahwistic material in Proverbs and later material that received a Yahwistic editing has been judged as overstated. As Fox claims, "The flaw with McKane's chronological distinctions is that both religious and secular maxims are found throughout ancient Near Eastern Wisdom literature, and there is no reason to suppose that the first Israelite compilers were restricted to the secular."[25] What's more, criticism of the modern binary that distinguishes sharply between the secular and religious—which has been applied to premodern thought and on which McKane's analysis in part depends—is also now so common it is almost banal to mention it.[26] Likewise, scholars have recognized that it is important not to overstate the religious and theological uniqueness of ancient Israel within its West Asian and Egyptian context. Just as wisdom literature has strong parallels in texts from ancient Mesopotamia and Egypt, so do the Bible's creation accounts, its legal traditions, its psalms, its notions of covenant, and its modes of prophecy.[27] It is all "foreign," even as it also carries unique Israelite and Judahite accents.

23. Cf. Perdue, *Wisdom and Creation*.
24. See, e.g., Schipper and Teeter, *Wisdom and Torah*; cf. Carr, *Formation of the Hebrew Bible*, esp. 403–31; and Schipper, *Proverbs 1–15*, 36–39.
25. Fox, *Proverbs 10–31*, 482.
26. See the keen discussions of Sherwood, *Biblical Blaspheming*.
27. Cf. the similar observation of Plöger, *Sprüche Salomos*, xxxii–iii: "Die Verbindung alttestamentlicher Schriften mit der analogen Literatur in der altorientalischen Umwelt ist Gewiss nicht nur innerhalb des Weisheitsberieches erkennbar" (The connection of Old Testament

If some of the missteps or failures in Proverbs research have been remedied, others have started to be rectified more slowly. For instance, the idea that Proverbs offers a simplistic, mechanical view of ethics is still heard both inside and outside scholarly circles. Most Proverbs scholars recognize that viewing the act-consequence nexus in Proverbs "too mechanistically" or "too simplistically" is not quite right. Simple exegetical observations demonstrate that there is no iron-clad retributive system at work in the book. Many verses in Proverbs reveal that the ancient sages who composed and compiled the text knew that things like prosperity and status do not inevitably follow virtuous acts (e.g., 13:23; 16:8; 21:6; 28:6). They knew the "limits" of their wisdom, as von Rad puts it; and they recognized exceptions to the act-consequence rule, even if they believed that the rule itself was more or less valid.[28] A further exegetical observation that has mollified strong claims about Proverbs' act-consequence view of reality is the recognition that Proverbs' programmatic prologue identifies simple youth (1:4) as a primary audience for the book's instruction. To promise good things like wealth, status, and health to those who follow the book's teachings makes good rhetorical sense if one wants to motivate such an impressionable audience to adhere to instruction—even if such rhetorical promises were likely never meant to be taken in strict literal fashion.

A related response to the supposedly facile (or ideologically suspect) ethics of Proverbs is to regard the book's promises of things like riches, long life, and honor to those who attain wisdom as symbolic claims, rhetorical formulations designed to present wisdom and the life of virtue as the most desirable and valuable thing readers and hearers might acquire.[29] This approach recognizes not only that Proverbs is addressed to simple youth who may be well motivated by literal-sounding guarantees of reward; it also accounts for the fact that the book speaks to advanced students, to wise and understanding persons (1:5)—those who might be skeptical of such promises when understood in too straightforward a fashion. Words like "a slack hand causes poverty, but the hand of the diligent makes rich" (10:4) can thus be heard, on the one hand, in plain-sense terms as the exhortation of a youth to pursue the virtue of diligence, which will pay off, and to avoid laziness, which will not. On the other hand, such a statement can also be heard as a figurative articulation of the book's larger claims about the ultimate value that wisdom and virtue hold in securing human well-being and about the

---

writings with analogous literature in the ancient Near Eastern environment is certainly recognizable within the realm of wisdom).

28. Von Rad, *Wisdom in Israel*, 97–110.
29. See especially Sandoval, *Discourse of Wealth and Poverty*.

detrimental effects of particular vices to that pursuit. Proverbs' older, more experienced, or "wise" readers would likely have appreciated these sorts of more nuanced moral notions. Indeed, even if it is obviously the case that Proverbs' "wisdom prosperity axiom" could never always prove literally true, it nonetheless constitutes what might be called the wisdom mythos of the ancient sages.[30] It provides what Newsom, taking a cue from MacIntyre's work on narrative, calls an iconic story:

> Iconic narratives encode fundamental commitments, social roles, and profiles of virtue that constitute the community. These narratives make meaningful—and therefore possible—certain forms of action. That is, only within the contours of such narratives do certain kinds of action acquire meaning and so become the things one does or refrains from doing. These narratives ring true because they define the horizon of meaningful action within an already given social and moral world.[31]

Still, if Proverbs' motivational rhetoric can be understood figuratively as a kind of iconic narrative and not as literal guarantees that rewards will accrue to the just and wise, this is certainly not the end of the meaning and import of the book's promises of good things. The book's figurative rhetoric depends to an extent on the truth of its literal statements. A symbolic level of meaning does not completely eclipse a text's literal instruction. Rather, both levels function together, for as Paul Ricoeur explains, metaphorical meaning or "secondary signification" emerges only "by means of, or through, the literal one."[32] Proverbs, even when its figurative dimensions are appreciated, still insists that possessing certain virtues and clinging to particular values, living in this way and not another way, can and *ought* to lead to a eudaemonia that entails the attainment and enjoyment of real, exterior or secondary social and material goods—such as wealth, health, and social status (cf. chap. 3). The "problem" of rewards does not completely disappear with appeals to the figurative nature of Proverbs' promises of good things.

Modern Presuppositions

Despite the helpful revision of many scholarly views that undervalued Proverbs' moral discourse, descriptions of the book's moral rhetoric over the last

30. Sandoval, *Discourse of Wealth and Poverty*, 32 and passim.
31. Newsom, *Book of Job*, 123.
32. Ricoeur, *Interpretation Theory*, 55.

half-century have often been somewhat ambiguous. To a large extent this is because Proverbs has not been considered by many to be an ancient virtue-oriented work. More specifically, however, the ambiguity emerges from the kind of ethical language commentators use to describe the character and extent of Proverbs' teaching, especially its retributive or act-consequence rhetoric and logic, and how that ethical-analytical language is understood to function. Indeed, the nature of the ethical language many commentators use to describe and evaluate Proverbs' moral orientation has not always been fully articulated. This state of affairs begs several questions: What ethical systems or orientations provide a context for understanding the critical ethical vocabulary scholars use to explicate Proverbs? Do the ethical terms facilitate understanding Proverbs' moral vision as akin to ancient virtue-oriented traditions, or to some other ethical system? Are any of the ethical systems by which the language of Proverbs is sometimes described and evaluated regarded as more legitimate or more normatively acceptable than others? If so, what are these traditions and why are some of them preferred? Finally, why did such an ambiguity in descriptions of Proverbs' moral vision arise at all? What conditions made it difficult for biblical scholars to describe Proverbs fully as a kind of ancient virtue-oriented moral discourse?

In response to these queries, I suggest that despite Proverbs' ancient provenance—which might have led scholars to consider it more fully in light of similar ancient virtue traditions—interpreters have typically analyzed the book through the frameworks and presuppositions of modern moral systems. At least two Enlightenment strands of ethics have typically been brought to bear on the modern interpretation of Proverbs: utilitarian and deontological modes of thought.[33] This does not mean that the virtue-oriented nature of Proverbs' moral discourse has always been missed or wrongly depicted and subsequently disparaged. But it does mean that the book's moral orientation has sometimes almost systematically been ambiguously described, and consequently its moral worth at times ambivalently appreciated.

Utilitarian Perspectives

Utilitarianism is a complex phenomenon with a long history. Different thinkers have emphasized and elaborated elements of the basic position for centuries. A full presentation of this ethical system is impossible here. Instead,

---

33. For a sketch of philosophical concerns and orientations brought to bear on the modern study of wisdom literature that is not unrelated to what follows here, see Kynes, *Obituary for "Wisdom Literature,"* 82–104.

I will describe only a few of the key characteristics of utilitarian moral discourse that have impacted Proverbs scholarship.

Most basically, utilitarianism is a form of consequentialism, a mode of moral thinking that emphasizes the results or consequences of actions, laws, and policies.[34] Utilitarian ethical thought asserts that one should act in a way that maximizes utility. The quality of moral acts is determined by the usefulness of their outcomes as determined rationally.[35] But utility for what? To what end or consequence? Jeremy Bentham (1748–1832) locates the utility of acts in their ability to maximize an individual's pleasure and minimize pain.[36] John Stuart Mill (1806–73), by contrast, focuses on maximizing overall happiness in the world by insisting that moral agents act rightly when their deeds result in the greatest good for the greatest number.[37] Importantly, for utilitarian thought what constitutes an individual's pleasure or the general happiness is not necessarily objectively or naturally given. It is the subjective determination of liberal or autonomous rational actors.

In classic utilitarian moral reasoning, then, individual humans ought to deploy their rationality to act in ways that maximize utility, although what is maximized may be understood variously—whether pleasure (Bentham), happiness (Mill), or personal preferences, as a more contemporary theorist like Peter Singer (b. 1946) might say.[38] A typical way that humans pursue their own subjectively conceived view of happiness or pleasure, or strive to minimize pain, is to acquire things with clear utility vis-à-vis achieving those ends, things such as wealth, health, and social status—topics that are also quite important to a wisdom book like Proverbs. If the rhetoric of Proverbs, especially when literally or straightforwardly read, appears to promise such desirable things to those who follow wisdom's way, then it might well be considered by many in the modern world to offer a utilitarian moral perspective. Things that help a person achieve a pleasurable and successful life would be a primary motivation for morality. If the reader of Proverbs wants the things of great utility for securing happiness that the book appears to promise—whether riches, honor, or something else—it makes sense that the reader will decide to act in accordance with the book's teaching in order to attain them. It is "rational"

---

34. See Sinnott-Armstrong, "Consequentialism."
35. A convenient and accessible presentation of utilitarian thought is Driver, "History of Utilitarianism."
36. Bentham's position is presented in his *Introduction to the Principles of Morals and Legislation*.
37. Mill's classic formulation is called *utilitarianism*. See Mill, *Utilitarianism*.
38. Singer is well known for his writings on matters such as abortion, animal rights, and euthanasia. Cf. Perry, *God, the Good, and Utilitarianism*.

that such a person would heed the pedagogical impulse of sayings such as Proverbs 20:13 and 22:4.

> Do not love sleep, or else you will come to poverty;
> open your eyes, and you will have plenty of bread. (20:13)

> The reward for humility and fear of the LORD
> is riches and honor and life. (22:4)

If Proverbs' addressees desire material well-being, status, and a long life—all of which might prove eminently useful for securing someone's idea of happiness—they do well to act diligently, in humility, and with religious piety.

Deontological Perspectives

Like utilitarianism, deontological approaches to ethics are varied and complex. I will only discuss the main ideas that have impacted Proverbs scholarship.

In contrast to utilitarianism, a deontological approach to ethics emphasizes rule following or obedience to law. Kant's approach has been most influential in modernity.[39] While utilitarianism emphasizes acts that maximize utility in achieving happiness, Kant says that one should act out of duty to the universal moral law that can be rationally determined. His famous "categorical imperative" suggests that when one acts, one should do so in such a way that the action could be universalized, translated into a rule or maxim that would be valid for everyone, everywhere.[40] Of course, many biblicists are not self-avowed Kantians but theists who sometimes hold strong commitments to divine-command theories of morality. Kant opposes theistic approaches to ethics because for him (Enlightenment thinker that he is), it is the liberal subject's own rationality, not God, that gives us the law—the rules to follow. To follow divine commands would be to give up our autonomy. Yet, divine-command theories of ethics are also obviously deontological; and presupposing the existence of God can give humans—theists anyway—effective reason to believe that the moral law can and ought to be fulfilled. In any case, the immense influence of Kant inspires and informs modern ethical perspectives, theistic and otherwise, that prioritize law or rule following. This is so even if some thinkers—including biblicists—might reject Kant's confidence in the ability of human rationality to lead to right conduct on theological grounds (e.g., the fundamental sinfulness of humans).

---

39. A convenient and accessible introduction to Kant's moral philosophy is Johnson and Cureton, "Kant's Moral Philosophy."

40. On the categorical imperative, see Kant, *Groundwork for the Metaphysics of Morals*.

Importantly, for deontological streams of thinking, a utilitarian perspective—acting morally because I *get* something from it—may not only appear wrongheaded; it can prove scandalous. It may profoundly unsettle a person's deepest, even if unarticulated, (deontological) moral convictions. To do the right thing simply because one gets the *goodies* for doing so smacks of selfishness and greed. Instead, one should do the right thing because it is one's rational duty to do so, or because one ought to obey the rules set down by a legitimate authority like God, even if there is no obvious benefit from doing so. As Julia Annas notes, Kant "sees morality as standing in the sharpest possible contrast with happiness, indeed sometimes only to be achieved by sacrificing happiness."[41]

Virtue-Ethics Perspectives

In contrast to utilitarian and deontological approaches to ethics, neither following the rules of reason or of a legitimate lawgiver nor pursuing acts of utility that might effectively increase a rational actor's subjectively determined view of happiness are central for virtue ethics. What *is* primary is a life characterized by virtue, certain "excellent" qualities of character. The virtues are key because it is only through a virtuous life that people might achieve the final, natural end or telos of human beings: the attainment of a genuine, even objectively valid, eudaemonia or flourishing—though other nonmoral or external goods (e.g., material well-being, social recognition, and so forth) are also typically and intuitively thought to be necessary for a full, happy life (see chap. 3).

Of course, virtue, an ethical notion at the heart of character ethics, is not a foreign concept to other moral systems. It is simply not as central to them, or understood in the same way, as in virtue-oriented moral thought. With character ethics a person's appropriate desires and emotions are intimately related to the virtues. Yet as Annas says, "A common modern view, deriving from Kant, is that virtues are *correctives* to our feelings, and consist essentially in the strength of will to overcome feelings."[42] For Kant, as Thomas Hill and Adam Cureton say, virtue is essentially "a kind of strength and resoluteness of will to resist and overcome any obstacles that oppose fulfilling our moral duties."[43] The emphasis here is hardly on the qualities of character that constitute a good moral agent as in virtue traditions; instead, it centers on a person's singular ability to act rightly in consistently obeying legitimate laws and rules.

41. Annas, *Morality of Happiness*, 449.
42. Annas, *Morality of Happiness*, 53 (emphasis original).
43. Hill and Cureton, "Kant on Virtue," 263.

What is more, just as there is a place for virtue in deontological schemes, so there is a place for laws and rules in virtue ethics. But just as virtue has a different status in deontological thought than in character ethics, so acting rightly by obeying rules is not as central to virtue ethics as it is in deontological thought. One reason for this is because virtue ethics keenly recognizes that in "real life" there might arise any number of situations calling for moral decision and action for which there are no applicable laws or rules. Nonetheless, ethical rules may be quite helpful, especially in leading the moral novice to fuller virtue. As Annas says, "We can give rules to help the learner [of virtue]"—though she adds, "Obviously there is no foolproof recipe or guarantee of success."[44] What is more, as Nussbaum says, because "we are not always good judges," rules can also provide moral agents "constancy and stability in situations in which bias and passion might distort judgment."[45] Still, the "perception of particular cases" that a person's settled good character enables "takes precedence, in ethical judgment, over general rules and accounts."[46] The qualities of one's character and one's way of life, which make possible a life of flourishing, simply are more fundamental than obedience to specific moral precepts.

Deontological schemes thus have a place for virtue, and virtue ethics has a place for rules. Similarly, as in utilitarianism, virtue-oriented moral theories involve the exercise of intellect and human reason to know exactly what constitutes eudaemonia or happiness. Yet, for virtue ethics this is not a subjective undertaking. Instead, it is grounded in an understanding of and reflection on what sort of being humans naturally, and so objectively, are reckoned to be (chap. 3). In contrast to modern utilitarian and Kantian deontological schemes, character ethics considers the self to be naturally and inextricably embedded in and dependent on a broader community. The self is not primarily a "liberal," rational, autonomous individual. Virtue traditions thus see a person's quest to achieve well-being or happiness as an effort that simultaneously seeks the well-being of a larger social entity. Although some moderns may consider this an ideological justification for selfishness, the

---

44. Annas, *Morality of Happiness*, 71. The Stoic elaboration of Aristotelian views especially finds a clear place for rules in the life of the ethical beginner. It is basically correct to say that "the Aristotelian beginner follows the example or takes the advice of a mature and virtuous person; the Stoic beginner follows the rules such a person imparts" (*Morality of Happiness*, 109). Yet, "Aristotle in fact has not thought through the place of rules in the virtuous person's thought." Do rules emerge from the virtuous person's virtuous thinking, which may take "the form of bringing situations under moral rules, so that his reasoning will be 'rule case' reasoning"; or should they be regarded as "rules of thumb, extracted ex post facto from the virtuous person's intuitive judgements rather than leading him to them"? *Morality of Happiness*, 93–94. The latter seems more likely.

45. Nussbaum, *Fragility of Goodness*, 304.
46. Nussbaum, *Fragility of Goodness*, 294.

matter is more complex. For virtue ethics—given that humans are fundamentally social beings—an individual's well-being by necessity depends on the flourishing of others with whom one must exist. My happiness is bound up with the flourishing of those around me. Modern moral subjects formed largely by deontological perspectives might with some justification regard *utilitarian* pleasure seeking as scandalous and suspiciously self-centered because of its concern with a liberal moral subject acting in ways that augment personal pleasure or happiness. Such suspicion directed toward virtue ethics, however, is less warranted. Virtue-oriented moral perspectives, for which a socially embedded individual's eudaemonia is central, should not be collapsed into modern utilitarian or consequentialist thought that is concerned with a liberal subject's happiness.

The eudaemonic emphasis of premodern virtue traditions is, in fact, hardly as egocentric or self-centered as is sometimes thought when these traditions are not adequately distinguished from utilitarian perspectives. Ancient traditions of virtue ethics are certainly formally agent-centered (or "self-centered"). But this does not make them self-centered in content; indeed, "they hardly ever" are.[47] As Annas insists, "Charges of egoism made against ancient ethical theories because of their eudaimonistic form miss the mark completely."[48] One source of this misunderstanding is the tendency of modern ethics to equate morality with the happiness of others and not our own happiness. As Annas again explains, modern ethical thought sometimes suggests that practical reasoning takes two distinct forms: "Prudential where only my own interests are concerned, and moral, when I, separately, bring the interest of others into my reasoning." However, ancient virtue theories, which "allot the interests of others space in the framework of that agent's own happiness," "do not permit this kind of split to develop. Reasoning about my own interests differs neither in kind nor in sphere from reasoning about the interests of others."[49] For ancient virtue ethics, what is necessary in the pursuit of happiness is not a rational determination of actions that will ultimately increase my pleasure or make me (or most of us) happy. Instead, what is key is understanding what "goods" contribute to the thriving or eudaemonia of humans (including me), how they do so, and what virtues must guide efforts to achieve those goods.

Given the important place of utilitarian thought in the modern world and the fact that both ancient virtue traditions and utilitarianism are intimately concerned with the happiness or eudaemonia of individual moral agents and

---

47. Annas, *Morality of Happiness*, 220.
48. Annas, *Morality of Happiness*, 322.
49. Annas, *Morality of Happiness*, 323.

with the role of various goods in securing a person's happiness, it is not hard to understand how ambiguous descriptions of Proverbs' moral orientation arose. As we shall see on the one hand, some of Proverbs' rhetoric—its concern with virtue, "goods," and so forth—might seem to resonate with ancient virtue perspectives. Yet on the other hand, its rhetoric of reward and punishment for good and bad conduct might be understood by modern interpreters as entailing a kind of utilitarian perspective. On this second view, a person can be motivated to act in certain ways because the consequences of those actions enable the attainment of goods that augment personal pleasure or increase one's subjectively determined happiness. If such a utilitarian description of Proverbs' morality emerges, it is easy to discern why modern interpreters influenced by Kantian or theistic deontological ethics would consider such moral rhetoric to be not completely desirable or legitimate, if not downright scandalous.

The utilitarian and deontological ethical frames of reference prominent in modern studies of Proverbs are likely largely responsible for the inability of scholars—at least until the last two decades or so—to recognize how the text can be considered a book of character ethics. The intellectual-ethical context of modernity makes it difficult for commentators to imagine how the goods that the book "promises" to those who follow wisdom's way—whether material well-being, social recognition, or something else—can be part of a *legitimate* virtue-oriented moral tradition that is something other than utilitarian pleasure seeking (at best) or a crass pursuit of personal (or class) advantage (at worst).

Ambiguous Description, Ambivalent Appreciation

If Proverbs' moral rhetoric is regarded, even unconsciously, as a kind of self-interested utilitarianism, modern interpreters who are broadly oriented toward deontological modes of thought—whether Kantian or theistic—may well become suspicious of its moral worth. This is what seems to have happened in much of the early twentieth century: Proverbs' moral orientation was seen as utilitarian or consequentialist, and its ethical value was questioned. As Zoltán Schwáb, who has studied a range of early twentieth-century works on Proverbs, concludes, "It seems that by far the greatest ethical problem for the interpreters of Proverbs before the '30s was that it apparently bases its counsels about right behavior on how profitable that behavior is for the individual."[50]

50. Schwáb, *Toward an Interpretation of the Book of Proverbs*, 15. In this context Schwáb quotes a number of nineteenth-century and early twentieth-century commentators. Cf. further Schwáb's extended discussion in the section entitled "Utilitarianism; Retribution," 15–17.

C. H. Toy's influential commentary from the turn of the twentieth century is a good example of this phenomenon; it also illustrates the manner in which Proverbs' moral discourse has been ambiguously described. Toy speaks of Proverbs with a vocabulary that would be at home in premodern virtue traditions. Most significantly, he notes the book's concern with an individual's eudaemonia. For virtue ethics, eudaemonia constitutes the final "end" or telos of human life and is attainable only through a virtuous life, even if some external goods are necessary for thriving as well. However, like other modern interpreters discussed below, Toy tends to deploy this moral language in a distinct, even pejorative fashion. He both identifies eudaemonia in Proverbs with modern, utilitarian understandings of happiness or pleasure seeking and, just as Annas notes many moderns have done, he does not seem fully to appreciate the other-regarding nature of traditions of virtue ethics. Subsequently, he passes a negative verdict on what he considers Proverbs' undue emphasis on the importance of material and social goods, such as wealth and status. He writes disparagingly that the motivation Proverbs offers "for good living is individualistic utilitarian or eudaemonistic—not the glory of God, or the welfare of men in general, but the well-being of the actor."[51] Although there is little explicit evidence that Toy disparages the book's ethics because of his own adherence to a deontological perspective, his status as a Christian (originally Baptist) interpreter in a post-Kantian age that valued deontological ethics makes it a real possibility.[52]

By the 1970s Gerhard von Rad's *Wisdom in Israel* offered a more appreciative evaluation of Proverbs' theological ethics. Nonetheless, he ambiguously describes the nature of Proverbs' moral discourse. On the one hand, he uses modern, post-Enlightenment language to describe Proverbs' moral rhetoric. He deploys expressions such as the "universality of the human intellectual faculty," the "rational search for knowledge," "sound human reasoning," "enlightened intellectuality," and so forth.[53] On the other hand, von Rad—the expert exegete, Christian theologian, and learned scholar of the ancient world—also recognizes in Proverbs a moral-theological rhetoric that belongs less to any Enlightenment strand of moral reflection and more to something akin to classical virtue traditions. He speaks of Proverbs' wisdom in terms of "a whole way of life"; of the natural grounding of morality; and even of Greek *aretē* (or virtue), as well as the "good," understood "as a force which promotes

---

51. Toy, *Proverbs*, xiv.
52. Olbricht, "Toy, Crawford Howell." Toy was problematically also a product of nineteenth-century critical (Christian) biblical scholarship, which tended to see Proverbs as a "late" Jewish text that offered a view of ethics decidedly inferior to the Christianity that Jesus would inaugurate.
53. Von Rad, *Wisdom in Israel*, 58–59.

both the individual life and community life."[54] However, von Rad's strong concern to incorporate wisdom literature into his broader Old Testament theology, and especially his effort to view it as a moral-theological resource for people of a secular modern age (who surely resonated more with post-Enlightenment strands of ethics than they did with, say, Aristotle), seems to have precluded him from drawing fuller conclusions about the virtue-oriented nature of Proverbs' ethics.

Toy, then, is representative of how some past and present readers of Proverbs have been critical of Proverbs' "utilitarian" morality, while von Rad's work illustrates efforts to interpret Proverbs' theological ethics more appreciatively and as a constructive resource for communities and individuals who consider the Bible a theological and ethical authority. What is common to both Toy and von Rad's work, however, is an ambiguity in the way they depict Proverbs' moral discourse. Both use a moral vocabulary central, though not exclusive, to virtue ethics, and this rhetoric is juxtaposed with typically modern moral-philosophical terminology. But neither makes explicit the larger ethical orientations or systems that inform or "fill out" the meaning of the language they use to describe Proverbs' ethics.

This ambiguity in Toy's and von Rad's description of Proverbs' ethical orientation is also evident among many other interpreters in the late twentieth and early twenty-first centuries—at least among those who do not self-consciously read the book as a kind of ancient virtue ethics (cf. introduction). As with Toy and von Rad, these commentators sometimes deploy a moral rhetoric that could be understood as belonging to two or more moral systems. Scholars might describe Proverbs' moral orientation with an ethical vocabulary that resonates significantly with one ethical system—such as virtue ethics—and then juxtapose that language with an ethical terminology more at home in a different approach to ethics, such as deontological or utilitarian traditions. This all happens without any explanation of what connotations should be ascribed to such terminology.

We have already seen how Barton's earlier work characterizes Proverbs' moral discourse in ways quite similar to Toy's descriptions (cf. introduction above). A similar ambiguity characterizes the ethical language Bruce Waltke uses to describe Proverbs' moral orientation in his important two-volume commentary on the book. Like most others, Waltke speaks of the virtues in Proverbs and the moral character of good and bad agents in the book—an ethical vocabulary at home in, but not exclusive to, virtue-oriented moral traditions. Yet with respect to the book's cause-and-effect rhetoric, especially

---

54. Von Rad, *Wisdom in Israel*, 80.

its promises of "life" (which he believes point to a concept of immortality), Waltke also intimates that in Proverbs God does not reward virtue immediately. Why? So that the book's addressees would not "confound pleasure with piety, using piety and ethics to satisfy his prurient interests." For Waltke, a real danger implicit in Proverbs' rhetoric is that the addressee (and one might assume subsequent readers) will think it legitimate to "substitute eudaemonism (i.e., the system of thought that bases ethics on personal pleasure) for the true virtues of faith, hope, and love."[55] Regardless of the extent to which Proverbs may or may not prioritize the sorts of virtues that Waltke regards as "true" and that obviously become central to Christianity, it is clear that like Toy and the early twentieth-century interpreters of whom Schwáb speaks, Waltke reckons eudaemonism in Proverbs to have more in common with modern utilitarian pleasure seeking than it does with the good and flourishing life with which ancient virtue traditions are concerned.

In his erudite and informative introduction to wisdom literature, the eminent scholar James Crenshaw also ambiguously describes Proverbs' moral discourse. For example, he writes that for the sages who authored books like Proverbs, "hedonism in its classical sense received divine sanction";[56] and in their texts the sages "appealed to a sense of self-interest."[57] Both of those statements might aptly be thought to describe Proverbs in terms of certain ancient traditions of virtue ethics. The hedonism of Epicureanism, for instance, emerged from concerns for the eudaemonia of individuals that broadly characterized those strands of Hellenistic moral philosophy that developed and supplemented Aristotle's ethical views.[58] At the same time, Crenshaw's mention of "self-interest" in wisdom's teaching can be heard not merely as the concern of virtue-ethical traditions with an individual's happiness, but as the sort of critical evaluation of the "eudaemonism" (utilitarianism) that scholars like Toy, the earlier Barton, and Waltke also find in Proverbs.

Crenshaw's ethical terminology for Proverbs' moral perspective is ambiguous in other ways. For instance, he suggests that the Bible's sapiential works indicate that people are capable of "securing their [own] well-being."[59] Such a turn of phrase could again evoke a virtue-ethics discourse and a concept like eudaemonia. Yet "well-being" and the eudaemonia it may suggest also find a place in the lexica of modern reflections on ethics, such as utilitarianism. Adding to the ambiguity of Crenshaw's discussion is his comment that the

55. Waltke, *Proverbs*, 109.
56. Crenshaw, *Old Testament Wisdom*, 11.
57. Crenshaw, *Old Testament Wisdom*, 12.
58. Annas, *Morality of Happiness*, esp. 188–200, 236–44.
59. Crenshaw, *Old Testament Wisdom*, 11, 15, cf. 68–82.

ancient sages "believed that rules of conduct could be ascertained by careful observation, and they devoted considerable energy to spelling out these rules by which to live." This terminology sounds primarily deontological, rather than utilitarian or virtue oriented. Crenshaw goes on to suggest that "the primary concern" of wisdom works "is moral development."[60] Again, moral development and education are key components of virtue ethics (cf. introduction), though they are hardly absent from other moral perspectives.[61]

Roland Murphy's erudite publications often helpfully describe the nature of Proverbs' moral discourse, but they too are ultimately ambiguous. Although Murphy's moral rhetoric is less deontological and more aligned with virtue ethics, he does not explicitly describe Proverbs fully as a virtue-oriented work or in terms of another moral discourse. He relates his own critical ethical vocabulary neither to character ethics nor to another moral system.

Murphy, for instance, recognizes that it is common for scholars "to characterize the Book of Proverbs as a compendium of ethics"—by which he seems to mean a moral code or set of rules in the vein of deontological ethics. Yet Murphy appropriately recognizes that the book's "real intent" is "to form character." As he says, "It does not command so much as it seeks to persuade, to tease the reader into a way of life."[62] Murphy also acknowledges that the relationship between act and consequence in Proverbs is not an ironclad impersonal force. Nonetheless, he suggests that in the main for Proverbs "there is simply the dogged insistence that virtue will prevail," a statement that describes well the wisdom mythos of the book that I mentioned earlier.[63] Whatever the case, Murphy is not explicit about the kind of "virtue" he has in mind, whether a Kantian fulfilling of one's duties to act rightly or something more akin to the classical tradition's moral agent whose virtuous mode of existence is necessary to eudaemonia. However, something close to the latter seems to be the case since he suggests that for the sages who produced

---

60. Crenshaw, *Old Testament Wisdom*, 82n1. In his consideration of wisdom's ethics, Crenshaw also suggests that the sages "achieved an amazing breakthrough: the recognition that virtue is its own reward" (15). He may be thinking here of the book of Job, not only Proverbs. But in any case, the idea that virtue is its own reward suggests that the kind of virtue he has in mind is not precisely the Kantian strength to fulfill one's duty or the "excellencies of character" of Aristotle (and his peripatetic philosophical successors). Instead, Crenshaw sounds somewhat Stoic, reflecting that ancient school of thought that believed virtue alone was sufficient for happiness. Cf. Annas, *Morality of Happiness*, 388–411.

61. On the role that ideas of moral development have in Kant, see Kleingeld, "Kant, History, and the Idea of Moral Development." Kleingeld notes at the outset (59) that "to many commentators, the very idea of moral development has seemed inconsistent with" some "basic Kantian tenets."

62. R. Murphy, *Tree of Life*, 15.

63. R. Murphy, *Proverbs*, 262.

Proverbs, "one is urged to be just/wise in order to live longer, to prosper, to succeed in coping with life."[64] This language seems to prioritize, as do virtue traditions, the moral agent's way of life over obedience to commands, as well as the eudaemonia virtuous living enables. At the same time, Murphy suggests that Proverbs' rhetoric often functions to motivate adherence to the book's instruction. Consequently, to modern ears, the prosperity and success to which he suggests Proverbs' teaching leads can sound distinctly utilitarian, a rather straightforward exhortation to "selfish" (my term) pursuit of one's own pleasure or happiness by adhering to instruction. Indeed, Murphy almost apologetically concludes that "the motivation [Proverbs often offers] may not be as 'pure' as some wish."[65] He appears to concede that Proverbs does, in fact, sometimes seem to promote a crude utilitarianism, though he believes it is "a mistake . . . to deem" the sages' utilitarian-sounding discourse as "simplistic" or to regard Proverbs as a book "of unreality" in which good consequences unproblematically follow adherence to the text's instruction.[66] And finally, despite the shortcomings he discerns in Proverbs' moral vision—and perhaps in a deontological nod to a legitimate lawgiver—Murphy insists that the text's instruction is not "simply to be neglected, for it also involved a relationship to the Lord."[67]

In his valuable commentary, R. N. Whybray also offers a full and subtle, though still ultimately ambiguous, description of Proverbs' moral orientation:

> No distinction is made in Proverbs between the pursuit of happiness and prosperity on the one hand and attachment to moral virtues and religious faith and practice on the other: wisdom embraces both. Morality and religion are presented as essential features of the pursuit of wisdom because they lead to prosperity; but they achieve this because they are in themselves intrinsically good and desirable. This unitary view of life, in which there is no awareness of the modern distinction between "religious" and "secular," is not confined to Proverbs but is characteristic of the Old Testament . . . and . . . much of the ancient Near East.[68]

As a general depiction of the structure of Proverbs' moral rhetoric, Whybray's words offer little to quarrel with. And like so many others, he describes Proverbs with a vocabulary that is central, though not exclusive, to virtue-oriented moral traditions: happiness, prosperity, virtues, the good and

64. R. Murphy, *Proverbs*, 268.
65. R. Murphy, *Proverbs*, 268.
66. R. Murphy, *Proverbs*, 264–65.
67. R. Murphy, *Proverbs*, 268.
68. Whybray, *Proverbs*, 4.

desirable. But also like others, Whybray does not indicate explicitly that he understands Proverbs as an ancient virtue-oriented moral discourse (or in terms of some other moral system). One might wonder how and in what sense he thinks morality and religion—a virtuous life—lead to prosperity for Proverbs. He simply suggests that "they achieve this because they are in themselves intrinsically good and desirable."[69]

Although it is true that for virtue-oriented traditions, virtue itself is good and desirable, for Aristotle and others "wisdom" or virtue holds this status in part because it is necessary to guide one's understanding of and efforts to attain other (external) goods that are also necessary for eudaemonia or thriving. Whybray does not say if this is how he understands virtue and its relationship to "prosperity" in Proverbs. He suggests only that the "unitary view" of Proverbs, which holds the pursuit of prosperity and the pursuit of morality and religion together, results from the fact that Proverbs does not distinguish between secular and religious realms and pursuits—unlike many people today. As true as Whybray's claim about the lack of a secular-religious split in Proverbs is, and despite his use of a moral rhetoric at home in virtue ethics, his description of Proverbs' moral orientation remains somewhat opaque. It is close to but not quite consonant with the way virtue-oriented moral discourses would see the relationship between wisdom/virtue and other human goods.[70]

Still other scholars display ambiguity in the ethical rhetoric they use to describe Proverbs' moral orientation. Tremper Longman speaks of Proverbs' concern with "character and virtue," which is a "calling for something above and beyond the call of duty defined by law," and he speaks of a distinction between "wisdom and law," both of which "make demands upon a person's life and behavior."[71] This opposition of law with virtue suggests that Longman understands Proverbs' moral teaching largely as a kind of character ethics. Dianne Bergant, too, describes the book's moral rhetoric with the language of virtue ethics—of vice and virtue, character or "interior dispositions," and the goal of a "happy and successful" life.[72] Like other commentators, Longman and Bergant each also recognize that for Proverbs a life of virtue and wisdom is closely tied to the attainment of external goods. But it remains

---

69. Whybray, *Proverbs*, 4.
70. Likely this is due to the fact that Whybray regards the "wisdom" of Proverbs not as a kind of full Practical Wisdom akin to *phronēsis* in the classical tradition, but "always" as "life-skill" (*Proverbs*, 4). On the analogy of "wisdom" or being wise as a kind of *technē*, but not identical to the exercise of a skill, see chap. 8 below.
71. Longman, *Proverbs*, 80–81.
72. Bergant, *Israel's Wisdom Literature*, 82, 86, 102.

somewhat unclear in their writing whether what the wise person "gets" in attaining wisdom is the eudamonia of a good and flourishing life that virtue ethics is concerned with, or if it is simply external goods that constitute "prosperity." If the latter, the motivational structure of the book's instruction is easily regarded as utilitarian, whereby one acts to attain what is of most use to achieving one's own pleasure or happiness.

Other scholars, however, are far from ambiguous in their insistence that Proverbs offers no simplistic "utilitarian" ethic. Leo Perdue plainly states that Proverbs does not peddle an "individual utilitarianism or a crass eudemonism limited to the well-being of one's own particular fortune," as he suggests some wrongly believe it does.[73] Holger Delkurt similarly insists that "die These, die Ethik der Weisheit sei im weitesten Sinne opportunistisch, eudämonistisch und utilitaristisch, erwist sich als unzutreffend" (The thesis that the ethic of wisdom is in the broadest sense opportunistic, eudaemonistic, and utilitarian turns out to be incorrect).[74] Instead, Delkurt underscores for his readers the other-regarding dimensions of Proverbs' ethics—something we have said is typically an essential element of ancient virtue thought as well: "Vielmehr möchte die Weisheit gemeinschaftsdienstliches Verhalten um Gottes und des Mitmenschen willen" (Wisdom much more desires community-serving behavior for the sake of God and fellow human beings).[75] Yet beyond such critical remarks that insist Proverbs is *not* a utilitarian tract, neither Perdue nor Delkurt explicitly indicates that Proverbs might constructively be understood as a species of ancient virtue ethics or considered analogous to some other moral system.

The mixed and imprecise manner in which scholars have deployed a critical ethical vocabulary to describe the nature of Proverbs' moral orientation surely goes a long way in accounting for why the book's moral orientation has sometimes been only ambiguously apprehended and its moral worth subsequently only ambivalently appreciated. The scenario emerges because many modern interpreters have largely sought to understand the book's rhetoric and moral perspectives via a critical ethical vocabulary that belongs in part to ancient character ethics but, at the same time, is present in significant post-Enlightenment ethical discourses. When the critical terminology used to analyze Proverbs is not clearly identified as belonging to one or another moral theory or tradition, uncertainty emerges. Descriptions of Proverbs from some late twentieth- and early twenty-first-century scholars sound as if the

73. Perdue, *Proverbs*, 42.
74. Delkurt, *Ethische Einsichten*, 148.
75. Delkurt, *Ethische Einsichten*, 149.

book may represent a virtue-oriented tradition. Yet modern readers tend to understand the book's promises of good things to individuals who achieve a life of wisdom as a kind of utilitarian pleasure seeking. And these latter interpreters, many of whom have surely been deeply formed by modern deontological ethical cultures, are suspicious of the sort of utilitarianism they perceive in Proverbs.

A Long Story Made Short

If Proverbs' moral orientation has often been described ambiguously and its worth ambivalently appreciated, then one might ask how this state of affairs came about in the first place? Why—even when they consider the moral vision of an *ancient* text like Proverbs—have scholars been slow to turn fully to *premodern* virtue-oriented traditions of ethics to understand it? And why has the rhetoric of virtue ethics so often ended up intertwined with *modernist* moral discourse in helter-skelter fashion? The answers to these questions have to do not only with the rise of modern ethical systems but also with the ruptured relationship of the modern world and its ethics with premodern moral thought and natural philosophy.

The simple version of the story goes something like this: the modern world has suffered from what Alasdair MacIntyre describes as a kind of confused and sharply fragmented appropriation of premodern moral systems, discourses, and modes of thought.[76] MacIntyre begins his foundational work, *After Virtue*, by asking readers to imagine a world where modern science's texts and theories have suffered "the effects of a catastrophe" so that everything is destroyed except fragments. From these broken pieces of scientific discourse others later try to restore the scientific endeavor, a task that inevitably results in abundant half-truths and misconceptions. He writes: "The hypothesis I wish to advance is that in the actual world which we inhabit the language of morality is in the same state of grave disorder as the language of natural science in the imaginary world which I described."[77] Ted Clayton explains that for MacIntyre morality in the modern world is constituted by "bits and pieces of philosophies which are detached from their original pre-Enlightenment settings in which they were comprehensible and useful."[78]

In the small slice of modernity called biblical studies—and, more narrowly, Proverbs studies—evidence for MacIntyre's claims can be fairly easily

---

76. MacIntyre, *After Virtue*; MacIntyre, "How Moral Agents Became Ghosts."
77. MacIntyre, *After Virtue*, 1–2.
78. Clayton, "Political Philosophy."

discerned. Proverbs scholars (as just discussed) deploy an ethical vocabulary that is at home in virtue ethics but also evident in other moral systems, without making clear what sort of ethical discourse should inform the meanings of such rhetoric. Biblicists like Toy, Waltke, and (the early) Barton, for example, use an ancient moral concept like eudaemonia as a kind of shorthand expression for what they perceive as the book's consequentialist thought. A significantly more complex example is von Rad's *Wisdom in Israel*, where not only the terminology but a real appreciation for ancient ethics appears in his articulation of ancient Israelite wisdom thinking.

Von Rad characterizes the premonarchic epoch of Israel's history as an era of ancient "pan-sacralism," where every significant event "was encompassed by rites and sacral ordinances," a way of life that left little space for a "rational search" for knowledge.[79] This pan-sacralism gave way in the Solomonic era to an "Enlightenment," where human reason played a leading role in the development of proverbial wisdom that articulated the "rules" for coping with life (*Lebensbewältigung*).[80] With this story of wisdom in ancient Israel, von Rad was concerned to bring about a Gadamerian *Horizontsverschmeltzung* ("fusion of horizons") between the *Horizontsverstehen* of his own mid-twentieth-century European context and the *Horizontsverstehen* implicit in ancient Israel's wisdom literature.[81] However, as an heir of modernity's fractured moral discourse, which MacIntyre describes, von Rad's analysis of a text like Proverbs is only able to gesture toward the categories of ancient virtue thought, which are submerged in modern philosophical and moral concepts. On von Rad's own Gadamerian terms, virtue-oriented moral thinking constitutes a significant feature of Proverbs' *Horizontsverstehen*. Yet it is one to which von Rad did not—or, in light of MacIntyre's analysis, could not—fully attend when mediating a fusion of horizons with his own modern European context. As a result, von Rad in a sense simply "rewrites" the early history Israelite wisdom as the story of modernity, where unproblematic, premodern faith in the divine and a numinous cosmos gives way to an enlightened, reason-filled human reality that need not posit the existence of God—only in von Rad's account of ancient Israel's quest for wisdom, there is no fall away from faith in the divine or failure to acknowledge the deity's action in

---

79. Von Rad, *Wisdom in Israel*, 58–59.

80. Others use similar rhetoric to describe Proverbs' moral discourse, though without deploying as fully as did von Rad the ethical terminology most at home in virtue ethics. Plöger, e.g., notes that wisdom, with its interest in the everyday life of individuals, "bemüht sich ... um Verhaltensregeln, um das Leben möglichst erfolgreich zu gestalten" (strives to design rules of conduct to make life as successful as possible). Plöger, *Sprüche Salomos*, xxxiv.

81. See Van Leeuwen, "*Weisheit* in the Intellectual Context."

the world, as in modernity: "The process of secularization which definitely began in the early monarchy does not, in the teachings of the wise men [of Proverbs], go hand in hand with a disintegration of faith in Yahweh's power. That would be a simple and, to us, familiar process."[82]

Consequently, in von Rad's hands a wisdom book like Proverbs becomes a theological exhortation to modern persons, if not a rebuke. It declares that religion and faith in God, on the one hand, and reason and Enlightenment, on the other, are not mutually exclusive but can and ought to complement one another: "The idea of life completely embedded in sacral ordinances has gone. But this has by no means affected faith in Yahweh. It, rather, has become part of a completely new form of understanding reality."[83]

With von Rad's account of Israel's wisdom literature, we glimpse how descriptions of virtue-oriented aspects of Proverbs, when paired with modern ethical-philosophical categories, give way to the emergence of a "wisdom kerygma" (my term) that announces the possibility of successfully negotiating typically modern preoccupations and problems of faith and reason. Though undoubtedly a sophisticated hermeneutic and important theological achievement, von Rad's *Wisdom in Israel* also serves as a subtle but significant example of MacIntyre's account of modernity's ruptured relation with the premodern past and the confusion or ambiguity it precipitated in ethical discourse.

A longer story of how and why post-Enlightenment ethical theories led to ambiguity and ambivalence with respect to Proverbs' moral discourse relates to a fuller version of MacIntyre's account of modernity's rupture with the premodern past. It also relates to a cognate tale about the rise of the historical-critical method in biblical scholarship. In both stories the rise of modern science plays a leading role.

The Rise of Modern Science and Aristotelian Decline

One particular characteristic of the modern world that underwrote the rise of the historical-critical method in biblical studies and contributed to the difficulty that modern commentators have had in recognizing the virtue-oriented character of Proverbs' moral discourse is the emergence of modern science.[84] The most significant feature of modern science for the present discussion is

---

82. Von Rad, *Wisdom in Israel*, 61; cf. 98.
83. Von Rad, *Wisdom in Israel*, 61.
84. On the rise of early modern science, see especially Harrison, *Bible, Protestantism, and the Rise of Natural Science*. The discussion that follows is indebted to Harrison's account.

its rejection of a hitherto intellectually dominant Aristotelian natural philosophy. By the early seventeenth century, Francis Bacon (1561–1626) had famously banned Aristotelian metaphysics from the emerging scientific enterprise of his day. Such a development had enormous consequences. Once people started understanding the world more fully in scientific terms, the worth of premodern natural philosophies, which presumed an intrinsically meaningful or "enchanted" cosmos, was minimized.[85] Although most prominent representatives of the new scientific worldview in early modern Europe could still, through their Christian religion, acknowledge the divine creation of the universe, Aristotle's natural philosophy—hitherto the preeminent intellectual framework for understanding the cosmos—came to be regarded as belonging to an earlier and now intellectually suspect age.

In particular, Bacon rejected aspects of Aristotelian causality as incompatible with the principles and procedures of modern science. Aristotle famously spoke of four types of causes for every activity:[86]

1. a material cause ("that out of which" something emerges—e.g., the bronze out of which a statue might be fashioned);
2. a formal cause (an "account of what it is to be"—e.g., the shape of the statue);
3. an efficient cause (the "primary source of change or rest"—e.g., the artisan who shapes the statue); and
4. a final cause (the end or "that for the sake of which a thing is done"—e.g., decoration as the end of a statue or health as the end of a surgical tool).

For Bacon, Aristotle's formal and final causes were to be jettisoned in the project of modern natural science. Only material causes and efficient causes could be reconciled with an emerging Enlightenment rationalism (Descartes; 1596–1650) and empiricism (Bacon), which were both central to early modern science. As the scientific method of Bacon and others was refined and became dominant, it birthed a mechanical view of the workings of the natural world, perhaps culminating in Isaac Newton's laws of physics. Natural science, with its strong empiricist concerns, would also become the model for "scientific" investigation in other realms, including ethics and the study of the Bible.

---

85. Cf. Taylor, *Secular Age*.
86. See Aristotle, *Physics* II 3; *Metaphysics* V 2. For a convenient discussion of Aristotle's views, which I draw on here, see Falcon, "Aristotle on Causality."

In terms of the study of Proverbs, one point about the rise of the natural sciences and its impact on other fields needs to emphasized. Once Aristotle's intellectual status waned and he was no longer regarded as a preeminent academic authority, the way was open for other moral-philosophical perspectives to gain ascendency in the emerging (European) modern world. With the decline of Aristotle's natural philosophy, his conception of ethics that privileged virtue also suffered in reputation. Eventually, as noted above, utilitarianism and Kantian deontological ethics came to prominence. Understandably, then, when biblical scholars in the modern era have attempted to understand Proverbs' moral rhetoric, ancient conceptions of virtue like that promulgated by Aristotle were not—and, again, could not be—much accessed as apt analogues for understanding that book. Scholars working in this modern context were able only haltingly, as MacIntyre explains, to recognize and understand the ancient virtue perspectives that a text like Proverbs presupposes and represents. Instead, modern, scientifically trained students of the Bible quite naturally described and analyzed Proverbs through the lenses of the prominent utilitarian and deontological moral discourses of their own day.

The Historical-Critical Approach

The rise of modern science and the eclipse of Aristotle paved the way for the emergence of ambiguous descriptions of Proverbs' moral orientation and a subsequent ambivalent appreciation of its moral worth. But another factor also played a role: the rise to prominence of a typically modern way of reading the Bible. Early modern scientific discourse had a role to play in this phenomenon as well.

The development of historical-critical approaches to the study of the Bible will be well known to readers of a book like this and so won't be rehearsed here.[87] Suffice it to say it involves biblical studies' relationship to larger historical movements and forces that include Renaissance concerns to return *ad fontes*, to the sources, of the classical and biblical past; Reformation challenges to entrenched ecclesial authority that resulted in the eclipse of earlier allegorical and typological modes of Bible interpretation; the subsequent rise of authoritative literal or plain-sense interpretation of Scripture;[88] the emergence of a robust Enlightenment individualist rationality, coupled with a strong historical consciousness; and, as we said, the rise of natural science—a

---

87. See, e.g., Reventlow, *Authority of the Bible*; and Rogerson, *Old Testament Criticism*, esp. 15–27, 147–57.
88. A classic account of this hermeneutical shift is Frei, *Eclipse of Biblical Narrative*.

discourse that would make strong claims about the mechanistic workings of the universe that could be discovered by empirical observation.

Together these intellectual movements resulted in seismic epistemological shifts. In the shorthand of Eurocentric historiography, these shifts have resulted in the separation of modern from premodern European civilization. Although it did not happen overnight and there were attempts in the early modern period to reach epistemological compromises, the forces of emerging modernity fueled the emergence of historically oriented, critical, and scientific biblical studies. And *that* discourse tends to locate the true, and really the only legitimate, meaning of a text with its historically original and plain singular sense.[89]

Such hermeneutical concerns—with singular historical and plain-sense meanings of texts—were not only a feature of historical-critical approaches to the Bible. They also could be inflected in more theological approaches to biblical interpretation, since Protestant interpreters in particular tended to privilege plain-sense readings of Scripture. In both cases, however, the Bible's language, including Proverbs' moral rhetoric, is understood primarily in literalistic terms—and this sometimes despite a text's own hints that readers shouldn't read it that way (chap. 2).[90] If a text like Proverbs literally or straightforwardly seems to suggest a simple retributive view of ethics (even with some exceptions to the rule)—for example, that riches (and other goods) await those who acquire wisdom—then that is its meaning, whether understood merely as its historically original meaning or in terms of theological ethics as "Word of God." Klaus Koch's 1955 formulation of a nearly mechanistic act-consequence nexus in the Bible fits this intellectual climate.[91] Of course, an essentially literal or straightforward reading of Proverbs' "cause-and-effect" discourse, in which reward appears to flow easily from virtue, can also be taken to fit nicely with modernist, utilitarian moral rhetoric in which individuals

---

89. On the complicity of biblical studies with the European colonial and imperial projects of modernity, see Cuéllar, *Empire, the British Museum, and the Making of the Biblical Scholar*.

90. Much of biblical studies has moved beyond reading the Bible in only straightforward, literal ways or primarily with historical concerns and methods in mind. Instead, interpreters regularly recognize how the figurative dimensions of biblical texts, their literary and rhetorical structures, and the concerns readers bring to the act of reading all contribute to the Bible's multiple meanings. See the helpful sketch of recent approaches to the Bible in McKenzie and Kaltner, *New Meanings for Ancient Texts*. When it comes to Proverbs, certainly most studies appreciate well the book's poetic discourse and the figurative devices it deploys, its tropes and metaphors. On this topic see especially Stewart, *Poetic Ethics in Proverbs*.

91. And this despite its emergence in a post-Newtonian world inaugurated by Albert Einstein's "new physics," which appeared at the turn of the century. See Koch, "Is There a Doctrine of Retribution."

pursue those things that are of most utility in achieving their own pleasure or subjectively determined conception of happiness.[92]

However, as we shall next see, significant evidence suggests that Proverbs' moral rhetoric should not be read only or so fully in straight, literal terms; it can also be understood as symbolic discourse. A close look at Proverbs' prologue reveals not only how much Proverbs prizes virtue—especially social virtue and Practical Wisdom (see chaps. 7 and 8–9, respectively); its emphasis on the figurative dimensions of Proverbs also lays the hermeneutical groundwork for recognizing how the text uses images of real, nonmoral "goods"—whether wealth, status, health, or something else—in symbolic fashion, first in relation to the book's act-consequence rhetoric (chap. 2) and then in the text's efforts to direct its addressees' desires for various goods toward a yearning for wisdom or virtue itself (chap. 5).

---

92. The most significant exceptions to plain-sense, literal-leaning readings of Proverbs are found in feminist analyses of passages that speak of the prominent female figures of Prov. 1–9—Woman Wisdom, Woman Folly, and the strange or foreign woman. The bibliography on these figures is extensive, but see esp. Camp, *Wisdom and the Feminine* and "What's So Strange"; Yee, "'I Have Perfumed My Bed'"; Maier, *Die fremde Frau in Proverbien 1–9*; and Newsom, "Woman and the Discourse of Patriarchal Wisdom." See also Goering, "Honey and Wormwood"; and Sandoval, *Discourse of Wealth and Poverty*. The last two studies are not focused on the female figures in Proverbs but tend rather fully to the literary and figurative dimensions of Proverbs' poetry.

2

The Prologue as Hermeneutical Key

Categories of Virtues and Figurative Language

Several scholars, including myself, have pointed to the importance of the prologue of Proverbs (1:2–7) for understanding the book's moral goals.[1] The prologue is commonly regarded as the hermeneutical key for reading the book.[2] It constitutes the text's own articulation of its purposes and the nature of its instruction.[3] Most important for the present work are two points about Proverbs' opening lines: (1) the way they sketch key categories of virtue—intellectual, practical, and especially moral social (vv. 2–4)—that are at the heart of the book's virtue-oriented moral discourse, and (2) how they make clear that much of the instruction in the book should not be read only or merely in straightforward, literal ways but instead should invite fuller, sometimes figurative modes of interpretation. Both points are significant for subsequent discussions that contend Proverbs can to a large extent be regarded as a premodern, virtue-oriented moral discourse.

Recognizing that Proverbs itself firmly suggests its moral discourse should not always be regarded as straightforward instruction opens up possibilities

---

1. Brown, *Character in Crisis*, 23–30; and Sandoval, "Revisiting the Prologue."
2. E.g., R. Murphy, *Tree of Life*, 16; and Fuhs, *Das Buch der Sprichwörter*, 12, 37.
3. See Sandoval, "Revisiting the Prologue," in particular.

for recognizing (in this chapter) how premodern notions of causality might inform our understanding of Proverbs' act-consequence rhetoric, especially how and why in that rhetoric certain images of good and valuable things in the book function as figures of flourishing. A consideration of Proverbs' prologue, however, will also pave the way for recognizing other figurative aspects of the book's discourse; in chapter 5 below we will see how, by way of literary symbolism, the text seeks not to eliminate but to train its readers' desires for various goods while promoting a yearning for wisdom or virtue itself—an ethical exercise that is central to virtue-oriented moral theories. Chapters 7–9 will subsequently explore how Proverbs elaborates on the sorts of virtues the prologue highlights.

The Prologue (1:2–7)[4]

Proverbs begins with a superscription that gives the book its Hebrew name—*Mishlei* (proverbs)—and associates the text's instruction with Israel's legendary wise king, Solomon (1:1). The prologue proceeds as follows:

> For learning about wisdom and instruction,
>   for understanding words of insight,
> for gaining instruction in wise dealing,
>   righteousness, justice, and equity;
> to teach shrewdness to the simple,
>   knowledge and prudence to the young—
> Let the wise also hear and gain in learning,
>   and the discerning acquire skill,
> to understand a proverb and a figure,
>   the words of the wise and their riddles.
> The fear of the LORD is the beginning of knowledge;
>   fools despise wisdom and instruction. (1:2–7)

Proverbs' Virtues

These opening lines of Proverbs highlight the book's moral purposes through a series of infinitive constructions. The text wants to instill in its audience intellectual virtues ("wisdom," "insight"; 1:2), moral-social virtues ("righteousness, justice, and equity"; v. 3), and practical virtues ("shrewdness," "prudence" or cunning; v. 4). The literary design of the poem, not always evident in

---

4. This section draws much from Sandoval, "Revisiting the Prologue."

English translations, suggests that the book especially prizes the moral-social virtues of verse 3, which stands at the pinnacle of the prologue's structure.[5]

The Purpose of Proverbs (1:2–4)

A. To instill intellectual virtues (v. 2)
    (2a) for (לְ) knowing wise instruction
    (2b) for (לְ) understanding words of insight
  B. To instill social virtues (v. 3)
    (3a) for (לְ) gaining instruction in wise dealing
    (3b) righteousness, justice, and equity
C. To instill practical virtues (v. 4)
    (4a) for (לְ) giving to the simple cunning
    (4b) to (לְ) the youth, knowledge of shrewdness

The Invitation (1:5–6)

A. The call (in the jussive) to the one who would be wise (v. 5)
    "let the wise . . . gain in learning"
B. The tasks of the one who takes up the call (v. 6)
    "to understand a proverb and a figure . . ."

As the outline above indicates, both halves of Proverbs 1:2 begin with the Hebrew letter *lamed* and underscore the book's concern with intellectual virtues. Both stichs of 1:4 also begin with *lamed*, while highlighting the important role of practical virtues in Proverbs' moral program. Proverbs 1:3 breaks this literary pattern. Although verse 3a likewise begins with *lamed*, the second half of the line (v. 3b), significantly, does not. In essence verse 3b defines for the hearer or reader of the book what precisely and fundamentally the "wise dealing" (הַשְׂכֵּל, sometimes rendered "success") at the end of verse 3a consists of—namely, righteousness, justice, and equity (rectitude).[6] The shift in the prologue's literary structure at verse 3 sets this verse apart from the others and points to Proverbs' emphasis on moral-social virtue. Verse 5 subsequently

---

5. Brown (*Character in Crisis*) also makes this point, though via somewhat different literary observations.
6. For the rendering of מֵישָׁרִים as "rectitude" in 1:3, see Fox, *Proverbs 1–9*, 60. On the literary pattern of the prologue, its ancient West Asian and Egyptian parallels, and other matters, see Sandoval, "Revisiting the Prologue," where I understand the presence of the preposition *lamed* to be the key to analyzing the prologue's structure, rather than its disjointed infinitive structure, as do Brown and others.

serves as an invitation to any hearer/reader of the book to assume the position of one who would become wise by following Proverbs' instruction, and verse 6 points to the broadly figurative nature of the wisdom discourse that a reader will need to negotiate to fully absorb the work's wisdom. The final line in the prologue (v. 7), sometimes called the book's motto, asserts that the religious virtue of "fear of the LORD" undergirds and supports the book's broader social-ethical concerns.

Although rendering הַשְׂכֵּל as "success" in Proverbs 1:3 (as do some commentators and translations) is defensible, it is better translated "wise dealing" (so NRSV). The decision to translate the term as "success" is probably related to the sorts of ambiguous understandings of Proverbs' moral orientation discussed above, where the text is thought to reflect a kind of utilitarian ethical perspective rather than being understood as a book of character ethics.[7] If one does render הַשְׂכֵּל as "success," Proverbs should be understood as (re)defining this notion for its audience. Wisdom constitutes the key to flourishing, not the path to mere acquisition and accumulation of desirable, lesser goods (e.g., wealth or status), which many wrongly believe can ensure their happiness. Although external goods in virtue-oriented moral discourse are hardly irrelevant to one's happiness, "success" for Proverbs fundamentally entails thriving via the attainment of virtue. The moral-social virtues of which the second half of verse 3 speaks are likely especially prized, as the prologue's design suggests, because intellectual and practical virtues, when considered abstractly, can be reckoned as morally neutral. They gain their moral status and worth only in the contexts of their exercise; one can use intelligence or cunning for good or bad purposes. Consequently, for the ancient sages, the intellectual and practical virtues contribute to genuine "wisdom" only when they are rightly ordered and understood in relation to the moral-social virtues of justice, righteousness, and equity. As we shall see more fully below (chaps. 8–9), the wise and just person for Proverbs is the one who possesses a robust Practical Wisdom that is used to appropriately integrate and exercise a full range of virtues to understand and pursue goods, including exterior goods, that contribute to human thriving.

Besides valuing intellectual, practical, and social-moral virtues, the prologue of Proverbs also suggests that both simple youth *and* advanced sages (cf. 1:4–5) can be instructed in these virtues and thereby travel the "way" or path of wisdom and justice. This makes sense in terms of ancient virtue-oriented ethics. On the one hand, the book does not offer its moral beginners—the

---

7. That is, if Proverbs offers a simple, act-consequence guide to prosperity, reckoned largely as economic prosperity, then following its instruction results in something that holds great utility for individuals who seek to increase their own pleasure or happiness.

young and simple—strategies by which to solve ethical quandaries, which Julia Annas explains is a key concern for some modern conceptions of ethics. Instead, Proverbs will show itself to be a text like other ancient virtue-oriented systems. Such discourses should not be "seen *primarily* as mechanisms for answering ethical questions at all; they arise from the reflection provoked in an intelligent person about the shape and course of his life, not from the presumption that the intelligent agent will find lots of ethical questions facing him and will require a theory to answer them for him."[8]

In virtue traditions novices are instructed first in ethical problem-solving but are invited into a way of life where those more advanced in the moral life—the wise and just—serve as examples and guides to be followed (cf. chap. 9). Ancient virtue theories "assume that correct decisions are reached by agents who have accepted and lived by the theory."[9]

On the other hand, because the virtues constitute a way of living that is developed in order to improve one's life "as a whole," morally mature agents, such as those mentioned in Proverbs' prologue, will also regularly reflect on their life journeys. They will consider afresh the nature of the virtues they have valued and exercised in efforts to decide and act well—or for the good—in various life contexts. Indeed, for virtue traditions "the pressure to revise initial judgements in the interests of consistency and unification of the agent's life will be strong"; even accomplished moral subjects may at points decide to make key "course adjustments" regarding the paths they travel.[10] The text of Proverbs, with its early invitation to the "wise" to "hear and gain in learning," provides a site for this sort of ongoing, mature, reflective, intellectual-moral work, a matter we will return to in the conclusion.

Proverbs' prologue, however, also insists that the one who follows the "right" way will come to know wisdom by learning to understand a "proverb" (or trope), a "figure," and "riddles" (1:6). These words might be thought to designate specific literary forms used in the book. A "proverb" (מָשָׁל) in the Bible can refer to the kind of short sayings found in Proverbs 10–29. However, it can denote other literary forms too—for example, a taunt (Isa. 14:4 and elsewhere); a prophetic oracle (Num. 23–24 passim); or an allegory (Ezek. 17:2; 24:3). The Hebrew term מְלִיצָה, rendered above as "figure," similarly does not seem to refer to a unique literary form. Instead, it more broadly suggests a mode of speech (Hab. 2:6; cf. Gen. 42:23; 2 Chron. 32:31; Job 16:20; 33:23). A genuine riddle (חִידָה), though certainly known in the Hebrew Bible (Judg. 14:12–19), is probably not to be found in Proverbs, although some have

---

8. Annas, *Morality of Happiness*, 443 (cf. 334–35) (emphasis original).
9. Annas, *Morality of Happiness*, 125.
10. Annas, *Morality of Happiness*, 114.

suggested that riddles might lie behind some numerical sayings of Proverbs 30. All the terms of Proverbs 1:6—individually and especially when considered together—thus connote some sort of figurative language or discourse in need of interpretation.[11] Rather than naming specific forms of speech in the book, they more probably together describe the nature of the book's moral discourse and of the project of acquiring, understanding, and advancing in the wisdom the text proffers. Following wisdom's way means gaining intellectual, moral-social, and practical virtue as Proverbs 1:2–4 claims—certainly. But reckoning with Proverbs' presentation of wisdom's way is not a simple activity. Understanding the book's articulation of the wisdom that one should pursue will demand some hard interpretive work, like the unraveling of a riddle or the exploration of a trope or figure.

The final verse of Proverbs' prologue introduces another important and much discussed concept for biblical wisdom literature: the fear of the Lord (1:7; see also 8:13; 9:10; Job 1:1; 28:28; Eccles. 12:13). As Fox recognizes, the expression can refer to a certain awe and respect for the holy Other. However, the notion of the fear of the Lord also retains traces of literal fear of a powerful deity, a fear that can motivate adherence to wisdom's way, as do the promises of reward and punishment elsewhere in Proverbs.[12] As Proverbs 22:23 notes, those who stray from wisdom's way and rob the poor (22:22) ought to expect retribution from Adonai:

> for the LORD pleads their [the poor's] cause
> and despoils of life those who despoil them.

The emphasis on fear of the Lord as the beginning of wisdom (or knowledge) at the end of Proverbs' prologue thus places the intellectual, moral-social, and practical virtues of wisdom's way (cf. 1:2–4) in intimate connection with a fundamental religious virtue—although ancient writers/readers would not have distinguished moral and religious dispositions or presuppose a religious-secular split in the sharp way many contemporary people do. As Carol Newsom aptly notes, "Wisdom literature is centrally concerned with the nature of the proper moral and religious conduct of an individual and with the relation of such conduct to personal and communal well-being."[13] All the virtues that Proverbs knows belong to wisdom (Practical Wisdom; cf.

---

11. See Sandoval, "Revisiting the Prologue," for a discussion of the three terms, which occasionally appear in pairs in the Hebrew Bible in different combinations (e.g., Pss. 49:5 [49:4]; 78:2; Ezek. 17:2; Hab. 2:6).
12. Fox, *Proverbs 1–9*, 69–71; cf. C. Yoder, "Forming 'Fearers of Yahweh.'"
13. Newsom, "Job," 326.

chaps. 8–9), which itself is intimately related to Adonai and Adonai's creation (cf. Prov. 8:22–31; chaps. 11–12).

However, if Proverbs' prologue serves as a hermeneutical key for the book, the precise nature and content of the virtues it signals as central to its moral vision—a vision that will require interpretive effort to understand fully—is introduced only sporadically in the book's early chapters (Prov. 1–9). They come to expression more fully in the later collections of short proverbial sayings (Prov. 10–31). Chapters 7 and 8–9 below will explore the prominent place that both social virtue and Practical Wisdom hold in traditions of character ethics and especially in Proverbs itself. However, in the next section, we will attend to the figurative or symbolic dimensions of the book's moral discourse, which the prologue tells us to be ready for. Chapter 5 will do this more extensively, exploring the way Proverbs strives to train its addressees' desires.

How the Prologue Informs the Book's Cause-and-Effect Rhetoric

When we recognize how Proverbs' prologue points both to the centrality of virtue in its instruction and to the figurative dimensions of that instruction, we begin to see how the book's cause-and-effect rhetoric is not completely compatible with modernist moral thought. We noted in chapter 1 that many of the intellectual, historical forces behind the modern world contributed not only to the eclipse of ancient moral theories; they also underwrote the rise of historical-critical and much theological interpretation of the Bible, privileging singular historical and plain-sense meanings of texts. Such literalistic reading of Proverbs' moral rhetoric enables a reading of the book that fits with a modern moral perspective like utilitarianism, but it goes against the book's own hermeneutical key (the prologue; 1:2–7) by largely ignoring the figurative dimensions of the text and misconstruing the role of virtues in the book's rhetoric. A "means-end" or "cause-and-effect" rhetoric is an important feature of Proverbs, and it can be explained in fresh ways when we do not valorize literalistic interpretations of the book and when we set aside modernist moral thought, recognizing instead that an ancient moral discourse like Proverbs has much in common with (other) premodern understandings of ethics—like that of the classical tradition descending from Aristotle. Proverbs' conceptual world is hardly identical to Aristotle's, but it is still more analogous to that sort of premodern thought than to modernist understandings of ethics.

Neither of the preeminent modern moral perspectives discussed earlier (utilitarianism and Kantian/theistic deontological ethics), precisely because they belong to modernity, can accommodate the full range of causal explanations presupposed in a premodern, moral-philosophical system like the Aristotelian tradition. But a full understanding of causality such as Aristotle offers can provide nuance for understanding the relationship of "rewards" (e.g., secondary or exterior goods such as wealth and status) and virtue in Proverbs in ways that are *not* informed primarily by modern moral frameworks or notions like Koch's Tun-Ergehen Zusammenhang (act-consequence nexus).[14]

MacIntyre has suggested that, for many in post-Enlightenment modernity, "to cite a cause is to cite a necessary condition *or* a sufficient condition *or* a necessary and sufficient condition as the antecedent of whatever behavior is to be explained."[15] Consequently, "as an observer, if I know the relevant laws governing the behavior of others, I can whenever I observe that the antecedent conditions have been fulfilled predict the outcome."[16] On this sort of modernist understanding, if Proverbs speaks of a virtuous act as a "cause" of something else—say, wealth—then it can be considered a necessary and/or sufficient cause of such riches. One might even think the sages were confident they could predict the level of external rewards a person might receive based on good/bad behavior—whether the agent who metes out the rewards is thought of as an impersonal cosmic force (as Koch suggests) or the deity (as many of his critics suggest).

It is rare to find a wisdom specialist today who thinks Proverbs' cause-and-effect rhetoric reflects the sages' belief that the moral workings of the cosmos functioned in such a mechanical fashion. The rejection of such a thoroughgoing perspective is largely due to simple exegetical observations: Proverbs itself notes exceptions to the act-consequence rule (e.g., 13:23; 16:8; 28:6) and acknowledges limits to the sages' knowledge (see chap. 1). Yet the shadow cast by Koch's programmatic essay on "retribution" in the Old Testament still firmly frames and informs many discussions of Proverbs' ethics. Much of Proverbs' cause-and-effect rhetoric, however, hardly needs to be understood so fully in terms of an act-consequence nexus—even in the modified, exception-filled form of many contemporary exegetes.

Two Types of Means-End Relations

In elaborating the Aristotelian moral-philosophical tradition, MacIntyre insists that in ancient virtue-oriented understandings of ethics, "the virtues are precisely those qualities which will enable an individual to achieve eudemonia

---

14. Koch, "Is There a Doctrine of Retribution," 57–87; cf. chapter 1, note 87 above.
15. MacIntyre, *After Virtue*, 82–83 (emphasis original).
16. MacIntyre, *After Virtue*, 84.

and the lack of which will frustrate" this "movement toward that telos." But as MacIntyre also suggests, "That description is ambiguous," since one can in fact "distinguish between two different types of means-end relationship"—even if Aristotle himself was not explicit about this. With the first type of means-end relations, we might suggest "that the world as a matter of contingent fact is so ordered that if you are able to bring about a happening or state or activity of the first kind, an event or activity of the second kind will ensue."[17] If I throw a rock in a pool of water, I will get a splash. That sounds a lot like the kind of act-consequence thinking so often ascribed to Proverbs—and somewhat like empirical, scientific understandings of cause-and-effect. It also coheres with Aristotelian material and efficient understandings of causality (discussed below). This notion may not be absent in Proverbs, but it is not the most diagnostically significant kind of means-end relationship for understanding, on the one hand, how virtuous living relates to the acquisition of secondary goods and, on the other hand, how wise living engenders human flourishing, which includes some enjoyment of secondary goods.

MacIntyre emphasizes an important characteristic of this first type of means-end relationship: namely, the means are external to the end.[18] MacIntyre says that "the means and the end can each be adequately characterized without reference to the other and a number of quite different means may be employed to achieve one and the same end."[19] For example, I might be able to get rich by being diligent, as a plain-sense reading of some parts of Proverbs suggests: "The hand of the diligent makes rich" (10:4); "Those who till their land will have plenty of food" (12:11); "In all toil there is profit" (14:23). But I also might acquire wealth in a number of other ways: stealing, getting lucky when I play the lottery, receiving a big inheritance, and so on. There is, in other words, more than one way a person might acquire significant riches, and neither diligence, stealing, nor anything else constitutes means that are uniquely and inherently related to that end.

This first sort of means-ends relationship is not adequate for understanding the relationship of virtue to flourishing. Consequently, MacIntyre identifies a second way of conceptualizing means-end relationships: the means are internal to the end in question. This sort of means-end relation, he contends, is more appropriate for discerning the relationship of virtuous living to a flourishing existence. The exercise of the virtues is not "a means to the end of the good" life in the same way as buying a winning lottery ticket can be said to be a cause of gaining significant wealth. This is because "what

17. MacIntyre, *After Virtue*, 148.
18. Knight, *Aristotelian Philosophy*, 134–37.
19. MacIntyre, *After Virtue*, 149.

constitutes the good" for a person is "a complete human life lived at its best, and the exercise of the virtues is a necessary and central part of such a life, not a mere preparatory exercise to secure such a life."[20] Occasional or isolated virtuous acts, or those done without appropriate emotions and desires (cf. chap. 5), do not make a fully virtuous life, and the attainment of any particular external good does not constitute the entirety of eudaemonia. Living virtuously or performing isolated virtuous actions should not be considered simply as a means to achieve only one or another facet of a good life, this or that "external" good.

MacIntyre's analysis of how virtuous living relates internally to the attainment of the good "end" of a flourishing life has implications for how Proverbs' act-consequence language might be understood. This is especially so when we remember how the book's prologue directs readers to attend to the symbolic dimensions of its discourse. If, for example, Proverbs presents a virtue such as diligence as a means to or cause of material wealth, a character-ethics understanding views the exercise of that virtue as one aspect of a larger virtuous life, and the "consequence" or reward—wealth—to be just one part of a broader cluster of goods, which—along with virtue—are necessary for happiness or flourishing. In other words, if "the hand of the diligent makes rich" (10:4; see also 12:11; 14:23), then the diligence that this saying promotes is not only a virtue that one should acquire to live a fully virtuous life; it is also a figure—a synecdoche—for that sort of full virtuous life itself. And if diligence is rhetorically said to "cause" or result in material rewards, these external goods (which certainly contribute to human flourishing) should likewise be regarded as synecdoches for the genuine thriving or eudaemonia that a full virtuous life enables—a thriving that includes some enjoyment of external goods.[21] The discrete virtues and the discrete "rewards" that Proverbs links to them must be understood in this symbolic way if the means they speak of (virtue) is to be considered internal to a good end to which those virtues are related (e.g., riches, status, etc.). If they are not so figuratively understood, the relation of means (virtue) to an end (some good "reward") in the book's rhetoric can only be described as external and so necessarily ambiguous. For again, as MacIntyre has made clear, in such a relation the end of good things might be achieved in any number of ways and is hardly uniquely related to the virtue that is rhetorically cast as the means to that end.

When such an ambiguity of means-end relations arises in Proverbs, it contributes to a problematic interpretation of the book that suggests virtuous acts

---

20. MacIntyre *After Virtue*, 149.
21. Sandoval, *Discourse of Wealth and Poverty*.

quite literally and reliably (if not "mechanistically") result in the attainment of secondary goods; this cause and effect is empirically suspect since, as most people know, virtuous acts are too often not rewarded. The accumulation of various external goods can be said to constitute a condition that can perhaps be reckoned as "prosperity" or "success," but it is *not* the eudaemonia of virtue ethics. For, again, the end of a genuine flourishing existence for traditions of character ethics is uniquely or internally tied to the means of a *full* virtuous life—one cannot get the one without the other. Isolated good acts or those done without rightly trained desires and emotions, though important and perhaps necessary steps for moral novices, are not sufficient for genuine, full flourishing.

Causality in Proverbs

MacIntyre's analysis of how, for virtue-oriented thought, virtuous living (a means) relates to the attainment of a flourishing life (an end) provides a fresh way to understand Proverbs' act-consequence rhetoric. It presents an alternative to the contingent, one-to-one approach of modern means-ends thinking where a particular kind of act (e.g., throwing a stone into water) produces a particular kind of result (a splash), so that if I want a splash, I should simply throw a stone. To consider Proverbs' act-consequence rhetoric only in that way—where a means is external to an end that might be achieved in different ways—is to ask only about what in the book constitutes the material and efficient causes of virtuous living. This would entail consideration of only those modes of causality that the science of the modern world was largely able to assimilate (see chap. 1). Yet with a premodern moral discourse like Proverbs, we should also inquire after something like the formal and final causes of living wisely—precisely those aspects of Aristotelian causality that Bacon and modern science jettisoned but that point to the internal relation of a means (a fully virtuous life) to an end (a flourishing existence).

Aristotle's material cause is the "that out of which" something emerges—for example, the bronze out of which a statue might be fashioned—while an efficient cause is the "primary source of change or rest" of an activity—for example, the artisan who shapes the statue. (In the rock-splash example, the rock hitting the water is the material cause of the splash, and my throwing the rock is its efficient cause.) By contrast, a formal cause of an activity entails an "account of what it is to be"—for example, the shape of the statue (or the size of the splash)—while a final cause concerns the end or "that for the sake of which a thing is done"—for example, decoration as the end of a statue, health as the end of a surgical tool, or cooling off my dog with water as the end of the splash.

For Proverbs, that which might be called the material cause (the "that out of which") of virtuous living is a person's natural desires and pursuit of goods that are necessary for well-being. These include yearnings for material well-being, social recognition, health, and so forth—all the sorts of things that, along with virtue, contribute to human flourishing (see chap. 3; cf. chap. 5) but that many people erroneously believe are singularly necessary for happiness. The efficient cause ("the primary source of change") of virtuous action in Proverbs can be understood simply as the human agent, the one who decides to act virtuously in seeking a flourishing existence.

Because these notions of causality—the material and efficient—cohere easily with the contingent, one-to-one understanding of causality typical of modernity, they are also the ones most commonly ascribed to Proverbs' rhetoric. And when Proverbs is considered exclusively in this light, it is once more easy to see how and why the book's moral perspective is so often characterized in terms of an act-consequence system and as entailing utilitarian ethical motivations (cf. chap. 1). If one desires a good that seems useful for happiness (a material cause), and if Proverbs presents such a good as a reward or consequence for acting in a certain way (an efficient cause), then a person does well to act in that way to attain the desirable good. On this view of Proverbs, the person who does the "good" gets the "goodies." And the book at points seems to suggest precisely this. As the sages say, "The hand of the diligent makes rich" (10:4)!

Yet understanding Proverbs' cause-and-effect rhetoric only in terms of efficient and material causes offers an incomplete description of the causality at play in an ancient moral discourse. The explanation lacks elaboration in terms of something like Aristotelian formal and final causality. When these aspects of causality are included, it is easier to see how Proverbs presents the means of virtuous living as internal to the end of happiness. Considering these kinds of causality also shows that the discrete virtues or virtuous acts spoken of in Proverbs function as figures for a broader life of virtue, and the particular consequences or "rewards" for virtue that the sages mention are symbols of a broader flourishing existence.

First, the formal cause (or "the account of what is to be") of virtuous living in Proverbs should be identified as the larger cluster of virtues that a wise or just person cultivates—what might be called the book's "profile of virtue" (cf. chap. 9 below). Like Aristotle's famous acorn that grows into a stately and sturdy oak, the moral novices of Proverbs, the book's young and simple addressees, will eventually become wise and just people if they follow the ways of wise and just people. They will possess and rightly exercise all of wisdom's virtues through their Practical Wisdom (cf. chaps. 8–9). They will not merely possess or occasionally exercise this or that virtue but otherwise stray from wisdom's path. They will likewise not merely know and do the good and appropriate thing. They will also come to desire living a fully wise and just life (cf. chap. 5). Indeed, although moral novices learn to live fully virtuous lives by doing discrete virtuous acts, for ancient virtue ethics the virtues are properly united; only the truly virtuous person acts truly virtuously—that is, with deeds, knowledge, emotions, and desires aligned in the doing of the good. Only upon arriving at such a state can the acorn that is the moral novice be acknowledged as the oak of a fully virtuous person who may enjoy genuine well-being.

Second, the final cause ("that for the sake of which'" something is undertaken) of virtuous living in Proverbs is something that comes close to the classical tradition's notion of eudaemonia. That this is the case is surely indicated by the cluster of external goods—health, wealth, status, "life," and so forth—that the book associates with the "right" way of the wise and just, since for traditions of character ethics, it is not just virtue but the enjoyment of some (unspecified) level of external goods that is necessary for a genuine flourishing (chap. 5). Proverbs' rhetoric of external goods as the consequence or reward for the exercise of discrete virtues implicitly acknowledges this aspect of well-being. Yet these promised rewards have often convinced commentators that the book's instruction is only designed to enable a student to achieve something like "success" or "prosperity."

This conclusion, however, is too narrowly drawn. It results, on the one hand, from a plain-sense or literal understanding of the book's rhetoric. On the other hand, it emerges from consideration of the rhetoric only in terms of something like Aristotelian material and efficient causes, which are similar to modern contingent, one-to-one notions of means-ends relations. However, any "success" or "prosperity" the book holds out on these terms cannot be regarded as a genuine eudaemonia or flourishing, which is the final cause of virtuous living for virtue ethics. Instead, it can only be narrowly regarded as an accumulation of external goods that a person might desire (a material cause) and conceived as the reward for particular virtuous actions a person might engage in (an efficient cause).

Causality Conclusions

When the full range of Aristotelian causality is brought to bear on Proverbs' act-consequence rhetoric in light of the book's figurative or symbolic interpretive possibilities, the deeper "means-end" logic of this rhetoric exceeds typical modern conceptions of cause-and-effect thinking (throw a stone in water and you get a splash). Indeed, when the book's causal and symbolic complexity is held together, several conditions are simultaneously in effect.

First, any particular virtuous action in Proverbs and its positive consequence are not related to one another in a contingent sense, where doing one particular thing results reliably in another particular event (throwing a rock in water inevitably makes a splash; diligence inevitably produces riches). Second, the relation between a certain means (virtuous conduct) and a certain end (some sort of good) should properly be regarded as not an external but an internal relation. When a means-end relation is conceived as external, there is more than one way to achieve the end (I can also throw a watermelon in a pool of gasoline to get a splash; I can steal to acquire riches). But when the relation is internal, the particular end is attainable only by the particular means, just as MacIntyre says the "means" of virtuous living is internal to the "end" of genuine flourishing. Consequently, for Proverbs any particular virtue that appears to be the means to some exterior good is both a disposition to be valued and a figure for the living of a fully wise and virtuous life. Similarly, any external good (wealth, status, life) that the text suggests results from or is the end of a virtuous act is symbolic of a full notion of human flourishing (to which that particular good might belong). The development of the intellectual, practical, and moral-social virtues that Proverbs' prologue underscores should be regarded as internally related to the final good of happiness or well-being to which various secondary goods can also contribute.

All this may not sound tenable to those unaccustomed to thinking about Proverbs' act-consequence rhetoric in terms of premodern notions of causality and who are not used to reflecting on the figurative dimensions of the book's moral rhetoric. Yet, as I contended earlier, when the plain-sense meanings of Proverbs have dominated interpretation and its act-consequence rhetoric has been viewed in the light of modern moral theories, the book's moral discourse has been ambiguously described and ambivalently appreciated. Consequently, it is not unreasonable to shift intellectual gears and so describe the book's moral orientation with a renewed sense of the figurative, symbolic dimensions of the book' teaching (about which the prologue speaks) and the assistance of ancient moral-philosophical theories. This is so even if it is obvious that Proverbs does not explicitly theorize the logic of its moral discourse the way I do here. That was not a concern of the sages. Yet, I suspect that if we were to interrogate them, they might explain the presuppositions and workings of their discourse in ways not unlike what I am doing here.

Considering Proverbs' figurative and symbolic dimensions not only serves an analysis of the text undertaken in light of notions of causality adapted from an ancient moral-philosophical tradition like Aristotle's; it also elucidates other aspects of the text that may more obviously point to how Proverbs constitutes a virtue-oriented moral discourse—whether these features relate to questions about the nature of the human being (chap. 3), the priority of agents over acts (chap. 4), or especially the way the book seeks to train its addressees' desires for a life of wisdom (chap. 5). It is to an exploration of these matters that the next few chapters turn.

3

The Anthropology of Proverbs

The Nature and Happiness of Human Beings

In the premodern tradition of virtue ethics that emerged from Aristotle, the final end or telos of humans is their happiness: eudaemonia. In book 1 of *Nicomachean Ethics*, Aristotle famously engages the debates of his day about what counts as happiness, since individuals have different views about what makes them happy—whether money, honor, pleasure, or something else. Aristotle's response is that happiness is that which "is chosen for its own sake and never because of something else."[1] Whereas one might seek goods like riches or sex to ensure happiness, no one pursues eudaemonia for some other reason, to achieve some other end; it is, simply put, a human being's "final end." What is more, Aristotle seeks an objective foundation for what constitutes human eudaemonia, grounding it in rational reflection about the kind of being humans naturally are. As MacIntyre explains, for Aristotle, "human beings, like the members of all other species, have a specific nature; and that nature is such that they have certain aims and goals, such that they move by nature towards a specific *telos*. Their final good end is defined in terms of their specific characteristics."[2] Humans long for the good of happi-

---

1. *NE* 1097b. Cf. Annas, *Morality of Happiness*, 39–40.
2. MacIntyre, *After Virtue*, 148.

ness and naturally yearn for those things that will help them reach it, even if these desires need to be appropriately tutored (see chap. 5).

For virtue-oriented moral traditions, then, the question of what sort of beings humans are is central, for only in knowing this can one rationally discern what would constitute such a being's happiness. A virtue-ethics approach to Proverbs consequently does well to ask what sort of being this wisdom book considers humans to be. Knowing this will clarify how the ancient sages understood, ordered, and believed individuals should pursue a range of different goods that are typically thought to contribute to happiness or well-being and that Proverbs' moral rhetoric so obviously associates with following the way of wisdom.

Proverbs' Anthropology

Proverbs says little directly about the nature of humans. The book's anthropology must be inferred from its imagery and rhetoric. What is clear is that Proverbs' anthropology, like Aristotle's, reflects a gender and class (and perhaps ethnicity) bias. It imagines able-bodied, heterosexual males of a particular social position (and from a particular place) as the norm for humanity. Alice Ogden Bellis notes that this is perhaps most clear in the way Proverbs prioritizes particular virtues that arguably support the construction of specific masculinities or male identities, as opposed to the identities of female or nonbinary moral subjects.[3] Yet despite the human animal's considerable diversity of sex, gender, ethnicity, and so forth, several characteristics that Proverbs ascribes to male people can be more universally understood and are fairly easy to discern.[4]

First, for Proverbs humans are fundamentally physical or material beings. We are bodies of flesh, bone, and innards (e.g., 3:8; 5:11; 15:30; 16:24; 18:8; 26:22), and these bodies have particular needs and produce particular desires. Food, sex, and forms of material sustenance are the most obvious instantiations of these needs and desires; their significance for Proverbs is evident from the attention given to instruction on such matters, as well as from the way the text motivates adherence to instruction with images of eating and with

---

3. Cf. Bellis, *Proverbs*, xlviii–lii, 43.
4. MacIntyre similarly notes that, despite Aristotle's ethnic prejudices for the Greek city-state, his account of the good in *Nicomachean Ethics* is "at once local and particular—located in and partially defined by the characteristics of the polis—and yet also cosmic and universal" (*After Virtue*, 148). To this short description of Aristotle's prejudices one might add other exclusions and hierarchies related to sex, gender, and social status, as well as physical and intellectual ability, that his metaphysical biology presupposes. Cf. conclusion below.

erotic and economic rhetoric (cf. chap. 5). The centrality of these needs and desires is also evident in the many instances where Proverbs promises life or death as outcomes of particular ways of being (e.g., 1:19; 2:18–19; 3:2, 16, 18; 5:5). Indeed, the embodied human of Proverbs, like humans and other animals in the classical traditions, is naturally inclined to self-preservation. The pursuit of sustenance and material goods is one way by which individuals of the species strive to preserve their lives; sexual reproduction is another, though indirect, means.

"Life" in Proverbs consequently is a robust symbol of flourishing. Although the term can be collocated with words for external goods like riches and honor (3:16; 22:4), it is wisdom (4:13, 22; 6:23; 8:35; 9:11; 10:17; 13:24; 15:24; 16:22) and justice/righteousness (10:11; 11:30; 12:28; 16:31; 21:21) that are more often associated with life. So, too, are other key virtues that belong to a life of wisdom and justice: fear of the Lord (10:27; 19:23; 22:4), healing or appropriate speech (15:4; 18:21), and kindness (21:21).

Importantly, Proverbs also relates the attainment of life to the appropriate control of one's passions (14:30), including moderating desire for goods like wealth. As Proverbs 28:16 says, "One who hates unjust gain will enjoy a long life." It seems that enjoyment of such goods without virtue, without accepting wise instruction, does not entail the experience of a full life characterized by the shalom of which Proverbs 3:2 speaks:

> For length of days and years of life
>   and abundant welfare [שָׁלוֹם] they [a parent's teaching] will give you.

Regardless of what pleasure or contentment external goods may provide, they do not by themselves constitute the sort of genuine happiness that wisdom enables.

> She [Wisdom] is a tree of life to those who lay hold of her;
>   those who hold her fast are called happy. (3:18)

Any sort of "desire fulfilled" might also be reckoned as "a tree of life" (13:12), but for Proverbs, precisely how and what one desires is key to attaining the full "life" or happiness with which the book is most concerned (see chap. 5 below).

The embodied humans in Proverbs are not merely material creatures. They also possess a spirit (רוּחַ). The spirit of a person can be judged or weighed by God (16:2) and reveals a person's character: one who is quick of spirit shows anger (14:29); the person of elevated spirit is haughty (16:18); one of lowly spirit is humble (29:23). The spirit of people might also show them to be faithful or trustworthy (11:13). The human spirit can be controlled or directed so that it reflects a person's wisdom (16:32), not their folly (29:11). It can be crushed by sadness or despair (15:13; 17:22; 18:14), a fact that points to how humans in Proverbs are also viewed as psychologically complex beings, exhibiting a range of emotions associated with their desires—whether love, hate, anger, joy, or something else (e.g., 14:10, 13; 15:1; 18:14).[5]

A third assumption of Proverbs about humans is that they are deeply social, if not political, creatures. Fundamentally and importantly, they must exist with other people in families and social groups; the text's regular use of kinship terms (father, mother, child) and words for polities (towns, cities) makes this clear. However, it is not only with others of their kind that humans must coexist; human sociality extends to nonhuman creatures as well. Nonhuman animals are part of the human ecological niche in Proverbs, something not terribly remarkable for a text that emerges from a largely rural, agriculturally based milieu. Proverbs 27:23, for example, exhorts the reader or hearer to "know well the condition of your flocks, and give attention to your herds." This may allude to an individual householder and his animals or to a person's larger livestock-raising enterprise. Proverbs 12:10 insists that "the righteous" (or just person) will "know the needs of their animals." This perspective resonates with one of several "human capabilities" that Martha Nussbaum, working from the Aristotelian moral tradition, identifies as requisite for full human flourishing: the ability to show concern and be in relation to animals (as well as plants and other aspects of nature).[6]

The sociality of the human being in Proverbs also extends to the deity. Proverbs assumes that humans are created by God, and as such, they ought to stand in a particular sort of relation with this deity. This relationship is most fundamentally described as fear: "fear of the LORD." This moral-religious impulse finds expression throughout Proverbs (e.g., 1:29; 2:5; 3:7), most foundationally at the end of the book's programmatic prologue.

> The fear of the LORD is the beginning of knowledge;
>   fools despise wisdom and instruction. (1:7)

The fear of the divine in Proverbs is both a genuine psychological dread of another being that can potentially exercise arbitrary power over a person

---

5. On emotions in Proverbs, see C. Yoder, "Objects of Our Affections."
6. Nussbaum, "Women and Cultural Universals," 40–42. For a fuller discussion of Nussbaum's capabilities list in relation to the Woman of Valor of Prov. 31:10–31, see Claassens, "Woman of Substance" and cf. conclusion below. On human obligation to nonhuman animals in Proverbs, see Sandoval, "Morality of Non-Human Animals," forthcoming.

and a religious feeling of awe or wonder in the presence of a numinous other.[7] Because the deity in Proverbs is not only the maker of the heavens and the earth but also, as creator of humans, the ultimate guarantor of human morality, one who exhibits the virtue of "fear of the Lord" will assume a fundamental religious-moral and psychological posture of openness toward the book's ethical teaching.

Besides presenting humans as embodied, spiritual-emotional, and social beings, Proverbs' rhetoric depicts humans as rational or intellectual beings. The book's prologue highlights the importance for the sages of the closely related practical and intellectual virtues (1:2; cf. chap. 2 above), and the rhetoric of knowledge, understanding, and insight is ubiquitous in Proverbs. Proverbs 15:14 declares that "the mind of one who has understanding seeks knowledge," while Proverbs 23:12 exhorts the reader to "apply your mind to instruction and your ear to words of knowledge." Proverbs 21:11 knows that "when the wise are instructed, they increase in knowledge," and Proverbs 24:3 says that "a house is built" by wisdom, "and by understanding it is established." In such texts, humans are assumed to be able to acquire knowledge and deploy rationality to discern ways of achieving desired ends. Elsewhere in the Bible, wisdom as a kind of knowledge or know-how approximates Greek *technē*, itself often closely related to *epistēmē*, which Martha Nussbaum says is "usually translated 'knowledge,' 'understanding'; or 'science,' 'body of knowledge.'"[8] Most often in Proverbs, intellectual virtue should contribute to a person's Practical Wisdom (see chaps. 8–9 below) and so serve the task of living well, of discerning and choosing good and appropriate paths in life (cf., e.g., 2:11; 3:13; 8:9; 15:21; 16:23). Yet even the human capacity for knowledge and rationality in Proverbs implicates and underscores the fundamental social nature of humans. The assistance of others in various contexts—for example, parents or teachers who instruct (Prov. 1–9) or the anonymous communal insights of proverbial sayings (Prov. 10–29)—make possible advancement in rational abilities and Practical Wisdom.

The kind of being Proverbs assumes humans to be is thus something akin to MacIntyre's description of people as "dependent rational animals."[9] The term "dependent" in this characterization is key. As MacIntyre explains, "It

---

7. See Fox, *Proverbs 1–9*, 69–71; and C. Yoder, "Forming 'Fearers of Yahweh.'" Cf. the discussion of "fear of the Lord" in chap. 2 above.

8. Nussbaum, *Fragility of Goodness*, 94.

9. It also is consonant with C. Yoder's description of the human "self" in Proverbs as one that is "*in relation*" to a range of others, "*embodied*," capable of "*choice*," and "a *creation of God*." See *Proverbs*, xxx (emphasis original).

is most often to others that we owe our survival, let alone our flourishing."[10] Humans are the sort of animal whose biology and embodied existence mean that throughout our lives—most obviously as infants but also often in old age and in times of illness or disability—we are profoundly dependent on others and so fundamentally social. Although most humans can and should also develop our capacities to become individual rational moral agents and thereby attain a degree of independence, this independence is only made possible with the aid of others: parents, teachers, and various other guides in life. Any person's emergence as an individual rational moral agent should thus not, as Gilbert Meilaender says, "come at the expense of acknowledging our constant and continued dependence" on and obligations to others.[11]

The Goods of Happiness

What then constitutes the end or good life for a material, spiritual, rational, and fundamentally social animal like the human in Proverbs? The simple answer to that question is obvious: wisdom or virtue—living according to Proverbs' instruction—is what humans should strive for. As we will see fully in chapter 5, wisdom *is* what the sages regard as most valuable. But more complexly, what constitutes happiness or flourishing for Proverbs? Although the book does not explicitly theorize human happiness, it does identify or assume the value and desirability of several "goods," which virtue-oriented traditions consider natural objects of desire for people and necessary for eudaemonia. These goods include at least a degree of (1) material prosperity; (2) good health; (3) social recognition, status, or honor; (4) sexual fulfillment; (5) exercise of the intellect, with respect to theoretical concerns but more fundamentally to practical matters of living well; and above all, (6) a just social order within which these goods can be well and rightly pursued with others.[12]

That things like material well-being, health, and social status are features of a happy human life for Proverbs is obvious from the multiple ways the book promises such goods as motivation for people to choose wisdom (e.g., 3:16; 8:18; 16:24; 22:1). That the exercise of one's intellectual abilities is also an important good for Proverbs is clear not only from the number of verses already mentioned but also from the fact that a full conception of wisdom for

---

10. MacIntyre, *Dependent Rational Animals*, 4.
11. Meilaender, "Dependent Rational Animals."
12. As noted earlier, however, as with Aristotle and others in virtue-oriented moral traditions, Proverbs does not specify the baseline or minimum degree of external goods that are necessary for human happiness. Cf. Annas, *Morality of Happiness*, 381.

Proverbs is best regarded as a practical moral reasoning and knowledge—not unlike the *phronēsis* (Practical Wisdom) of the classical tradition—the regular exercise of which enables a person to discern, desire, and embark upon an appropriate course of action in any particular circumstance (see chap. 8 below).

Sexual fulfillment is also a foundational human good for Proverbs, although the book primarily expresses this conviction from a "straight" (in modern parlance) male's point of view. The good of sexual fulfillment is implicit especially in Proverbs 1–9's deep concern that its addressees express their sexuality in socially sanctioned relationships—within patriarchal marriage and not via adultery: "Keep your way far from her [the strange woman]" (5:8).[13] The text's concern with sex, moreover, is not limited to matters of procreation, social stability, and legitimate transfer of property across generations, as a text like Proverbs 5:8–10 might lead one to believe. It is also something that can and should be enjoyed. Indeed, the teaching voice in Proverbs also says, "Rejoice in the wife of your youth" (5:18; cf. 2:16; 7:4–27). The sages intuitively recognized, even if in narrow or parochial fashion, sexual expression as something that typically or potentially contributes to most (even if not necessarily all) adult persons' happiness.

If material well-being, physical health, social status, the exercise of one's intellect, and sexual fulfillment are reckoned as goods by Proverbs, it is not simply because they are things people might themselves think are central to their own pleasure or happiness. They are goods because they are necessary for the full flourishing of the sort of being the sages considered humans to be. They are, for Proverbs, natural goods.

Happiness, Virtue, and Vulnerability

As with other ancient virtue-oriented moral traditions, the goods that Proverbs assumes are necessary for human flourishing should not be chased by any and all means simply because they are good and desirable. Instead, their contribution to happiness should be understood via wisdom, and any pursuit of them should be carried out via the virtues the book promotes. Humans need to be morally trained by virtue in order to understand the role of goods in their lives and how best to pursue them (see chap. 5). J. E. Woodbridge, a creative mid-twentieth-century thinker in the Aristotelian tradition, puts it this way:

> If we ask, as we often do, for what purpose we exist, and consult the way we live in Nature for an answer instead of imagining one, then the answer is clear

13. On the female figures in Prov. 1–9, see chap. 5.

and definite. We exist, not to reproduce our kind, not to enjoy life and love, and not to be happy, *but to be provident and prudent in these matters*. . . . And that, interestingly enough, is something most of us dislike; we would much prefer to reproduce our kind, enjoy life and love, and be happy without any trouble. Our natural obligation to be provident and prudent haunts us like a guilty conscience. That natural purpose of our existence, however, is not altered by our preferences. *We are born to improve.*[14]

Woodbridge adds that "to be exceptionally teachable belongs to our natural status."[15]

But which virtues ought to be taught and cultivated to attain which goods? Although the relationship between distinct goods and the different virtues Proverbs highlights can be variously parsed, it is possible to suggest five plausible relations:

1. Diligence can be beneficial for achieving material well-being (e.g., 10:4).
2. A responsiveness to instruction (sometimes via reproof and discipline) and the attainment of knowledge promote the good of human intellectual or rational activity (e.g., 15:32; 21:11).
3. Moderation and knowledge might support the attainment of health (e.g., 23:4; 25:16).
4. Moral-social and religious virtues such as faithfulness, loyalty, humility, fairness, kindness, and fear of the Lord, which are frequently mentioned in Proverbs (see chap. 4 below), are indispensable for the establishment of a fair and just society, within which one might legitimately pursue some wealth, social recognition, and sexual fulfillment.
5. Practical Wisdom—the ability to size up situations, to know and desire what is good in any particular moment, and to exercise the appropriate virtues toward right ends—serves the attainment of all the goods named above (see chaps. 8–9 below).

This sort of Practical Wisdom for Proverbs is essential for a person to be truly wise and just. Indeed, it is an agent's *phronēsis* or practical moral reasoning ability that, for the sages of Proverbs as in classical traditions, underlies and unifies "all the virtues in the agent's practical thinking."[16]

However, if a full flourishing is not achieved by the acquisition of exterior goods alone but requires a life of virtue, neither does wisdom or virtue

---

14. Woodbridge, *Essay on Nature*, 14 (emphasis added).
15. Woodbridge, *Essay on Nature*, 14.
16. Annas, *Morality of Happiness*, 79.

guarantee access to such goods. Bad luck, human finitude, or the viciousness of others might result in the lack of key goods that virtue-oriented traditions recognize as necessary for most people's happiness. As Nussbaum says, "human good living, *eudaimonia*," is "vulnerable" to such matters.[17]

The relationship between virtue, exterior goods, and happiness for character ethics is thus obviously complex. Indeed, the notion of happiness in Aristotle entails two matters in tension with each other. Annas speaks of this tension in terms of (1) "the intuitive requirement," which involves taking pleasure in, or enjoying, external goods; and (2) "the theoretical pull," which focuses on the sufficiency of virtue. The intuitive requirement means that "happiness must involve our enjoying the good things of life. It must be a pleasant life, in which we have access to what in our society counts as affluence." The theoretical pull, however, means that "happiness must involve not just satisfying a state now . . . it must involve morality, which we praise and value for its own sake, and not because of its contribution to further ends."[18]

Consequently, a question much discussed in the classical traditions of virtue ethics is whether a wicked person with abundant exterior goods or a virtuous person living in misery might both be said to be truly "happy" merely by possession of their exterior goods or their virtue, respectively. For many thinkers, and probably for the composers of Proverbs, although a wicked person with exterior goods surely is able to enjoy those goods and derive real advantage from them, that person nonetheless must be said to be lacking something fundamental, even most important, to genuine eudaemonia—namely, virtue. But what of the virtuous person who possesses that which is considered most important for flourishing—virtue—but is not permitted to enjoy even a basic level of exterior goods (food, shelter, social respect)? Could such a person be said to be fully happy in the way most people think of happiness? The Stoics famously believed that virtue by itself was enough for happiness, relegating the external goods somewhat ambiguously to the category of "indifferents"—nice if you have them but constituting a fundamentally different category of good than the ("highest") good of virtue.[19] Other ancient thinkers in the classical tradition—probably like the composers of Proverbs—seemed to understand that for most people virtue, along with some degree of exterior goods, was necessary for genuine happiness.[20] As Aristotle suggests, "It is evident that

17. Nussbaum, *Fragility of Goodness*, 318.
18. Annas, *Morality of Happiness*, 365.
19. For a discussion see Annas, *Morality of Happiness*, 167–68, 405–6.
20. For MacIntyre, "we value the virtues both for their own sake and for the sake of eudaimonia (cf. *NE* 1097b2–4)." See MacIntyre, "Moral Rationality, Tradition, and Aristotle," 461–62. Knight explains that, for MacIntyre, to value the virtues "for the sake of eudaimonia

eudaimonia stands in need of good things from outside . . . for it is impossible or difficult to do fine things without resources."[21] When minimal enjoyment of such "good things from outside" is conspicuously lacking, no one's happiness will be full. Even the most virtuous person cannot be said to truly have eudaemonia on the torture rack.[22] However, as Annas notes, the baseline for the enjoyment of such goods was never really specified in the classical tradition; nor is it in Proverbs.[23]

That the sages of Proverbs understood that the attainment of external goods by themselves—without wisdom—is not constitutive of or sufficient for genuine thriving or "prosperity" is evident from their insistence that people erroneously believe it is. The exhortation of texts like Proverbs 24:1 and Psalm 37:1 (a wisdom psalm) point to this reality.

> Do not envy the wicked,
>   nor desire to be with them. (Prov. 24:1)

> Do not fret because of the wicked;
>   do not be envious of wrongdoers. (Ps. 37:1)

The logic of the lines depends on the recognition of texts like Psalm 73 that people might be tempted to envy the wicked and follow their way of life precisely because of the desirable exterior goods they possess—a matter to be explored more fully in chapter 5. For these texts, wicked wrongdoers might enjoy significant external goods but still lack something vital—namely, wisdom or virtue. Indeed, when the speaker of Psalm 73 "saw the prosperity of the wicked," he became "envious of the arrogant" (v. 3). Eventually, however, he was able to recognize a fundamental error in his longings and thinking:

> If I had said, "I will talk on in this way,"
>   I would have been untrue to the circle of your children. (Ps. 73:15)[24]

Upon reflection, the speaker of Psalm 73 was able to choose an appropriate path, one surely characterized by the sort of wisdom Proverbs venerates. He was able to recognize that absent virtuous living, the exterior goods a person might possess hold limited worth in securing authentic happiness.

---

is to value them precisely as 'essential constituents'" to flourishing (Knight, *Aristotelian Philosophy*, 138–39).

21. *NE* 1099a 31–33, cited in Nussbaum, *Fragility of Goodness*, 318.
22. Cf. *NE* 1153b 16–21.
23. See Annas, *Morality of Happiness*, 364–425.
24. For an insightful discussion of Ps. 73, see Newsom, "'If I Had Said . . .'"

In more opaque fashion, Proverbs 13:7 makes a similar point about the relation of virtue and exterior goods to flourishing.

> There is one who becomes rich [מִתְעַשֵּׁר] but has nothing;
> and one who is poor [מִתְרוֹשֵׁשׁ] but has great wealth.[25]

Most scholars take this verse as Raymond Van Leeuwen does: an ambiguous and ironic comment that censures "deception of self and of others."[26] Some translations even render the *hithpael/hithpolel* verbs as "pretend to be rich" and "pretend to be poor," respectively (cf. NRSV, NASB). There is no need to deny these possible levels of meaning, but there are good reasons to hear more too. Proverbs 13:7 offers the only example of the *hithpael/hithpolel* forms of the roots עשׁר and רושׁ in Proverbs (and the Hebrew Bible). In Ben Sira 11:18, however, the *hithpael* of עשׁר does not mean "pretend to be rich" but to "become rich."[27] Murphy is likely on the right track when he asks whether, beyond "the literal sense" of the line, one might be warranted in suggesting that in 13:7 the one who becomes rich but has nothing is in fact a person who lives by "another order of values" when compared to the ways of wise and just people.[28] Though the rich person apparently possesses much, the worth of it all in ethical terms—and so its ability to produce genuine flourishing—is nil, at least if virtue is not added to it. By contrast, the one who is poor may well possess that which for Proverbs is of most worth—wisdom or virtue.

Of course, as Proverbs 28:11 says, a rich person can be "wise" too—but only in his own eyes.

> The rich [עָשִׁיר] is wise in self-esteem [חָכָם בְּעֵינָיו],
> but an intelligent poor person [דַּל מֵבִין] sees through the pose.

A locution like "being wise in one's own eyes," as the Hebrew of 28:11 literally says, does not mean the rich person of the line is somehow deficient in intellect or practical abilities; he may be shrewdly intelligent. It is simply that the עָשִׁיר is not ethically wise according to the standards of Proverbs. The same verse also makes clear, as does 13:7, that an economically marginalized

---

25. The translation of the first line follows Schipper, *Proverbs 1–15*, 446; the second relies on Fox, *Proverbs 10–31*, 563.
26. Van Leeuwen, "Book of Proverbs," 131–32.
27. As Schipper (*Proverbs 1–15*, 446–47) also notes. In Beentjes, *Book of Ben Sira in Hebrew*, the MS A line is 11:16. "To become rich" appears as the typical meaning of the *hithpael* of the root in rabbinic Hebrew as well; cf. Jastrow, *Dictionary*, 1127.
28. R. Murphy, *Proverbs*, 96.

person can possess the virtues of wisdom. A poor person (דַּל) can be one who understands (מֵבִין). The last point is obvious from Proverbs 19:1 too.

> Better the poor [רָשׁ] walking in integrity [תֹּם]
> than one perverse of speech who is a fool.

In light of Proverbs 28:11 and 19:1, Proverbs 13:7—in addition to ironically and generally teaching that appearances can be deceptive—also clarifies one particular instance of social life where appearances may sometimes skew ethical evaluations. A person's possession of wealth—becoming rich—is neither a simple indicator of one's wisdom nor of a genuine thriving existence; a person's poverty is likewise no clear sign that the figurative "great wealth" of virtue (cf. chap. 5) is absent in that person's life. However, although poverty does not exclude someone from the category of the wise, it might well cast a shadow over even a virtuous person's ability to fully flourish. The rhetorical juxtaposition of good character (intelligence and integrity in 28:11 and 19:1, which is necessary for genuine flourishing) with a person's economic status as poor—something that Proverbs intuitively knows can hinder full thriving—gestures toward this fact, "for it is impossible or difficult to do fine things without resources."[29]

The Rich in Proverbs

Proverbs obviously conceives of "wealth" or "riches" as desirable and valuable things (e.g., 3:16; 8:18, 21; 10:15; 12:27; 18:11; 22:4; 24:4) that can contribute to human flourishing. But what is the status of the "rich" in the book? Wealth may be a prized "good" for the sages, yet the rich person (עָשִׁיר) in Proverbs is, as Roger Whybray says, "always regarded with hostility."[30] This characterization of the rich person has important consequences for how one understands the logic of the book's cause-and-effect or act-consequence rhetoric. If wealth is considered a straightforward reward for virtue, how is it that Proverbs so often negatively describes the rich—who by definition possess significant wealth? This conundrum has troubled many commentators. Van Leeuwen simply concludes that the sages are "very aware of exceptions" to the act-consequence nexus, such as the suffering of the righteous and the prosperity of the wicked.[31]

---

29. NE 1099a 31–33.
30. Whybray, *Wealth and Poverty*, 62–63. Cf. the discussion of the rich and "friendship" in chap. 7 below.
31. Van Leeuwen, "Wealth and Poverty," 31–32.

Many commentators take an approach similar to Van Leeuwen's and regard the existence of the less-than-virtuous rich in Proverbs as exceptions to the book's Tun-Ergehen Zusammenhang. However, it is more correct to understand "rich" in the book as primarily a moral category, not merely an economic one. The existence of the (wicked) rich in Proverbs is not so much an exception to an act-consequence logic as it is a different inflection of the book's moral discourse. The rich are regarded quite simply as vicious moral agents, the sort of person whose way of life the book's addressee ought to shun. Indeed, the rich in Proverbs are people with flawed character since they persistently, or typically, act aggressively, violently, and manipulatively for their own advantage, while at the same time they misunderstand the value of wealth and its place in a flourishing life.

The rich, for example, sometimes, or typically, lord their status and power over the poor and others in economically subordinated positions, even responding to the destitute person's petitions harshly, with "strength" (עַזּוֹת, 18:23), which the NRSV renders as "roughly."

> The rich rule over the poor,
>   and the borrower is the slave of the lender. (22:7)

> The poor use entreaties,
>   but the rich answer roughly [עַזּוֹת]. (18:23)

A rich person's way of life in Proverbs can be "crooked" (28:6), and such a person can be wise in their own eyes (28:11). What's more, the rich seek their security not in social bonds or the deity but in their wealth. As Proverbs 10:15 and 18:11 say, "The wealth of the rich is their fortress," and "The wealth of the rich is their strong city."[32] Consequently, the rich person likely also belongs to that class of individuals who anxiously seek to accumulate. The rich person is also surely one who gathers wealth "hastily" (13:11) and "augments wealth by exorbitant interest" (28:8).[33]

Proverbs' depiction of the (vicious) rich underscores the fact that, for the ancient sages, the possession of external goods is not evidence of virtue and the absence of external goods is not evidence of a lack of virtue. In the terms of chapter 2 above, riches or other goods—though not unimportant to thriving—are only externally related to virtuous living. The trappings of happiness—the enjoyment of a range of external goods—might make it appear that someone has attained a genuine flourishing existence even without

32. These lines, including their parallel stichs, will be discussed further in chap. 7.
33. Cf. Cho, "Wisdom's Wealthy."

a virtuous life. But as with character ethics, so for Proverbs: without wisdom or virtue, a person cannot authentically or fully flourish. Likewise, a serious lack of external goods in a virtuous person's life impedes well-being.

The Rewards of Virtue

For Proverbs, as in ancient virtue-oriented traditions like the Aristotelian tradition, virtue is both its own reward *and not*. One can derive pleasure from a range of activities, including living virtuously, and this may happen without the external goods that contribute to a flourishing life. But the pleasure derived from "acting virtuously for virtue's sake" does not equate to eudaemonia, either for Aristotle or for Proverbs—though, as noted earlier, it seems to for some later Stoics (and perhaps Cynics).[34]

The wisdom tradition to which Proverbs belongs recognizes (like its Aristotelian counterpart) that the wicked often prosper—in the sense of attaining things like wealth, status, and power—while the just may suffer many kinds of loss. In the Bible, the book of Job is the text that explores these dynamics most profoundly.[35] However, for such virtue-oriented moral traditions, the prosperity of the wicked and the "poverty" of wise and just people, though hardly desirable, are not merely exceptions to an act-consequence rule. The trials of the virtuous, especially, can be explained otherwise. Such difficulty can be evidence of what Nussbaum calls "the fragility of goodness."[36] One person's wickedness or injustice might impinge on another's efforts to flourish, a reality Proverbs certainly knows (e.g., 11:30; 14:31; 16:29; 24:15; 28:15; 29:2, 16). Or a person's misfortunes may result from simple human finitude or bad luck, what some call Fate. After all, we are all subject at times to accidental injury, unforeseen illness, or unexpected loss. As Qohelet knows, "No one can anticipate the time of disaster. Like fish taken in a cruel net, and like birds caught in a snare, so mortals are snared at a time of calamity, when it suddenly falls upon them" (Eccles. 9:12).

Theologically speaking, some might say ascribing misfortune to chance or others' wickedness ultimately places the blame for suffering and injustice, as well as the "prosperity of the wicked," at God's doorstep. Surely an all-powerful, good being should be able to prevent such happenings. For modern

---

34. As Striker notes, "The Stoics . . . tried to show that happiness is identical with virtue," relegating to the category of "indifferents" external goods that Aristotle and his followers intuited were also necessary for human happiness. *Essays on Hellenistic Epistemology and Ethics*, 178.

35. Cf., esp., Newsom's discussion of "the fate of the wicked" in *Book of Job*, 115–25.

36. Nussbaum, *Fragility of Goodness*; cf. Newsom, *Book of Job*, 243–44.

people especially, this all begs the question of theodicy—whether the ways of God in a world of pain and wickedness can be justified.[37] However, instead of only indicting a supposedly omnipotent, all-loving God for the woes of human existence, parts of the biblical wisdom tradition respond with another moral-theological logic—one emerging from ancient cosmology and accounting mythologically for the "fragility" of human experiences of goodness. On this view, the divine creates the cosmos out of a preexisting watery chaos. However, as the book of Job suggests, God does not completely dominate these precreation forces of chaos. Instead, God only limits or constrains the symbols of these chaotic forces (including the sea, the great beast Behemoth, and the sea monster Leviathan in Job 38–41). The imagery of chaos as a sea suggests that the boundaries God sets for this force (e.g., doors and bars; cf. Job 38:8–11) are somewhat permeable.[38] Although the coastline is a more or less stable border between an ocean's waters and terra firma, anyone who has spent time near the beach knows that waves at high tide can pummel the coast significantly more than at low tide, while severe storms transgress even farther onto the "dry land" (cf. Gen. 1:9) of creation.

In other words, in parts of the wisdom tradition, the occasional in-breaking of the waves of chaos into cosmos (lit. "order") is inevitable, despite the divine's creation of and rule over that cosmos. The same tradition also suggests, remarkably, that the forces of chaos can be objects of God's pleasure. Carol Newsom contends that in Job God *extols* the sea monster Leviathan; the divine's words are "a celebration of the awesome and terrifying power of Leviathan." Job, however, "has been unable to recognize the presence of the chaotic within God's design and governance of the world."[39] Even more striking is Psalm 104's view of Leviathan, which presents the symbol of primeval chaos as one of God's creatures fashioned either to sport in the sea that God made or as a creature with whom the divine itself might play: "There [in the sea] go the ships and Leviathan that you formed to sport in [or with] it" (Ps. 104:26).[40] In the tradition's mythological or cosmological logic, the divine is thus either unable to control completely the disruptive forces of chaos or is

---

37. The classic formulation of the theodicy question is Leibnez's *Theodicy*. The usual formulation of the issue poses four statements, at least one of which must be regarded as logically incompatible with the others: (1) there is a God; (2) God is all-powerful; (3) God is loving and good; (4) there is innocent suffering. For this formulation and a readable account of theodicy as a modern problem, see Long, *What Shall We Say?*, 1–39.

38. Newsom, "Job," 602.

39. Newsom, "Job," 623. For a more negative understanding of Leviathan in Job, see Levenson, *Creation and the Persistence of Evil*, esp. 47–49.

40. McCann says that for Ps. 104:26 "Leviathan is a creature who simply plays in the water. Or is Leviathan, in effect, God's water toy? The grammar is ambiguous" ("Psalms," 1098).

unwilling to do so for the sake of those chaotic forces, which—like humans—are also the object of divine care and delight.

Job's cosmological logic of containment or limitation of chaos is applied to social sources that also disrupt human well-being. Imagery in Job 38:12–15, for instance, makes clear that in the divinely created cosmos that this wisdom work imagines, wickedness is constrained but not eliminated: the dawn shakes out the wicked from the earth every morning—but night (and the wicked with it) will surely come again. In the poetry, "light is" likewise "withheld from the wicked" person, whose "uplifted arm is broken" (38:15); but the wrongdoer is not done away with.

Proverbs does not elaborate on these matters of cosmic justice as Job does, but it does in part share Job's cosmology (and perhaps implicitly the theodicy). Although the human being for Proverbs is thrown into such a world, Proverbs 8 develops its own view of the origins of the cosmos in ways that correspond to its virtue-oriented moral discourse (cf. chaps. 11 and 12 below).

For Proverbs, then, humans are material, spiritual, rational, and social beings whose thriving depends on some level of enjoyment of external goods and on the attainment and exercise of wisdom or virtue—even if a full good and happy life ultimately remains fragile. For the ancient sages, the human being is also the sort of being who is fundamentally teachable (cf. chap. 4 below). As with traditions of character ethics, a center of moral gravity for Proverbs lies not in deontological obedience to rules or in utilitarian pleasure seeking but with human moral agents who can augment their virtue and learn to choose to follow good life paths—the ways of wise and just persons. By following these paths, they increase the possibilities for advancing their own and others' genuine flourishing. And so it is to the depiction of moral agents and their ways in Proverbs that we next turn.

4

Proverbs' Way of Life

The Priority of Moral Agents over Right Acts

Besides being concerned with the nature of the human and what contributes to eudaemonia, ethical discourses that prioritize virtue are often more concerned with moral agents and the virtues they cultivate than with their adherence to rules (deontological ethics) or actions that promote people's subjectively determined happiness (utilitarian ethics).

In Proverbs the prominence of the virtues and vices is obvious. The book persistently alludes to the qualities it considers desirable or undesirable. As with other character-ethics traditions, Proverbs prioritizes moral agents and their way of life. This strong concern with virtuous agents is set in relief by the relatively rare appearance in the book of commands that demand its addressees fulfill particular precepts. Even in the instructional poems of Proverbs 1–9, where the imperative voice is most discernible, the exhortation is to follow wisdom's way generally, not to adhere to specific rules. Although Proverbs does occasionally insist on obedience to particular precepts (e.g., 3:27–31; cf. chap. 11 below), what is more common is the book's strategic and broad use of nouns, substantival adjectives, and participles ("one who does X") to refer to kinds of virtuous or vicious people. This is clearest in Proverbs 10–15, the collection of short, mostly antithetical sayings that begins the second major section of the book, but it is also evident in subsequent collections of proverbial sayings and in the book's initial chapters (Prov. 1–9).

Moral Types in Proverbs 10–15

The catalog of moral types or agents in Proverbs 10–15 is remarkable. Nearly every verse in these chapters identifies moral figures or kinds of characters: the wise, the foolish, the righteous, the wicked, the diligent, the lazy, the timid, the aggressive, the blameless, the generous, the good, the upright, the evil, the one who plans evil, the one who acts faithfully, the one who is clever, the scoffer, the treacherous, the upright, the faithless, sinners, the one who walks uprightly, the one who is devious, the perverse, the quick-tempered, the schemer, the one who plans evil, the one who plans good, the one slow to anger, the one who has a hasty temper, the proud, the one who is greedy.[1]

To this list of moral agents in Proverbs 10–15 one can note still more specific character types in these chapters: the one who trusts in riches, the one who troubles his household, the one who loves discipline, the one who tills the land, the one who follows worthless pursuits, the one who counsels peace, the one who guards his mouth, the one who opens wide his lips, the one who despises the word, the one who respects the commandment, a bad messenger, a faithful envoy, the one who ignores instruction, the one who heeds reproof, a faithful witness, a false witness, the one who despises neighbors, the one who is kind to the poor, the one who oppresses the poor, and the one who hates bribes.

The virtues or vices characteristic of these moral types are implicit in substantival grammatical forms: the generous person is one who freely and gladly shares with others; the diligent person is one who persistently exerts a best effort in their work; and so forth. The moral types, with their distinguishing virtues and vices, can also be collocated with one another to create a sketch of the virtues that are constitutive of wisdom and righteousness (and of folly and wickedness) and a catalog of the human characters who are wise and just (or wicked and foolish). For example, the broader categories of the wise, the righteous, the good, and the upright should be associated with characters like the faithful, the diligent, the trustworthy envoy, and the true witness, as well as those who are slow to anger, love discipline, counsel peace, guard the mouth, heed reproof, hate bribes, and are kind to the poor.

Though explicit mention of particular moral types outside of Proverbs 10–15 is less frequent, it does occur. For example, such nouns and substantival participles appear only somewhat less often in the next major section of the book (16:1–22:16) than in Proverbs 10–15. These chapters speak again of the just and the wicked, as well as the foolish and the wise, and a host of other agents that can be collocated with those principal moral types. By contrast,

---

1. Cf. the list offered by Schipper (*Proverbs 1–15*, 25), and see also Keefer's sketch of the book's moral types in *Proverbs 1–9*, 46–92.

nouns and participles representing the full range of moral agents in Proverbs are significantly less frequent in the collection of short sayings of Proverbs 25–29, where they are clustered in chapters 26, 28, and 29. In the diverse and distinct material of Proverbs 30–31, the character types typical of other parts of Proverbs likewise appear infrequently, except for the prominent example of the Woman of Valor (אֵשֶׁת־חַיִל) in 31:10–31 (cf. conclusion).

The moral agents so common in Proverbs 10–15 also do not appear often in the instructional material of Proverbs (chaps. 1–9; 22:17–24:34), but they are present. In the early chapters of the book, we also encounter another cluster of terms for a most significant character type or moral agent in Proverbs, one who is somewhat distinct from the other types: the text's addressee, "my child" (בְּנִי; e.g., 1:8, 10, 15; 2:1; 3:1, 11, 21; cf. "children" in 4:1 and 8:32). Later in Proverbs, "my child" appears primarily where the imperative voice is prominent—namely, in instructional material (23:15, 19, 26; 24:13, 21), as opposed to the collections of short sayings (but cf. 19:27; 27:11). The mention of children and the direct or indirect moral characterization of them either as generally wise or foolish (e.g., 10:1; 13:1; 15:20; 17:25; 19:26; 28:7; cf. 20:7; 29:3) indicate that the book's presumed young and simple audience (1:4) should be regarded as genuine moral agents, ethical novices developing particular moral identities. They are presumed able to advance in wisdom or pursue folly and vice, as noted earlier in the introduction. If they weren't, there would be no point instructing them.

The "my child" of Proverbs should also probably be related to the young (נַעַר) and simple (פֶּתִי) persons mentioned throughout the book, most prominently in the prologue at 1:4. Although the book's opening lines make clear that even advanced sages (the wise; the understanding person; 1:5) can benefit from studying the text's wisdom, the primary constructed audience of the instructional material is the person who is young and simple—youths susceptible to and in need of social-moral training. Fox suggests that, although certain characters in Proverbs appear incorrigible (e.g., the אֱוִיל, "fool") and unable to advance in morality, the פֶּתִי (simple person), who is typically young, is particularly teachable.[2] Though such youthful moral subjects do not always naturally or inevitably reveal an aptitude for wisdom (e.g., 7:7; 14:15; 22:3), they are corrigible (e.g., 8:5; 9:4, 6; 19:25; 22:6, 15).

At least two additional moral agents are prominent in Proverbs 1–9. These are the characters whose voices at different times proffer instruction to "my

---

2. Fox, *Proverbs 1–9*, 40. Yet as Newsom ("Models of the Moral Self," esp. 13) recognizes, even the "inveterate fool" was likely at some point a teachable "simple youth," but one whose failure to attain wisdom resulted in the hardening of his defective character.

child," the young, and the simple. Sometimes this is a parental (and patriarchal) voice, of both fathers and mothers (e.g., 1:8; 4:2–4; 6:20; 23:22; 31:1), heard explicitly in the "I" of 4:1–4. At other times, the instructing voice is Woman Wisdom (e.g., 1:20–33; 8:1–36). These characters are represented as virtuous moral agents whose roles as authoritative teachers confirm their advanced moral status. The parent in Proverbs 4 claims to offer "good precepts" (לֶקַח טוֹב) and to have been morally formed by his own parents (4:2–4). Woman Wisdom is represented in Proverbs as the personification of virtue (e.g., 8:12–16). She actively seeks to address those in need of instruction. She calls out and stations herself in public places in order to reach potential audiences (1:20–21; 8:2–5).

The limited number of particular precepts Proverbs offers, coupled with the sheer volume of nouns, substantival adjectives, and participles naming moral types, suggests that the book's moral concerns truly do lie primarily with the formation of moral agents, not with actions undertaken in obedience to moral precepts or with utilitarian purposes. But a tally of terminology is not sufficient to establish the book's priority on moral agents and their character-defining virtues and vices. To affirm this priority, we need to examine more broadly the place of these agents in the book's moral discourse.

The Two Ways

The priority Proverbs places on moral agents over rules or the utility of acts is related to the book's well-known metaphor of the two ways, a figure that illustrates the virtuous or vicious modes of existence of different sorts of moral subjects. The agents in Proverbs whose examples the reader/hearer should follow—or avoid—are easily identified in the rhetoric of the way or path throughout the book.

Terms for the "way" or "path" (אֹרַח, מַעְגָּל, דֶּרֶךְ) and associated images are especially prevalent in Proverbs 1–9, though hardly absent from other sections of the book.[3] I have elsewhere suggested that for Proverbs the reader or hearer of the book is asked to choose between two ways—the way of wisdom and righteousness on the one hand, and the way of folly and wickedness on the other.[4] Such a general formulation of Proverbs' discourse of the two ways is not incorrect; Proverbs does on occasion characterize the two ways in terms

---

3. The noun אֹרַח appears nineteen times in Proverbs, twelve times in chaps. 1–9; מַעְגָּל appears seven times, all in Prov. 1–9; the noun דֶּרֶךְ is attested seventy-four times, twenty-eight times in Prov. 1–9.

4. Sandoval, *Discourse of Wealth and Poverty*, 56.

of general moral categories such as wisdom and righteousness. Hence, we read about the "good path" (2:9) and the path/way of justice or righteousness (2:8; 8:20; 12:28; 17:23), as well as the path/way of wisdom, uprightness, insight, and life (e.g., 2:13; 4:11; 5:6; 6:23; 9:6). And by contrast, the wrong way is characterized as the way of evil (2:12; 8:13).[5]

However, to say the addressee of Proverbs is asked to choose between the way of wisdom and righteousness and the path of folly or wickedness is insufficiently precise, especially since Proverbs persistently speaks of a range of good and bad moral subjects. The choice that Proverbs' hearer/reader faces is not primarily between pursuing one generalized notion or following the path of another abstraction—whether wisdom/righteousness or folly/wickedness. It is between following the way of wise and righteous *people* or pursuing the path of wicked and foolish *persons*. Although the metaphor of the two ways in Proverbs might evoke static, binary conceptions—only one right way of wisdom and only one wrong path—the entailments of the metaphor correspond more flexibly to the complex and subtle differences in the ways virtuous and vicious people might choose to live.[6]

The path or way in Proverbs is most fundamentally a metaphor for the moral life of particular human moral agents, their mode of being or "form of life" through all the diverse experiences and desires that distinct human lives confront—whether in the legal realm (e.g., 18:17; 25:8), in the marketplace (e.g., 11:1; 16:11; 20:10), in agricultural pursuits (e.g., 3:9; 13:23; 14:4), or in household (e.g., 17:1; 24:27) and urban existence (e.g., 11:10; 29:8). Even if one might speak in a limited sense of the singular "way" of wisdom in Proverbs, the ways of life of various wise and righteous persons are not identical, though they are surely related because each person is guided by the exercise of wisdom's virtues. In other words, one should assume that for Proverbs there exists more than one sort of virtuous life, just as the lives of vicious people will be variously depraved. The book thus sometimes speaks of human ways

---

5. The adjectives in these verses can also be understood as substantives, referring to an evil person or moral agent; cf. the following discussion.

6. Proverbs also deploys the rhetoric of the way/path in more general terms. In 14:12; 15:10; 16:25; 19:2, 16; 21:16; and 23:19, such language speaks about the moral life generally. In 6:6; 30:19; 31:3, and 27, the rhetoric describes typical forms of action or existence of particular beings—humans and animals. In 5:21; 16:2, 7, and 9, the terminology insists that one's existence or the course of one's life is ultimately under the control of the divine. In 8:2 and 9:15, it refers immediately and literally to real pathways, but the rhetoric is closely associated with the metaphorical-moral use of the terminology. In 8:2, it points to the place where one of the book's most prominent moral agents, Woman Wisdom, stands, and in 9:15 to the path of another moral type, the simpleton, who might turn aside to the house of Woman Folly. Other terminology associated with the complex of the way (images of feet, verbs of motion, lying in wait, etc.) appears throughout Proverbs.

and paths in the plural. For instance, in Proverbs 2:13 wisdom can protect the addressee from those "who forsake the paths of uprightness to walk in the ways of darkness." And Proverbs 5:21 knows that "human ways are under the eyes of the Lord, and he examines all their paths."

All this is unsurprising and even expected in virtue-oriented moral discourse, because moral agents do not perform particular virtues in isolated or static social contexts. Instead, virtues such as diligence, honesty, kindness, and justice must be exercised in life's many contexts. Praiseworthy moral figures do not rotely follow particular commands and so perform particular acts that might simply be repeated by others. Instead, in and through the vagaries of human social existence, the virtuous demonstrate through their Practical Wisdom (cf. chap. 8)—through the perceptions that their settled dispositions afford them—how, when, and in what form they should act. Although Arthur Keefer is no doubt correct to suggest that the "character types" of which Proverbs speaks are "literary caricatures" or "idealized figures," they nonetheless serve to shape readers or hearers into real moral agents who must, as Nussbaum puts it, "be flexible, ready for surprise, prepared to see, resourceful at improvisation."[7]

The Ways of the Wicked in Proverbs 1–9

That the reader or hearer of Proverbs should avoid the ways of vicious agents is most fully and obviously articulated near the outset of the book. This is evident in the text's first vignette, which follows quickly on the book's prologue:

> My child, if sinners entice you, do not consent. If they say, "Come with us, let us lie in wait for blood; let us wantonly ambush the innocent; like Sheol let us swallow them alive and whole, like those who go down to the Pit. We shall find all kinds of costly things; we shall fill our houses with booty. Throw in your lot among us; we will all have one purse"—my child, do not walk in their way, keep your foot from their paths; for their feet run to evil, and they hurry to shed blood. For in vain is the net baited while the bird is looking on; yet they lie in wait—to kill themselves! and set an ambush—for their own lives! Such is the end [are the ways][8] of all who are greedy for gain; it takes away the life of its possessors. (1:10–19)

---

7. Keefer's conclusions (*Proverbs 1–9*, 72) are drawn in relation not only to positive character types, but vicious ones too. Nussbaum, *Fragility of Goodness*, 305.

8. The MT reads "paths" (אָרְחוֹת) and not "end" (אַחֲרִית). Both terms "fit" in the passage's imagery. "End," of course, is part of the metaphorical complex of the way or path—a journey has a destination, and one's way of life an outcome or conclusion. Hebrew אַחֲרִית also has a temporal sense, the end of a period of time, but even such a sense is related to the metaphor

In this passage, the instructing parental voice warns the addressee ("my child") against being enticed by "sinners" (חַטָּאִים), who are described as violent robbers who "lie in wait" to "ambush the innocent." The lines brim with terms related to the rhetoric of the two ways.[9] This is especially evident after the parental voice "quotes" the robbers' words in verses 11–14 and takes up his own admonition in verse 15.[10] As the instructing voice makes clear at the outset, however, it is actually the "sinners"—those who have "missed the mark" and strayed onto wrong ways—who first deploy the moral metaphor of "walking on a path" in Proverbs. They invite the addressee to "come with us" (v. 11). The addressee, however, should not simply avoid a way of folly and wickedness generally speaking; he should avoid the robbers' "way" and stay far from "their paths" since "their feet run" toward the evil of shedding innocent blood. "Their end" is their own death. The images of lying in wait and ambushing also belong to the broader metaphorical complex of the "way," since a person typically would have been literally vulnerable to such things while traveling a path or road.

Proverbs' opening vignette makes clear that the book's addressees should not follow the sinners in their violent robbing and murder. But features of the passage's depiction of the robbers' wanton wickedness also suggest that the account of the robbers functions as more than an object lesson. The sinners are also symbolic representatives of all who trod the wrong way. Indeed, the passage is placed in an important literary space at the very beginning of the book, almost immediately after the programmatic prologue, which hints at the book's figurative dimensions in its mention of a "proverb," "figure," and "riddles" (1:6; see chap. 2 above). The text's literary location is an initial signal that its significance for the book may exceed the literal instruction it offers.

There are other clues to this surplus of meaning in Proverbs 1:10–19. First, as noted, the words the robbers speak are not precisely their own but rather are placed in their mouths by the parent-teacher: "My son, if sinners . . . say" (v. 10). And the words that the instructing voice attributes to the sinners are hyperbolic. The robbers' invitation to steal and kill runs blatantly counter

---

of the way. Life is regularly regarded metaphorically as a "journey," and journeys involve not only paths traveled, but they also take time to complete. Though possible, the emendation of אָרְחוֹת to אַחֲרִית is not necessary. See the brief discussion in Schipper (*Proverbs 1–15*, 90) and cf. Waltke, *Proverbs*, 185.

9. These verses are also important for considering how Proverbs seeks to train a reader's desire toward virtue. This aspect of the passage will be considered in chap. 5.

10. Although the instructing voice mimics the rhetoric of the sinners who tempt the addressee, the words he ascribes to them are his own. The instructing voice's utterance here is thus similar to what Bakhtin would call a "dialogized interior monologue." See *Problems of Dostoevsky's Poetics*, 72–75. Cf. Kim, *Reanimating Qohelet's Contradictory Voices*.

to common, even universal, norms of justice.[11] The passage's rhetoric also generalizes from the sinners' violent robbing to "all" who are "greedy for gain," a rhetorical move that indicates the instruction's focus is not limited to warnings about engaging in violent theft but is interested in wrong desires and choices too.

Together these features of the text—the vignette's placement at the beginning of the book, the father's caricature of the sinners' speech and actions, and the text's generalizing rhetoric—suggest that it is a paradigmatic tale for Proverbs, not simply straightforward instruction. However, its figurative level of meaning does not eclipse its literal instruction. Both levels function together. As Paul Ricoeur explains, metaphorical meaning or "secondary signification" emerges only "by means of, or through, the literal one."[12]

At the outset of Proverbs' moral teaching, then, the young and simple addressee is not merely instructed to avoid murderous robbing. He is firmly warned, via descriptions of the most heinous of acts committed by wicked characters, against following the way of *any and all* suspect moral agents. Elsewhere in Proverbs 1–9, the addressee is directly warned against following the paths of these morally deficient subjects. Proverbs 3:31, 4:14, and 4:19 single out the ways of violent (חָמָס), wicked (רְשָׁעִים), and evil (רָעִים) people:

> Do not envy the violent
> and do not choose any of their ways. (3:31)

> Do not enter the path of the wicked,
> and do not walk in the way of evildoers. (4:14)

> The way of the wicked is like deep darkness;
> they do not know what they stumble over. (4:19)

In Proverbs 2:12–15 wisdom can save one

> from the way of the evil person,
> from those who speak perversely,
> who forsake the paths of uprightness
> to walk in the ways of darkness,

---

11. "Universal" is not always an unproblematic term. Yet as Nussbaum suggests, the universality of any particular virtue, such as justice, need not be tethered to the particular specification of that virtue in a particular time and place (or text). Rather, the universal quality of a virtue emerges from fundamental "grounding experiences," such as human sociability. In different times and places, a virtue such as justice will require different specifications or distinct articulations of the entailments of the virtue. See Nussbaum, "Non-Relative Virtues."

12. Ricoeur, *Interpretation Theory*, 55.

> who rejoice in doing evil
> and delight in the perverseness of evil;
> those whose paths are crooked,
> and who are devious in their ways. (2:12–15 NRSV modified)

This second passage characterizes the two ways as "paths of uprightness" or "ways of darkness" (v. 13), and the entailments of these images are suggestive, even if subtle. The verse metaphorically indicates that one path is desirable in that it seems sure and easy to walk. However, it is not the path of an "upright" moral agent (*yāšār*), as might be expected in Proverbs. Rather, it is the way of "uprightness" (*yōšer*)—a clear path upon which one might walk standing up; it is a path a person can easily navigate, not the sort of trail where a traveler must bend down to avoid obstacles like low-lying tree branches. By contrast, the darkness of the path in the second half of verse 13 would make any road dangerous. It can leave a person vulnerable to impediments, which are easily avoided in the light of day but at night can cause one to stumble, fall, and be injured.

Despite verse 13's description of the paths people travel, the focus of the larger passage remains on the agents who travel such ways. Verse 12 speaks of the way of "the evil person" and of people "who speak perversely" (מְדַבֵּר תַּהְפֻּכוֹת).[13] The paths of uprightness and of darkness in verse 13 are described via a complex syntax that names particular kinds of agents and the nature of their agency. In verse 13 those who forsake (הָעֹזְבִים, masculine plural participle) paths of uprightness do so in order to walk (לָלֶכֶת, infinitive construct) in the ways of darkness; verse 14 mentions those who rejoice (הַשְּׂמֵחִים, masculine plural participle/adjective) to do evil (לַעֲשׂוֹת רָע, infinitive construct) that they might delight (יָגִילוּ, imperfect) in perversity. Verse 15 mentions "those whose" (אֲשֶׁר, relative pronoun) paths are crooked and those who are devious (נְלוֹזִים, masculine plural participle)—that is, who turn aside on their paths.

The negative moral types in Proverbs 2 are surely akin to other negative moral types in the book's early chapters. The metaphor of the way is also applied to the scoundrel or villain of Proverbs 6:12. This sort of person walks (הוֹלֵךְ) with "crookedness of mouth" (עִקְּשׁוּת פֶּה) or, as the NRSV says, "goes around with crooked speech." Subsequent verses (vv. 13–15) sketch

---

13. The translation of 2:12a diverges slightly from the NRSV. Instead of "the way of evil," I render "the way of the evil person." Although רָע here might be regarded as an adjective modifying דֶּרֶךְ ("evil way"), it can also be understood as the substantival adjective "evil person" in a construct phrase ("an evil person's way"). This rendering is supported by the second, parallel stich of the verse, which refers to "the person who speaks perversity" (אִישׁ מְדַבֵּר תַּהְפֻּכוֹת), as well as by the passage's broader concern with moral agents.

further, via participial constructions, the continual or typical deceptive and disruptive nature of this person's mode of life; they also envision his abrupt demise:

> A scoundrel and a villain
> 	goes around with crooked speech,
> winking the eyes, shuffling the feet,
> 	pointing the fingers,
> with perverted mind devising evil,
> 	continually sowing discord;
> on such a one calamity will descend suddenly;
> 	in a moment, damage beyond repair. (6:12–15)

Other places in Proverbs' opening chapters use images from the metaphorical complex of "walking on a way" to portray the perverse planning of vicious agents. For example, in Proverbs 4:16 the wicked "trip up" others. Indeed, they

> cannot sleep unless they have done wrong;
> 	they are robbed of sleep unless they have made someone stumble.

The Strange or Foreign Woman

Related to the ways of wicked and evil persons in Proverbs 1–9 is another figure whose path Proverbs clearly presents as the wrong way: the strange or foreign woman.[14] In binary fashion not uncommon to patriarchal discourse, the strange or foreign woman (2:16–19; 5:3–14; 6:24–35; 7:1–27; cf. Woman Folly in 9:13–18) in Proverbs 1–9 is often contrasted with Woman Wisdom—a personified symbol of the virtues Proverbs insists anyone traveling "the right way" will possess.

Some scholars understand the strange or foreign woman in Proverbs in light of the socioeconomic, political context of Second Temple Judea, especially the so-called marriage crisis reflected in Ezra-Nehemiah (Ezra 9–10; Neh. 13).[15] On the literal level of the text, however, the strange woman is not necessarily foreign in an ethnic or political sense. She is simply an illegitimate and dangerous sexual partner for the book's imagined young male addressee. She is, as Fox forcefully contends, another man's wife and the social opposite

---

14. The literature on this figure is extensive. See, e.g., Camp, "What's So Strange," and the titles mentioned in note 15 below. Cf. Maier, "Wisdom and Women."
15. Cf. Washington, "Strange Woman"; Yee, *Poor Banished Children of Eve*, 135–58; Yee, "'I Have Perfumed My Bed.'"

of the legitimate wife the book's addressee should seek (cf. 5:15–20).[16] Fox rejects the views of those who relate Proverbs' strange or foreign woman to the marriage crisis and identity struggles of the golah community (returned exiles) in Ezra-Nehemiah. Yet Proverbs' rhetoric of strangeness, foreignness, and "woman" surely evokes a broader biblical discourse about foreign wives/women like that of Ezra-Nehemiah (and other texts; e.g., Num. 25), even if, as Fox insists, Proverbs' earliest young readers and hearers may have regarded the instruction to be mostly about avoiding adultery.

Whatever the case, Proverbs urges its male addressees to delight in their own spouses rather than consort with another man's wife (5:18). What is more, they should seek Woman Wisdom—that figure whose desirability is constructed in erotic terms associated with legitimate patriarchal marriage. Woman Wisdom can, in fact, save the addressee from the dangers of illicit sex (adultery) with the strange woman (e.g., 2:16–19; 6:24) and more generally from the illicit way of folly and wickedness. Although we will say more about the female characters of Proverbs 1–9 in chapter 5, the point here is that the binary relationship between Woman Wisdom and the strange or the foreign woman suggests that she should, like Woman Wisdom herself, be understood as a foundational trope for a particular way of life (in this case, what the text views as the "wrong way"). Just as the parent's teaching about the "sinners" in 1:10–19 serves not only to warn of the wanton, violent acts characteristic of the robbers but also to present these figures as potent symbols of all who travel the wrong way, so too the strange woman is not merely a character in the book's literal teaching about adultery. She is a figure for all who walk the wrong moral path. Proverbs not only describes her in terms that evoke the obviously symbolic character of Woman Folly in 9:13–18 but also explicitly connects with her "the way" several times in the book. In 2:18, the instructing voice claims that "her way leads down to death, and her paths to the shades." Proverbs 5:5–6 adds,

> Her feet go down to death;
>   her steps follow the path to Sheol.
> She does not keep straight to the path of life;
>   her ways wander, and she does not know it.

In Proverbs 7:6–27 the woman who approaches the simple youth—surely the strange or foreign woman of verse 5—is also imagined as one who is rebelliously "wayward" in relation to her house (v. 11).[17] Rather than dwelling

---

16. Cf. Fox, *Proverbs 1–9*, 134–41.

17. Hebrew סֹרָרֶת most fundamentally suggests stubbornness, but the larger imagery of the line warrants the NRSV's rendering "wayward." I would gloss "stubbornly wayward."

in her home, "her feet" roam.[18] "Now in the street, now in the squares, and at every corner" is where "she lies in wait," as did the sinners of Proverbs 1 (v. 12), who likewise followed their own paths rather than one commended by the patriarchal teaching voice. In 7:25–27 the instructing voice offers further admonition about the strange or foreign woman:

> Do not let your hearts turn aside to her ways;
>   do not stray into her paths.
> For many are those she has laid low,
>   and numerous are her victims.
> Her house is the way to Sheol,
>   going down to the chambers of death. (7:25–27)

The moral agency of the strange or foreign woman in Proverbs 1–9 thus emerges clearly in light of the metaphor of the way. She travels her own path and is reckoned by the male writers of the book as able to manipulate those who follow after her. However, the focus of Proverbs' instruction at this point is less on *her* person and character than it is on the developing character of the young male students whom the book addresses. The audience's ability to resist the temptation to follow the strange woman's paths—either literally by avoiding adultery or figuratively by avoiding the wrong path of any vicious agent—will be foundationally important to the development of his disposition. Depending on his choice to follow one path or another, his character will bend either toward wisdom and justice or in the direction of folly and wickedness. All of the addressee's particular choices to follow the right or wrong path shape his desires and so train his character for a life of wisdom and justice or of wickedness and folly (cf. chap. 5 below).

Of course, the book's teaching about wisdom and adultery, the two ways, and the development of the addressee's character in relation to two women—Woman Wisdom and the strange woman—is far from innocuous or innocent. Although Proverbs suggests some agency for both Woman Wisdom and the strange woman, it does so quite transparently through an enactment and inflection of the infamous "whore-virgin dichotomy" typical of patriarchal

---

18. Given that passages about the strange/foreign woman function as warnings to young men about the dangers of adultery, as well as the fact that the woman's path strays from her house (an important site of patriarchal control of a woman's sexuality), it is not impossible that the imagery of feet in some of these texts, though clearly associated with the moral metaphor of the way, serves a further rhetorical purpose. As is well known, "feet" in biblical discourse can be a euphemism for genitalia. In this case, the woman not only permits her literal feet to follow a morally problematic path, her feet/genitalia (a synecdoche for her sexuality) are precisely what stray. On these matters in relation to Prov. 5:5 in particular, see Newsom, "Woman and the Discourse of Patriarchal Wisdom."

discourse. As we suggest more fully below (chap. 5), the book presents virtuous Woman Wisdom as a legitimate object of men's erotic desire (cf. Prov. 4:5–9), while the strange woman's agency and sexuality are negatively marked, depicted as dangerous to the book's male audience. Contemporary readers of Proverbs need not uncritically adopt the prejudices of the ancient text here or at other points; one need not concede the rightness or "timelessness" of the book's conceptions of gender, justice, or anything else. Indeed, as will be suggested in the conclusion, readers of Proverbs are exhorted, ironically by features of the "text" itself and implicitly by the broader moral logic of the book's virtue-oriented discourse, to question its social and moral presuppositions and conclusions, many of which rather obviously represent historically contingent—and so contestable—perspectives.

The Paths of Simpletons

The addressee of Proverbs 1–9 is warned about the ways of "wicked" and "evil" persons and those most closely associated with them (e.g., the strange/foreign woman; the villain and scoundrel). Following the way of certain kinds of simpletons, a moral type mentioned ten times in Proverbs 1–9, is also problematic. Although certain moral characters in Proverbs may not be particularly susceptible to moral training, the simpleton is in fact teachable. As Fox puts it, this type of person is "open to learning and improvement."[19] Nonetheless, these malleable moral agents are also susceptible to choosing a "way" that entails rejecting instruction. In an early passage (1:20–33), for example, Woman Wisdom admonishes "simple ones," along with "scoffers" (לֵצִים) and dolts (כְּסִילִים), to heed her call (1:22). When these character types do not follow Wisdom, Proverbs ominously says, they "shall eat the fruit of their way and be sated with their own devices" (1:31).

Who precisely the simpletons are and what they exactly do are not explicitly spelled out in Proverbs 1–9. We learn of their refusal to heed Wisdom's counsel and reproof in Proverbs 1:25. Yet besides this, and being warned about sex with another man's wife (7:7–27), we read little in the book's early chapters of the specific instruction they might refuse or of other acts, choices, and modes of being that might characterize such moral agents. They are simply immature and prone to moral waywardness, even if not fully committed to a wrong life path. Despite being collocated with scoffers and fools in 1:22, elsewhere the simple are more positively described as capable of turning onto the right way. In Proverbs 9:4–6 Woman Wisdom optimistically invites the simple to her feast

---

19. Fox, *Proverbs 1–9*, 43.

and so to follow "the way of insight." Still, some simpletons may persistently reject Wisdom's instruction and accept Folly's desirable invitation to stolen water and secret meals (9:16–17).

As for the scoffers and the dolts in Proverbs 1:22, these moral agents make limited appearances in Proverbs 1–9. Proverbs 3:35 contrasts dolts (כְּסִילִים) with the wise, while in 8:5 they are again parallel with the simple, both capable of advancing in learning:

> O simple ones [פְּתָאיִם], learn prudence;
>   acquire intelligence, you who lack it [כְסִילִים]. (8:5)

The scoffer, on the other hand, is not only contrasted with the humble in Proverbs 3:34 and with the wise in 9:8, but such a person is also collocated in 9:7 with the wicked person (רָשָׁע), a moral subject whose settled character seems to make that person incorrigible. The status of the scoffer as corrigible or not in Proverbs 1–9 is thus ambiguous. He is sometimes associated with corrigible agents—the simple ones and dolts—while at other moments he is linked with an incorrigible wicked person. It may thus be that 1:22, which collocates the scoffer with dolts and simpletons, is pointing to the fact that a simple person's character—depending on the instruction he receives and the choices he makes—may from an early age start to bend in good or bad directions—if not toward wisdom and justice, then toward the ways of dolts and scoffers.

Whatever the precise features and inclinations of simple people's ways of life, Proverbs 1 makes clear that without Wisdom's assistance, they will, along with scoffers and dolts, suffer inevitable "calamity" (1:27). As Proverbs 1:28 says,

> Then they [simpletons, scoffers, dolts] will call upon me [Wisdom],
>   but I will not answer;
> they will seek me diligently, but will not find me.

Suffering through moments of disaster unaided by w/Wisdom[20] is, for the moral types who refuse wise instruction, "the fruit of their way" (1:31). The paths that some simpletons (and others) choose in rejecting Wisdom's call is thus a dangerous way, not unlike the path of darkness in 2:13 above. Although the primary addressees of Proverbs 1–9 may themselves be young, simple, and susceptible to moral education, they should take care not to follow the lead of other young simpletons whose character already may be tending toward

---

20. Here and throughout, "w/Wisdom" is occasionally deployed to signal that the text may be pointing not simply to a moral-intellectual notion of wisdom (lowercase "wisdom") but at the same time to personified Woman Wisdom (uppercase "Wisdom").

scoffing and stupidity. Indeed, for the addressee to adopt the way of doltish, simple scoffers is a first step to following still other morally suspect agents down their paths. The simple youth who follows another simpleton on the path of scorning wisdom runs the risk of becoming a full-blown incorrigible fool (אֱוִיל) or another wicked agent (רָשָׁע)—someone whose bad character has become fixed. In such instances, the young simple person will face significant consequences. Like the man who chooses adultery with the strange or foreign woman, his end is like death itself—dire and permanent. As the instructing voice of 2:19 says to "my child" (2:1), "those who go to her [the strange woman] never come back, nor do they regain the paths of life." Or in the words of 7:22, such a simple youth (7:7) "goes like an ox to the slaughter, or bounds like a stag toward the trap."[21]

The Ways of the Wise and Just in Proverbs 1–9

In Proverbs 1–9 the text's addressee is not only confronted with the ways of unsavory and vicious agents (or simpletons) against which he must define his own path of wisdom; virtuous agents, traveling desirable paths, are also presented in the book's opening instructional poems. It is the paths of these moral agents that the book's readers, especially the young and simple, should follow.

Contrasting with the way of the wicked, the way of morally laudable agents in Proverbs 1–9 is characterized as straight and secure. The instructing voice admonishes the addressee to follow virtuous agents down such paths. By attentiveness to traditional parental teaching, the young person's path will be safe and sure. By holding fast to "sound wisdom and prudence" (3:21), the hearer is reassured: you will "walk on your way securely and your foot will not stumble" (3:23). Or as Proverbs 4:12 says in relation to remaining on paths of wisdom and uprightness,

> When you walk, your step will not be hampered;
> and if you run, you will not stumble.

After Proverbs 6:22 similarly states, "When you walk, they [the parents' commands] will lead you," the text augments the images of safe travel with one of secure slumber:

> When you lie down, they will watch over you;
> and when you awake, they will talk with you.

21. On the difficult text and the emendation reflected in the NRSV, cf. Fox, *Proverbs 1–9*, 249–50.

To the promise of a safe and secure existence that wisdom can enable (though not guarantee), Proverbs 4:26–27 adds an admonishment not to stray from such ways.

> Keep straight the path of your feet,
>   and all your ways will be sure.
> Do not swerve to the right or to the left;
>   turn your foot away from evil.

For help in finding the promised smooth and straight paths, the addressees of Proverbs 1–9 can rely on Adonai. In a line that authorizes the parental instruction of Proverbs by linking the way of wisdom with the divine (cf. 2:6; 8:22–23), Proverbs 3:5–6 exhorts the young addressee:

> Trust in the LORD with all your heart,
>   and do not rely on your own insight.
> In all your ways acknowledge him.

If the reader/hearer does, Adonai "will make straight your paths" (3:6b). Proverbs 2:6–8 is similar. Not only does wisdom ultimately come from the divine, but the Lord also secures the path of the upright.

> For the LORD gives wisdom;
>   from his mouth come knowledge and understanding;
> he stores up sound wisdom for the upright;
>   he is a shield to those who walk blamelessly,
> guarding the paths of justice
>   and preserving the way of his faithful ones.

The rhetoric of texts like Proverbs 2:6–8 and 3:5–6 has the flavor of promises designed to motivate a hearer to choose a good path in life by associating such a life with the divine. Trusting or acknowledging the Lord (3:5) is a fundamental religious virtue and belongs to wisdom's way. It is close kin to fearing Adonai. Together these religious virtues sketch the contours of a piety that is foundational to Proverbs—a stance of openness, confidence, wonder, and when appropriate, even a genuine dread toward the divine who ultimately sanctions the book's moral teaching.[22]

---

22. For an elegant exploration of these sorts of matters, see Brown, *Wisdom's Wonder*. The rhetoric of 2:6–8 makes clear that the one who strays from the right path ought literally to fear the deity who can potentially cause a person harm. This is because Adonai, who is a guardian—a "shield" (2:7)—of those who follow the way of wisdom, might not only remove

Yet besides pointing to the role of the divine in the acquisition of virtue, these lines also place in relief something important about how Proverbs understands the moral selves of humans. The instructional poems (and the rest) of Proverbs imply that through openness to the book's instruction and acceptance of the accompanying discipline and reproof (cf. chap. 6 below), a person can achieve wisdom. With the exercise of this wisdom a person can refuse to travel a wicked course and understand how various human goods contribute to happiness and how to pursue those goods appropriately. In Carol Newsom's study of the types of moral selves in the Bible and early Jewish literature, the moral self usually presumed by Proverbs is "a self in control." Such selves have (or can develop) the capacity to make appropriate moral choices; their moral agency is not "under the control" of another agent or force.[23]

In Proverbs 3:5–6 and especially 2:6–8, however, Adonai's assistance might be considered necessary, not merely felicitous, for navigating life's paths via wisdom's virtues. The rhetorical promise, however, does not seem to imagine that the divine directly, immediately, or fully enables a person's acquisition of the wisdom needed to traverse a good moral path in life—though it does incline in that direction and in a fashion that may be consonant with aspects of the Thomistic-Catholic moral tradition's teaching about the necessity of divine grace to live truly virtuously. In Proverbs 2:6 the Lord gives wisdom, certainly. Adonai is regarded in some sense as the ultimate source of wisdom or at least as intimately associated with wisdom and its acquisition by humans (see 3:18–19, but cf. chaps. 11 and 12 below). And as the book's "motto" at the conclusion of the prologue reminds us (1:7), fear of Adonai is the beginning or best part of wisdom (NRSV "knowledge"). Yet the text does not seem to imagine more than that. As in Deuteronomy, with which aspects of Proverbs 1–9 resonate (cf. esp. Prov. 3:1–5; 6:20–24; 7:1–5; Deut. 6:6–9; 11:18–20), the divine does not seem to be the force that fundamentally enables humans to live rightly—whether in the form of obedience to covenant commands, through the exercise of virtues, or some combination of these.[24]

---

such protection; he can also punish wrongdoers. On the literal dread or fear of the Lord that Proverbs sometimes envisions, see the discussion of the prologue in chap. 2 above.

23. Newsom, "Models of the Moral Self," 10–12. The "self in control," Newsom claims, is the default model of the Hebrew Bible and is especially evident in Deuteronomic literature. The relationship between Proverbs' instruction and the torah of Deuteronomy is often discussed. See, e.g., several of the essays in Schipper and Teeter, *Wisdom and Torah*. Cf. further Carr, *Formation of the Hebrew Bible*, 403–31; and Schipper, *Proverbs 1–15*, 36–39.

24. Although a relationship between aspects of Prov. 1–9 and Deuteronomy seems clear, what is less obvious is the relative priority of the texts and the direction of "influence" between them. Schipper (*Proverbs 1–15*, 37) speaks of "allusions to Deuteronomy" in Prov. 1–9, suggesting Deuteronomy's priority and the influence of that book on Proverbs; see further Schipper, "'Teach Them Diligently.'" By contrast, Fox (*Proverbs 1–9*, 79; *Proverbs 10–31*, 951–53) explains

There is little sense in which Proverbs imagines anything like the divine's transformation of a human heart of stone into a heart of flesh, as in Ezekiel (36:26–27);[25] there is no "new" covenant where the Lord promises, "I will put my law within them [Israel], and I will write it on their hearts" so that "they shall all know me," as Jeremiah claims (31:31–34). The moral self implicit in Proverbs is also distinct from that presumed by Second Temple traditions that speak of subjects acquiring revealed, eschatologically oriented wisdom (e.g., 4QInstruction; the Enoch tradition). Although a verse like Proverbs 2:6, which speaks of knowledge and understanding coming from the Lord's mouth, resonates with the divine's revelation of torah, which itself can be regarded as "wisdom" (Deut. 4:6; cf. Sir. 24; chap. 13 below), the "self in control" of Proverbs has no place for the esoteric knowledge of some early Jewish texts, the possession of which ensures a future, even postmortem flourishing.[26] The addressees of Proverbs are instead regarded as perfectly capable of attaining this-worldly eudaemonia by advancing, via instruction and discipline, in the virtue promoted by the ancestral-parental voice of the book.[27]

Proverbs 1–9 elaborates on the safe and secure ways that 3:5–6 and 2:6–8 confidently believe addressees of the book can, perhaps with some help from the divine, travel. For example, Proverbs 2:20 says a person should "walk in the way of the good, and keep to the paths of the just." In contrast to the

---

the relation in opposite terms. Carr's work (*Formation of the Hebrew Bible*, 403–31), if correct, likewise suggests a relation of influence from Proverbs to Deuteronomy. On intertextual relations and the question of the "influence" of one text on another, see chap. 10 below.

25. On the moral self in Ezekiel, see Lapsley, *Can These Bones Live?*

26. Agur's wisdom in Prov. 30:1–4 may be an exception, but see the following note and cf. Sandoval, "Texts and Intertexts."

27. Schipper (*Proverbs 1–15*, 36–39) offers an alternative, complex, and nuanced view. Whereas much of the "oldest literary core" of Prov. 1–9, like Deuteronomy, offers a conception of human moral agency consonant with Newsom's "self in control," he sees in the redaction of the book a development of this position so that the latest strands of the text—the prologue with its emphasis on fear of the Lord and the initial lines of Prov. 30—suggest something different. Unlike, say, Prov. 2:1–5 where humans are regarded "as capable of attaining 'knowledge of God' through sapiential learning," the prologue offers a "a completely different view." For Schipper, it seems that as with Agur's words in 30:2–3, for the book's opening lines "sapiential instruction is now seen as coming from God," rather than human tradition. In my view, the prologue's emphasis on fear of the divine as the beginning of wisdom does not indicate a strong conception of wisdom as divinely given but can simply be regarded as a rhetorical insistence on the intimate link between religious and moral-social virtue in the book and the belief that the ultimate origin of all wisdom is with God (cf. 8:22–31). Agur's apparently esoteric "knowledge of Holy Ones" in 30:1–4 is distinct, but it does not represent a central perspective of the book. Indeed, 30:4 rhetorically, as well as critically and ironically, queries as to the sort of person who might legitimately claim the sort of wisdom to which Agur pretends: "Who has ascended to heaven and come down?" (NRSV). For those sages who produced and transmitted Proverbs, the implied answer is "no one." See further Sandoval, "Texts and Intertexts," 169–72.

darkness characteristic of the paths of the wicked (cf. 2:13; 4:19), the just person's way in Proverbs 1–9 is marked with a metaphor of light—a luminosity that enables one to see clearly and so travel safely:

> But the path of the righteous is like the light of dawn,
> which shines brighter and brighter until full day. (4:18)

Interestingly, in Proverbs 1–9 (and throughout the book) "the wise" are not often singled out as those who follow a path the addressee should emulate.[28] However, Proverbs 4:11 implies that the instructing parental voice is a wise voice that can reliably guide the hearer down the right path.

> I have taught you the way of wisdom;
> I have led you in the paths of uprightness. (4:11)

Proverbs 1:20–21 and 8:2 introduce the paths of another figure who might sagaciously guide the book's addressee: personified Woman Wisdom, who stations herself near the most bustling parts of the city—streets, squares, corners, entrances, ways, and crossroads.

> Wisdom cries out in the street;
> in the squares she raises her voice.
> At the busiest corner she cries out;
> at the entrance of the city gates she speaks. (1:20–21)
>
> On the heights, beside the way,
> at the crossroads she takes her stand. (8:2)

The cluster of terms that speak of locations where the personified, symbolic figure of virtue is present is part of Proverbs' central moral metaphor of life's two ways. The ones who desire w/Wisdom should heed her call as they travel various life paths. They should, in a sense, "find their way" to the places and the paths she frequents—which are obviously many. This not only underscores wisdom's accessibility but also points to the inevitable diversity of lives that human moral agents (young and simple, wise and just, dolts and others) will live and the variety of contexts that they should strive to negotiate sagely.

Other passages in Proverbs 1–9 take up the moral metaphor of the way in relation to Woman Wisdom even more clearly. Proverbs 3:17 speaks of the

---

28. However, a number of verses in the book gesture toward the paths wise people travel, sometimes by contrasting an aspect of their character with the way or path of another (sometimes negatively marked) character. See, e.g., Prov. 3:7; 12:15; 13:20; 15:10; 29:8.

desirability of Wisdom's path, and Wisdom herself insists in 8:20 that her way is a way of virtue, especially social virtue.

> Her [Wisdom's] ways are ways of pleasantness,
>   and all her paths are peace. (3:17)

> I [Wisdom] walk in the way of righteousness,
>   along the paths of justice. (8:20)

Wisdom also intimates that her teaching constitutes a necessary and trustworthy path by which one might attain flourishing.

> And now, my children, listen to me:
>   happy are those who keep my ways. (8:32)

> Happy is the one who listens to me,
>   watching daily at my gates,
>   waiting beside my doors. (8:34)

Indeed, as the parental teaching voice in Proverbs 1–9 also claims,

> Happy are those who find wisdom,
>   and those who get understanding. (3:13)

Much of Proverbs 1–9 thus suggests, as do premodern, virtue-oriented moral systems, that the desirable end of a good human life—happiness, flourishing, well-being, or "success"—is achieved not by individuals pursuing their own subjective conceptions of happiness, following their "own ways" and deciding what makes them most happy or affords the most pleasure. Rather, the proper end of human life is a happiness or eudaemonia that emerges through a particular way of life that wise and just agents have traveled. It is a way that has been judged most capable of producing well-being for the sort of social, spiritual, material, and rational beings human are thought naturally—and so objectively—to be.

For Proverbs the best way for a person to satisfy natural desires for various goods that contribute to happiness is to follow the ways of wise and just moral agents. There is no genuine flourishing or happiness for those who cannot follow such paths; there is no true "life" apart from w/Wisdom or a virtuous existence (cf. 1:19; 2:19; 3:2, 16, 18, 22; 4:13; 22; 6:23; 8:35). In fact, quite the opposite is the case. As Wisdom herself says in Proverbs 1:32, "Waywardness kills the simple, and the complacency of [dolts] destroys them."

Moral Agents and Their Ways in Proverbs 10–31

Proverbs 10–31 similarly contrasts the way or path of virtuous figures with that of vicious persons. Given the high frequency of nouns, substantival participles, and adjectives in Proverbs 10–15 that name particular sorts of moral characters, it is not surprising that these chapters also allude frequently to the way or path of such agents. The ones who walk in virtuous ways—the blameless, the upright, and so forth—are contrasted with those who follow perverse ways—the wicked, fools, the faithless, and the lazy. At other points the path of particular agents is set in parallel with other agents or moral traits, but not precisely in contrast to the "way" of these other agents or traits.

In the following verses from Proverbs 10–15, rhetoric that most pertains to moral agents and their ways is italicized:

> *Whoever walks in integrity walks securely,* but *whoever follows perverse ways will be found out.* (10:9)

> *The righteousness of the blameless keeps their ways straight,* but *the wicked fall* by their own wickedness.[29] (11:5)

> *Those of crooked mind*[30] are an abomination to the LORD, but *those of blameless ways* are his delight. (11:20)

> *The way of fools* is right in their own eyes,[31] but *the wise* listen to advice. (12:15 NRSV modified)

> *The righteous* gives good advice to friends,[32] but *the way of the wicked leads astray.* (12:26)

> Righteousness guards *one whose way is upright,* but sin overthrows *the wicked.* (13:6)

---

29. Fox explains that בְּרִשְׁעָתוֹ יִפֹּל here "can mean 'because of his wickedness' or 'into his wickedness,' the latter picturing wickedness as a pit into which the evildoer stumbles" (cf. 26:27a). *Proverbs 10–31*, 532 (emphasis original).

30. The first four words of this translation diverge from the NRSV, which renders עִקְּשֵׁי־לֵב as "crooked minds." However, the masculine singular adjective in construct with a noun is a construction identical with the second half of the verse (תְּמִימֵי דָרֶךְ). The NRSV's rendering of those words—"those of blameless ways"—reveals the line's concern with moral agents and warrants translating עִקְּשֵׁי־לֵב as "those of crooked mind."

31. NRSV renders, "Fools think their own way is right."

32. The MT of 12:26a is difficult. The NRSV rendering above appears to capture the sense. However, other ways of understanding the text are also possible; cf. Schipper, *Proverbs 1–15*, 434; and Fox, *Proverbs 10–31*, 559.

Good sense wins favor, but *the way of the faithless* is their ruin.³³ (13:15)

The perverse get what their ways deserve, and *the good*, what their deeds deserve.³⁴ (14:14)

The way of the wicked is an abomination to the LORD, but he loves *the one who pursues righteousness*. (15:9)

There is severe discipline for *one who forsakes the way*,³⁵ but *one who hates a rebuke* will die. (15:10)

The way of the lazy is overgrown with thorns, but *the path of the upright* is a level highway.³⁶ (15:19)

Beyond the confines of Proverbs 10–15, a number of other verses in the second half of the book highlight the paths of particular moral subjects and set these figures in parallel with other agents or moral traits—though again they do not always precisely contrast to the "way" of the initial agents or traits. In the following proverbs from chapters 16–29, rhetoric that most pertains to moral agents and their ways is again italicized:

The highway of the upright avoids evil; *those who guard their way* preserve their lives. (16:17)

The violent entice their neighbors, and *lead them in a way that is not good*. (16:29)

Those [the one] who keep the commandment will live; *those who are heedless of their ways* will die.³⁷ (19:16)

---

33. The final word in the MT of 13:15 is אֵיתָן ("unchanging"), which the NRSV and many commentators emend to אֵידָם ("ruin, destruction") in order to have the line reflect a clear antithetic parallelism, as in most other lines in Prov. 10–15. Schipper (*Proverbs 1–15*, 452–53), however, argues compellingly for the MT, translating 13:15b as "but the way of the treacherous is lasting."

34. "The MT's *wmʿlyw* 'and from upon him' is clearly an error (haplog.) for *wmmʿlyw* 'and from his ways'" (Fox, *Proverbs 10–31*, 578). So, too, Schipper, *Proverbs 1–15*, 474, who cites further Meinhold, *Die Sprüche*, 1:234n59.

35. As Fox (*Proverbs 10–31*, 592–93) also notes, it is only here in Prov. 15:10 that אֹרַח ("way") is not further modified as some sort of particular way or as the way of a particular kind of person or persons; cf. דֶּרֶךְ in 23:19.

36. Cf. further 15:24 and 12:28. The first of these verses speaks of "the path of life" but closely associates this with "the wise"; the second mentions "the path of righteousness." Proverbs 14:12 similarly speaks of the "way" that seems right to a person but ends in death. On this last line (and similar lines), cf. chap. 8 below.

37. The NRSV captures well the sense of 19:16b. Fox (*Proverbs 10–31*, 655–56), however, finds the MT's "despises his ways [*drkyw*]" to be obscure and offers two emendations to the line, rendering it "He who guards a precept guards his life, while he who despises a word will die."

A person's way may be crooked, [even] while his deeds are pure and upright.[38] (21:8)

Whoever wanders from the way of understanding will rest in the assembly of the dead. (21:16)

The wicked put on a bold face, but *the upright give thought to their ways*. (21:29)

Thorns and snares are in *the way of the perverse*; *the cautious will keep far from them*. (22:5)

Make no friends with *those given to anger* [בַּעַל אָף], and do not associate with *hotheads*, or *you may learn their ways* and *entangle yourself in a snare*. (22:24–25)

Better to be poor and *walk in integrity* than to be *crooked in one's ways* even though rich.[39] (28:6)

Those who mislead the upright into evil ways will fall into pits of their own making, but *the blameless* will have a goodly inheritance. (28:10)

One who walks in integrity will be safe, but *the one who twists about on two ways will fall* by one of them.[40] (28:18 NRSV modified)

In Proverbs 1–9 a patriarchal instructional voice occasionally admonishes his "child" to attend well to the way the young person chooses to travel. At points later in the book, this same kind of addressee and his path are the explicit concerns of a teaching voice. The instruction of Proverbs 23:19 and 26, for instance, echoes the book's earlier concern that "my child" follow a parent's ways (see also 19:27; 20:7; 24:13, 21; 27:11; cf. 31:28).

---

38. The MT of 21:8 is difficult. The first half of the above translation is mine; the second half follows Fox (*Proverbs 10–31*, 682), who omits MT's וָזָר as "a dittograph of the nearly identical" וְזַךְ and who supplies יָשָׁר with the conjunction *waw*, which was "lost by near-dittography."

39. Though as noted in chap. 3 (cf. chap. 7), the terminology of the "rich" in Proverbs is a moral as well as an economic designation. Here the contrast with the "poor" indicates that economic connotations are primary. Nonetheless, the rich person in 28:6 is associated with morally deficient conduct.

40. The NRSV renders 28:18b as "but whoever follows crooked ways will fall into the Pit." The final word of 28:18 in the MT is בְּאֶחָת, which means "in one." The NRSV and many commentators emend this to בְּשַׁחַת ("in a pit"). However, the MT deploys a dual form of דֶּרֶךְ (cf. 28:6) to speak of the one who follows "two ways" (*dərākayîm*), perhaps suggesting the "double-mindedness" of such a person. That person will fall by his double-mindedness on one of the two ways.

> Hear, my child, and be wise,
> and direct your mind in the way.[41] (23:19)

> My child, give me your heart,
> and let your eyes observe my ways. (23:26)

Finally, if Proverbs 1–9 speaks of Adonai but not his way (דֶּרֶךְ; but cf. 8:22), at least one verse in the latter chapters highlights the path of this divine agent. Proverbs 10:29 says,

> The way of the Lord [דֶּרֶךְ יְהוָה] is a stronghold for the upright,
> but destruction for evildoers.[42]

Though an isolated allusion to the "way" of the Lord, this naming of the divine's path authorizes Proverbs' view of wisdom. Not only is the instruction of human teachers or communities thereby associated with the deity, the allusion to Adonai's way also gestures toward the security or well-being that the sages believe a life of wisdom makes possible. Proverbs 10:29 also resonates with other lines in the collections of Proverbs, both those that closely associate the Lord with the ways of virtuous characters—the blameless, the ones who pursue righteousness, those who please the Lord—and those that speak of the character and paths of others, which are rejected by the deity and so can be called an "abomination."

> Crooked minds are an abomination to the Lord,
> but those of blameless ways are his delight. (11:20)

> The way of the wicked is an abomination to the Lord,
> but he loves the one who pursues righteousness. (15:9)

> When the ways of people please the Lord,
> he causes even their enemies to be at peace with them. (16:7)

The book's addressees are to follow the paths of virtuous human agents, and these figures themselves follow the way of Adonai. The path of wisdom is thus the way of Adonai (10:29) because it is sanctioned by the deity; subsequently, it is characterized as a way of safety and security, a reliable path to secure one's well-being. As Proverbs 18:10, similar to 10:29a, says,

---

41. Cf. note 35 above.
42. For alternative ways of construing this proverb, see Fox, *Proverbs 10–31*, 528.

> The name of the LORD is a strong tower;
> the righteous run into it and are safe.[43]

Through its rhetoric of the ways of morally laudable people, placed in contrast to the ways of suspect agents, the later chapters of Proverbs, like Proverbs 1–9, thus reveal an important facet of the book's moral orientation. The sages are not primarily concerned with specific acts of obedience to particular precepts and rules. Nor are they interested in promoting people's pursuit of their own subjectively reckoned ideas of happiness and what form of life might enable them to achieve that happiness. Instead, the book's discourse privileges moral agents and their mode of existence—those whose virtue makes them most likely to achieve genuine thriving for the sort of being humans are imagined to be, and those whose character frustrates the attainment of flourishing. The manner in which the text strives to convince its audience that the way of the virtuous—the wise and just—is a desirable path and is the best route to securing the goods people naturally desire for happiness is the question to which we next turn.

---

43. Cf. Prov. 14:26. On 18:11 and the related 10:15, which together serve to negatively characterize the "rich," see chap. 7.

5

The Training of Desire for a Life of Flourishing in Proverbs

Virtue-oriented moral discourses see humans as naturally inclined to pursue certain goods, but the mere acquisition and accumulation of the goods humans naturally desire cannot alone ensure a person's happiness. The role of the various goods in flourishing, their relation to one another, and how a person rightly attains them must be properly understood with the help of the virtues (chap. 3). A person's desires for certain goods must be appropriately tutored or trained and directed toward a yearning for virtue itself. For traditions of character ethics, the virtuous person ought not to act in appropriate ways simply because she might receive a desirable reward; nor should fear of punishment or some bad consequence motivate her conduct. She should act in particular ways because she desires and chooses to live virtuously—to do the good—for itself. As Alasdair MacIntyre explains, for virtue ethics what needs to be accomplished in character development is "a transformation" of a person's "motivational set, so that what were originally external reasons" for acting "become internal."[1] Proverbs presents humans as fundamentally corrigible—at least initially. Humans tend to be teachable and trainable until they reach young adulthood, at which point one's character begins to settle, either virtuously or viciously. If Proverbs seeks to train (especially young) people's desires and natural inclinations for a range of goods toward a more fundamental yearning for a life of virtue along the lines that

---

1. MacIntyre, *Dependent Rational Animals*, 87.

MacIntyre speaks of, we can be more confident that the text represents a kind of virtue-oriented moral discourse. At the same time, we can gain further clarity about the contours of the book's character ethic.

Anne Stewart has perhaps most fully and elegantly explored the dynamics, psychology, and poetry of desire in Proverbs.[2] Like others she recognizes how the text deploys a rhetoric of yearning to motivate its addressees to choose the path of wise and just individuals and to avoid the ways of wicked and foolish people.[3] Stewart also helpfully unpacks how desire and Proverbs' discourse of desire are complexly structured. First, she notes that "at the heart of desire is a paradox between satiation and want" as that which can bring "both pleasure and pain."[4] She also recognizes, as I suggest below, that the "formation of the moral self," with which Proverbs is so concerned, is "more than an intellectual project"; it entails the appropriate cultivation of one's cognitive, emotional, and aesthetic sensibilities.[5] Proverbs seeks to train its hearers to "desire rightly," shaping the yearnings of its addressees "as it patterns various desires and desirers over the course of the [book's] poems and proverbial sayings."[6]

Stewart's study of desire in Proverbs also recognizes that the book's discourse of desire largely centers around two types of rhetoric—the rhetoric of valuable riches and the rhetoric of erotic yearning.[7] In the following pages, I emphasize two things somewhat more than Stewart: (1) the symbolic dimensions of the rhetoric of sex and wealth in training the desires of the book's addressees; and (2) the fact that the desires of both good and bad moral agents in Proverbs fundamentally derive from their yearnings for the sorts of goods that typically contribute to the full and happy lives for which humans naturally long. Of course, for the androcentric and patriarchal book of Proverbs, the place of erotic yearning is articulated exclusively in terms of male desire for women.

Training Desire in Proverbs: Honor and Health

Before turning to the symbols of wealth and woman in Proverbs, it is important to mention two other significant "goods" that the book understands

2. Stewart, *Poetic Ethics in Proverbs*, 102–69.
3. Cf. Sandoval, "Training Desire in Proverbs."
4. Stewart, *Poetic Ethics in Proverbs*, 131.
5. Stewart, *Poetic Ethics in Proverbs*, 152; 161–62.
6. Stewart, *Poetic Ethics in Proverbs*, 144–45.
7. Cf. Sandoval, *Discourse of Wealth and Poverty*, 71–113; Sandoval, "Training Desire in Proverbs."

humans to naturally desire: honor and health. Proverbs does not speak of health and status as robustly as it does sex and wealth. Still, the images are important in the book's efforts to train its audience's yearnings toward wisdom. The sages intuitively recognized that some positive recognition by others and enjoyment of bodily and psychic integrity are typically necessary for robust human flourishing. By associating the desirability of social status and health with the way of wisdom, the text subtly directs the addressees' desires toward the truly valuable life of virtue.

For example, in Proverbs 1–9 positive social status is promised to those who find w/Wisdom. As 3:35a says, "The wise will inherit honor" (cf. 3:16; 4:8; 8:18). Since honor is a good that virtue-oriented moral traditions know humans naturally desire, it is not surprising to find the sages collocating social recognition with other goods people prize—for example, life and riches (3:16; 8:18). Unsurprising, too, is Proverbs' insistence that high social status not be assigned to those who lack moral insight. For example, the "dolt" (כְּסִיל) of 26:1 and 8 is not worthy of public praise.

> Like snow in summer or rain in harvest,
>   so honor is not fitting for a dolt. (26:1)

> It is like binding a stone in a sling
>   to give honor to a dolt. (26:8)

In addition to associating honor with wisdom and insisting it is inappropriate for dolts, Proverbs also indicates that social recognition accrues to those who attain particular virtues that belong to wisdom's way. For example, high status should belong, somewhat ironically, to those whose lives are characterized by humility. As Proverbs 18:12 says (cf. 15:33; 29:23),

> Before destruction one's heart is haughty,
>   but humility goes before honor.

A degree of social status is associated with other virtues that the sages highly prize too, whether justice/righteousness and kindness or fear of the Lord.

> Whoever pursues righteousness and kindness
>   will find life and honor. (21:21)

> The reward for humility and fear of the LORD
>   is riches and honor and life. (22:4)

Proverbs' collocation of terms for positive social status with particular virtues represents an effort to invert typical social hierarchies of value. The book's rhetoric of honor, for instance, makes clear that valuable social esteem ought not to accrue to the wealthy or powerful—the usual recipients of public esteem—simply on account of their wealth or power. Instead, it should be ascribed to the wise on account of their virtue (cf. conclusion). Indeed, the ones who follow the way of wisdom are those who understand the place of social esteem in a full constellation of the goods that produce human flourishing. Hence, they do not overvalue it or pursue it for its own sake, knowing that

> it is not good to eat much honey,
> or to seek honor on top of honor.[8] (25:27)

The full life or thriving that Proverbs hopes its addressees can secure entails more than attaining a degree of social recognition. It also includes some enjoyment of genuine mental and physical health. The sages believed the significant absence of bodily and psychic well-being limits or detracts from the various ways in which humans might flourish.[9] As with honor, images of physical well-being in Proverbs are directly associated with wisdom or with particular virtues of wisdom's way. In Proverbs 4:22 "healing" is paralleled with the "life" that the instructing voice's teaching leads to:

> For they [the teacher's words] are life to those who find them,
> and healing to all their flesh.

And in Proverbs 3:8, healing (and bodily refreshment) is collocated with the virtue of trust in the divine:

> It [trusting Adonai] will be a healing for your flesh
> and a refreshment for your body.

Elsewhere Proverbs says having a "tranquil mind" ("a heart of healing") or a "cheerful heart" provides "life to the flesh" or constitutes "a good medicine"

---

8. The second half of the line is difficult. It might be rendered, "And the seeking out of their honor is honor." The NRSV appears to reflect a plausible emendation of the Hebrew consonantal text (חקר כבוד מכבד to חקר כבדם כבוד) that might literally be translated as "nor is the seeking out of honor honorable"—taking the מכבד as a *piel* participle and understanding the negation of the first stich to do double duty in the second half of the verse. Still other proposals are also possible. See Van Leeuwen, "Proverbs XXV 27 Once Again"; cf. Fox, *Proverbs 10–31*, 790.

9. The sages did not seem able to imagine that different impairments or disabilities could enable other forms of flourishing. This failure of imagination represents a further area around which readers of Proverbs today need critically to engage the book (cf. conclusion).

(14:30; 17:22). In these cases, a person's character and choices to act in a particular way enable their attainment of the good of corporal and psychological well-being. Yet it may also be the case that the lines mean to suggest that the character of such people promotes the bodily and psychic thriving of others too. This well-being of others might result from a wise and just person's good speech (16:24) and otherwise reliable character (13:17). As Proverbs 12:18 says,

> Rash words are like sword thrusts,
> but the tongue of the wise brings healing.

Proverbs recognizes that some degree of both social esteem and bodily and mental integrity typically contribute to the possibilities for happiness. They are natural and desirable goods for the sort of being humans are understood to be. But they are not by themselves constitutive of well-being, and they are not as desirable as w/Wisdom itself. Consequently, when desirable honor and health are associated with wisdom's virtues, a reader's yearnings for those goods are simultaneously directed toward a life of virtue. Still, Proverbs' concern to acknowledge the desirability of certain goods and to train a person's desires for those goods by (re)directing them toward w/Wisdom is most evident in the book's patriarchal and androcentric discourse of riches and sex, wealth, and woman.

Training Desire and the Symbol of Wealth in Proverbs 1–9

Proverbs 1–9 certainly contains some direct instruction, even commands, about concrete economic matters (e.g., regarding surety in 6:1–5). However, by and large these chapters broadly employ the language of wealth and precious material goods—those things that possess obvious worth in real economic terms—to describe the desirability of wisdom's nonmaterial way of virtue over the way of folly and wickedness. In so doing, the chapters teach the book's audience that wealth, though clearly valuable, is not to be pursued for its own sake, as if it alone, or most fundamentally, constitutes the key to happiness. For Proverbs, wisdom, or a life of virtue, holds a more crucial position in human efforts to thrive.

We saw above that Proverbs 1:10–19—the book's opening vignette about murderous robbers—is most basically concerned with offering concrete instruction to the book's addressees about avoiding vicious conduct and associates. Yet the sinners' invitation to rob and murder for material gain also contains hints of a broader, figurative level of meaning. The passage presents its robbing sinners as paradigmatic figures, symbols of all those who travel the wrong path of life (cf. chap. 4).

The lines about the robbers and their ways in Proverbs 1 can be regarded as figurative and symbolic discourse in another way too. They constitute the first passage to employ a rhetoric of wealth to ascribe value to the two ways that Proverbs metaphorically imagines as structuring the moral possibilities of human lives. The rhetoric of desire is already discernible in the first line of the pericope. In 1:10 "sinners" are imagined as "enticing" (פתה) the addressee to engage in brutal conduct (vv. 11–12). The enticement involves the appeal of joining peers rather than patiently submitting oneself to the patriarchal hierarchy or social order represented by the instructing voice, as Carol Newsom demonstrates.[10] A further enticement for the addressee is the promise of material gain or הוֹן יָקָר ("costly things" or "precious wealth") and שָׁלָל ("booty") in verse 13. The sinners attempt to lure the addressee onto their path with the promise of real, desirable wealth.[11] On a literal plane, then, the text warns against the dangers of gangs and the immorality of pursuing riches through violence and injustice (vv. 11–12). But the wealth language in this passage also functions as a broader symbol of the potential desirability of the ways of life chosen by any suspect moral agent.[12]

The sinners' way in Proverbs 1:10–19, however, is not a bona fide option that the instructing voice places before the hearer. Although the robbers' promise of wealth articulates the perceived desirability of their way, in quick measure the passage proclaims that their path provides no advantage to the addressee, economic or otherwise. The sinner's way actually leads to death, where the "paths" of all who pursue unjust gain end (v. 19).[13] The "wrong way" may secure certain goods humans naturally desire—in this case, material wealth—but in the end it actually frustrates attainment of a full, flourishing life. In Proverbs 1:10–19, the sinners who rob and murder for gain are likely intelligent and shrewd in their planning of evil. However, they do not comprehend rightly the value of material goods in relation to the central role of human sociality in constituting a person's well-being; they are not able to grasp the relevant relationship between the good of material wealth and their own and others' status as naturally social creatures. Subsequently, the sinners yearn for riches inordinately and pursue wealth by any means. Not virtue but untutored desire directs their steps.

---

10. Newsom, "Woman and the Discourse of Patriarchal Wisdom," 143–57.
11. Cf. Sandoval, *Discourse of Wealth and Poverty*, 71–76.
12. Even as this figurative level of meaning does not eclipse the literal instruction; cf. Ricoeur, *Interpretation Theory*, 55.
13. On the emendation of אָרְחוֹת ("paths") to אַחֲרִית ("end"), see chapter 4, note 8 above.

Proverbs 1:10–19 is a discursive first step in the book's efforts to restructure the hearer's desire *away from* the way of fools and the wicked via a rhetoric of wealth. The next step will be to direct this desire *toward* a life of virtue—a life lived on the right path. To do this, Proverbs 1–9 progressively escalates the force of its rhetoric of riches to build a compelling depiction of the exceeding value of wisdom.

Initially, the instructing voice of Proverbs 1–9 does not employ the same wealth language used by the sinners in 1:10–19. But in the final pertinent passages of Proverbs 1–9, the text co-opts the sinners' own language of riches; and it does so to proclaim the enduring worth of wisdom, while simultaneously undermining the sinners' wrongheaded claims about the desirability of their way of life.[14] Hence, in Proverbs 2:4–5 wisdom's worth is first said to be valuable "like" silver and treasures. In Proverbs 3:14–16 personified Wisdom is described not merely as "like" precious metals but "better than" silver and other valuable goods. In Proverbs 4:5–7, w/Wisdom is said to be so valuable that the addressee should use whatever possessions (קִנְיָן) he has to acquire or "buy" (קנה) her, metaphorically speaking.[15] Then Proverbs 8:10–11 deploys the rhetorical strategy of personification to have the larger-than-life Woman Wisdom herself—rather than the instructing parental voice—command the addressee to take her instruction "and not silver" (אַל־כָּסֶף), so superior is her worth to material goods.[16]

All these passages use familiar images of valuable material wealth to ascribe worth and desirability to wisdom's way. The text's explicit use of similes, comparative constructions, metaphorical wordplays, and the personification of wisdom as a woman together point to the figurative use of the rhetoric of riches—something for which 1:6 of the book's prologue has prepared readers (chap. 2). In Proverbs 1–9, a desire for riches is associated with, and so rhetorically (re)directed toward, even more valuable wisdom. The images of wealth and wisdom help transform a reader's natural inclination for attaining the good of material well-being into a desire for wisdom and the virtues by which the desire for wealth itself can be more adequately understood and riches themselves appropriately pursued.

---

14. The term הוֹן, which the sinners use in 1:13 and which Woman Wisdom deploys in 8:18, is otherwise attested in Prov. 1–9 only in 3:9 and 6:31. In 3:9 it appears in the context of offering gifts, presumably to the temple. In 6:31 the text again speaks of robbers. Thieves who are caught will be forced to hand over all the הוֹן they possess.

15. Although the root קנה generally means "to acquire," in many instances it has the sense of "to buy." Since in the second half of 4:7 קִנְיָן means "possessions" and the verb קנה is deployed with the *bet pretii* (or *bet* of exchange), the Hebrew קְנֵה חָכְמָה וּבְכָל־קִנְיָנְךָ קְנֵה בִינָה is best rendered as "buy wisdom; in exchange for all your possessions, buy understanding."

16. I analyze these passages more fully in *Discourse of Wealth and Poverty*, 76–101.

It is, however, only in Proverbs 8:18, with personified Wisdom's own words, that we reach the pinnacle of Proverbs 1–9's rhetorical efforts to train the addressee's desires via a rhetoric of wealth. Here Wisdom claims, "Riches and honor are with me, enduring wealth and prosperity." The riches and honor here hold obvious worth in economic and social terms, respectively. However, the passage might be constructing an image that is primarily economic in nature since the word כָּבוֹד ("honor") is occasionally used as a synonym for wealth. It is also possible that עֹשֶׁר ("riches") and כָּבוֹד together function as a hendiadys, meaning something like "honorable riches."[17] Whatever the case, Wisdom's possession of עֹשֶׁר and כָּבוֹד belong to the economy of images in Proverbs 1–9 that underscore her (Wisdom's) worth or desirability in terms of the sorts of external goods (e.g., wealth and status) humans are naturally inclined to seek as they pursue eudaemonia.

For the sages, however, wisdom's value cannot be reduced to material reward. Proverbs 8:18 invites readers to look beyond the literal material (and social) plane of its rhetoric. Unlike other passages that figuratively associate wisdom with valuable material goods, in Proverbs 8:18 personified Woman Wisdom is herself now actually said to possesses עֹשֶׁר and כָּבוֹד (cf. 3:16). She claims they are "with me" (אִתִּי). Some readers might assume that the one who finds w/Wisdom could thus also expect to find, quite literally, material and social rewards (or socially appropriate material rewards—"honorable riches"). That is, the pursuit of wisdom for Proverbs may, after all, turn out to be fundamentally externally motivated, with students exhorted to pursue Wisdom primarily for the "success" or material-social benefits she makes available. Certainly, young and simple addressees of Proverbs may have been inclined to understand the rhetoric of valuable wealth and high social status in that sort of straightforward sense, even as it contributes to the book's wisdom mythos (chap. 1)—confidence that virtue is somehow rewarded. Still, in Proverbs 8:18 what Woman Wisdom holds is not only riches and honor but הוֹן עָתֵק or "enduring wealth."[18] This is the verse's key expression since it contrasts Woman Wisdom's riches with the sinners' promise of הוֹן יָקָר ("costly things"; "precious treasure" NJPS) in Proverbs 1:13. The enduring quality of Woman Wisdom's wealth indicates that its worth is distinct from that of

---

17. Fox, *Proverbs 1–9*, 277. The close association of the terms underscores a regular fact of social life—namely, the close relationship between social status and material wealth.

18. As Fox (*Proverbs 1–9*, 277) notes, "'*āteq* . . . is usually understood to mean 'old' (Malbim) or 'venerable' (Delitzsch), equivalent to '*attîq* 'ancient,' hence 'enduring.'" Fox continues, "The ability to endure, demonstrated by something's antiquity," is here in Prov. 8:18 "transposed into the future." Cf. the discussion of Hurowitz in "Two Terms for Wealth" (esp. 254), who notes, based on Akkadian parallels, that the expression might mean "traveling silver/property."

the sinners' valuable wealth—and similarly distinct from the worth of other precious metals that describe the value of wisdom throughout Proverbs 1–9.

Moral philosophers have long contended that material wealth is by nature of limited value. It is ephemeral, easily and quickly lost—whether to theft, death, or other factors. Proverbs itself recognizes this characteristic of wealth, as does the broader biblical wisdom tradition (e.g., Prov. 23:4–5; Job 15:29; Eccles. 5:13; cf. the hastily acquired riches of Prov. 13:11). By contrast, the wealth that Woman Wisdom in Proverbs 8 holds and offers is long lasting. Importantly, it is also "held" not by a real person but by a personification of virtue (8:12–14). Wisdom's wealth in Proverbs 8:18 is thus best understood symbolically as the riches of virtue, the value of those character traits that enable one to rightly understand the place and pursuit of the goods necessary for human flourishing. This sort of wealth (i.e., virtue), because it is internal to a person—a part of one's character—cannot be easily lost. It is appropriately characterized as enduring, and its worth regarded as superior to that of literal, material wealth.

Wisdom's הוֹן עָתֵק ("enduring wealth") in Proverbs 8:18 is also paralleled with a term that NRSV/NIV and NJPS, respectively, render rather strangely as "prosperity" and "success." The lexeme in question, צְדָקָה, is typically translated as righteousness or justice. Philological and semantic reasons offered for the uncommon translation here in Proverbs 8:18 are not compelling. As Fox bluntly concludes, "There is no need to ascribe a special sense" to צְדָקָה in the verse.[19] The term should be rendered as "justice" or "righteousness," as it nearly always is and as it is translated just two verses later (v. 20) by NRSV/NIV and NJPS.[20] Others have understood הוֹן עָתֵק and צְדָקָה to form a second hendiadys in the verse, parallel to that of עֹשֶׁר and כָּבוֹד

---

19. Fox, *Proverbs 1–9*, 277–78.
20. Exactly why several prominent English translations of the Bible render צְדָקָה as "prosperity" or "success" is an interesting question. Translations in other modern languages avoid this. For example, the Spanish translation Reina-Valera (1602), ultimately following the (Roman Catholic) Vulgate's *"iustitia,"* renders *"justicia."* The Louis Segond French translation (1871) likewise translates *"justice,"* while the Protestant Luther Bible (1545) reads *"Gerechtigkeit."* Even the King James Version (1611) renders the term as "righteousness," as does the Roman Catholic New American Bible. Although deeper investigation is needed to understand the reasons for this state of affairs, my hunch is that it has to do with the fact that the capitalist English Industrial Revolution, along with utilitarian modes of ethical thought, did not gain steam until the eighteenth century. Subsequent to these social-economic and moral-philosophical movements, Proverbs came to be interpreted as a utilitarian sort of discourse (see chap. 1), a kind of simple guide to "success." Such a rhetoric in capitalist ideology carries strong connotations of economic prosperity, and in capitalist cultures the quest for such prosperity constitutes a central pursuit of many individuals (capitalists at least). Once Proverbs was regarded fundamentally as a kind of utilitarian guide to success in a capitalist epoch, the rhetoric of "justice" in a verse such as Prov. 8:18 was revised—and, ideologically speaking, almost *had* to be revised—to mean "prosperity."

(8:18a), so that the "enduring wealth" Wisdom offers in 8:18b can be viewed as a "material gain" that endures because it is "justly" acquired, as opposed to wealth that is hastily gained and so ephemeral (cf. 13:11).[21] However, the salient conceptual distinction at work in the passage is between the external good of material wealth, which is valuable but inherently ephemeral, and the riches of character, which endure because they are internal to a person and are thereby of more worth. In the symbolic economy of Proverbs 8, צְדָקָה in effect stands in apposition to הוֹן עָתֵק and thus defines it.[22] The "enduring wealth" that Wisdom holds is the "true" wealth of virtue. The verse's "justice" or "righteousness"—one of the moral-social virtues of primary importance for Proverbs (cf. 1:3)—functions as a synecdoche for the entire range of virtues that constitute wisdom's way.[23] As the New English Bible (Revised English Bible) recognizes in its rendering of צְדָקָה at 8:18, what Wisdom offers is "the rewards of virtue."

If Proverbs 8:18 does not unequivocally suggest that the promise of gain for those who acquire Wisdom is to be taken in strict literal terms, it certainly assumes that wealth is a good that humans regularly seek in pursuit of happiness; and in contrast to the sinners' robbing and murdering in Proverbs 1, it surely imagines the one who is wise will only seek to acquire it in legitimate ways—of course. Yet, the fundamental point for Proverbs here is not that acquiring wisdom, or acting rightly, results unproblematically in material rewards, but that the value of wisdom exceeds the worth of material goods. The external motivation of Proverbs 1–9 for cultivating a virtuous life—hinted at by its association of wisdom with material wealth—gives way to an internal motivation: the value of virtue itself.[24] What the text affects is, again, essentially a reordering of typical hierarchies of value. Wealth and status (and other goods) are indeed "good" and of significant worth in human efforts to flourish. But they do not constitute the highest good. If they did, that might justify their pursuit in excessive ways— for example, by agents whose most valued "excellencies" of character would be covetousness and shrewd ruthlessness. Instead, for Proverbs the most valuable of goods is internal to a person, the virtues of "wisdom," with its strong inclination toward social virtue (cf. chap. 7).

21. Cf. Fox, *Proverbs 1–9*, 277.
22. In the same way, in the book's programmatic prologue (1:3) צֶדֶק וּמִשְׁפָּט וּמֵישָׁרִים ("justice, righteousness, and equity") stands in apposition to and so defines הַשְׂכֵּל ("wise dealing" [NRSV] or "success" [NJPS]; cf. chap. 2).
23. Indeed, as we saw in chap. 2 above, in a moral discourse like Proverbs the relation between any particular virtue and any particular good thing associated with the attainment of that virtue evokes all the virtues of a good person and a full notion of the eudaemonia such a person might enjoy.
24. Cf. Sandoval, *Discourse of Wealth and Poverty*, 92–98.

In a kind of denouement to this section of Proverbs 8, the passage further associates wealth language and the rhetoric of social virtue with Woman Wisdom. Proverbs 8:19 first reinforces Wisdom's desirability by again comparing her to material goods—"My [Wisdom's] fruit is better than gold." Next, verse 20 reinforces verse 18's emphasis on social virtue as the center of Proverbs' moral vision by having Woman Wisdom proclaim, "I walk in the way of righteousness, along the paths of justice." Finally, in verse 21 Wisdom describes her actions as "endowing with wealth those who love me, and filling their treasuries." In this last line, Wisdom promises to bequeath (לְהַנְחִיל) to her lovers (אֹהֲבַי) what the NRSV translates as "wealth" (יֵשׁ), indicating that she will fill their storehouses. As in verse 18, which depicts Wisdom as possessing riches and honor, here the book's young and simple audience especially might assume that anyone who attains w/Wisdom will also acquire real riches. The rhetoric can certainly be heard literally, expressing a simple cause-and-effect logic. But as we said in chapter 2, the relation of means to end in such act-consequence language should be regarded otherwise, as an "internal," not "external," relation. Indeed, what is at issue in the verse is the nature and status of the wealth that Wisdom promises.

Because earlier lines in the passage operate at a figurative level, Wisdom's promises in verse 21 should not be interpreted in an overly literal fashion. Woman Wisdom throughout Proverbs 8 is a literary personification of virtue and not a real person. She cannot fill the storehouses of anyone with anything, except metaphorically. Moreover, the term that the NRSV renders as "wealth" is not one of the usual terms for wealth or riches in Proverbs or in the rest of the Bible. It is not הוֹן or עֹשֶׁר but יֵשׁ.[25] In classical Hebrew the word is usually the particle of existence, "there is." However, Sirach 42:3 may use the term in the sense of riches and in conjunction with נַחֲלָה ("possessions"). Victor Hurowitz contends that יֵשׁ is the semantic equivalent of Akkadian *bušu*, a term derived from a root meaning "to exist" or "to be in existence" and which apparently refers to movable wealth.[26] Although יֵשׁ may have developed the meaning of "riches" in the late Second Temple period, the absence of the expression with such a meaning in biblical Hebrew, except (perhaps) in this metaphorically rich passage, suggests the term signals something more, if not something quite different.[27] Rather than indicating merely that Wisdom holds and promises any sort of literal material wealth—an external reward—to

---

25. The NJPS version renders the term as "substance."
26. Hurowitz, "Two Terms for Wealth."
27. Fox (*Proverbs 1–9*, 278) points to the Sirach evidence and argues that "the phrase *wʾl yš lh* 'and upon that which is hers' in Sir 25:21 shows the intermediate step between *yēš* as an existential particle and as a noun meaning possessions."

those who follow her way, the evocative term יֵשׁ ("there is") can also, from a virtue-ethics reading, point more subtly to the sort of full "existence" or genuinely happy mode of being that the acquisition of wisdom enables. It evokes the possibility of attaining, through virtue, a good and flourishing life.[28]

Through the rhetorical and figurative operations just explored, Proverbs 1–9 seeks to train a reader's or hearer's untrained or undisciplined desires for any lesser good toward truly valuable wisdom. The eudaemonia Proverbs 1–9 envisions is thus no mere crass economic advantage. Yet the text's heavy reliance on a rhetoric of desirable riches surely suggests that the book's vision of a happy human life is one that includes a degree of material well-being. If the sages of Proverbs recognized that a person's natural desire for happiness, for eudaemonia, entails something of a desire for material well-being, such desires must in some sense be reckoned as legitimate yearnings for the sort of embodied beings humans are. It is simply that a person who would arrive at moral maturity, the one who would become wise, must first learn that although wealth is valuable and some level of enjoyment of it is necessary for thriving, it is not that which is most valuable; its worth must be subordinated to virtue's value. The one who would be wise will shun evil and pursue the good not merely out of fear of punishment or by the hope of gaining valuable external rewards, but from an internal desire to do so, from a yearning for the good "riches" of virtue or wise living itself. Indeed, for Proverbs, a truly wise person with well-trained yearnings for a genuine good such as material wealth will also understand that she is the sort of material, spiritual, rational, and social being whose own well-being depends on living well and fairly with others. She will understand what place a good like wealth has in a constellation of other goods necessary for human flourishing—whether a just social order, the acknowledgment by others of one's social worth, the exercise of (practical) intellect, or something else, such as the gratification of one's sexual yearning, which Proverbs 1–9 engages forthrightly, though exclusively from the perspective of men who are sexually attracted to women.

Training Desire and the Symbol of Woman in Proverbs 1–9

The training of desire so important to character ethics is evident in Proverbs 1–9 in more than the text's manipulation of wealth images. It is also apparent

---

28. Cf. Sandoval, *Discourse of Wealth and Poverty*, 98–101. Alternatively, because יֵשׁ is paired with נחל and נַחֲלָה in Prov. 8:18 and Sir. 42:3, respectively, it may stand more firmly in parallel with הוֹן עָתֵק and indicate "enduring, stable property" (cf. Fox, *Proverbs 1–9*, 278) and hence point to the enduring, stable, and so not easily lost "riches" of virtue that Wisdom holds.

in the way the book's opening pages present several female figures. Yet the manner in which images of women function in these chapters is somewhat more complicated than the way images of wealth do. The two prominent figures in the book's early chapters, the strange or foreign woman (זָרָה, נָכְרִיָּה) and Woman Wisdom, operate basically at different levels of meaning. The strange or foreign woman is presented as a real woman with whom the addressee might commit adultery.[29] Woman Wisdom, by contrast, is a metaphorical figure, a personification of wisdom's virtues, and is even described in mythological and cosmic terms (e.g., Prov. 8:22–31). Similarly, the (potential) wife of the addressee (5:15–20) is imagined as a real woman, while another female literary personification, Woman Folly, appears in Proverbs 9:13–18.

As most commentators recognize, while the strange or foreign woman is conceptually distinct from Woman Wisdom, certain passages depict this real, strange woman in language similar to that used for Woman Wisdom. For example, the description of Woman Wisdom in 1:20–21 and 8:1–3 resonates with the image of the woman in 7:10–13, who is clearly a/the strange or foreign woman (cf. 7:5). In these passages both female characters are in public places and address (young) males directly. In addition, Woman Wisdom is an obvious foil to the strange woman in Proverbs 7:5, where Wisdom is said to be able to save or keep (שׁמר) the hearer from the foreign woman. All this suggests that in some sense Woman Wisdom and the strange or foreign woman are parallel figures in Proverbs.

Proverbs 9 strengthens this association, but it does so in a roundabout way. Proverbs 9:1–6 and 9:13–18 neatly contrast Woman Wisdom with Woman Folly.[30] As Schipper says, "The unit on Dame Folly is the contrasting foil to what was said about Lady Wisdom."[31] Yet Woman Folly herself in 9:13–18 is also described in terms that recall the strange or foreign woman, for example, in 7:7–23. Both figures bustle about in public; each is "restless" (הֹמִיָּה; cf. 7:11 and 9:13);[32] and both address a "simpleton" (פְּתָאיִם/פֶּתִי; cf. 7:7 and 9:16).[33]

However, passages depicting the strange or foreign woman as a real woman do not limit her to only being a real figure. Ricoeur claims that a figurative level of textual meaning is arrived at via literal signification and does not eliminate the literal.[34] Therefore, the literary association of Woman Folly and the strange/

---

29. Fox, *Proverbs 1–9*, 134–41.
30. On the abstract "attributive genitive" כְּסִילוּת (9:13), see Schipper, *Proverbs 1–15*, 320, 335; and Fox, *Proverbs 1–9*, 300–301.
31. Schipper, *Proverbs 1–15*, 335.
32. On the term, see esp. Schipper, *Proverbs 1–15*, 335.
33. Woman Folly herself is called "inexperienced" (פְּתַיּוּת) in 9:13b.
34. Ricoeur, *Interpretation Theory*, 55.

foreign woman (and each one's pairing with Woman Wisdom) suggests that the strange/foreign woman should not be conceived only as a real figure, a literal object of warning for the text's male addressees. She is also a symbol of folly. The sages' instruction to avoid the strange woman is not only an exhortation to avoid sex with another man's wife—however alluring Proverbs imagines that to be for its primarily male audience. It is also instruction to avoid all that belongs to the sometimes desirable-looking "wrong way" that she represents and that stands in contrast to the virtuous way Woman Wisdom symbolizes. One need not be a full-fledged Ricoeurian reader to recognize this basic symbolic structure of the text. Indeed, a number of historically minded scholars (e.g., Whybray, Murphy) also conclude that whenever the text mentions the figure of the strange woman (and Woman Folly) in Proverbs 1–9, it evokes her personified opposite, Woman Wisdom, as well.[35]

The "wrong way" in Proverbs 1–9 is thus symbolized for the book's young, male audience not only through the personification of Woman Folly but also in terms of an adulterous erotic encounter with a real woman. As with the sinners' promise of desirable but illicit wealth in Proverbs 1:10–19, the initial chapters of Proverbs also speak of illicit sex with a strange or foreign woman in order to make clear to its male addressees that the "wrong way" of life can appear alluring. Analogously, the addressee's real wife in Proverbs 1–9 is collocated with the symbolic figure of Woman Wisdom. To desire and cling to one's wife (5:15–23)—and so avoid adultery—is one particular instance of following the right way of virtue. It is the most obvious or "real" way that wisdom (and so personified Woman Wisdom) can save the young addressee from the strange woman—that is, from committing adultery with her (7:5), an act that itself would constitute a step down a wrong, and so dangerous, moral path.

Significantly, like the strange woman, Woman Wisdom herself can be described in erotic terms. This description constitutes an important effort by the text to channel the addressee's natural desire for sex—illicit sex with a strange or foreign woman in particular—toward a strong desire for Wisdom and virtue itself. In contrast to the depiction of a young man's yearning for adulterous sex with a strange or foreign woman, however, Proverbs describes the desirability of Woman Wisdom in terms of erotic longings for a legitimate wife. Proverbs 4:5–9 is the key text:

> Get wisdom; get insight: do not forget, nor turn away
> from the words of my mouth.

---

35. Whybray, *Proverbs*, 89; R. Murphy, *Proverbs*, 282.

The Training of Desire for a Life of Flourishing in Proverbs

> Do not forsake her, and she will keep you;
>   love her, and she will guard you.
> The beginning of wisdom is this: Get wisdom,
>   and whatever else you get, get insight.
> Prize her highly, and she will exalt you;
>   she will honor you if you embrace her.
> She will place on your head a fair garland;
>   she will bestow on you a beautiful crown [עֲטֶרֶת תִּפְאָרֶת].

The passage enjoins the addressee to "get" w/Wisdom (v. 5, קְנֵה) and not to "forsake her" (v. 6, אַל־תַּעַזְבֶהָ)—an injunction that contrasts with the strange or foreign woman's forsaking (עזב) "the partner of her youth" (אַלּוּף נְעוּרֶיהָ) in 2:17, a phrase that may refer to the woman's husband.[36] Just as Proverbs elsewhere commands the addressee to rejoice in the wife of his youth and to avoid the embrace (חבק) of another woman (5:20), here it exhorts him to desire w/Wisdom with a related rhetoric. He should "love her" (אֲהָבֶהָ, 4:6), spare no expense to acquire her (קנה, v. 7; see below), and "prize her highly" (סַלְסְלֶהָ, v. 8), so that she may guard and exalt him (vv. 6, 8).[37] Indeed, if the addressee "embraces" (חבק, v. 8; cf. 5:20) Wisdom, she will bring him honor (תְּכַבֵּדְךָ, 4:8; cf. 8:18), a social status like the being "known [נוֹדָע] in the city gates" that the husband of the Woman of Valor in Proverbs 31:10–31 (herself a figure that evokes personified Wisdom) can enjoy because of his wife (31:23; cf. conclusion).

The presentation of Wisdom as a desirable wife in Proverbs 1–9 is evident in other ways. In Proverbs 4:9 the graceful wreath and the crown that Wisdom will bestow on the one who loves and prizes her likely constitute marriage imagery.[38] Fox (among others), however, rejects the notion that Woman Wisdom in Proverbs 1–9 is reckoned as a wife, viewing her more as a matron figure.[39] Schipper, too, does not believe the rhetoric of 4:9 and especially עֲטֶרֶת תִּפְאָרֶת (a beautiful or magnificent crown) constitute wedding images. Instead, such a crown is simply "a sign of honor."[40]

---

36. The precise meaning of אַלּוּף in 2:17 is debated. Fox contends that in the Bible the term likely means "friend, companion" and "connotes intimacy and affection" (*Proverbs 1–9*, 120). But it is hardly exclusively used to speak of a marriage partner. The expression "friend" of one's "youth," however, also appears in Jer. 3:4 in a passage where Adonai is imagined as Israel's husband (Jer. 3:1).

37. As C. Yoder notes, the root עזב is sometimes used for "an abandoned or divorced woman" (cf. Isa. 54:6–7; 60:15; 62:4) and is cognate to "Akkadian *ezēbu*, 'to abandon a wife/husband, to divorce.'" *Wisdom as a Woman of Substance*, 95.

38. Cf. Song 3:11; Clifford, *Proverbs*, 61–62.

39. Fox, *Proverbs 1–9*, 173–74.

40. Schipper, *Proverbs 1–15*, 173.

There is no question that the images of the wreath and the "beautiful crown" in 4:9 point to items that were sometimes used to bestow honor on a person. The question is which social context(s) in which honor is bestowed is being evoked. In Song 3:11, a crown is bestowed on Solomon when he is honored as bridegroom. The daughters of Jerusalem are exhorted to come out and look at King Solomon,

> at the crown [עֲטָרָה] with which his mother crowned him [שֶׁעִטְּרָה־לּוֹ]
> on the day of his wedding,
> on the day of the gladness of his heart.

Because it is Solomon's mother who bestows the crown in Song 3, it might in fact be thought that Wisdom in Proverbs 4 is a matron figure, as some maintain. Still, Proverbs 4:9 imagines its addressee *receiving* a crown, as does the bridegroom Solomon in Song 3.

Isaiah 62:1–5 also uses the image of a crown in a passage with explicit marriage imagery. When the divine restores Israel/Judah, Isaiah says the people will be in the hand of the Lord like a "crown of glory" (עֲטֶרֶת תִּפְאֶרֶת, v. 3)—a phrase identical to that of Proverbs 4:9. Although it might appear that the divine will take the crown that is in his hand to place on "Israel," this is not explicitly stated. Instead, the crown appears (as is likely in Song 3 and Prov. 4) to belong to the (divine) bridegroom. It is bestowed on the deity who takes Israel/Judah as wife, a wife who will, not unlike Wisdom in Proverbs 8:30–31, bring Adonai not merely honor but delight:[41]

> You [Israel/Judah] shall be called My Delight Is in Her,
> and your land Married [בְּעוּלָה];
> for the LORD delights in you,
> and your land shall be married [תִּבָּעֵל]. (Isa. 62:4)

The prophet continues by noting that

> as a young man marries a young woman,
> so shall your builder marry you,
> and as the bridegroom rejoices over the bride,
> so shall your God rejoice over you. (Isa. 62:5)

When the crown language and marriage terminology of Song 3 and Isaiah 62 is added to the economy of images in Proverbs 4:5–9—with its rhetoric of

---

41. However, the precise rhetoric of delight and rejoicing in the two passages is not identical.

embracing, loving, and not divorcing—it makes sense that the social esteem, represented by the crown, that is promised for acquiring w/Wisdom is like the (androcentrically conceived) honor bestowed upon a bridegroom when he takes a wife.

The fact that Proverbs' addressee should call Wisdom "sister" (7:4) is further indication that w/Wisdom in this book is symbolically imagined as a legitimate bride. Israelite and Judahite (and related) textual traditions use such kinship terminology to speak of a man's wife—for example, in the ancestral narratives (Gen. 12:13; 20:12; 26:7); Song 4 and 5; Tobit 5:21; 7:11, 15; and the Aramaic texts from Elephantine.[42] Finally, although the verb קנה likely means something like "buy" in Proverbs 4:7 (with *bet pretii*), in verse 5 it may also evoke a different sort of acquisition—namely, a man's acquisition of a wife. An enigmatic verse in the book of Ruth (4:5) may use the root in such a context: "Then Boaz said, 'The day you acquire the field from the hand of Naomi, I will acquire Ruth the Moabite, the widow of the dead man, to maintain the dead man's name on his inheritance" (NRSV modified).[43]

There is much discussion about this difficult verse—whether, for example, to read with the *ketiv* or the *qere*, or whether various emendations ought to be adopted. In all likelihood, the verse has Boaz announce to the "closer redeemer" of Elimelech's land that upon the redeemer's appropriation of that land, Boaz will acquire (קנה) Ruth, "the widow of the dead man" as a wife.[44] Although the usual expression for marriage in the Hebrew Bible is לקח followed by a personal name, in the context of the story of Ruth, Boaz's assertion that he will acquire (קנה) Ruth surely means that he will marry her; indeed, the two have already shared an ambiguously erotic encounter at the threshing floor (Ruth 3:6–13), an event that itself seems to have motivated Boaz's meeting with the closer redeemer. In any case, the redeemer relinquishes his claim to Elimelech's land probably because any offspring of a Ruth-Boaz coupling might subsequently lay legitimate claim to the land, compelling the redeemer to abandon it. Boaz's manipulation of a complicated social-economic scenario means that he marries an אֵשֶׁת חַיִל (3:11), as does the husband of the Woman of Valor (אֵשֶׁת חַיִל)—herself reminiscent of Woman Wisdom (cf. conclusion)—in Proverbs 31:10–31.

All this suggests that Woman Wisdom in Proverbs 1–9, like the strange or foreign woman, is depicted for its male audience as a sexually desirable woman. It reinforces the parallel, if also contrasting, roles that (marriageable)

---

42. C. Yoder, *Wisdom as a Woman of Substance*, 95.
43. Unlike the NRSV, I am reading the *ketiv* (קניתי) instead of the *qere* (קניתה).
44. Cf. Linafelt and Beal, *Ruth and Esther*, 67–70.

Woman Wisdom and the (adulterous) strange/foreign woman play in the book. For Proverbs, what an adulterer, like the sinners in Proverbs 1:10–19, misunderstands is the place of one particular human good—in this case, sexual satisfaction (and companionship, perhaps)—in relation to other goods, such as social (and familial) stability and peace. Such a person does not know how to properly pursue each good in a quest for happiness or eudaemonia.

Recognizing the symbolic dimensions and associations of the female figures of Proverbs 1–9 thus permits one to see how the text attempts to train its male addressee's desires and inclinations toward the virtues of wisdom that are necessary for human flourishing.[45] It does so by seeking to transform not only his natural (though undisciplined and wide-ranging) desire for sexual satisfaction into a desire for his own wife alone; it also seeks to restructure and channel this desire into a desire for w/Wisdom itself, a yearning for a life of virtue. The addressee should not avoid adultery simply because of the possible negative consequences of such behavior or because his erotic desires can be slaked with pleasurable sex with his own wife—true as all that might be for the instructing voice. He should also avoid pleasurable sex with another man's wife because to do so is to choose to travel what is emerging in the book as the likewise alluring way of w/Wisdom.

The symbolic training of desire in Proverbs, whereby a strong natural desire for sex is redirected or integrated—at least in part—into a desire for a life of virtue or w/Wisdom itself, constitutes, when achieved, a further transformation of a person's motivational set. In the logic of the images in Proverbs 1–9, the addressee's erotic yearning for the strange or foreign woman is analogous to a desire for illegitimate wealth, such as that offered by the sinners in Proverbs 1. Yet, just as Proverbs does not deny but affirms the worth of material wealth, so too the book does not deny but affirms the desirability of sexual experiences. It is simply that this fundamental human urge must also be properly tutored. In the book's moral vision, the adequate fulfillment of sexual desire, like the attainment of some material prosperity, is regarded as typically vital to a good and flourishing life for the sort of being Proverbs understands humans to be. Of course, the book's instructions both about how sinners pursue their wealth and about the strange woman's allure remain valid literal instructions for the real life of its addressees. Its message is easily

---

45. For some commentators, like Fox (*Proverbs 1–9*, 252–62), although the addressee's erotic yearnings for adulterous sex should be redirected to his own wife, his desires are not necessarily regarded as trained more fundamentally toward w/Wisdom's virtuous way. Such a view is, of course, not wrong, but it probably does not say enough. The various literary-symbolic connections between the female figures of Prov. 1–9 constitute a more complex and subtle set of textual associations and collocations.

rendered in straightforward, even deontological terms: Don't rob or plunder. Don't commit adultery. That level of meaning hardly disappears, even as one starts to discern in and through that teaching the more subtle and symbolic contours of Proverbs' discourse of desire. The symbolic moral work of the text—the transforming of a hearer's desire—is accomplished via its literal instruction, without eliminating its plain-sense teaching.

For virtue-oriented thinking like that which we are discovering in Proverbs, when a transformation of a person's motivational set occurs, the enjoyment of natural human goods like wealth and sex can indeed contribute to human happiness. In such cases, they cease to be the mere pleasures of untutored passions, the chasing after of which may actually thwart eudaemonia or genuine human thriving. As Proverbs 1:10 makes clear, although the sinners' frenzied pursuit of precious wealth may in fact (and perhaps often does) yield real riches, this comes at the cost of any real social stability and solidarity, since others are brutally attacked and murdered in the sinners' quest for their own benefit. The unbridled pursuit of unjust gain, it turns out, takes the life of those who act in such a way—sometimes literally for sure, but certainly always in moral symbolic terms, given that such a way of life can never produce a full thriving existence for the sort of embodied, rational, spiritual, and social being Proverbs imagines humans to be. The same is true when it comes to Proverbs' teaching that a man should avoid sex with another man's wife. The encounter may well be imagined as both possible and pleasurable for the book's male addressees. However, it too can result in social strife and even the adulterer's literal death, if a cuckolded man seeks full vengeance (cf. Prov. 6:32–35). What the pursuit of untutored sexual desire can never produce, and indeed frustrates, is a full flourishing life, for which humans naturally yearn.

What is regularly problematic for many contemporary readers of Proverbs in all this is that the book's instructions, though presented as universally valid teaching, are offered from the historically contingent and exclusionary view of ancient males of a particular social status. This is particularly troublesome in the text's teaching on adultery, not simply because sexual expression within the context of marriage may not be as valued, or valued in the same ways, by some today as it was by the ancient sages. It is troublesome most fundamentally because the book's counsel offers only a male perspective and emerges from obviously androcentric and patriarchal arrangements that depend on a strict policing of female sexuality. For the ancient sages, a woman's sexuality belongs within the boundaries of a patriarchal household and is reckoned as the property, and so properly under the control, of particular males in her life—whether her father initially or her husband subsequently.

Consequently, Proverbs' moral discourse demands ethical-critical engagement. Some readers will want to question the ongoing legitimacy of the book's sex, gender, and marriage concepts and perhaps read against the grain of the text's straightforward instruction by, say, ascribing *positive* agency to the strange, adulterous woman of Proverbs 7, whose sexuality is depicted as a threat to young men. For others, such critical engagement may prove scandalous—at least initially so—because Proverbs is an authoritative religious text. However, to read in this way, *on the side of* the strange woman and *with* some feminist interpreters, would not be to glorify adultery or to sanction the throwing off of all sexual norms, as some might fear. It would rather be to imagine and celebrate this strange woman as an active subject who claims control over her own sexuality in the midst of a patriarchal culture that dictates her choice of sexual partners and regularly values her primarily in terms of her ability to mother sons. It would be to ask if, and how, the Proverbial tradition of virtue can, even through its often contingent and exclusionary rhetoric, prove a liberative moral resource in contexts where individuals and communities strive to eliminate toxic legacies of patriarchy and sexism. The grounds on which such an interpretive task might be warranted will be explored further in the conclusion.

Training Desire in Proverbs 10–31

Proverbs' efforts at shaping its addressees' desires and emotions are not limited to the book's initial nine chapters. Verses in Proverbs 10–31 also point to ways in which the text is concerned with the proper tutoring of human yearnings.

The Desires of the Wicked

In Proverbs 12:12, 21:10, and 21:26, for example, the sages speak forthrightly about the wicked person's desires. The lines read:

> The wicked covet the snare of evildoers,
>   but the root of the righteous gives [favor]. (12:12, author's translation)
>   חָמַד רָשָׁע מְצוֹד רָעִים וְשֹׁרֶשׁ צַדִּיקִים יִתֵּן [חֵן]

> The souls of the wicked desire evil;
>   their neighbors find no mercy in their eyes. (21:10)
>   נֶפֶשׁ רָשָׁע אִוְּתָה־רָע לֹא־יֻחַן בְּעֵינָיו רֵעֵהוּ

> All day long the wicked covet,
>   but the righteous give and do not hold back. (21:26)
>   כָּל־הַיּוֹם הִתְאַוָּה תַאֲוָה וְצַדִּיק יִתֵּן וְלֹא יַחְשֹׂךְ

The initial words of each of these verses present the book's basic position regarding the wrong desires of those on the wrong way. In 12:12, the wicked person desires the sorts of actions—"the snare of evildoers"—that may result in some gain for himself but will likely harm others, just as the fowler's trap benefits the hunter but hardly the bird! As 21:10 says, the soul or appetite (נֶפֶשׁ) of the wicked person is misdirected, desiring evil. The MT of 21:26a intimates something similar, but the text is difficult. On the one hand, it speaks of someone desiring "desire" (הִתְאַוָּה תַאֲוָה); on the other hand, the only available subject for the verb in the clause is the sluggard of the previous verse (v. 25), which fits the sense of the line only awkwardly. The LXX, which the NRSV follows, supplies *asebēs*—the wicked or impious person—as the subject and introduces the term *kakos* ("evil, bad") to describe the nature of the "desire" that constitutes the object of the (wicked) person's yearnings.

> ἀσεβὴς ἐπιθυμεῖ ὅλην τὴν ἡμέραν ἐπιθυμίας κακάς.[46]
> The impious longs for wicked desires all day long. (21:26a NETS)

Although LXX Proverbs, well known for its moralizing in relation to Hebrew Proverbs, may not represent the best reading of the line in text-critical terms, it captures well the sense of the verse. In the Hebrew of 21:26a, the repetition of the root אוה as a *hithpael* verb and its object (הִתְאַוָּה תַאֲוָה; "he goes about desiring desire")—together with the statement that the (wicked) person's desiring is perpetual ("all day long")—makes clear that part of what is at issue is covetousness, excessive desire, or desire that is undisciplined. The characterization of this desiring as κακάς in LXX reveals that, like the wicked person's appetite for evil in 21:10 and for the snare of evildoers in 12:12, the yearning of the (wicked) person in 21:26 is likewise misdirected. Together the three verses make clear that for Proverbs, persistent, excessive, and misdirected desire is characteristic of those who most fundamentally follow a wrong moral path, the wicked (רָשָׁע). The ways of such people the text's addressees must shun.

Neither 12:12 nor 21:10 and 26, however, indicate what exactly the "wicked" desire or covet. The first two lines simply speak generically of evil or "snares of evildoers" as the object of the wicked person's longings. The second halves of these verses, however, permit an inference as to the object of their desires. For example, 21:10b describes the wicked as those who show no mercy to others, while 21:26b contrasts its implied (vicious) subject to "righteous" people (צַדִּיק) who do not covet but instead "give and do not hold back." In 12:12b, the just person is characterized similarly. The final word

---

46. Cf. Fox, *Proverbs 10–31*, 690–91, 1027–28.

of the line—the verb יִתֵּן without an object—is syntactically unexpected. It may be a shorthand or "proverbial" way to express the idea that unlike the wicked person who covets that which results in his own advantage (e.g., a snare of evildoers), a just person (like the צַדִּיק of 21:26b) is generous—"he [simply] gives." Still, the verb without an object is odd. Fox (following Toy) emends יִתֵּן ("he gives") to אֵיתָן ("secure," "firm," "enduring")—"the root of the righteous" does not "give" but is "secure."[47] It may be simpler, while also producing a stronger parallel with the line's first half, to imagine that the word חֵן has dropped out of the text. As Schipper notes, the verb נתן with חֵן is not unexpected, appearing for example in Genesis 39:21; Exodus 3:21; 11:3; 12:36; and Psalm 84:12, while the precise expression יִתֶּן־חֵן "occurs in Proverbs 3:34 . . . and 13:15, and in 3:34 it comes at the end of the verse," as is the case with יִתֵּן here in 12:12.[48] While the untutored desires of the wicked profit themselves but likely harm others, the desires of the just are different. They seek not only their own advantage but augment the favor others might enjoy, for as Fox says (in relation to 3:34), "To 'give (*natan*) favor' means to make someone attractive to others."[49]

For Proverbs when a person's pursuit of happiness entails an unbridled "desiring of desire" that seeks to quench undisciplined yearnings for natural human goods without the full guidance of wisdom's virtues, such a quest inevitably moves one onto a path that only the wicked trod; indeed, it might be said actually to "make" one wicked. For a virtue-oriented discourse like that which Proverbs appears more and more to constitute, the goods necessary for human flourishing are legitimate objects of desire because they can genuinely contribute to eudaemonia. But they are so only when yearning for them is well tutored, when their place within a constellation of other goods is well comprehended, and when they are appropriately pursued with a wisdom that acknowledges one's dependence on and responsibility to seek the well-being of others. Through a generative way of life and generosity, the just person (צַדִּיק) of 12:12 and 21:26, one can infer, understands and does precisely this. The covetous, merciless, wicked person does not. The desires of the one are well trained; the yearnings of the other are not.

The "wicked" in the above lines are thus those in whom a virtue like loyalty, which Proverbs 19:22 knows is more valuable for human flourishing than any secondary good acquired by self-serving behavior (e.g., prevarication), is not to be found.

47. Fox, *Proverbs 10–31*, 553.
48. Schipper, *Proverbs 1–15*, 425–26.
49. Fox, *Proverbs 1–9*, 169.

The Training of Desire for a Life of Flourishing in Proverbs

> What is desirable in a person is loyalty,
>   and it is better to be poor than a liar. (19:22)

Elsewhere Proverbs speaks of the desires of other moral types that can easily be collocated with the wicked mentioned in 12:12, 21:10, and 21:26. Proverbs 13:2 says,

> From the fruit of their words good persons eat good things,
>   but the desire of the treacherous is for wrongdoing.[50]
> מִפְּרִי פִי־אִישׁ יֹאכַל טוֹב וְנֶפֶשׁ בֹּגְדִים חָמָס

The syntax and meaning of the first half of 13:2 in the MT are difficult. Unlike the NRSV's rendering, which may be influenced by the LXX, it says, "From the fruit of the mouth of a person he eats good (things)." Fox captures the literal sense more concisely: "From the fruit of his mouth a man will eat good things."[51] The line is intriguing, if not odd. The imagery reverses a literal process of eating, whereby (good) food goes into a person's mouth and down into them; the line also leaves unexplained how one "eats" or consumes the "good" that seems to constitute the fruit that "comes out" of a person's mouth. What is more, one might wonder what is the fruit of a person's mouth. One plausible suggestion is that the fruit is a figure for their words. As such, the line might simply be saying that one's fine words or ethical discourse can be counted on to produce benefits for a person. As Whybray says, every person "has a chance of eating good as a result of his words."[52]

However, the second half of 13:2 does not speak of an agent being satisfied with good things but instead refers to the desire or appetite (נֶפֶשׁ) of a certain class of people, the treacherous (בֹּגְדִים). And what such people desire is violence (חָמָס). This is an obvious characterization of what Proverbs regards as a misdirected yearning of those who have chosen to follow the wrong path of life. But the line likely entails a fuller and more subtle moral perspective.

The treacherous are not thoroughly characterized by Proverbs. They are, however, paralleled with the wicked and contrasted with the just and upright in 2:22 and 21:18; they are also presented as those who, to their own detriment, follow wrong ways in life (13:15; 22:12). Elsewhere in the Bible, forms of the root בגד describe people who fail to live up to their promises and obligations—for example, in the context of marriage or covenants (e.g.,

---

50. Cf. the similar first stichs in 12:14 and 18:20.
51. Fox, *Proverbs 10–31*, 561.
52. Whybray, *Proverbs*, 201.

Jer. 3:20; Mal. 2:10–11).⁵³ This suggests the treacherous in Proverbs are similarly inconstant. Indeed, Proverbs 25:19 knows a בּוֹגֵד, like "a bad tooth or a lame foot" that inhibits chewing or walking, can't be depended on. Similarly, Proverbs 23:27–28—although in part exonerating male בּוֹגְדִים for their bad behavior vis-à-vis their marriages by speaking of the dangerous sexuality of women—knows that a prostitute or adulteress "increases the number of the faithless." The treacherous, it seems, lack the loyalty that 19:22 so highly prizes.

Yet, the very failure of בֹּגְדִים to be true and reliable with respect to social compacts and obligations indicates that, like all humans, they, too, naturally and fundamentally desire sociality—meaningful relations with others that will contribute to their well-being. However, the בֹּגְדִים misunderstand how association with others might authentically promote their own happiness. They are unable to acknowledge that certain institutions, with their responsibilities and boundaries, structure human relations in ways that promote the relationality for which they yearn. Instead of submitting to institutional demands, the faithless or treacherous seek their own advantage outside of and in disregard for their own promises and commitments to those institutions. Even if a person might, through critical, practical moral reasoning (cf. chaps. 8–9 below), recognize that the institutional structuring of human relations (e.g., in matrimony and other social arenas) is often unequally and unjustly carried out—and so should be reformed (cf. conclusion)—the faithless for Proverbs are those who shun the difficult work of self-denial in the construction of a mutuality that should genuinely benefit both them and their fellows. Consequently, as Proverbs 11:6 says,

> The righteousness of the upright saves them,
>   but the treacherous are taken captive by their schemes.

While the justice, or appropriate social and institutional engagement, of the upright benefits them, the treacherous (בֹּגְדִים) may themselves be "taken captive" or hindered in their pursuit of happiness by their own ill-trained desires (הַוָּה), what the NRSV renders as "schemes."⁵⁴ The actions and decisions of faithless people, however, may not merely result in negative consequences for themselves; they can contribute to the erosion of social institutions. In pursuit of their own advantages and happiness outside the guardrails of established institutions, such people may seek to dominate others and rely on coercion in their relations, thereby spawning social disruption. Such a person's appetite might aptly be characterized, as it is in 13:2, as a treacherous longing for violence.

---

53. Cf. Erlandsson, "בָּגַד."
54. Proverbs 11:6, including the difficult word הַוָּה, will be discussed more fully in chap. 8.

The Desires of the Rich and Powerful

Proverbs 23:1–8, which exhorts the hearer not to envy the position and possessions of socially and economically powerful people, also makes clear that the second half of Proverbs is concerned that the desires of its audience are rightly directed. The passage belongs to the section of Proverbs that is famously parallel to the Egyptian Instruction of Amenemope.[55] Although there is little doubt that the genealogy of the Proverbs passage traces to Amenemope, the moral accents of the biblical text are distinct.[56]

> When you sit down to eat with a ruler,
>   observe carefully what is before you,
> and put a knife to your throat
>   if you have a big appetite.
> Do not desire the ruler's delicacies,
>   for they are deceptive food.
> Do not wear yourself out to get rich;
>   be wise enough to desist.
> When your eyes light upon it [wealth], it is gone;[57]
>   for suddenly it takes wings to itself,
>   flying like an eagle toward heaven.
> Do not eat the bread of the stingy;
>   do not desire their delicacies;
> for like a hair in the throat, so are they.
>   "Eat and drink!" they say to you;
>   but they do not mean it.
> You will vomit up the little you have eaten,
>   and you will waste your pleasant words. (23:1–8)

This passage offers practical advice on how the addressee should conduct himself in the presence of a social superior, first a "ruler" (מוֹשֵׁל, v. 1) and then one with an "evil eye" (רַע עָיִן, v. 6)—that is, a stingy person or, more broadly, one whose intentions in interacting with others are typically for his

---

55. For early publications on Amenemope, see Budge, *Facsimiles of Egyptian Hieratic Papyri*; Erman, "Eine ägyptische Quelle der 'Sprüche Salomos'"; Gressman, "Die neugefundene Lehre des Amen-em-ope"; cf. Bryce, *Legacy of Wisdom*; Römheld, *Wege der Weisheit*; and Washington, *Wealth and Poverty*.

56. For a convenient comparison of Amenemope with certain verses in Prov. 22:17–23:11, see Fox, *Proverbs 10–31*, 707–33. Cf. further Longman, *Proverbs*, 422–24, on the relation of 23:1–5 to Egyptian works.

57. The text in the first half of v. 5 is difficult. The antecedent of the pronoun in the prepositional phrase בּוֹ is absent. Here it is assumed to be something like wealth or riches, based on the use of the *hiphil* infinitive לְהַעֲשִׁיר ("to get rich") in v. 4.

own advantage.⁵⁸ If the addressee has a "big appetite" or is the "lord of an appetite" (בַּעַל נֶפֶשׁ, v. 2), he should sooner take his own life than desire a ruler's fare, since such nourishment is "deceptive food" (v. 3). Neither should the addressee yearn for the delicacies of the wealthy but stingy person's table. Although these dainties are clearly desirable, the pleasure is short lived and will end in illness (v. 8).

These lines surely exhort their addressee to social decorum, as is likely the case in the parallel lines from the earlier Amenemope and in the later analogous Sirach 31.⁵⁹ However, several features of the text suggest deeper concerns too. In Proverbs 23:1–5 the ruler's deceptive food, for which the addressee may be hungry, is called literally the "food of lies" (v. 3). What this לֶחֶם כְּזָבִים is, however, is not entirely clear. The warning about the ruler's food may simply reflect a rhetorical effort to make plain the futility of seeking social and political advancement through close association with the rich and powerful. As Richard Clifford says, "luxurious meals" may have constituted occasions "of later regret for young and ambitious courtiers."⁶⁰ But there is also the implication that the delicacies the ruler enjoys—and which the hearer might share—are a kind of ill-gotten gain, a form of wealth acquired through deception (lies) and perhaps through the covetous or frenzied desire for advantage that the "desire for desire" in Proverbs 21:26 gestures toward. The very next verses exhort the hearer not to "wear yourself out to get rich" (23:4), since material wealth is ephemeral (v. 5) and so can hardly be of sufficient worth to pursue in the deceptive manner the ruler presumably does. In fact, the ruler in Proverbs 23:1–5 appears to have a wrong understanding about the role and value of both material and social goods in human flourishing. Not only is his prosperity, signaled by his delicacies (מַטְעַמּוֹת, v. 3), likely a result of ill-gotten gain (לֶחֶם כְּזָבִים, "a food of lies"); he also seeks to leverage his wealth through manipulation of social space in the institution of the banquet. Occasions of feasting in the ancient world were designed to reinforce the host's social and economic superiority over others—a practice that is a far cry from the basic "equality" (מֵישָׁרִים) that Proverbs' prologue highlights as a key aspect of the social virtue the book values (1:3).⁶¹ The hearer should not yearn to emulate such a "ruler." He should not desire to follow his "way."

---

58. As Fox (*Proverbs 10–31*, 726) says, "'bad of eye' (also in 28:22)" is "the opposite of 'good of eye' (22:9), that is, generous."

59. Fox, *Proverbs 10–31*, 722; cf. Plöger, *Sprüche Salomos*, xxxiii.

60. Clifford, *Proverbs*, 208–9. For a similar reckoning of the line, cf. McKane, *Proverbs*, 382.

61. For a fuller study of food and eating in the Hebrew Scriptures, see, e.g., MacDonald, *Not Bread Alone*.

It is not, however, simply the case that the addressee should not at all yearn for what the ruler desires—namely, material and social goods. Rather, the hearer should not long for what the ruler desires in an excessive, untutored fashion, as the ruler presumably yearns for his goods. Instead of striving inordinately for wealth and status—seeking his own advantage at the expense of others, wearing himself out to get rich—the addressee should "be wise enough to desist" (23:4). And he should do so not merely out of a basic practical concern to avoid falling victim to the ruler in some way—a real enough danger—but because the ruler's way of life is a morally wrong path to follow.[62]

The logic of Proverbs 23:6–8, where the "evil-eyed," stingy person takes center stage, is similar to that of the chapter's initial lines. On a basic level, verses 6–8 are also a piece of practical instruction to the book's readers and hearers regarding interaction with a social superior and any accompanying hopes for personal advantage. That the stingy person is of high social-economic status seems clear both from the fact that the food (לֶחֶם) he offers consists of delicacies (מַטְעַמֹּת, v. 6) and from the invitation he holds out to feast ("Eat and drink!") with him (v. 7). The addressee should not desire the tasty delicacies of the stingy person (v. 6), since efforts to ingratiate himself to such a person by sharing his table ultimately will not succeed—"you will waste your pleasant words" (v. 8). The invitation of stingy persons to share their bounty is insincere or, perhaps better, deceptive in its implicit promise to satisfy. "'Eat and drink!' they say to you; but they do not mean it" (v. 7). Like the robbers' invitation to the addressee in Proverbs 1:10–19, the summons to the stingy person's banquet is a specious bidding. The table fellowship offered turns out to be no genuine opportunity to pursue social and economic advancement through social intercourse with a benevolent superior. It is, likewise, surely no occasion to give or receive expressions of mutuality. Not unlike the "snare of evildoers" in 12:12, the stingy person's banquet is a trap that can lead to the hearer's demise. It does so, first, by reestablishing (rather than transforming) the hearer's subordinate social position vis-à-vis an individual who characteristically seeks his own advantage and, second, by tempting him to emulate a "wicked" and "foolish" (though the passage does not employ those precise terms) moral agent with a skewed understanding of how best to attain human thriving.

All of the things the stingy person possesses and enjoys are desirable, good things that typically can contribute to a person's happiness. But by characterizing

---

62. Literally and conceptually, Prov. 23:4–6 does double duty. The lines conclude the preceding instruction about the "ruler," and they introduce the subsequent teaching about the person with the "evil eye."

their consumption as leading to vomiting (23:8), the text indicates that it is misguided to pursue and value such goods the way a stingy person does. Both the ruler and the stingy person of 23:1–8 hold, and presumably continue to pursue, the trappings of happiness—in particular, the wielding of social and economic power. And this may make it appear that they have attained a "good life." But because their desires have not been shaped by wisdom's virtues, the valuable things they pursue and possess are surely wrongly acquired, and their place in a constellation of goods that contribute to flourishing is plainly misunderstood. Any appearance of genuine well-being is thus fundamentally illusory (cf. chap. 3 above).

Beyond the Desires of Sinners and the Wicked

Just a few verses after Proverbs 23:1–8 warns about desiring the goods that the ruler and stingy person possess, verses 17–18 reiterate that moral impulse through a rhetoric of desire (in this case "envy," but also a "future" and "hope"):

> Do not let your heart envy sinners,
>   but always continue in the fear of the LORD.
> Surely there is a future,
>   and your hope will not be cut off. (23:17–18)

Proverbs 24:1 and 14 add to this rhetoric:

> Do not envy the wicked,
>   nor desire to be with them. (24:1)

> Know that wisdom is such [like honeycomb] to your soul;
>   if you find it, you will find a future,
>   and your hope will not be cut off. (24:14)

Proverbs 23:17 and 24:1 in particular are clear in their assertion that the addressee's desires should be trained away from the path of sinners and the wicked (what *they* have and do) and toward a life of virtue, expressed in 23:17 by the book's fundamental religious virtue, fear of the Lord (cf. 1:7; etc.), and in 24:14 by the mention of wisdom. The internal and central good of living a wise life is what ought to motivate the hearer's actions, not a yearning for anything the sinners or wicked people may hold. As with 12:12, 21:10, and 21:26, however, the lines do not say what the sinners or wicked have or do that the addressee might yearn for or what constitutes the future and hope that the reader is promised. Yet based on the description of those other "sinners" in 1:10–19 and what the book says about the wicked and other negative moral agents (e.g., the ruler and stingy person of 23:1–8), it is easy enough to imagine what the wicked/sinners in 23:17 and 24:1 possess that the addressee might well envy: exterior goods like social status, power, or riches.[63]

Some readers/hearers of Proverbs, however, may also have been susceptible to envying the manner by which the vicious attain those goods and their way of life or character. Recognizing, for example, that a just person's generosity (cf. 21:26) may diminish the good wealth such persons themselves can enjoy, readers might envy the wicked person's merciless or unsentimental harsh dealing with others (cf. 21:10). If certain politically and socially elite figures, or even "sinners" (cf. 23:1–8; 1:10–19), unflinchingly deploy a calculated use of power and aggression to secure their own advantage, such a mode of existence might well be perceived as the best "way"—worthy of emulation—of attaining goods that might be thought to ensure happiness. Of course, for Proverbs, to think in these ways is a mistake. It is to misunderstand the role various goods play in securing human flourishing; and such misunderstanding signals that a person's desires for natural goods have not been appropriately trained toward a life of wisdom.

The hope and future promised to the one who fears the Lord and who gains knowledge of wisdom in 23:18 and 24:14 thus surely entails an expectation of some enjoyment of precisely those external goods for which people might envy "sinners." But if so, this is because Proverbs knows that such goods typically contribute to the happiness for which people long. What most fundamentally constitutes the hope and future the text promises is this sort of eudaemonia or full flourishing, not simply the pleasures that can be derived from external goods. What both 23:17 with its allusion to fear of the Lord and 24:14 with its explicit rhetoric of "wisdom" insist on, moreover, is that the hoped-for, authentic flourishing that the text imagines, including enjoyment of some external goods, is internally related to, and so only possible via, a life of virtue (cf. chap. 2). As Proverbs 10:28 says, with explicit mention of two of the book's key moral types and the "ends" related to these people's characters,

> The hope of the righteous ends in gladness,
>   but the expectation of the wicked comes to nothing.

Of course, the sort of virtuous existence to which Proverbs 23:17 and 24:14 allude is in some sense regarded as desirable in and of itself; it is pleasurable even without external goods that Proverbs recognizes typically contribute to

---

63. Cf. the similar point made in the discussion of Prov. 24:1 and Ps. 37:1 in chap. 3 above.

happiness. As 24:14 says, "wisdom" itself is sweet like honeycomb. Still, such a virtuous existence without some enjoyment of exterior goods does not—at least for most people—constitute full happiness. But wise persons understand that eudaemonia is ultimately unattainable without the tutoring of one's broader yearnings that virtue affords. As Proverbs 19:2 says,

> Desire without knowledge is not good,
>   and one who moves too hurriedly [אָץ] misses the way [חוֹטֵא].

The second half of this verse, with its image of hurried movement leading one to "miss the way," is not simply a general observation that moving too quickly may cause one to stray from a path, as the NRSV suggests. It also evokes a person's covetous character; elsewhere in Proverbs the verb אוץ describes inappropriate quests for wealth. In Proverbs the person in a hurry tends to be in a hurry to acquire material advantage for themselves; such a person is excessively acquisitive. Because for the sages a hurried person is typically morally suspect, that person may well be disciplined for their faulty character or perhaps for the illegitimate ways their untutored desires drive them to seek gain. As the second half of Proverbs 28:20 says, "One who is in a hurry to be rich [אָץ לְהַעֲשִׁיר] will not go unpunished." In 19:2 the one who is in a hurry is called a sinner (חוֹטֵא), as are the robbers in Proverbs 1:10–19 (v. 10), who also aggressively and immorally seek profit.[64]

Although in "real life" the vice of covetousness might result in the accumulation of significant external goods, it can never be the means to arrive successfully at the end of genuine human flourishing—that hoped-for status which surely and most fundamentally motivates a person's quest for valuable goods in the first place. Consequently, in a verse like Proverbs 21:5, "the plans of the diligent" may result in an increase or advantage (מוֹתָר), but a person's hurried pursuit of material goods ends, ironically, in "want" (מַחְסוֹר)—sometimes literally so, because of carelessness perhaps, but always in terms of the pursuit of genuine eudaemonia.

Still, like other verses in the book, Proverbs 19:2 recognizes that the pursuit of those things humans typically desire is not inevitably or always bad or misguided. A main moral point of the verse is simply that human appetites need to

---

64. Proverbs 29:20, by contrast, speaks of one who is hurried with his words. This is probably primarily a general warning to be cautious in one's speech. However, given the other usages of אוץ in Proverbs, it may also signal that one who speaks quickly to a situation or hastily engages another person in conversation is in fact hoping his oral interaction with that person will result in some advantage. The connotation of hurried actions in the service of gain is also somewhat evident in Exod. 5:13, where the Egyptian taskmasters speak urgently, demanding that the Hebrew slaves complete their work quickly.

be trained, not eliminated. Indeed, "knowledge," a central intellectual virtue for Proverbs (cf. 1:2), is the key term in the verse. The saying insists that the hearer's desires or natural inclinations ought to be shaped by this important wisdom virtue. What the "sinner" in 19:2 needs to "know" is that he ought to slow down and learn the actual worth of external goods in producing flourishing, how they are to be ranked, and which virtues are necessary for rightly accessing and enjoying them.

The Desires of the Righteous

The sentence sayings of Proverbs 10–31 speak not only of the desires of negative moral agents; these chapters also allude, as already evident in Proverbs 12:12 and 21:26, to the appropriately directed longings of the just. Proverbs 10:3, 24, and 11:23, for example, speak of the desires of righteous people, while also expanding a bit what constitutes the misdirected yearnings of the wicked (cf. above) with whom the just are often contrasted.

> The LORD does not let the righteous go hungry,
> but he thwarts the craving of the wicked. (10:3)[65]

> What the wicked dread will come upon them,
> but the desire of the righteous [תַּאֲוַת צַדִּיקִים] will be granted. (10:24)

> The desire of the righteous [תַּאֲוַת צַדִּיקִים] ends only in good;
> the expectation of the wicked in wrath. (11:23)

These NRSV renderings reinforce a view of Proverbs that understands the book to operate by a literal act-consequence logic. The virtuous (the just) will receive positive benefits on account of their virtue; their desires will be granted and lead only to good. By contrast, the wicked will rightly find their evil ways turned back upon them; at their end they will find that which they dread, an appropriate punishment.

The basic optimism of Proverbs' wisdom mythos (see chap. 1)—that virtue is sure to be rewarded—is on full display with verses like 10:24 and 11:23; this confidence is perhaps the most fundamental effect of the rhetoric. What is more, there is no need to deny the pedagogical efficacy of the promises of reward and punishment for Proverbs' young and simple addressees; when

---

65. The term הַוַּת (רְשָׁעִים הַוַּת) here and in Prov. 11:6 and Mic. 7:37 may mean desire; cf. Schipper, *Proverbs 1–15*, 367–68. Or הַוַּת might be emended to חַיַּת ("desire"), as Fox (*Proverbs 10–31*, 512) suggests. Cf. the discussion of 11:6 in chap. 8.

literally understood, they can motivate novice students to follow the book's teachings. Yet the moral contours of the verses are also more subtle and rich than this. The second half of 10:24 and the first half of 11:23 may, in fact, speak of the completed transformation of a virtuous person's desires in the manner envisioned by MacIntyre noted at the outset of this chapter. That is, the just persons in each verse can be said to be people who already possess good and fully developed moral characters; and their settled dispositions mean they are not tossed to and fro by any natural-but-untutored desires for riches, status, or any other lesser good.

To see this most clearly, one must resist understanding the lines as only expressing something like the magical workings of a cosmic act-consequence nexus, where the good rewards of the one who follows wisdom's morality are easily and usually granted. Instead, one should first simply ask of Proverbs 10:24 and 11:23, "What is it that just people desire?" What is the תַּאֲוַת צַדִּיקִים of which both lines speak? For what does the appetite of the righteous (נֶפֶשׁ צַדִּיק) hunger in 10:3? For virtue-oriented discourses, next to happiness—that which one pursues for its own sake—what good moral agents will most earnestly desire is to live a life of virtue, something they know to be indispensable for authentic well-being. This sort of yearning can be satisfied simply through living a just life. Consequently, as 11:23 seems to know, what the just person seeks is only the "good" itself—something that is clearer when the verse is translated more literally than it is in the NRSV. The NJPS captures well the sense of the line:

> What the righteous desire can only be good. (11:23a NJPS)
> תַּאֲוַת צַדִּיקִים אַךְ־טוֹב

This short saying does not parse fully what the desired "good" consists of. In the context of the book, however, the yearning of these צַדִּיקִים obviously includes an inclination to pursue justice through the virtues that Proverbs persistently highlights (צֶדֶק, צְדָקָה; cf. chap. 7 below) and that give the just person his name! Yet the "good" that the line envisions just people yearn for can hardly be limited to the book's concern with social virtue. It surely entails desire for good or rightly conceived sexual relations, as well as appropriate yearning for and pursuit of social status, health, and wealth—all topics and images that abound in Proverbs and that the sages believe contribute to an individual's happiness. To the extent that just persons not only hunger for the "good" but actually live virtuously, what they desire can be reckoned as something they persistently attain. As 10:24b says, "The desire of the righteous will be granted." Or as Proverbs 10:3a suggests, Adonai will not starve

(יַרְעִיב) the appetite (נֶפֶשׁ) of the righteous since what they hunger for is consistent with the Lord's own way (cf. 10:29). What is more, if the just in verses like 10:3, 24, and 11:23 are those whose moral motivations and desires for natural human goods have been appropriately trained and transformed, they can provide examples for others—not unlike Aristotle's fully virtuous people who see matters truly and judge rightly because of their good character.

In contrast to an interest in the longings of "just people," Proverbs 10:3, 24, and 11:23 are also concerned with the "craving of the wicked" (10:3), "what the wicked dread" (10:24), and their "expectation" or hope (11:23). An expectation or hope is essentially a form of desire, a longing for something to happen or come to pass. A sense of dread is a kind of negative hope, the desire that something *not* come to pass within a context of fear that it will. If in Proverbs 11:23a, then, the just person is said to desire only what is good, the second half of the line asserts something like the opposite. The NRSV's rendering of 11:23b, "the expectation of the wicked [ends] in wrath," is of course possible. It may, as Fox suggests, constitute a "paradoxical and facetious" statement, "for the wicked do not really hope for this." It only appears that they do since their evil deeds "will inevitably bring wrath upon them."[66] Yet this again interprets the Hebrew in terms of a fairly strong act-consequence logic. By contrast, the NJPS's rendering of the half-verse, "What the wicked hope for stirs wrath," perhaps better captures the sense. That is, "whatever the wicked desire" (which is not precisely stated in the line) results in someone's anger. This might be God's wrath, but it also may be some person's anger. That is, because the wicked are not guided by wisdom, what they typically want usually leads them to do things that cause social strife, a state of affairs naturally at odds with the high value the sages place on social virtue and the social harmony such virtue should produce.

From other lines in Proverbs it is easy to sketch the sorts of behavior wicked people engage in that would stir the sort of wrath of which 11:23 speaks. For example, a number of verses focus on the wicked person's speech, which conceals violence (10:6, 11), articulates what is perverse (10:32; 15:28), and offers unreliable or wicked counsel (12:5, 26). Other verses describe the wicked as shameful (13:5) and haughty (21:4). They covet (12:12; 21:26), accept bribes (17:23), and lack mercy (12:10; 21:10; cf. 12:6). All these activities would surely stir up strife and make others angry. Still, as Fox says, the "hope" of the wicked is not literally *for* wrath—of course. Who would desire that for themselves? Rather, what the wicked presumably most fundamentally

---

66. Fox, *Proverbs 10–31*, 541.

yearn for in 11:23 is precisely that for which others hope: their own happiness. What is distinct is the manner in which the wicked pursue their hopes and desires, the way of life they follow. They seek to satisfy their drive for happiness not by wisdom but via the calculations of their own vicious characters; and that inevitably results in strife and others' anger. Their hope can thus poetically be described in 11:23 as a hope for wrath. Consequently, in 10:24 that which "the wicked dread" coming upon them may be divine punishment for their conduct, for as 10:3 says, the Lord "thwarts the cravings of the wicked." But what the wicked dread may also be reprisals from other humans whose wrath they stir up. In any case, what the wicked surely also fear, even if not consciously so, is never attaining the genuine happiness they hope the secondary goods they excessively desire and pursue will secure.

Like Proverbs 10:3, 24, and 11:23, Proverbs 13:25 also speaks of the desires or appetites of both a just person, one whose desires are already properly tutored and whose motivational set is fully transformed, and a wicked person, whose bad character is likewise well-settled:[67]

> The righteous have enough to satisfy their appetite,
> but the belly of the wicked is empty. (13:25)
> צַדִּיק אֹכֵל לְשֹׂבַע נַפְשׁוֹ וּבֶטֶן רְשָׁעִים תֶּחְסָר

Understanding Proverbs from a straightforward Tun-Ergehen point of view, the saying simply motivates righteous living with a promise of good rewards and the threat of bad consequences: the satisfaction of one's hunger or appetite, on the one hand, or persistent hunger, a belly that always lacks food, on the other. There is no reason to reject fully a reading that focuses on that level of meaning.

However, the verse can also be rendered slightly differently than the above NRSV translation. The just person in the first part, as Fox says, simply "eats till his appetite is sated," likely with the sense that this person "eats just enough to satisfy his appetite."[68] The second stich can be translated as "but the belly of wicked people (continually) lacks," the ongoing nature of the verbal action signaled by the imperfect verb form (תֶּחְסָר). The just person is described as moderate in satisfying his desire for food. By contrast, the wicked person, whose belly is never quite sated, is characterized by immoderate habits of consumption—always eating, never getting enough.

---

67. With similar rhetoric, Prov. 13:4 speaks of the appetite of the lazy that continually craves and that of the diligent, which is "richly supplied."

68. Fox, *Proverbs 10–31*, 571.

The righteous person in Proverbs 13:25, however, is not simply "rewarded" with a satisfied appetite *because* he is righteous. Rather his appropriately controlled appetite and his moderation also evidence an already well-tutored or transformed desire for a basic human need.[69] MacIntyre's words on the virtue of moderation are aptly applied to the verse: "Someone who has become temperate will have come to enjoy moderation and to find excess disagreeable and even painful. She or he will no longer practice moderation in spite of a desire for the pleasures that belong to excess but because desire itself has been transformed."[70] Likewise, the wicked person's empty belly in the verse is not a simple punishment for vice. Neither Adonai nor an impersonal retributive mechanism of the cosmos is starving him. Instead, his stomach is always "empty" because his untrained appetite is never long satisfied.

On a basic level, then, the rhetoric of Proverbs 13:25 promotes the virtue of moderation in eating. However, it is surely also concerned to offer a further moral point. After all, the line speaks not merely of any person's appetite but the *just* person's "soul" (נֶפֶשׁ) and the *wicked* person's belly (בֶּטֶן); and, of course, the ability or inability to moderate one's food consumption does not alone make someone completely virtuous or vicious. The ethical lives of real human beings are more complex and nuanced than that. The just person's נֶפֶשׁ and the wicked person's belly in 13:25 thus also serve as tropes for the broader sets of desires and appetites of each moral type, which are rightly trained and tutored, or not. The just person's controlled appetite is a sign of his wise character more broadly conceived. Similarly, the person of insatiable hunger does not merely overeat and otherwise lives well and justly. He is instead the paragon of vice in Proverbs. His immoderation is a symptom and symbol of a more comprehensive failure to appropriately train a broader set of natural inclinations and desires. The just and wicked persons' respective moderate or immoderate appetites (for food or anything else) signal the settled nature of their characters, for better or worse.

Other verses in the later chapters of Proverbs also point to the book's concern that the desires of people who follow the paths of the wise and just be rightly tutored and trained into a life of virtue. Consider, for example, Proverbs 21:17.

---

69. Proverbs 13:4—"The appetite of the lazy craves, and gets nothing, while the appetite of the diligent is richly supplied"—uses rhetoric similar to 13:25. Over and beyond the literal instruction the verse offers, it might be thought to express a point analogous to 13:25. The desires of the diligent person, like those of the just person in 13:25, are appropriately trained and so are regularly satisfied, while the longings of the lazy person, like those of the wicked, have not been transformed and so are perpetually experienced.

70. MacIntyre, *Dependent Rational Animals*, 89.

> Whoever loves pleasure will suffer want;
> whoever loves wine and oil will not be rich.

This verse certainly knows that a person can use economic resources to enjoy the finer things in life—here oil and wine. But it also suggests that spending significantly on such pleasures may prevent a person from getting ahead financially. And *that* may be the fundamental, practical message of the verse for the book's young and simple audience. As Van Leeuwen concludes, the saying may be "an ancient parallel to 'You can't have your cake and eat it too.'"[71] It may be a warning about spending above one's ability, something that might lead to poverty, as Longman similarly notes.[72] However, if this is the case, the verse does not merely reflect the insight that enjoying much oil and drink can exhaust one's resources and for that reason should be avoided. At issue, too, is excessive desire or the "love" of the sort of pleasure that oil and wine might provide. A symbolic understanding of Proverbs' rhetoric of wealth and poverty, as I offered in an earlier study,[73] might suggest that because the text associates such a way of life with poverty, it considers it of little moral worth. Though such a view is not incorrect, it also does not say quite enough.

Many readers in fact also sense in 21:17 a larger moral point and regard the verse as an exhortation to avoid a life of profligacy. Besides a warning about spending, Longman also takes the line to be censuring "overindulgence" and the "pursuit of pleasure."[74] Murphy similarly believes not only that the proverb "comments on one reason for poverty" but that such poverty is related to "an extravagant indulgence."[75] Indeed, that the issue in Proverbs 21:17 is not only a practical, financial one but an ethical matter arises from the clustering of the terms for oil, wine, and pleasure. By themselves, none of these words necessarily implies luxurious or extravagant living. But together they perhaps do, as is likely the case in Ecclesiastes 9:7–8 (cf. Eccles. 8:15). The command of Proverbs 23:20–21, which deploys a cognate rhetoric to that of 21:17, is similarly concerned with censuring the same sort of extravagant or gluttonous living (cf. 23:29–35):

> Do not be among winebibbers,
> or among gluttonous eaters of meat;
> for the drunkard and the glutton will come to poverty. (23:20–21)

---

71. Van Leeuwen, "Book of Proverbs," 194.
72. Longman, *Proverbs*, 395.
73. Sandoval, *Discourse of Wealth and Poverty*.
74. Longman, *Proverbs*, 395.
75. R. Murphy, *Proverbs*, 160.

Oil, wine, and meat, especially when collocated together, can be understood as luxury goods, the excessive consumption of which is implicitly associated with the economic elite. Proverbs 21:17 and 23:20–21, consequently, both hint at the potential dangers of wealth for virtuous living. Though the sages recognize that some level of material wealth contributes to well-being, this is not the case without wisdom, when desires for certain goods are untutored and the goods themselves are inordinately pursued and consumed.[76]

It is obviously not the case that profligate living always produces poverty, though certainly it might. Living an extravagant lifestyle actually demands full and reliable access to significant resources. But if the scenarios sketched in the lines above (coming to want, dispossession) are not always literally true, they *are* always true for Proverbs in a moral sense. The excessive consumption of goods, the chasing or "love" of pleasure untutored by wisdom's virtues, can never slake a more fundamental natural desire for well-being that, again, surely motivates the pursuit and enjoyment of goods like wine, oil, and meat in the first place. When it comes to authentic happiness, even if people possess and can partake of luxury goods, without the guidance of wisdom's virtues they will always be people of lack (מַחְסוֹר, 21:17); they will always be dispossessed (יוֹרִישׁ, 23:21) and will never sufficiently prosper (לֹא יַעֲשִׁיר, 21:17) in ways that permit a genuine thriving life.

Proverbs 30:15–16 also seems to allude to people whose desires have not been properly trained and who subsequently wrongly and inordinately seek external goods in their quests to secure their own happiness.

> The leech has two daughters;
>   "Give, give," they cry.
> Three things are never satisfied;
>   four never say, "Enough" [הוֹן]:
> Sheol, the barren womb,
>   the earth ever thirsty for water,
>   and the fire that never says, "Enough" [הוֹן].

The lines present images of things that characteristically appear insatiable. The leech continually sucks the blood of its host, parched land never stops absorbing the water poured on it, and fire continuously consumes its fuel; and in the more gendered rhetoric of a contingent cultural bias, the "barren" womb represents the imagined persistent desire of a childless woman for offspring. What is intriguing in the passage, however, is that the rhetoric

---

76. On Prov. 21:17 and 23:20–21, see further Sandoval, *Discourse of Wealth and Poverty*, 168–71.

of insatiability—"enough"—associated with these images of consumption is literally the language of wealth—הוֹן. The sages of Proverbs know that some people, in their desires for various goods, are like J. D. Rockefeller, who reportedly expressed his insatiable craving for riches by responding to the question about how much money is enough with the quip, "Just a little bit more."

Given that Proverbs 30:15–16 is immediately preceded by two verses that criticize the proud and those who "devour the poor from off the earth," it is not far-fetched to think that insatiable desire for riches here is a further characterization of precisely those people. And in Proverbs such figures are to be collocated not only with the wicked but the rich too, whom we saw persistently overvalue wealth and pursue it wrongly (chap. 3; cf. chap. 7). They are those who can never say "enough," who are unable to realize that they possess a level of wealth sufficient for human well-being. Consequently, they continue to immoderately and unjustly pursue it. Such people are aptly characterized by the ancient text, as in some contemporary idioms, as "leeches" (30:15). Their motivational sets are never adequately transformed and their desires never sufficiently directed to the internal good of virtue and a life of wisdom. Their character, though surely once malleable and trainable, has been hardened in the *longue durée* of their ill-conceived pursuit of those goods, which can in fact contribute to human thriving—when pursued by virtue. Even if such people believe themselves to be happy and look to others as if they are, they cannot be said to experience a genuine flourishing life for the sort of embodied, spiritual, intellectual, and social being Proverbs reckons humans to be. They lack the most valuable and essential good needed for eudaemonia—wisdom or virtue.

Given Proverbs' full and extensive rhetoric of desire, it is safe to say that, like other virtue-oriented moral discourses, this book is robustly interested in the yearnings of its audiences, whether they are well trained or not, directed toward wisdom or toward some lesser good. Yet also like traditions of character ethics, the sages are further interested in the relationship of a moral agent's desires to their intellect and the relation of knowledge to goodness. It is to these questions that we turn before considering more fully how Proverbs speaks of the key virtues of sociability (chap. 7) and Practical Wisdom (chaps. 8–9).

6

Desire, Knowledge, and Goodness

Beyond Wise and Just, Foolish and Wicked

Throughout the pages of Proverbs, the ancient sages point to an intimate connection between moral and intellectual capacities. If one is just, one is surely also wise; if one is a fool, there is a good chance that person also travels wicked paths. For Proverbs, as scholars have sometimes noted, the "wise person" and the "just person" are by and large coreferential terms, as are the "fool" and the "wicked"—they denote one and the same object/type of person.[1] Though not wrong, the linguistic phenomenon of coreferentiality does not say quite enough about the relationship between the wise and just, or knowledge and goodness, in Proverbs. Premodern traditions of ethics can again help us moderns think through Proverbs' moral discourse—in this case, its understanding of the relationship between human moral and intellectual abilities.

The relationship between ethical and intellectual virtue in Proverbs is probably not quite analogous to the Socratic view—"to know the good is to do the good"—as some have suggested.[2] Instead, the book's concern with training

---

1. Coreferentiality is a concept invoked, e.g., by Heim, *Like Grapes of Gold Set in Silver*, 81–82 and passim; Lyu, *Righteousness in the Book of Proverbs*, 33 and passim; and Keefer, *Proverbs 1–9*, 48–49.

2. Fox, *Proverbs 10–31*, 940–42; cf. Newsom, "Models of the Moral Self," 12.

one's desires hints that the relationship between intellectual and moral virtue in Proverbs is more akin to Aristotelian conceptions.[3] For Aristotle, one can know a good and right course of action but choose to act otherwise because of the compelling nature of one's untutored or incompletely trained yearnings. Certainly, something like this may sometimes be the case for the young and simple figures that Proverbs addresses, as well as for the book's other moral types whose dispositions may not be as fully settled as the "character" of just (and wicked) persons. Still, as MacIntyre explains, for the Aristotelian tradition "excellence of character and intelligence cannot be separated," a fact that MacIntyre contends is at odds with dominant modern conceptions like those of Kant, for whom "one can be both good and stupid"—that is, by having a "good will" that is able to follow the moral law but not "knowing how to apply general rules to particular cases." By contrast, for Aristotle a person "'cannot have practical intelligence [*phronēsis*] unless he is good.'"[4] That is, a particular sort of intellectual capacity and knowledge of the good is required for one to exercise genuine practical moral reasoning or what in Proverbs might be called Practical Wisdom, a concept that we will explore more fully in chapters 8–9.

Aristotelian Moral Types and Proverbs

The Aristotelian tradition of virtue ethics in part accounts for the relationship between intellectual and moral virtue—the question of whether knowing the good inevitably entails doing the good—by considering the cases of those who intellectually know the good and appropriate thing to do and still choose not to do it, a situation ruled out by the Socratic dictum "To know the good is to do the good." In these situations, the Aristotelian tradition recognizes the significant role of desire in people's moral lives. For understanding how Proverbs reckons with the relationship of desire to moral and intellectual virtue, Aristotle's description of enkratic and akratic persons can prove quite helpful—even if Proverbs has no equivalent terminology for these Aristotelian moral agents and even if the analogies that can be drawn must remain somewhat imprecise.[5]

---

3. Ansberry in particular argues that Proverbs' moral discourse is more akin to that of Aristotle than it is to Socrates. See "What Does Jerusalem Have to Do with Athens?" Others who study the book in light of virtue ethics also tend to invoke the Aristotelian tradition. See, e.g., C. Yoder, "Objects of Our Affections"; Stewart, *Poetic Ethics in Proverbs*; and Keefer, *Book of Proverbs and Virtue Ethics*.

4. MacIntyre, *After Virtue*, 154–55, citing *NE* 1144a 37. As MacIntyre says, "For Aristotle stupidity *of a certain kind* precludes goodness" (155, emphasis added). On these matters and a fuller discussion of Practical Wisdom in Proverbs, see chaps. 8–9 below.

5. Aristotle treats these issues especially in book 7 of *Nicomachean Ethics*. Cf. the more technical discussion in Kraut, "Aristotle's Ethics."

For Aristotle, enkratic people know that they ought or ought not to do something, and despite a desire to follow the wrong way, they overcome their yearnings and choose a good and appropriate course of action. By contrast, the genuinely virtuous person not only understands what constitutes a good and right course of action and chooses it, but such a person also desires such a moral course. Their "motivational set," of which MacIntyre speaks (cf. chap. 5), has been transformed. The enkratic person, as Annas says,

> can do the morally right thing, but in an important respect doing the right thing is not what matters most of all to him since he has desires which do not go along with his deliberation. The fully virtuous person, on the other hand, is unified in motivation and deliberation. He does not have to summon up the willpower to do what he sees to be the right thing, for he does not have to fight down countering desires.[6]

In Proverbs, as we have just seen, one often reads of wise and just people where the text's rhetoric suggests their desires or yearnings have been transformed. The rhetoric of other lines, however, does not explicitly indicate that wise and just people have experienced a fundamental reorientation of desire. For example, Proverbs 10:30–32 repeatedly speaks of the צַדִּיק but mentions nothing of this person's desires:

> The righteous will never be removed,
>   but the wicked will not remain in the land.
> The mouth of the righteous brings forth wisdom,
>   but the perverse tongue will be cut off.
> The lips of the righteous know what is acceptable,
>   but the mouth of the wicked what is perverse.

Are the righteous persons in such lines fully virtuous, with transformed desires and emotions? Or are they perhaps merely enkratic? Unlike Aristotle, Proverbs does not obviously or systematically make clear these sorts of fine distinctions.

The situation is analogous with vicious and akratic persons. For Aristotle vicious agents not only intellectually believe they should take a wrong and wicked moral course (e.g., as an expedient way to attain a good), but they have also come to desire that course of action and so understandably choose it. Akratic persons, by contrast, are weak willed, and though they perhaps know or think they should or should not do something, they surrender to their desire and follow a wrong or wicked path. In Proverbs, just as the

---

6. Annas, *Morality of Happiness*, 369.

depictions of wise and just persons do not always speak of their desires, no strong yearning is consistently ascribed to wicked and foolish people either (e.g., 10:11, 32; 12:5–7). In the same way that it does not draw a bright line between virtuous and enkratic individuals, Proverbs also does not draw a bright line between truly vicious agents and merely akratic ones in the manner Aristotle does.

Still, even if in Proverbs the nature of the desires of the wise/just and the yearnings of the wicked/fool are not always clearly (or even implicitly) stated, they often are. These moral types probably should be thought to represent people with settled good or bad moral dispositions. Consequently, they can be correlated to the primary positive and negative moral types in Aristotelian traditions of virtue ethics. They are the virtuous and the vicious, respectively, though especially the wise and just person in Proverbs is likely an ideal figure whose pure character is rarely found unadulterated among real people in real life. As Annas suggests, for Aristotle, too, the fully virtuous person is probably "a normative ideal to which we aspire."[7]

Proverbs, however, also speaks of a host of other agents who, though not called חָכָם or צַדִּיק, are said to follow the paths of wise and just people. And what the text says about these people also does not always reveal explicitly whether their fundamental desires have been transformed or if they are instead driven to right behavior by the force of their wills and the strength of their rational deliberations. Likewise, the book does not always make clear whether moral agents who are characterized by only one particular vice are ignorant of the fact that the wicked and foolish path they choose to follow is not good, or if they know it is a wrong path but are led by their desire to follow it nonetheless. Beyond the wise and just and the wicked and foolish, other moral agents in Proverbs can thus be described as either akratic or enkratic or, perhaps more heuristically accurate, as akratic-like or enkratic-like. They are those who, in any particular moment and context, may know the good and appropriate course of action but whose desires for certain goods that contribute to human well-being are not (yet) well or fully trained; they are those whose dispositions are not (yet) well or fully settled as vicious or virtuous. This is hardly unexpected since, as we have seen, Proverbs strives to train the desires of those it addresses toward wisdom and virtue so that their character will, in fact, finally become settled as wise and just.

Proverbs does not provide sufficient information about all its character types to discern unequivocally how each might relate to Aristotelian categories. Still, the sages say enough about a handful of moral types beyond the

---

7. Annas, *Morality of Happiness*, 91; cf. 125.

wise and just or wicked and foolish to offer some tentative observations and suggestions about how they are akratic- or enkratic-like.

The Akratic-Like in Proverbs

A few of the primary types of moral agents in Proverbs are figures who typically follow the wrong way but are nonetheless somewhat corrigible. The akratic nature of these people usually seems to get the best of them. For example, the כְּסִיל, "dolt," often translated "fool," appears at times to be akratic-like. For Fox, however, such a person is "morally perverse by reason of his obtuseness"; it is a lack of knowledge that prevents him from choosing wisdom.[8] If he were truly to *know* the good, he would surely *do* the good, as Socrates predicted.

Although the dolt's fundamental and usual problem may be presented by the sages as an intellectual one—a lack of knowledge or rational failure—this is not necessarily the only thing that impedes the dolt from living wisely and virtuously. For example, the dolt's untrained desire for certain goods appears to be operative at points too, as in Proverbs 10:23 and 18:2.

> Doing wrong is like laughter [שְׂחוֹק] to a dolt,
> but wisdom is pleasure to a person of understanding.[9] (10:23)

> A dolt takes no pleasure in understanding,
> but only in expressing personal opinion. (18:2)

And 21:20 knows that

> precious treasure remains in the house of the wise,
> but the dolt devours it.

In these lines the dolt's untutored desires that he chooses to satiate are likely what lead him down the wrong path, at least in part.[10] In Proverbs 10:23 the wrongdoing of this sort of person provokes his laughter (שְׂחוֹק), a fact that suggests such conduct pleases him. Proverbs 18:2 is similarly explicit that the dolt delights in thoughtlessly speaking his mind, while in 21:20 the appetite of

---

8. Fox, *Proverbs 1–9*, 41–42.

9. The שְׂחוֹק ("laughter") of the first half, though absent in the second clause, should be assumed to be operative in the syntax of both halves; here it is translated as "pleasure."

10. Cf. further 13:19; 14:24; 15:14; 18:2; 19:10; 21:20; 26:8, which use a rhetoric of desire or desirable goods to gesture toward the yearning of the dolt that is regularly not well trained.

the כְּסִיל for desirable things is surely what drives him to "devour" (בלע) any "precious treasure" he might encounter. The contrast with the understanding and wise person's desires that are well trained—he takes pleasure in "wisdom" and does not voraciously consume his valuables—underscores the untutored character of the dolt's yearnings. Although a dolt's mode of being may also be characterized as folly (אִוֶּלֶת; cf. 12:23; 13:16; etc.), this sort of "fool" is not an אֱוִיל, a person of fully settled negative character who "vacates (yᵉḥasser) his mind from choosing good and rejecting evil."[11] Granted that though there may not be *much* hope that the dolt will "wise up" and change his ways so that he might be rightly tutored by virtue, he nonetheless apparently remains somewhat teachable. As Proverbs 8:5 (cf. 1:22–23) says,

> O simple ones, learn prudence [עָרְמָה];
> acquire intelligence [הָבִינוּ לֵב], O dolts.

The dolt's basic corrigibility is probably the reason he remains subject to discipline (18:6; 19:29; 26:3).

All this suggests that the dolt in Proverbs is one who may be able to understand what is good (for himself or others) but does not choose it because he desires some aspect of the wrong way. He does not always simply or only lack knowledge; he sometimes "hates" it (1:22)—a reaction that suggests some comprehension of it. The dolt is not always simply ignorant of the good; he sometimes appears weak willed (akratic-like) when it comes to deliberations on his way of life. Although he should "instruct" his mind or "acquire intelligence" (8:5; cf. NJPS, NRSV), he "trusts in [his] own wits"—choosing not to walk "in wisdom" (28:26). And because of this inability to choose wisdom, he sometimes "utters slander" (10:18) when a just person, by contrast, might choose the good of making his fellow attractive to others (12:12).[12] Or the dolt may give "full vent to anger," while the wise person "quietly holds it back" (29:11).

What makes a dolt a dolt, then, is not intellectual or rational deficiency alone. When faced with decisions or action, he lacks the ability to let his intellect and rationality be guided by virtue. Any knowledge of what is good for people, to which he may have been exposed, can sometimes be inhibited by his insufficiently trained desires. Recall MacIntyre's note that, for the virtue ethics of the Aristotelian tradition, "excellence of character and intelligence cannot be separated." The dolt in Proverbs can be said to be "stupid" because he does

---

11. Moshe ben Ḥayyim Alsheikh, cited in Fox, *Proverbs 1–9*, 40; cf. 429.
12. See the discussion of Prov. 12:12 in chap. 5 above.

not exercise any genuine practical moral reasoning (chaps. 8–9) whereby his intellect is guided by his virtue. Indeed, the contrast between the wise person and the dolt in Proverbs has centrally to do with the ability of the one, but not the other, to bring one's virtuous character (with its well-tutored desires) to bear on intellectual and rational activities and thereby discern appropriate paths in any particular context of decision or action.

Similar to the כְּסִיל in Proverbs is the חֲסַר־לֵב, the one who lacks sense. This person is also not incorrigibly foolish or wicked, but he likewise tends to follow the way of folly and wickedness. His problem is again presented as an intellectual one. He lacks heart (or "mind"), which surely in part means he does not always understand what is authentically good for himself given the kind of (human) being he is. But his intellectual lack is, like the dolt's, also not unrelated to his desires. The one who lacks heart, for instance, is also one who is tempted by sex with a woman who is not his wife, as in Proverbs 6:32. This is also the case in 7:7, where the youth addressed is both collocated with the simple person and said to lack heart. In 15:21 the חֲסַר־לֵב can also be said to pursue folly. But this too is not a function merely of ignorance since the folly is said to be pleasurable (שִׂמְחָה). And in 9:16 the one who lacks heart (again collocated with the simple) is not merely intellectually deceived by Woman Folly; he also is clearly tempted by the desirable (though wrongly acquired) things she, as well as the life path she represents, offers—sweet (stolen) water and pleasant bread (secretly enjoyed).

As Fox notes, a person who lacks heart is also prone to laziness (24:30),[13] but this too does not mean merely that he fails completely to understand that a life of diligence is better for him. It may also suggest he is unable to resist the appeal of leisure. Likewise, the empty or useless things the חֲסַר־לֵב chases in 12:11 may reveal a fundamental misapprehension regarding what is worth striving for, but the fact that he pursues them indicates that he yearns for them too. Similarly, the חֲסַר־לֵב may unwisely guarantee a loan (17:18), but the inclination to do so may be motivated by a desire for economic gain since, as Fox says, for Proverbs "remunerative surety" likely constitutes the form of the practice with which the book is most concerned.[14] In the end, because the one who lacks heart is, like the dolt and simple person, somewhat teachable, he seems to possess some cognitive and rational understanding of what a life of virtue entails. What he lacks is the strength of will to consistently let his practical reasoning in various life contexts be guided by wisdom's virtues.

13. Fox, *Proverbs 1–9*, 40.
14. Fox, *Proverbs 1–9*, 215; cf. Sir. 29:14.

Still another, perhaps more fully akratic figure in Proverbs—whose negative-leaning character may be more settled than that of either the כְּסִיל or the חֲסַר־לֵב—is the לֵץ. The "scoffer" seems mostly unteachable. As Proverbs 14:6 says, the לֵץ only in vain seeks wisdom. Yet, as we have seen earlier (chap. 4), Proverbs 1:22 mentions the scoffer alongside the akratic-like and corrigible כְּסִיל, as well as the פֶּתִי/פְּתָאיִם, a quite corrigible character type in Proverbs whose status as akratic- or enkratic-like is fluid (discussed below). In any case, the לֵץ character type can be "both arrogant and scornful"[15] (21:24) and prove to be an "abomination" to others (24:9), rebelliously resisting chastisement. Scoffers abuse and hate those who rebuke them (9:7–8; 15:12) and simply do not heed correction (13:1). Even harsh discipline may not prove effective in molding the scoffer's character (19:25, 29; 21:11); hence, for the sages, it may sometimes be necessary to "drive out" such a person from full participation in a community (22:10). The scoffer's obstinate refusal to conform to the norms of wise instruction, however, may ironically suggest that, more than the dolt or the person who "lacks heart," the scoffer actually comprehends instruction. He knows that he should or should not act in certain ways but nonetheless regularly, tenaciously, and arrogantly refuses to bend to authority and emend his ways. Although it is not at all explicit to what extent the scoffer's desires inhibit his choosing wise and just paths, the very rejection of instruction might imply that he considers his own intellect, yearnings, and affective inclinations more relevant for achieving happiness than the sages' teachings.

The Enkratic-Like in Proverbs

Unlike the akratic-like character types of Proverbs who likely understand—even if only incompletely or occasionally—what paths in life are good but who, because of their desires, often will choose not to follow such ways, a few other primary moral types in Proverbs seem typically to know the right way *and* to be able to choose it. However, the extent to which their desires and emotions positively incline them to follow such a way is unclear. The מֵבִין ("understanding person") and the נָבוֹן ("discerning person") in Proverbs are, for instance, obviously characterized by their intellectual virtue, and the נָבוֹן can also be positively paralleled to the "wise" (1:5; 17:28; 18:15). Unsurprisingly, these two moral types usually follow the paths of the virtuous (cf. 8:9; 10:13; 14:6, 33; 15:24; 16:21; 17:10, 24; 18:15; 19:25; 28:7). However, we hear

---

15. Fox, *Proverbs 1–9*, 42.

almost nothing specifically of their desires to follow the good and appropriate ways of wisdom.[16]

Given Proverbs' silence regarding the emotions and desires of the מֵבִין and נָבוֹן and the fact that both are frequently (but not exclusively) contrasted with akratic figures—whether the scoffer (14:6; 19:25), the one who lacks heart (10:13), or the dolt (14:33; 15:14; 17:10, 24)—the understanding person and the discerning individual in Proverbs might be regarded as something like enkratic figures in Aristotelian terms.[17] By contrast, two other figures who are also rhetorically characterized by their intellectual virtue, the אִישׁ תְּבוּנָה ("person of understanding"; 10:23; 11:12; 15:21; 17:27; 20:5) and the מַשְׂכִּיל (the one who acts "wisely"), are probably more akin to fully virtuous people. Not only does each possess a range of virtues that characterize the wise and just (e.g., diligence, right speech), in 21:12 the just person (צַדִּיק) is characterized as acting wisely (מַשְׂכִּיל) vis-à-vis a wicked person's household, while the אִישׁ תְּבוּנָה is said not only to possess wisdom (חָכְמָה) but to desire it (10:23); he is also paralleled with a person of high religious character, the one who trusts in the Lord (16:20). In any case, although the emotions and desires of the מֵבִין and נָבוֹן are perhaps not always or fully aligned with their intellectual virtue and knowledge of good ends—as the fully virtuous are (whether the wise and just, the אִישׁ תְּבוּנָה, or the מַשְׂכִּיל)—it is likely that the strength of their wills and ability to deliberate rationally will enable them to "know" and also to choose the ways of wise and just persons. It is consequently quite possible that they will develop a settled wise and just character, including the cultivation of right emotions and desires, which together with their knowledge of wisdom will most fully incline them toward virtuous living.

Another type of moral agent in Proverbs, the עָרוּם or "clever person," likewise appears enkratic-like in Aristotelian terms. Clever persons, Proverbs says, act by means of the knowledge they possess.

> The clever do all things intelligently [בְּדַעַת],
>   but the dolt displays folly. (13:16)
>
> The simple are adorned with folly,
>   but the clever are crowned with knowledge [דָּעַת]. (14:18)

---

16. However, Prov. 28:7 speaks of an understanding son who keeps instruction (תּוֹרָה) in contrast with זוֹלְלִים, who might be gluttons (cf. 23:20–21); this might suggest the understanding child here is one whose desires are well moderated.

17. In 28:2 the מֵבִין is contrasted with rulers in a rebellious epoch, while a poor מֵבִין is contrasted in 28:11 with a rich person, a moral type whose vicious character is well annotated in Proverbs (see chap. 3 above; cf. chap. 7). In 17:28 the נָבוֹן is contrasted with the inveterately foolish אֱוִיל.

> The simple believe everything,
>   but the clever consider their steps [יָבִין לַאֲשֻׁרוֹ]. (14:15)

An עָרוּם, however, can also (typically in Proverbs?) make appropriate choices about the "way" he walks by purposefully aligning his intellectual abilities with the moral-social virtues and knowledge of what is good for people that are so central to the book's "wisdom."

> It is the wisdom of the clever to understand where they go [חָכְמַת עָרוּם הָבִין דַּרְכּוֹ],
>   but the folly of fools misleads. (14:8)

As with the מֵבִין and the נָבוֹן, Proverbs says essentially nothing about the desires of clever persons, although perhaps 14:15 plays on the consonants *aleph-shin-resh* ("to go straight," "to pronounce happy") to suggest not only that clever persons reflect on their way of life or "steps" but also understand something of what constitutes their happiness (cf. 29:18). In Proverbs 12:23, moreover, the clever person "conceals knowledge" (כֹּסֶה דָּעַת), an expression that likely points to this person's modest character and disposition, which does not desire recognition upon recognition (cf. 25:27) that might be secured by placing one's knowledge on public display.[18] The עָרוּם will also conceal shame (כֹּסֶה קָלוֹן) in 12:16, a turn of phrase that perhaps suggests such a person will, when it is prudent to do so, "ignore an insult," as the NRSV renders the Hebrew. And this "self-control" itself might suggest a clever person's emotions are often well aligned with his virtuous actions or decisions. The enkratic-like nature of the clever person is also perhaps intimated by the fact that this moral type, like the understanding (מֵבִין) and discerning person (נָבוֹן), is typically contrasted with akratic-like figures, especially the dolt (12:23; 13:16; 14:8) and the simple person (14:15, 18; and the essentially identical 22:3 and 27:12, discussed further in chap. 9).

Akratic/Enkratic Simpletons

Somewhat distinct from the acratic- and enkratic-like moral agents in Proverbs is the book's פֶּתִי, or simple person. The text regularly imagines this figure as young (cf. 1:4; 7:7) and hence probably on the same moral-rhetorical plane as that other young addressee, "my child" (cf. chap. 4). These sorts of persons—who are both corrigible and constitute one of the book's primary

---

18. Cf. Fox, *Proverbs 10–31*, 557; and Schipper, *Proverbs 1–15*, 432.

audiences—sometimes appear akratic-like but other times appear more enkratic-like.

In terms of their knowledge and intellectual capacity, for instance, simple ones can be collocated with the one who lacks heart (7:7); and lacking strong discernment abilities, such a person might even "believe everything" (14:15). As regards their desires, they "love being simple" (1:22), and as Fox says, they may "have a proclivity for backsliding (1:32) and even for the deep corruption of *'iwwelet* [folly]" (14:18).[19] Consequently, one might think they are largely akratic-like. Still, the simple in Proverbs are also able to respond positively to instruction and so progress in wisdom, though they are typically—and unsurprisingly—motivated by external factors, the promise of some reward or fear of punishment (8:5, 10–11; 9:4, 6; 19:25; 21:11). The simple thus also appear like enkratic people, capable of knowing and choosing the right path even if their desires are not fully trained toward wisdom.

In the end, it seems that if the simple, as enkratic-like people, often enough choose to follow the paths of wise and just persons, they should eventually come to desire the good; as a result they may well become fully wise and just. If, however, like akratic persons, their untutored desires lead them too consistently to choose what they know to be the wrong path, their bad character may eventually settle and harden, shaping them into wicked and foolish people. Many simple ones, however, may not progress much beyond any akratic or enkratic state, sometimes following the ways of the just, sometimes those of the wicked, but never with desires and emotions fully aligned with their knowledge of either life path.

Wisdom's Discipline

If the book of Proverbs reveals a deep concern that a person's natural inclinations for various goods be rightly tutored to desire a life of wisdom and virtue (see chap. 5), one may ask more specifically how it understands this transformation to come about for the corrigible akratic- and especially enkratic-like agents in the book. We have already seen how Proverbs symbolically and rhetorically redirects its readers' fundamental yearnings for natural goods toward a desire for wisdom and virtue. Yet such literary-symbolic efforts alone could never "in real life" affect the sort of fundamental transformation in a person's motivational set of which MacIntyre speaks, where a person comes to live well and virtuously because of a desire for the good itself and not out of hope for an external reward or fear of punishment. Indeed, a

---

19. Fox, *Proverbs 1–9*, 43.

person learns the right way of wisdom and justice not merely by studying a book, not even one as concerned with virtue as Proverbs (cf. chap. 8 below). More is needed. The text of Proverbs consequently implies that the moral-social education it literally offers to shape its audience's desires and character is, and should be, supplemented by practices of chastisement, rebuke, and discipline—sometimes of a physical sort.

The key term in Proverbs' discourse of discipline is מוּסָר, which appears some thirty times in the book. It is a noun derived from the root יסר, which most fundamentally means "to punish."[20] In Proverbs the word often carries this connotation and is at points paralleled with both תּוֹכַחַת ("chastisement"; 3:11; 5:12; etc.) and גְּעָרָה ("rebuke"; 13:1). As Fox explains, although מוּסָר in Proverbs "can refer to the substance of the teaching conveyed by correction" (e.g., 4:13), it is most fundamentally a form of punishment "to correct a moral fault." It may take the form of "a verbal reprimand and warning" (12:1; 13:18), but it also may be corporal correction—a beating (e.g., to the back; 26:3) with the "rod of discipline" (13:24; 22:15; 23:13).[21] The sages believe firmly that the book's akratic-like figures—including young students whose desires are not fully trained and whose abilities to deliberate rationally on their choices are not sufficient to goad them onto virtuous ways—can be directed to right paths by stern practices of discipline. At Proverbs 22:15 (cf. 3:11 and passim), for example, we read,

> Folly is bound up in the heart of a boy,
>   but the rod of discipline drives it far away.

Proverbs also recognizes that enkratic-like moral agents—intelligent, understanding, and clever people who "know" and typically do what virtue requires but whose desires may not (yet) be completely trained—can sometimes be guided to (stay on) the paths of the wise and just by chastisement. As Proverbs 17:10 says,

> A rebuke strikes deeper into a discerning person [מֵבִין]
>   than a hundred blows into a fool.

The learning of wisdom and the training of desire in Proverbs are not, as we noted at the outset of chapter 5, merely intellectual endeavors; they are not simply a matter of cognitive assent to a teacher's oral/written instruction about how one should or should not live or what one should or should not

---

20. Fox, *Proverbs 1–9*, 34.
21. Fox, *Proverbs 1–9*, 34–35.

yearn for. Proverbs assumes that its moral-pedagogical task, which includes the training of a person's desire, is sometimes accomplished through disciplinary action upon the very bodies of the material, spiritual, social, rational, and moral subjects the book presumes its addressees to be.

Of course, raw discipline, even when coupled with the book's symbolic effort to train its readers' desires, may also prove insufficient to mold someone into a robustly wise or virtuous person. For that sort of broad and deep moral development, neither the study of a book like Proverbs alone nor one coupled with a strict מוּסָר would be sufficient. Rather, what is also needed are real-life ethical models whom an individual might emulate and to whom one might even be apprenticed. To advance fully in wisdom, to attain that quality of character the Greek tradition calls *phronēsis*—the ability to discern, desire, and do the good and right thing in any particular situation—a student of Proverbs needs genuine moral exemplars, people whose ethical lives offer models for the student's own life journey. But before turning to Proverbs' concern with Practical Wisdom and moral exemplars in chapters 8–9, we will first consider key qualities of character that the sages expect morally exemplary people will embody—namely, the social virtues.

7

The Centrality of Social Virtues for Flourishing

In his book *Dependent Rational Animals*, Alasdair MacIntyre argues that although many philosophical accounts of the nature of humans recognize our "dependence on others . . . in a general way," an "acknowledgment of anything like the full extent of that dependence and of the ways in which it stems from our vulnerability and our afflictions is generally absent."[1] For MacIntyre, however, the human being's radical dependency on others is central to ethics. This fundamental reliance on others—so obvious in infancy and old age, as well as in moments of illness or disability—establishes the priority and universality of human sociality.[2] Martha Nussbaum, who like MacIntyre elaborates the Aristotelian tradition of ethics, likewise contends that humans are fundamentally social beings. She explains how "once we recognize how thoroughly sociability permeates our lives, we will . . . acknowledge that any search for the good life must go on inside a context of relatedness" with and in light of other moral agents.[3] For the character ethics of both MacIntyre

---

1. MacIntyre, *Dependent Rational Animals*, 2–3.
2. This grounding of ethics in human biology is important for MacIntyre since in *After Virtue* he rejects Aristotle's metaphysical biology and seeks to ground human morality sociologically with a concept of "practice." With *Dependent Rational Animals*, MacIntyre revises his thinking: "Although there is indeed good reason to repudiate important elements in Aristotle's biology, I now judge that I was in error in supposing an ethics independent of biology to be possible" (x). We will return to MacIntyre's concept of a "practice" in chap. 13, as it is also helpful in understanding Proverbs' moral discourse.
3. Nussbaum, "Aristotle on Human Nature," 108.

and Nussbaum, then, virtues such as justice, which promote and safeguard human sociability, are legitimately elevated in importance.[4]

Like MacIntyre and Nussbaum, Julia Annas makes clear that for ancient virtue-oriented moral discourses social virtue is central to human flourishing. She notes, however, that for moral discourses that give significant weight to individuals' eudaemonia, some account is required as to *why* people who strive for well-being must possess other-regarding character traits. These discourses "must make some attempt to show" that social virtues like justice are ones "the agent needs in his attempt to achieve overall happiness."[5]

As we have seen, Proverbs, like other traditions of character ethics, grounds the necessity of justice and other social virtues for human happiness in its understanding of the sort of material, spiritual, rational, and fundamentally social being humans are (chap. 3). For the ancient sages, it is not simply the case that existing with others is necessary for our survival. In order to flourish, one must live well with others. Like other virtue-oriented traditions of ethics, for Proverbs a person's own thriving can never be divorced from the well-being of others in the communities in which one's life is inextricably embedded. Subsequently, although traditions of character ethics are fundamentally concerned with the virtues that individuals possess and less centrally concerned with the structures of human social organization, it is wrong to believe that a virtue-oriented discourse like Proverbs would hold little or no concern with "the relation of the individual to the common good, or to the justice of institutions."[6] Indeed, the social virtues Proverbs values—though typically cast in paternalistic and patriarchal terms—are not unrelated to the institutions within which humans typically exist and through which their life together is structured—for instance, the legal realm or marketplace.

As we saw in chapter 2, both William Brown and I demonstrate the important place Proverbs' prologue (1:2–7) holds for understanding the book's ethical program.[7] For both of us, the literary shape of the opening lines points to the book's moral center of gravity: a concern for virtues, and especially the virtues of sociability—justice, righteousness, equity—of which Proverbs 1:3 speaks. The contours of this concern, as we will next see, are developed throughout Proverbs via a wide-ranging discourse of social justice.[8]

4. Cf. Nussbaum, "Non-Relative Virtues," esp. 266.
5. Annas, *Morality of Happiness*, 291; cf. 298.
6. Annas, *Morality of Happiness*, 292.
7. Brown, *Character in Crisis*, 23–30; Sandoval, "Revisiting the Prologue."
8. In *Discourse of Wealth and Poverty*, 29–70, I discuss the "sub-discourse of social justice" in Proverbs.

Kindness to the Poor

Proverbs' concern for social virtue is perhaps most evident in the sages' insistence that wise and just individuals show kindness to the poor and ensure that the economically destitute, along with widows and orphans, not fall victim to gross injustice and oppression. Proverbs 14:31 and 21:13 provide a sample of this concern (see also 15:25; 17:5; 22:9; 23:10–11; 28:27):

> Those who oppress the poor insult their Maker,
>   but those who are kind to the needy honor him. (14:31)

> If you close your ear to the cry of the poor,
>   you will cry out and not be heard. (21:13)

The sages are also concerned that royal figures and other political elites fulfill their obligations to establish paternalistic social justice in their realms. Proverbs 16:12, 29:4, and 29:14 provide examples (see also 25:4–5; 28:16; 31:8–9):

> It is an abomination to kings to do evil,
>   for the throne is established by righteousness. (16:12)

> By justice a king gives stability to the land,
>   but one who makes heavy exactions ruins it. (29:4)

> If a king judges the poor with equity,
>   his throne will be established forever. (29:14)

It is not only the political institution of kingship that is subject to the sages' justice demands. Proverbs also insists that the rights of the poor are to be protected in legal proceedings, such as those that occurred in the gates of ancient towns and cities.

> Do not rob the poor because they are poor,
>   or crush the afflicted at the gate. (22:22)

> The righteous know the rights of the poor;
>   the wicked have no such understanding. (29:7)

Besides exhorting its readers to kind and fair conduct with respect to the poor in their individual lives, in politics, and in legal proceedings, Proverbs also places a premium on justice in the marketplace—the use of accurate weights, measures, and balances. As Proverbs 11:1 and 16:11 (cf. 20:10, 23) make clear, the sages considered these practices to be essential and believed the divine is intimately interested in the affairs of exchange:

> A false balance is an abomination to the LORD,
> but an accurate weight is his delight. (11:1)

> Honest balances and scales are the LORD's;
> all the weights in the bag are his work. (16:11)

The mention of the Lord in these lines is an apt reminder that for Proverbs the demands of sociality are not merely about people's interactions with fellow human beings. Instead, as we saw in chapter 3, human sociality includes relations with the divine. A person's obligations to do justice extend even to the nonhuman animals with whom people share an ecological niche. As Proverbs 12:10 says,

> The just know the needs of their animals,
> but the mercy of the wicked is cruel.

In light of these sorts of verses, Brown can aptly summarize Proverbs' concern with social justice as "not unlike that of the classical prophets in many instances."[9] As Brown well understands, for the ancient sages "the way in which the poor are treated provides nothing short of a litmus test for determining the community's character."[10] Like the prophet Amos (cf. chap. 10 below), Proverbs can even insist that the demands of justice outweigh cultic obligations:

> To do righteousness and justice
> is more acceptable to the LORD than sacrifice. (21:3)

Limiting Strife

Besides concerns for the poor, fairness in the marketplace, and right relations with nonhuman others, Proverbs' keen interest in sociability is evident in

---

9. Brown, *Character in Crisis*, 47. Delkurt has made similar observations in *Ethische Einsichten*. Cf. chap. 10 below.

10. Brown, *Character in Crisis*, 47. Brown is, of course, right about this. Yet he would surely agree that Proverbs' particular view of social justice, what Nussbaum would call the book's "specification" of this universal human virtue, is one that is obviously paternalistic and patriarchal. On these matters, see briefly below and cf. Nussbaum, "Non-Relative Virtues," and the conclusion below.

other ways. For example, the book sharply censures social or familial strife and those who sow it.[11] As Proverbs 15:18, 20:3, and 28:25 say,

> Those who are hot-tempered stir up strife,
> but those who are slow to anger calm contention. (15:18)[12]

> It is honorable to refrain from strife,
> but every fool is quick to quarrel [גלע]. (20:3)[13]

> The greedy person stirs up strife,
> but whoever trusts in the LORD will be enriched. (28:25)

Although these sayings are cast as indicatives, their rhetorical thrust about avoiding social strife and pursuing tranquility suggests that for the sages responsible for Proverbs, unnecessary discord and conflict, as well as those who instigate it, ought to be avoided. The "hot-tempered" person (15:18), the fool (20:3), and the greedy person (28:25) are all figures who travel the "wrong way." By contrast, those who are forbearing, patient, and pious—those who are "slow to anger" (15:18), "refrain from strife" (20:3), and "trust in the LORD" (28:25)—reveal themselves to possess virtues that belong to the ways of the wise and just. Their mode of being nourishes the sort of interaction with others that robustly social beings like humans need and desire.

For Proverbs, prosocial, other-regarding virtues—though counterintuitive to some—ultimately serve the well-being of the individual. The ability to "calm contention" or "refrain from strife" (15:18; 20:3)—and not, say, the ability to provoke and prevail over others in agonistic contests and contexts—is what is of most value to social creatures like humans. Indeed, such cooperative virtues are what ought to inspire the esteem of others (20:3). For the sages, a person "will be enriched" (28:25) not by striving for advantage over others but through confidence in the deity and via traditional moral dispositions, which Adonai sanctions. The phrase "will be enriched," however, does not reflect a form of עשר, which might suggest primarily or merely economic advantage. It translates דשן, a root which means "to grow fat," an image that in Proverbs can function as a metaphor for what Fox recognizes as a more profound sort of "prosperity and happiness."[14]

---

11. For Proverbs' widespread concern that its addressees avoid social strife, see also 10:12; 13:10; 16:28; 17:1, 19; 18:6; 22:10; 23:29; 26:21; 28:25; 29:22; 30:33.

12. On the "type" of the hot-tempered person mentioned in Prov. 15:18 and its possible relation to Egyptian wisdom, see Schipper, *Proverbs 1–15*, 504; cf. Fox, *Proverbs 10–31*, 598–99.

13. The meaning of the rare root גלע in 20:3 is not certain, but it appears to refer to "outbreaks of anger" (Fox, *Proverbs 10–31*, 664). Cf. Prov. 17:14 and 18:1.

14. Fox, *Proverbs 10–31*, 831.

By contrast, the ways of life of the negative moral agents in the above verses inhibit genuine sociality and indeed damage relations with others. The hot-tempered, the fool, and the greedy person misunderstand how their social relations can best be pursued to contribute to the genuine well-being for which they themselves yearn. Consequently, the relationships they pursue in their natural quest for happiness are not characterized by a mutuality that entails concern for others. Instead, they produce conflict, not the shalom that characterizes the full "life" spoken of in Proverbs 3:2 (cf. 3:17; 12:20). Rather than cooperating with others to achieve the good of a robust and just sociality that both they and others might enjoy, they become angry (15:18), are thoughtless (20:3), and seek their own advantage (28:25).

Generosity

Proverbs 11:24–25 comprises two further verses that subtly underscore Proverbs' concern with a social virtue, which is also a key element in the kindness people should show to the poor—namely, generosity (cf. 21:13):[15]

> One person gives generously and adds still;
>   others withhold what is due, and only suffer want.
> A generous person enjoys prosperity,
>   and one who gives water will get water. (NJPS modified)

What these verses make clear through an ironic rhetoric of "gaining by giving" is that, for the sort of social creature Proverbs reckons humans to be, to be robustly other-regarding—here via generosity—is to simultaneously seek one's own thriving as well.

The phrase "adds still" in verse 24 and especially the words "enjoys prosperity" in verse 25, however, may suggest to some that a generous person will primarily or merely find economic advantage as a kind of reward for their virtue. As we have said before, there is no need to deny the efficacy of such cause-and-effect language or logic in motivating Proverbs' young and simple students to choose the way of wisdom. What is more, the lines certainly suggest that if a person is generous to others, that person can expect others to be generous in return. But that is not the only sort of "payoff" that virtue here, and elsewhere in Proverbs, results in. A person's virtuous actions or decisions

---

15. On the structurally similar 11:26 ("The one who withholds grain will be cursed by the people, but blessing is for the head of the one who dispenses it"; adapted from the NJPS and NRSV), which censures the vice of economic hoarding and promotes the social virtue of appropriately distributing goods, see Sandoval, *Discourse of Wealth and Poverty*, 171–73.

do not merely or reliably result in an increase of material goods (cf. chap. 3). Instead, what it "adds" is more elementary to thriving human existence. Living virtuously (in this case, by assisting others in need) not only enables a person to live more *humanely*; it is a way to live more authentically *humanly*—that is, in a fashion that is natural for the sort of social being humans are imagined to be. However, without the guidance of wisdom most of us will incline toward egoism, perhaps attaining for ourselves an abundance of external or secondary goods. But the living of such a self-centered mode of existence means the chances of genuine happiness for a social being like the human quickly evaporate. Indeed, behind the words "enjoys prosperity" in verse 25 is again not a form of עשׁר, "to grow rich," but דשׁן, "to grow fat"—a word we said in regard to Proverbs 28:25 points not only to real material goods but can function as a metaphor for a full or profound sort of thriving.[16]

Friendship and Kinship

The centrality of sociability for Proverbs is also, perhaps even more, evident in sayings that highlight the value of friendship and kinship. These verses implicitly or explicitly ask the one who would be wise and righteous to cultivate social virtue in the form of social solidarity and mutual assistance.

> A friend loves at all times,
>   and kinsfolk are born to share adversity. (17:17)

> Some friends play at friendship
>   but a true friend sticks closer than one's nearest kin. (18:24)

> Do not forsake your friend or the friend of your parent. (27:10a)

Maintaining robust and positive social connections is so important for Proverbs that one should even at times overlook another's faults:

> One who forgives an affront fosters friendship,
>   but one who dwells on disputes will alienate a friend. (17:9)

Preserving strong social bonds in various ways, including when it is not to one's immediate advantage to do so, is important for Proverbs not only because communal ties are vital for the sort of social being the book presumes humans to be. It is important also because the sages understand the difficulty

---

16. Fox, *Proverbs 10–31*, 831 and cf. 543.

of repairing the bonds of fundamental relations once they have been destroyed. As Proverbs 18:19 says,

> Kin [אָח] offended is stronger than a city;[17]
> such quarreling is like the bars of a castle.

Other sayings in Proverbs that do not obviously or immediately promote friendship or fraternalism but speak of how wealth and power might undermine foundational social ties also indirectly value the virtues of sociability.

> The poor are disliked even by their neighbors,
> but the rich [עָשִׁיר] have many friends. (14:20)

> Wealth brings many friends,
> but the poor are left friendless. (19:4)

> Many seek the favor of the generous [נָדִיב],
> and everyone is a friend to a giver of gifts. (19:6)

> If the poor are hated even by their kin,
> how much more are they shunned by their friends![18] (19:7)

These lines are not prescriptive or normative moral formulas but ironic descriptions of a particular kind of social reality.[19] Although they indicate that wealth can attract companions to those who possess it, a person should not strive after wealth and then use those riches to "buy friends." In fact, the descriptions of rich people and their acquaintances in the first three of these verses imply that the social relations of the עָשִׁיר are not based on others' genuine affection for them, a sense of mutuality or solidarity, or the excellence of the rich person's character. Rather, they rely on the much more ephemeral and weak bonds that the rich person's wealth might create—for example, the hope that riches might be shared or that the rich person's social power might be deployed on one's behalf.[20]

---

17. The NRSV renders אָח as "an ally"; the NJPS, "a brother."
18. The final stich of 19:7, which the NRSV renders as "when they call after them, they are not there," is not included here. The words are exceedingly problematic and difficult to translate. Fox (*Proverbs 10–31*, 651) calls them "meaningless" and suspects they may be "the mangled fragment of a lost couplet."
19. Here and in the following discussion, cf. Sandoval, *Discourse of Wealth and Poverty*, 155–204, esp. 188–201.
20. Cf. the discussion of the ruler and stingy person of Prov. 23:1–8 in chap. 5 above.

In these lines, however, only 14:20b explicitly mentions the "rich" (עָשִׁיר). Yet "wealth" in 19:4a functions as a metonym for a rich person whose significant possessions increase the number of apparently positive social ties that such a person, like the עָשִׁיר of 14:20b, enjoys. The נָדִיב of 19:6a may be a person of high social status or a generous person or both, as Fox notes.[21] But the fact that the line, like 14:20 and 19:4, speaks of friends that accrue to this "man of gifts" (אִישׁ מַתָּן) seems to indicate his status as a kind of "rich" person who uses what Proverbs knows to be the efficacy of gifts or bribes for his own benefit (cf. 17:8; 18:16; 21:14). Yet whatever the precise case may be with 19:6, the verse surely suggests that if a person has no wealth or his wealth vanishes, close acquaintances will grow scarce too, proving as hostile and absent as the poor person's kin and friends in 14:20a, 19:4b, and 19:7.

In real life (including the social contexts the sages knew) the poor are all too regularly despised and left friendless, as the above lines suggest. Proverbs' other teaching on the value of reliable acquaintances, however, and the book's clear and broad concern with promoting sociability suggest that among wise and just persons it should not be so. The destitute ought not to be left in their need without intimate companions who might provide succor. Proverbs 14:20, 19:4, and 19:6–7 not only suggest that the social ties wealth creates are weak; they also imply that riches can actually undermine what are typically firmer and more reliable social bonds based on genuine friendship and kinship. In the case of 14:20, for example, the very next line offers a critical evaluation of the state of affairs just described. If it is true that the poor are disliked by their neighbors, Proverbs 14:21 insists that

> those who despise their neighbors are sinners,
> but happy are those who are kind to the poor.

Although the rich may truly have many friends, their faulty character means that the social relations they secure—their friendships—are not robust and contribute little to their own or others' well-being. Their way of life with others is not a path the book's audience should follow.

Other Social Virtues

The juxtaposition of Proverbs 14:20 and 14:21 illustrates a broader logic at work throughout the literary work of Proverbs. It is a logic that assimilates into the text's larger patterns of moral reasoning those proverbs whose sense

---

21. Fox, *Proverbs 10–31*, 650.

appears to contradict central aspects of the book's moral vision—if read in isolation from their broader literary-moral context or divorced from the larger complex "utterance" (cf. introduction) that constitutes the whole of Proverbs. This assimilation of disparate sayings into Proverbs' moral vision, moreover, is *not* dependent on the juxtaposition of lines (such as 14:20 and 21) or even on "proverb clustering."[22] We see it throughout and between different sections of Proverbs too. Consider, for example, 10:15 and 18:11, two lines also concerned with promoting social virtue but separated by seven chapters of text.

> The wealth of the rich is their fortress;
> the poverty of the poor is their ruin. (10:15)

> The wealth of the rich is their strong city;
> in their imagination it is like a high wall. (18:11)

The identical initial words of the two verses (הוֹן עָשִׁיר קִרְיַת עֻזּוֹ) is what initially invites, even demands, that readers bring the proverbs into conversation with one another to compare and contrast their senses.[23] Proverbs 10:15 belongs to a subcollection of sayings marked by its persistent use of antithetical parallelism. When read in isolation, the verse offers a straightforward observation about the social advantages that accrue to those who possess wealth—in this case, the rich—and the social disadvantage that poverty brings. Wealth provides a degree of protection from the vagaries of social life. The rich can subsequently regard it as their "fortress." The poor who lack material wealth do not enjoy such security. Their poverty is not merely a material shortfall, however; it translates more fundamentally into a social vulnerability that appears inevitably to result in their "ruin"—a grave state of non-well-being.

Some readers of Proverbs might think 10:15 reflects the book's upper-class ideology—that is, the notion not only that the sages observed the realities of social and economic inequity but that what they say about social arrangements reflects the way they believed the world actually does and should operate, in their own favor.[24] However, by attending to the central concerns and virtues

---

22. For proverb clustering, or the way in which groups of Proverbs are thought to be (usually intentionally) placed close to one another based on shared themes, key words, sounds, wordplays, and so forth, cf. Van Leeuwen, *Context and Meaning*; and Heim, *Like Grapes of Gold Set in Silver*.

23. On the phenomenon of repeated proverbs in Proverbs, see Snell, *Twice-Told Proverbs*; and Heim, *Poetic Imagination in Proverbs*.

24. See, e.g., the subtle ideological analyses of Bergant in *Israel's Wisdom Literature*, 78–107. Cf. Pleins, *Social Visions of the Hebrew Bible*, 457, cf. 452–83; Pleins, "Poverty and the Social World of the Wise," 69; and Pleins, "Poor, Poverty."

that the entire book promotes—such as social justice, concern for the poor, and a right understanding of the value and desirability of wealth—a better conclusion emerges. Although Proverbs 10:15 describes well what is often a social reality (rich people trust in the security their wealth provides), *that* social reality does not correspond to the moral vision the book promotes.[25]

As it turns out, Proverbs 18:11 responds quite directly to the observation of social reality in 10:15 regarding how the world often seems to work in favor of those who possess abundant wealth. In contrast to 10:15, however, Proverbs 18:11 reveals that the rich tend to misunderstand the worth of their wealth. They believe it provides a full and secure protection, which the second half of 18:11 reveals to be an illusion. The wealth of the rich is a "high wall" indeed—but only in their imaginations.[26] For Proverbs, although some enjoyment of material goods is important for a person's well-being, the exercise of (social) virtue, such as showing generosity with one's material wealth, is the true key to achieving the authentic flourishing humans naturally seek. For Proverbs, it is quite possible for a person who possesses much wealth to follow the way of the wise and just; but a rich person, whom the sages regard as a type of moral agent with a settled negative character (chap. 3), cannot. This is so even if to some—like the rich themselves—the claim that wisdom, and not an exterior good like wealth, is key to happiness might seem naïvely foolish.

This implicit criticism in 18:11 and 10:15 of the rich for their misplaced trust and overvaluing of wealth is extended when these verses are placed in dialogue with still other lines in Proverbs. Proverbs 18:10, for example, deploys images from the domain of military life—fortresses and protections—just as 18:11 does. By doing so, verse 10 expands and deepens the critical point of verse 11, a fact easy to see when the lines are juxtaposed.

> The name of the LORD is a strong tower;
> the righteous run into it and are safe. (18:10)

> The wealth of the rich is their strong city;
> in their imagination it is like a high wall. (18:11)

---

25. Proverbs 13:8—"Wealth is a ransom for a person's life, but the poor get no threats," as the NRSV renders it—is sometimes thought to concede the social value of wealth but also, subtly and perhaps with ironic humor, to critique such arrangements. However, the NRSV's translation of the second stich is probably not correct. The words וְרָשׁ לֹא־שָׁמַע גְּעָרָה more likely mean "but a poor person does not heed a rebuke," a turn of phrase that does not form a neat parallel with the line's first stich. These words were likely "mistakenly copied from the end of 13b," as Fox suggests (*Proverbs 10–31*, 564).

26. As Fox (*Proverbs 10–31*, 642) explains, "The exact meaning of *maśkît*" in the word *bemaśkîtô* "is not certain." However, here it is best regarded as something like "'imaginings.' The rich man mentally pictures his wealth as a fortress city with a high wall."

In Proverbs 18:10, in contrast to 10:15 and 18:11, it is not wealth that is imagined as providing protection, but the name of the Lord. It is a particular devotion to, and confidence in, Adonai (cf. 3:5) that provides true security; this is surely not unrelated to the book's central religious virtue, "fear of the Lord." This divine protection, based on trust in the deity, is not the sort of security after which the rich strive. But it is what the righteous earnestly and actively seek. They "run into it and are safe."

Together Proverbs 10:15, 18:10, and 18:11 thus contrast the rich with the righteous. Each character type seeks security—a natural inclination of humans to self-preservation and happiness. But the rich are cast in a decidedly negative light. They seek security and happiness primarily in wealth and not in strong social bonds of faithful companionship—whether with humans or the divine.

The deity in whom the just in Proverbs trust, however, is not simply a being like other humans with whom the book's audience ought rightly to interact. The divine is also the source and foundation of human social bonds. As Proverbs 22:2 says,

> The rich and the poor meet,[27]
> the LORD is the maker of them all. (NRSV modified)

The saying offers no simple or crass ideological justification for the existence of distinct economic and social class positions in ancient Israel; it does not imply that such distinctions are part of the divine's ordering of, or "natural" design for, creation. Instead, it augments Proverbs' concern for the socially and economically marginalized by insisting that social-economic distinctions ought not to overdetermine one's status in a wise and just community. Because typically those with wealth enjoy more social power and prestige than people who lack material abundance, the verse reveals an impulse toward social equality—at least for those (adult males) who are full members of the community the ancient sages had in mind. Rich and poor are creatures of the same deity; they share a fundamental equality and stand in relations of obligation to one another.

Proverbs 22:2, however, functions not merely as a theological dictum about human equality. It also more subtly, but forcefully, warns against the exploitation of social and economic differences by those with significant social and economic power. As Roland Murphy says, "the 'meeting'" of the rich and poor in the verse "is not casual."[28] Yong Hyun Cho likewise argues that the

---

27. The Hebrew root פגש here likely has to do with a physical encounter; hence the rendering "meet" instead of the NRSV's "have this in common."
28. R. Murphy, *Proverbs*, 165, cf. 261.

imagined encounter of the rich and poor in an ancient, agriculturally based society was likely not often by chance or always innocent.[29] Instead, such a meeting may often have been initiated by one or the other party. On the one hand, a rich person may seek out an encounter because of a desire to secure some economic or social advantage over the destitute person—for example, to (re)establish their status as patron of the poor.[30] (Recall the perhaps analogous intentions of the ruler and stingy person that the addressee is warned about in Prov. 23:1–8; cf. chap. 5). Or more sinisterly, the rich person may seek a meeting with a poor person specifically to extract—on whatever grounds— wealth from that person.[31] On the other hand, a poor person may seek out a rich person to petition for protection or support, or to renegotiate the status of an already existing economic relationship, or perhaps even publicly to complain or plead for mercy.[32] As the very close parallelism of Proverbs 29:13 to 22:2 makes clear, the rich person can also be an oppressor of the poor.

> The poor and the oppressor meet:[33]
> the Lord gives light to the eyes of both. (29:13 NRSV modified)

What is more, it sometimes happens that

> the poor use entreaties,
> but the rich answer roughly. (18:23)

Although these last lines may speak of possible, even typical, social interactions between economically and socially powerful persons and the poor, they are again not ultimately observations justifying that status quo or implying the sages' resignation to the way the world so often works. Rather, Proverbs 22:22 and 29:13 together censure certain injustices or acts of social viciousness that might arise in the encounters of those occupying fundamentally different socioeconomic positions. Any tendency for one person to take advantage of another because of these differences—to "lord it over" another, act as oppressor, or respond harshly to a fellow's petition—evokes the rebuke of the theological claim that the divine is creator and sustainer of all.

29. Cho, "Wisdom's Wealthy."
30. On patronage in ancient Israel, see Houston, *Contending for Justice*, esp. 44–48.
31. For considerations of economic systems and relations in ancient Israel and Judah, see, e.g., Boer, *Sacred Economy*; and Houston, *Contending for Justice*.
32. Cho, "Wisdom's Wealthy"; cf. Fox, *Proverbs 10–31*, 694–95. On public complaints in the Psalms, see Sheppard, "'Enemies' and the Politics of Prayer."
33. As in 22:2, the NRSV renders the Hebrew root פגש not as "meet" but as "have this in common."

Sociability Conclusions

At the very outset of the book Proverbs announces the priority of social virtue for the text's moral vision (1:3), and its preeminence becomes evident throughout the rest of the book. It is clear that an emphasis on sociability, like that which MacIntyre, Nussbaum, and Annas highlight in the Aristotelian tradition of character ethics, is amply evident in Proverbs too. For example, Proverbs' conceptions of friendship, though not theorized to the same extent as in other virtue-ethics discourses, importantly share significant affinities with them. For instance, as Frederic Schroeder explains, Aristotle reckoned friendships in three ways: (1) "character friendship or friendship that is grounded in virtue"; (2) "friendship grounded in pleasure"; and (3) "friendship grounded in utility."[34] The second and third forms of friendship that Aristotle identifies are comparable to the sorts of false friendship Proverbs associates with the rich and those who "play at friendship" (18:24). They are not grounded in affection, commitments to mutuality, or trust. By contrast, Aristotle's "character friendship" entails an altruistic love for another and resonates with the "true," other-regarding friendship (and kin relations) Proverbs promotes as belonging to the way of wisdom (e.g., 14:21; 17:17; 18:24; 27:10).[35]

However, just as we have seen in regard to Proverbs' discourse of desire and its representation of female figures, the book's moral vision of justice or social virtue is contingent and parochial. It is not merely paternalistic; it is also clearly patriarchal and androcentric in scope. These characteristics of Proverbs' discourse of justice are clear first from the fact that what stands at the heart of the book's justice instruction is the expectation that full and able-bodied members of the community should, like a good father providing for his household, care for and defend the poor, as well as others whose status in the community is secondary (e.g., widows, orphans, and so forth; cf. 15:25; 23:10). In doing so these community members demonstrate their virtue, revealing themselves to be wise and just individuals or at least people who sometimes follow the ways of life of the virtuous. Ironically, however, it is likely that the poor and needy, for whom Proverbs' male addressees ought to care (like a father), were themselves male heads of households who also had obligations to care for others. Yet any hint of a robust egalitarianism, like that prized by many moderns formed by liberal ideals of equality and freedom, is not strong in Proverbs. Though the poor may be heads of their

---

34. Schroeder, "Friendship in Aristotle," 37.
35. Schroeder, "Friendship in Aristotle," 43. Cf. Whiting, "Nicomachean Account of Philia." For an account of Aristotle's view of friendship in relation to the book of Job, see Vesely, *Friendship and Virtue Ethics in the Book of Job*, esp. 50–73.

own "father's house" (בֵּית אָב) and so potentially full members of the ancient polity, they largely remain those who should be paternalistically cared for by other heads of households.

The paternalistic, androcentric, and patriarchal character of the book's vision of social virtue is evident in other ways too. A cluster of sayings that esteem domestic tranquility within households evidences this limited moral-social vision. Although the text considers a good wife to be a divine gift that might contribute to a man's happiness (18:22; 19:14), the sages make clear that some wives might be irksome and quarrelsome, provoking the sort of strife the writers of Proverbs regard as detrimental to the well-being of their male addressees. As Proverbs 21:9 says (cf. 19:13; 21:19; 25:24; 27:15),

> It is better to live in a corner of the housetop
> than in a house shared with a contentious wife.

The sages, of course, make no mention of the household strife and its detrimental effects that husbands might provoke. The nature and scope of "proper" domestic relations in Proverbs is plainly constructed from an exclusively male point of view.

Given these limitations to Proverbs' understanding of social virtue, if the book is to be engaged as a source for normative ethical reflection today, such aspects of the text's virtue-oriented ethics—like its views of sex, gender, and marriage (cf. chap. 5)—ought to be identified and critically assessed. How readers of Proverbs today might be warranted in constructively engaging and resisting the book's contingent and parochial moral claims is a question we will return to in the conclusion. It is, moreover, a matter that is intimately related to the sort of practical moral reasoning Proverbs imagines genuinely wise and just moral agents will be able to exercise. It is thus to a consideration of the book's conception of Practical Wisdom that we next turn.

8

Practical Wisdom in Proverbs

At the outset of chapter 7, we noted Alasdair MacIntyre's argument that the human experience of radical dependency on others establishes the priority and universality of human sociality. In the same work, *Dependent Rational Animals*, MacIntyre further explains that it is only via relationships with other people—moral agents such as parents, teachers, and friends who serve as moral exemplars—that one is able to learn the virtues, the full and integrated exercise of which constitutes Practical Wisdom. The classical tradition called this *phronēsis*: the rational ability to "size up" any particular situation and to desire and do the good and appropriate thing in that moment.[1] For MacIntyre, learning Practical Wisdom or becoming what he calls "independent practical reasoners" comes only through people's relationships and in everyday life. Daily life is where the excellencies of other moral agents help define for us a good and right way of life that is necessary for attaining eudaemonia. He writes, "Just as the virtues are exercised in the whole range of our activities, so they are learned in the same range of activities, in those contexts of practice in which we learn from others how to discharge our roles and functions first as members of a family and household" and then in other contexts.[2] Martha Nussbaum likewise contends that an emphasis on Practical Wisdom is a key feature of a character ethic.[3] As she explains, for Aristotle any good human life must in a

---

1. MacIntyre, *Dependent Rational Animals*. See chapter 7, note 2 above.
2. MacIntyre, *Dependent Rational Animals*, 88–89.
3. Nussbaum, "Non-Relative Virtues," esp. 266.

real sense be one that we each authentically and fully engage for ourselves. It must thus include an element of choice by which a moral agent discerns and chooses this good form of life over some other way of life; hence, it entails an exercise of Practical Wisdom.[4] Julia Annas similarly underscores the centrality of Practical Wisdom in traditions of virtue ethics emerging from the classical tradition. As she says, *phronēsis* "underlies and unifies all the virtues in the agent's practical thinking."[5]

The emphasis MacIntyre, Nussbaum, and Annas—all leading interpreters of the Aristotelian tradition of ethics—place on Practical Wisdom evidences the key place this virtue holds in traditions of character ethics. If it can be demonstrated that Proverbs likewise prioritizes Practical Wisdom, we can gain still more clarity about the book's moral shape and further certainty regarding its status as a virtue-oriented moral discourse. In this chapter, I make my case for the existence of Practical Wisdom in Proverbs, and in the following chapter I discuss how Proverbs depicts the limitations of Practical Wisdom—the frontiers of its efficacy and the expectation for readers to search outside the text for moral exemplars of Practical Wisdom.

Difficulties with Identifying Practical Wisdom in Proverbs

If the virtues of sociability are key for Proverbs (cf. chap. 7), they are not the only virtues the book values. As noted in chapter 2, Proverbs' prologue also highlights the book's interest in intellectual (1:2) and practical virtues (1:4), which are specified as knowledge or understanding, on the one hand, and shrewdness or cunning, on the other. The book further hints that the wise person will be able to rightly order and integrate the full range of moral-social, intellectual, and practical virtues and embody them in the vagaries of social life. However, the centrality for Proverbs of this Practical Wisdom, what again the Greek moral tradition calls *phronēsis* and often translated as "prudence," is more difficult to demonstrate than is the importance of virtues promoting sociability.

There are several related reasons why identifying the presence and importance of a robust conception of Practical Wisdom in Proverbs is difficult. First, there is no exact congruence between terms and concepts in the classical tradition of virtue ethics and the moral vocabulary of (Hebrew) Proverbs. The intellectual, social, and practical virtues to which Proverbs' prologue points

---

4. Nussbaum, "Aristotle on Human Nature," 119. Cf. Nussbaum, *Fragility of Goodness*, 290–316.
5. Annas, *Morality of Happiness*, 79.

do not correspond precisely to the distinctions in the Aristotelian tradition between terms like *phronēsis, technē, sophia*, and more.

For example, *sophia* (wisdom) is for Aristotle theoretical knowledge.[6] It is a combination of *nous* (intuitive understanding of first principles) and *epistēmē* (scientific or demonstrable knowledge). In its highest form, *sophia* is achieved through contemplation of the divine.[7] On the other hand, *technē*, as Stephen Halliwell explains, was "the standard Greek word both for a practical skill and for the systematic knowledge or experience which underlies it."[8] Consequently, Aristotle could use the concept as an analogy for understanding the life of virtue. As we will see in chapter 13, in the Bible, terms derived from the root חכם sometimes closely approximate the meanings of *technē*.

In contrast to *sophia* and *technē*, *phronēsis* is a "reasoned and true state of capacity to act with regard to human goods."[9] *Phronēsis* provides the capacity to develop and rightly deploy those virtues required for eudaemonia. As C. D. C. Reeve writes, for Aristotle, "the practically wise man possesses a complex array of well-entrenched and stable capacities to be richly aware and effectively responsive to all the good and bad things salient in any situation, and all the considerations bearing on them."[10] In more straightforward terms, in regard to any action or decision, *phronēsis* enables people "to determine the right amount, the right means, the right goal, the right time, the right situation, the right person," and so forth. For "what is suitable" is always "relative to the person, the circumstances, and the object."[11] As John Casey further suggests, "[*Phronēsis*] is the ability to 'see' what is at stake where the application of rules may not be at all obvious, and to know how to respond." Subsequently, one can rightly describe the person of "practical wisdom as having moral imagination."[12]

Besides the fact that the moral terminology of Proverbs corresponds only imprecisely to conceptions in the classical tradition of virtue ethics, it is also difficult to identify and trace a robust conception of Practical Wisdom in Proverbs because no single word in the Hebrew of Proverbs clearly connotes "Practical Wisdom" the way *phronēsis* does in Greek moral literature. The Hebrew term most likely to indicate something like Practical Wisdom is *chokmah* (חָכְמָה). But the situation is complicated by the fact that "wisdom" (חָכְמָה) in

6. *NE* 1141a 18–19.
7. Cf. Reeve, "Aristotle on the Virtues of Thought," esp. 199–202.
8. Halliwell, *Aristotle's Poetics*, 44.
9. *NE* 1140b 20–25.
10. Reeve, "Aristotle on the Virtues of Thought," 213. Cf. MacIntyre, *After Virtue*, 154–56.
11. Grier, *Virtue of Non-Violence*, 69; cf. *NE* 1122a 25–26.
12. Casey, *Pagan Virtue*, 147.

Proverbs is regularly associated with a cluster of other lexemes such as "knowledge" (דַּעַת) and "insight" or "understanding" (תְּבוּנָה, בִּינָה). This collocation of terms, all of which can function, as Fox writes, as "near-synonyms," naturally impacts how one might finally parse Proverbs' conception(s) of wisdom.[13] Each lexeme can individually or in combination connote straightforward intellectual virtue(s), a kind of mental acuity or power of "intelligence" that "exists as knowledge" and rationality.[14] But wisdom (חָכְמָה) in Proverbs is also sometimes obviously personified in cosmic and mythic terms (e.g., Woman Wisdom in Prov. 8). Consequently, if *chokmah* in Proverbs is not always simply to be equated with intellectual virtue or with cosmic wisdom, neither can it be said to serve consistently as an unambiguous sign for a notion of Practical Wisdom understood as something like *phronēsis*. Careful consideration of the distinct usages of the term in Proverbs is required.

There is another important, and related, consideration to keep in mind when striving to discern a notion of Practical Wisdom in Proverbs: namely, the necessity of distinguishing the book's practical *virtues*, such as cunning (עָרְמָה), shrewdness (מְזִמָּה), and resourcefulness (תַּחְבֻּלוֹת)—all mentioned in the prologue at 1:4–5—from a broader concept of Practical *Wisdom*. Like the intellectual virtues to which they are close kin, the practical virtues of Proverbs will inform, or form a necessary piece of, Practical Wisdom. But without the guidance of a genuine Practical Wisdom or *phronēsis*, the practical virtues will not necessarily aid anyone in living well or choosing the good in any particular moment or context. In fact, without the guidance of Practical Wisdom, the practical virtues can easily be deployed to vicious ends. As many people know from personal experiences, unsavory characters often prove more intelligent, shrewder, and more resourceful in achieving their ignoble ends than noble people can be in striving for their good goals. As MacIntyre says, "The exercise of practical intelligence [Practical Wisdom] requires the presence of the virtues of character; otherwise it degenerates into or remains from the outset merely a certain cunning capacity for linking means to any end rather than to those ends which are genuine goods." In Proverbs, as we said in chapter 6, the coreferentiality of the terms "wise" and "just" is not a mere linguistic phenomenon. It points to a key aspect of the relationship of moral and intellectual virtue in the book too. A "genuine practical intelligence [Practical Wisdom] . . . *requires* knowledge of the good, indeed itself *requires*

---

13. Fox, "What the Book of Proverbs Is About," 155. Fox includes in his tally of near-synonymous wisdom terms שֵׂכֶל and לֵב as well.

14. Fox, *Time to Tear Down*, 72–73. Although Fox is describing Qohelet's "wisdom" in Ecclesiastes, his words also describe well intellectual virtue in Proverbs.

goodness of a kind in its possessor."[15] Although in Proverbs the practical virtues are typically presented positively, regarded as (already) rightly integrated into a cluster of other virtues and directed toward a good end, it is not always the case that they are so positively marked. As Proverbs 12:5 says,

> The thoughts of the righteous are just;
>   the resourcefulness [תַּחְבֻּלוֹת] of the wicked is treacherous. (NRSV modified)

Finally, what is also symptomatic of and contributes to the confusion about how Proverbs constructs a concept of Practical Wisdom and distinguishes it from discrete practical virtues is the fact that an English translation of Proverbs like the NRSV sometimes translates practical virtues like מְזִמָּה as "discretion" (e.g., 8:12) and עָרְמָה as "shrewdness" (e.g., 1:4).[16] But elsewhere it uses "prudence"—that common English rendering of *phronēsis*—to translate both מְזִמָּה (1:4; 2:11; 3:21; 5:2) and עָרְמָה (8:5, 12; verbal form in 15:5; 19:25). Adding still further to the terminological and conceptual muddle is that for much modern moral discourse, as Annas explains, practical reasoning "actually takes two distinct forms, namely *prudential* where only my own interests are concerned, and moral, when I, separately, bring the interests of others into my reasoning."[17] For ancient virtue ethics, however, practical reasoning is not so bifurcated. As we noted in chapter 1, although premodern virtue traditions are formally concerned with the happiness of individuals, they are also regularly quite fully other-regarding in content; and as we have already seen in the discussion of social virtue in Proverbs, the same holds true for the ancient scribes who composed the book. In any case, the disparate renderings of Proverbs' moral terminology in modern Bible translations not only betrays the difficulty of translating ancient moral concepts into contemporary languages; it also likely constitutes further evidence for MacIntyre's claim, discussed in chapter 1, that the modern world inherited only fragments—bits and pieces—of premodern moral discourse and that this state of affairs has hampered contemporary efforts to speak (and interpret certain ancient texts, perhaps) in a morally coherent fashion.

Despite all these difficulties and ambiguities, a broader concept or category of wisdom as a kind of *phronēsis* can be discerned in Proverbs, in both the poems of chapters 1–9 and the short sayings in Proverbs 10–29. Wisdom in the book regularly appears to be more than either simple intellectual and

---

15. MacIntyre, *After Virtue*, 154, 155, citing *NE* 1144a 37 (emphasis added).
16. Cf. Prov. 12:2 and 14:17 for the evil and foolish אִישׁ מְזִמּוֹת and 24:8 for the בַּעַל־מְזִמּוֹת.
17. Annas, *Morality of Happiness*, 323 (emphasis added).

practical virtue or moral-social virtue. Wise and righteous persons appear as those who possess both knowledge, rationality, and intellectual acuity—along with shrewdness and resourcefulness—*and* a range of social-moral virtues. This constellation of dispositions enables a kind of ethical reasoning that results in the ability to know, desire, and choose a good way forward in the myriad of different contexts that demand human moral decision or action.

Identifying Practical (Woman) Wisdom in Proverbs 1–9

As we have already suggested, Proverbs' prologue closely aligns intellectual, practical, and moral-social virtues, while also signaling the priority the sages place on the last of these (chap. 2). This is a first indication that for Proverbs a person's intellectual-practical abilities ought to be exercised in service of the moral-social virtues—justice, righteousness, equity (cf. 1:3)—that are indispensable in establishing the good life for the sort of being Proverbs believes humans to be. Although Proverbs distinguishes intellectual, practical, and moral-social virtues, an integrated exercise of them all constitutes the book's full conception of wisdom, wisdom as Practical Wisdom. A truly wise and just person—a person of genuine Practical Wisdom—will possess, integrate, and appropriately exercise all of Proverbs' virtues.

Although wisdom in Proverbs is famously personified as a woman (1:20–31; 8:1–36), Woman Wisdom herself is not obviously described in such a way that she is easily or precisely identified as a personification of *Practical Wisdom* (in the sense of *phronēsis*). Nonetheless, her words in Proverbs 8:12–14 do construct a somewhat coherent, even if poetic, conception of Practical Wisdom. The clustering in this passage of terms associated with the intellect—wisdom, understanding, knowledge (חָכְמָה, דַּעַת, בִּינָה)—in close juxtaposition with a group of terms connoting practical virtues—cunning, discernment, resourcefulness (תּוּשִׁיָּה, מְזִמּוֹת, עָרְמָה)—gestures toward Proverbs' conception of Practical Wisdom.

> I, Wisdom [חָכְמָה], dwell with cunning [עָרְמָה],
>   I attain discerning knowledge [דַּעַת מְזִמּוֹת].
> The fear of the LORD is hatred of evil.
> Pride and arrogance and the way of evil
>   and perverted speech I hate.
> I have counsel [עֵצָה] and resourcefulness [תּוּשִׁיָּה];
>   I am Understanding [בִּינָה], I have strength.[18] (8:12–14)

18. The translation is my own but at points follows the NRSV and Fox, *Proverbs 1–9*, 263.

Importantly, Wisdom in Proverbs 8:12–14 is not only closely associated with those intellectual and practical virtues that constitute key components of Practical Wisdom; her desires and emotions are, like those of other virtuous agents in the book, also rightly formed (chap. 5)—a fact revealed by her longing to avoid the vices of pride, arrogance, and duplicitous speech. Indeed, she "hates" all that belongs to "the way of evil" (v. 13). For Wisdom, to hate the wrong way means, positively, to possess Proverbs' central moral-religious virtue—"fear of the LORD" (v. 13), which can here be regarded as a synecdoche for all of the book's moral-social virtues. What is more, the "counsel" (עֵצָה) Wisdom possesses in verse 14 (cf. 1:25, 30) is the highly prized discernment and advice that a wise person throughout Proverbs both offers and heeds (12:15; 19:20; 20:5, 18; cf. 27:9). Even Adonai possesses such counsel, which can override the best laid human plans (19:21; 21:30). Woman Wisdom, finally, is also characterized in 8:12–14 as one who possesses both the resourcefulness and the "strength" (v. 14) or capacity necessary to embody or live out a life of virtue. She not only holds intellectual, practical, and moral-religious virtue, she also is willing and able to exercise these. She is, in other words, the personification of that "understanding" (v. 14) that wise and just people typically deploy to good ends in different contexts; and this is well called Practical Wisdom.

The following two verses of Proverbs 8 (vv. 15–16) name figures who execute their duties "by Wisdom," and in doing so they further reveal the contours of the book's conception of Practical Wisdom. In these lines Woman Wisdom explains:

> By me kings reign,
>   and rulers decree what is just [יְחֹקְקוּ צֶדֶק];
> by me princes rule,
>   so too nobles, all who judge justly [שֹׁפְטֵי צֶדֶק]. (8:15–16)[19]

By introducing the rhetoric of justice (צֶדֶק), this passage recalls the priority Proverbs places on social virtue. By associating this rhetoric with kings, princes, and nobles, it invokes a larger biblical, ancient West Asian, and ancient Egyptian ideology of kingship that insisted royal figures ruled legitimately only to the extent that they ensured (paternalistic) social justice in their realm (cf. chap. 7). For Proverbs, as we said in chapter 3, the attainment of eudaemonia for the sort of beings humans are is only possible within just social-political and institutional arrangements where individuals can choose to exercise virtues

---

19. The translation of v. 16 is mine.

in pursuit of those goods necessary for human flourishing—whether material well-being, social recognition, sexual satisfaction, or something else.

The point of Proverbs 8:15–16, as Fox recognizes, is not that kings, princes, rulers, and judges somehow *always* rule wisely or inevitably "mandate righteous laws."[20] Nor does the text necessarily suggest that political elites are granted their positions by heavenly Wisdom, like some sort of cosmic and divine appointment. Though it is possible—perhaps even likely—that the sort of rhetoric 8:15–16 articulates might have been used by some as ideological justification for a ruling class, it most fundamentally points to the crucial importance of Practical Wisdom for those who govern. The actual pursuits or duties of these named figures—the legitimate reign of kings, the appropriate decreeing of rulers, and the judging of princes and nobles—would have been characterized by a plethora of unforeseeable situations. No single law, rule, principle, or proverb—all forms of ethical discourse that typically hold important deposits of moral wisdom—would have provided sufficient practical moral guidance for every circumstance that required judgment and action. Rather, to negotiate the demands of their offices well and virtuously—that is, to ensure justice—these political elites would require not only good laws to consult; they would also need fine intentions and appropriate values. They would have to possess intellectual acumen and practical institutional abilities, as well as a clear conception of the good end of justice they were charged to ensure. They would need, in other words, a wisdom that Proverbs 8, via a literary strategy of personification, reveals to be a full and robust sort of Practical Wisdom. For traditions of virtue ethics, the practically wise person can direct due attention to the stable and universal components of morality that are often settled in laws and principles. But such a person will also attend to the "mutability, indeterminacy," and "particularity" that characterize each context or case they might confront.[21] Only a significant ability to reason in practically moral fashion prepares people, as Nussbaum says, "to meet the new with responsiveness and imagination, cultivating the sort of flexibility and perceptiveness that will permit [them] to 'improvise what is required.'"[22]

Practical Wisdom in Proverbs thus involves understanding weighty moral and social matters that impact human thriving, and it includes the ability and willingness to act effectively on that understanding. Most significantly, it entails the ability to deploy a range of virtues in order to discern and carry out actions directed toward good ends in the various contexts in which humans

---

20. Fox, *Proverbs 1–9*, 274.
21. Nussbaum, *Fragility of Goodness*, 302.
22. Nussbaum, *Fragility of Goodness*, 303.

find themselves. In other words, Practical Wisdom is more than a matter of possessing a certain kind of knowledge or clever know-how; it goes well beyond any sort of pragmatic skill necessary to attain "success" or to achieve whatever one's own ends might be. For that sort of thing, the exercise of a more limited set of intellectual and practical *virtues*—ingenuity, intelligence, shrewdness, and so forth—would suffice.

Identifying Practical Wisdom in Proverbs 10–29

As with Woman Wisdom's self-presentation in Proverbs 8, the short sayings in Proverbs 10–29 also reveal the importance Proverbs places on the attainment of Practical Wisdom. William Brown has suggested that studying the sayings in Proverbs 10–29 enables readers or hearers to "develop practical wisdom, to cultivate what Aristotle would identify as the chief virtue, prudence."[23] The leading example Brown offers to support this claim is the famous, paradoxical juxtaposition of Proverbs 26:4 and 5.

> Do not answer fools according to their folly. . . .
> Answer fools according to their folly. . . .

Certainly, knowing that one need not always answer a fool may be regarded as a form of practical knowledge. But that, in and of itself, probably does not constitute Practical Wisdom in a full sense of the concept. By contrast, knowing how to respond to a fool in a particular moment of real life in a way that achieves some good and desirable end, and then actually answering that fool (or not)—*that* would constitute an exercise of Practical Wisdom. Nonetheless, it may be that extended reflection on these two sayings about responding to fools—say, recalling and imagining contexts when the first or second proverb was or might be apt—could be an exercise of moral practical reasoning. Reflection on how any of the short proverbs in the book might be true or useful in a particular context would constitute an exercise of moral practical reasoning in this sense. To this extent one can happily concur with Brown.

The Question of Folk Sayings

Brown, however, ultimately seems to be suggesting a stronger link between the study of Proverbs' sayings and the cultivation of Practical Wisdom. As he puts it, the sayings of Proverbs are best understood as "situation oriented,

---

23. Brown, *Character in Crisis*, 14.

open-ended sayings, designed to exercise one's mental and moral faculties and thereby enable the moral agent to size up ethically demanding situations and to act appropriately."[24] For Brown, as for many Proverbs scholars, it seems the short sayings primarily function like oral folk proverbs, which paremiologists (those folklorists who study proverbs) have long taught are regularly uttered or performed to illumine or give guidance to action in particular concrete contexts of life.[25] Simply learning and studying the sayings written down in an anthology like Proverbs, however, is not quite the same thing as actually performing folk proverbs in the various contexts of life or taking from such a performance a cue for a good and right course of action.

There is a long scholarly debate about whether the sayings of Proverbs ought to be regarded, in Fox's schematization, as folk sayings emerging from the "farm" or as the literary constructions of scribes associated with the "court."[26] In their final form, the sayings of the *book* of Proverbs are almost certainly a scribal literary product. But the nature of this proverbial discourse is complex. The short sayings written down in Proverbs are surely in some sense related to folk proverbs too. They do minimally evoke for the reader the form and function of folk sayings—though ultimately, as I will suggest, both the form and function of the sentences in the book are distinct from the form and function of oral folk proverbs. It is not the case that the "poetic artistry" of proverbs written down in Proverbs exceeds that of oral folk sayings, a fact that, if true, perhaps could serve as evidence for their origins as scribal literary products. Indeed, folk proverbs themselves regularly reveal the poetic sophistication of their collective, oral authors. What is more, some of the written sayings in Proverbs very possibly originally emerged in an oral folk milieu.[27] Certainly, any number of phrases or "half-verses" in the book resonate with the sorts of folk proverbs that might have been regularly performed in different contexts in ancient Israel. For example, in isolation, either half of a verse like Proverbs 18:6 sounds like oral folk wisdom.

> A fool's lips bring strife,
> and a fool's mouth invites a flogging.

---

24. Brown, *Character in Crisis*, 14.

25. For the vast field of paremiology, see Mieder, *Proverbs*; and Hrisztova-Gotthardt and Varga, *Introduction to Paremiology*.

26. Fox, "Social Location." Important studies on the issue include Westermann, "Weisheit im Sprichwort" and *Roots of Wisdom*; Golka, *Leopard's Spots*; Hermisson, *Studien zur Israelitischen Spruchweisheit*; Naré, *Proverbes salomoniens et proverbes mossi*; and Akoto-Abutiate, *Proverbs and the African Tree of Life*.

27. Cf. Akoto-Abutiate, *Proverbs and the African Tree of Life*; cf. Sandoval, "Orality of Wisdom Literature."

Together, however, the two half-verses sound more like a literary maxim.[28] Folk proverbs—like those that appear elsewhere in the Bible itself and in different cultures throughout history—are often short, "one-line" sayings.[29] The sentences of Proverbs are, by contrast, regularly two-line utterances, which use the different sorts of parallelism well known to students of biblical Hebrew poetry. As Schipper similarly notes, "Proverbs does not contain a single example of a general proverb" like the short utterances of Ezekiel 16:44 or Judges 8:21. Instead, what "predominates" is "the two-part proverb," which Schipper (not unlike Brown) suggests "leads to further creative and critical reflection."[30]

Besides often taking a more concise form than Proverbs' sentences, folk sayings do not refer as regularly or fully as the sayings of Proverbs do to strong moral types and categories—for example, the wise and foolish, the wicked and righteous, and so forth.[31] The relatively long and often overtly ethical sayings of Proverbs can, unlike folk sayings, also only awkwardly or artificially be orally performed afresh in new contexts. Although orality surely played a key role in the transmission of the literary text of Proverbs (see chap. 10 below), the book's two-line sayings likely were never intended to be orally performed or recontextualized by the addressees of Proverbs in the same fashion that most folk proverbs are.[32] Instead, the sentences overtly function to articulate and value a range of virtues that will characterize a wise and righteous person's way of life (and a range of vices that characterizes wicked, foolish people). They sketch a set of dispositions and characterizations of significant concern to a particular group of people who were able to compose, read/perform, and transmit long and complex literary works—primarily well-placed (though not necessarily economically or politically elite) scribes or sages, members of ancient Israel's and Judah's intellectual class.

---

28. Cf. Sandoval, "Orality of Wisdom Literature," 276–77.

29. Though, of course, not always. But note the utterances in biblical narrative (Judg. 8:2, 21; 1 Sam. 16:7; 24:14; 1 Kings 20:11) discussed by Fontaine, *Traditional Sayings in the Old Testament*; see further, 1 Sam. 10:12; 19:24; Ezek. 18:2.

30. Schipper, *Proverbs 1–15*, 30. The "general proverbs" of Ezek. 16:44 and Judg. 8:21 are "Like a mother (is) her daughter" (כְּאִמָּה בִּתָּה) and "As a man is, so is his strength" (כָּאִישׁ גְּבוּרָתוֹ).

31. Note, however, 1 Sam. 24:13.

32. Even today, although some religious people who place a high value on Scripture (e.g., Bible-centered evangelicals) will occasionally quote verses from Proverbs to comment on particular contexts and situations, these utterances hardly reveal the same level of mastery (e.g., in terms of memorization of a broad range of sayings and agility in apt performance) that utterers of traditional folk proverbs in largely oral cultural contexts demonstrate. Interestingly, Fox (*Proverbs 10–31*, 485) reports, albeit anecdotally, that when Hebrew-speaking Israelis quote the book of Proverbs, it is typically only the first lines that are uttered.

Still, it is important that portions of some individual sayings in Proverbs evoke the form and function of folk sayings. It implies that the wise utterances in Proverbs may sometimes offer close (re)presentations of a folk wisdom that was broadly current in ancient Israel and Judah. This state of affairs suggests an affinity between Proverbs' ultimately *scribal* moral vision with that of the broader rural, agricultural population in Israel/Judah, among whom folk sayings would have also, perhaps especially, enjoyed currency.[33] Proverbs' emphasis on paternalistic social justice, with its strong focus on care for the poor and marginalized, for example, might be imagined as one instance of overlapping moral vision between (mostly) urban scribes and rural agriculturalists. As Gale Yee explains, with increased political and economic centralization in Israel and Judah in the period of the monarchy (and indeed a shift from a "familial" to a "Native-Tributary" mode of economic production), the justice responsibilities of the *pater familias* or village elders likely would have shifted somewhat to officials in the civil-royal bureaucracy, who themselves were in service to that royal figure—the king—who could be reckoned as a "father" to the entire people.[34] In such a scenario, the rhetoric of justice at home in small settlements and towns could have been adapted and applied to a larger polity where ideologies of kingship also insisted that political elites serve justice.[35]

Practical Wisdom Manifested in Appropriate Action

If the sayings of Proverbs 10–29 share some characteristics with folk proverbs but ultimately are distinct in form and function from them, this probably means that a person will *not* progress much toward a full or robust Practical Wisdom simply by studying the book's short sayings. Knowing that showing kindness to the poor or being faithful in friendship are prized virtues and actually concretely showing kindness and being faithful to others at appropriate moments are quite different matters. Nonetheless, a significant number of verses in Proverbs 10–29 do reveal the sages'

---

33. This is so even if one would also expect that in certain respects the perspectives of the two distinct social formations would vary precisely as a function of their different social-economic positioning.

34. Yee, *Poor Banished Children of Eve*, esp. 59–79. It would be incorrect, however, to imagine modes of production like those just mentioned to succeed one another in a strict chronological fashion. As Gottwald and Boer each explain, dominant modes of production tend to coexist to some extent with the economic system they displaced, while traces of emerging modes of production might also be detected in present arrangements. See Gottwald, "Sociology"; Boer, *Sacred Economy*.

35. For a similar notion, see Washington, *Wealth and Poverty*, 171–202, esp. 185.

concern that the book's addressees develop a genuine Practical Wisdom; these verses speak rather clearly of the reflective activity of those who follow wise and just paths and whose virtue enables them consistently to desire and pursue good and right courses of action. Such sayings also hold implications for how Proverbs understands a person might in fact come to acquire Practical Wisdom, including the role moral exemplars might play in this development.

Of the lines in Proverbs 10–29 that allude to the practical moral reasoning carried out by virtuous moral actors, consider the following:

> The integrity [תֻּמָּה] of the upright guides them,
>   but the crookedness of the treacherous destroys them. (11:3)
>
> Deceit is in the mind of those who plan evil,
>   but those who counsel peace have joy. (12:20)
>
> Those who are hot-tempered stir up strife,
>   but those who are slow to anger calm contention. (15:18)
>
> The wicked put on a bold face,
>   but the upright give thought to their ways.[36] (21:29)

As Proverbs 11:3 makes clear, it is the character or integrity (תֻּמָּה) of upright people that serves as their moral-social compass; it is what enables them to identify good ends in any particular situation and directs their practical reasoning. As 21:29 adds, "the upright" person understands or gives good thought to their ways. In Proverbs 12:20 and 15:18, moreover, "those who counsel peace" and "those who are slow to anger"—both of whom are surely to be collocated with the wise, just, and upright in Proverbs—choose courses of action that bring about explicitly positive or good social ends. The counselors' considered recommendation of peace enables both them and others to experience the joy of shalom, while those who patiently keep their anger in check, or "hold their peace," limit the social strife that detracts from everyone's experience of social harmony.

By contrast, the character of the negative moral types in the above lines impedes their ability for practical moral reasoning. The crooked character of the treacherous in Proverbs 11:3 means they cannot thoughtfully and well

---

36. In 21:29b, the *qere*, which suggests the upright person "understands" or considers well (יָבִין) his way, is to be preferred to the *ketiv*, which suggests the upright person prepares (יָכִין) his way. As Fox (*Proverbs 10–31*, 692) notes, the latter "does not complement the first line well."

imagine good ends in the range of contexts that will confront them in life.[37] Hence, even if they are the brightest and most clever of people, they will not be able to exhibit a genuine Practical Wisdom. Their character cannot direct their actions well, certainly not in the way the moral disposition of the upright "guides" them. Instead, their vicious character "destroys them," where the third-masculine plural pronoun "them" may refer either to the treacherous themselves (and so accord with an act-consequence logic) or perhaps obliquely to the "upright" of the verse's first stich, emphasizing the socially disruptive ways of the vicious. Similarly, in 12:20 those who plan for wicked ends don't seem to lack raw intelligence or knowledge; what they are deficient in is virtue, that which can appropriately guide their practical rationality. Instead of thoughts of justice or wisdom, "deceit is in the mind of those who plan evil." Likewise, the character of the hot-tempered person in 15:18 means he has no time or intellectual-emotional space for virtuous reflection on a situation. Instead of calming conflict, as the practically wise typically will do, he only provokes strife.[38] Similarly, in 21:29, all that the wicked person can muster in confronting unstated situations is a "bold face," a countenance that projects confidence and strength but which is a poor substitute for action emerging from genuine practical moral reasoning.

For Proverbs, then, a person of Practical Wisdom is able to order their practical and intellectual virtues under the moral-social virtues and can typically marshal them all appropriately when confronted with the variety of situations that demand action and decision in life. The moral-intellectual deficit of others means they cannot reason practically in ways that aim for and enable good and just results. As Proverbs 14:8 thus says,

> A shrewd person's [עָרוּם] wisdom [חָכְמָה] consists in understanding his way;
> while the folly of dolts is deceit.[39]

The practical and intellectual abilities of the enkratic-like עָרוּם (cf. chap. 6) are here (and typically in Proverbs) guided by virtue or wisdom. Such a person may not only reason well and shrewdly in different contexts; he can rationally consider "his way" in light of his knowledge of the full range of moral-social and religious virtues that ought to characterize the wise and just.

---

37. On the term for "crookedness" (סֶלֶף), see Schipper, *Proverbs 1–15*, 394; and Fox, *Proverbs 10–31*, 532.

38. On the "type" of the hot-tempered person mentioned in Prov. 15:18 and its possible relation to Egyptian wisdom, see Schipper, *Proverbs 1–15*, 504; cf. Fox, *Proverbs 10–31*, 598–99.

39. The translation follows Fox, *Proverbs 10–31*, 575.

The dolt is unable to do this (cf. chap. 6). Any limited practical reasoning such a figure undertakes, because it is done without the moral-social wisdom Proverbs prizes, is inevitably wrongheaded. It thus entails a kind of deceit or "misleads," as the NRSV says.[40]

Still other lines in Proverbs that are often thought to reflect the book's simple act-consequence logic might be marshaled as evidence for the claim that Proverbs' wise and just individuals typically exercise a robust Practical Wisdom. Consider Proverbs 11:6 and 12:6, for instance:

> The righteousness of the upright saves them,
> but the treacherous are taken captive by their schemes [בְּהַוַּת].[41]
> (11:6)

> The words of the wicked are a deadly ambush,
> but the speech of the upright delivers them. (12:6)

In these lines, Proverbs is clearly urging its readers or hearers to choose a life path that provides "life-saving" advantage over another way that leads to deadly trouble. But what precisely is it about the upright that delivers or saves them? What is it that results in advantage for them? It is surely nothing other than their virtue, their character. As 11:6 states clearly, it is the "righteousness" or justice of the upright that saves them, while 12:6 understands the (character-revealing) speech of such a person to rescue them.

Still, one might wonder, in what sense can one's character or virtuous words "save" a person? Are we not left with a version of the act-consequence connection, where good and bad conduct is thought to be regularly (if not always) appropriately rewarded? Perhaps on one level—the level of the book's wisdom mythos—yes. But in another sense perhaps not, at least if one can again

---

40. As Schipper (*Proverbs 1–15*, 471) says, "Verse 8b can be understood to mean either that fools store up 'deceit' (מִרְמָה) for anyone who comes to them or that fools ultimately deceive themselves."

41. As Fox (*Proverbs 10–31*, 533) notes, some scholars believe the term הַוָּה ("schemes") in 11:6b might be a by-form of Hebrew אַוָּה ("desire"), while others regard it as cognate to Ugaritic *hwt* and Akkadian *awātu* and so render it as "word," as perhaps one might do in Job 6:30. Kselman seizes on both possibilities, suggesting that the line represents a case of "deliberate ambiguity," whereby the verse's rhetoric means two things at once. "The treacherous will be ensnared by their greedy desire, as well as by their malicious words; and ensnared, they will fall inevitably into disaster" ("Ambiguity and Wordplay," 545). Given the prologue's suggestion that Proverbs' instruction will be offered via tropes, figures, and "riddles" (cf. chap. 2), Kselman may well be right. The fact that the treacherous here can be imagined as articulating the desires they pursue warrants the NRSV's rendering of the term in this context as "schemes." Cf. further Schipper (*Proverbs 1–15*, 395–96), who takes הַוָּה to mean "craving," citing Prov. 10:3 and Mic. 7:3—though in Prov. 10:3, it may be better to emend *hawwat* to *ḥayyat* (cf. Fox, *Proverbs 10–31*, 512).

conceptually bracket any strong version of an act-consequence connection as a fundamentally defining concept for Proverbs' moral vision and think more in terms of what character-ethics discourses prioritize. If so, one can readily surmise that rather than salvation coming as a kind of automatic reward for the just, simply because they are just, their deliverance instead is something like the fruit of their exercise of Practical Wisdom. It is the upright's ability to bring their virtue or their character—their justice or wise speech—to bear on different situations that saves them.

That a saying like Proverbs 11:6 is concerned with a person's practical moral reasoning is evident first from the fact that it spotlights two specific and contrasting moral types, the upright and the treacherous. The upright person possesses justice—that key social virtue in Proverbs that here, as elsewhere, functions as a synecdoche for a person's full virtue. Because his character is well formed, the upright person is in the position to exercise intellectual acuity toward good ends. He has the tools necessary for authentic Practical Wisdom. Although verse 6a is not explicit about the upright person engaging in rational planning or thinking, that this should be assumed is evidenced by the line's second half, which speaks of the "schemes" of the treacherous. The treacherous are not here intellectually deficient but clearly possess a shrewd and strong mind that enables them to "scheme." Although the just and upright can deploy their intellect to the end of some intentional activity just as the treacherous do, the ways each moral type exercises their intellectual and practical abilities are not the same. The key distinction is that the treacherous do not possess the sort of virtue that would enable them to marshal their intellectual power in authentically, practically wise fashion, toward good ends. As a result, what they do or say typically concludes negatively, for themselves and likely for others too (e.g., those who may fall into the ambush of the wicked in 12:6).[42] By contrast, the thoughts of the upright are guided by virtue (i.e., their just character), and this enables them to deliberate rationally with some good end in mind, one that here "saves them." As MacIntyre explains, as mentioned above, for virtue ethics authentic Practical Wisdom "requires knowledge of the good, indeed itself requires goodness of a kind in its possessor."[43]

Proverbs 11:6 and especially 12:6 suggest further that the sages also knew that one's Practical Wisdom, or lack thereof, often manifests itself through one's "speech," the shrewd words one speaks in a particular context.[44] As Proverbs 11:9 (cf. 11:8; 13:6), with rhetoric similar to 11:6 and 12:6, says,

---

42. Proverbs 11:8 ("The righteous are delivered from trouble, and the wicked get into it instead"), a line rhetorically similar to 11:6 and 12:6, likely makes the same point as those lines.

43. MacIntyre, *After Virtue*, 154–55 (citing *NE* 1144a 37).

44. Though the rhetoric of speech is not explicit in 11:6, cf. note 41 above.

> With their mouths the godless would destroy their neighbors,
> but by knowledge the righteous are delivered. (11:9)

In this verse, "godless" persons destroy their neighbors with their words; they undo the social bonds necessary for human thriving. Righteous people, by contrast, by means of their "knowledge," are able appropriately to address a situation detrimental to their own well-being (e.g., the destruction that the discourse of the impious in the first half of the verse precipitates). The saying does not state what the godless actually say or what practically wise course of action—oral or otherwise—the knowledge of the righteous leads them to decide upon. No hard and fast rule can be formulated for responding to the destructive utterances of godless people. The precise nature of any good and appropriate response—including the uttering of real words—depends more narrowly on "the who, the what, the where," and so forth of a particular situation. Nonetheless, based on other descriptions of the wise and just in Proverbs, one might imagine the just person's response to the destructive words of the godless would be characterized by things like patience, as well as careful and shrewd efforts to ensure that fairness and justice carry the day. Through an ability to bring their knowledge of wisdom and what constitutes the good to bear on a particular situation, the צַדִּיקִים of 11:9 can thus, like the upright of 11:6 and 12:6, be said to "deliver" themselves—and perhaps others too. They can restore or preserve a well-being that would be diminished if the destructive words of the vicious, instead of the social virtue of the wise and just, constituted the norms of people's relations with their neighbors.

Practical Wisdom Manifested in Wise Speech

We have started to see that for Proverbs, Practical Wisdom, or its absence, often manifests itself in words (Prov. 11:6, 9)—pleasing and effective speech on the one hand and perverse utterances on the other. Wise and just people—and those who follow their paths—understand how prudent words can affect and shape positive outcomes. Such people know what to say, when to say it, and how to say it so that some good end imagined through one's virtue-informed intellect might be reached. Other lines in the book make this clear too. Several verses clustered in Proverbs 16, for example, point to the fact that Practical Wisdom for the ancient sages manifests in a person's speech.

> The wise of heart [חֲכַם־לֵב] is called perceptive [נָבוֹן],
> and pleasant speech [מֶתֶק שְׂפָתַיִם] increases persuasiveness [לֶקַח].
> (16:21)

> The mind of the wise [לֵב חָכָם] makes their speech judicious [יַשְׂכִּיל פִּיהוּ],
> and adds persuasiveness [לֶקַח] to their lips.
> Pleasant words [אִמְרֵי־נֹעַם] are like a honeycomb,
> sweetness to the soul and health to the body. (16:23–24)

Both Proverbs 16:21 and 23 associate an enkratic or virtuous person's intellectual acuity or intelligence with speech that is rhetorically intentional and effective—pleasant (i.e., "sweet"; מֶתֶק) or judicious (שֵׂכֶל) and persuasive (לֶקַח). However, practical virtue or the intellectual ability that permits one to be rhetorically effective requires no particular moral orientation. Many people can effectively use fine words or blandishments to ignoble ends.

The נָבוֹן of 16:21, however, is an enkratic-like figure who in Proverbs typically follows the "right" way of the wise and just (cf. chap. 6). That which enables this "perceptive" person to speak pleasantly and effectively is thus probably not mere oratorial ability or raw intelligence; knowledge of virtue, which inclines the person to deploy rationality toward some good end, is surely also a factor. Indeed, the נָבוֹן in 16:21 is said to be חֲכַם־לֵב, "wise of heart," an interesting locution that suggests the intellect works under the influence of wisdom. Fox calls it a "predisposition for wisdom."[45] Such a person (חֲכַם־לֵב), as 10:8 says, "will heed commandments" (cf. 11:29). The character of this נָבוֹן, however, is perhaps not as fully settled as that of the wise person (חָכָם) in 16:23, whose intellect (לֵב) appears to be fully aligned with wisdom's virtues so that what this wise person utters is more reliably sagacious or judicious than the speech of the נָבוֹן. Still, the "perceptive" person of 16:21 is well on the way to achieving the sort of moral-intellectual status of a חָכָם.

The next verse in the above cluster of verses, Proverbs 16:24 does not explicitly mention figures such as the חָכָם or the נָבוֹן, but it similarly suggests that Practical Wisdom manifests itself through speech. The verse insists that certain kinds of discourse are, like the taste of honeycombs, pleasing to others. Such words appear to constitute what people, at different moments, yearn to hear and so are said to be "sweet to the soul" (מָתוֹק לַנֶּפֶשׁ). The verse suggests that such pleasant and desirable words—likely those typically uttered by the sorts of intelligent and wise people mentioned in verses 21 and 23—serve not only the speaker's advantage; they are plainly well-considered words, uttered to achieve a good end that contributes to others' flourishing too. When pleasant and effective, a person's speech can serve the healing of people's bodies or bones (מַרְפֵּא לָעָצֶם), a turn of phrase in 16:24 that indicates not merely the soothing of a physical malady but also the promotion of a full

---

45. Fox, *Proverbs 10–31*, 619.

psychological well-being (bones as metonym for a person). As Bruce Waltke says, the image points to "the restoration of the entire person or community, both the immaterial and material aspects."[46]

Together, the above observations regarding pleasant and effective words uttered by moral agents who incline to virtuous ways of life suggest that these verses presume the workings of a rather full conception of Practical Wisdom. The practical moral reasoning these agents engage in is evident in their speech: what they say in a range of unstated situations constitutes (good) responses that might affect good ends.

Other lines in Proverbs also suggest that prudent speech reveals the Practical Wisdom of moral agents whose dispositions are more fully settled than those of the נָבוֹן (and the חֲכַם־לֵב). The following sayings allude to the utterances of the just or righteous (צַדִּיק) as well as to the words of the wise (חָכָם), as does Proverbs 16:23.

> The wise lay up knowledge,
>   but the babbling of a fool [פִּי־אֱוִיל] brings ruin near. (10:14)
>
> The lips of the righteous know what is acceptable,
>   but the mouth of the wicked what is perverse [תַּהְפֻּכוֹת]. (10:32)
>
> Rash words are like sword thrusts,
>   but the tongue of the wise brings healing. (12:18)
>
> The teaching of the wise is a fountain of life,
>   so that one may avoid the snares of death. (13:14)
>
> The mind of the righteous ponders [יֶהְגֶּה] how to answer,
>   but the mouth of the wicked pours out evil. (15:28)

These lines make clear that the words the wise and just use to respond in appropriate and effective fashion to a range of contexts emerge from their considered reflection on matters in ways that are intimately related to their character. Proverbs 15:28, for instance, notes that the just person "ponders" (הגה) or meditates upon his response to situations. So too the just person's lips "know" what is acceptable (10:32). The wise person's words are tailored to produce good ends; they bring "healing" (12:18; cf. 16:24) and appear as a flowing fountain—a potent symbol of life—in contexts where the flourishing existence people desire is at risk of disappearing into the "snares of

---

46. Waltke, *Proverbs*, 30.

death" (13:14). Proverbs 10:14 also refers to a wise moral agent, but it does not mention the words such a person speaks or the good end that an expression of her "knowledge" might bring about. However, this person's speech and the efficacy of her moral reasoning in achieving a good end are evoked in the contrast with the verse's second half. There the "babbling," literally the "mouth of," an inveterate "fool" (אֱוִיל) provokes a terrible outcome (cf. 13:16; 15:7; 18:7).

In contrast to wise and just people, the foolish and wicked moral agents in the above lines lack the Practical Wisdom of virtuous figures, something that is evident from the fact that their words do not contribute to finding good and appropriate ways to resolve difficult situations. Instead, their sometimes "rash words" are likened to destructive "sword thrusts" (12:18a). Although this half-verse does not explicitly name a negative moral agent, the contrast with the "wise" in verse 18b makes clear that words that promote conflict belong to the vicious. The speech of such people perverts and confuses matters, overturning everything, as the term תַּהְפֻּכוֹת (derived from הפך, "to turn or overthrow") in 10:32's description of wicked people's words implies.

Given Proverbs' concern with how Practical Wisdom (or its lack) might manifest itself in speech, Proverbs 15:1 and 23 summarize well the sage's perspective on the ethical implications of speech:

> A soft answer turns away wrath,
> but a harsh word stirs up anger. (15:1)

> To make an apt answer is a joy to anyone,
> and a word in season, how good it is! (15:23)

Proverbs 15:1, especially when understood in isolation from the rest of the book's moral discourse, may be thought to point merely to practical virtue—the ability to talk one's way out of a situation (v. 1a) or to create conflict in the service of one's own immediate, and not necessarily good, ends (v. 1b). Yet for Proverbs it is wise and just people who will regularly be guided in their thinking by virtue and will have good ends in mind when they "speak to" different contexts. By preferring a "soft answer" over a "harsh word," they will, for example, minimize the deterioration of social bonds, seek to repair broken relations, and diffuse situations of conflict. As 15:23 knows, a considered and well-timed word ("a word in season"; דָּבָר בְּעִתּוֹ) articulated by a practically wise agent contributes to some such "good" end, even if only the psychological well-being or "joy" of others.

A wise and just moral agent, however, is not explicitly named as the one who utters the soft and apt answers of Proverbs 15:1 and 23. Nonetheless, in light of what we have been discovering about speech and Practical Wisdom in Proverbs, it is safe to say that for the sages such a practically wise agent will be most capable of producing such pleasant and efficacious speech. Others, with ill-formed characters, will likely devise plans and deploy speech to reach ends that serve only their own narrowly conceived advantage, which may cause social relations to deteriorate dangerously. For example, with respect to the wicked, Proverbs 24:2 says,

> Their minds devise violence,
> and their lips talk of mischief.

And as 26:24–25 suggests about those who despise others,

> One who hates [שׂוֹנֵא] dissembles in speaking
> while harboring deceit within;
> when an enemy speaks graciously, do not believe it,
> for there are seven abominations in his mind [בְּלִבּוֹ]. (NRSV modified)

What is more, as Proverbs 17:14a knows, "Starting strife is (like) releasing water."[47] Once water is running it is difficult to stop and essentially impossible to store once again. (In modern parlance, one can't put the toothpaste back in the tube.) So, too, are contentious words once unleashed. Consequently, unlike the vicious who trade in conflict, the wise and just person will heed 17:14b's advice: "So before a quarrel breaks out, leave off!"[48]

Practical Wisdom Manifested in Silence

Although the words of wise and just individuals might reveal their capacity for appropriate moral reasoning, it is also the case for Proverbs that remaining silent can be the clearest evidence of Practical Wisdom. Silence can be the best way to respond to others in unforeseen situations and in ways that promote good ends. Consider Proverbs 11:12 (cf. 12:16) and 17:27 (cf.

---

47. This is Fox's translation (*Proverbs 10–31*, 631).
48. This is Fox's translation (*Proverbs 10–31*, 631). Other lines in Proverbs also suggest that one's speech can signal possession of Practical Wisdom, or not. Although not all of the verses speak of good or bad ends that a person's words might promote, the moral language (the fool, the just, hatred, trespass, etc.) of Prov. 10:18–21, for instance, makes clear that the speech of moral agents can be a guide to evaluating their relative abilities to reason morally.

14:29), which deploy key proverbial terms for knowledge (דַּעַת, תְּבוּנָה) or its absence (חֲסַר־לֵב):

> Whoever belittles another lacks sense [חֲסַר־לֵב],
> but an intelligent person [אִישׁ תְּבוּנָה] remains silent. (11:12)
>
> One who spares words is knowledgeable [יוֹדֵעַ דָּעַת];
> one who is cool in spirit has understanding [אִישׁ תְּבוּנָה]. (17:27)

In Proverbs 11:12a, the belittling or despising words of those who lack sense characterize that negative moral agent. Their derisive speech quite plainly does not promote the good of sociability that Proverbs so fully values. The understanding person (אִישׁ תְּבוּנָה) deploys no such words; in moments where others might speak harshly, she stays silent. Indeed, the one who "spares words" (17:27) is one who is "cool of spirit" (reading the *ketiv*, קַר־רוּחַ); she is not easily angered and so is unlikely to verbally disparage her neighbors.[49] One might reckon the "person of understanding" merely as an enkratic-like figure and not a wise and just person whose character is fully settled (cf. chap. 6). However, the parallel construction of the first half of the line suggests this "knowledgeable" figure (יוֹדֵעַ דָּעַת), like the נָבוֹן elsewhere, knows and seems regularly to choose the ways of the wise and just—here a quiet path.[50] As Proverbs 19:11 says, though without the precise rhetoric of "speech," a person with good practical insights (שֵׂכֶל) understands that responding to different situations in one's immediate anger is not usually wise. The line instead exhorts the reader of Proverbs to "overlook an offense."

> Those with good sense are slow to anger,
> and it is their glory to overlook an offense. (19:11)

Verses like 11:12, 12:25, and 19:11 promote strategies of engagement with others that surely would prevent the escalation of disputes. Such wise engagement can (and for Proverbs surely ought to) curry esteem from others who experience or witness a person's silence and magnanimity—it is "their glory" (19:11). This type of strategy, however, should always be balanced with the need to "speak up," to oppose injustice, to ensure fairness, or to defend the marginalized. When complemented in this way, the patience and

---

49. Cf. Fox, *Proverbs 10–31*, 637.
50. That the אִישׁ תְּבוּנָה is an enkratic-like moral type seems evident from the fact that he is easily contrasted with akratic-like figures—e.g., the כְּסִיל in 10:23 and the חֲסַר־לֵב in 15:21. Cf. chap. 6.

willingness to sometimes set aside, in silence, what may be one's own legitimate claims constitute a Practical Wisdom that contributes to the sort of robust sociality Proverbs prizes. So fully does Proverbs know that not speaking can sometimes signal Practical Wisdom that it even says those with settled vicious characters—and thus manifestly unable to reason well morally—can *appear* as ethically intelligent when they keep their mouths shut!

> Even fools [אֱוִיל] who keep silent are considered wise;
>   when they close their lips, they are deemed intelligent. (17:28)

The Practical Wisdom Proverbs envisions as something evident in a wise person's strategic silence surely also includes the ability of virtuous agents to listen and weigh the advice of others.

> Fools think their own way is right,
>   but the wise listen to advice. (12:15)

> By insolence the heedless make strife,
>   but wisdom is with those who take advice. (13:10)

Others, like the fool of 12:15, are wrongly overconfident in the worth of their own opinions and so sometimes—even regularly—respond to different situations that demand decision or response in inappropriate fashion (cf. 13:10). In contrast, the wise, when confronted with weighty matters, listen to others and reason with them to discern the best ways forward; they "take advice" or are willing to be counseled (13:10).[51]

Practical Wisdom Manifested in Finding Good Paths

Several sayings in Proverbs 10–29 that employ the idiom "to find (the) good" (מצא טוב)—Proverbs 16:20, 17:20, and 19:8—may also gesture to the important role Practical Wisdom plays in the collections of short sayings in the book. Though this expression might be understood as simply linking wise actions or discernment to successful living, with a virtue-ethics lens one can also reckon the lines to intimate how Practical Wisdom necessarily entails practical reasoning undertaken with some good end in mind.

---

51. It is tempting here to add to the discussion Prov. 27:17, which according to the NRSV states, "Iron sharpens iron, and one person sharpens the wits of another." Though such an understanding of the verse has ancient roots, it is not a certain rendering of the line. See Fox, *Proverbs 10–31*, 811.

Those who are attentive to a matter will prosper,
and happy are those who trust in the Lord. (16:20)
מַשְׂכִּיל עַל־דָּבָר יִמְצָא־טוֹב וּבוֹטֵחַ בַּיהוָה אַשְׁרָיו

The crooked of mind do not prosper,
and the perverse of tongue fall into calamity. (17:20)
עִקֶּשׁ־לֵב לֹא יִמְצָא־טוֹב וְנֶהְפָּךְ בִּלְשׁוֹנוֹ יִפּוֹל בְּרָעָה

To get wisdom is to love oneself;
to keep understanding is to prosper. (19:8)
קֹנֶה־לֵּב אֹהֵב נַפְשׁוֹ שֹׁמֵר תְּבוּנָה לִמְצֹא־טוֹב

Behind the NRSV's rendering of "prosper" in these verses is the Hebrew expression "to find (the) good." This is a more morally charged expression than the typical economic עשׁר, which a reader might suspect lies behind the English translation "prosper." What "good" is found is not directly stated in the lines and so must be inferred. Typically, as with the NRSV's rendering, the good that will be "found" is thought to be some sort of success or material gain, an exterior good understood as the prize for right action.[52] As Longman says in relation to 16:20, "The reward mentioned in the proverb was likely understood as material."[53]

There is no reason to reject a material understanding of the expression "to find (the) good." Again, one does not need to deny the efficacy of the rhetoric of reward and punishment to motivate the young, morally malleable audience of Proverbs to follow wisdom's way. Yet, another possibility emerges for interpreting these verses if one reads them divorced from a strong expectation of finding only, or primarily, a Tun-Ergehen logic at work in the book and instead imagines Proverbs' teaching more in terms of virtue-oriented instruction. This interpretation expands and nuances an understanding of both the sort of "good" outcome a virtuous person will "find" and such a person's moral agency in producing that "good." The lines intimate that the virtuous person who possesses Practical Wisdom is the one who is attentive to a matter (16:20) or who keeps or "guards" understanding (שֹׁמֵר תְּבוּנָה, 19:8). As a result, that person "finds" (in the sense of reaching or arriving at) a "good" resolution to any particular circumstance that might require choosing one or another course of action. By contrast, the "vicious person"—the one of crooked mind and perverse tongue

---

52. Proverbs 18:22a also deploys the expression "to find the good," but it does so in a considerably less ambiguous fashion than in other instances, since what it describes as "good" is explicitly articulated. The man who finds a wife, says the patriarchal text, "finds a good thing" (מָצָא טוֹב). Here, the good that is found obviously does not refer narrowly to some sort of economic prosperity, though marriage in ancient contexts certainly had significant economic implications.

53. Longman, *Proverbs*, 335.

(17:20)—lacks practical moral reasoning ability and hence in the same sorts of situations finds no good way forward; things subsequently end badly for him.

In Proverbs 16:20 in particular, the one who considers well or "is attentive to" (מַשְׂכִּיל) a matter may not simply be exercising an intellectual virtue that enables reaching one or another end or achieving some advantage. Instead, the מַשְׂכִּיל may be engaging in genuine moral practical reasoning—Practical Wisdom. This reasoning is the careful, virtue-guided reflection that people who follow the right way in Proverbs undertake to discern and arrive at some good end. This is evident first from the fact that in the second half of 16:20, this person is paralleled to the one who "trust[s] in the Lord." The reflective person is closely linked to, probably even identified with, the one who confidently relies on the deity. This type of person appears quite fully virtuous throughout Proverbs, like the צַדִּיק with whom the מַשְׂכִּיל is identified in 21:12 (cf. chap. 6).

That Proverbs 16:20, with its rhetoric of finding the good, speaks not of practical-intellectual *virtue* but of Practical Wisdom might also be discerned by recalling what the book elsewhere describes as "good." Proverbs 2:9 describes a way or path as "good" (מַעְגַּל־טוֹב), while 4:2 speaks of an instruction or a "lesson" (לֶקַח) as good (4:2), and in 12:25 a word (דָּבָר) is considered good.[54] All these expressions fill out what is meant by the generic good thing that a person with practical moral reasoning abilities finds in 16:20 (and 19:8; and what is not found by the "crooked of mind" in 17:20). Because the "matter" in question in Proverbs 16:20 (as in 12:25) is expressed as דָּבָר ("word"), the verse may also point to the fact that one's Practical Wisdom, for Proverbs, can regularly be expressed in speech. Whatever the case, as an exercise of Practical Wisdom, the intelligent reflection of a virtuous (or enkratic) moral agent in relation to some situation unsurprisingly ends well, according to the second half of the verse. The one who is "attentive to a matter" and who is characterized by virtue—trusting in Adonai—will in some sense be rewarded—"Happy is he" (אַשְׁרָיו), says 16:20b. Yet the sort of "happiness" that Proverbs is most concerned with, as we have been suggesting, is no mere attainment of economic prosperity or "external goods"; it is a genuine human thriving or well-being that includes some enjoyment of exterior goods for which a person may legitimately strive, if that striving is guided by the exercise of a full range of virtues—that is, via Practical Wisdom.[55]

---

54. On לֶקַח as "instruction" or "lesson," see Fox, *Proverbs 1–9*, 62–63; and cf. Schipper, *Proverbs 1–15*, 67.

55. The expression אַשְׁרֵי and related locutions in Proverbs are almost always intimately associated with the life of virtue. Those who are declared "happy" include not only the robustly virtuous Woman of Valor of Prov. 31 (v. 28) but also those who find wisdom (3:13), attend to Woman Wisdom's instruction (8:34), are kind to the poor (14:21), trust in the Lord (16:20), are cautious (or fear) (28:14), and keep instruction (29:18).

Proverbs 17:20 expresses the same point as 16:20 but in opposite terms. The person who is "crooked of mind" (עִקֶּשׁ־לֵב) will not find (the) good (לֹא יִמְצָא טוֹב). Such a person, collocated with the one who is "perverse of tongue" in the second verse-half, is clearly characterized as not wise; he does not possess the sort of virtuous character that is prerequisite for appropriate moral reasoning. Importantly, this sort of person is not one who is merely a חֲסַר־לֵב. He does not "lack" intellectual or rational capacities but may very well possess a kind of shrewdness and use his intellect in purposive ways. Yet because of his lack of virtue, he is incapable of proper—"straight," not "crooked"—practical moral reflection. He cannot imagine genuinely good ends to which he can better or appropriately apply his intellectual and practical capacities; consequently, as he traverses life's paths, he "falls" into something bad (רָעָה, a "calamity").

Proverbs 19:8 contains the last instance in the book of the idiom "to find (the) good." The line's second stich is syntactically difficult but can be analyzed similarly to 16:20.[56] Alongside the rhetoric of the good, terms expressing intellectual acuity ("possessing a mind"; קֹנֶה־לֵּב) in the first half of the verse and a rhetoric of wisdom (here called "understanding"; תְּבוּנָה) in its second stich suggest the verse as a whole is concerned with a person's "moral" intellect. The second half of the line especially need not imply simply that wisdom is regularly rewarded; rather, it shows that one whose intellectual capacities are guided by virtue can find a way forward toward good and appropriate ends or outcomes in whatever context one might face. The one who guards understanding (שֹׁמֵר) is able to find a morally suitable response to any sort of situation; he will "find" the good.

A further point about Proverbs 19:8 is also important. If the good that one might find in 19:8b need not be considered merely the reward of some exterior good (like "prosperity"), the notion that a virtuous person's exercise of intellectual virtue ("possessing a mind"; קֹנֶה־לֵּב) entails "loving oneself" (19:8a) suggests something similar. The exercise of practical reasoning toward some good end may certainly result in some "real" tangible benefit. That is undeniable, even if it is not inevitable. Reading with a virtue-ethics lens, however, the rhetoric of this line suggests something more thoroughgoing—namely, that by living wisely and justly one is in fact seeking one's own well-being. For modern readers who think of the moral life as acts that "I" perform on behalf of others because it is the right thing, or my duty, to do so, such talk of self-interest or loving oneself in ethics may sound suspect (chap. 1). However, for virtue-

---

56. The difficulty revolves around the infinitive expression לִמְצֹא־טוֹב. Fox (*Proverbs 10–31*, 651) believes the construction expresses a "certain result"—the one who "keeps good sense will surely find good fortune."

oriented thought and a book like Proverbs, it is not illegitimate. Pursuing one's own full thriving by living virtuously is not the same as striving primarily or narrowly for some secondary good that might enhance one's pleasures and advantages in life. Despite the fact that many deploy their intellectual and *practical virtue* toward precisely such ends, that sort of egoistic existence can never be the final end or goal of the exercise of a genuine *Practical Wisdom*. A wise and just life for the sort of being Proverbs understands humans to be demands not only that one embody other-regarding social virtue (say, to gain a reward); it also requires one to comprehend that the well-being of others is inextricably linked to one's own happiness and that secondary goods hold a limited—though real—place in establishing human well-being.

None of this discussion of the expression "to find (the) good" in Proverbs denies that the proverbs can or should be understood in more or less literal fashion. As noted, we can still understand 16:20, 17:20, and 19:8 as discourse that effectively motivates the book's young audience to strive after wisdom by rhetorically promising good things to those who follow the book's teachings (and bad things to those who reject it). However, we should also remember that Proverbs' audience includes advanced students too; the wise and discerning are invited to increase their learning by interpreting the subtle contours of the book's figurative or symbolic moral discourse (chap. 2; see 1:5–6). Might not such readers conclude that the good a person of virtue finds need not always or simply be regarded as the reward of an external good but can also be the good end toward which a person's Practical Wisdom is directed?

If so, it nonetheless remains important to remember that the sages do recognize that any authentic human thriving will necessarily include some enjoyment of external goods. It is thus not surprising that in speaking of the book's key social-moral and religious virtues, verses like Proverbs 21:21 and 22:4 also suggest a virtuous person will find and enjoy particular external goods.

> Whoever pursues righteousness and kindness
> will find life and honor. (21:21)
> רֹדֵף צְדָקָה וָחָסֶד יִמְצָא חַיִּים צְדָקָה וְכָבוֹד

> The reward for humility and fear of the Lord
> is riches and honor and life. (22:4)
> עֵקֶב עֲנָוָה יִרְאַת יְהוָה עֹשֶׁר וְכָבוֹד וְחַיִּים

Fox rightly understands that the message of 21:21 is that "the pursuit of ethical virtues, which benefit others, will reward the pursuer as well."[57] A

---

57. Fox, *Proverbs 10–31*, 688.

similar conclusion can be drawn in relation to 22:4. The sages believe this, however, not simply because of their confidence in an act-consequence moral mechanism at work in the cosmos. The statement of 21:21 (and 22:4 too) is more subtle and sophisticated than that, at least when understood in terms of virtue ethics.

The riches and honor mentioned in these verses are external goods, the possession of which to some degree contributes to "life"—what one might gloss in both verses as a full or thriving existence. Exercising wisdom's virtues for Proverbs is both beneficial and praiseworthy. What must be understood, however, is how goods like riches and recognition by others fit together with other goods to contribute to a more fundamental good, the "end" of human flourishing. Those who attain a full Practical Wisdom—who rightly understand the nature and role of external goods in human well-being, who are guided by virtue in the pursuit and enjoyment of such goods, and who know how to embody virtue on behalf of others—such people are in the prerequisite position to genuinely flourish. Such a position must remain "prerequisite," since even for such wise and just people full flourishing cannot be guaranteed given humans' vulnerability to misfortunes—whether disease, injury, or the viciousness of others (cf. chap. 3).

Nonetheless, verses like Proverbs 21:21 and 22:4 do seem to imply that, unlike those who misconstrue the worth of external goods and pursue them excessively and even unjustly (cf. the sinners of 1:10–19), the virtuous in some sense *deserve*—in social-ethical terms—such external goods. What is implicit here and in much of Proverbs' discourse is an effort at a symbolic and ideological inversion of the ways social and economic goods are typically distributed and how this distribution is justified. Even if the wicked or greedy, because they are rich or powerful, may in "real life" be those who often enjoy significant economic wealth and social status, this is not how it should be (cf. conclusion). It is the wise and just who ought to receive and control such goods, not simply as rewards for their virtue but because they understand the real worth of such things and how appropriately to pursue them. They possess the Practical Wisdom necessary to know how such goods (and the quest to attain them) might contribute to, and at times frustrate, their own and others' pursuit of abundant "life."[58]

Although the workings of practical virtue and especially the virtue of Practical Wisdom are key concerns for Proverbs, the exercise of neither is imagined by the sages as always and everywhere completely effective. Thus, it is to the limitations of practical (moral) reasoning in Proverbs that we now turn.

---

58. Most translations and commentators, like the NRSV above, omit the second mention of justice (צְדָקָה) in the second half of Prov. 21:21, judging it an instance of dittography with the word in the first half.

9

The Efficacy and Limitations of Practical Wisdom in Proverbs

In the previous chapter, I demonstrated that Proverbs exhibits a relatively full notion of Practical Wisdom and discussed why this is so important for the virtue-oriented work that Proverbs seems to be. However, the book does not insist that the exercise of such practical reasoning—whether the workings of practical and intellectual virtue or a full Practical Wisdom—will always be 100 percent effective in leading moral agents to their desired ends. Not only does Proverbs raise questions about the efficacy of Practical Wisdom, it also fails to provide readers with a clear picture of moral exemplars whose lives reflect a full Practical Wisdom. This last fact constitutes a significant lacuna in the book's virtue-oriented moral discourse since traditions of virtue ethics highly prize such models for the character formation of moral novices. It is to these two limitations of Proverbs' depiction of Practical Wisdom that we now turn.

The Limits of Practical Virtue and Practical Virtue's Efficacy

Proverbs obviously prizes practical (moral) reasoning but does not claim it will always be effective in leading moral agents to their desired ends. Proverbs

11:14, 20:18, and 24:6 (cf. 15:22), for instance, all extol the need for and efficacy of planning and counsel in preparation for war.¹

> Where there is no guidance, a nation falls,
>> but in an abundance of counselors there is victory. (11:14 NRSV modified)

> Plans are established by taking advice;
>> wage war by following wise guidance. (20:18)

> For by wise guidance you can wage your war,
>> and in abundance of counselors there is victory. (24:6)

Since explicit moral language is absent in these lines—there is no talk of the wise or just, the wicked or foolish, justice or evil, or ends that contribute to thriving—these texts are best viewed as speaking of the exercise of practical and intellectual virtue (cf. 16:22; 20:5), not Practical Wisdom. The "*wise guidance*" of 20:18 and 24:6, like the simple "guidance" of 11:14 in the above NRSV translations, renders an unmodified תַּחְבֻּלוֹת, a term that Fox says is best conceived as a sort of "design" or "plan." It is the fruit of a person's intellectual and practical virtue that might be formulated for good or bad purposes.² The exercise of practical-intellectual virtue, to which these verses allude, is imagined as regularly efficacious in the waging of war. Yet as Proverbs 19:21 and 21:31 (cf. 16:1) make clear, such beneficial outcomes are not guaranteed.

> The human mind may devise many plans,
>> but it is the purpose of the LORD that will be established. (19:21)

> The horse is made ready for the day of battle,
>> but the victory belongs to the LORD. (21:31)

That these verses are also concerned with practical virtue and not a full moral Practical Wisdom is again evident from the absence of an explicitly ethical terminology. For example, 19:21 speaks only of the plans of a "human mind" (לֶב־אִישׁ) instead of something more morally charged—such as the plans of the just (12:5), the plans of an evil person (or "evil plans"; 15:26), or even the plans of the diligent (21:5). Though potentially (and perhaps typically) effective, the fruits of human practical and intellectual virtue are

---

1. The book's concern with war plans provides further evidence for its androcentric nature, since in ancient West Asian cultures the practice of warfare was typically an exclusively male pursuit. See Smith, *Poetic Heroes*, 76; cf. conclusion below.

2. Fox, *Proverbs 1–9*, 37. The term, as Fox puts it, is "ethically neutral."

ultimately subject to the divine will. As Fox says, "However many plans" a person may conceive, "they may be overridden by a single decision of God."[3]

The limited efficacy of practical virtue is probably also alluded to in Proverbs 14:12 and 16:25. But the rhetoric of these identical verses is ambiguous and might be understood in more than one way.

> There is a way that seems right to a person [אִישׁ],
> but its end is the way to death. (author's translation)

The most straightforward understanding of the line might be as follows: even what seems to be the best exercise of human practical virtue might not, for unpredictable reasons, yield the hoped-for outcomes but instead may produce something quite different. This understanding of the verse is possible. However, the moral language of the "way" and of something that is "upright" or "straight" suggests that the lines are speaking not of practical virtue but of the Practical Wisdom of a virtuous person that is typically but not inevitably efficacious. Still, the agent who strives to discern a correct way in the texts is described in morally generic terms as simply a (male) person: אִישׁ. This person is not characterized further as virtuous; he is not described as wise or just—the sort of person who, because of his rightly formed character, would genuinely be able to reason effectively about the good ends to strategically pursue in various contexts.

If Proverbs 14:12 and 16:25 are not concerned with a virtuous person's Practical Wisdom, perhaps the generic "man" of which the lines speak is better imagined as the corrigible and enkratic-like (or akratic-like) person who obliquely surfaces throughout Proverbs—neither entirely and reliably wise and just, nor hopelessly wicked and foolish (chap. 6). If so, because such a person's character is not *fully* settled as virtuous, that person's practical moral reasoning abilities may not be as persistently reliable as the judgments of the fully wise and just person. Although such an enkratic person may make a sincere effort to consider the good end of a particular situation and how best to promote it, his less-than-fully-formed character may lead him astray on some matters. What he thought was a good way forward in some contexts turns out to be a deadly wrong way.

The Limits of Practical Wisdom's Efficacy

It may not prove surprising that for Proverbs the exercise of practical virtue and the efforts at genuine practical moral reasoning by less-than-fully virtuous

---

3. Fox, *Proverbs 10–31*, 658.

agents are not always or uniformly efficacious. What is more intriguing, however, is that even what appears to be the exercise of a robust Practical Wisdom by virtuous agents in Proverbs likewise may not be always reliable. Like practical virtue, Practical Wisdom for the sages remains in some sense always subject to the sometimes-mysterious divine will. Proverbs 21:30, for instance, says,

> No wisdom, no understanding, no counsel,
> can avail against [לְנֶגֶד] the Lord. (21:30)

Some translations and commentators take the line to be referring to wise (i.e., shrewd and intelligent) plans that are inimical to the divine. As Fox somewhat hyperbolically states, "This verse is universally understood among scholars to refer to wisdom *hostile* to God."[4] Proverbs certainly knows that humans might set their intellect in opposition to the deity, as when people blame the Lord for the bad outcomes that result from their own flawed character and decisions.

> One's own folly leads to ruin,
> yet the heart rages against the Lord. (19:3)

The sages likewise understand that few people are *completely* immune from vicious thoughts and acts.

> Who can say, "I have made my heart clean;
> I am pure from my sin"? (20:9)

However, in Proverbs 21:30, as Fox notes (and Whybray before him), the expression לְנֶגֶד does not actually mean "against" but "before" or "opposite" in a spatial sense (Whybray: "face to face"). However, it also "can mean 'before' mentally, as in Habakkuk 1:3. . . . The phrase in the present verse is thus equivalent to 'in your sight.'"[5] It does not, as Van Leeuwen says, "merely have in view wisdom that opposes God." Instead, "its purpose is simply to contrast human wisdom, whether good or bad with God's."[6] Still, the piling up of key wisdom terminology in Proverbs 21:30—wisdom, understanding, counsel—points not simply to any kind of human knowledge but most fully to the ethical wisdom much of the rest of the book valorizes; it suggests that the "wisdom" in question in the verse is a full "moral" Practical Wisdom. The verse consequently

---

4. Fox, *Proverbs 10–31*, 693. For this sort of view, see Longman, *Proverbs*, 400. Others plainly do not adopt such a position: cf., e.g., Whybray, *Proverbs*, 317; and Van Leeuwen, "Book of Proverbs," 195.
5. Fox, *Proverbs 10–31*, 693; Whybray, *Proverbs*, 317.
6. Van Leeuwen, "Book of Proverbs," 195.

The Efficacy and Limitations of Practical Wisdom in Proverbs

highlights the limits of human intellectual and practical virtue, generally speaking; it also points to the limits and subordinate status of even the wisest and most just person's exercise of practical moral reasoning vis-à-vis the divine.

Consequently, for Proverbs any exercise and articulation of a person's Practical Wisdom ought to be characterized by a deep humility that is not unrelated to that central religious virtue in Proverbs, "fear of the Lord"—awe in the presence of that being who not only may punish and bring catastrophe but whose own wisdom does not always or precisely correspond to even the best practical reasoning of the best persons. Yet, if "all our steps are ordered by the LORD," the sages rightly query, "how then can we understand our own ways?" (20:24). The answer to that rhetorical question is, we can't. At least not in absolute terms.

Despite Proverbs' concern to remind its addressees that even the soundest practical moral reasoning must not be simplistically identified with the divine will, none of the lines just discussed censures people's efforts to reason in practical fashion out of their (good) characters, a practice of regular concern in Proverbs. Instead, these verses point to the ultimate inscrutability of the divine and the ultimately unpredictable nature of human existence. They also reiterate that Proverbs' picture of wise and just moral agents is an ethical ideal. Both the mysterious ways of God and (limited) human moral capacities might impact human efforts to discern which paths are good to follow in a multitude of challenging and changing situations. Besides demanding humility about the efficacy of one's own wisdom, such realities also mean people should be open to revising their own moral reasoning and conclusions when necessary and appropriate, a matter we will return to in the conclusion. As we have already seen, practically wise people in Proverbs know not only how to reason rationally through their good character and in light of good ends; they also know when to be silent and accept the counsel of others.

A final saying in the second half of Proverbs is also worth discussing when considering how the book articulates a concern with practical moral reasoning and its limits. It is also a verse that introduces the question of the role of moral exemplars for the sages. Proverbs 14:16 says,

> A wise person is diffident [יָרֵא] and turns aside from evil,
> but a dolt becomes angry and falls.[7]
> חָכָם יָרֵא וְסָר מֵרָע וּכְסִיל מִתְעַבֵּר וּבוֹטֵחַ

---

7. Author's translation. The final two words of Prov. 14:16 are difficult to make sense of and are rendered variously by commentators. The above translation takes מִתְעַבֵּר as the *hithpael* of עבר II, which seems to mean "to become angry," though the etymology of the root is not clear. בוֹטֵחַ is reckoned as the masculine singular participle not of בטח I ("trust") but of בטח II ("fall down").

The line's clear and full moral rhetoric (e.g., the wise person, an "evil person" [or misfortune, רָע]) suggests much. First, like other lines discussed in Proverbs 10–29, it probably means the verse is not designed primarily to be performed orally to illumine different specific situations in distinct ways. Its robust moral rhetoric would permit little more than heavy-handed moralizing in such moments. If performed, the saying's general sentiment would be appropriate to almost any context in which the speaker believed the listener should not take a particular course of action.

Significantly, however, the line's pronounced ethical terminology articulates something like a general moral principle or warrant. The first stich says what a person of wise character typically does—and why—in contexts that demand action or decision. Such a person "turns aside from evil" because she "fears" (יָרֵא)—likely an abbreviated expression not for timidity but for cultivation of the moral-religious virtue of fear of the Lord (*pace* NJPS's "diffident" and NRSV's "cautious"). Indeed, as Proverbs 16:6b says with rhetoric very similar to 14:16a, "By the fear of the LORD one avoids evil [וּבְיִרְאַת יְהוָה סוּר מֵרָע]."[8] This fear of the divine—alluded to in shorthand in 14:16—underscores the fundamentally virtuous character of the practically wise person. His moral disposition allows him to use his intellect to determine good ends and appropriate courses of action in different moments. In the case of 14:16a, an otherwise unspecified "evil" situation is recognized, and a simple strategy to avoid it (turning aside) is enacted.

Proverbs 14:16, however, is helpfully read alongside Proverbs 22:3:

> The clever see danger and hide;
> but the simple go on, and suffer for it. (22:3)
> עָרוּם רָאָה רָעָה וְיִסָּתֵר וּפְתָיִים עָבְרוּ וְנֶעֱנָשׁוּ

While Proverbs 14:16 is concerned with Practical Wisdom, Proverbs 22:3 seems to be more narrowly concerned with practical virtue. Notice first that 22:3 does not deploy the same robust level of moral rhetoric as 14:16. The first part of the line speaks only of the enkratic clever person (עָרוּם) who sees (רָאָה) danger or a bad situation (רָעָה) and hides (וְיִסָּתֵר, *ketiv*). By contrast, 14:16a alludes to the wise person (חָכָם) who fears (יָרֵא) and so turns aside (וְסָר)—a term associated with the "way" throughout Proverbs—from evil (מֵרָע). What is more, the second half of 14:16 is concerned with the dolt

---

8. For fear of the Lord and "turning aside from evil," see further Prov. 3:7 and cf. 4:27; 8:13; 14:27; 16:7; as well as Job 1:1. Commentators are, however, divided on whether יָרֵא in 14:16 is a way to express "fear of the Lord." Fox (*Proverbs 10–31*, 578–79) and Schipper (*Proverbs 1–15*, 475) do not take it as such; Longman (*Proverbs*, 301–2) and Waltke (*Proverbs*, 595) do.

(כְּסִיל)—a well-known moral type in Proverbs, whose character is well described as akratic-like, though such a person is sometimes corrigible (chap. 6). In Proverbs 14:16 the dolt's untutored angry emotions (מִתְעַבֵּר) get the best of him, causing him to fall—a further image in the line related to the moral metaphor of the way. By contrast, the probably young simpletons (פְּתָיִים) of 22:3b, likely because they are inexperienced and do not know any better, "cross over" (עָבְרוּ)—presumably toward the danger of which the first half of the verse speaks. They subsequently "suffer," given that they have not developed the slightest bit of practical virtue that would otherwise afford them minimal protection, as it does the clever person in the first half of the line, who at least knows to hide in the face of danger.

The difference between the wise person and the clever person in Proverbs 14:16 and 22:3 is a subtle disparity in their practical reasoning abilities, which itself may be a function of their respective virtuous or enkratic moral dispositions. The wise person's "turning aside" from evil (14:16a) is a considered course of action; it can be thought to emanate from her fully developed "wise" character. By contrast, the clever person in the first half of 22:3 is not explicitly described as following the way of a virtuous agent. Instead, he is said only momentarily, and shrewdly, to protect himself from a harmful situation by hiding. This is obviously a better course of action than the simple person's thoughtless encounter with harm in 22:3b. Yet, one might well wonder if, in the same situation, the practical rationality of fully wise persons would have led them to conclude, as did the clever person, that ensconcing was the best and most appropriate way forward. It may well have, especially given that the enkratic-like clever person in Proverbs typically chooses to follow wise paths (chap. 6). But it is also possible that the Practical Wisdom of a fully virtuous agent may have led to a different response to the danger from which the עָרוּם in 22:3 hides. Indeed, the virtuous person will know that there are moments when danger is appropriately confronted. The person of Practical Wisdom will understand when this is the better course of action, rather than shrewd avoidance of a situation. She will know when, for example, a virtue like courage is called for and how she should best "cross over" to aptly address a potentially harmful situation.

The Necessity and Absence of Moral Exemplars in Proverbs

Like most of the other lines in Proverbs 10–29 that allude to a virtuous person's practical moral reasoning, Proverbs 14:16 also—and rather obviously—offers readers only very limited information about the context of the virtuous person's exercise of Practical Wisdom. Especially when read in conjunction with texts like Proverbs 22:3, this verse and others like it beg certain questions. For example, one might wonder: To what extent does a practically wise person, in any particular situation that demands decision or action, actually pause for considered reflection on the best ends to pursue and how best to pursue them? Does such a person engage in a full, conscious form of deliberation, or does he "just act" in more immediate fashion and, because of his settled good character, can be counted on to do so appropriately?

Proverbs hardly provides answers to such questions. However, as Annas explains, for Aristotle it sometimes seems that a "virtuous agent" in fact "has to work out what to do before deciding to do it." Yet, at other points, Aristotle suggests that a "fully virtuous person embodies such harmony of thought and feeling that she does not have to work out what to do: she is immediately sensitive to it." For Annas the ambiguity in Aristotle's position can best be resolved, first, by recognizing that *a virtuous learner* might well need to puzzle out appropriate responses to situations he might face, whereas the intellect and affect of *the fully virtuous* person enables her to respond more immediately to circumstances. But more than this, Aristotle also understood that "problems" for practical reasoning are sometimes not a function of the agent's abilities but are "created by bad or inadequate information, uncertainties, [and] difficulties in interpreting empirical aspects of situations." Hence, even a fully virtuous person at any particular moment "may have a lot of problem-solving and working out to do." Still, the "*phronimos*," or authentically, practically wise person, is the one who is "best at deliberating" and will importantly "have the right framework within in which" a host of factors impinging on decision and action might be judged.[9]

Besides such theoretical matters regarding the workings of practical moral reasoning in different sorts of agents, a reader of Proverbs 14:16 might also wonder about other more basic questions. For example, what situations or persons in real life might be regarded as רַע ("evil") and hence require "fear" to engage well and appropriately? How and toward what, exactly, does one turn aside in such situations? And who, in real life, is the "wise person" who does this?

If reflection on and performance of sayings from Proverbs 10–29 can produce Practical Wisdom in a person, as some suggest, this moral development could arise only partially, slowly, and very cerebrally. As we noted, however, for virtue-oriented moral discourses the actual process of "making" a wise person—for example, by training a person's desires—comes not merely

---

9. Annas, *Morality of Happiness*, 91.

through reading about wisdom in a book. For Proverbs the role of reproof as well as discipline and punishment—מוּסָר—is also needed to train individuals to choose the "right way." Yet for traditions of character ethics, it seems that even textual study, together with real practices of rebuke and discipline, is not necessarily sufficient for the formation of moral character. What is also foundational for the cultivation of virtue in most people are habitually undertaken moral practices carried out in emulation of moral exemplars whose "ways" of life have some narrative shape by which their estimable character—their authentic Practical Wisdom—can actually be discerned. Consequently, if Proverbs is to be considered a virtue-oriented moral discourse, it is important to ask whether and how the book conceives of the role of moral exemplars in a person's ability to advance in a life of wisdom.

As we saw in chapter 4, Proverbs is fundamentally interested in moral agents and their characters. These agents' ways of life result in a kind of "profile of virtue" of wise and just people whose dispositions readers of the book would do well to imitate. (Similarly, the ways of negatively characterized moral agents result in a profile of vice that Proverbs' audience should shun.) The profile of virtue that percolates up through the book's thirty-one chapters includes such character traits as righteousness or justice, diligence, faithfulness, self-control, and kindness to the poor. Proverbs is clear that the book's audience should imitate parents, teachers, and others who possess such traits. As the instructing voice of Proverbs 23:26 says,

> My child, give me your heart,
>   and let your eyes observe my ways.

Proverbs 13:20 and 15:31 make similar points:

> Whoever walks with the wise becomes wise,
>   but the companion of fools suffers harm. (13:20)

> The ear that heeds wholesome admonition
>   will lodge among the wise. (15:31)

However, even these lines, which allude to the examples of virtuous people that might be followed, do not say much about how the wise and just deliberate and choose to act in specific moments and under various conditions of "real life." One might thus continue to wonder, How can a person follow the examples of these wise and just literary figures when the text has no real narrative arc or texture? Without accounts of virtuous people's virtuous conduct in concrete contexts—stories by which their typical habits and modes of being can be reckoned both as imitable and worthy of emulation—one might think the book's profiles of virtue are incomplete. The poem extolling the Woman of Valor in Proverbs 31:10–31 constitutes perhaps the fullest account of a virtuous life that readers might emulate. However, as we shall see in the conclusion, that poem's celebration of a virtuous *woman* presents special problems for Proverbs' *male* addressees.[10] If critical reflection on Proverbs' sentence sayings—imagining when and how they might well be performed—is a valuable but insufficient method for a hearer/reader of the book to progress much in a full sort of Practical Wisdom, so too the book's literary shape is not adequate to that task.

Brown, even as he suggests that study of the short sayings of Proverbs 10–29 contributes to Practical Wisdom, knows well that "Proverbs is not, generically speaking a narrative" that might reveal more fully the habits and modes of being of the book's virtuous characters. Nonetheless, in *Wisdom's Wonder* he seeks to identify something like a metanarrative shape to Proverbs. The simple youth the book addresses in early chapters "moves out from the household to the Grand Central Stations of urban life," until finally "in the last chapter of the book"—with "the profile of the 'woman of strength'" and her husband (31:10–31)—a "narrative-like resolution" to the story of this character's moral formation is offered. For Brown, "the book of Proverbs began with a silent son," and after chapters and chapters of instruction, "it ends with an adult male who has successfully fulfilled these responsibilities by marrying well and finding his place among the elders."[11]

Although the sort of narrative arc Brown discovers in Proverbs is certainly conceivable and has proven compelling to some, it is not a particularly obvious feature of the text. The seams and breaks in the anthology are more prominent than the youth-to-adult story to which Brown points. Anne Stewart, who also attempts to understand Proverbs as a book of virtue ethics, finds no narrative plot in Proverbs. In fact, she wishes more fundamentally to question the important place notions of narrative and "narrative rationality" play in the virtue-ethics systems of thinkers like Stanley Hauerwas and MacIntyre (cf. introduction). She contends that "both narrative and non-narrative modes [of rationality] have integrity as means to view the moral life" and that the

---

10. The vignette that describes the violent, robbing sinners that opens the book in 1:10–19 (cf. chap. 4 above) is a similar, quite limited story of what constitutes vicious behavior. The actions of a virtuous person are not much articulated in those lines. Instead, the presumably young and simple addressee ("my child") is forcefully but simply instructed to avoid the ways of the vicious.

11. Brown, *Wisdom's Wonder*, 64–65. Brown nonetheless recognizes that the patriarchal nature of the text and its vision of the developing male requires feminist and cultural critique of the text. See the conclusion below for an exploration of the warrants Proverbs itself offers for engaging in such critique.

book of Proverbs "provides a non-narrative way of articulating character . . . revealed in discrete moments and particular situations."[12] Although Stewart concedes that such a view of Proverbs ultimately means the book's moral vision "bears some resemblance to a rule-based ethic that privileges acts, not character," she insists that the emphasis in Proverbs nonetheless remains, as in virtue-oriented discourses, "on the quality of the agent rather than the act itself."[13]

Despite Stewart's compelling argumentation and elegant analysis of Proverbs, most virtue ethicists will probably continue to insist on the key role that narrative and narrative rationality play in conceptualizing and revealing the more or less virtuous or vicious lives of humans. It may thus be better simply to concede that, although one can discern clusters of virtues that wise and just people possess and that the text's addressees should seek to acquire and embody, Proverbs' lack of narrative discourse means it ultimately does not paint an adequate picture of moral exemplars a person might emulate to truly cultivate and advance in virtue and Practical Wisdom.

Importantly, the sort of overarching narrative structure to Proverbs that Brown describes in *Wisdom's Wonder* is a somewhat different response to the problem posed by the book's nonnarrative shape to a virtue-ethics analysis of the text than what he offers in earlier work. In *Character in Crisis*, not unlike Stewart, Brown points to the fact that despite the central place narrative holds for character ethics, it nonetheless has real space and place for other sorts of discourse. As Brown notes, "There are countless factors and diverse 'genres' that can make moral conduct intelligible and shape the capacity for intentional actions."[14] Quoting Hauerwas, Brown aptly remarks, "Though moral principles are not sufficient in themselves for our moral existence, neither are stories sufficient if they do not generate principles that are morally significant."[15] Annas would surely agree, for in speaking of the multifaceted nature of virtue-ethics discourses, she says, "Moral progress is too complex and involves too much of an agent's personality to be guaranteed merely by adopting one form of [ethical] reasoning rather than another."[16]

It may be, then, that more than any effort to discern a metanarrative shape to Proverbs, Brown's earlier view represents a more compelling, if partial,

---

12. Stewart, *Poetic Ethics in Proverbs*, 206–7.
13. Stewart, *Poetic Ethics in Proverbs*, 213.
14. Brown, *Character in Crisis*, 18. Among others, Ansberry also identifies a kind of literary shape to the book. See his *Be Wise, My Son*. Cf. the discussion in Stewart, *Poetic Ethics in Proverbs*, 210–11.
15. Brown, *Character in Crisis*, 19; Hauerwas, "Self as Story," 89.
16. Annas, *Morality of Happiness*, 108.

response to the problem that Proverbs' nonnarrative literary shape poses for reading the book as a virtue-oriented discourse. If it remains certain that narrative rationality and the narrative shape of the lives of moral exemplars constitute important features of many virtue-oriented ethical reflection, it is not essential (as Stewart, Brown, and others sense) for a moral discourse to appear in a narrative form—and through that form to reveal the contours of moral agents' character over time—for that discourse to be judged "virtue oriented." There is warrant in calling even a nonnarrative work a virtue-ethics discourse if a sufficient number of other character-ethics features can be identified—like those discussed above in relation to Proverbs (e.g., a particular understanding of anthropology, a concern with human happiness, the privileging of agents over acts, the importance of training desire, the prioritizing of the virtues of sociality and Practical Wisdom). What is more, as I shall suggest further in chapter 11, for a moral discourse to count as a virtue-oriented work, it need not reduce all other normative concepts to virtues and vices; instead, one only needs to indicate plausibly how in that discourse other normative concepts can be explained in terms of character ethics and how virtue itself ought not to be subordinated to some other ethical notion.

Still, the question remains: If Proverbs lacks a narrative shape, where shall the moral exemplars so critical to actual virtue acquisition be found by its readers/hearers? The answer is simple: in the world outside of the text. Proverbs presupposes that in the social world of its addressees there exist real and adequate moral exemplars, the narrative arc of whose lives reveal their "ways" to be wise and just. These "extratextual" figures are moral exemplars the book's addressees must seek out, and perhaps apprentice themselves to, to advance in a full Practical Wisdom and thereby augment their chances at attaining the genuine well-being a life of virtue enables.

In the end, despite all the ways the literary text of Proverbs represents virtue-oriented moral teaching that might contribute to the formation of its audience's character, readers and hearers of Proverbs would never have been able to transform themselves into the sort of independent, rational, moral animals (MacIntyre) the text imagines humans might become (cf. chap. 3) only through study of the book's "discourse."[17] To truly advance in Practical Wisdom—to know when to hide from danger and when to courageously confront it, to understand how and why to act with justice or kindness, or to comprehend in what contexts to utter wise words or remain quiet—Proverbs' addressees will need to lift their eyes from the pages of that book and learn from the lives of real wise and just individuals.

17. Cf. MacIntyre, *Dependent Rational Animals*.

It is now time to rest my case that the book of Proverbs can profitably be read via character-ethics hermeneutics and that to a large extent it actually constitutes an ancient virtue-oriented moral discourse. What remains to be done is to consider some implications of reading and understanding Proverbs this way for broader questions in the study of Proverbs, including the relation of the book's teachings to other moral discourses in the Bible (chap. 10 below), the manner in which the book's ethics are related to its creation theology (chaps. 11–12), and how Proverbs' wisdom is understood as the sort of moral tradition readers are invited to take up, revise, and expand (chaps. 13–14; conclusion). These are the tasks of part 2.

PART 2

The Implications of Proverbs as Virtue-Oriented Moral Discourse

10

Proverbs' Virtue Ethics beyond Proverbs?

The Shared Moral Discourse of Proverbs and Amos

If Proverbs is, to a significant extent, a virtue-oriented moral discourse, one might wonder just how widespread its character-focused moral vision may have been in ancient Israel and Judah. This is an especially apt question if one agrees with John Barton that the Hebrew Bible presents primarily a "deontological rather than a virtue-based ethic," or if one recognizes with Hava Tirosh-Samuelson that, despite much in the Scriptures that resonates with classical virtue traditions, "the Bible . . . is usually adduced as an example of deontological ethics, whose major modern exponent was Immanuel Kant."[1]

Two matters with long, complex histories in the modern study of Proverbs help answer the query about the reach of Proverbs' virtue-oriented teaching in the biblical epoch. The first has to do with the nature and extent of the influence of a book like Proverbs on other moral discourses in the Hebrew

---

This chapter is an expanded and revised version of Timothy J. Sandoval, "Prophetic and Proverbial Justice: Amos, Proverbs, and Intertextuality," in *Second Wave Intertextuality and the Hebrew Bible*, edited by Marianne Grohman and Hyun Chul Paul Kim, RBS 93 (Atlanta: SBL Press, 2019), 131–51.

1. Barton, *Understanding Old Testament Ethics*, 70; Tirosh-Samuelson, "Virtue and Happiness," 711.

Bible. The second matter has to do with the possible existence and character of "schools" in ancient Israel and Judah, since such institutions may well have been a primary mechanism by which the moral discourse of Proverbs might have come to impact other biblical literature.

In this chapter I focus on the question of wisdom's influence on or relation to the prophetic book of Amos. My contention is that although Amos and other parts of the Bible might best be described as theistic, deontological discourse—focusing on obedience to the commands of a legitimate authority (in this case, a prophet and the God for whom that prophet claims to speak)—the underlying moral vision of the book of Amos (and perhaps other books) may have emerged from its composers' contact with, perhaps in an ancient educational context, the "character ethics" of a text like Proverbs.

Proverbs and Amos

In an erudite 2014 article, John McLaughlin revisits a question over which more than a few Hebrew Bible scholars have puzzled: Did the prophet Amos belong to the circle of the wise?[2] As McLaughlin explains, the thesis that Amos belonged to the wise was first robustly argued by Hans Walter Wolff in his short book, *Amos' geistige Heimat*, though he was anticipated in this endeavor by Samuel Terrien.[3] These scholars identify what they believe to be features of Amos and wisdom literature that suggest a relationship between the two.[4] Both Terrien and Wolff contend that Amos's words and thoughts in some sense belong to or borrow from the social-historical context of those early clan leaders whose oral, wise notions and rhetoric came to be enshrined in books like Job and especially Proverbs.

McLaughlin's article systematically reviews the main arguments put forward by Terrien and Wolff regarding the geographical links between Amos

---

2. McLaughlin, "Is Amos (Still) among the Wise?"
3. Terrien, "Amos and Wisdom"; Wolff, *Amos' geistige Heimat*, translated as *Amos the Prophet*. Many of Wolff's claims about Amos and wisdom are also in his *Joel and Amos*. Subsequent studies on Amos and wisdom include Crenshaw, "Influence of the Wise"; and Soggin, "Amos and Wisdom." Scholarly investigations of wisdom's impact on prophetic works in the twentieth century are usually traced back to Fichtner's "Jesaja unter den Weisen," translated as "Isaiah among the Wise." Wisdom influence has often been detected in other biblical works as well. See Crenshaw, "Method in Determining Wisdom Influence." Sheppard (*Wisdom as a Hermeneutical Construct*) argues wisdom scribes redacted much of the Hebrew Bible.
4. A number of scholars have recently questioned the coherency of the concept of a "wisdom tradition," focusing instead on questions of genre classification, literacy, text production, and education in the ancient world. See Sneed, *Was There a Wisdom Tradition?*; and Kynes, *Obituary for "Wisdom Literature."*

and wisdom traditions, the presence of wisdom forms in Amos, wisdom terminology that the prophet employs, and wisdom ideas in Amos that suggest sapiential influence on the prophet—and then deems them unconvincing. Here I do not explicitly defend either Terrien and Wolff or McLaughlin regarding the influence of wisdom circles on Amos. Rather, in order to demonstrate that the underlying moral vision of the book of Amos (and perhaps other biblical texts) may well have emerged via contact with a virtue-oriented moral discourse like Proverbs, I reframe the way relations between wisdom books and the text of Amos have been posed. Because the modernist, critical terminology of "influence" has become problematic in light of contemporary discussions of (inter)textuality, I build on a set of ideas and critical terms developed by Mikhail M. Bakhtin (and his interpreters) having to do with authors, discourse, and intertextuality to demonstrate a relationship between the books of Amos and the wisdom book of Proverbs in particular. Via this Bakhtinian orientation, I suggest that the distinct utterances or discourses of Amos and Proverbs are related to each other, especially in regard to their articulation of a moral-theological vision in which justice rhetoric plays a key role. I contend that the ethical vision of each book draws on a broad, shared moral discourse that each text accentuates and inflects in its own ways, toward its own particular rhetorical ends and in its own distinct social-historical context. But more than this, I suggest that we can make warranted historical claims about the character of educational institutions in ancient Israel and Judah that may well have mediated the shared moral-social vision that Amos and Proverbs take up in their own ways. It should subsequently also be possible to offer sketches of potential real historical relations between Amos and Proverbs. I conclude that it is conceivable that Amos was, in fact, influenced by a wisdom work like Proverbs; but the opposite is also possible: that Proverbs was actually influenced by Amos. In either case, the way that one understands "influence" shifts significantly from the way Terrien, Wolff, and McLaughlin have understood it.

The "Influence" of Terrien, Wolff, and McLaughlin

The arguments Terrien and Wolff present regarding Amos's relatedness to wisdom or the wise are often complex and are largely offered as responses to the critical orthodoxy of the mid-twentieth century about the provenance of Amos's thought and language. At that time, the background to the prophet's ethical-religious outlook was generally believed to be in covenant or cultic-legal traditions and social circles.⁵ If a relation between Amos and Proverbs existed, it was thought that the eighth-century prophet influenced the wisdom book, which was regularly dated to the Second Temple period. Terrien, however, entertains the thought that instead of the early book of Amos influencing a historically subsequent Proverbs, perhaps early wisdom circles and traditions influenced the prophet.

Wolff makes similar claims. His arguments about the influence of wisdom circles on Amos, however, are significantly more thoroughgoing and polemical than Terrien's. Wolff is more concerned than Terrien to upend the thesis that Amos belonged to covenant-oriented, cultic-legal circles. Like Terrien, however, Wolff assumes a late date for the book of Proverbs and suggests that Amos belonged to or was influenced by the early oral wisdom traditions of Israelite clan life, which was apparently discernible in later wisdom texts like Proverbs. Neither Terrien nor Wolff, however, say much about the method by which one might discern early clan wisdom in the literary expression of texts like Proverbs, which in the form that we have them surely were produced and transmitted in a somewhat later period by learned urban scribes who were likely associated with Israel's and Judah's central institutions of court and temple.⁶

Few commentators wholly accept Terrien's and Wolff's claims, though some occasionally affirm aspects of their arguments.⁷ Others, like McLaughlin, are less receptive, viewing the connections that Terrien and Wolff identify between Amos and wisdom works as tenuous, superficial, and often too general (i.e., belonging too broadly to Amos's social-historical context) to warrant the claim that the prophet belonged to circles of the wise or that early clan wisdom directly influenced his words.

Terrien and Wolff try to identify in Amos the possible sites and sorts of wisdom "influence"—genres, terms, ideas, and so forth—that could have been derived or taken over from wisdom circles and thought. On the first two pages of McLaughlin's article critiquing Terrien's and Wolff's position, the term "influence" appears twelve times (including the abstract)—a textual tick that gestures toward the modernist theoretical terms upon which all these scholars explore questions of the literary and ideological relations between Amos and wisdom. On this understanding of textual relations, authors (here Amos) intentionally cite or otherwise clearly allude to the works of other authors/

---

5. Terrien, "Amos and Wisdom," 113; and Wolff, *Amos the Prophet*, 1–5.

6. A version of this methodological problem continues in Proverbs studies in the debate over whether the origin of the sentence sayings of Prov. 10–29 "was the scribal school or village life." See Fox, *Proverbs 1–9*, 7. Cf. chap. 8 above.

7. See Crenshaw, "Influence of the Wise," 51.

sources and so can be said to be substantively influenced by them. I suggested in part 1 that the virtue-oriented nature of Proverbs' moral discourse has not been clearly recognized because the book has so often been evaluated via the lenses of modern ethical systems (chap. 1). It may be that the wisdom work's relation to a prophetic text like Amos has been misapprehended because of analogous commitments to modern theoretical presuppositions about how texts can be best said to relate to one another.

Influence and Intertextuality

Though the term "intertextuality" is now widely employed in a range of academic disciplines, including biblical studies, it is variously used. It can function as a simple gloss to describe the modernist quest to discover the influence of one text/author upon another. That sort of intertextuality discerns a precise literary "source" for one author's text in the work of another author, or in less explicit fashion, it describes the way one text alludes to or echoes another.[8] Such a view is quintessentially modern in that it presupposes self-contained subjects as authors who embed intended meanings in texts that unproblematically refer to things beyond the literary work. Such texts and authors can thus sometimes be thought purposely and substantively to influence each other.

The chief debates in this way of understanding relations between authors/texts are methodological. As Jay Clayton and Eric Rothstein explain, scholars investigating the influence of one text on another regularly worry about "how to discriminate genuine influences from commonplace images, techniques, or ideas that could be found in almost any writer of a given period."[9] Unless there is explicit acknowledgment in one text (by one author) of influence by another text (author), or a critic finds something close to a verbatim citation of one text in a second text, disputes over influence are inevitable and interminable. Where one critic of a work claims influence and hears allusion to a second text, another critic will insist that any similarity is due not to the influence of one author/text on another but, for example, to a common context or shared world of ideas.

This is precisely how the debate about wisdom's influence on Amos takes shape. As Soggin says in his own contribution to the question, "The problem ... seems to me to be one of method: if a wisdom text and a non-wisdom text use the same idiom, does it automatically follow that the latter has been

---

8. Cf. Clayton and Rothstein, "Figures in the Corpus."
9. Clayton and Rothstein, "Figures in the Corpus," 5.

influenced by wisdom?"[10] Indeed, Wolff does not see in the author/text of Amos sufficient evidence to conclude that the prophet was directly or substantively influenced by cultic-legal thinking and rhetoric, as others suspect. Instead, he discerns a substantive and clear influence of wisdom ideas and rhetoric on Amos. Yet others, including McLaughlin, reject this argument, claiming that the commonalities between the two discourses can be explained otherwise, admitting at most that Amos and wisdom works might have shared a common cultural background.

On the typical modernist understandings of influence upon which Terrien and Wolff carry out their project (and upon which McLaughlin engages their work), there is little to quibble with in McLaughlin's critique. McLaughlin is right—or at least it's hard to say that Wolff and Terrien unambiguously demonstrate that Amos belonged among the wise. Yet one might wonder why Terrien and Wolff discern a relationship between Amos and wisdom works in the first place, especially since their efforts to demonstrate this relationship seem to have failed, rather spectacularly so according to McLaughlin. I suspect Terrien's and Wolff's deep familiarity with the language, forms, and ideologies of a wide range of biblical books—including Proverbs—triggered their exegetical instincts regarding a relation of influence between Amos and the wise, even if they were unable to prove it on the modernist theoretical terms available to them.

Yet it may be that other theoretical tools can be employed to rehabilitate and revise their thesis. Perhaps other notions of intertextuality, which move beyond questions of "influence," can reframe questions and arguments about the relations between books like Amos and Proverbs. If so, we may be in a position to see how even a deontologically oriented discourse like the book of Amos is intimately related to the character ethics of Proverbs.

Textuality and Intertextuality

Rather than focusing on sources and influence, contemporary discussions of intertextuality often involve thoroughgoing claims about textuality in general, thereby shifting considerably the discussion of intertextuality itself. Robust postmodern articulations of (inter)textuality that insist on inevitable relations between texts are usually associated with such theoretical heavyweights as Julia Kristeva, Jacques Derrida, Roland Barthes, and others.[11] Deriving from

---

10. Soggin, "Amos and Wisdom," 122.
11. Key texts include but are hardly limited to Kristeva, "Word, Dialogue, and Novel"; Barthes, *Writing Degree Zero*; Barthes, "Death of the Author"; Barthes, *S/Z*; and Derrida, *Of Grammatology*.

Kristeva's encounter with Bakhtin's work and poststructuralist critiques of Saussurean linguistics, the conception of (inter)textuality that emerges recognizes that, as signified slides under signifier, authors vanish into sites of discourse, multiplicity of meaning bursts the bonds of simple claims about reference and truth, and all texts are revealed to be intertextually related to all other texts. As Simon Dentith puts it, "This version of intertextuality seeks to do away with our common-sense ideas of authors and texts and replace them with a sense of the underlying productiveness of writing itself; from the perspective of 'textuality' any actual text is merely a particular density among a myriad [of] codes or discourses, whose origins cannot be traced and which stretch to the horizon in all directions."[12]

Despite these claims about intertextuality from the world of critical theory, modernist, diachronically oriented critics may continue to see the influence of one author or text on another—Amos intentionally alluding to or echoing wisdom teaching, for instance. As Dentith explains, "There is nothing wrong with this kind of criticism" for explaining relations between works "except that it does not go nearly far enough."[13] By contrast, synchronically minded, postmodern intertextual critics might simply insist theoretically on the inevitable intertextual relationship between Amos's language and the rhetoric of wisdom works and then identify some of the available intertexts. Regardless of any demonstrable, direct, historical relationship between wise clan elders (or the book of Proverbs) and Amos, according to this model all that is really necessary to identify and warrant claims of intertextual relations between Amos and wisdom traditions is a reader who points to them.

However, for many critics the "high theory" notions of intertextuality articulated by Kristeva, Barthes, and others turn out to be not all that helpful for practical study of literary works. As Clayton and Rothstein say in relation to Barthes's views in particular, such theories "do not provide the critic with a particularly effective tool for analyzing literary texts."[14] Wielding this sort of critical instrument alone, one doesn't learn much about specific works and the relation between texts except that they are (inevitably) intertextually related and can be said *not* to mean what one might have, in an earlier epoch, thought their authors intended them to mean. Historically minded biblical scholars might reach the conclusion (warranted or not) that such intertextual work shows a lack of rigor in a critic's textual analysis; or they might suspect a renunciation of any concerns with history and the history

12. Dentith, *Bakhtinian Thought*, 95.
13. Dentith, *Bakhtinian Thought*, 95.
14. Clayton and Rothstein, "Figures in the Corpus," 22–23.

of texts—whether or not good arguments for skepticism about different historical projects and diachronic relations between literary products are articulated.[15] In short, for some this version of intertextuality grants too little theoretical space for recognizing real, material, social actors, whose subjectivity and texts may not be as unified and coherent as once thought, but whose utterances are nonetheless articulated in specific social and historical contexts that matter.

It will not do, however, simply to refuse the postmodern and return cheerfully to modernist views and practices of interpretation and the "intertextual" search for sources and influences. One can't unring the bell of poststructuralism or undo the announcement of inevitable textual relations. How, then, to proceed with a notion of intertextuality that is both useful for understanding specific works and relations between them and which has learned—or at least has been critically informed by—the lessons of Derrida, Kristeva, and Barthes regarding textuality?

One way forward is to (re)turn to Bakhtin.[16] In articulating a foundational notion of intertextuality, Kristeva draws on and famously alters aspects of Bakhtin's musings by wedding them to French poststructuralism.[17] Indeed, as Dentith (among others) notes, Kristeva's work is focused differently than Bakhtin's. The criticism of the modernist or "the 'classic realist' text" associated with Kristeva and French poststructuralism is largely epistemological; it is concerned "to show the impossibility of the 'truth-speaking' authorial voice escaping the same deconstructive considerations which afflict all language."[18] By contrast, Dentith observes that for Bakhtin the "deconstruction of the apparent unities of authorship, or the apparent obviousness of reference is always towards the heterogeneity of the historical process, and never towards the paradoxes that can be generated by considering epistemology in the abstract."[19]

In a Bakhtinian mode of reflection, real authors are not superfluous, no mere useful fictions or stand-ins for the intersection of various discourses. However, an "author's intentions" are "always refracted through one or more historically specific languages" that a writer activates by engaging other dis-

---

15. Cf. Sommer, "Exegesis, Allusion and Intertextuality."
16. I say "(re)turn" to Bakhtin as Bakhtin's oeuvre largely appeared prior to that of the critical theorists already noted. Culler suggests another way forward: limiting intertextual relations to those emerging from logical and pragmatic presuppositions in a text. See Culler, *Pursuit of Signs*, 100–118. Cf. Clayton and Rothstein, "Figures in the Corpus," 24–25.
17. Cf. Dentith, *Bakhtinian Thought*, 95–98; and Clayton and Rothstein, "Figures in the Corpus," 17–21.
18. Dentith, *Bakhtinian Thought*, 94.
19. Dentith, *Bakhtinian Thought*, 95.

courses that are also historically and socially situated.[20] For a Bakhtinian perspective on intertextual relationships, heteroglossia (the different varieties of any single language—regional dialects, class inflections, etc.) and polyphony (the multiple points of views and perspectives of others that are already present in any[one's] utterance) are key concepts. As Bakhtin explains,

> At any given moment, languages of various epochs and periods of socio-ideological life cohabit with one another. . . . At any given moment of its historical existence, language is heteroglot from top to bottom: it represents the co-existence of socio-ideological contradictions between the present and the past, between differing epochs of the past, between different socio-ideological groups in the present, between tendencies, schools, circles and so forth, all given a bodily form. . . . Therefore, languages do not exclude each other, but rather intersect with each other in many different ways.[21]

Superficially, such a Bakhtinian understanding of relations between discourses might sound less "postmodern" and more fully (and ironically) as if it has not moved too far from notions of textual "influence" or shared cultural background that critics of an earlier generation (like Wolff and Terrien) and others still use today to describe relations between texts.

However, both the resonances with and the distinctions between Bakhtin and typical modernist and postmodern approaches to intertextuality are significant. On the one hand, a Bakhtinian perspective regarding relations between texts "radically transforms the question of sources, making them a matter not of individual influences or borrowing but of the socially located languages that each and every text manages in its own particular way."[22] Different authors/texts (sometimes struggling against other voices) accent or inflect already-at-hand, socially marked languages in ways appropriate to each one's particular rhetorical ends. "Dialogue" (or dialogism or the dialogic), not influence, thus best describes the nature of relations between texts. Bakhtin writes:

> Each word tastes of the context and contexts in which it has lived its socially charged life. . . . The word in language is half someone else's. It becomes one's "own" only when the speaker populates it with his own intentions, his own accent, when he appropriates the word, adapting it to his own semantic and expressive intention. Prior to this moment of appropriation, the word does not exist in a neutral and impersonal language . . . but rather it exists in other

20. Dentith, *Bakhtinian Thought*, 91–92.
21. Bakhtin, *Dialogic Imagination*, 291.
22. Dentith, *Bakhtinian Thought*, 95.

people's mouths, in other people's contexts, serving other people's intentions; it is from there that one must take the word, and make it one's own.[23]

On the other hand, Bakhtin's insistence upon the particularity of such social-historical language also refuses an interminable slide into intertextuality (at least provisionally) and instead warrants efforts to speak of the historical and social conditions, contexts, and institutions associated with particular discourses.[24] Bakhtin points not to "the unstoppable indeterminacy of 'textuality'" but to an irrepressible dialogism, moments in the history of which criticism can gesture:

> There is neither a first nor a last word and there are no limits to the dialogic context (it extends into the boundless past and boundless future). Even *past* meanings, that is those born in the dialogue of past centuries, can never be stable (finalized, ended once and for all)—they will always change (be renewed) in the process of subsequent, future development of the dialogue. At any moment in the development of the dialogue there are immense, boundless masses of forgotten contextual meanings, but at certain moments of the dialogue's subsequent development along the way they are recalled and invigorated in renewed form (in a new context).[25]

The Discourse of Justice in Proverbs and Amos

As noted earlier, Wolff was concerned to demonstrate the influence of early clan wisdom on Amos in a variety of ways. His argument regarding geographical connections is the most speculative part of his case and thus the least compelling. In light of Bakhtinian notions of texts and their relations, however, the relations Wolff suggests between Amos and wisdom in regard to literary forms, terminology, and especially motifs merit further consideration.

Wolff dedicates nearly eight pages of his little book on Amos and wisdom to exploring the specific motif and language of justice and righteousness (including fair marketplace practices); he adds an additional five pages analyzing other themes that also belong to the biblical discourse of justice—concern for the "poor and needy" and the censuring of "an extravagant life."[26] Given what we have seen to be Proverbs' priority on social virtue (cf. chaps. 2 and 7), all this suggests that the best chance of a productive reconsideration of

23. Bakhtin, *Dialogic Imagination*, 293–94.
24. Dentith, *Bakhtinian Thought*, 95.
25. Bakhtin, *Speech Genres*, 170 (emphasis original).
26. Wolff, *Amos the Prophet*, 70–75.

Proverbs' Virtue Ethics beyond Proverbs?

the relations between Amos and Proverbs is through a review of each text's moral rhetoric of social justice.

To demonstrate that Amos was influenced by the wise, Wolff points especially to the pairing of the important words "justice" and "righteousness" in Amos (three times) and the appearance of "justice" by itself on one further occasion.

> Ah, you that turn justice [מִשְׁפָּט] to wormwood,
> and bring righteousness [צְדָקָה] to the ground! (Amos 5:7)

> But let justice [מִשְׁפָּט] roll down like waters,
> and righteousness [צְדָקָה] like an ever-flowing stream. (5:24)

> But you have turned justice [מִשְׁפָּט] into poison
> and the fruit of righteousness [צְדָקָה] into wormwood. (6:12bc)

> Hate evil and love good,
> and establish justice [מִשְׁפָּט] in the gate. (5:15a)

Wolff believes that the justice and righteousness rhetoric of Amos 5:15 appears within a "wisdom type of exhortation speech," while in 6:12 it is expressed within a "wisdom didactic question."[27] However, he is most concerned to point out that Amos's terminology of justice and righteousness appears not only in wisdom forms but is a rhetoric frequently attested throughout wisdom books. Though Wolff cites only Proverbs 16:8, the term צְדָקָה appears eighteen times (צֶדֶק = nine times) in Proverbs, while מִשְׁפָּט occurs twenty times. In Proverbs 1:3, 2:9, 8:20, 16:8, and 21:3, the terms appear together (מִשְׁפָּט with either צֶדֶק or צְדָקָה). In Proverbs 18:5, 21:15, and 31:9, forms of the two roots (e.g., צַדִּיק, "the just person")—if not both the substantives "justice" and "righteousness"—also appear together.[28]

Wolff likewise thinks Amos's concern for honest weights, measures, and balances was influenced by early wisdom's similar concerns, as preserved in Proverbs. While the oppressors in Amos 8:5 claim, "We will make the ephah small and the shekel great, and practice deceit with false balances," verses such as Proverbs 11:1 (cf. 16:11; 20:23) insist, "A false balance is an abomination to the LORD, but an accurate weight is his delight."[29] So too for Wolff, wisdom's prioritizing of justice over cultic activity likely shaped the prophet's words.[30]

---

27. Wolff, *Amos the Prophet*, 60.
28. Wolff, *Amos the Prophet*, 62.
29. Wolff, *Amos the Prophet*, 62–63.
30. Wolff, *Amos the Prophet*, 63. On the relation of cult to ethics, cf. Klawans, *Purity, Sacrifice, and the Temple*, esp. chap. 3.

For example, just before calling down justice and righteousness in Amos 5:24, in verses 21–22 the prophet has the Lord proclaim,

> I hate, I despise your festivals,
>   and I take no delight in your solemn assemblies.
> Even though you offer me your burnt offerings and grain offerings,
>   I will not accept them;
> and the offerings of well-being of your fatted animals
>   I will not look upon. (Amos 5:21–22)

Similarly, Proverbs 21:3 (cf. 15:8 and 21:27) states,

> To do righteousness [צְדָקָה] and justice [מִשְׁפָּט]
>   is more acceptable [נִבְחָר] to the LORD than sacrifice. (Prov. 21:3)

Wolff also highlights the concern with the poor and needy in both Amos and wisdom contexts. In Amos, the דַּל (2:7; 4:1; 5:11; 8:6), the אֶבְיוֹן (2:6; 4:1; 5:12; 8:4, 6), and the עָנִי/עֲנָוִים (2:7; 8:4) are all mentioned, sometimes in word pairs (2:7; 4:1; 8:4, 6). Wolff is keen to point out that this same terminology is also regularly found in Proverbs, sometimes also in pairs (e.g., Prov. 14:31; 22:22; 30:14).[31] Finally, Wolff points to both Proverbs' and Amos's warnings against extravagant living.[32] For example, he highlights Amos 2:8, 4:1, 5:11, and 6:6, the last of which rebukes those "who drink wine from bowls, and anoint themselves with the finest oils." Amos's sentiments, Wolff believes, are shared by verses such as Proverbs 21:17 (cf. 23:20–21, discussed with 21:17 in chap. 5), 23:29–35, and 31:4, which warn the reader/hearer against becoming an excessive lover of wine and other fine things.

McLaughlin examines Wolff's arguments and is persuaded that none of them necessarily indicates wisdom influence on the prophet. The features of Amos's justice rhetoric described by Wolff may be traced instead to the influence of biblical legal works, to other prophetic texts, or perhaps to broad literary and ethical traditions in ancient West Asia.[33] There is no unambiguous relation of influence between wisdom and Amos. When it comes to Amos's view of justice, on the modernist terms of the debate sketched above, McLaughlin successfully rebuts Wolff's arguments that Amos was "under the influence" of the wise.

However, on the terms of the distinct, postmodern discourse of intertextuality discussed above, another ironic conclusion is possible. McLaughlin's

---

31. Wolff, *Amos the Prophet*, 70–73.
32. Wolff, *Amos the Prophet*, 74–75.
33. McLaughlin, "Is Amos (Still) among the Wise?," 296–97.

rebuttal of Wolff's claims on the grounds that the supposed wisdom elements of Amos need not be traced only to sapiential texts but also appear in a range of other works points to a robust set of intertextual relationships that Amos has with any number of other texts. In other words, McLaughlin's work reveals that Amos's discourse of justice represents the sort of intertextuality Dentith describes as "a particular density among a myriad [of] codes or discourses, whose origins cannot be traced and which stretch to the horizons in all directions"—whether to the Pentateuch, other prophets, or cognate texts in the world of ancient West Asia.[34]

Amos and Proverbs in Bakhtinian Dialogue

Besides arguing about influence and pointing to signs of (inter)textuality, there is a third way to explore the (intertextual) relations between Amos and Proverbs: the Bakhtinian route that understands dialogic relations between texts to include not only points of agreement or similarity but the ways in which social-historical voices or discourses disagree or struggle with one another, the manner in which each accents a broader historically and socially grounded discourse that authors or speakers find at hand. On modernist terms, such dialogic *differences* between texts like Amos and Proverbs might be regarded as support for the claim that Amos did not substantively fall under the influence of wisdom. For a Bakhtinian mode of intertextual analysis, they clarify the complex nature of the dialogic relations between the works.

Despite similarities between Amos's and Proverbs' justice rhetoric, significant differences between their moral discourses are also evident. Most obvious is the near complete absence in Amos of a central feature of Proverbs' moral rhetoric: its discourse of "two ways," each populated by particular moral types (cf. chap. 4). One path in Proverbs is trod by the wise and righteous (and others aligned with such types); on the second path, one finds the foolish and wicked (and others aligned with those figures). In Amos, none of the three common wisdom terms for the way or path—דֶּרֶךְ, נְתִיבָה, אֹרַח—appears. Wolff identifies only a single term in Amos, employed only once, that might be said to belong to this aspect of Proverbs' moral discourse. But he makes much of it. Although Wolff is correct that "a man can betray what his cultural home is with a single characteristic word," it is not as clear that the single word he identifies in Amos 3:10—נְכֹחָה ("right," "straight")—is so revelatory.[35] Wolff claims that it "occurs frequently in wisdom," but it is attested

34. Dentith, *Bakhtinian Thought*, 95.
35. Wolff, *Amos the Prophet*, 56.

only twice in Proverbs (8:9; 24:26) and once in Sirach (11:21; MS A 11:19), though Wolff believes the word's appearances in Isaiah may also be wisdom contexts (at least 30:10; cf. 26:10; 57:2; 59:14).[36] The term certainly belongs within the frontiers of a wisdom rhetoric of the morally right way—and in Amos 3:10 one can identify other terminology important to wisdom texts—but its isolated appearance in Amos underscores the distinct characters of the two discourses more than wisdom's impact on the prophet.

As we have seen earlier (throughout part 1), terminology derived from roots such as חכם, בין, אול, כסל, צדק, and רשע clearly mark Proverbs' moral discourse.[37] Proverbs' understanding of justice is linked closely to the way of life of certain virtuous and vicious characters described by this rhetoric—the wicked and the just, the foolish and wise. Human subjects are reckoned as just (and wise) or wicked (and foolish) precisely insofar as they embody wisdom's virtues, including the social virtues of justice and righteousness. Together, different verses in Proverbs sketch brief profiles of virtue and vice corresponding to the characters of just and wicked persons. For example, the just are teachable (9:9); they possess a wise practical rationality (10:32; 11:9) that includes the ability to speak both honestly and appropriately at particular moments (10:11, 20, 21, 31; 13:5); and they care well even for nonhuman members of their community (12:10). Their desires and thoughts are also rightly ordered (11:23; 12:5; 15:28), and hence they correctly understand the value of wealth (11:28); they are generous (21:26; 22:9), just toward the poor (29:7), and rightly oriented to the divine (15:29), as well as toward contexts of justice and iniquity—rejoicing in the one (21:15) and abhorring the other (29:27). In short, they are people of integrity (20:7) or Practical Wisdom in that they possess and are consistent in their exercise of a full range of virtues toward good ends.

By contrast, the wicked, who often stand in parallel to the just in Proverbs, are typically characterized in opposite moral terms. They are iniquitous evildoers (5:22; 14:32; 19:28) who don't listen to rebuke (9:7). Their desires are wrongly structured (11:23; 12:12; 21:10), and their (practical) moral reasoning ability is lacking (10:20; 12:5), something evident in their morally problematic utterances (10:6, 11, 32; 11:11; 12:6, 26). They are religiously suspect (15:8–9, 29; 21:27) and full of vice, characterized as cruel (12:10), unreliable (13:7), haughty and proud (21:4), violent (21:7), and merciless (21:10). They don't understand the rights of the poor (29:7) and even take bribes to pervert justice (17:23).

Proverbs, of course, is considerably longer than Amos (with more than three times the number of words), so it would be surprising to discover the

---

36. Wolff, *Amos the Prophet*, 58–59.
37. Terms derived from צדק appear 94 times; רשע, 87 times; חכם, 103 times; בין, 48 times; אול, 42 times; כסל, 51 times.

same terms attested in the same numbers in both books. Yet even when controlling for this difference in length, most of Proverbs' key moral terminology is conspicuously sparse in Amos. The righteous (or just) person (צַדִּיק) appears only twice in Amos (2:6; 5:12; צְדָקָה is attested three times), while the figure of the wicked (רָשָׁע) is completely absent. Words derived from the other roots noted above are likewise not attested. What's more, the emphasis in the prophetic book is not on the quality of a just person's character but on particular subjects who act in particular negative ways against the just (and others). The צַדִּיק in Amos, in other words, is inflected differently than in Proverbs. Such a person is less the morally rotund individual of the wisdom book and more simply an "innocent" person, associated with the "needy" (אֶבְיוֹן), whom others unjustly afflict in the social-economic realm.[38] As Amos 2:6 (cf. 5:12) says, "They [Israel] sell the righteous for silver, and the needy for a pair of sandals."

The moral-theological discourse of Proverbs is distinct from that of Amos in other ways too. The wisdom book's teaching, though variously associated with the divine (e.g., the fear of the Lord) and grounded in creation (3:19–20; 8:22–31), is cast primarily as human teaching—as instructional poems uttered by teachers or parents to children or students or as short sayings that evoke communal, folk wisdom, even if such sayings equally, or ultimately, are the product of a group of urban scribes.[39] By contrast, the book of Amos is cast as the prophet's report of divine visions and messages. The book's superscription speaks of Amos's prophetic "seeing" (חזה), and in 7:12 he is called a "seer" (חֹזֶה), perhaps alluding to the visions recounted elsewhere in the book, which are described with forms of ראה (7:1–9; 8:1–3; 9:1–4). The prophet's own utterances are cast as divine words (כֹּה אָמַר יְהוָה/נְאֻם יְהוָה) against the nations, including Israel (2:6–16, etc.). Such revelatory terms are not absent in Proverbs, but they are rare. Only in Proverbs 29:18 do we find חָזוֹן in the sense of a prophetic vision (though the root with the usual meaning "to see" is more common); נְאֻם appears a single time, introducing Agur's somewhat enigmatic words in Proverbs 30:1.[40]

If there is a central or controlling moral term in Amos's discourse, it is arguably פֶּשַׁע—"transgression"—a word that is not central to Proverbs' ethical rhetoric. The root appears twelve times in Amos and is largely used to connote broad and severe political and social outrages. Most of the "crimes against humanity" in the initial oracles against the nations are described as transgressions,

---

38. Of course, Proverbs deploys צַדִּיק in the sense of "innocent" as well. Cf. 17:26; 18:5.
39. See note 6 above and cf. Sandoval, "Orality of Wisdom Literature," 272–78.
40. On the figure of Agur in Prov. 30, see Fox, *Proverbs 10–31*, 850–62; and Sandoval, "Texts and Intertexts."

as is Israel's social-economic failing (1:3, 6, 9, 11, 13; 2:1, 4, 6; 3:14; 5:12; cf. the two verb forms in 4:4). According to Wolff, all of the nominal forms of פשע appear "in authentic oracles of Amos," except for 1:9, 1:11, and 2:4.[41] The root is hardly unknown in Proverbs, with a nominative form appearing twelve times and a verbal form twice. However, only in Proverbs 18:19, 28:2, and 29:16 are political connotations easily discernible; and only in the last instance (29:16) does the term point to the sort of political or social-economic moral failing that Amos associates with the word. All its other usages in Proverbs suggest a more individualized conception of ethical failure (e.g., Prov. 10:19; 12:13).

Although other differences between Proverbs and Amos might be discerned, enough has been said to illustrate that the broader moral-theological rhetoric of the two books is distinct. These differences, however, do not necessarily imply no intertextual relation between the moral-theological vision of the two works. Rather, they invite further description of the full range of dialogic relations—similarities, agreements, and other points of difference—between the two books.

One obvious way to conceptualize how Amos and Proverbs inflect in unique ways an already-at-hand socially and historically specific moral discourse is to say that Proverbs, as an ancient instruction, and Amos, as prophetic utterance, are directed toward distinct rhetorical situations. Though the precise moral language of "the way" of the just and the wicked, which is so prevalent in Proverbs, is absent in Amos, the underlying vision of justice (and wickedness) in the two books is not unrelated conceptually or in terms of each text's broader moral rhetoric. Through its descriptions of the wicked, the righteous, and their respective modes of life and destinies, Proverbs is concerned to morally form those who are not (yet fully) virtuous, to motivate and train them to follow the paths of wise and just individuals. These latter figures will embody a range of virtues, including social virtues like kindness and generosity toward the poor, fairness in economic practices, and so forth, all of which can be gathered under the sign(s) of righteousness and justice. Amos, by contrast, announces divine judgment on humans whose (wrongly formed) characters and whose lack of social virtue have resulted in them oppressing the poor and dealing deceptively and treacherously with others in the marketplace.

Although Amos doesn't use the word רָשָׁע, his upbraiding of his audience paints them in hues very close to what one finds in the portrait of the wicked (and other travelers of the wrong path) in Proverbs. In their domination of the poor and through their cheating in the market, those whom Amos addresses, like the wicked in Proverbs, have not only failed to walk a path characterized

---

41. Wolff, *Hosea and Amos*, 152.

by social virtue; they also, again like Proverbs' wicked, do not heed the exhortations and rebukes they are offered (Amos 5:4–6, 10, 14–15), are religiously suspect (2:12; 4:4–5; 5:21–25; 8:5), and can easily be characterized as haughty, violent, and merciless (1:3–2:3; 2:7; 3:9–10; 4:1; 5:11; 6:3; 8:4, 6).[42] The wisdom text of Proverbs exhorts readers and hearers to cultivate social virtue, highlighting the value of this wisdom for enabling human well-being.[43] The prophet Amos rails against precisely the absence of justice and righteousness among those in his social world who ought to embody it but don't. Such individuals, instead, anxiously strive to satisfy their own untutored desires for the sorts of goods (like wealth) that the sages believed contribute to, but do not constitute, happiness. In failing to understand the worth of riches in an economy of other goods that support human flourishing, those whom Amos addresses impede others' chances at flourishing, and if Proverbs is right, they surely also frustrate their own chances to authentically thrive as the sort of material, spiritual, rational, and social being the sages reckon humans to be (cf. chap. 3).

Further Points of Dialogic Relation

A few further characteristics of Amos and Proverbs can be added to the data one considers when discerning how the character-ethics discourse of Proverbs and the prophetic preaching of Amos might be in dialogue. Wolff briefly mentions some of these points of connection, and although McLaughlin does not much contest them, they surely could be dismissed on the same modernist terms by which he rejects other suggestions of Amos's dependence on wisdom. Nonetheless, with a Bakhtinian conception of intertextuality, they remain worth considering.

Wolff, for example, notes that Amos condemns certain of his hearers for their extravagant lifestyle. One aspect of this concern that Wolff doesn't emphasize, but which might suggest that the prophetic text stands in a positive dialogic relation with Proverbs, is Amos's characterization of those who pursued such a lifestyle as feeling "at ease" (שַׁאֲנָן) and "secure" (בטח).

> Alas for those who are at ease in Zion,
>   and for those who feel secure on Mount Samaria,
> the notables of the first of the nations,
>   to whom the house of Israel resorts! (Amos 6:1)

---

42. Wolff, *Amos the Prophet*, 44–53.
43. As discussed in chap. 3, the value and desirability of wisdom is expressed primarily via the rhetoric of desirable human goods, whether health and status or especially wealth and sexual gratification. Cf. Sandoval, *Discourse of Wealth and Poverty*, 71–100; Stewart, *Poetic Ethics in Proverbs*, 102–69.

Words formed from the root בטח, "to trust," are fairly common in Proverbs, appearing fourteen times, mostly in contexts that alert readers to dependable and deceptive loci of trust. The Lord (3:5; 28:25; 29:25) and wisdom's virtues (3:23; 10:9; 11:15; cf. 28:26) provide genuine security, while relying too much on one's intellect (לֵב; 28:26) and riches (עֹשֶׁר; 11:28) is suspect. As noted earlier (cf. chaps. 3 and 7), throughout Proverbs the "rich"—like those against whom Amos preaches—are not only merciless, extravagant in their lifestyle, arrogant, and greedy (18:23; 21:17; 22:7; 28:11, 20, 22; cf. 23:20–21, 29–35); they are also people whose trust is misplaced.[44] On the one hand, the advantages or security that riches provide are acknowledged, likened to city fortifications that surely would have adorned places like Samaria and Jerusalem: "The wealth of the rich is their fortress" (10:15; cf. 18:11). On the other hand, the refuge of wealth is described as illusory and stands in contrast with the genuine security Adonai provides:

> In their [rich persons'] imagination it [wealth] is like a high wall. (Prov. 18:11b)[45]

> The name of the LORD is a strong tower;
> the righteous run into it and are safe. (Prov. 18:10)

Proverbs 1:33, however, most fully represents a dialogic relation with Amos 6:1, since the wisdom text employs both of the key terms the prophet uses. For Proverbs 1:33, it is not an apparently secure existence in Zion or Samaria, attained via "a reign of violence" (Amos 6:3), that can ultimately put one at ease or secure well-being. Instead, it is an attainment of wisdom, a life of virtue. As Woman Wisdom herself proclaims:

> Those who listen to me will be secure [בֶּטַח]
> and will live at ease [שַׁאֲנַן], without dread of disaster. (Prov. 1:33)

A further intertextual connection between Amos and Proverbs that Wolff does not emphasize appears in Amos 3:8, where the prophet connects the inevitability of his prophesying the divine word with the dread one might feel upon hearing a lion's roar.

---

44. As Whybray says, "The rich man (ʿāšîr) is always regarded with hostility" in Proverbs. See *Wealth and Poverty*, 63.

45. The expression וּכְחוֹמָה נִשְׂגָּבָה בְּמַשְׂכִּיתוֹ is difficult. For a discussion and a defense of the above sense of the line, see Fox, *Proverbs 10–31*, 1018–19.

> The lion has roared;
> > who will not fear?
> The Lord GOD has spoken;
> > who can but prophesy? (Amos 3:8)

Although Wolff recognizes that "the fear of God" was an "ultimate characteristic of wisdom," he does not believe the prophet was "aware of the theme" among the early wise.[46] Wolff's modernist understanding of the nature and extent of the evidence necessary to establish one text as the source of or source of influence upon another text surely cut short his analysis of this possible point of connection between the prophet and wisdom. The fact that the root ירא appears only once in Amos (3:8), and only to characterize divine speech, was apparently not sufficient evidence for Wolff to claim (or explore) wisdom's influence on the prophet when it came to the motif of fear of the divine.

Yet with a Bakhtinian approach to intertextuality, it may be worth considering more fully a dialogic relationship around the rhetoric of fear and the divine in Amos and Proverbs. Proverbs, for example, twice says (19:12; 20:2) that a king's anger is similar to the "growling of a lion," and Proverbs 24:21–22 exhorts one to "fear the LORD and the king . . . for disaster comes from them suddenly, and who knows the ruin that both can bring?" Such an assertion calls to mind Amos's fearsome announcements of the Lord's "day" (5:18–20), with its severe punishments on Israel (e.g., 1:7–8, 14–15; 2:13–16; 3:14–15; 5:16–17; 9:1–4), and it also evokes Proverbs' confidence that the wicked will face disastrous consequences for their immorality.

Although fear of the Lord in Proverbs entails a pious respect or religiosity, it surely also includes genuine physical-emotional trepidation of the divine as the powerful guarantor of the moral vision the book proffers (cf. chap. 2). As Yoder notes, the concept includes "dread of God's disapproval or punishment."[47] A fearful stance toward a potentially terrifying deity helps motivate the adherence of especially young, moral novices to the book's instruction; it is said to ensure protection from death and security from harm (19:23). By contrast, wrongdoers, those who one might say do not "fear" God, are promised destruction (or something close to this). Throughout Proverbs one reads of the inevitable demise of the wicked and sinners. In 1:18–19 the robbing sinners lose their lives. Elsewhere the wicked will be "cut off from the land" or "rooted out of it" (2:22; cf. 10:30); they will "not go unpunished"

---

46. Wolff, *Amos the Prophet*, 76.
47. C. Yoder, *Proverbs*, 69–71; Yoder makes similar observations about the "real fear" (70) involved in Proverbs' conception of fear of the Lord. Cf. the brief discussion of this topic in chap. 2 above.

(11:21) and will be repaid for their iniquities (11:31), condemned by God (12:2), "overthrown" (12:7), "filled with trouble" (12:21), and so on (cf. 14:32; 15:6; 15:10; 16:4; 18:12; 21:7; 29:1). When Proverbs' concerns for fairness in the marketplace and right treatment of the poor are related to its emphasis on fear of the Lord and to the punishments awaiting the wicked who "fear not," it is not a big step from the wisdom book's moral vision to Amos's proclamation of imminent divine judgment and destruction of Israel for its social-economic misdeeds.

In Bakhtinian terms, all these sorts of rhetorical and conceptual similarities *and differences* between Proverbs' and Amos's moral rhetoric constitute each work's inflection of a historically and socially anchored moral discourse that intersect most obviously in each book's rhetoric of (social) justice. Again, none of this is to suggest that one can prove Proverbs' direct "influence" on Amos along the lines that Wolff and McLaughlin pursue the matter. It is rather to say that the two works stand in Bakhtinian dialogic relation to each other; they thus can appropriately be said to be intertextually linked.

Proverbs as Early Education Text

Still, if one makes certain assumptions about the relative priority of Amos and Proverbs—which book came first—it is possible on a Bakhtinian understanding of intertextuality and the social-historical nature of discourse to speak in a limited sense about the "influence" of one text on another. But not quite in the way Wolff, McLaughlin, and others imagine such influence. As noted above, it is not a matter of determining whether the rhetoric and themes of one text/author reflect the direct and substantive impact of another text/author. It is not even a matter of arguing over what counts as evidence of influence. Rather, if either Proverbs or Amos were demonstrably chronologically prior to the other, it would not be unreasonable to think that the inflections of the moral discourse of the later text might be dialogically *responding* to the accentuations of the moral discourse of the earlier work (and to other socially-historically situated voices too)—whether via contestation, agreement, extension, or some other relation with the earlier text's arguments and rhetoric. If one wishes to call this "influence," then so be it—so long as one also recalls that theoretically this sort of intertextual relation is distinct from the way biblical critics typically have employed the term.

But can we make warranted claims about the relative priority of Amos and Proverbs? Perhaps—but certainly not uncontested ones. The question is complicated by the long and complex redactional histories of both works.

Occasionally, the essential unity and eighth-century-BCE date of most of Amos is asserted, as when John Hayes claims, "Amos's preaching at Bethel probably lasted only a single day at the least and a few days at the most . . . just prior to the fall festival beginning the year 750–749."[48] Hayes eschews complex theories of prophetic schools and redactions and believes "it is easier to assume either that Amos wrote his own words, whether before or after delivering them, or more likely, that they were written down by someone in the audience . . . [for] additions and glosses to the text are minimal."[49] Most often, however, scholars try to discern which passages of the book go back to the prophet or his earliest followers and which are later accretions. Wolff identifies "three eighth-century literary strata, all of which for the most part derive from Amos himself and his contemporary disciples," while "three additional strata can be recognized as later interpretations" emerging in subsequent centuries.[50] Proverbs, by contrast, is self-evidently an anthology of collections of sayings and poems, likely composed at different times and perhaps with later collections joined to early core compilations.[51]

David Carr contends that much of Proverbs is reminiscent of ancient West Asian oral-written educational texts that would have been used for training intellectual and religious elites, including priests, scribes, and others. Students in ancient West Asian educational contexts, he explains, would have memorized and recited or performed large sections of the collections of poems, proverbs, and other material recorded in certain "long-duration" compositions that formed the core of an ancient curriculum.[52] By memorizing and reciting long stretches of a curriculum that included works like Proverbs, students progressed not only in literacy; they were also formed morally through deep engagement with the social-ethical visions of the texts they studied. This work of social-moral enculturation, the "writing on the tablet of the heart" (cf. Prov. 3:3; 7:3), would contribute to the production of moral subjects characterized by the virtues and values prioritized by the works themselves. Given Proverbs' emphasis on social virtue and Practical Wisdom, one would expect the study of such a text to goad individuals into becoming robust practical moral reasoners inclined to practices of justice and righteousness.

Carr suggests that an early version, or core, of Proverbs may have been used early in ancient Israel's educational contexts, analogous to those in other

---

48. J. Hayes, *Amos*, 38.
49. J. Hayes, *Amos*, 39.
50. Wolff, *Joel and Amos*, 107.
51. Cf. Schipper, *Proverbs 1–15*, 923–33.
52. Carr, *Writing on the Tablet of the Heart*, 5 and passim.

ancient West Asian societies, perhaps within the households of master scribes.[53] Like others he dates significant portions of Proverbs to the preexilic period, even if the final form of the Hebrew book was not achieved until the late Persian or Hellenistic epoch.[54] For example, he believes that the Amenemope section of Proverbs likely was included in a Proverbs scroll in the preexilic period; so too Proverbs 25–27, the sayings associated with King Hezekiah. Other proverbs in the second half of the book (chaps. 10:1–22:16) may have formed an even earlier preexilic core to which these already-mentioned sections were appended.[55] Carr more controversially suggests that much of the instructional poetry of Proverbs 1–9 may also be early, preexilic material. For Carr, any dating of the poems based on claims that the length and complexity of their wisdom speculation precludes the possibility that they were composed early is suspect. Such arguments, he avers, may well fall into an evolutionist conceptual error characteristic of some earlier practices of form criticism, where it was thought that short, conceptually straightforward texts are early, while longer, more intellectually complex ones must be later. Carr further notes that the instruction form of the early chapters of Proverbs is based on quite ancient Egyptian prototypes. And although this fact doesn't prove those texts were written early, he is not convinced, as some are, that the language of Proverbs 1–9 is obviously Late Biblical Hebrew (LBH), a point others, like Fox, also concede.[56] Subsequently, for Carr it is likely that an early textual form of much of what would become the book of Proverbs emerged somewhat early during the monarchial period, where it formed part of ancient Israel's, and especially Judah's, educational curriculum.[57]

Because Carr thinks an early version of a fairly full Proverbs scroll may well have been a key educational text in ancient Israel and Judah, he believes that subsequent biblical texts would have been composed by educated individuals who had been morally and literarily formed by the most ancient portions of that wisdom book. Put otherwise, Proverbs at points affected the composition of other biblical books. Carr, for example, contends that portions of

---

53. Carr, *Writing on the Tablet of the Heart*, esp. 19; *Formation of the Hebrew Bible*, esp. 403–31. On the long-contested question of literacy and "schools" in ancient Israel, see Davies, "Were There Schools"; Fox, *Proverbs 1–9*, 6–12; and the bibliographies in both. For Carr's statement on earliest literacy in Israel, see *Formation of the Hebrew Bible*, 355–85.

54. Cf. Carr, *Formation of the Hebrew Bible*, 408–13; Fox, *Proverbs 1–9*, 6, 48–49; and Fox, *Proverbs 10–31*, 499–506.

55. Carr, *Formation of the Hebrew Bible*, 411; Fox believes most of Prov. 10–29 is preexilic but favors a late eighth or early seventh century date for the collections (*Proverbs 10–31*, 505).

56. "The language [of Prov. 1–9] is neither clearly late nor early" (Fox, *Proverbs 1–9*, 48). Carr also rejects C. Yoder's arguments (*Wisdom as a Woman of Substance*, 15–38, esp. 20–21) that Prov. 1–9 is LBH.

57. Carr, *Writing on the Tablet of the Heart*, esp. 403–31.

Deuteronomy and Isaiah depend on wording and expressions derived from Proverbs.[58] If Carr's arguments are on target, Amos (and other prophetic texts) might also reflect the same sort of wisdom "influence." It may have been composed under the impact of an oral-written educational curriculum anchored by an early Proverbs scroll. If so, one other of McLaughlin's critiques of Wolff's arguments could ironically turn out to be not far from the truth—namely, if early wisdom influenced Amos, then all the prophets should be said to fall under wisdom's influence.

Carr's attempts to demonstrate how certain verses in later biblical books show dependence on Proverbs suggest his view of textual relations is similar to that of Wolff, Terrien, and McLaughlin. However, his broader model for understanding the production and use of ancient texts appears to imagine relations between works in a way that is akin to a Bakhtinian perspective. Although Carr does not put it this way, it is as though the authors/tradents of works like Deuteronomy and Isaiah, which he discusses (and possibly Amos, which he doesn't), made use of, as Bakhtin might say, an already-at-hand moral discourse, which (early editions of) Proverbs also inflected and so in part represented. The educated individuals who penned Isaiah and Deuteronomy did not "quote" or directly copy from a Proverbs scroll. Instead, in ways appropriate to their own social-historical contexts and rhetorical needs, they recalled and rearticulated aspects of the educational discourse represented by the oral-written text of an early Proverbs scroll, which already had been "written on the tablet of their hearts."

If Carr is correct in dating large sections of Proverbs to the period of the early monarchy, it is possible to understand Amos, the mid-eighth-century prophet and/or the earliest tradents of the prophet's words, to have engaged Proverbs' wisdom teachings—as Terrien and Wolff, in their own ways, long ago sensed. All that is required for this to be a real possibility is for Amos and/or his earliest tradents to have been the kind of person(s) who would have been literarily and morally trained via deep engagement with an early version of an oral-written Proverbs text. It may be difficult to imagine a humble shepherd from Tekoa as such a person. Yet, as is well known, Amos belonged to the class of נֹקְדִים (perhaps "sheep breeders"; 1:1); and he shares that designation with the king of Moab (2 Kings 3:4), who is said to have delivered to Israel a thousand lambs and the wool of a hundred thousand rams.[59] Based on

---

58. E.g., Isa. 59:7 is dependent on Prov. 1:16, and Deut. 19:14 on Prov. 22:28. See Carr, *Formation of the Hebrew Bible*, 415–25. For other views on Proverbs' relationship to Deuteronomy, see Schipper, *Proverbs 1–15*, 36–39. More generally, on wisdom's relationship to Torah, see Schipper and Teeter, *Wisdom and Torah*.

59. In Amos 7:14, the prophet is called a "herdsman" (בּוֹקֵר).

Ugaritic texts that use the same Semitic root, Hayes also suggests that a sheep breeder like Amos was perhaps "a type of official associated with temple/court service."[60] Although hardly assuredly demonstrated, it could be that Amos was less a simple caretaker of livestock and sycamore trees (7:14) and more a wealthy landowner or an official responsible for livestock associated with the temple/court.[61] These sorts of social and economic identities—if inhabited by Amos—may have meant the prophet had access to the kind of literary-moral education Carr discusses.

Such an argument is similar to but also distinct from Wolff's and Terrien's assertions about how Amos may have come into contact with wisdom traditions. It is, however, not an appeal to the direct impact on Amos of some hypothetical, oral clan wisdom, thought to be preserved in Proverbs; instead, it is an argument based on well-documented, ancient West Asian educational practices, the quite possible early use in Israel of a version of Proverbs as an oral-written educational text, and the likelihood that Amos and his earliest disciples might have been educated through such a text. This view presents one way to negotiate the messy methodological question mentioned above, which Terrien and Wolff never directly address: How can one discern in Amos a wisdom most at home in the scribal wisdom that the book of Proverbs, in the final instance, represents? However, it begs another set of contested questions over the dating of different sections of Proverbs.

Carr's arguments that Proverbs (or an early Proverbs scroll) was a key part of ancient Israel's educational curriculum are largely compelling. Yet there are good reasons to be suspicious of an early preexilic dating of much of Proverbs that would permit us to claim that Amos responds dialogically to a historically earlier wisdom literary tradition. Despite the evidence that Carr marshals for a degree of literacy in earliest Israel, other data suggest it is not all that likely that a significant educational curriculum would have emerged in Israel/Judah much before the second half of the eighth-century BCE.[62]

Arguments against dating much of Proverbs to the early preexilic period are related to debates in Syria-Palestinian or "biblical" archaeology. The so-called minimalists suggest that the archaeological record for early preexilic Israel and Judah does not witness to, for example, the presence of significant monumental architecture that would indicate they would have needed or been able to support a significant scribal apparatus that might have produced and used a complex work like Proverbs. Rather, the material record points to the

60. J. Hayes, *Amos*, 44.
61. See esp. Steiner, *Stockmen from Tekoa, Sycamores from Sheba*.
62. Carr, *Formation of the Hebrew Bible*, 355–85.

eighth (or perhaps late ninth) century BCE as the earliest period for such social formations.[63]

What is more, Bernd Schipper contends that after the Middle Bronze Age, the influence of Egypt and its institutions on the highland culture of the Levant would not have been significant until the second half of the eighth century at the earliest.[64] If so, it is unlikely that the sorts of Egyptian texts Carr believes served as prototypes for the instructional poems of Proverbs 1–9 would have been available or studied at a much earlier preexilic time in places like Shechem (1 Kings 12:25), Tirzah (1 Kings 15:33), Samaria, or Jerusalem—political-religious centers where scribes may have been requisite.

It may be that an early, oral-written version of Proverbs' virtue-oriented moral vision would not have anchored Israel's educational curriculum until closer to the second half of the eighth century. Aspects of Proverbs might thus be said dialogically to engage, or respond to, the moral vision and justice rhetoric of Amos. However, it may be safer to think that both texts emerge at essentially the same moment so that one can't say which "came first." In any case, regardless of relative priority and despite any desire we might have to speak unequivocally of the historical direction of interaction between the discourses of Amos and Proverbs, the two texts stand in intertextual—that is, Bakhtinian dialogical—relationship with each other.[65]

Conclusions

If the prophet Amos and the core collections of his preaching appear roughly at the same time as certain key instructions and collections of Proverbs, then one would be warranted in considering possible historical as well as literary and conceptual relations between the two texts. As we have seen above, in certain respects the moral center of gravity in Amos is distinct from Proverbs, and in other ways the prophetic text resonates with the wisdom work. The two texts represent what might be called a Bakhtinian dialogic relation of difference and congruence. On the one hand, Amos speaks to

---

63. Jamieson-Drake, *Scribes and Schools*. Cf. Davies's critique of Jamieson-Drake in "Were There Schools," 207–9.

64. Schipper, "Egypt and Israel."

65. Carr develops several methodological points that guide his analysis of the relationship of particular verses in Proverbs with other works. It should be possible to apply his criteria in a heuristic way to the question of the relative priority of Amos and Proverbs. My initial informal exploration of the matter affirms, tentatively, the slight priority of an early oral-written core of Proverbs over the prophetic book. However, a definitive answer to the question must await the full analysis of a further study.

a particular moment with a particular urgent rhetoric that is essentially a divine-command moral discourse—"thus says the Lord!" Proverbs, on the other hand, presents a character ethics that focuses on the virtues that will enable individuals to understand well, and rightly pursue, the goods that produce human flourishing and happiness; and such a thriving state for the kind of being Proverbs takes humans to be demanded the robust exercise of other-regarding social virtue. In other words, Proverbs is concerned to morally form precisely the sort of person that Amos so keenly recognizes as absent in and around Samaria in the middle of the eighth century. Those against whom Amos rails and to whom he promises destruction are precisely the sort of wicked and "rich" people that Proverbs also claims will not long live securely in the land.

What this all suggests is that the moral vision of Amos, with its divine commands and unique prophetic, political moral accents, was forged in and through a virtue-oriented moral discourse like Proverbs. The prophet simply gives expression to the core virtues and values of "wisdom" in a rhetorical context distinct from that of the wisdom instruction. One might even say that Amos's moral discourse reflects the sort of Practical Wisdom Proverbs so highly esteems (chaps. 8–9). The prophet was able to size up and speak to his context in a morally appropriate and rhetorically compelling fashion. Unlike the instructing voices in Proverbs, for Amos it would not do to teach the social-political elites in and around Samaria in the mid-eighth century BCE about the value of wisdom or to explain to them how wisdom's virtues allow kings to reign rightly and rulers to decree what is just (Prov. 8:15–16). These figures, by their acts, had already revealed their settled, flawed characters. What then might be left to one, like Amos perhaps, who was trained in the way of wisdom? Perhaps not much more than to avoid becoming a byword to whom a saying like Proverbs 25:26 might be disparagingly applied:

> Like a muddied spring or a polluted fountain
>   are the righteous who give way before the wicked. (Prov. 25:26)

It appears that Amos is not one who yielded to the wicked. In holding his ground, he surely recognized that

> whoever says to the wicked, "You are innocent,"
>   will be cursed by peoples, abhorred by nations;
> but those who rebuke the wicked will have delight,
>   and a good blessing will come upon them. (Prov. 24:24–25)

In all this Amos likely drew on a wisdom tradition like Proverbs, as well as on a range of other moral-religious perspectives and discourses—whether covenant-legal traditions, or West Asian ideologies of kingship and social justice, or something else. The particular intersection of these discourses in and around Samaria in the mid-eighth century BCE, which Amos instantiates, constitutes the preaching of the prophet.

Given the intertextual and ethical relations between Proverbs and Amos and the foundational role an early Proverbs scroll likely played in Israelite/Judahite education, Proverbs again turns out not to be the sort of moral outlier in the Hebrew Bible canon that it has sometimes been taken to be (cf. chap. 1). The virtue-oriented moral discourse of the book can be intimately, though dialogically, related to other biblical discourses, like that of the theistic, deontologically oriented rhetoric of the famous prophet of social justice, Amos.

However, it is here we must leave aside further reflection on the relation of the man from Tekoa with Israel's wisdom tradition, as well as the broader issue of the relation of Proverbs' virtue ethics to other biblical literature. Instead, we turn to an equally vexing matter: the role of personified Woman Wisdom in Proverbs' account of creation and whether the cosmogony of Proverbs 8:22–31 is consonant with the virtue-oriented moral discourse we have suggested is present in much of the rest of the book.

11

A Virtue-Ethics Approach to Cosmogony in Proverbs (Part 1)

Reconsidering the Interpretive History of Natural Law, the Orders of Creation, and Empiricism in Proverbs

In his book *Wisdom's Wonder*, William Brown notes a central unresolved tension in the study of wisdom literature, especially Proverbs—namely the relationship between those who understand the heart of wisdom literature to be about ethics and right (or good) living and those who emphasize the centrality of creation theology in the tradition.[1] Brown proposes to mediate this tension via the category of "wonder." For Brown, "the prominent themes of character and creation pervade" the sages' discourse "in ways that are intended to elicit wonder, and consequently, cultivate wisdom."[2] Brown's erudite work is compelling in many ways. However, I want to attempt to mediate the tension between wisdom as ethics and wisdom's emphasis on creation theology in a related but nonetheless somewhat distinct manner: through a reconsideration of how Proverbs 8:22–31, that famous poem on Woman Wisdom's role in creation, might reflect or undergird, in poetic, pretheoretical, and indeed mythological fashion, a notion of natural law. In so doing I hope to show that Proverbs' cosmologic vision not so much underwrites

---

1. Brown, *Wisdom's Wonder*, 4–5.
2. Brown, *Wisdom's Wonder*, 19.

conceptions of the book's ethics in deontological terms but instead is more fully consonant with understanding it as a virtue-oriented discourse.

When considering Proverbs 8:22–31, scholars interested in the theological and moral worth of Proverbs often invoke some conception of natural law to understand how Woman Wisdom, so clearly associated with Adonai's creation of the world in this passage, relates to those other parts of the book more directly concerned with questions of ethics or conduct.[3] Proverbs 8 suggests to some that the book's moral perspective, as ethicist David VanDrunen notes, "points toward a conception of natural law as natural moral order." Such a view is consonant, VanDrunen says, with "most classical natural law theories," which hold that "the world has a real, objective, and meaningful nature that communicates moral obligations to human beings."[4] However, I want to consider Proverbs 8 and the relationship of ethics to the cosmos not in terms of a "natural moral order" that Proverbs may seem to presume, but instead, as fully as possible, in terms of moral thinking that prioritizes the character of virtuous agents. If this reconsideration is successful, we will have further evidence for how the book of Proverbs represents and is best interpreted as a premodern, virtue-oriented moral discourse.

The notion that for Proverbs "the world has a real, objective, and meaningful nature" that is morally relevant is not difficult to acknowledge in a broad sense. It is consistent, as Charles Taylor notes, with the fact that premodern natural philosophies and worldviews presumed an intrinsically meaningful or "enchanted" cosmos.[5] Or as theologian David Kelsey explains, in affirming the (Christian) doctrine of creation, "one not only claims that the world is intelligible but also implies that one has and cultivates the disposition actively not only to pay attention to it in delight but also to understand it."[6]

What is more difficult to assimilate into a specifically character-ethics reckoning of Proverbs is the claim that the book, and Proverbs 8 in particular, imagines a cosmos that "communicates moral obligations to human beings" and "points toward a conception of natural law as natural moral order." This sort of understanding of Proverbs typically entails the idea that a natural moral order can be discerned in and through the God-created orders or the orderliness of the natural world. As Brown says, wisdom texts recognized

---

3. On the somewhat broader question of "natural theology" in the Bible, including some limited comments on wisdom works, see Barr, *Biblical Faith and Natural Theology*. Collins considers the place of natural theology in the wisdom literature in "Biblical Precedent for Natural Theology."

4. VanDrunen, "Wisdom and the Natural Moral Order," 153–54.

5. Cf. Taylor, *Secular Age*.

6. Kelsey, "Doctrine of Creation," 179.

"that moral conduct was informed and shaped by the world's order and that the world's order, in turn, was established and sustained by right conduct."[7] Indeed, "the ancient sages discerned a natural world that was orderly and hence meaningful and instructive."[8] The cosmos is "comprehensibly didactic."[9]

Others similarly characterize Proverbs' view of the created natural world in relation to its ethics. James Crenshaw claims that for the sort of wisdom tradition Proverbs represents, "God had created the universe orderly, bestowing on that creation the necessary clues to enable humans to assure their continued existence."[10] He says that "Israel's sages seem to have discerned a fundamental order hidden with the universe"[11] and "believed that rules of conduct could be ascertained by careful observation" of God's world, so they "devoted considerable energy to spelling out these rules by which to live."[12] Or, as Arndt Meinhold puts it, "Die theologische Grundlage weisheitlichen Denkens liegt in der Überzeugung, dass der Mensch und die Welt, in die er gehört, ihr Dasein der Schöpfergottheit verdanken und dass der Schöpfung und der Gesellschaft eine Ordnung zugrundeliegt, der sich der Mensch einzufügen hat und die infolgedessen wietgehend erkennbar ist." (The theological basis of wisdom thinking lies in the conviction that humans and the world to which they belong owe their existence to the Creator deity and that creation and society are based on an order to which humans have to submit and which is consequently largely recognizable.)[13]

Raymond Van Leeuwen also points to a kind of natural moral order in Proverbs. He associates the rhetoric of חקק ("cut" or "inscribe") in Proverbs 8:27 (בְּחוּקוֹ) and 8:29 (בְּחוּקוֹ, חֻקּוֹ) with Jeremiah 31:35–37. Subsequently, he suggests somewhat more directly than Brown or Crenshaw that "the stable decrees of nature" point to "the social order and obligations that obtain between Yahweh and Israel." He further says, "For Israel, the order of divine creation set limits and determined the norms for human activity."[14] In alluding to the work of Helmer Ringgren, Bernd Schipper also believes that a play on חקק in Proverbs 8:22–31 "evokes the notion of divine statutes," implying that "God establishes not only the physical boundaries of creation but also the laws governing the world and humanity."[15]

---

7. Brown, *Wisdom's Wonder*, 5.
8. Brown, *Wisdom's Wonder*, 17.
9. Brown, *Wisdom's Wonder*, 17.
10. Crenshaw, *Old Testament Wisdom*, 11.
11. Crenshaw, *Old Testament Wisdom*, 55.
12. Crenshaw, *Old Testament Wisdom*, 82n1.
13. Meinhold, *Die Sprüche*, 1:38.
14. Van Leeuwen, "Book of Proverbs," 94, 97; cf. Loader, *Proverbs 1–9*, 356.
15. Schipper, *Proverbs 1–15*, 311; Ringgren, "חָקַק *ḥāqaq*." Briefer comments of others seem also to regularly gesture toward the notion of a natural moral order in Proverbs. Cf. R.

This rhetoric of obligation—of decrees and laws—would seem to subordinate what we have seen to be Proverbs' broader virtue-oriented moral discourse to deontological moral thought. Indeed, the typical emphasis on the orders of the cosmos that relate creation and ethics in Proverbs places a good deal of stock in the human ability to learn from and articulate social, moral perspectives not in terms of understanding human nature and the virtues that shape the good character of agents pursuing human flourishing but as duties or precepts that ought to be accepted because they are thought to be derived from the divine's well-ordered creation—and so ordained by God. To borrow language from Robert Johnson and Adam Cureton on the work of that preeminent modern deontological thinker, Kant, on this view it is as if human beings for Proverbs "inevitably feel" the moral law "as a constraint on their natural desires, which is why such Laws, as applied to human beings, are imperatives and duties."[16] When discussing "character and creation," Brown approvingly quotes Kant: "Two things fill the mind with ever new and increasing admiration and reverence, the more often and more steadily I reflect upon them: the starry heaven above me and the *moral law* within me."[17]

Natural Law in Proverbs?

When considering natural law in Proverbs or the book's relation of ethics to creation, one can surely affirm in terms of virtue ethics that for Proverbs the created cosmos has a real, objective, and morally meaningful nature. What may need to be jettisoned is the conception that *for Proverbs* the natural, orderly structures of the created world communicate divine obligations and laws for society and individuals—whether or not that be true for other biblical discourses or as a theological-moral claim established on other grounds.

There is no need to dispute that Adonai's setting limits to the primordial waters in Proverbs 8:27–29 is a kind of ordering of the cosmos. Nor need one deny that the rhetoric of חקק in the passage, especially חק in 8:29, "evokes the notion of divine statutes."[18] But the divine "command" here is directed primarily to the primordial waters; *they* must "obey" the boundary God has decreed for them. It is not necessary to insist that the passage primarily and effectively implies that God, in and through creation, establishes not only the physical boundaries and

---

Murphy, *Proverbs*, 266, 277; Dell, *Book of Proverbs in Social and Theological Context*, 128–29; and Davis, "Preserving Virtues," 197.

16. Johnson and Cureton, "Kant's Moral Philosophy."

17. Kant, *Critique of Practical Reason*, 133, cited in Brown, *Wisdom's Wonder*, 5–6 (emphasis added).

18. Schipper, *Proverbs 1–15*, 311.

orderliness of creation but also the precepts or natural laws that should govern and order human society and the lives of individuals. Even the claim in 8:15 that "by me [Wisdom] . . . rulers decree what is just" is, as we noted in chapter 8, an allusion to the Practical Wisdom that ought to characterize the "good governance" of political elites; it is not a claim that any given ruler's precepts are derived from the natural moral order of God's created world.

One can likewise concede that the virtue-oriented moral vision Proverbs promotes relates in some general sense to the divinely determined structure of the cosmos. For example, the regularity of the seasons and the consistent movements of celestial bodies might be said to mirror the integrity of wise and just persons. The reliably good lives of virtuous people can be said to conform to nature's perceived orders and regularities. But this is not the same as saying that the virtuous have learned to be wise and just by discerning obligations and rules from "a natural world that was orderly."[19]

In any case, to say that for Proverbs humans can discern moral and social obligations and precepts from the orderliness of the natural world God created is not to deny that aspects of Proverbs resonate with deontological conceptualizations of ethics. Commands or rules have a place in virtue-oriented moral thought; and obligations and precepts need not always be regarded as arbitrary inventions uttered by authoritative law givers. They can also be formulated through reflection on the good habits and estimable conduct of wise and just people whose ways of life consistently contribute to their own and others' well-being: "To be good, just, and happy . . . , do X and don't do Y." Given this and in light of Proverbs' concern with creation, it is possible to discover in the book a limited articulation of a kind of "natural moral law." But this natural law is distinct from the concept of natural law that depends on claims that humans derive moral obligations from a consideration of the structures or orderliness of creation.

Although one can legitimately concede some conception of natural law in Proverbs and acknowledge the presence of deontological rhetoric in the book, this is no reason to abandon prioritizing the virtue-oriented nature of Proverbs' moral discourse in one's analysis of the book. As Rosalind Hursthouse and Glen Pettigrove explain, "A virtue ethical account need not attempt to reduce *all* other normative concepts to virtues and vices. What is required is simply (i) that virtue is *not* reduced to some other normative concept that is taken to be more fundamental and (ii) that some other normative concepts *are* explained in terms of virtue and vice."[20] A (re)consideration of "natural

19. Brown, *Wisdom's Wonder*, 17.
20. Hursthouse and Pettigrove, "Virtue Ethics," 22 (emphasis original).

law and Proverbs"—or the relation of ethics to creation in the book—that begins from a robust virtue-ethics orientation will thus insist that the right place to focus is not on what are usually regarded as the observed, empirically known orders of the natural world and how moral obligations of humans derive from and conform to them; instead, focus should be on questions about what sort of being humans are naturally thought to be in the book, what constellation of goods contributes to their final end of flourishing, and what virtues need to be exercised to attain and rightly order those goods necessary for the happiness of that particular part of God's creation called humanity. Premodern reflections on natural law in fact tend to be intimately related to virtue-oriented moral discourses that are concerned with such matters. As Ronald Garet suggests, premodern "natural law" theory most fundamentally associates and develops "claims about the ordering of basic social relations with claims about *human nature*."[21] This focus on human nature is evident in the reflections of that preeminent natural law thinker, Thomas Aquinas. As Mark Murphy explains, for Aquinas natural law has much to do with the practical rationality of the human creature:

> The precepts of the natural law are binding by nature: no beings could share our human nature yet fail to be bound by the precepts of the natural law. This is so because these precepts direct us toward the good as such and various particular goods (ST IaIIae 94, 2). The good and goods provide reasons for us rational beings to act, to pursue the good and these particular goods. As good is what is perfective of us given the natures that we have (ST Ia 5, 1), the good and these various goods have their status as such naturally. It is sufficient for certain things to be good that we have the natures that we have; it is in virtue of our common human nature that the good for us is what it is.
>
> ... [Human knowledge of the natural law] is exhibited in our intrinsic directedness toward the various goods that the natural law enjoins us to pursue, and we can make this implicit awareness explicit and propositional through reflection on practice.[22]

Although different conceptions of natural law vary in important ways, Murphy further explains that the social and moral claims of this sort of thinking might be reckoned in either derivationist or inclinationist terms. With "derivationism" humans "can derive from a metaphysical study of human nature and its potentialities and actualizations the conclusion that certain

---

21. Garet, "Natural Law and Creation Stories," 218 (emphasis added).
22. M. Murphy, "Natural Law Tradition," §1.2.

things are good for human beings, and thus that the primary precepts of the natural law bid us to pursue these things." By contrast, with "inclinationism" a person's "explicit grasp of the fundamental goods follows upon but is not derived from one's persistent directedness toward the pursuit of certain ends, which directedness involves an implicit grasp of these items as good." If "human beings exhibit a tendency to pursue life, and knowledge, and friendship, and so forth," then "reflection on this tendency occasions an immediate grasp of the truth that life, and knowledge, and friendship, and so forth are goods."[23]

Inclinationism and derivationism, however, are not mutually exclusive. Murphy continues:

> It may well be that one way of knowing can supplement and correct the other. There may be some goods that are easier to recognize when taking the speculative point of view, the point of view of the observer of human nature and its potentialities, and some that are easier to recognize when taking the practical point of view, the point of view of the actively engaged in human life.[24]

Indeed, in Proverbs both modes of reflection are likely operative, though the inclinationist view probably dominates since the sages both understand humans to be quite naturally directed toward things like wealth, social recognition, and sex, and they recognize these as "good" for the sort of creatures we are.[25]

Order in Proverbs?

That scholarship on wisdom literature has been (pre)occupied with the idea of order is well known. Decades ago Roland Murphy named "order" as one of the "assured results" of wisdom scholarship, even as he (along with a few others) contested the centrality of the notion in wisdom books (and hence the scholarly conclusion about its centrality).[26] For Murphy, such scholarly claims

---

23. M. Murphy, "Natural Law Tradition," §2.2.
24. M. Murphy, "Natural Law Tradition," §2.2.
25. Yet the central role God and personified Wisdom play in Proverbs' moral discourse also suggests a place for derivationist rational operations. Humans are seen to derive their being and their ability "to know" from the divine realm—from the creator God and primordial Wisdom. They thus naturally do well to pursue, with reverence and awe, those goods whose worth is consonant with the characters of those metaphysical realities in the book—Adonai and Wisdom—which constitute the center of value for humans. Indeed, we saw above (chap. 2) that the paths of wise and just people in Proverbs are intimately related to an understanding of Adonai's "way" or character.
26. R. Murphy, "Wisdom—Theses and Hypotheses," 35. See, too, Westermann's criticism in *Wurzeln der Weisheit*. Cf. the helpful overview of the debate by Loader, *Proverbs 1–9*, 19–28, as well as the discussion and bibliography noted in Fox, "World Order and Maʿat."

about wisdom and order were a "modern reconstruction," based largely on "an over-reliance upon the parallelism between Egyptian *Maat*," regarded as a cosmic principle of order, "and Hebrew *ḥokmâ*."[27] More recently, Fox has called into question the correctness of the idea of *ma'at* as world order. He concludes that without the "crooked parallel" of *ma'at* (understood as world order) to a conception of wisdom in Proverbs, the robust place the idea of order has in Proverbs scholarship would never have arisen.[28]

Still, despite these protests, the notion that God's creation in Proverbs—especially in 8:22–31—is an orderly one that "establishes not only the physical boundaries of creation but also the laws governing the world and humanity"[29] is so commonplace in Proverbs studies that it may seem fundamentally wrongheaded to question it. One reason it is so widespread is because it is not completely wrong. Though surely sometimes overplayed by scholars, the concept of "order" is not nonexistent or unimportant in Proverbs. In Proverbs 8:22–31 creation is in fact characterized by a kind of order and orderliness; the deity forms the known world by constructing a series of limits or boundaries for the primordial waters out of which the cosmos takes shapes. Likewise, the centrality of social virtue in the book points to the importance of an appropriately organized or ordered society that places restraints and obligations on social actors (cf. chaps. 2 and 7). The question we are concerned with, however, has to do with the relationship of the first sort of order *in creation* to the second sort of *social or moral* order. Does Proverbs suggest that the relationship between the orderliness of creation (the "statute" or limit decreed by God for watery chaos [חֻקּוֹ, 8:29]) and the moral order is one in which ethical obligations and precepts for humans (statutes [חֻקּוֹת]) are derived from the natural world so that the book reflects a conception of natural law as natural moral order (as discussed above)? Does Proverbs intimate that the deity offers binding moral obligations and rules through creation in ways that mean what appears to be Proverbs' virtue-oriented moral discourse should actually be interpreted in deontological terms?

I do not think it does. Later Jewish works draw significant connections between Wisdom and its relation to an ordered cosmos, on the one hand, and divine law, whether Torah or an esoteric moral law, on the other, in ways that

---

27. R. Murphy, "Wisdom—Theses and Hypotheses," 41n4. However, Murphy accepts that ascribing to wisdom works a search for order might be "correct" (ibid.); cf. Loader, *Proverbs 1–9*, 20.

28. Fox, "World Order and Ma'at," 47–48. Schipper (*Proverbs 1–15*, 13–14 and passim) offers a brief sketch of *ma'at* in Egyptian wisdom thought as both "educative" (offering "instructions for life") and as "cosmotheistic knowledge" ("knowledge of how the universe functions"). Cf. Assman, *Ma'at*.

29. Schipper, *Proverbs 1–15*, 311; see also Ringgren, "חָקַק *ḥāqaq*."

indicate those discourses do consider the cosmos not merely to be ordered but also to entail a natural moral order. Sirach famously associates cosmic personified Wisdom with Torah (e.g., Sir. 24). And because, as Christine Hayes says, "wisdom was identified with law on the one hand and creation on the other, it served as a bridge for the transference of properties between the two and in both directions."[30] A work like 1 Enoch, too, facilitates a "transference of properties" between a conception of divine law, creation, and wisdom. This text speaks of things like the progressions of seasons and the regular movements of heavenly bodies as the natural world's obedience to the deity's commands that they "behave" in such fashion (e.g., 1 En. 41:5–6; 18:15–16; 21:1–10). The obedience of aspects of creation to the divine's decrees can subsequently serve as a foil to denounce human failure to follow God's commands, conformity to which can also be reckoned as wisdom, as in 1 Enoch 2:1–2 and 5:2–4. As Hayes similarly contends, "1 Enoch's explicit characterization of the laws of nature as divine decrees facilitates an even more radical transference of legal attributes to the realm of the created order than is found in Sirach's 'torah-fication' of wisdom."[31]

All these sorts of later associations of divine law with the orderliness and "obedience" of nature, especially with a w/Wisdom that is also related to the natural world, can result in a notion of the cosmos as not only well ordered but as holding a discernible natural moral order, a kind of natural law.[32] The various relations between Torah, Wisdom, and nature or creation that some texts draw constitute early Judaism's varied and complex efforts to come to terms in the Hellenistic epoch with the relation of Torah to Greek notions of natural law. Although, as Hayes explains, the idea of a natural moral order of creation is already evident in Heraclitus's (535–475 BCE) linking of "a universal reason or *logos* that govern[s] the unified cosmos ... to law," a full notion of natural law (as natural moral order) does not fully develop in the Greco-Roman world until later.[33] It was only after the Stoics' notion of the cosmos's "rational order" (*logos*) gained intellectual traction across the Hellenistic world that Jews reflected on the relation of Torah to Greek ideas of natural law, which is "unwritten, universal, eternal,

---

30. C. Hayes, *What's Divine about Divine Law?*, 97. However, C. Hayes also says, although for Sirach "both the cosmic order and the Torah are separately identified with Wisdom (in the sense of correlation rather than strict logical identity), the two are not *directly* identified with one another. The realm of law is not *directly* identified with the realm of creation, and the law is not a comprehensive cosmic law but the particular Torah of Israel" (ibid., emphasis original).

31. C. Hayes, *What's Divine about Divine Law?*, 99.

32. C. Hayes discusses other texts that work in analogous fashions—e.g., Jubilees and certain Qumran scrolls, especially 1QS. See *What's Divine about Divine Law?*, 101–5.

33. C. Hayes, *What's Divine about Divine Law?*, 55.

and unchanging."[34] Proverbs does, of course, imagine wisdom in terms of ethics, with Wisdom existing in an ordered cosmos. It does not, however, make the same conceptual links as some early Jewish works—for example, the ideas of the natural world as obedient to divine commands or w/Wisdom directly associated with Law/Torah. It is best, then, not to interpret (probably anachronistically) chapter 8's understanding of the relation of ethics to creation—Wisdom to cosmos—in the natural-law-leaning direction of later works.

Instead, if the moral vision of Proverbs can rightly be said to be "realist" and objectively grounded in the nature of God's creation, the best place to look first for this natural foundation is in *human* nature, with the sort of being Proverbs understands humans to be, not in the orders or orderliness of God's construction of the cosmos. The distinction may seem slight between a morality grounded in and discernible from the cosmos's orders and a morality grounded in and discernible via rational reflection on the sort of being humans are; one may even claim that the created nature of humans is an instance of the divine ordering of creation. So be it. Still, the difference between the two perspectives is important, not least because one view tends to "rewrite" Proverbs as a deontological moral discourse, while the other is consonant with the virtue-oriented character of Proverbs' rhetoric that I suggest is on display throughout the book.

The Orders of Creation?

There is likely another important hermeneutical-ideological phenomenon that helps explain why Proverbs' ethics are typically thought to derive from human observation of the natural world. If until relatively recently interpreters have not much considered how Proverbs might be a species of ancient virtue ethics and instead have studied it on the terms of modernist moral orientations, whether utilitarian or deontological (cf. chap. 1), this phenomenon also has to do with the character of the modern study of Proverbs' ethics.

Few would dispute the invaluable contribution German-language scholarship has made on biblical studies in the modern world, especially in the nineteenth and twentieth centuries. It has left a deep and enduring imprint on the discipline's structure and discourse. Names like de Wette, Wellhausen, Gunkel, Noth, and von Rad litter handbooks on exegetical "method" and histories of biblical interpretation. Although not all scholars publishing in German during this time were Lutheran, many of the major

---

34. C. Hayes, *What's Divine about Divine Law?*, 59.

theological centers that produced biblical scholarship in Germany were (so too in other places closely related to German biblical scholarship, such as Scandinavia).[35] Hermeneutically speaking, it would not be surprising if seminal nineteenth- and twentieth-century European biblical scholarship was impacted by the theological context in which it was produced. And, in fact, a particular feature of the Lutheran theological landscape in the modern epoch may have indirectly shaped interpretations of the relationship between creation and ethics in Proverbs: namely, the specifically Lutheran conception of natural law embodied in the teaching of the "orders of creation" (*Schöpfungsordnungenslehre*).

The idea of the orders of creation originates in the writings of Martin Luther himself in his doctrine of three "fundamental forms of life which God has provided for human existence." Luther, "keeping with tradition," calls these three forms of life—the family, state, and church—"'orders' (*Stände*)."[36] The developed notion of the Schöpfungsordnungenslehre essentially claims that basic forms of human society and relations are grounded in God's creation. As Carl Braaten explains the teaching, "God has placed all human beings in particular structures of life such as nationality, race, sexual identity, family, work, or government that in some form or other are simply givens of creaturely existence. The law and commandments of God are revealed through these common created structures of existence."[37]

Although the roots of the Schöpfungsordnungenslehre are in the Reformation, the doctrine was "primarily the product of nineteenth-century neo-Lutheranism."[38] According to Nathan Howard Yoder, among those who contributed to the doctrine's development were scholars intimately concerned with the theological study of the Bible, including J. C. K. von Hoffman (d. 1877)—a prominent figure in the history of biblical interpretation.[39] Although the Schöpfungsordnungenslehre was a significant feature of nineteenth-century Lutheran theology, according to Yoder the doctrine did not reach "its high water mark" until the mid-twentieth

---

35. Rogerson, *Old Testament Criticism*, e.g., 15, 79–80, and esp. 141–44.
36. Bayer, "Nature and Institution," 127, citing Luther, *Luther's Works*, 13:369–71.
37. Braaten, "God in Public Life," §1. The quotation continues: "and function apart from and in tension with the special revelation of God in the gospel of Jesus Christ." Ryan Tafilowski says the doctrine is "a theological designation of the institutional exercise of God's 'left-hand rule' through the social structures of marriage and family, legal and economic systems, and the state." See Tafilowski, "Reappraisal of the Orders," 288.
38. Tafilowski, "Reappraisal of the Orders," 289.
39. N. Yoder, "Ordnung in Gemeinschaft," 2. As Rogerson (*Old Testament Criticism*, 104) says in his account of nineteenth-century biblical criticism in England and Germany, Hoffman (to whom he devotes half a chapter; 104–20) was "by far the most adventurous thinker among the Confessional Lutherans of the mid-nineteenth century."

century in the work of Erlangen theologians Werner Elert (d. 1954) and Paul Althaus (d. 1966).[40]

Certain non-Lutheran moral-theological traditions also affirm some conception of divinely ordained orders of creation. This is especially true of more conservative (evangelical) Christian faiths that hold very high views of the authority and divine inspiration of Scripture. More conserving strands of the Reformed tradition might be included here as well, although the most influential twentieth-century Reformed voice—Karl Barth—vigorously rejected the doctrine. In any case, it is in Lutheran theology that the theological notion of the orders of creation has held most currency.

The potential problems with a doctrine like the Schöpfungsordnungenslehre are easily discernible, and the tragic moral failures it facilitated in mid-twentieth-century Europe are well documented. Most obviously the teaching can easily judge particular historically contingent social formations to be natural, immutable, God-given, and eternal arrangements—just like the rest of the nonhuman aspects of creation. As Tafilowski explains, not only might the doctrine "sanction authoritarian politics," it can sometimes also justify "an implicitly hierarchical ethnic taxonomy."[41] About this theological position Reinhold Niebuhr concludes, "Reformation moral theory led to confusion when it sought to deal with historic structures and institutions such as marriage and the state as belonging to the 'order of creation.'"[42] Karl Barth likewise condemns the Schöpfungsordnungenslehre as "a catastrophic basis for Christian ethics, especially in questions of politics. For Barth, Lutheran teaching on the ordinances of creation *necessarily* and *inevitably* reinforces oppressive and unjust societal structures. He thus called it 'the most evil of all theological doctrines.'"[43] Barth concedes that the sphere of creation as well as the spheres of reconciliation and redemption "within which the ethical encounter takes place might very well be called orders (*Ordnungen*)." But if so, "there would then exist the permanent possibility of 'misunderstanding them as laws, prescriptions and imperatives.'"[44] The Christocentric Barth, for whom the Word of God (and no natural theology or virtue ethics) was theologically central, thus distinguishes

---

40. N. Yoder, *"Ordnung in Gemeinschaft,"* 2.
41. Tafilowski, "Reappraisal of the Orders," 288.
42. Niebuhr, *Faith and History*, 208, cited in Tafilowski, "Reappraisal of the Orders," 288.
43. Barth, "Basic Problems of Christian Social Ethics," 48, cited in Tafilowski, "Reappraisal of the Orders," 289 (emphasis original). In Barth's Christocentric theology, the preeminence of the Word of God could not be easily reconciled to any sort of natural theology; but cf. further Nimmo, "Orders of Creation," who traces the development of Barth's use of distinct theological rhetorics of "order." For efforts to rehabilitate the doctrine of the orders of creation, see Braaten, "God in Public Life"; and N. Yoder, *"Ordnung in Gemeinschaft."*
44. Nimmo, "Orders of Creation," 30, citing Barth, *Church Dogmatics* III/4, 29.

his own notions from the Lutheran conception of Schöpfungsordnungen: "The distinction between this [Barth's conception of] order and what is customarily called 'order of creation' elsewhere is clear and irreconcilable.... We do not in some way read off this order where we just think we find it. We do not understand it at all as an order which can be discovered by us."[45]

Given the impact of the biblical scholarship emerging from Lutheran theological centers in the nineteenth and twentieth century, it is not far-fetched to think that the Lutheran teaching of the orders of creation (and its variations in other traditions) directly or indirectly impacted that strain of the modern interpretation that insists Proverbs' moral and social teaching is intimately related to God's creation of a well-ordered cosmos. Of course, even if Proverbs scholarship was influenced by the teaching, that does not mean Proverbs itself does not reflect something like the Lutheran doctrine. Still, one may well suspect that the historical hermeneutical phenomenon treated in part 1 above is again at play: namely, the tendency in the modern study of Proverbs to analyze its moral vision in terms of dominant modernist ethical theories—in this case, the theistic, deontological doctrine of the orders of creation—and consequently to misread or fail to recognize its virtue-oriented character.

To what extent a notion like the Schöpfungsordnungenslehre can be said to correlate with typical scholarly claims about God's ordered creation and ethics in Proverbs is impossible to say. What is certain, however, is that the language biblical scholars use to describe the relationship between ethics and creation in Proverbs often resonates deeply with the rhetoric of Schöpfungsordnungen. As noted above, Van Leeuwen calls attention to "the stable decrees of nature" that he believes points to "the social order and obligations that obtain between Yahweh and Israel,"[46] while Schipper (following Ringgren) suggests creation in Proverbs 8:22–31 is an orderly one that "establishes not only the physical boundaries of creation but also the laws governing the world and humanity." Later in the same context he even deploys the precise rhetoric of Schöpfungsordnung, concluding that "according to [Proverbs] chapter 8, the divine law can be conceived of as part of the order of creation [Schöpfungsordnung] that applies to both the physical world and humanity."[47] Even von Rad, whose analysis of Proverbs and wisdom often suggests that he senses the virtue-oriented nature of its ethics (cf. chap. 1), falls back on some idea of the orders of creation. As I will suggest shortly, von Rad tends (but ultimately fails) to see Wisdom in Proverbs as immanent in creation in a way that would support a virtue-ethics understanding of the book's moral discourse. For him,

---

45. Nimmo, "Orders of Creation," 30, citing Barth, *Church Dogmatics* III/4, 45.
46. Van Leeuwen, "Book of Proverbs," 94.
47. Schipper, *Proverbs 1–15*, 312 = Schipper, *Sprüche (Proverbia) 1–15*, 530.

Wisdom in Proverbs 8, finally, is a kind of ordering principle of creation, and this "Weltordnung herrscht ebenso in der Natur wie durch das Sittengesetz (wie wir sagen würden) über die Menschen." (The world order rules in nature as it does through the moral law [as we would say] over men.)[48]

Although the importance of a concept of order for Proverbs has been overstated and overplayed by biblical critics, it remains true that for the ancient sages the world or creation has a real, objective, and meaningful nature that is morally significant for human beings. It is simply that the morally meaningful aspects of nature are to be discerned first in the nature of the human rather than in the orderly construction of the cosmos. To further clarify this, we turn briefly to the question of Proverbs' moral epistemology—how the sages can be said to know what they claim to know about the moral life or the way of wisdom.

Empiricism in Proverbs?

Scholars often describe Proverbs' moral epistemology as "empirical" in some sense, and this perspective is closely related to claims that humans can discover natural, binding, moral-social obligations within and as part of God's well-ordered creation. Such scholars almost always invoke a terminology of "experience" and "observation" in discussions of how the sages know what they claim to know. As Brown notes, scholars have long insisted that the "epistemological distinctiveness of biblical wisdom" is "its appeal to experience."[49] Proverbs' pervasive means-end or cause-and-effect rhetoric is also regularly highlighted in descriptions of the sages' empirical epistemology—when X is done, one can see or observe that Y will follow. This is so even as most Proverbs specialists refuse a strong version of Klaus Koch's famous thesis about an act-consequence nexus in the book (cf. chap. 1).[50]

However, not all understand the book's empiricism as a bare or simple empiricism, "as if Proverbs envisions human beings as blank slates, who observe the world and automatically deduce proper moral conclusions."[51] Instead, some recognize that learning what to do from the orderliness of nature and social life also involves rational reflection on what is observed and experienced. Thus, scholars sometimes regard the moral epistemology of the sages

---

48. Von Rad, *Weisheit in Israel*, 208 = von Rad, *Wisdom in Israel*, 159.
49. Brown, *Wisdom's Wonder*, 19.
50. Koch, "Is There a Doctrine of Retribution." According to Koch's thesis, the consequences of deeds proceed nearly automatically from the particular actions themselves, not from the hand of a free divine agent.
51. VanDrunen, "Wisdom and the Natural Moral Order," 159.

as inductive: the sages infer an order—both natural and moral—in the cosmos. They do so through various particular observations and experiences of the world, in a kind of quasi-empiricist way. However, Proverbs' empiricist epistemology also admits of a formulation in deductive terms: the sages begin with the affirmation that the divine created a wise and orderly cosmos, like that described in Proverbs 8:22–31; and from this starting point, they reckon their particular experiences and observations of nature and the social and moral dimensions of existence as specific manifestations of the fundamental wisdom of God's creation. In either case, this viewpoint considers human morality, or wisdom, as ultimately naturally given, discoverable, and authoritative because it is grounded objectively in the orderliness of the cosmos that God wisely fashioned.

Scholars cite a cluster of verses to support claims about the empirical nature of Proverbs' epistemology. Among these is the famous exhortation in Proverbs 6:6–8 to "go to the ant" and learn diligence by observing and thinking about that creature and its activities.[52] The verses immediately following, which claim a lazy person's proclivity to sleep is productive of poverty, are nearly as (in)famous (6:9–11; cf. 24:30–34.) These lines offer a lesson about diligence that some take to be based on the observation of a lazy person's field and some reflection about it and the character of its owner. Proverbs 7:6–23, which recounts how that poem's wise instructing voice witnessed a male youth caught in the snares of adultery, is likewise regularly marshaled as prime evidence for Proverbs' empirical epistemology.

The second half of Proverbs 30 is a further piece of evidence scholars use for Proverbs' apparent empirical epistemology and for the view that the book understands the created, natural order of the world to be deeply imbricated with the social and moral order. This collection of sayings (largely of the ascending numerical parallelism sort, "three things, even four . . .") makes extensive use of images and observations of the nonhuman natural world to describe the nature of wisdom. For example, Proverbs 30:24–28 says,

> Four things on earth are small,
>   yet they are exceedingly wise:
> the ants are a people without strength,
>   yet they provide their food in the summer;
> the badgers are a people without power,
>   yet they make their homes in the rocks;

---

52. For a full and helpful discussion of the verses, which acknowledges that for some scholars Prov. 6:6 may be "a reference to the divine order of nature," see Schipper, *Proverbs 1–15*, 224–26 (citing Keel and Schroer, *Schöpfung*, 69–70).

> the locusts have no king,
> > yet all of them march in rank;
> the lizard can be grasped in the hand,
> > yet it is found in kings' palaces.

Some think that humans, by observing and reflecting on the animals and their activities mentioned in these verses, have been or will be able to discern the natural importance for themselves of diligence and discipline, cooperation and cleverness.

Proverbs 30:21–23 likewise draws on images of the natural world in proffering its wisdom. These verses presume certain political, moral, social, and gender hierarchies, which the text insists are "natural." Because of this, the passage also underscores some of the problems many modern individuals, formed so deeply by important liberal values of equality and freedom, often have with natural-law thinking in general—namely, the reification and justification of historically and socially contingent relations and categories. Indeed, the verses seem to highlight the sort of realist, natural-law-as-natural-moral-order perspective some think is at work in Proverbs. The lines appear to some as evidence that a conception similar to the orders of creation is at work in Proverbs. This happens despite some interpreters not affirming such teaching as normative but evaluating the passage as an ancient example of the naturalistic fallacy, the unwarranted extrapolation of an "ought" from an "is."[53]

> Under three things the earth trembles;
> > under four it cannot bear up:
> a slave when he becomes king,
> > and a fool when glutted with food;
> an unloved woman when she gets a husband,
> > and a maid when she succeeds her mistress. (30:21–23)

Some think the disruptive effect of these "reversals" of fortune, power, expectation, and status were observed by certain individuals and described as literally "earth shaking," an overturning of the (divinely ordained) orders of creation.

A number of other texts in Proverbs are also regularly (and rightly) regarded as teachings that analogically draw conclusions about social and moral life in light of observations of nature. Three good examples are Proverbs 25:23, 26:11, and 30:33.

---

53. Cf. VanDrunen, "Wisdom and the Natural Moral Order," 159.

> The north wind produces rain,
> and a backbiting tongue, angry looks. (25:23)
>
> Like a dog that returns to its vomit
> is a fool who replicates his folly. (26:11)
>
> For as pressing milk produces curds,
> and pressing the nose produces blood,
> so pressing anger produces strife. (30:33)

Whether such lines ultimately should be said to witness to a strong connection between the orders of creation and the social-moral realm is not as certain as their analogical structures. Nonetheless, Brown's view regarding these sorts of sayings is representative of much Proverbs scholarship. Not only did "the bond between the natural and the social" worlds supply the sages with "rich possibilities for constructing analogies," but these sorts of proverbs also "testify to the sages' perception that the natural and social realms are an interconnected whole."[54] As Brown's comments intimate, the sort of analogical thinking evident in these verses plausibly fits with the sort of empirical epistemology and realist, natural-law-as-natural-moral-order perspective often attributed to Proverbs.

There is, however, good reason to reconsider the extent of Proverbs' empirical epistemology. This reevaluation may impact how one reckons with Proverbs' understanding of the relation between creation and ethics and, hence, the book's relation to conceptions of natural law. Just as some scholars offer objections about the centrality of "order" to wisdom works, other scholars occasionally dissent regarding Proverbs' supposed empirical epistemology. Most notably, Michael Fox cites Proverbs 20:22, 20:20, and probably 22:29 to insist that "many proverbs are assertions of consequences that do not even hint at an experiential basis."[55] He also believes those passages in Proverbs noted above that speak of an individual's observation of ants, fields, or sexual liaisons are not accounts of empirical observations from which moral conclusions have been derived. They are instead rhetorical devices that promote or illustrate the sages' already-held social and moral views.[56] (Such an evaluation surely can be aptly applied to Prov. 30:21–23 too, those infamous lines that reflect the sages' traditional views toward the social order). As Fox recognizes, the composers of Proverbs by and large believed that "the structure of society as

---

54. Brown, *Wisdom's Wonder*, 18.
55. Fox, *Proverbs 1–9*, 964–65.
56. Fox, *Proverbs 1–9*, 965–66.

they knew it was fundamentally the right one."[57] But to say this is not necessarily to claim this view was grounded in observation of the immutable orders and orderliness of creation. (Indeed, it might well be based on rational reflection and one's understanding—albeit limited and prejudiced from a modern perspective—of the nature of human beings.) Fox, in any case, buttresses his claim that Proverbs' epistemology should not be regarded as empirical by averring that much of what the book teaches constitutes moral perspectives that simply could not have been developed through critical observation of the world. For example, he notes that verses such as Proverbs 10:3, 12:21, and 16:7—which speak of the good that will befall the just and the evil that pursues the wicked—are "statements of faith, not abstractions from experiential data."[58] Fox claims that "nowhere does a sage discover truths about the moral realm by observing the workings of nature."[59]

Fox's criticisms have themselves been criticized as overstated. Brown, for instance, seems not fully to accept them and seeks to preserve for Proverbs, via a notion of perception, something of the observational-empiricist epistemology that Fox criticizes.[60] As Brown explains, perception "involves the selective internalization and integration of events and aspects of life" that thus give "shape to the way people experience events and render them meaningful. Perception involves the way one selects, interprets, and evaluates events by means of certain fundamental symbols." Although Brown believes that "the sages considered themselves keen observers of the world around them," this observation was "filtered through and informed by their theological convictions (and their theological convictions informed by their experiences)."[61] The composers of Proverbs, in other words, worked both inductively and deductively with their observations and experiences.

Brown's appeal to the notion of perception is significant, and it would be hard to quarrel with the claim that people often assimilate diverse experiences and observations of reality to their prior understanding of how reality operates. It's not hard to recognize that experiences that do not conform to a person's deeply held conceptions about the true nature of things, especially in the social and moral realms, can be explained away, regarded as anomalies, and, importantly, given little explanatory weight in describing reality. To offer

---

57. Fox, *Proverbs 10–31*, 652; the comment is in relation to 19:10, which Fox evokes when discussing 31:21–23 (874).
58. Fox, *Proverbs 10–31*, 964.
59. Fox, "World Order and Ma'at," 48.
60. Brown, *Wisdom's Wonder*, 19n105: "Fox unnecessarily minimizes the role of perception, which is by nature slanted and selective, in the acquisition of knowledge."
61. Brown, *Wisdom's Wonder*, 19.

a trite example: I know prayer works because several times I prayed for a good parking spot and one became available; the many other times I prayed for such a space but did not find one have little explanatory weight for me vis-à-vis my core belief about the efficacy of petition to the divine. I can either sift them out of that stock of experiences that "count," or I can explain them away as consonant with my broader worldview: God wanted me to park further away so I could help that older person load their groceries. People typically see their experiences of the world in the way they want and are accustomed to see reality. Brown is right to remind us that the ancient sages sometimes surely did too.

Still, Fox may be on the right track with his forceful rejection of an empiricist epistemology in Proverbs. Even if one need not deny fully the presence of any "empiricism" in Proverbs, the book's teaching nonetheless is not primarily or fundamentally epistemically grounded in experience or observations. It is rather offered as traditional, intergenerational teaching. This is explicitly the case in Proverbs 1–9, which persistently addresses "my son," and implicitly so with the wisdom of the short sayings of Proverbs 10–29, which—though passed through a scribal lens—remain marked by the traditional moral vision of rural, agricultural communities (cf. chap. 8).

Other objections to the claim that observation and empiricism are epistemologically central for Proverbs can be noted too. For instance, the analogical thinking evident in many sayings in Proverbs may reflect some form of "empiricist" observation, certainly. However, the role of observation or empiricism in these cases need not be fundamental to Proverbs' moral epistemology; the sort of observation and empiricism Proverbs envisions need not fund a view of the book's moral perspectives as a kind of natural moral order anchored in the observable orderliness of God's created world.

The analogical thinking in sayings like Proverbs 25:23, 26:11, and 30:33 (noted above), for instance, is surely evidence for the workings of a rational intellect, but it primarily grounds a certain moral perspective by constructing an analogy to some typical occurrence. Although the terminology deployed in the analogies refers to things that one might "observe" in the world (e.g., windy days, dogs and dog vomit, fists to faces), the validity of such rational analogical thinking is not dependent on the typical occurrence happening in a well-ordered natural world that entails a natural moral order too; it is only contingent on a perceived regular happening. To coin two versions of a proverb with a similar moral point: "A righteous person is as reliable as rain in the winter"; or "A righteous person is as reliable as a Swiss train." The first version of the invented saying might be thought to be anchored in observations of the orders of creation. It certainly presumes some knowledge of regular—one might say "ordered"—meteorological phenomena and seasons. The second version of the proverb is grounded in a recognizable and regularly occurring social fact: Swiss trains typically arrive and depart according to schedule. What is relevant rhetorically and epistemologically in both cases is the regularity to which the analogy draws attention in order to describe the constancy of a just person's character. Neither version of my proverb requires a further claim about divinely created orders of the cosmos (or for that matter the "natural" punctuality of Swiss nationals) to anchor its moral-rhetorical point. What is more, although a just person may in fact be reliable *like* a Swiss train or *like* rain in winter, Swiss trains and regular rains on their own could never truly and fully teach a person to be dependable, nor could they teach that it is a good thing to possess such a virtue. To know *that*, the just person would have to turn someplace else. Certain laws or rules might insist that it is right to live with integrity; and it might be thought "good" to do so, say, because an authoritative figure commands it. For a virtue-oriented discourse like Proverbs, by contrast, to be a reliable person would be considered something good for the sort of social being people naturally are; it would be thought to contribute in some fashion to genuine human happiness.

If the instruction Proverbs offers is "empirical" or based on "observation," it is not so much a product of people's scrutiny of nature or the consequences of different sorts of discrete deeds; instead, it emerges most fully from a community's rational reflection on its long experience with human natural inclinations toward certain goods, as well as its extended observations of how and why certain (wise and just) people are happy and others are not. Observations of the natural world, analogies drawn from the same, and claims about the "rewards" that (ought to or usually) accrue to different sorts of "good" and "bad" individuals can illustrate and promote a community's already-held moral knowledge and convictions. Such convictions and knowledge, however, are not necessarily or likely derived primarily from scrutiny and consideration of the orders or orderliness of creation.

Natural Law and Character Ethics in Proverbs

A proper virtue-ethics approach to the question of natural law or the relation of cosmos to ethics in Proverbs should focus on questions about the sort of being humans are understood to be in this text. Before turning to a more detailed consideration of how Proverbs 8:22–31 conceptualizes the relation between morality and cosmos in a way that is distinct from the usual scholarly approaches that depend rather fully on concepts like the orders of creation, we should recall what was noted in part 1 about the book's implicit anthropology (chap. 3). For Proverbs, humans are first and fundamentally material beings created by Adonai, possessing bodies with certain natural physical needs, inclinations, and desires. Second, humans for Proverbs are deeply social creatures—the kind of animal that must exist and can only flourish with others of its kind. Humans are also beings with a spirit and emotions, as well as a rational intellect.[62] Proverbs also identifies, or assumes, several "goods," the attainment and right ordering of which are normally essential for many forms of human flourishing (see chap. 3). The means to achieve the goods that Proverbs assumes necessary for human flourishing is the right exercise of particular virtues that the book persistently highlights, whether of an intellectual, practical, or moral-social sort (1:2–7). These virtues include at least diligence, moderation, discretion, faithfulness, loyalty, humility, fairness, kindness, fear of the Lord, and knowledge (in the sense of understanding the nature and importance of certain things), as well as "openness to instruction" (in the form of reproof, discipline, and counsel) and, most importantly, a full and robust Practical Wisdom—the ability to integrate all the virtues appropriately and consequently to "size up" diverse situations of life and to know, desire, and carry out good and appropriate courses of action in them.

If one starts with the understanding of the nature of the human being with which the sages begin, certain precepts or rules might be rationally discerned and formulated that can be considered natural law for such a creature. These precepts will, however, regularly be of a minimal sort—the usual and most general formulations of natural law, such as "don't kill or violently attack innocents," "don't lie, steal, or cheat," "don't commit adultery," all motifs of social-moral instruction that are of significant concern to Proverbs. So, too, a few other second-order precepts might be developed. Yet all these rules will also easily be recognized as useful in character formation or habituating subjects, especially ethical novices, into the moral and social virtues most important for the flourishing of the kind of being the sages understood humans

---

62. As the following reconsideration of Prov. 8:22–31 will indirectly demonstrate, for Proverbs the rationality or "wisdom" humans naturally possess is logically shared with other parts of creation, like nonhuman animals. Because human wisdom is wisdom appropriate to humans in particular, it can be regarded as unique in its capacities and potential for development. Just so, however, the sort of wisdom that Proverbs implies nonhuman animals possess ought to be considered unique in its capacities and potential for development in those creatures. Put otherwise, for Proverbs, w/Wisdom's relation to creation implies that human wisdom-rationality-intellect is not fully distinct from that of other creatures. Its uniqueness lies mainly in the fact that it is *human* wisdom, a rationality and intellectual capacity that gains its particular characteristics from its instantiation or embodiment in the particular sort of being that humans are. Cf. Sandoval, "Morality of Non-Human Animals."

naturally to be. Although the above sorts of "laws" are not the primary moral idiom of a virtue-oriented text like Proverbs, they will not be completely shunned. As Brown says, "Moral rules and principles" constitute "an integral part of the comely dynamic of moral formation by contributing to the community's task of constructing particular concepts of the good by which character is formed."[63] For example, since Proverbs fundamentally imagines humans to be social creatures, the kind of being that in order to flourish must live fully and well with others of its kind, the book not only highlights the virtues of justice and the "ways" of just persons; it also issues clusters of commands like those articulated at the end of Proverbs 3.

> Do not withhold good from those to whom it is due. . . .
> Do not say to your neighbor, "Go, and come again . . ."
>   —when you have it with you.
> Do not plan harm against your neighbor
>   who lives trustingly beside you.
> Do not quarrel with anyone without cause. . . .
> Do not envy the violent
>   and do not choose any of their ways. (3:27–31)

Similar formulations are elsewhere in the book. In Proverbs 22, near the opening of the Amenemope collection of sayings, we find the following statements:

> Do not rob the poor because they are poor,
>   or crush the afflicted at the gate. (22:22)
>
> Make no friends with those given to anger,
>   and do not associate with hotheads. (22:24)
>
> Do not remove the ancient landmark
>   that your ancestors set up. (22:28)

The consistent keeping of these sorts of commands, especially by moral novices, will help produce profoundly prosocial moral subjects characterized by virtues like honesty, fairness, restraint, loyalty, and kindness. And all this will contribute to the achievement of the good of a stable and just social order. The commands contribute to the formation of good character, both personal and communal. But because such precepts simply can't be adequate to every situation that might arise in the life of an individual (or community), they ultimately are subordinated to the Practical Wisdom that a just and wise

---

63. Brown, *Wisdom's Wonder*, 15.

person might exercise in any particular context of moral decision-making (cf. chap. 8). Thus, despite room for such commandments or rules, which might legitimately constitute a kind of natural law, Proverbs' moral vision remains decidedly virtue oriented rather than command focused.

What a close (re)consideration of Proverbs 8:22–31 in the next chapter will further help to demonstrate is that any natural law one might discover in Proverbs—like the sorts of precepts just discussed—does not emerge from something like the ancient sages' discernment of a natural moral order in Adonai's well-designed creation. The natural-law character of Proverbs' moral discourse does not lie in the book's similarity to conceptions of natural law as natural moral order. Instead, Proverbs' precepts of "natural law" and the realist, natural, and objective character of its moral discourse are best regarded as grounded in the ancient tradition's rational reflection on the nature of the human being and the conditions for the flourishing of such a being in the world God created.

The Cosmology of Proverbs 8:22–31

Still, if all the foregoing is so, how should we regard a passage like Proverbs 8:22–31, which so closely associates God's creation of a "well-ordered" cosmos with a personification of wisdom's virtues? The question is significant, for as we have seen, many erudite and ethically minded readers regularly regard this passage as signaling Proverbs' affinities to a deontological-leaning, realist, natural-law perspective whereby the orders and orderliness of the cosmos communicate binding moral duties and obligations to humans.

I have already offered one response to this inquiry: the prevalence of virtue-oriented moral discourse in Proverbs suggests that Proverbs 8 should not be quickly or easily assimilated to deontological conceptions of ethics, especially since the book's deontological features are easily accounted for in terms of a virtue-ethics approach to the book's moral discourse. The precepts and rules Proverbs formulates can be understood as emerging from reflection on the nature of humans and what produces their happiness, as well as from a consideration of the variety of good lives lived by wise and just individuals. If notions like the orders of creation or natural law as natural moral order were central to Proverbs, we would have to revise our evaluation of the book's moral logic, its implicit way of "thinking" ethically. Such a revision would suggest that the sages first and foremost consider people wise and just because they dutifully obey important moral commands proffered by legitimate lawgivers—parents and teachers, for example—whose words ultimately derive from the obligations the divine legislator embeds in and makes available to humans through observation of God's well-structured cosmos. I have been suggesting, however, the essence of ethics for Proverbs lies not as it does for Kant (and many modern people) with "the moral strength of a *human being's* will in fulfilling his duty" to obey rules or precepts.[64] It has much more to do with the excellent character and good ways of life of wise and just people who pursue a thriving existence appropriate to human beings. Ascribing to Proverbs a perspective of natural law as natural moral order contradicts this essence of ethics in the book.

The second answer to the question of how we should understand Proverbs 8:22–31 in light of the tendency to interpret its cosmology in ways that support deontological understandings of the book is more complex. We need not emphasize Adonai's creation of an orderly cosmos in Proverbs 8 "by Wisdom," understood in an instrumental sense. Such a perspective might well be discerned in Proverbs 3:19–20 (cf. Ps. 104:24) and in later wisdom works such as Sirach (e.g., Sir. 24). In Proverbs 8 itself, however, we should place more weight on the creative work Adonai carries out "in Wisdom," understood in a more literal, local, and immanent, if also profoundly mythological, sense. If we can understand Adonai's creation of the cosmos in Proverbs 8 in this way, the subsequent cosmogony results in humans (and other aspects of creation) that are beings created *in*, and so *with*, a wisdom that is natural and appropriate to our kind—a moral, spiritual, social, practical, and rational-intellectual capacity. And as I said, for a virtue ethics reading of Proverbs it is precisely with questions about the kind of being humans are "naturally" imagined to be that we should start our analysis of the relationship of the book's creation theology to ethics and the possible affinities of its ethics to natural-law thinking. To support especially this second response to the tendency to interpret the cosmology of Proverbs 8 in deontological terms, we now turn to a close reading of Proverbs 8:22–31.

---

64. Johnson and Cureton, "Kant's Moral Philosophy," quoting Kant, *Metaphysics of Morals*, in *Kants gesammelte Schriften* (Berlin: De Gruyter), 6:405.

12

A Virtue-Ethics Approach to Cosmogony in Proverbs (Part 2)

Reading Proverbs 8:22–31 as a Test Case

The number of both major and minor exegetical difficulties related to Proverbs 8:22–31 is well known.¹ However, it is not necessary to treat all of these issues in depth here to see how Proverbs' realist and objectivist moral discourse is grounded in creation but not unduly aligned to modern deontological presuppositions and understandings of the book. There is, for example, no need to take a strong position on even the most contested matters in the passage—namely, the meaning of קנה in 8:22 and of אָמוֹן in 8:30. Still, despite no direct interest in tackling some of the most disputed aspects of the passage, my reading will offer suggestions and arguments about these (and other) questions. No doubt some will wish to contest these arguments. When offering a "new take" on a passage like Proverbs 8:22–31, it could (and should) hardly be otherwise. My aim is not to establish *the* definitive reading of the passage but to point to a way it might be appreciated as a text that is consonant with a virtue-ethics-informed reading of the book—in particular, how the cosmology it presents aligns with the book's virtue-oriented ethical orientation. In so doing I hope to contribute to broader conversations about how its origins and meanings might be understood. Most centrally I

---

1. For a thorough sampling, see the discussions of the passage in Fox, *Proverbs 1–9*; Loader, *Proverbs 1–9*; and Schipper, *Proverbs 1–15*.

claim that in the cosmogony put forward and presupposed by the passage, the precreation watery matter (תְהוֹם) out of which Adonai creates the heavens and the earth is infused with and even animated by Wisdom prior to Adonai's acts of creation. This means that the known cosmos, as the Proverbs text conceives it, is a creation "in Wisdom"—not in an instrumental sense but in a kind of literal, though profoundly mythological, way.

Such a perspective is hardly widespread among commentators. It is, however, close to a view Gerhard von Rad articulates about wisdom and creation in *Wisdom in Israel*. For von Rad, the notion of Adonai creating "in wisdom"— for example in Proverbs 3:19—does not simply suggest Wisdom is an attribute of the Creator used to make the cosmos. Rather, Wisdom "could also be understood as an attribute of the earth" or the "world."[2] Wisdom should be regarded as "immanent in the world."[3] For von Rad, however, Wisdom is also intimately related to what he variously, and so ambiguously, calls "'primeval order' or 'mysterious order' or 'world reason.'"[4] As this language indicates, von Rad also links the powerful idea of the immanence of Wisdom in the world with a conception of an orderly creation. This suggests that ultimately von Rad's view is consonant with efforts to relate the cosmology of Proverbs 8 to the sort of realist, objectivist, and deontologically inclined natural-law position described in the previous chapter, where the orders of creation are thought to permit humans to discern moral law via careful attention to God's cosmos.

Nonetheless, von Rad's exegetical instinct regarding the immanence of wisdom in the cosmos is worth preserving. Although in the form that it appears in the MT, Proverbs 3:19–20 probably imagines a divine "instrumental" use of wisdom in the creation of an ordered cosmos, those lines do not represent the only, or in my view the central, cosmogonic tradition of Proverbs. The cosmogony of Proverbs 8:22–31, articulated by personified Wisdom herself, is longer, more complex, and more broadly influential in the history of the book's reception.

It has sometimes been suggested that Proverbs 8:22–31 is an originally independent composition redacted into Woman Wisdom's speech, which makes up the rest of the chapter (vv. 4–21, 32–36). This is quite possible, since, as Whybray says, "if it [vv. 22–31] were omitted, the rest of Wisdom's speech would constitute a self-contained unit with a satisfactory logical structure: Wisdom commends herself to her audience as honest, truthful, immensely influential and an invaluable companion and adviser (vv. 5–21), and then

---

2. Von Rad, *Wisdom in Israel*, 155.
3. Von Rad, *Wisdom in Israel*, 157. Others, of course, also hint at conceptions of Wisdom's immanence in creation. See, e.g., Collins, "Biblical Precedent for Natural Theology."
4. Von Rad, *Wisdom in Israel*, 157.

concludes her speech by offering all these qualities to those who are ready to listen to her and to devote themselves to her (vv. 32–36)."[5]

My own hunch, however, is that 8:22–31 was composed for its context by Judahite scribe-theologians (probably in the monarchic period) who were interested in developing their own conception of w/Wisdom (cf. 1:20–33; 3:13–20) and did so by mediating a robust dialogic encounter of their own Israelite/Judahite traditions with ancient West Asian, especially Egyptian, cosmogonic and mythological discourses. Demonstrating this—or even pointing to an acceptable level of plausibility for the claims—is difficult. Methodologically, for example, it entails drawing on a range of conceptions and texts with geographically and chronologically distant provenances. There is no fully satisfactory solution to such a matter. Still, given the cultural contact between especially Egypt and Syria-Palestine starting in the eighth century BCE, I assume certain Judahite scribes were in a position to dialogically engage a range of Egyptian traditions. Some of the traditions that may have informed their own cosmologic reflection, however, may not have been central to Egyptian life or religious-theological speculation in the Twenty-Fifth and Twenty-Sixth Dynasties (eighth to sixth centuries BCE), while the sages of Proverbs may have held only rudimentary understandings of others. Still, the reflexes of especially Egyptian mythological ideas on Proverbs 8:22–31 have long been noted and warrant further exploration as to the extent and nature of such "influence" (cf. chap. 10) on that text.

In the end, I want to suggest through a study of these most famous lines in Proverbs that the cosmology of 8:22–31 is one in which God creates the known world out of the already-existing Wisdom-infused watery deeps. Because humans, like all of creation, are formed in and through the primordial waters, they can be said to be created with a wisdom, or natural capacity for wisdom, appropriate to their kind. This capacity for wisdom—an aptitude for moral, social, spiritual, and rational-intellectual development—when rightly tutored can guide humans in acquiring the goods we naturally long for, and so this ability to advance in wisdom is essential to our happiness, the final end humans desire. The cosmogonic vision in Proverbs 8 can, consequently, be said to correspond best to a virtue-oriented conception of the book's ethics, not a deontological one.

Exegeting Proverbs 8:22–31

There is no need to reject completely the notion that in Proverbs 8:22–31 God is imagined, in some general sense, as undertaking the divine creative work

---

5. Whybray, *Proverbs*, 121–22.

"by wisdom" in an instrumental fashion. Like a "wise" craftsperson, the divine shapes and structures the cosmos.[6] Yet the vestiges of mythological, especially goddess, imagery associated with Woman Wisdom in Proverbs 8 is well known. The traces of this rhetoric in the passage mean it can also be understood to suggest that the divine creation of the known cosmos occurred in and through Wisdom in a literal if also deeply mythological sense.[7] The passage reads as follows:

> [22]The LORD created me at the beginning of his work,
>   the first of his acts of long ago.
> [23]Ages ago I was set up,
>   at the first, before the beginning of the earth.
> [24]When there were no (deep) oceans,[8] I was brought forth,
>   when there were no springs abounding with water.
> [25]Before the mountains had been shaped,
>   before the hills, I was brought forth—
> [26]when he had not yet made earth and fields
>   or the world's first bits of soil.
> [27]When he established the heavens, I was there,
>   when he drew a circle on the face of the deep,

---

6. On conceptions of wisdom elsewhere in the Bible, which include the skill and activities of craftspeople, see chap. 13 below.

7. It is possible that Prov. 3:19–20 represents a cosmogonic vision that originally was consonant with the view of 8:22–31 developed here, where God creates "in wisdom" in a literal, though mythological, sense. If so, the lines have been normalized to a subsequent, early Jewish view of creation like that of Sirach, where God is imagined as using (God's own) wisdom to fashion an orderly cosmos (cf. Sir. 1; 24). The terms for "wisdom" and "understanding" in Prov. 3:19, standing in synonymous parallelism, can together refer to a full conception of Wisdom rather than to distinct intellectual virtues. (Note personified Wisdom is the topic of the immediately preceding lines.) The *bet* preposition on both terms, however, need not initially be regarded as instrumental—expressing the means by which God created earth and heaven. Instead, the verse could be expressing a cosmogonic-mythological picture of the locus of creation: in the midst of Wisdom/Understanding. The main problem with seeing the prepositional constructions in 3:19 as anything other than an instrumental expression is that the parallel prepositional construction in the first stich of v. 20 does not say that the divine creates "by knowledge"—where knowledge might be regarded as a further synonym for some full allusion to a mythological Wisdom "in which" God fashions the known world. Instead, it says Adonai created "by *his* knowledge," which almost certainly must be regarded in an instrumental sense. Yet the LXX does not represent the third-masculine singular suffix of v. 20, which may indicate it was rendering a text in which it was absent. Regardless of the LXX's *Vorlage*, the use of the dative τῇ σοφίᾳ ("by Wisdom") in LXX v. 19 suggests, unsurprisingly, that the later Greek text itself understands the divine to be creating the cosmos by means of the divine's own Wisdom.

8. The NRSV translates the Hebrew תְּהֹמוֹת here as "depths"; for an explanation of my rendering, see the discussion below.

²⁸when he made firm the skies above,
   when he established the fountains of the deep,
²⁹when he assigned to the sea its limit,
   so that the waters might not transgress his command,
when he marked out the foundations of the earth,
   ³⁰then I was beside him, like a master worker;
and I was daily his delight,
   rejoicing before him always,
³¹rejoicing in his inhabited world
   and delighting in the human race. (8:22–31, author's translation)

²²יְהוָה קָנָנִי רֵאשִׁית דַּרְכּוֹ קֶדֶם מִפְעָלָיו מֵאָז
²³מֵעוֹלָם נִסַּכְתִּי מֵרֹאשׁ מִקַּדְמֵי־אָרֶץ
²⁴בְּאֵין־תְּהֹמוֹת חוֹלָלְתִּי בְּאֵין מַעְיָנוֹת נִכְבַּדֵּי־מָיִם
²⁵בְּטֶרֶם הָרִים הָטְבָּעוּ לִפְנֵי גְבָעוֹת חוֹלָלְתִּי
²⁶עַד־לֹא עָשָׂה אֶרֶץ וְחוּצוֹת וְרֹאשׁ עַפְרוֹת תֵּבֵל
²⁷בַּהֲכִינוֹ שָׁמַיִם שָׁם אָנִי בְּחוּקוֹ חוּג עַל־פְּנֵי תְהוֹם
²⁸בְּאַמְּצוֹ שְׁחָקִים מִמָּעַל בַּעֲזוֹז עִינוֹת תְּהוֹם
²⁹בְּשׂוּמוֹ לַיָּם חֻקּוֹ וּמַיִם לֹא יַעַבְרוּ־פִיו בְּחוּקוֹ מוֹסְדֵי אָרֶץ
³⁰וָאֶהְיֶה אֶצְלוֹ אָמוֹן וָאֶהְיֶה שַׁעֲשֻׁעִים יוֹם יוֹם מְשַׂחֶקֶת לְפָנָיו בְּכָל־עֵת
³¹מְשַׂחֶקֶת בְּתֵבֵל אַרְצוֹ וְשַׁעֲשֻׁעַי אֶת־בְּנֵי אָדָם

A good starting point for arguing the case that in Proverbs 8:22–31 Adonai creates the known world out of the Wisdom-infused primordial deep is the scholarly consensus on two aspects of the passage. The first point of agreement is that Wisdom is in existence—is acquired, begotten, or created (קנה)—in Proverbs 8:22 prior to the creation of the cosmos, even if scholars have long argued over the appropriateness of one or another of the meanings for קנה (see below). The second consensus opinion is that Wisdom in Proverbs 8 is also somehow intimately present with Adonai and the world at the time of the cosmos's creation. Beginning with verse 27, Wisdom is both present at the moment of God's fashioning of the world and located in the world. When Adonai took up the various acts of creation, Wisdom says in verse 27, "I was there." Wisdom was, as verse 30 notes, "beside him" (אֶצְלוֹ). Verses 30–31 make clear that Wisdom's "delight" and her rejoicing occur "in the presence of" the Lord (לְפָנָיו) and "in" or "upon" his inhabited world—בְּתֵבֵל אַרְצוֹ. As the תֵּבֵל is the proper, "solid ground" dwelling place of humans, Wisdom's rejoicing is also said, in parallel fashion, to be "with" (אֶת) the בְּנֵי אָדָם—that is, on earth.⁹ When creation happens, Wisdom is clearly and intimately located deep in the mix of it all.

---

9. Cf. Schipper, *Proverbs 1–15*, 310. For the presence of Wisdom on earth and with humans, see below.

Wisdom's Emergence: Proverbs 8:22–26

Despite these points of scholarly consensus, further attention to the logic of the two-stage cosmogonic account's imagery is needed to warrant the more specific claim that Adonai in Proverbs 8 creates the cosmos out of the Wisdom-infused primordial deeps. These two stages are Wisdom's emergence in primordial time in verses 22–26 and the creation of the cosmos in verses 27–31.

Acquired, Created, or Begotten?

It is not particularly important for my argument to favor one or another meaning of קנה in verse 22—whether acquire, create, or beget.[10] As Fox notes, the term basically means "to acquire" but in particular contexts can carry the other connotations.[11] The ambiguity of the term in Proverbs 8:22 is obvious—whether or not it reflects an ancient scribe's "intention" to produce a multivalent text; all the possible senses of the term in some sense fit the context of the passage. They all also cohere with the reading of the lines that I am developing. In the literary context of Proverbs 1–9, for example, קנה understood as "to acquire" makes good sense. Just as the young and simple addressees of earlier chapters are urged to acquire w/Wisdom to navigate well the journey of their lives (cf. esp. 4:5), now in Proverbs 8 the divine does exactly that too; Adonai, a divine moral exemplar of sorts, acquires Wisdom at the outset of "his way" (דַּרְכּוֹ).[12]

Adonai in Proverbs 8:22, however, can also be said to create (קנה) rather than acquire Wisdom. This rendering, which avoids any implication that Adonai acquires (perhaps as a consort) an already-existing goddess-like being, fits well with the monotheistic inclinations of some exilic and postexilic Judahite theological reflection (e.g., Isa. 40–66) and with the explicit monotheistic claims of later forms of Judaism and Christianity. It is, however, somewhat anachronistic to think that the writers of Proverbs 8 were particularly concerned to protect the monotheistic character of their religion. This is especially so if Proverbs 8 is essentially a preexilic composition.[13] The notion of Adonai

---

10. On the various proposals for rendering the term, see Schipper, *Proverbs 1–15*, 308.
11. Fox, *Proverbs 1–9*, 279.
12. Many of the major commentaries rehearse the proposals for understanding דַּרְכּוֹ in Prov. 8:22, including W. F. Albright's suggestion that it be related to Ugaritic *drkt* ("dominion"); most conclude it simply means "his [Adonai's] way." See, e.g., Loader, *Proverbs 1–9*, 350; Fox, *Proverbs 1–9*, 280–81; and Schipper, *Proverbs 1–15*, 308.
13. Cf. chap. 10 and the contentions of Carr noted there, as well as Fox's concession that the language of Prov. 1–9 is not necessarily Late Biblical Hebrew. Carr, *Formation of the Hebrew Bible*, esp. 403–31; cf. Fox, *Proverbs 1–9*, 48. By contrast, Schipper dates Prov. 8 to "the late Persian period at the earliest" (*Proverbs 1–15*, 292). This claim is based in part on his belief

"creating" Woman Wisdom in a nonmonotheistic context—or "begetting" her, another possible gloss for קנה—fits well with the primarily Egyptian mythological discourses that have left a mark on the passage—even if it is difficult to point unequivocally to a particular textual or theo-mythological tradition from Egypt as directly "influencing" Proverbs 8 (see below).[14] As should become clear, in my view, the Yahwistic writers of Proverbs 8 have not woodenly taken over but have dialogically encountered and uniquely accented for their own purposes Egyptian theological-mythological discourses in the composition of their Judahite cosmology. For example, the sexual connotations of a male deity's acts of creation (or with a consort), which are sometimes evident in mythological texts of Israel's neighbors, have in Proverbs largely been displaced by an emphasis on Adonai's identity as an independent, transcendent creator. Still, traces of these connotations can be detected in Proverbs 8 (e.g., when קנה is understood as "beget"). What is most important to recognize at this point is the consensus view that Wisdom in Proverbs 8 is in existence—acquired, created, begotten—prior to the creation of the heavens and the earth.

Woven Together or Poured Out?

After קנה in Proverbs 8:22, the next significant and contested term in Proverbs 8:22–31 is נִסַּ֫כְתִּי in verse 23. Unlike קנה, for the reading being developed here there is a bit more at stake in discerning the meaning of this term. The word as it appears in the MT of 8:22 represents the only instance of the *niphal* of the root *n-s-k* in the Hebrew Bible. Consequently, various proposals about the lexeme have been offered. The most common and compelling of these suggestions is that the MT's *nissaktî* (*niphal*, first common singular of נסך, "I was poured out") should be emended/repointed to the *niphal* of

---

that Prov. 1:20–33 and 3:13–20 presuppose Prov. 8:22–31, a view not shared by all (cf. Lenzi, "Proverbs 8:22–31," 694–96; and Whybray, *Proverbs*, 121). It is also related to Schipper's belief that the image of Wisdom in Prov. 8 is likely influenced by later Greek Isis aretologies (292–94), as well as his larger, complex arguments regarding Deuteronomy's influence on Proverbs. For Schipper, "(1) That which originally described the *torah* in Deuteronomy 30 was (2) applied to personified Wisdom in Proverbs 8 . . . , before (3) the attributes of personified Wisdom were 'inverted' and applied to the sapientially conceived *torah* in Psalms 19 and 119" (291–92). If forced to draw a conclusion about the priority of texts, I would suggest that Proverbs influenced Deuteronomy. But I would prefer to say that the intertextual relations between Proverbs and Deuteronomy are best understood as distinct inflections of a shared, at-hand, moral discourse and concede that questions of priority and directions of influence between the texts probably can never be assuredly and finally established.

14. On the question of "influence" and other possible intertextual relations, cf. chap. 10 above.

סכך (II)—nəsakkōtî—meaning "I was woven together."[15] This rendering, it is thought, produces a better parallel to קנה of verse 22, at least when *that* word is understood as "create" or "beget" (cf. Ps. 139:13, where the two roots appear together).

Nonetheless, there is good reason to preserve the MT's *nissaktî*. First, the parallelism of *nəsakkōtî* with קנה is not as strong when the latter is reckoned as "acquire" and not "create" or "beget." Second, the typical repointing of the text's consonants, *nissaktî* to *nəsakkōtî*, lacks strong textual support and itself is derived from a root that is rare in the Hebrew Bible.[16] What is more, although commentators often struggle with making sense of the idea of Wisdom being "poured out," that this entity could be dispatched in this manner resonates with similar mythological images in certain ancient Egyptian texts.

The root נסך has fundamentally to do with the idea of "pouring out" a liquid in the way we normally think of it. This is clear from forms of the root associated with "drink offerings." A person, for instance, can be said to "pour out" (נסך) a *nesek* ("drink offering"; e.g., Jer. 7:18; 19:13). Given the range of uses of נסך in the Bible, it may also be legitimate to render the term in Proverbs 8:23 as "I was formed" or even "I was set up" (NRSV), as perhaps in Psalm 2:6 where the *qal* is used to speak of the deity's establishment of a Davidite king: "I have set [נָסַכְתִּי] my king on Zion, my holy hill." Both of these connotations of נסך, however, are related to the notion of "pouring out" a liquid since both are suggestive of artisanal activities of metal working and crafting idols (Isa. 40:19; 44:10; cf. מַסֵּכָה, "image; cast idol"; Isa. 30:1). Indeed, as Keel notes, "In Ägypten wurden Götter und Könige gerne als kostbare Standbilder aus Edelmetall beschrieben und ihre Entstehung folgerichtige als ein Gegossen werden geschildert" (In Egypt, gods and kings were readily described as costly statues made of precious metal, and their emergence consequently portrayed as a pouring out). For Keel, in Proverbs 8:23, "Da es sich bei der Weisheit ähnlich wie bei Göttern und Königen um eine Gestalt des numinosen Bereichs handelt, trifft das vornehme <<gegossen>> den gemeinten Sachverhalt vielleicht noch besser als das allgemein menschlich <<geflochten werden>>" (Because Wisdom, like

---

15. Cf. Fox, *Proverbs 1–9*, 281; Loader, *Proverbs 1–9*, 351; and Schipper, *Proverbs 1–15*, 309.

16. The LXX's ἐθεμελίωσέν με ("he founded me") is in the active voice, with the divine as subject, and points neither to the Hebrew root נסך or סכך but to יסד ("establish," "found"), perhaps reflecting a rare *kaph-dalet* interchange (Fox, *Proverbs 1–9*, 412). However, according to Fox, Symmachus reads "*prokecheirismai* for *prokechrismai* 'anointed before,'" which would likely mean that the translator(s) of that work understood the Hebrew root as נסך. As Loader notes, this term in 8:23 might "refer to anointing and state that wisdom was appointed for a special function," which he suggests also is the direction "traditional rabbinic interpretations went" (*Proverbs 1–9*, 351).

gods and kings, is a figure of the realm of the numinous, the distinguished "poured out" fits the intended meaning somewhat better than the generally human "to be woven together").[17] In any case, a later text like 1 Enoch 49:1, although speaking of wisdom in a very different context, captures well the image here in Proverbs when it says, "Wisdom is poured out like water." One might also note Isaiah 29:10, where the divine is said to "pour out" (נסך) not Wisdom but a likewise intangible "spirit of deep sleep" upon humans (cf. Joel 3:1 [2:28], with the verb שׁפך).

Hence, if one reads Proverbs 8:23 with the MT's pointing and understands נסך in its typical way, the mythological picture of Wisdom's origins starts to emerge. Wisdom is first acquired or created/begotten by Adonai, and subsequently she is poured out either by the deity or, in a reflexive sense, by herself. But poured out over, or into, what? The root נסך is sometimes accompanied by a prepositional phrase to indicate either that upon which something is poured out—usually *'al* or *bet* (e.g., Gen. 35:14; Exod. 25:29)—or by a *lamed* that points to the entity to or for which something is poured out. With drink offerings this indirect object is typically Adonai (e.g., Num. 28:7; 2 Sam. 23:16) or other gods (e.g., Jer. 7:18; 44:17–19).

Proverbs 8:23 does not state that toward which Wisdom is poured. Yet the logic of the mythological and poetic images in the passage suggests that the place where Wisdom is poured is the eternally existing primordial watery deeps—the same watery deeps out of which the divine so clearly creates the cosmos in the second half of the passage (vv. 27–29). The book of Sirach, in a couple of passages clearly dependent on Proverbs 8, deploys a similar rhetoric. Sirach 1:9 speaks of how God "poured out" (ἐκχέω // שׁפך) Wisdom, while Sirach 24:3–6 notes that Wisdom came forth (ἐξέρχομαι) from the divine and encircled and moved about over the vault of heaven and the depths of the abyss.[18] Von Rad, too, says Sirach's image of the divine pouring out of Wisdom over creation is an apt description of what is occurring in Proverbs 8. It can, von Rad says, "scarcely be understood as a free, poetic, figurative representation, but rather as the description of a real, cosmological process,

---

17. Keel, *Die Weisheit spielt vor Gott*, 17–18.
18. Sirach 24:3–6 reads:
   I came forth from the mouth of the Most High,
       and covered the earth like a mist.
   I dwelt in the highest heavens,
       and my throne was in a pillar of cloud.
   Alone I compassed the vault of heaven
       and traversed the depths of the abyss.
   Over waves of the sea, over all the earth,
       and over every people and nation I have held sway.

namely as the bestowal of something special on creation, something which ... now mysteriously inhabits it."[19]

Yet despite this rhetoric that is so similar to Proverbs, Sirach seems to imagine Wisdom's being poured out and her moving about *not* as precosmos phenomena as in Proverbs 8, but as postcreation happenings, or perhaps as the last step or a final overlay of creation. In Sirach 24:3–6, when Wisdom comes forth from "the mouth of the Most High" and moves about, the "vault of heaven" (v. 5; cf. Prov. 8:27–28) is already in place and "earth" is already inhabited, it seems, by peoples and nations (Sir. 24:6). Sirach 1:9–10 is even more explicit that Wisdom is a kind of final overlay of creation: "[The Lord] poured her [Wisdom] out upon all his works, upon all the living according to his gift; he lavished her upon those who love him." Sirach's view of Adonai's creative work is closer than Proverbs 8:22–31 is to the notion that the divine used God's own wisdom (cf. Prov. 3:19–20) instrumentally to create an orderly cosmos. Not only is there for Sirach "but one who is wise, greatly to be feared, seated upon his throne—the Lord" (Sir. 1:8); the Wisdom that is poured out over creation in that book is clearly an attribute of the divine—it proceeds from God's mouth (24:3).

Sirach's view of Wisdom's relationship to God and the created cosmos means that for that text humans might be able to derive some ethical obligations and precepts from the divine wisdom of the cosmos. If God lavishes God's wisdom on that which God creates, and if Wisdom has "held sway" "over every people and nation," such a cosmological vision might well be consonant with a deontologically inclined understanding of natural law as natural moral order. But to view Proverbs in this way is too quickly to assimilate the more ancient, mythologically inflected cosmology of Proverbs 8:22–31 to the views articulated in the later book of Sirach, in which Torah has also become a prominent motif. It does not sufficiently consider how Proverbs might be different, how its reckoning of the relationship of ethics and cosmos might be consonant with a virtue-ethics perspective where certain limited formulations of natural law can be said to emerge not from study of the orders of creation but from a consideration of the sort of being humans naturally are.

Brought Forth or Whirled About?

The next important term in Proverbs 8 for my argument about how Adonai creates the known world out of the Wisdom-infused watery deeps is חוֹלָלְתִּי in verses 24 and 25. As with *nissaktî*, my claim about the passage is enhanced

---

19. Von Rad accepts the MT's *nissaktî* in Prov. 8:23 but makes no mention of it in this particular discussion of Sirach (*Wisdom in Israel*, 151, 156).

if a particular, though in this case not usual, understanding of the term can be accepted for at least one of its two attestations. Almost universally חוֹלָלְתִּי is regarded as the *polal* of חיל and translated "I was born" or "I was brought forth." Such a rendering has much to commend it. The root is used similarly in other contexts: Isaiah 23:4; 51:2; Psalm 90:2; Job 15:7; and especially Deuteronomy 32:18. It also forms a strong parallel with קנה in Proverbs 8:22, if that term is again understood as "create" or "beget." Similarly, it works well with the emendation in verse 23 of *nissaktî* to *nəsakkôtî*, "I was woven together." However, the parallel with verse 23 is not so strong if one accepts the MT's *nissaktî*, "I was poured out."

Although חוֹלָלְתִּי can be well understood as "I was born" or "I was brought forth," it is curious that an identical term appears twice within the space of two verses. This is perhaps especially so since in all five of the clearly analogous texts mentioned above, the root חיל is never repeated, while a form of ילד is persistently introduced as a parallel. The multiple expressions used to refer to primordial time in verses 22–23 make clear that the scribal poet of Proverbs 8 was learned and had a good vocabulary; hence, one might wonder about the motives that resulted in the repetition of a word like *ḥôlāltî* when a very good, and even expected, parallel term was readily available.

Proverbs 8:22–31 duplicates other terms too, a fact that might suggest one should not make too much of the repetition of *ḥôlāltî*. But the other terms that are repeated are relatively minor and common, and they are not verbs (e.g., אֶרֶץ, תֵּבֵל); or they can be accounted for as graphic errors in text-critical terms (e.g., בְּחוּקוֹ in vv. 27 and 29).[20] Some might wish to appeal to the literary design of Proverbs 8:22–31 and, say, regard the two occurrences of *ḥôlāltî* as a rhetorical strategy (inclusio) to emphasize wisdom's birth in a primordial epoch.[21] Though all this is possible, it is probably better to look for another way to account for the duplication of the term. One reasonable explanation is to suggest we have here not a simple stylistic repetition of terms but a wordplay—the sort of sophisticated use of language that Proverbs' prologue

---

20. The repetition of v. 27's בְּחוּקוֹ (preposition *bet* with the *qal* infinite construct and third masculine singular suffix, "when he inscribed") in v. 29 likely represents a graphic error. Fox and others are surely correct when they suggest that the second attestation of בְּחוּקוֹ ought to be emended to בְּחַזְקוֹ and rendered "when he strengthened." The *waw-zayin* (ו-ז) confusion in ancient Hebrew scripts is not uncommon; the miswriting of the verb in v. 29 can be explained by the influence of חָקַק just a few words earlier in v. 29 and בְּחוּקוֹ in v. 27. The emendation also fits with v. 28's image of "making firm" the sky and the broader creation scene of v. 29. What Adonai is inscribing or strengthening in the verse is the foundations of the earth. Yet, as Fox indicates, foundations are not so much inscribed as laid firmly and reinforced (*Proverbs 1–9*, 285). Loader objects, claiming that at the very beginning of the construction of a building, lines tracing where foundations will be laid are inscribed on the ground (*Proverbs 1–9*, 356).

21. Cf. R. Murphy, *Proverbs*, 52.

(1:6) hinted would at points characterize the book's teaching. It seems the root חִיל, "to be in pain, writhe, labor, or give birth," and the apparently semantically related root חוּל, "to whirl about or dance," should be distinguished, as they are by several major lexicographical projects (e.g., *HALOT, DCH, TDOT*). If one distinguishes between חִיל and חוּל in Proverbs 8, the parsing of חוֹלָלְתִּי in verses 24 and 25 becomes ambiguous. In isolation, neither word *must* be analyzed as the *polal* first common singular perfect of חִיל—"I was born" or "I was brought forth"—though both could be. Either attestation of the term might just as well be parsed as the *polal* or, in this context, the *polel* first common singular perfect of חוּל and be translated as "I danced" or "I whirled about." Such a rendering offers no obvious parallel with any of the typical understandings of קנה in verse 22 or with the emendation of verse 24's *nissaktî* to *nəsakkōtî*, "I was woven together." It does, however, fit with the MT's *nissaktî*, "I was poured out."

If one renders the second instance of חוֹלָלְתִּי as the first common singular *polel* of חוּל, the broader movement of the poetry of Proverbs 8:22–31 would suggest that after being acquired, begotten, or created by Adonai in verse 22, Wisdom in verse 23 is poured out. Subsequently, in parallel with the earlier verbs—קנה and נסך, respectively—she is said in verse 24 to be "brought forth" (understanding חוֹלָלְתִּי in this line to be derived from חִיל, "to be born") and, finally in verse 25, to "whirl about" (understanding חוֹלָלְתִּי in this case as derived from חוּל). As with Wisdom's being poured out in verse 23, her whirling about or dancing can be understood as taking place in or upon the primordial deeps. That is, just as one can speak poetically (in English at least) of a liquid, when poured out, as "dancing" upon the surface of what it was poured on to, so Wisdom might be said to dance upon the formless matter of the primordial deep. As already noted, Ben Sira understands something similar in a passage that is clearly dependent on Proverbs 8. After Wisdom is poured out in Sirach 1:9, in 24:3–6 (v. 5) she "moves about" in creation.

Although understanding one of the two חוֹלָלְתִּי forms in Proverbs 8 as "I whirled about" might technically work, there are some difficulties with such a view, though hardly insurmountable ones. The first difficulty was already addressed—namely, the evidence from key parallel texts for understanding the term as "I was brought forth." Second, although the substantives מָחוֹל ("dance") and מְחֹלָה ("dancing") are fairly well attested in the Hebrew Bible (six times and eight times, respectively), and finite verbal forms of חוּל in the *qal* also occur (e.g., Hosea 11:6; Mic. 1:12), no finite verbal forms in the *polel* are attested in the ancient sources. Only the participle is found, and assuredly only once (Judg. 21:23). However, a warranted emendation of 1 Kings 1:40 based on the Greek and a less assured emendation of Psalm 87:7 would constitute a second and third instance of the *polel* participle.²² Third, although the image of Wisdom dancing like a liquid poured out upon something is generally comprehensible—again, think of the English metaphor of dancing waters—the Bible does not appear to attest a further comparable image of a liquid, in whatever form, being said to dance. However, certain liquid substances, like the water of rivers, can be described metaphorically, as when the river in Job 40:23 is said to "oppress" (עשק) Behemoth or freezing waters "become hard like stone" (כְּאֶבֶן מַיִם יִתְחַבָּאוּ) in Job 38:30. Finally, as with נסך, finite forms of חול in *qal* in classical Hebrew (or *polel* in later texts) are also regularly accompanied by a prepositional phrase, commonly ʿ*al* (e.g., 2 Sam. 3:29) or *bet* (e.g., Judg. 21:21). Things and people usually whirl about or dance "upon" or "in" something. Still, the logic of the mythological images of Proverbs 8:22–31 warrants the inference that in 8:23 Wisdom is poured out, and that on which or in which she is poured—and that upon or in which she now in verse 25 whirls or dances about—is the primordial deeps.

In any case, the emphasis in Proverbs 8:25 likely lies less on the image of Wisdom's dancing about like a poured-out liquid *upon* something and more on the fact that it is *Wisdom herself* that whirls about. Indeed, the image of Wisdom whirling or dancing is consonant with her other activities in the passage. Wisdom's "delights" (שַׁעֲשֻׁעִים) and "rejoicing" (or "dancing"; מְשַׂחֶקֶת, the *piel* participle of שחק) before/in the presence of (לִפְנֵי) Adonai in 8:30–31, for instance, are sometimes reckoned as expressions of her childlike joy, a view that is largely based on understanding the enigmatic אָמוֹן in 8:30 (discussed below) as "little child," "nursling," or some similar term for a juvenile. The root שחק is attested in the Hebrew Bible in descriptions of playful children (e.g., Zech. 8:5). However, as is well known, Christa Kayatz and others such as Othmar Keel long ago suggested that the mythological background to the image of Wisdom rejoicing and delighting before the Lord in Proverbs 8:30–31 is in Egyptian sources, where goddesses are depicted as dancing and rejoicing before other deities in order to please or delight them.²³

---

22. In 1 Kings all that is required is a slight emendation to the MT's account of the people following Solomon מְחֹלְלִים בַּחֲלִלִים (*məḥalləlîm baḥălîlîm*)—"playing on pipes"—to מְחֹלְלִים בִּמְחֹלוֹת (*məḥōləlîm bimḥōlôt*)—"whirling about with dancing." This is a small change that is supported by LXX's ἐχόρευον ἐν χοροῖς. In Ps. 87:7, it is similarly possible to emend חֹלְלִים (*ḥōləlîm*, "flautists") in the phrase וְשָׁרִים כְּחֹלְלִים (*wəšārîm kəḥōləlîm*, "singers and flautists alike") to מְחֹלְלִים ("dancers," so "singers and dancers alike"). Yet in this case there is no textual support from the LXX.

23. Kayatz, *Studien zu Proverbien 1–9*; Keel, *Die Weisheit spielt vor Gott*. Kayatz points especially to Maat's status as daughter of Re to suggest that Wisdom plays like a child in front of Adonai in Prov. 8, though calling someone a child (a daughter or son) of someone does not necessarily mean they are imagined as a very young child. Cf. further Fox's criticism ("World Order and Maʿat," 44) of Kayatz's particular suggestion that Maat is a likely direct *Vorbild*

Even within the Hebrew Bible one can find acts of dancing and rejoicing in close connection with the deity. A key text is Jeremiah 31:4, which addresses the Judahites who, like Wisdom in Proverbs 8, are personified as a woman. "Virgin Israel" shall take "tambourines, and go forth in the dance [מָחוֹל] of the merrymakers [מְשַׂחֲקִים]" (*piel* participle of שׂחק). To this passage can be added the accounts of David's famous dancing "before the Lord" in 2 Samuel 6 (vv. 5, 12, 14, 21) and its parallels in 1 Chronicles 13 (v. 8) and 15 (v. 29). Although the terminology for David's dancing is not derived from חול, his activity is closely linked with rejoicing in a religious or cultic context (before [לִפְנֵי] the divine; in relation to the ark) that is expressed in part via the *piel* of שׂחק, which is itself regularly rendered as "dancing" in these texts (cf. the NRSV and NJPS of 2 Sam. 6:5, 21; 1 Chron. 13:8; 15:29).

In light of the Bible's use of שׂחק to express joyful dancing, the term's deployment in Proverbs 8 thus also supports the reasonableness of regarding one of the חוֹלָלְתִּי of verses 24–25 as Wisdom announcing, "I danced" or "I whirled about"—the sort of action she later in the passage explicitly carries out before the Lord. Yet one further key conclusion about חוֹלָלְתִּי and the logic of the movement of the images in Proverbs 8:22–26 is warranted. Since Wisdom in these lines can be said to be acquired and then poured out, to be brought forth (חוֹלָלְתִּי) and then to whirl about (חוֹלָלְתִּי) upon the watery deeps, it is possible to imagine her as indwelling that formless watery matter out of which the divine will subsequently fashions the cosmos (vv. 27–31). One can thus say that in Proverbs 8 the world that Adonai creates is fundamentally fashioned "*in* Wisdom," understood somewhat literally but also in a deeply mythological sense. If so, then everything that exists, including humans, possesses naturally—from its originary relations to the Wisdom-infused primordial deeps—a wisdom appropriate to its particular kind of being.

Wisdom-Infused Deeps: The Mythological Background

Further important comparative evidence from within and beyond the Bible supports understanding Wisdom as also animating the primordial deeps in Proverbs 8:22–31. This enlivening of the primordial waters in some sense enables the emergence of the known world that Adonai fashions in the midst of the waters in the second half of the passage (vv. 27–31).

---

for Wisdom in Prov. 8, though he accepts the broader argument of Egyptian influence on the depiction of Wisdom. Schipper (*Proverbs 1–15*, 292–94) believes Isis aretologies and not Maat images more likely influenced Prov. 8. Though female gods tend to be described with quite similar attributes, as I note below, Mut may be the best suggestion for the goddess who most immediately influenced the picture of Wisdom in Prov. 8.

Ancient Egyptian and West Asian cosmogonies, including biblical ones, are not easily categorized. Nonetheless, they are sometimes classified into two types: (1) the divine conflict or cosmic battle that involves a deity's overcoming threatening watery chaos and (2) those that are more concerned with the emergence of the world and life from the primordial deeps.[24] The divine conflict model is best known from Mesopotamian and Canaanite texts such as Enuma Elish and the Baal cycles of Ugarit. The second type is more commonly associated with Egyptian mythological traditions. Traces of both types are present in the Bible, though features of both cosmogonies are not always strictly segregated.[25] Scattered throughout the Psalms, for instance, are imagery and rhetoric that are rather easily collocated with the cosmic battle cosmogony (e.g., Pss. 29, 68, 74, 89). Genesis 1, however, resonates not only with the conflict model of Enuma Elish but with other mythological texts that recount the emergence of the world out of the watery deeps, even as it also possesses its own distinctive features and emphases (e.g., creation in six days in response to divine speech). Proverbs 8:22–31 is likewise no pure exemplar of one or the other type of cosmology. The images of setting boundaries and limits for the watery depths in verses 27–29 may point to West Asian cosmogonic models. Other features of the passage resonate more fully with Egyptian mythological traditions.

None of the ancient West Asian (including biblical) or Egyptian parallels with Proverbs 8 is exact or reflects a strict "influence" of one particular mythological text upon the Bible.[26] They do, however, testify to widespread or common cosmogonic concepts and motifs that form a context for understanding Proverbs 8. In what follows I explore a full range of possible dialogic contacts between Proverbs 8:22–31 and the cosmologic mythologies of ancient West Asia and especially Egypt. Some suggestions build on the long-argued views of different scholars; others point to contacts that are admittedly somewhat speculative. Given the importance I place on the ancient sages' dialogic accenting and appropriation of cognate cosmologic traditions, this full effort is warranted, even if acceptance of the general thrust of the argument is not incumbent on acceptance of all my suggestions.

The Genesis 1 cosmogony resonates with Proverbs 8:22–31 in describing the close encounter of the divine realm with the deeps prior to creation.[27] Verse 2

---

24. See Oden, "Cosmogony, Cosmology," esp. 1164–65.
25. Levenson underscores the importance of the conflict model in biblical creation accounts. See *Creation and the Persistence of Evil*.
26. On questions of "influence" between texts and notions of intertextuality, cf. chap. 10.
27. For a fuller comparison of Gen. 1 with Prov. 8, see Bauks and Bauman, "Im Anfang war . . . ?"

of the Bible's initial creation account, however, speaks not of Wisdom being poured out or whirling about over and in the primordial deeps. It instead mentions the divine spirit that flutters upon the face of the waters: וְרוּחַ אֱלֹהִים מְרַחֶפֶת עַל־פְּנֵי הַמָּיִם. The words reflect a well-known conundrum for those who see Genesis 1:2 not as a brief description of precreation mythological "reality" but as God's first act of fashioning the heavens and the earth, a view that helps ground a doctrine of creatio ex nihilo in Scripture. However, this understanding of the line is unlikely given the logic and movement of the passage. "The waters" and even the "formless" earth (mentioned earlier in v. 2) are clearly already in existence before God creates the known world in subsequent verses.[28] Indeed, "dry land" emerges only later, on creation's third day, suggesting that the formless earth itself is already present within the primordial deeps, emerging only after the waters are displaced from upon it: "And God said, 'Let the waters under the sky be gathered together into one place, and let the dry land appear'" (v. 9).

Jon Levenson hears in the earliest lines of Genesis 1, as well as elsewhere in the chapter and other biblical texts, significant echoes of the West Asian motif of a primordial battle between a creator god and the watery forces of chaos.[29] True as that may be, Genesis 1 also evokes the Egyptian emergence model of creation when it speaks of the dry land (יַבָּשָׁה) appearing out of the primordial waters (1:9). What Levenson himself says of the receding waters after the flood in Genesis 8:13 holds equally well for Genesis 1:9: "The image of creation as dry land emerging from the waters of creation is . . . suggestive of some Egyptian material."[30]

The Egyptian emergence model echoes in subsequent verses of Genesis 1 too. For instance, on the same day that dry land emerges from the primordial waters, life upon the once-water-covered אֶרֶץ appears as well: "Then God said, 'Let the earth put forth vegetation: plants yielding seed, and fruit trees of every kind on earth that bear fruit with the seed in it.' And it was so" (v. 11). Likewise, on day five we read of the creation of swarms of living creatures and birds from the waters, and on day six of creatures from the earth (vv. 20–21, 24–25). Although the biblical writer is careful to insist that the earth and living creatures come forth not on their own but because of the word uttered by the creating God, in Genesis 1, as theologian Catherine Keller provocatively puts it, "God has the waters and the earth . . . do their own producing (vv. 20, 24)."[31] Proverbs 8:27–31 is not as full an account of creation as the first

---

28. See the discussion of Keller in *God and Power*, 137–40.
29. Levenson, *Creation and the Persistence of Evil*, 1–25.
30. Levenson, *Creation and the Persistence of Evil*, 74.
31. Keller, *God and Power*, 145.

chapter of Genesis. However, it also speaks generally both of the emergence of the earth from the primordial deeps via the divinity's construction of limits for the waters and the appearance of this earth's human inhabitants—surely assuming the creation of other life forms in its focus on human presence in the inhabited world.

Several cosmologies that Richard Clifford identifies in his work on ancient Mesopotamian and Egyptian creation accounts are also intriguing comparisons with Proverbs 8:22–31 and its imagery of a heavenly Wisdom poured out on the deeps. This is true especially of those cosmological accounts that imagine a vital force introduced by divine figures into watery, precreation matter, an act that precedes (and apparently enables) the emergence of the inhabitable world and the life that exists in it. In what Clifford calls the Eridu tradition of Sumerian cosmogonies, Enki, the god of fertility and wisdom and the personification of underground springs, participates in creation via his insemination of waters that then give life to the world (Mesopotamia). Through his ejaculation, Enki fills the Tigris River with "sparkling water," which ensures fertility for the earth. Despite fragmentary textual evidence, the complexity of the cosmologies, as well as the confusing manner by which the myths mark primordial and postcreation temporality, Clifford believes that such creation accounts "may intend to attribute all life to Enki's interventions."[32]

Yet perhaps the most apt comparisons for Wisdom's role in creation in Proverbs 8 come from the cosmogonic texts of Egypt. In the Hermopolis tradition, the Ogdoad—or the four gendered pairs of primordial gods—represent, as Clifford puts it, the "conditions before creation." Included in the Ogdoad are Nun and Naunet, the deities of the primeval waters. Images of a primordial egg, "from which all things were born," and of the lotus, the first living thing to emerge in creation, are also significant features of this complex mythology. One ritual text in this tradition presented by Clifford also alludes to the gods' "insemination" of Nun, the watery, formless, primordial deeps: "You (the Ogdoad) made a seed from a fluid expelled from you, and you poured over the (lotus) this seed, while spilling the seminal fluid; you put it in Nun [the primordial waters]."[33]

A second text that Clifford highlights speaks further of the primordial egg and also mentions the Great Pool of Hermopolis. In this tradition Hermopolis was reckoned as the geographical site of creation, while the Great Pool of the city was symbolically identified with Nun, the watery deeps. This text speaks

---

32. Clifford, *Creation Accounts*, 35.
33. Clifford, *Creation Accounts*, 112, citing his own translation of the text presented in Sauneron and Yoyette, "La naissance du monde."

of the time "when the land was still immersed in Nun, for it is the place of the birth of all the gods who began to exist at the beginning, for it is in this spot that every being was born, . . . and there also are all the beings that issued from the egg."[34] The divine generative forces that produce created life in these texts are, like Wisdom in Proverbs 8, intimately connected with the primordial waters. Yet even more interesting and significant for Proverbs 8 than the tales of the Ogdoad are the Egyptian creation traditions associated with the deity Amun, the "hidden one."

Amun

Amun is known from early Egyptian texts. Like Nun and Naunet, Amun, together with Amunet, belonged to the ancient Ogdoad. However, his cult became prominent in Thebes only during the Eleventh Dynasty, growing in importance in the New Kingdom and Third Intermediate period. Devotion to Amun was reinvigorated by the so-called Nubian pharaohs of the Twenty-Fifth Dynasty, who were perhaps concerned to legitimate their rule by appealing to indigenous Egyptian traditions. Importantly, as Schipper notes, it is precisely during the Twenty-Fifth and Twenty-Sixth Dynasties (the late eighth to seventh centuries) that the most significant contact between Egypt and Syria-Palestine, which included the central highlands of Judah, took place.[35] The Bible knows of Amun in the name used for Thebes, that god's principal city—No-amon (נֹא אָמוֹן; Nah. 3:8; cf. Jer. 46:25). Dating biblical texts is often difficult, but Nahum 3:8 is surely preexilic, probably from the seventh century, around the time of the fall of Nineveh (612 BCE). Christopher Hays also demonstrates the significant presence of the cult of Mut—the mother goddess who replaces Amunet as Amun's most familiar consort—in Judah as early as the late eighth century.[36] The texts of Proverbs 1–9, including 8:22–31, are typically considered postexilic, yet as we saw in chapter 9, Carr compellingly argues that an early Proverbs scroll, including much of Proverbs 1–9, may have existed in the period of the monarchy, where it formed part of ancient Israel and Judah's early educational curriculum.[37] If Carr is correct (and given the likely preexilic connections between Jerusalem and Egypt, as well as the recognizable Egyptian mythological undertones of Prov. 8),

---

34. Clifford, *Creation Accounts*, 113.
35. Schipper, "Egypt and Israel." However, recall that Schipper (*Proverbs 1–15*, 292) dates Prov. 8 "to the late Persian period at the earliest."
36. Hays, "Egyptian Goddess Mut."
37. Carr, *Formation of the Hebrew Bible*, esp. 403–31.

traditions about Amun and his creation of and immanence in the cosmos might shed light on the cosmogony of Proverbs 8:22–31. They may, in particular, illumine Wisdom's role in the Israelite and Judahite understanding of the creation of the cosmos.

Amun's characteristics have sometimes been compared to traits possessed by Adonai. To one conversant with the Psalms and the doxological material of the Bible, much in the hymns to Amun sounds familiar. Amun is praiseworthy, attends to the poor, and so forth. Most importantly, like Adonai, Amun is a creator god. James Allen even speaks of Amun's creative activity under the rubric of "Genesis in Egypt."[38]

The traditions associated with Amun as creator are complex and multiple. They can't all be brought to bear on Proverbs 8:22–31 here. Yet a few things can be noted. Compared with Adonai, for instance, Amun is equally transcendent vis-à-vis the created world; he is the cause of all that is. As Allen says, "Amun is 'the principle of the creator who begets himself and all beings.'"[39] However, the creator god's immanence in creation is more obvious and profound in Egyptian works than is Adonai's relation to the physical world in the Bible. The Israelite/Judahite tradition appears to have been more concerned than its Egyptian counterpart to preserve the creator deity's distance from that which the god creates. As Allen explains, "Amun is one as the single ultimate cause of all existence, but many in its realization. He is transcendent as the preexisting creator, but immanent in his creation."[40] Indeed, Amun was called "the hidden one" who was thought to invisibly indwell aspects of the created world, especially the wind. "His body is of air, the sky is over his head," says the Great Amun Hymn.[41] "You [Amun] are 'Sacred of Manifestations' as the four winds of heaven, so (you) are called, when they come forth from the mouth of his majesty."[42]

Besides the wind, Amun is said to be immanent in other aspects of nature. Indeed, Amun is the divine animating force of creation. He "enters into the earth" and "enters into every tree with the result that the branches come alive." He "endures in all things" and is "the Life-force (*'nh*) from whom one lives, eternally."[43] As Klotz says, the deity in the Invocation Hymn to Amun-Re "does not simply manifest himself as the elements; rather, the elements are specific physical discharges of Amun."[44] The Hymn, for example, says of the

---

38. Allen, *Genesis in Egypt*.
39. Allen, *Genesis in Egypt*, 48.
40. Allen, *Genesis in Egypt*, 48.
41. Translated by Klotz, *Adoration of the Ram*, 79.
42. Klotz, *Adoration of the Ram*, 60.
43. Klotz, *Adoration of the Ram*, 40, 60.
44. Klotz, *Adoration of the Ram*, 50.

god's third Ba (or unique cluster of traits): "It is in allowing throats to breathe that he spits out wind," and his name is "Amun-who-endures-in-all-things," an epithet that expresses the god's "all-pervasiveness."[45]

For our consideration of Proverbs 8 in light of Amun traditions in Egypt, what is most significant in the Egyptian texts' articulation of Amun's immanence in the cosmos is the god's relation to the primordial watery deeps (Nun). As Klotz explains, like other Egyptian creator gods, Amun can be said to "emerge from these primordial waters."[46] Indeed, the Great Amun Hymn says, "It is from the water surface (*m-nt*) that you appear in the hidden egg (*swh.t imn.t*), Amunet (*'Imn.t*) being with you."[47] Amun emerges through the deeps, stirring up the waters of Nun, to bring forth the cosmos. Yet Amun is also sometimes regarded as the progenitor of the deeps themselves. Through a sexual image reminiscent of the Enki traditions mentioned above, Amun is called "the bull who ejaculates Nun." That is, Amun's ejaculate does not merely animate Nun (as Enki's did the Tigris); it is the animating watery deep itself, that from which land and all life will emerge. Nun, the primordial deeps, can also be said to bear "his [Amun's] mysterious image."[48] As Amun is a divine principle, he can be identified with other deities, but as such a principle he does not eliminate the presence of other gods.

In the cosmogony of Proverbs 8, Adonai is less immanent than Amun, while his deeds are not described in (as) sexualized terms as the Egyptian god's sometimes are. Adonai does not emerge from the deeps, but just "is." He does not produce the watery depths through ejaculation; the primordial deeps just "are." The closest Proverbs 8 comes to a sexualized image in relation to Adonai is with the verb קנה in verse 22, since that term can be used in the context of sexual reproduction—as in Genesis 4:1, when Eve recounts that she has conceived and bore Cain, saying, "I have gotten [קנה] a man with [the help of] the LORD."[49] In Proverbs 8:22, the text thus might opaquely hint that Adonai "begets" Wisdom. But this meaning for the root in 8:22 is neither obvious nor the only possible one.

If in the Egyptian sources Amun can sometimes be said to create the deeps and to emerge from the same, in Proverbs 8 Adonai neither creates nor emerges from the waters; he fashions the cosmos in the midst of them. If Amun's ejaculate can constitute and animate the watery masses from which land and life emerge, in Proverbs it is Wisdom who is poured out (perhaps implicitly by

---

45. Klotz, *Adoration of the Ram*, 28.
46. Klotz, *Adoration of the Ram*, 23.
47. Klotz, *Adoration of the Ram*, 102.
48. Klotz, *Adoration of the Ram*, 79.
49. Author's translation.

Adonai, or perhaps she pours herself out) upon the deeps. If Amun stirs up the waters as he emerges from the deeps before he brings forth the cosmos, in the Judahite wisdom book it is Wisdom who dances or whirls about on the ancient waters out of which the Lord creates the known world. Although the Judahite Yahwistic text does not say so explicitly, in the economy of images of Proverbs 8, Wisdom can be thought to be functionally analogous to the enlivening, vital nature of Amun's presence in some of the Egyptian works. She can be thought to infuse and animate the waters out of which Adonai will make the known world appear—a creation that takes the form, on the one hand, of establishing the canopy of the heavens and other boundaries for the watery deeps and, on the other hand, of establishing the foundations for the pillars upon which the dry land of the inhabited world will rest over the waters (8:27–29).

The Primordial Hill

Amun's immanence in creation and his involvement in the watery deeps is also evident in the god's relation to what the Egyptian sources call the primordial mound or hill, a concept that is complexly presented in various traditions but that is usually regarded as the precreation "site" of the emergence of the cosmos. Amun, in fact, rises "from Nun within the primeval mound."[50] As the Great Hymn to Amun puts it, "Your ancient throne is the mound of Hermopolis."[51] Elsewhere, in the Hymn to the Ba's of Amun, we read that Amun is actually identified with the Memphite god Tatjenen—the name for the primordial mound that rises out of the churning waters of Nun. As Tatjenen, Amun is the one "who came about in the beginning. You are the one who built his body with his own hand."[52] As Geraldine Pinch summarizes, "The Primeval Mound was the place where the spirit of the creator could take on form and begin the work of creation."[53] It was "the place where creation began," "the very place in which the creator first brought forth life."[54]

Traces of this conception of a primordial mound might well be found in the Bible. Levenson hears echoes of it "in Ezekiel's oracles against the king of the island-state Tyre, who says in his arrogance, 'I am a god: I sit enthroned like a god in the heart of the seas'" (Ezek. 28:2).[55] In Proverbs 8:22–31, of

---

50. Klotz, *Adoration of the Ram*, 54.
51. Klotz, *Adoration of the Ram*, 102. "The mound is likely also symbolized by the *benben* stone of Heliopolis." Pinch, *Egyptian Mythology*, 180.
52. Klotz, *Adoration of the Ram*, 54.
53. Pinch, *Egyptian Mythology*, 180.
54. Pinch, *Egyptian Mythology*, 12, 22.
55. Levenson, *Creation and the Persistence of Evil*, 74.

course, there is no explicit mention of a primordial mound. Yet because we are seeing more and more how the passage stands in dialogic relation with a range of ancient Egyptian mythological language and concepts, it is worth considering if traces of this rhetoric and thinking might still be discerned through the imagery of the Israelite/Judahite creation poem. And, in fact, in the midst of the passage's mythologically laden poetry at least one peculiarity of the wisdom cosmogony might be a vestige of the Egyptian conception of a primordial mound. Consider Proverbs 8:23–26.

> [23] Ages ago I was poured out, at the first, before the beginning of the earth.
> [24] When there were no (deep) oceans *I was brought forth*,
>   when there were no springs abounding with water,[56]
> [25] before the mountains had been sunk [into their foundations].
>   Before [in the presence of] the hills, *I whirled about*,
> [26] when he [Adonai] had not yet made the earth or fields,
>   or the first of the dust of the world. (NRSV modified)
>
> [23] מֵעוֹלָם נִסַּכְתִּי מֵרֹאשׁ מִקַּדְמֵי־אָרֶץ
> [24] בְּאֵין־תְּהֹמוֹת חוֹלָלְתִּי
>   בְּאֵין מַעְיָנוֹת נִכְבַּדֵּי־מָיִם
> [25] בְּטֶרֶם הָרִים הָטְבָּעוּ
>   לִפְנֵי גְבָעוֹת חוֹלָלְתִּי
> [26] עַד־לֹא עָשָׂה אֶרֶץ וְחוּצוֹת
>   וְרֹאשׁ עָפְרוֹת תֵּבֵל

The poetry of this passage is complicated. We have already noted the wide-ranging temporal expressions in the opening lines (v. 23; cf. v. 22); we have also called attention to the repetition of חוֹלָלְתִּי in verses 24 and 25 as a sophisticated wordplay. What is also evident is that the poem does not trade extensively in simple parallelism between two half-stichs of binarily constructed lines, as is common in much other biblical poetry, including elsewhere in Proverbs. Its verses are more freely composed. The structure of the lines is, in fact, not obvious and can be variously analyzed. As the layout of the poem above indicates, I understand the חוֹלָלְתִּי in verse 24 and verse 25 not as forming a kind of *inclusio* for a short subsection of the poem, but as anchoring initial clauses in a string of three poetic stichs.

The key to discerning the vestige of the conception of a primordial mound in the poem is to pay attention to the expressions of time and space in these three-clause clusters. In verse 24 and the first phrase of verse 25, Wisdom "is

---

56. On the identification of the תְּהֹמוֹת with the seas and other sources of water known to humans in the midst of the created cosmos, see below.

born" when the deeps and the springs did not exist (בְּאֵין) as well as before (בְּטֶרֶם) the mountains were sunk (into their foundations). In the following phrases of verse 25, Wisdom is said to whirl about or dance before the "hills" (גְּבָעוֹת), "when [Adonai] had not yet made earth and fields," nor earth's first soil.

It is this mention of hills that may reflect the mythological conception of the primordial mound that plays an important role in various Egyptian cosmological texts. Several things suggest this. First, as we have been indicating, the passage is deeply, even if broadly, impacted by Egyptian mythological conceptions and rhetoric. Recall the Egyptian background to the images of Wisdom's dancing and delighting in Proverbs 8:30–31, as well as the various proposals that suggest the figure of Wisdom in Proverbs 8 is modeled on an Egyptian goddess, whether Maat, Isis, or another. (My analysis will suggest Mut is the most likely candidate.)

Second, there is a curious shift from temporal expressions in verses 24 and 25a (בְּטֶרֶם; בְּאֵין) to a locative expression in verse 25b (לִפְנֵי). Wisdom is born or brought forth (חוֹלָלְתִּי) "when" key aspects of the known world did not exist. But in verse 25 she is said to whirl about (חוֹלָלְתִּי) "before" or "in the presence of" (לִפְנֵי) the hills. The term לִפְנֵי, of course, can unproblematically be used as a temporal expression. For example, Amos 1:1 speaks of the time "two years before the earthquake" (שְׁנָתַיִם לִפְנֵי הָרָעַשׁ) to chronologically situate the prophet's preaching. But the temporal usage of "before the face of" still evokes the word's potential locative usage, which appears just a few lines later in 8:30 (and in the other attestation of the term in Prov. 1–9; 4:3).[57] The line might thus also be read as saying that Wisdom whirled about in front of, in the presence of, the hills. She may thus in some sense be "present" there as Amun is similarly present on (or as) the primordial mound in the Egyptian traditions noted above.

The main problem with understanding Wisdom to be dancing about (חוּל) in the presence of (לִפְנֵי) the hills in verse 25—at least on the usual understanding of the line—is that according to a typical understanding of the logic of the passage, these hills do not yet exist! The actual creation of the known world is recounted only in the second half of the passage (vv. 27–31); the earlier lines (vv. 22–26) speak of what happens *prior to* Adonai's cosmos-creating work. A simple solution, of course, is the one typically adopted: to understand לִפְנֵי in a temporal sense, parallel to the other unproblematic temporal expressions

---

57. The Greek of Prov. 8:25 also renders לִפְנֵי with *pro*, the usual rendering of the temporal expression בְּטֶרֶם, though it too can express location; typically, however, the LXX will render לִפְנֵי as a form of ἔναντι or ἐναντίον or a similar locution of place (e.g., ἐνώπιον; or more literally, πρόσωπον).

in the passage, especially verse 25's בְּטֶרֶם הָרִים ("before the mountains")—"before the mountains . . . before the hills, I [Wisdom] was brought forth."

However, in Egypt the emergence of the hill from the deeps and Amun's presence in or through it are precosmos or precreation events, happenings that occur just prior to creation. The mound is like a primordial prerequisite site for creation. Though it may be a manifestation of Amun, it is itself usually a key element of the precreation reality out of which the known cosmos emerges. In a sense, the mound's appearance marks the beginning of the end of primordial time. The hill is not so much the first element of the created and known cosmos, but more like the platform upon which the creation of the earth and the life that will inhabit it materialize. Only subsequent to the hill's manifestation does the land of the known world emerge from the deeps.

Even if one can't be certain about how Judahites would have comprehended and adapted Egyptian traditions, if one understands such Egyptian mythological-cosmological speculation about Amun and the primordial mound as a pertinent context for interpreting aspects of the cosmogonic rhetoric of Proverbs 8, then Wisdom's whirling about upon or in the presence of the hills (לִפְנֵי גְבָעוֹת) can likewise be regarded as a precreation act analogous to Amun's presence in and on the primordial mound. In this case, the pre/postcreation logic of the movement of 8:22–31 is preserved without having to regard לִפְנֵי as a temporal expression. In the first cluster of three clauses in 8:24–25a, the temporal expressions are all forms constructed with the preposition *bet*—בְּטֶרֶם, בְּאֵין, בְּאֵין. However, after locating Wisdom at the hill(s) (לִפְנֵי גְבָעוֹת), the last verse of the precreation account of Wisdom in Proverbs 8 returns to an obvious temporal expression to make clear that Wisdom's whirling about in the presence of the hill(s) was a primordial act. But now verse 26 deploys a different sort of temporal expression than did the earlier verses (vv. 24–25). Wisdom's dancing before the primordial hill(s) happened עַד־לֹא עָשָׂה אֶרֶץ וְחוּצוֹת וְרֹאשׁ עָפְרוֹת תֵּבֵל—"when he [Adonai] had not yet made the earth or fields, or the first of the dust of the world."[58]

It might well be objected that the Egyptian sources speak of a primordial mound or hill in the singular, not "hills" in the plural as in the Hebrew of 8:25. This is easily explainable in terms of the processes of dialogical encounter with, and transposition of, Egyptian mythological discourse—its rhetoric and concepts—into a cosmological key that would resonate in Hebrew and in an Israelite-Judahite context. Mountains and hills are a fixed word pair in

---

58. The expression עַד־לֹא is somewhat strange. It likely means "when" or "before" and is analogous to phrases such as עַד אֲשֶׁר לֹא in Eccles. 12:1: "Remember the days of your youth, before (עַד אֲשֶׁר לֹא) the days of trouble come. . . ."; cf. Fox, *Proverbs 1–9*, 283.

classical Hebrew. They regularly occur together in the Hebrew Bible (some forty times) in a range of texts whose poetry is characterized by *parallelismus membrorum*. However, as Bauks and Baumann recognize, although mountains and hills independently are attested in cosmological contexts (Ps. 90:2; Job 15:7), "Im Zusammenhang der Weltschöpfung ist die Erwähnung des Wortpaares in Prv 8, 25 singulär" (In the context of the creation of the world, the mention of the word pair is unique to Prov. 8:25).[59] The obvious question is, of course, Why? Why does the word pair appear here in Proverbs 8?

One answer is that the Judahite scribes who penned Proverbs 8:22–31 simply obscured an allusion to the primordial mound in those Egyptian cosmological discourses that conceptually resourced their own creation composition. When these sages—well versed in Hebrew literature and the techniques of parallelism, and whose indigenous cosmogonic traditions had no place for a primordial hill—sought to "translate" aspects of the cosmological discourses of Egypt to the theology and ideology (and language) of Yahwism, the mention in verse 25 of the "mountains" (הָרִים) of the "not-yet-created world" triggered the use of the plural expression גְּבָעוֹת to render what was an allusion to a single primordial hill in the mythological discourse that the poets were dialogically engaging. The account of Wisdom's existence prior to the creation of the known world's "mountains," on the one hand, and her whirling about in the presence of the primordial hill, on the other hand, thus morphed into an account of Wisdom's existence prior to the creation of the (fixed word pair) "mountains" and "hills."

The arrangement of the lines in Proverbs 8:23–26 presented above thus indicates the likely mythological logic of the poetry. Although the bold portions of the verses—בְּטֶרֶם הָרִים הָטְבָּעוּ and חוֹלָלְתִּי גְּבָעוֹת לִפְנֵי—have been regularly reckoned as standing in strict parallelism to one another, they may be better said to point to the genealogy of different aspects of the passage's cosmogonic concepts—namely, Wisdom's temporal existence prior to the created cosmos and her (original) local presence upon a primordial hill in the midst of the deeps. Syntactically, in verses 24 and 25 בְּאֵין־תְּהֹמוֹת, בְּאֵין מַעְיָנוֹת, and בְּטֶרֶם הָרִים are subordinate clauses governed by חוֹלָלְתִּי, the first common singular *polal* perfect of חִיל ("I was brought forth") in verse 24. In verses 25b and 26a, לִפְנֵי גְּבָעוֹת and the longer clause that begins with עַד־לֹא are likewise governed by a חוֹלָלְתִּי, though in this case the first common singular *polel* perfect of חוֹל—"I whirled about" in verse 25. Wisdom "was brought

---

59. They add, "Jedoch erscheinen 'Berge' und 'Hügel' je für sich in diesem Kontext erstere in Ps 90, 2 und letztere in Hi 15, 7." (However, "mountains" and "hills" each appear separately in this context, the former in Psalm 90:2 and the latter in Job 15:7.) See Bauks and Baumann, "Im Anfang war . . . ?," 39–40.

forth" (חוֹלָלְתִּי) prior to the creation of key aspects of the known cosmos, when the (deep) oceans and springs (see below) did not yet exist, as well as before (temporally) the world's mountains were sunk. Wisdom's temporal preexistence, however, is matched in the last part of verse 25 by her presence, understood locally, *in* the precreation reality. She whirls about upon or in the primordial waters more broadly, but also in the presence of the primordial hill(s), which again, in Egyptian mythology, emerges from the deeps prior to the creator's full bringing forth of the humanly known world.

One should acknowledge that although verse 25 may well obliquely allude to the (primordial) hill(s) of Egyptian mythologies, there is no hint that the hill is in any way a manifestation of Adonai in the way that the primordial mound in Egypt can be regarded as an appearance of Amun. The Judahites again appear to have been much too concerned to preserve Adonai's transcendence for that. Nor is the hill(s) in Proverbs 8 to be regarded precisely as a primordial manifestation of Woman Wisdom in a way that would also be analogous to Amun's appearance on and through the primordial mound. Nonetheless, Wisdom's whirling about upon or in front of the hill(s) is resonant of the mythological discourse used to describe Amun's presence in/on the primordial mound in Egyptian texts. Wisdom's whirling about in front of the hill(s) may thus be a literary-conceptual vestige of Egyptian mythological-theological discourses involving Amun. Like the description of Wisdom being poured out upon the watery deeps, the image gestures toward her divine, Amun-like indwelling of and vivifying relation to the primordial waters and so to the world that Adonai will create in the midst of those waters.[60]

Wisdom's Primordial Priority

In West Asian and Egyptian creation stories, the known world is fashioned in the midst of the eternally existing deeps, whether this creation results from a deity's victory in cosmic battle against watery chaos or more placidly emerges from the ancient waters. One potential objection to the above exegetical scenario, which underscores Wisdom's existence in primordial time and space, has to do with the idea that Wisdom in Proverbs 8:22–31 might be understood as acquired/created/begotten *prior to* the creation or existence even of the primordial formless deeps out of which the world obviously emerges in verses

---

60. The image is also not unlike Gen. 1:2 (discussed above), where the divine spirit flutters about עַל־פְּנֵי הַמָּיִם ("over the face of the waters"), a fact that might further intimate the affinities of that creation account not merely with West Asian conflict cosmogonies but with Egyptian-style emergence accounts.

27 to 31. Indeed, in Proverbs 8:22–31 Wisdom's existence—Adonai's acquiring, creating, or begetting of her—is mentioned prior to any allusion to the watery depths. The key verse is 8:24, where Wisdom says, "When there were no depths I was brought forth, when there were no springs abounding with water."[61] Schipper believes the verse points "to a time 'when there were no depths,'" to "Genesis 1, verse zero."[62] Fox similarly notes that the formation of the deeps "is a step in creation, apparently the first after wisdom's."[63] If the word תְּהֹמוֹת ("deeps") and its parallel term מַעְיָנוֹת ("springs") in verse 24 refer unequivocally to the primordial watery deeps, it would be hard to deny that Wisdom was acquired or created by Adonai prior to the creation or existence of the primordial waters. Consequently, one could hardly say she was poured out, whirled about upon, and indwelled (8:23, 25) such (not-yet-created) deeps. In that case, she might better be regarded as "woven together" and "brought forth" in primordial time (cf. above).

There are good reasons, however, for rejecting the view that Wisdom in Proverbs 8 is created before the primordial deeps come to be. For one, if Wisdom in Proverbs 8 were created prior to the תְּהֹמוֹת, understood as an undifferentiated, watery, primordial matter in the midst of which the known cosmos is fashioned, that would be a somewhat unique perspective in the Hebrew Bible and hardly consonant with the majority of ancient West Asian and Egyptian cosmogonic texts.[64] What is more, if there were for Proverbs 8 a time when the primordial deeps did not exist, this *also* would entail, as Fox intimates, understanding Adonai as the creator of the ancient waters. And *that* would mean Proverbs reflects a kind of thoroughgoing and literal creatio ex nihilo (cf. the discussion of Gen. 1:2 above). Though such a view is perhaps attractive to some because of its compatibility with normative claims of later theological traditions, it is thoroughly anachronistic.

---

61. Whether *nikbaddê māyim* should be emended to *nibkê māyim*—that is, from "springs heavy" or "abounding with" water to the "sources of waters"—is not vital for my argument. See Fox, *Proverbs 1–9*, 264, 283.

62. Schipper, *Proverbs 1–15*, 310.

63. Fox, *Proverbs 1–9*, 282. Fox, however, concedes that the deeps in Prov. 8:24 may refer to "the ordinary seas," as I argue here.

64. For some of the different emphases distinct biblical creation texts place on the deeps' relation to the divine's creation in the Bible, see Levenson, *Creation and the Persistence of Evil*. Of course, one might claim that Proverbs' implication that Wisdom exists prior to the deeps is poetic hyperbole, that the point of the passage is to suggest nothing more than the idea that "Wisdom is as old as the Abyss," as Loader (*Proverbs 1–9*, 353) puts it. This is possible, but it is a view that perhaps does not take seriously enough Wisdom's independent status in the context of the text's mythological images; it regards the images as mere figures rather than expressions of religio-philosophical, if mythological, expressions of cosmic reality.

Several exegetical observations related to the larger passage also indicate that the תְּהֹמוֹת and מַעְיָנוֹת in Proverbs 8:24 do not refer to the ancient watery deeps but rather to the seas and other sources of water familiar to humans in the known world.[65] If so, then the possibility that Wisdom in Proverbs 8:22–26 is imagined as existing prior even to the primordial deeps evaporates. As R. N. Whybray rightly contends, the mention of the deeps in verse 24 "is probably not an allusion to the primeval ocean . . . but to the existing terrestrial oceans."[66] Since מַעְיָן commonly denotes normal terrestrial spring waters (e.g., Josh. 15:9; 2 Chron. 32:4; Prov. 5:16) and refers to the primordial waters only in cosmogonic contexts (e.g., Gen. 7:11; 8:2), I focus the following discussion on the terms תְּהוֹם/תְּהֹמוֹת, which often obviously refer to the primordial deeps, in order to make clear that the waters of Proverbs 8:24 are seas and springs of the known, created world.

A first reason to understand תְּהֹמוֹת in Proverbs 8:24 as a term that here connotes not primarily the watery matter of the primordial epoch but waters known from the created, inhabitable world is the cluster of images in the first movement of Proverbs 8:22–31. As noted earlier, essentially all commentators agree that verses 22–26 focus on the (primordial) time before creation of the known world, and they do so by speaking of those features of the created cosmos that were *not yet* fashioned when Adonai first acquired or created Wisdom. These not-yet-created aspects of the cosmos include the earth generally, but also mountains (v. 25; on "hills" see above), as well as fields and the dust or dirt of the inhabitable world, the תֵּבֵל (v. 26).[67] The seas and springs of verse 24 are thus also best understood not as the formless matter of the primordial deeps but as part of that inhabitable world that comes into existence only with God's creative work beginning in verse 27 and, hence, after the appearance of Wisdom. Indeed, תְּהוֹם/וֹת (and the rhetoric of "springs") does not always and everywhere in the Bible refer simply to the primordial waters.[68] This is most clear from Deuteronomy 8:7:

---

65. See Emerton, "'Spring and Torrent,'" 126n2. Cf. Loader, *Proverbs 1–9*, 352–53; and Fox, *Proverbs 1–9*, 282.

66. Whybray, *Proverbs*, 132.

67. Despite efforts to discover in the passage an orderly upward and downward progression of creation that begins in the deeps in v. 24, such a movement is imprecise and general at best, as noted by Loader, *Proverbs 1–9*, 351–52.

68. There does not seem to be any full or clear distinction in the use of the singular or plural (תְּהוֹם/תְּהֹמוֹת) of the term in the Bible. At points both refer unambiguously to the primordial deeps (e.g., singular in Gen. 1:2; plural in Ps. 33:7). However, when the substantive is used to describe the sources of water known in and from the created world, the texts may tend toward the plural (e.g., Exod. 15:5, 8; Deut. 8:7; Pss. 78:15; 106:9; Isa. 63:13), as in Prov. 8:24.

For the LORD your God is bringing you into a good land, a land with flowing streams, with springs [עֲיָנֹת] and underground waters [תְּהֹמֹת] welling up [or "going forth"] in valleys and hills.[69]

Here the various sources of water are clearly located in the geography of the created world, the good land with valleys and hills, which the Israelites will inhabit. They do not refer to the primordial deeps.

Besides Deuteronomy 8:7, a number of texts that describe or allude to the crossing of the Red/Reed Sea also use תְּהֹום/ות in a way that must—at least in part—refer to the real waters of the real Red Sea and not only to the mythic, primordial deeps. These verses include Exodus 15:5 and 8, Isaiah 51:10 and 63:13, as well as Psalm 106:9, which reads as follows:[70]

> He rebuked the Red Sea, and it became dry;
> he led them through the deep [תְּהֹמֹות] as through a desert.

That the retellings of the Red Sea crossing reverberate with mythic motifs of creation out of threatening watery chaos need not, and ought not, be denied. However, the more literal reference to the real Red Sea likewise ought not to be elided in these allusions to the ancient deeps. Like Deuteronomy 8:7, the Red Sea passages suggest that תְּהֹום/ות can occasionally refer not merely to primordial waters but also, sometimes at the same time, to the known waters of the created cosmos.

None of this is particularly surprising given Israel's vision of a three-tiered cosmos. Although the picture of this cosmos is not completely unified across biblical passages, what the texts suggest is that the earth is supported on pillars in the midst of primordial waters; God bounds the mythological sea by holding back the primordial deeps from all around the dry land, while also deploying the vault of heaven to restrain the waters above the earth. Various "windows" and "doors" permit the falling of rain and dew from the waters in the heavens above, while subterranean channels allow springs and bodies of water to bubble up from the deeps below the earth. The postcreation waters of the inhabited world—the rains, seas, and springs—can thus be seen as controlled participations in the primordial deeps in the midst of which the world exists.

One might object to understanding תְּהֹמֹות in verse 24 as referring to the waters of the created world and not the primordial sea on the grounds that the

---

69. In contrast to the NRSV, one might understand עֲיָנֹת and תְּהֹמֹת here to form a hendiadys: "a land of flowing streams, of deep springs welling up in valleys and hills."

70. To these verses a few others might be added, e.g., Jon. 2:5. See Emerton, "'Spring and Torrent,'" 126.

same word in verses 27 and 28 undoubtedly does refer to the watery deeps—though in these subsequent verses the form is singular rather than plural.[71] One might well wonder whether a sophisticated theo-mythological text like Proverbs 8:22–31 would use the same word in short order with two different senses. We have already contended in relation to חוֹלָלְתִּי that it surely would and that such sophisticated wordplay contributes to the theo-mythological force of the passage. What is more, the different connotations of תְּהוֹם/תּ in these lines of Proverbs 8 are also easily explained by recognizing that the second half of the passage moves from an account of the divine's acquisition of Wisdom *before* the formation of features of the inhabitable world to assertions about Wisdom's presence *in and during* the creation of that cosmos. When verse 27, for example, speaks of the drawing of a circle (חוּג) on the face of the תְּהוֹם, this is obviously the act of constructing "the horizon, the border between earth and sky," as Fox puts it.[72] This vaulted horizon of the heavens holds back from the earth the primordial waters (תְּהוֹם) from which the cosmos emerges, just as they (תְּהוֹם) are damned up by the limits assigned to the sea in verse 29. In verse 28, the image of springs (עִינוֹת) "growing" or, better, "being made strong" is the endowing of these waters with the power to surge up through the earth to become precisely the springs (מַעְיְנוֹת) of verse 24. The תְּהֹמוֹת and מַעְיְנוֹת of the first half of the passage are thus quite clearly the oceans, seas, and springs that humans know in the created world.[73]

Despite the ambiguous rhetoric of deeps and springs in 8:24, Wisdom in Proverbs 8:22–31 is thus *not* acquired or created prior to the watery formless matter that most other biblical and ancient West Asian and Egyptian cosmogonies also imagine as preexisting the creation of the heavens and the earth. Rather, Wisdom is first created or acquired by Adonai and is then poured out over and dances in or upon the formless matter of the deeps (and perhaps originally "before" a primordial hill). She subsequently can be said to infuse the תְּהוֹם. The conceptual and rhetorical (re)sources deployed by the Israelite-Judahite text of Proverbs 8:22–31 in this poetic "wisdom cosmogony" are primarily to be discerned in Egyptian mythological texts associated with Amun. The Israelite-Judahite theological appropriation and accenting of these discourses—hardly a strict or straightforward adoption of Egyptian notions—preserves not only an opaque trace of the previously

71. See note 63 above.
72. Fox, *Proverbs 1–9*, 284.
73. Fox, *Proverbs 1–9*, 285. The *qal* infinitive in v. 28 in the phrase *baʿăzôz ʿînôt*, "when the springs of the deep grew strong," probably should be emended, following the LXX, to the *piel* infinitive with third masculine singular suffix, *baʿazzəzô ʿînôt*, "when he [Adonai] made strong the springs."

spoken "word" (as Bakhtin might say; cf. chap. 10) of the Egyptian conception of the primordial hill; it has also more fundamentally and creatively aligned Amun's transcendence as creator with Adonai's transcendent creative work and merged Amun's characteristic immanence and relation to the primordial waters with the divine goddess-like figure of Wisdom whom Adonai acquires/creates/begets at the beginning of "his way" (v. 22). In being poured out and dancing upon or in the primordial waters, Wisdom now indwells and, as a kind of vital force within the primordial watery mass that serves as the site of creation, animates those deeps, the "stuff" from which the Lord, like Amun in Egypt, brings forth the world.

'Āmôn Is (or Was) Amun

Traces of Egyptian mythological discourse associated with the god Amun, which elucidate the way Proverbs 8 understands Wisdom to infuse and animate the primordial deeps, are likely evident in the text in at least one additional way—namely, the problematic term אָמוֹן ('āmôn) in Proverbs 8:30. The debate regarding the meaning and possible emendations to 'āmôn is one of the most famous in biblical criticism. As the major commentators on Proverbs all explain, there is a cluster of typical (and a few less widely adopted) proposals regarding how to understand the term.[74] Some exegetes emend 'āmôn to 'ommān and translate "artisan" or "master workman" (NRSV), sometimes appealing to an Akkadian term, *ummānu*, that refers to the postdiluvian sages of Mesopotamian mythology. This translation underscores Wisdom's active role in creation. Other commentators understand the term to be an infinitive absolute of the root אמן ("to trust"), render it as the adverb "faithfully" or "constantly," and understand Wisdom in Proverbs 8 as a faithful or constant presence in relation to the divine. Still others understand 'āmôn to be derived from אמן II, a root that means "to nurture," and so translate the term as "pedagogue" or "ward" or as "growing up with." Depending on how other key terms and imagery in Proverbs 8:22–31 are understood, all these possibilities make some sense. Yet they are also all to some extent unsatisfactory.[75]

---

74. The discussion in this paragraph primarily follows Fox, *Proverbs 1–9*, 286–87; cf. Loader, *Proverbs 1–9*, 356–60; and Schipper, *Proverbs 1–15*, 312–15.

75. With regard to the first proposal, as Fox (*Proverbs 1–9*, 286) says, "MT's *'āmôn* is not compatible phonologically or orthographically with *ummānu*. The attested Hebrew cognate (possibly a loanword) is *'ommān*." Hence "the analogy with *ummānu* requires an emendation, but the only justification for the emendation is the analogy, which is not a close one." Although a translation such as "pedagogue" could be explained "by parsing *'āmôn* as a rare

One possibility for understanding the word *'āmôn* in Proverbs 8:30, which is only rarely mentioned and even more seldomly argued for, may ironically turn out to offer the best solution to the famous textual conundrum, especially in light of the already identified traces of Egyptian mythological discourse in the passage. This solution is simply to regard the term as the personal name of the Egyptian deity Amun. Its appearance in Proverbs 8 reflects a relatively incomplete assimilation (at least from later biblical and normative Jewish and Christian perspectives) of Egyptian mythological-cosmological discourse to an Israelite-Judahite theological-ideological context. That is, Proverbs 8:22–31 preserves the vestiges of an early Israelite-Judahite attempt to appropriate Egyptian mythological rhetoric and concepts into a Yahwistic context at a time and place when and where the monotheistic concerns of later tradents were simply not at play. The term *'āmôn* in verse 30 is merely the most unrefined of these mythological remnants.

The resonances between Adonai's and Amun's characters as high gods and creator deities, as well as the analogy between Wisdom's immanence in the watery deeps from which the cosmos emerges in Proverbs 8 and Amun's immanence in primordial space evident in the Amun tradition of Egypt, are the first reason to consider *'āmôn* in Proverbs 8:30 as a vestigial allusion to the god Amun. A second reason emerges if one recalls that by the late eighth century significant contact between Egypt and Jerusalem was well underway; such contact is evident from the presence of the cult of Amun's consort, the goddess Mut, in Judah by this time. The material remains of amulets and the onomastica from the late preexilic era point to Mut's influence in the area.[76] What is more, the Bible itself testifies to the Judahites' direct appeals to Egypt for assistance in complex international affairs of the time (e.g., Isa. 31). The "ways of cultural contacts," as Schipper puts it, that surely resulted in some level of Egyptian fertilization of Judahite theological and religious

---

(or Aramaizing) *nomen agentis* of the *qatol* pattern," it seems "the picture of Wisdom either carrying or instructing (whom?) during creation has no place in Prov. 8." "Ward" or "nursling" are also possible renderings of *'āmôn*. If the Hebrew word is parsed as an infinite absolute that functions as "an adverbial complement" (so Fox; cf. Schipper, *Proverbs 1–15*, 313), no emendation of the text is necessary, but one needs to decide the sense of the adverbial expression—e.g., "faithfully," "constantly," or "growing up with" (so Fox). This last solution relies exegetically on understanding the "story" of Wisdom in the passage to be something like the creation or begetting of a being that develops or grows up and, subsequently, plays before Adonai like a child. As we have seen, however, the nature of Adonai's acquisition (קנה) of Wisdom in 8:22 is not necessarily primarily or only that of begetting a child or even the creation of a being, which as it grows up will play like a child. What is more, the rhetoric of rejoicing and dancing that follows in 8:30–31 need not evoke child's play; it also sometimes carries a significant ritual or cultic sense and is appropriate to a female deity's actions directed toward a high god.

76. Hays, "Egyptian Goddess Mut."

speculation was thus well established in the late monarchic period.⁷⁷ Third, unlike some other proposals, understanding *'āmôn* as an allusion to the god Amun requires no emendation/revocalization of the Hebrew text of 8:30. The references to this god's city (*Nō' 'Āmôn*) in Nahum 3:8 (cf. Jer. 46:25) make clear that the Hebrew spelling and vocalization of his name was likely *'āmôn*, as in Proverbs 8:30.

Understanding *'āmôn* as a vestigial allusion to the god Amun, however, does require a particular understanding of the syntax of the phrase וָאֶהְיֶה אֶצְלוֹ אָמוֹן in Proverbs 8:30. *'Āmôn* here is regularly regarded as a reference to, or an attribute of, Wisdom. "I [Wisdom] was beside him [Adonai] as an artisan/nursling/faithful one." However, the term can also be said to stand in apposition to אֶצְלוֹ; subsequently, it need not be regarded as a predicate of Wisdom but of the referent of the third masculine singular possessive suffix of אֶצְלוֹ, which most take to be Adonai. Cleon Rogers marshals "several examples" of just such "a noun in relation to a preceding suffixed personal pronoun in Hebrew" and contends that in Proverbs 8:30 "the word אָמוֹן would describe the Lord in His role as the world's 'master builder' or 'architect.'"⁷⁸ Yet, instead of insisting, as Rogers does, that אָמוֹן carries a contested meaning like "master builder," on the understanding of the line's syntax that he promotes, the phrase וָאֶהְיֶה אֶצְלוֹ אָמוֹן can be rendered simply as "then I [Wisdom] was beside him, [that is,] Amun." Though a minority scholarly voice when it comes to the question of *'āmôn* in Proverbs 8:30, as Loader notes, P. E. Bonnard similarly regards "אָמוֹן" as an apposition to the suffix in "אֶצְלוֹ" and likewise sees in 8:30 some direct reflex of the divine name Amon/Amun: "as Ma'at is the companion to Amon, so Wisdom is the companion of Yahweh, the only true 'Amon' (consolidator)."⁷⁹

Other observations and arguments likewise suggest that *'āmôn* in Proverbs 8:30 is a vestigial reference to the god Amun. It has already been noted that some scholars, such as Kayatz and Keel, point out how Wisdom's rejoicing and dancing in Proverbs 8 is reminiscent of the images of Egyptian goddesses delighting a high god. Within the Hebrew Bible, such dancing and celebrating (שׂהק), like that which David does, are appropriate acts to perform before the divine. To these general observations regarding "religious dancing" and Wisdom's relation to Egyptian goddesses, one can also note how rejoicing

---

77. Schipper, "Egypt and Israel." The phrase "ways of cultural contacts" appears in the subtitle of Schipper's article.

78. Rogers, "Meaning and Significance," 208–21.

79. Loader, *Proverbs 1–9*, 358n139. See Bonnard, "De la Sagesse personifieé," 121–22. In contrast to Bonnard (and Kayatz, upon whose work Bonnard in part draws), I regard Mut, rather than Maat, as a more likely model for Wisdom in Prov. 8. Cf. Fox, "World Order and Ma'at," and Schipper, *Proverbs 1–15*, 292–94, for some of the problems with the Wisdom-Maat parallel.

before Amun in particular is explicit in certain Egyptian texts. For instance, one hymn to Amun notes that "while worshipping your [Amun's] face . . . the gods come (. . .) they say: 'Awake in peace!' (. . .) The goddesses shake the *sistra*. . . ."[80]

When considering cultic activity performed for Amun, mention should also be made of the God's Wives of Amun, who likewise ritually rejoiced before the deity.[81] The office of the God's Wife was a prestigious and powerful position regularly occupied by royal women. The institution is attested as early as the Middle Kingdom and gained in significance by the Eighteenth Dynasty. It was revitalized during the Twenty-Fifth Dynasty—the historical time of renewed and increased Egyptian-Judahite cultural contact. The God's Wife of Amun was likely symbolically identified with Amun's consort, the goddess Mut, whose cult we noted appears to have reached Judah by the late eighth century. Mut by this time had displaced Amun's primordial female divine counterpart Amunet, who belonged to the Hermopolian Ogdoad—the divine figures of the primordial epoch or precreation age with which Proverbs 8:22–26 also concerns itself.

One of the key responsibilities of the God's Wife of Amun was to perform certain ritual actions in the cult of Amun, including shaking the *sistrum* before the deity. Mariam Ayad explains that this action was designed probably not to arouse the deity sexually, as some believe, but to delight or entertain the god. Iconographic representations of the God's Wives and their rituals show these cultic figures carrying out their pleasure-provoking rites in proximity to Amun—even, one might say, "beside him" (cf. Prov. 8:30).[82] If the figure of Woman Wisdom in Proverbs 8 is regularly thought to be constructed in part from ancient goddess imagery, then the goddess in question may thus not be Maat, Isis, or even Asherah—the usual suggestions—but Mut.[83]

Like certain goddesses and the God's Wives of Amun in Egypt, Wisdom too apparently acts to please a creator deity (Prov. 8:30–31). In Proverbs 8, however, there are questions about whether Wisdom's "delights" in verse 30 ought to be understood objectively or subjectively. Does she provoke the pleasure of Adonai? Or does *she* delight in God? In verse 31, is she herself rejoicing in creation, including delighting in humans? Or does *she* delight humanity or (again) the deity? The lines might be understood in any of these

---

80. Klotz, *Adoration of the Ram*, 70. The *sistrum* (pl. *sistra*) was a percussion instrument often alluded to in ritual texts.

81. On the God's Wives of Amun, see esp. Ayad, *God's Wife, God's Servant*.

82. Ayad, *God's Wife, God's Servant*, esp. 34–51; cf. the images on pp. 68, 74, 111.

83. Such a suggestion must remain only a possibility, however, as ancient female deities, because they are so often assimilated to one another, are regularly described in quite similar terms.

ways. However, in an ancient mythological and poetic context like Proverbs 8, it is best to understand Wisdom's delights in both verses 30–31 as that which pleases the deity:

> I was daily his delight,
>   rejoicing before him always,
>   rejoicing in his inhabited world
>   and delighting in the human race.
> וָאֶהְיֶה שַׁעֲשֻׁעִים יוֹם יוֹם מְשַׂחֶקֶת לְפָנָיו בְּכָל־עֵת
> מְשַׂחֶקֶת בְּתֵבֵל אַרְצוֹ וְשַׁעֲשֻׁעַי אֶת־בְּנֵי אָדָם

Understanding the syntax of וָאֶהְיֶה שַׁעֲשֻׁעִים and the meaning of שַׁעֲשֻׁעַי is difficult; it is another of the well-known, but second-order "*cruces*" of the passage, taking its place behind the major questions surrounding the meaning of קנה in verse 22 and *'āmôn* in verse 30. The term שַׁעֲשֻׁעִים is a substantive that only appears in the plural. Although after the verb "to be" in verse 30 one might expect something like a feminine singular participle to indicate more clearly what Wisdom was "doing" day by day at the dawn of the cosmos, such clarity is not forthcoming. Instead, she says only "I was delights." The expression is probably roughly equivalent to the English idiom in which someone is called a "delight," meaning that the presence and actions of the person please others. As Fox says, "To be one's *ša'šu'im* is to be a *source* of delight to him (cf. Isa. 5:7; Jer. 31:20; Ps. 119:24). God, rather than Wisdom, is the one experiencing the delight here."[84] The LXX, too, makes clear that Wisdom is Adonai's delight when it says, ἐγὼ ἤμην ᾗ προσέχαιρεν ("I was the one in whom he rejoiced").

In Proverbs 8:31, however, the term "*my* delights" (שַׁעֲשֻׁעַי; the substantive with the first common singular possessive suffix) in the phrase וְשַׁעֲשֻׁעַי אֶת־בְּנֵי אָדָם may refer to Wisdom's own pleasure. Schipper believes the text "should be understood to mean that Wisdom has joy 'in' humanity," as does the NRSV rendering above.[85] This is quite possible since, as Fox notes, in seven of the ten occurrences of שַׁעֲשֻׁעִים with a suffix, the possessive suffix "refers to the one who feels the pleasure."[86] Nonetheless, Fox believes that the syntax of the line makes this sort of understanding unlikely and suggests another interpretation: "the delight I *give* is found with (*'et*)—felt by—humans."[87] That is, if God experiences Wisdom's delights in verse 30, in verse 31 humans do.

---

84. Fox, *Proverbs 1–9*, 287 (emphasis original).
85. Schipper, *Proverbs 1–15*, 314.
86. Fox, *Proverbs 1–9*, 288.
87. Fox, *Proverbs 1–9*, 288 (emphasis original).

The movement of the passage, however, suggests that it is again the deity who takes pleasure from "my [Wisdom's] delights." Recall that in verse 27 Wisdom was "there" (שָׁם), at creation, and her rejoicing or dancing in verse 30 is "before" (לִפְנֵי) the Lord, while in verse 31 it is "in" (בְּ) "the inhabitable world of [God's] earth" (בְּתֵבֵל אַרְצוֹ); then finally and also in verse 31, "my [Wisdom's] delights" are said to be "with" (אֵת) humanity. Given the local sense of שָׁם in verse 27 and of לִפְנֵי in verse 30, the *bet* of בְּתֵבֵל should likewise be taken as expressing location; subsequently, the following preposition אֵת is also well understood in its usual locative sense. The אֵת, that is, refers to the company in which Wisdom's delighting the deity takes place. Wisdom's delighting of, and rejoicing *before*, the Lord (v. 30), which is designed to please this God, happens in the midst of creation, *in* (בְּ) the inhabitable world (תֵבֵל) of God's earth (אַרְצוֹ). But because that is precisely where humans dwell, the delight Wisdom gives to Adonai can also be said to be "with" humans, creatures who likewise might be thought to provoke the creator deity's pleasure. Commenting on Proverbs 8:30, Schipper points to an Egyptian hymn that constitutes an interesting point of comparison. In this text not only do "deities that are lower than the creator god but above humanity praise the creator god"; humans do too.[88]

> The gods are crowing: "Let us pray to our ancestors!"
> The humans: "Let us delight our creator in his name,
> The-one-who-has-made-our-flesh."[89]

What is more, this hymn dates from the Libyan period (c. 750 BCE)—that time when the matrices of cultural contact between Judah and Egypt had started to wax, suggesting again that the period of the monarchy conceivably formed the context within which Judahite scribal theologians creatively and dialogically engaged Egyptian traditions in composing Proverbs 8:22–31.

Finally, one further reason for understanding *'āmôn* in Proverbs 8:30 as originally an allusion to the Egyptian deity Amun might be mentioned. It is well known that in ancient West Asian and Egyptian cultures particular deities could be manifest in different places and also could be identified with other deities in a syncretistic manner. Many of the distinctive characteristics of El and Baal of the Canaanite pantheon come to be identified with Adonai.[90] In Egypt, the high god Amun was likewise understood as incorporating in himself all other divinities, without canceling their existence. As Klotz explains,

---

88. Schipper, *Proverbs 1–15*, 313.
89. Quoted in Schipper, *Proverbs 1–15*, 314.
90. Cf. Cross, *Canaanite Myth and Hebrew Epic*; and Smith, *Early History of God*.

"Amun-Re travels through various cult centers of Egypt, inhabiting several local forms of himself" and appearing in many forms.[91] As already noted, certain texts identify Amun not only as emerging from the primordial deeps or as the cause of such deeps, but also as Nun himself. So, too, Tatjenen, the god who is the primordial hill, can be identified with Amun.

Although Bonnard, we saw, acknowledges an allusion to Amun in Proverbs 8:30, he finally concludes that monotheistic concerns prevented a direct identification of Adonai with the Egyptian deity in that line. It is certainly true that some ancient Judahite tradents prior to the exile became increasingly concerned with asserting Adonai's unique status as the one and only God for Israel, with some eventually insisting on a monotheistic understanding of the biblical God. However, other internationally aware and intellectually elite scribes in a monarchic context, like that from which Proverbs 8 conceivably emerged, probably would not have held such theological scruples; and given the cultural contact with Egypt, including the diplomatic exigencies of the international political context of the monarchic period (cf. Isa. 28, 36), they also quite likely would have been somewhat familiar with versions of Egyptian myths and literature.[92] For at least some Judahite literati, there would thus likely have been little surprising or much objectionable in a theological-religious conflation of two creator gods—Amun with Adonai—like that to which Proverbs 8:30 attests.[93] For these thinkers, Wisdom, created/begotten/acquired by Adonai—the creator god of the minor polity called Judah—could be said to be "beside him," that is, beside Amun—the creator deity of the culturally and politically influential Egyptian monarchy. In Proverbs 8:30, the Judahite deity is merely being identified with the Egyptian god.

Like the rest of Proverbs 8:22–31, the allusion to Amun in Proverbs 8:30 thus reflects early scribal efforts to assimilate and appropriate Egyptian mythological-cosmological rhetoric and concepts to a Judahite, Yahwistic ideological context and moral-theological discourse. However, because of the various ways to understand the meaning and syntax of the letters אָמוֹן that were available to later readers of the poem—a diversity that the history of research on the term makes abundantly clear—the subsequent tradition was able to pass on faithfully the ancient text. Only now it had to be understood

---

91. Klotz, *Adoration of the Ram*, 51.
92. The clearest evidence for this is, of course, Proverbs' use of Instruction of Amenemope in Prov. 22:17–23:11. For a reasonable account of how such a text may have been transmitted from Egypt to Judah, see Fox, *Proverbs 10–31*, 764.
93. Though the biblical texts privilege voices that insist on devotion to Adonai alone, the very fact that the Bible alludes to Israel's significant struggles with devotion to Adonai likely points to a real religious diversity in the ancient context.

in a fashion consonant with Adonai's (new) status as the only God for Israel (and later as the only true God). Consequently, *'āmôn* becomes a problem for exegetes to solve, instead of constituting, as it did for the Judahite intelligentsia who composed Proverbs 8, a resource for theological-cosmological speculation about Wisdom, which holds implications for understanding the sages' view of the relation of ethics to creation.

Conclusions

With Proverbs 8:22–31, then, we find ourselves deep in a complex dialogic encounter and appropriation by ancient Judahite scribes of nonindigenous mythological language and concepts. In Proverbs 8 ancient West Asian, and especially Egyptian, cosmogonic discourses stand in intriguing dialogical relationship with the theological-ethical wisdom traditions of Israel and Judah. The passage consequently is broadly expressive of the idea of a divine, vital force animating the primeval waters from which the cosmos and presumably the various kinds of beings that populate the world emerge. Ancient mythological-cosmological texts and notions from West Asia and Egypt provide much of the conceptual-rhetorical raw material for Proverbs' articulation of its own "wisdom cosmogony," where Woman Wisdom herself is poured out upon and animates the deeps prior to Adonai's creation of the cosmos out of those waters. Proverbs certainly imagines Adonai's creative work as happening by the Lord's own intellect or sage plan and practical ability—that is, by Adonai's instrumental use of the deity's own, however acquired, "wisdom." Yet God's creation in Proverbs 8 should also be understood in a more literal and mythological sense. What is fashioned by Adonai is created out of the midst of the Wisdom-infused deeps so that all that "is" can be imagined as created "in Wisdom."

To come full circle from where we started in chapter 11, Wisdom's relation to creation in Proverbs 8 ought not to be understood primarily, as it often is, as implying that moral precepts and principles can be discerned from the observable orders and orderliness of God's wisely fashioned creation. Such a view is consonant with that deontological-leaning, realist perspective where natural law is thought to derive from a natural moral order (chap. 11). Instead, for Proverbs the cosmos is better regarded as created "in Wisdom" so that humans (and, logically, other creatures) are fashioned with a wisdom that is natural to their kind. For the sort of embodied, spiritual, intellectual-rational, and social creature that the human being is, this wisdom entails a certain capacity for practical moral-intellectual understanding, reflection, training, and development. It is better to think of the sort of "created-in-Wisdom" being, which humans in Proverbs are, less as those who can discover (and sometimes obey) the wise moral orders of the natural world and more in terms of the sort of wise creature Frederick Woodbridge describes: "We exist, not to reproduce our kind, not to enjoy life and love, and not to be happy, but to be provident and prudent in these matters. . . . We are born to improve." Indeed, "to be exceptionally teachable belongs to our natural status."[94]

Clearly what Woodbridge has in mind with these words is not merely the human ability to learn and heed the commands and precepts of legitimate authorities—even those that might be discovered in the moral orders of creation. Rather, he is pointing to a natural human capacity to arrive at a "prudence" (*phronēsis*/Practical Wisdom) that enables humans to thrive as humans. For the virtue-oriented book of Proverbs, though, no one is born a sage; since we are created in wisdom, we naturally have the potential to become truly or fully wise, to attain a genuine Practical Wisdom that enables authentic human flourishing. The sort of wisdom humans possess by virtue of being created in Wisdom is one that must be developed and nurtured by humans themselves.

Still, as we have seen (chap. 11), the virtue-oriented moral discourse of Proverbs does have a place for the formulation of certain limited and basic precepts, and some of these might be fairly regarded as natural law. But these natural laws are not derived from some natural moral order or the orders of creation, which are grounded in the unchanging orderliness of God's creation. Instead, they emerge from the rationally drawn conclusions of accomplished practical moral reasoners who reflect on the nature of humans and what is thought to be good for them—whether always and everywhere or in particular historically and socially contingent contexts.

The relationship between ethics and creation in Proverbs, or the manner in which the book might be said to reflect or promote natural law, thus reveals further how the book's virtue-oriented moral vision is distinct from important modern ethical orientations, whether utilitarian or deontological (either rationalist or theistic). When people are appropriately tutored in paths of virtue—as is quite natural for the of sort of "created-in-wisdom" being humans are—these moral agents should be able via a robust Practical Wisdom to identify and desire good and appropriate pursuits and courses of action in life. They should be able to navigate life in this fashion within constantly shifting social, economic, cultural, and political contexts, where a striving after one's own subjectively determined view of happiness or the

---

94. Woodbridge, *Essay on Nature*, 14.

following of particular rules, precepts, or laws will not always prove fully morally adequate.

To emphasize a contextually sensitive and also flexible Practical Wisdom in Proverbs, however, is not to say that the settled, and sometimes historically contingent, moral counsel, orientation, and assumptions that the book reflects—or the precepts and rules of other traditions, for that matter—are unimportant. Quite the contrary. They remain examples of the fruit of the moral and religious reasoning of earlier generations that may yet prove ethically relevant. Indeed, "one who listens to counsel is a wise person" (Prov. 12:15, author's translation), whether that counsel is ancient or contemporary. An emphasis on Practical Wisdom is rather simply to insist that for a virtue-oriented discourse like Proverbs such expressions of wisdom ought never to be reified; they should instead remain open to evaluation and revision by the tradition itself. Put in the Aristotelian terms that Alasdair MacIntyre develops, a life of wisdom ought to be understood as a "practice" that can always be extended and enhanced by the those who have become expert in, or masters of, the tradition.

We thus now turn to a consideration of the various conceptions of wisdom or being wise in the Bible in order to understand how the wisdom of Proverbs might be regarded as a practice in the way MacIntyre deploys the term.

13

Wisdom as Practice (Part 1)

Overview of Biblical Concepts and MacIntyrian Terms

The multiplicity of biblical concepts of wisdom is well known. But this diversity of senses for the term *chokmah* and other words derived from the root חכם should not be surprising. As we saw in our discussion of Amos and Proverbs—and Bakhtin—words can be accented or inflected in a range of ways when uttered by distinct speakers or writers in different contexts. Indeed, in the Bible, as Job 11:6 says, "wisdom is many-sided"!

In this chapter, I first explore the various conceptions of wisdom and being wise in the Bible.[1] Then I explain the concept of practice in the sense in which Alasdair MacIntyre, one of the leading interpreters of the Aristotelian tradition of virtue ethics, has developed the notion. These two parts lay the necessary groundwork for the next chapter, in which I will consider whether these various biblical conceptions of wisdom and Proverbs' own "moral" vision of wisdom in particular can well be regarded as kinds of practices in the MacIntyrian sense.

Wisdom as Practical Skill or Know-How

Far from referring to a kind of moral sagacity as in Proverbs, "wisdom" or "being wise" in different parts of the Bible entails not much more than prac-

---

1. Most major commentaries on Proverbs and the significant handbooks on wisdom literature regularly address the various biblical concepts of wisdom. See, e.g., Crenshaw, *Old Testament Wisdom*, 1–21; and Schipper, *Proverbs 1–15*, 14–17.

Wisdom as Practice (Part 1)

tical ability. It is a kind of skill or know-how, sometimes involving a clear technical aspect. Consider Jeremiah 9:16 [9:17], for instance:

> Thus says the Lord of hosts:
> Consider, and call for the mourning women to come;
>   send for the skilled women [הַחֲכָמוֹת] to come.

Here the term "skilled" renders nothing other than a form of the root חכם ("to be wise"). The women who are skilled are "wise." They appear to be experts in rituals of lamentation; they possess a particular kind of practical ability. Any moral aspect of these women's character is not overt and may not even be regarded as relevant to the appropriate exercise of the practical skill of lamenting.

Besides the professional mourners of Jeremiah, the description of craftspeople who engage in the work of building and furnishing the tabernacle in Exodus 31–36 are leading examples of a biblical conception of wisdom that seems to be essentially a practical ability, skill, or know-how. Consider, for example, Exodus 31:1–7 and 35:25–26.

> The Lord spoke to Moses: See, I have called by name Bezalel son of Uri son of Hur, of the tribe of Judah: and I have filled him with divine spirit, with ability [חָכְמָה], intelligence [תְּבוּנָה], and knowledge [דַּעַת] in every kind of craft, to devise artistic designs, to work in gold, silver, and bronze, in cutting stones for setting, and in carving wood, in every kind of craft. Moreover, I have appointed with him Oholiab son of Ahisamach, of the tribe of Dan; and I have given skill [חָכְמָה] to all the skillful [חֲכַם־לֵב], so that they may make all that I have commanded you: the tent of meeting, and the ark of the covenant, and the mercy seat that is on it, and all the furnishings of the tent. (Exod. 31:1–7)

> All the skillful [חַכְמַת־לֵב] women spun with their hands, and brought what they had spun in blue and purple and crimson yarns and fine linen; all the women whose hearts moved them to use their skill [חָכְמָה] spun the goats' hair. (Exod. 35:25–26)

As with the Jeremiah passage, the NRSV's language of "skill" and "ability" in these passages translates the language of wisdom—forms of the Hebrew root חכם, "to be wise." Though significant and sophisticated, the artisanal skills or wisdom of the tabernacle builders is a kind of know-how and not obviously of an ethical sort. Likewise, the rhetoric of "intelligence" (תְּבוּנָה) and "knowledge" (דַּעַת), terms that refer to mental capacities, relates directly to the know-how of the skilled workers, not to a moral Practical Wisdom like one encounters in the book of Proverbs.

Wisdom as (Political) Shrewdness

Closely related to wisdom as practical ability or know-how in the Bible is the idea of wisdom as shrewdness. This sort of wisdom is most clearly on display with certain Machiavellian actions of political leaders. Two good examples are Pharaoh in Exodus 1:10 and Solomon in 1 Kings 2:5–9.

In Exodus 1:10 the Pharaoh who "knew not Joseph," out of fear that the Hebrew slaves would rebel and take up arms against Egypt, says to his people, "Let us deal shrewdly" with the Hebrews. The Hebrew word for "deal shrewdly" is again simply a verbal form of the root חכם, "to be wise." What Pharaoh intends to do shrewdly is increase the oppression of the Hebrews to maintain exploitative control over them—a far cry from the wisdom and justice with which Proverbs is so often concerned.

The same sort of "wisdom" or ruthless political shrewdness that Pharaoh articulates is also on display in 1 Kings 2:5–9. Here David commends his son Solomon as wise because Solomon will know how, and know *that* it is necessary, to eliminate David's (and now Solomon's) political adversaries. In regard to Joab, who had murdered Abner and Amasa "in a time of peace for blood that had been shed in war," David says in verse 6: "Act therefore according to your wisdom [חָכְמָה], but do not let his gray head go down to Sheol in peace."

Similarly, in regard to Shimei, who had cursed David when he was forced to flee before Absalom, the old king exhorts his son with these words: "Therefore do not hold him guiltless, for you are a wise man [אִישׁ חָכָם אָתָּה]; you will know [וְיָדַעְתָּ] what you ought to do to him, and you must bring his gray head down with blood to Sheol" (1 Kings 2:9). As with Pharaoh in Exodus 1:10, Solomon here is not merely imagined as exercising a morally neutral practical skill, as might the lamenting women of Jeremiah or the tabernacle builders of Exodus. Rather, his "wise" policy of oppression and domination runs counter to the primary moral impulses of wisdom texts like Proverbs, which centrally value social virtue (e.g., Prov. 1:3) and insist that political figures deal justly and benevolently, even if paternalistically, with subjects (e.g., 8:15–16; 29:4, 14; cf. chap. 7 above). David's counsel to Solomon—to exact revenge on David's adversaries and thereby eliminate political rivals—may well express a common, "practical" (i.e., pragmatic or expected) political "wisdom" of monarchs and political elites in different times and places. Nonetheless, it is distant from the profile of the wise and just person in the paradigmatic Israelite wisdom work of Proverbs.[2]

---

2. Both critical and more positive evaluations of the portrait of Solomon in 1 Kings are widespread. See Dell, *Solomonic Corpus of "Wisdom."* I sketch my own view of the 1 Kings material that treats Solomon in "Reconfiguring Solomon."

Just as the wise artisans of Exodus and the mourners of Jeremiah possessed a certain kind of knowledge—the know-how or expertise of their craft—the wisdom that Pharaoh and Solomon hold is also reckoned in terms of an intellectual acuity. However, in the cases of both Pharaoh and Solomon, the practical, shrewd exercise of political power involves, at least implicitly, the exercise of a fuller or more robust rationality than what appears to be demanded of artisans—except, as we shall see, when it comes to the likes of Bezalel and Oholiab. The sort of rationality and intellectual acuity the rulers possess permits them to analyze situations and devise plans that most effectively achieve their particular ends. Indeed, in 1 Kings Solomon is not only described by his father as one who will be able to negotiate a dangerous political landscape; elsewhere in the book he also plans and oversees a complex administrative apparatus through which he manages his minor imperium (cf. 1 Kings 4–5, 9–10).

It is not only powerful men in the Bible who possess and exercise the sort of shrewd political wisdom of Pharaoh and Solomon. Two wise women, associated with particular locales—Abel and Tekoa—also appear to be practically wise in a political sense. The wise woman of Tekoa (2 Sam. 14) is recruited by Joab, David's general, to affect a change in David's thinking about the need to eliminate his treasonous son, Absalom. In the plan Joab hatches, she is to play the part of a woman mourning the death of her son, who was killed by her other son. This association with mourning may in part explain the text's decision to call her wise (cf. Jer. 9:17).[3] But if so, she is also more than a mourner. Her words and acts, though directed by Joab, paint her as a shrewd or wise political actor. She is able through the ruse of her child's death at the hand of a "brother" (2 Sam. 14:6) to convince David to change his stance toward Absalom. Not unlike the prophet Nathan in the incident of David's adultery with Bathsheba and murder of Uriah, she manipulates David into passing a verdict on himself regarding the situation with Absalom (cf. 2 Sam. 12:1–13).

The wise woman of Abel is likewise introduced in the narrative of 2 Samuel 20 in relation to political events involving David and Joab. The context is the rebellion of a certain Sheba against David and the hunting down of Sheba by Joab. Sheba flees to a town called Abel for safe harbor and perhaps—we are not told—to take his stand there. However, as Joab begins to besiege the city in order to capture Sheba, a wise woman of the city negotiates with David's general to save her town, promising to present Sheba's head to him in exchange for Joab's withdrawal.

---

3. Cf. the discussion of McCarter, *II Samuel*, 345.

Wisdom as Knowledge and Intellectual Acuity

Having wisdom or being wise in the Bible is also sometimes regarded as an accumulation of knowledge, facts, or information, accompanied by a mental acumen, ability, or ingenuity not unlike the political shrewdness noted above. The description of Solomon and his wisdom in 1 Kings 5:9–14 [4:29–34] is perhaps the most well-known example of this sort of wisdom.

> God gave Solomon very great wisdom [חָכְמָה], discernment [תְּבוּנָה], and breadth of understanding [רֹחַב לֵב] as vast as the sand on the seashore, so that Solomon's wisdom [חָכְמָה] surpassed the wisdom [חָכְמָה] of all the people of the east, and all the wisdom [חָכְמָה] of Egypt. He was wiser [חכם] than anyone else, wiser than Ethan the Ezrahite, and Heman, Calcol, and Darda, children of Mahol; his fame spread throughout all the surrounding nations. He composed three thousand proverbs, and his songs numbered a thousand and five. He would speak of trees, from the cedar that is in the Lebanon to the hyssop that grows in the wall; he would speak of animals, and birds, and reptiles, and fish. People came from all the nations to hear the wisdom [חָכְמָה] of Solomon; they came from all the kings of the earth who had heard of his wisdom. (1 Kings 5:9–14 [4:29–34])

Here Solomon is able to set his mind to composing thousands of proverbs and songs, showing his capacity to control intellectually complex information and a wide range of facts about the natural world.

Wisdom as Esoteric Understanding

Related to the notion of wisdom as knowledge in the Hebrew Bible is wisdom that is a kind of esoteric or revelatory insight. In Proverbs itself, Agur in Proverbs 30 is likely an example of one who possesses this sort of wisdom. Agur, it appears, rejects or refuses traditional wisdom—"I do not have human understanding [בִּינַת אָדָם]" (v. 2b); "I have not learned wisdom [חָכְמָה]" (v. 3a)—in favor of a revealed knowledge that includes insights into esoteric matters—"but knowledge of holy ones [דַּעַת קְדֹשִׁים] I [do] know" (v. 3b).[4]

---

4. On Prov. 30:3b, cf. Sandoval, "Texts and Intertexts," 166–67. Most commentators read the two halves of Prov. 30:3 as standing in synonymous parallelism and thus understand the negative adverb לֹא of the first stich to do "double duty" in the second stich: "I have not learned wisdom, nor have I knowledge of the holy ones" (NRSV). Also, the expression "knowledge of holy ones" (דַּעַת קְדֹשִׁים) is often taken as an allusion to the Holy One (God), or more generally to heavenly things. But "holy ones" is not unambiguously attested as a gloss for God elsewhere in the Hebrew Bible; it is, however, a well-known locution for angelic beings, especially in Second Temple texts, where such beings are mediators

Agur's wisdom rhetoric evokes the knowledge discourses of emerging apocalyptic traditions in the Hellenistic age, the epoch during which this penultimate chapter of Proverbs likely was composed (cf. introduction). However, the broader context of Agur's words, especially the rhetorical questions of 30:4, indicates that the tradents of Proverbs questioned the worth of Agur's brand of wisdom. These traditional sages are skeptical of the wisdom of those whose "knowledge of holy ones" requires that they ascend to heaven and return again. Who is the person who can do that? "What is the person's name?" they sardonically ask (30:4). The producers of Proverbs 30 favor the traditional virtue-oriented wisdom of most of the rest of the book. This traditional wisdom, moreover, is likely regarded as quite consonant, ethically speaking, with what in the Hellenistic era was an increasingly prominent "Torah Wisdom"; indeed, the instruction of Proverbs 30:5–9 at points resonates significantly with Deuteronomic rhetoric.[5]

Elsewhere Joseph's and Daniel's interpretations of dreams in the later chapters of Genesis and in the tales of Daniel 1–6 are key examples of wisdom as esoteric knowledge. As Pharaoh at one point says of Joseph, "I have heard it said of you that when you hear a dream you can interpret it" (Gen. 41:15). Indeed, "there is no one so discerning [נָבוֹן] and wise [חָכָם] as you [Joseph]" (v. 39). Daniel, for his part, is accounted as one of the "wise men of Babylon [חַכִּימֵי בָבֶל; Aramaic]" (Dan. 2:18), who are also expected to be able to know and interpret dreams.

Joseph and Daniel are interesting wise figures because both seem also to embody other conceptions of wisdom besides esoteric knowledge related to dream interpretation. Joseph is a shrewd and effective political leader who is able to affect a transfer of land wealth from the population of Egypt to Pharaoh's holdings, while Daniel is described along with his friends as possessing "knowledge [מַדָּע] and skill [שֵׂכֶל] in every aspect of literature and wisdom [חָכְמָה]" (Dan. 1:17, cf. 1:4). He also responds to precarious circumstances with "prudence and discretion" (2:14).

---

of esoteric, heavenly wisdom. Reading the second half of Prov. 30:3 as adversative to the first half is not only possible but syntactically unremarkable. As Fox (*Proverbs 10–31*, 855) says, "Since the negative [in v. 3b] is not explicit, the [second] clause could also be read as affirmative, hence adversative to the preceding: 'but I do have knowledge of'" holy ones, which Fox takes as "the Holy One."

5. The differences between the "human" wisdom of traditional wisdom and the "word of God" (Prov. 30:5) of Deuteronomic discourse should not be overstated. Ethically, the two discourses are not much in conflict, and traditional wisdom's human-centered moral epistemology, in my view, was never "secular"; like Torah it always acknowledged a place for the divine, via conceptions of the fear of the Lord or Wisdom's own heavenly origins. For more on the relationship of Torah and Wisdom, cf. the following paragraphs.

Nonetheless, the wisdom of both Joseph and Daniel is most fully associated with their abilities as dream interpreters, and the interpretations they receive are explicitly said to be revealed to them from the divine. As Joseph says, "It is not I; God will give Pharaoh a favorable answer" (Gen. 41:16). And as Daniel says in 2:23, when he learns the king's dream and its meaning,

> To you, O God of my ancestors,
>   I give thanks and praise,
> for you have given me wisdom [חָכְמְתָא] and power,
>   and have now revealed to me [הוֹדַעְתַּנִי] what we asked of you,
> for you have revealed to us [הוֹדַעְתֶּנָא] what the king ordered.

Daniel's knowledge and skill in literature is also said to be a gift from God (Dan. 1:17), though this ability is not represented as explicit revelation in the way his wisdom in dream interpretation is said to be.

Wisdom as Morality

Finally, at different points in the Hebrew Bible wisdom can also be conceived, as in Proverbs, as correct ethical action, right social ordering or justice, and as a kind of religious piety—the fear of the Lord. Although only very brief examples can here be offered, wisdom terminology with this sense is associated not only with the teachings of Torah but is found also in the oracles of the Prophets. At different points it is embedded in the poetry of the Writings too.

In the Pentateuch, for example, Deuteronomy 4:6 states,

> You must observe them [the statutes and ordinances] diligently, for this will show your wisdom [חָכְמָה] and discernment [בִּינָה] to the peoples, who, when they hear all these statutes, will say, "Surely this great nation is a wise [חָכָם] and discerning [נָבוֹן] people!"

Deuteronomy 4 reckons as wisdom the statutes and ordinances Moses relates to the people, commands that are often of a social-ethical nature. The question of Deuteronomy's relation to wisdom literature, especially Proverbs, has often been discussed. Moshe Weinfeld, for example, identifies a variety of overlapping concerns and content between Deuteronomy and Proverbs.[6] More recently, David Carr suggests that Proverbs' moral discourse, which in some form likely constituted a key early educational text in Israel/Judah, could largely be a preexilic work and may have influenced aspects of Deuteronomy

---

6. Weinfeld, *Deuteronomy and the Deuteronomic School*.

(cf. chap. 10).[7] By contrast, in a series of publications Bernd Schipper understands Deuteronomy to have influenced Proverbs.[8] In any case, scholars are increasingly recognizing the rhetorical and conceptual relations between the small-*t* torah of wisdom teaching (e.g., Prov. 1:8; 3:1; and eleven more instances) and the instruction of capital-*T* Torah in the Pentateuch.[9] Of course, the later wisdom tradition more robustly identifies wisdom with Torah, Ben Sira most famously (Sir. 24).

In regard to the wisdom of the prophets, we already saw (chap. 10) how the moral perspectives of Proverbs and Amos might be intertextually related. Other prophets, too, deploy the rhetoric of wisdom in important ways.[10] Here we briefly consider an example of Hosea's occasional but noteworthy evocation of terminology reminiscent of Proverbs. In Hosea 14:10 [14:9] the text says,

> Those who are wise understand these things;
>   those who are discerning know them.
> For the ways of the LORD are right,
>   and the upright walk in them,
>   but transgressors stumble in them.

The verse is often regarded as a secondary gloss, and it may well be. Yet C. L. Seow demonstrates that the lines are hardly unrelated to much of the rest of the book. The "'Hoseanic composer' or an editor," he says, might well have produced the line as an appropriate "conclusion to the book."[11] Just prior to these words, Hosea makes clear that what the wise will understand most immediately has to do with Israel's disastrous turn to idols: "O Ephraim, what have I to do with idols?" (14:9 [14:8]). The people's religious apostasy is a major motif in the book, and the moral components of the people's covenant failure are obvious. The central virtue of parties to a covenant—loyalty or faithfulness to the covenant partner—is what the prophet insists is lacking among the people. As the (in)famous initial chapters of the book reveal, Hosea reckons Israel to be like an unfaithful wife deserving of punishment from her betrayed husband.[12] Yet "the ways of the LORD" in which

---

7. Carr, *Formation of the Hebrew Bible*, 403–31.
8. Schipper, *Proverbs 1–15*, 36–39; Schipper, "'Teach Them Diligently to Your Son!'"; and Schipper, *Hermeneutics of Torah*.
9. Cf. Schipper and Teeter, *Wisdom and Torah*; and Schipper, *Proverbs 1–15*, 36–39.
10. See chapter 10, note 3 above.
11. Seow, "Hosea 14:10."
12. Works that critically engage the language and concepts of Hosea 1–3, especially feminist engagements, are abundant. See, e.g., the still apt rhetorical analyses of the marriage metaphor in Hosea and other prophets by Weems in *Battered Love*.

"the upright walk" and upon which "transgressors stumble" points not only to covenant faithfulness (or its lack) narrowly conceived. The "right paths" rhetoric also evokes the broader "wisdom-like" moral aspects of the prophet's preaching—for example, his denouncement of wickedness, iniquity, and lies (e.g., Hosea 7:2–3, 13; 10:13, 15; 12:1 [11:12]). The people's failures to keep covenant with the deity in Hosea also entail failures in the realm of social justice and as such resonate not only with Torah but with Proverbs' discourse of social virtue. The wisdom of which Hosea speaks is thus, like the wisdom of Proverbs, also of a robust moral sort.

Among the Writings, Psalms 37:30 and 111:10 offer two examples of a conception of wisdom in the Bible that is also more than practical ability, shrewd rationality, intellectual acuity, or knowledge (esoteric or otherwise); it is a moral vision that can ground a way of life.

> The mouths of the righteous utter wisdom,
>   and their tongues speak justice. (Ps. 37:30)

> The fear of the LORD is the beginning of wisdom;
>   all those who practice it have a good understanding. (Ps. 111:10)

Both Psalm 37 and Psalm 111 are sometimes categorized as wisdom psalms—a somewhat ambiguous and contested scholarly designation. The category, as well as the particular psalms that might be exemplars of the "genre," has often been disputed.[13] Since the central criteria for determining whether a psalm is a wisdom psalm have been the nature and extent of its affinities to an "undisputed" wisdom book like Proverbs, Job, or Ecclesiastes, it is hardly surprising that there is disagreement about which psalms are wisdom psalms and which are not.[14] In Psalm 111, for example, only verse 10 sounds anything like wisdom literature. Though the psalm is obviously at this point drawing on a rhetoric prominent in a book like Proverbs, it is perhaps better designated a hymn or psalm of praise; it, in fact, begins with the word "hallelujah" ("praise the Lord"), as is typical for such psalms (cf. Pss. 146–50). Psalm 37, by contrast, is a more certain exemplar of a wisdom psalm—if one were to accept such a category. Several literary features of the psalm suggest a full and close relation to the discourse of texts like Proverbs and Job (e.g.,

---

13. Cheung identifies and reviews the major contributions in the debate about wisdom psalms in *Wisdom Intoned*, 1–19. The category and disputes over what psalms belong to such a designation raise the question of whether or how "wisdom" might be an adequate term for analyzing and categorizing biblical texts. Cf. Kynes, *Obituary for "Wisdom Literature."*

14. As noted earlier, describing books like Proverbs, Job, and Ecclesiastes as "wisdom literature" itself is hardly uncontested. Cf. again Kynes, *Obituary for "Wisdom Literature."*

the rhetoric of the way, a concern for the poor, the "better than" proverbial form, the problem of the prospering wicked, etc.). Hence, this composition might well be the product of scribes and sages that were fluent in the tradition of discourse attested in books like Proverbs and Job. By contrast, the single verse 10 in Psalm 111 is easily regarded as a gloss, inserted by just such a "wisdom" scribe. In any case, as with Hosea, the point here is that especially in Psalm 37—and other psalms not discussed (e.g., 19, 51, 90, 105, 119)—the "wisdom" that is invoked is often of a robust moral sort akin to the discourse of Proverbs.

Of course, the most significant example of a moral conception of wisdom in the Bible comes from the book of Proverbs. In the next chapter, we will consider how Proverbs' virtue-oriented understanding of wisdom discussed in part 1 and the entire range of biblical conceptions of wisdom might (or might not) be understood as practices in a MacIntyrian sense. However, it is first necessary to consider what precisely MacIntyre means by the term.

So what is a practice? Or more specifically, what is the MacIntyrian idea of practice that can inform an understanding of Proverbs?

MacIntyrian Concept of a Practice

What one means by the term "practice" can vary considerably. For instance, it might refer to an action done over and over to gain proficiency—as a child might "practice" piano. Although the conception of a practice that I am interested in, which MacIntyre develops, does include repeated attempts to hone one's skills and abilities, it is not a synonym for such activity. A practice is also not just a mode of action or a particular series of acts that a person physically engages in that can be distinguished from reflections on or "thinking about" such acts. It is not simply "doing" something as opposed to theorizing about what we are doing or why and how we do it. Rather, it is more akin to the notion of praxis—a practical application of theory where the actual doing of something also informs the theorization of the activity. But it is more and other than this too.

MacIntyre paints his portrait of a practice, derived from the Aristotelian tradition of ethics, in several publications, but perhaps most famously in his book *After Virtue*.[15] It is a concept that has been taken up and critiqued or rejected by scholars in a host of disciplines, including theological and biblical studies. MacIntyre's definition of a practice is thus not unsurprisingly widely cited:

---

15. McIntyre, *After Virtue*, esp. 187–203.

By a 'practice' I am going to mean any coherent and complex form of socially established cooperative human activity through which goods internal to that form of activity are realized in the course of trying to achieve those standards of excellence which are appropriate to, and partially definitive of, that form of activity, with the result that the human powers achieve excellence, and human conceptions of the ends of goods involved are systematically extended.[16]

That's a philosophical mouthful, and so it can be helpful to consider a few examples. These examples should illustrate (1) how certain biblical conceptions of wisdom (just discussed) may or may not resonate with MacIntyre's notion of a practice and (2) how the wisdom of Proverbs discussed in part 1 certainly does.

Examples of Practices

MacIntyre himself offers chess as an illustration of the sort of coherent and complex activity he has in mind when he talks about a practice. Chess has a particular set of characteristics that make it a practice: it involves learning certain rules and complicated strategies; it demands significant time and study with others to gain proficiency; its more accomplished practitioners gain deep satisfaction from engaging in it; and institutions, such as chess clubs and chess tournaments, develop to support it. By contrast, games that are comparatively simple, such as tic-tac-toe, do not share these sorts of characteristics. Whereas chess clubs and associations abound, there is no AATTTP ("American Association of Tic-Tac-Toe Players")!

Others expand the range of useful examples for understanding MacIntyre's notion of practice. Sometimes sports examples are invoked. The act of striking someone out of anger could never be called a practice; but anyone who seriously trains their body and mind in the "sweet science" of boxing may well be involved in a practice in MacIntyre's sense. So, too, to be able to throw a ball fast and accurately on a consistent basis requires significant skill and hard work, but in and of itself, it does not constitute a practice. However, the pitching of a baseball in a baseball game by a baseball player, who through much effort and coaching knows how to strike out a hitter by throwing three fast balls in a row followed by a curveball, is a practice.

Other examples could easily be offered. The work of physicians or musicians can also be well conceived as practices. Giving someone a couple of aspirin or placing a bandage on a cut do not by themselves qualify as practices of healing. But a person who has significant understanding of anatomy, body

16. MacIntyre, *After Virtue*, 187.

chemistry, and the compositions of medicines and who, on the basis of this knowledge, is able to diagnose illness or injury and prescribe appropriate and effective treatment (including the giving of aspirin or the application of bandages) is involved in a practice. Likewise, being able to produce a sound by blowing air through a brass instrument would not by itself constitute a practice in MacIntyre's sense. A jazz trumpeter, however, who has studied long and hard with others to know well a range of rhythms and how deftly to change keys in a performance may well be involved in a practice. Such a person will know how to imitate the great jazz masters and when to improvise on her own; she will also know how to combine her own skills with others to produce new, complex music and may also come to inspire and teach others to master their own instruments.

These sorts of examples are helpful for initially understanding what a practice is in the sense I am borrowing the concept from MacIntyre. But to understand more fully MacIntyre's notion of a practice and to be able to discern how it contributes to an understanding of Proverbs, a few further matters should be discussed.

Practices, Virtue, and Internal and External Goods

One of the key features of MacIntyre's conception of a practice is that practices provide a context for the exercise of virtue. Virtues, as the standard definitions go, are qualities of excellence that allow for the proper attainment of goods and hence different modes of human flourishing. Boxers, baseball pitchers, and quarterbacks exercise and cultivate certain virtues, such as diligence and discipline, when they daily "work out" their bodies to enhance their physical abilities, which are necessary to their practices, or when they regularly study opponents' tactics. When in light of this training and study they hone their skills and strategies by rehearsing with and against trainers and teammates, they also exercise and cultivate intellectual and practical virtue. This sort of work entails a kind of rationality distinct from merely learning an opponents' typical tactics, since such drills develop proficiency in bout or game management or good decision-making in the different, ever-shifting scenarios inherent to the actual "doing" of the practices. And all this is undertaken so that the boxers, pitchers, and quarterbacks may become more proficient boxers, pitchers, and quarterbacks, that they may flourish as—and even expand conceptions of what it means to be—excellent boxers, pitchers, and quarterbacks.

Consider further the example of medical doctors or jazz musicians and how the practices they engage in demand the exercise of appropriate virtues. Like athletes, medical doctors must use their intellectual ability in studying things like anatomy and biochemistry and for learning the typical symptoms of a range of diseases. But bringing all that learning to bear on the diverse symptoms with which various patients might present, as well as correctly diagnosing and effectively treating each person's ailments, is the exercise and cultivation of a further, complex, practical-intellectual virtue—a sort of "healer's rationality." Jazz musicians, too, engage in the intellectual work of learning to read musical notes and jazz charts. But composing a jazz composition requires a kind of practical jazz reasoning, the ability to bring one's knowledge of instruments, jazz music, history, and performances to bear on the formation of an original piece of music.

What all the above figures—doctors, musicians, athletes—share when they heal, play music, or engage in sport is the exercise of particular virtues in order to pursue better, flourish in, and expand the conceptions of what it means to be good at their practices.

Practices also generate what MacIntyre calls internal and external goods. Internal goods refer, as Mark Banks writes, to the "rewards that can only be attained through immersion in the particular practice in question."[17] They are only achieved by an immersion in the character of the practice, its "specific demands, rhythms, and standards."[18] They can be enjoyed only through an application of the virtues that are required of any particular practice. The goods internal to a practice, however, can benefit more than individual practitioners; they are potentially available to all who engage in the practice. For example, the satisfaction of mastering the curveball and developing a way to throw it better are pleasures only a pitcher can know; they are goods internal to the particular practice of baseball pitching. But this pitcher's new way of throwing a curveball is the sort of good that can also be appreciated by others who have seriously tried their hand at throwing baseballs to batters in baseball games. What's more, the pitcher's efforts and new skills enhance the broader practice of pitching; it makes it more complex, opens new avenues for thinking about pitching strategy, and can in principle be taught to and perhaps modified by other pitchers.

Similarly, the pleasure of joining one's voice or instrument with others in a performance is the sort of good that can be enjoyed only by those who engage in practices of music. Yet when a jazz quartet gains its own style, improvises on the jazz standards in significant new ways, and produces its own compositions, it enhances not only its own status as a jazz quartet but contributes to

---

17. Banks, "MacIntyre," 70.
18. Banks, "MacIntyre," 70.

the entire practice of jazz. So, too, the physician who develops a new medical technique and teaches it to others knows not only the satisfaction of her own ingenuity and the pleasure of mentoring others; she also expands the broader practice of healing.

In MacIntyre's thinking, however, a practice can also produce external goods. The concept of external goods in relation to practices is perhaps easier to grasp than is the notion of internal goods since external goods tend to be closely related to the rewards commonly associated with certain activities. The two leading examples of external goods that a practice might generate, and which resonate with important aspects of Proverbs' moral rhetoric, are the rewards of material wealth and high social status or esteem.

Achieving a certain kind of excellence in boxing or quarterbacking, in music or medicine, might very well enable a person to enjoy significant levels of external goods—wealth and fame—that typically accrue to many accomplished athletes, doctors, and musicians. What distinguishes a practice's external goods from its internal goods is the fact that the external goods are also obtainable through other means. The external rewards or goods of any particular practice are not contingent upon that practice in the way internal goods are inseparable from the practices that generate them. One may get quite rich and enjoy a mountain of social esteem by becoming a doctor, a music star, or a champion athlete. But doctoring, music performance, and athletics aren't the only ways to achieve those external goods. My wealth, for example, might come from my luck at picking the ponies or playing the lottery; it might come from an inheritance that my great-uncle left me; it might even be the fruit of my ability to dupe others in a pyramid investment scheme! Likewise, the social status or respect I enjoy may not derive from my excellent work as a physician, but from my family's wealth and power or our already established "good name"—especially if I'm not a very good doctor.[19] What's more, in contrast to internal goods that benefit all who engage in a practice, external goods are regularly exclusive goods. That is, they "tend to be accrued at the expense of their availability to others."[20] The attainment of external goods tends to be a zero-sum game. My big salary and the status

---

19. See further below and cf. the discussion above in chap. 2 regarding premodern forms of causality and Proverbs' act-consequence rhetoric. There we note that the final end of living wisely—namely, a flourishing life—is best conceived as an effect that is internal, or inextricably linked, to the practice of living virtuously—you can't get one without the other. Virtuous living is thus inextricably linked to well-being, but it ought not be thought of as simply causing the effect of external goods, such as riches or status. These goods, of course, to some degree are necessary for eudaemonia but obviously can be attained in a variety of ways, including profoundly vicious ways.

20. Banks, "MacIntyre," 71.

I enjoy mean you won't enjoy as much material bounty or be held in quite the high regard as I am.

Finally, although it is often very possible that one's pursuit of this or that practice will result in the attainment of external goods, these external goods may ironically turn out to "be detrimental to maintaining the integrity of the practice," as Banks puts it.[21] The external goods of a practice may corrupt the practice. This is easy to see in terms of a person's motivation to engage in a practice. The baseball player no longer pitches for "the love of the game," but for the paycheck. The heart surgeon takes a new position not because it provides better and more occasions to contribute to healing, but for the professional prestige a university research hospital affords. In such cases the external goods that might accrue to one engaging in the practice can prove detrimental to the practice in a variety of ways. They may stifle the complex manner that individuals engage in and so contribute to a practice. The physician who excels at heart bypass surgeries but is motivated primarily by the profits of performing such procedures may come to focus her work solely on that one activity. That work, of course, continues to demand a high degree of knowledge and skill; and it will still regularly serve the end of restoring health. But such a focus on an external good may also mean that this physician is no longer actively exploring better and more adequate ways to prevent and diagnose heart disease; or she may not be as devoted to mentoring young physicians or discovering alternative and better modes of treatment—all of which would serve the good end of the practice of healing more robustly.

Practices, Rules, Standards, and Change

Practices in the MacIntyrian sense also regularly require that those who engage in them submit themselves to aspects of the practice itself. To engage in a practice means accepting its rules and standards and taking the posture of apprentice to those who are masters or experts in the practice. As MacIntyre puts it, "A practice involves standards of excellence and obedience to rules" and not only "the achievement of goods." He continues: "To enter into a practice is to accept the authority of those standards and the inadequacy of my own performance as judged by them. It is to subject my own attitudes, choices, preferences and tastes to the standards which currently and partially define the practice."[22]

These features of a practice are easy enough to recognize in the examples I've been offering: the musician who wants to play jazz trumpet must heed the

21. Banks, "MacIntyre," 71.
22. MacIntyre, *After Virtue*, 190.

instruction of her teacher about the movement of her fingers over the valves or the positioning of her mouth on the mouthpiece, as well as the instructor's judgment regarding the quality of the sound that emerges from the horn's bell. Eventually, the music student will be required to learn and imitate the traditions and modes of excellence set out by jazz greats like Dizzy Gillespie or Miles Davis. The medical doctor must pass board exams and also be apprenticed to other doctors through medical school rotations and residencies. The best boxers, quarterbacks, and pitchers learn from their coaches and other accomplished boxers, quarterbacks, and pitchers, who open gyms and schools or offer camps to train and teach novice athletes—using varying degrees of discipline and rebuke.

The fact that the person who engages in a practice must submit to the standards and authorities of the practice and its accomplished practitioners might make such practices sound heavily authoritarian and the product of closed systems that leave little room for any change, development, or critique from either inside or outside. This, perhaps, is a real danger in MacIntyre's conception of a practice; as such it demands that we exercise a hermeneutics of suspicion about any sort of human practice, but especially in relation to the moral practice of wisdom that I am suggesting Proverbs promotes since, for many people, attending to the voices of the biblical text is an important step in arriving at their own moral-theological conclusions.

MacIntyre himself seems to recognize that the practices of which he speaks might be regarded as closed systems of authoritarian control since he insists that practices are, in fact, not static or overly confined by the prescribed standards of a few experts or a venerable tradition. Those who engage in a practice, learn its standards and rules, apprentice themselves to experts in the same practice, and are motivated by a practice's internal goods also become "agents of change" (my term). They are not bound inexorably to the traditions of the practice, to its rules and standards, or to its traditional experts. Rather, they themselves become active shapers of the practices they perform. They become innovators of its standards and architects of the next stage of the practice's living and unfolding tradition. Those who excel in a practice can affect changes to it.

The possibility of change and innovation in MacIntyre's account of a practice is due to the fact that there should be no blind, unyielding commitment to the standards and experts of a practice or, as we will see in a moment, to the shape of institutions that support it. If some different, innovative means of engaging in the practice emerges, then so be it—provided the enhancement of human capacities and flourishing that the practice promotes continues or is expanded. The character of a practice can and ought to change in such a situation. Carlos Santana surely studied great guitar players like Muddy Waters. He also engaged the Latin styles of music of his Mexican and Mexican American cultures, and he understood the psychedelic music scene of 1960s San Francisco. Yet he did more than imitate and remain safely in the bounds of any particular style of guitar playing, and that resulted in his producing a distinctive sound that both remains easily recognizable and continues to impact the broader practice of guitar playing. Similarly, anyone familiar with the history of basketball or American football is well aware of how significantly the actual playing of those sports at the highest levels has changed over the last seventy-five years. These transformations are primarily due to innovations introduced by the sports' most accomplished practitioners, who have subsequently been imitated by others. And, of course, physicians no longer try to heal by using leeches to let blood!

When considering how practices can be changed and shaped by those who engage in them, it is important to mention the role of competition. MacIntyre distinguishes between what he calls emulative competition and market competition. The difference is that market competition views external goods as ends in themselves, while "emulative competitors see achieving the standards of excellences and internal goods as paramount, with external goods valued primarily as resources for further contributions to the practice."[23] The emulative practitioner of jazz who makes a successful jazz recording cuts that record not primarily to enjoy the external good of music royalties but for the love of making and performing music. But when those royalties accrue, they can be reinvested to facilitate the musician's further engagement in the practice. The external good of the paycheck makes possible more focus on the practice itself. With (more than) sufficient income, the musician can shower attention on the music and not on the part-time job that would otherwise be needed to pay the bills. So, too, the medical doctor who enjoys significant material rewards but remains committed to the practice of healing does not focus on acquiring more wealth and status. Rather, she finds ways to reinvest those external goods to support and enhance the practice of healing—for example, by engaging in efforts and supporting institutions that promote physical and other sorts of well-being in new, better, broader, or more accessible ways.

Yet since practices are not closed systems involving just a very few enthusiastic individuals who possess specialized skills and exercise them for the pure sake of doing so, they need institutions in order to survive and thrive—firms, clubs, societies, schools, and so forth. The practice of jazz, for instance, does not just involve musicians who learn to play or sing in a particular style in

---

23. Banks, "MacIntyre," 72.

light of particular standards of jazz masters. It also involves the recording companies and clubs that provide performers opportunities to actually play jazz. These institutions often compensate musicians, and this compensation, as we said, in part enables the continued existence and flourishing of the practice. The practice of jazz involves other sorts of institutions too: music schools where accomplished musicians can instruct novices or associations of artists that can act on behalf of the musicians and publicly acknowledge the accomplishments of its individual members. A variety of music styles and a range of sports all have their halls of fame!

When it comes to practices, then, institutions provide "necessary economic resources" and administer the standards or established rules and norms of the practice (what counts as good chess, boxing, quarterbacking, doctoring, or jazz).[24] No less important, they also cultivate the communities within which the practice can be recognized, developed, and refined. The irony of it all, however, is that although practices—which prioritize internal goods—need institutions to flourish, the institutions themselves must often focus on securing external goods in order to survive. They need money and buildings and certain hierarchies to support and promote the practice with which they are associated. This often, perhaps inevitably, brings practices into tension with their related institutions. Indeed, the standards, ideals, and creativity of a practice regularly face the danger of being eroded or deformed by a supporting institution and that institution's need to maintain its own existence. As MacIntyre explains, a practice is "always vulnerable to the acquisitiveness" and "competitiveness" of the institution that is "responsible for the cooperative care of common goods of the practice."[25]

With this overview of MacIntyre's conception of a practice in hand, we turn next to consider to what extent various biblical conceptions of "wisdom"—including that of Proverbs—might be said to constitute a MacIntyrian practice.

---

24. Banks, "MacIntyre," 72.
25. MacIntyre, *After Virtue*, 194.

14

Wisdom as Practice (Part 2)

How MacIntyrian Practice Informs an Understanding of Proverbs' Virtue Ethics

In the previous chapter, we explored various conceptions of wisdom and being wise in the Bible, and I introduced the way Alasdair MacIntyre has developed the notion of practices. This laid the necessary groundwork to consider how biblical concepts of wisdom and, more importantly, Proverbs' virtue-oriented understanding of wisdom might be regarded as a "practice" in a MacIntyrian sense. By recognizing how Proverbs' conception of wisdom fits with MacIntyre's understanding of a practice, which itself ultimately derives from Aristotle, we will see further how and why Proverbs is well regarded as, at least in part, a premodern, virtue-oriented moral discourse. But more than this, the analysis of the wisdom of Proverbs in terms of MacIntyrian practices will begin to open space for constructive, ongoing criticism and new appropriation of Proverbs' own tradition of ethics—a task that may be of interest especially to those individuals and communities who claim Proverbs as Scripture. In what sense, then, might the various expressions of wisdom or being wise in the Bible that were considered in the previous chapter be regarded as practices in the MacIntyrian sense?

The Practice of Tabernacle Artisans?

We first noted that wisdom or being wise in the Hebrew Scriptures is sometimes a practical ability, technical skill, or artisanal know-how. We considered the

Wisdom as Practice (Part 2)

professional mourners of Jeremiah and, especially, called attention to those in Exodus who were involved in the construction of the tabernacle and its furnishings. The texts of Exodus 31 and 35, which speak of the wisdom of the tabernacle builders, make at least two, perhaps three, distinctions among the persons involved in the construction of the sanctuary. Attending to these subtle distinctions can elucidate whether, or in what sense, the "wisdom" of these figures—their skillful tabernacle building—can be said to be a practice in a MacIntyrian sense.

Bezalel is the most prominent figure named in the tabernacle-building accounts. Several explicit and implicit aspects of the character of his work indicate that what he is engaged in is, in fact, a practice in the MacIntyrian sense. First, he undertakes a complex, creative activity—planning and overseeing the overall work on the sanctuary, as well as specific aspects of it. Bezalel is obviously a master craftsperson, who serves as the project's director. He has expertise "in every kind of craft" and is accomplished "in cutting stones for setting, and in carving wood, in every kind of craft" (Exod. 31:3, 5). But he is also able to exercise creative rationality, "to devise artistic designs [לַחְשֹׁב מַחֲשָׁבֹת], to work in gold, silver, and bronze" (31:4; cf. 35:32). Bezalel is able to discern what is appropriate to the design and decor of any particular project he may encounter, including surely the tabernacle—even if the basic plan of that structure and its utensils is revealed by the divine architect (25:9). To achieve this sort of expertise and creativity as an artisan, Bezalel obviously had to cultivate and exercise a range of virtues like those we mentioned in relation to other practices—diligence, discipline, study, humility (a virtue necessary to submit oneself to others' expertise and judgment), as well as a practical rationality necessary to discern how best to bring one's skills and practiced techniques to bear on any particular complex project.

It is also significant that the work Bezalel is focused on is not just any sort of construction project, but tabernacle building. The work is not his personal hobby or something contracted primarily to enrich himself or enhance his reputation. That is, he is not motivated by external goods that might accrue to him—or at least the text doesn't explicitly ascribe to him such profit or status-seeking concerns. Rather, the work is directed toward a broader end or good: the designing and construction of sacred space that will be the locus of the community's encounter with the divine and a central institution of its life together. The tribes will camp around it (i.e., around the tent of meeting) in a specific order (Num. 2), and it will be the site where a range of community activities, including sacrifices, take place (Exod. 40:5, 28–29).[1] All

---

1. On the question of the relationship of the tent of meeting to the tabernacle, see Sommer, "Conflicting Constructions"; Meyers, *Exodus*, 222–26.

this implies that Bezalel in some sense ascribed significant worth to much of what a wisdom book like Proverbs values—a range of social and practical-intellectual virtues and also something close to the fundamental religious posture of fear of the Lord.

Bezalel's relations to others also suggest he is involved in a practice. He collaborates closely with Oholiab, who is either an immediate subordinate, a second-in-command, or perhaps the project's co-coordinator.² But more than just working together, Bezalel and Oholiab also pass their skills on to others. Exodus 35:34 says God "inspired" Bezalel "to teach, both him and Oholiab." If the divine "inspired" Bezalel and Oholiab to teach others, then their expert abilities and character surely also inspired others to apprentice themselves to them, to seek to conform their own work to the master artisans' standards. Working closely with and teaching and inspiring others also requires the exercise of particular virtues—social virtues of cooperation, obviously, but also patience and the practical wisdom of knowing when and how to effectively reprove and correct others, activities that are likewise central to Proverbs' teaching.

Although Oholiab is only briefly mentioned in the tabernacle-building texts, he, like Bezalel, appears to be engaging in a kind of complex practice. As noted, he is appointed with Bezalel to oversee the tabernacle project, and hence the roles he carries out are analogous to Bezalel's. As we just saw, like Bezalel, Oholiab teaches others, though unlike Bezalel, he is not said "to devise artistic designs." Still, the divine has filled not only Bezalel but also Oholiab "with skill to do every kind of work done by an artisan or by a designer or by an embroiderer in blue, purple, and crimson yarns, and in fine linen, or by a weaver—by any sort of artisan or skilled designer" (Exod. 35:35; cf. 38:23).

It seems perfectly warranted, then, to regard both Bezalel and Oholiab as involved in a complex practice of tabernacle building. They are expert craftspeople, planners, overseers, and teachers whose creative efforts, directed toward appropriately achieving an end that benefits others and not just themselves, require the exercise of a range of virtues. Their artisanal activities and abilities are examples of what it might mean to flourish fully as an artisan. And importantly, when Exodus speaks of Bezalel's (and Oholiab's) character and activities, it rhetorically turns to a piling up of "wisdom terms"—intelligence or understanding (תְּבוּנָה), knowledge (דַּעַת), and wisdom (חָכְמָה) (cf. Exod. 35:31)—that in Proverbs carry connotations not merely of artisanal distinction but of moral excellence.

2. Cf. Propp, *Exodus 19–40*, 489. Meyers (*Exodus*, 252) calls Oholiab Bezalel's "assistant."

The tabernacle-building texts in Exodus speak also of "all the skillful" (31:6) and "all the skillful women" (35:25) whose efforts contributed to the sanctuary's construction. The NRSV's term "skillful" in 31:6 reflects the Hebrew construction חֲכַם־לֵב, which is also attested four times in Proverbs. It is grammatically masculine but surely entails a collective, mixed-gender referent; by contrast, in 35:25 "skillful" renders חַכְמַת־לֵב, a grammatically feminine form that thus refers explicitly to female artisans.[3] Both expressions might literally be rendered "wise of heart" or "wise of mind." In the tabernacle-building passages of Exodus, both also allude to a certain kind of practical ability or knowledge since the heart in ancient Israelite anthropology was considered the seat of the intellect. The wise of heart working on the tabernacle in Exodus are specifically those who *know how* to work well with gold, silver, bronze, wood, textiles, and other material (cf. Exod. 35:32–35), and in the case of the women who were wise of heart, the spinning of yarn and linen (cf. Exod. 35:25–26). To be wise of heart (or mind) thus means to have a particular kind of ability, skill, and knowledge needed to accomplish *something* that could not be accomplished, or only inadequately achieved, without the requisite skill and knowledge—whether tabernacle building or something else (including following wisdom's moral path; cf. Prov. 11:29; 16:21).

Whether this sort of artisanal wisdom or practical skill and know-how—being wise of heart—can properly be regarded as a practice in MacIntyre's sense is difficult to say without knowing more about the relative complexity of the distinct activities themselves, how individuals learned the work, what communities (or institutions, such as guilds) supported the activity, and how those institutions proffered support to those engaged in a task, as well as what levels of creativity were permitted or demanded of those involved in the activity, what ends it was thought to support, and so forth. It is certainly possible that in ancient Israel and Judah, especially in later epochs with more complex social and economic organization, the activity of craftspeople like what we hear about in the tabernacle work could be described as a practice. The passages in Exodus, however, introduce the phrase "wise of heart" in a way that suggests perhaps we should make a distinction between Bezalel's and Oholiab's complex practice of tabernacle building and the more basic artisanal work of others in other contexts. That is, it may be that being wise of heart on its own refers not to a kind of practice in the sense MacIntyre speaks of, but merely points to a basic competency or a particular practical virtue—the simple possession of some know-how or skill.

---

3. Gafney in various venues emphasizes the importance of recognizing possible mixed-gender referents in grammatically masculine forms. See, e.g., *Womanist Midrash*, 10 and passim.

If this is so, what is significant about the activities of the "wise of heart" in the tabernacle-building passages is precisely what the broader context permits us to infer about their work on the sanctuary and how this might be distinguished from the work of craftspeople in other contexts. The craftspeople in the tabernacle-building texts obviously exercise a particular practical ability or skill. They cut stones, sew, and so forth. But in the broader narrative, they cannot be reckoned *merely* as those who possess a particular practical knowledge or technical, artisanal know-how. This is because what they are engaged in is more than an isolated exercise of a single practical skill on a routine project for the usual rewards. What they contribute to is no ordinary work, and what they receive is no ordinary wage.

The book of Exodus notes not only that the skilled workers of the tabernacle building, both male and female, are wise of heart or mind; it also indicates, in the NRSV rendering of 31:6, that the divine has "given skill to all the skillful." This translation, however, obscures the rather complex Hebrew syntax: וּבְלֵב כָּל־חֲכַם־לֵב נָתַתִּי חָכְמָה—a phrase that literally says "in the heart [or mind] of all who are wise of heart, I [Adonai] have set wisdom." A similar but perhaps even more complex syntax lies behind the NRSV's translation of 35:26, "All the women whose hearts moved them to use their skill spun the goats' hair." The Hebrew in this line does not use the precise phrase חָכְמַת־לֵב, as in 35:25, yet the sense of the line is similar: וְכָל־הַנָּשִׁים אֲשֶׁר נָשָׂא לִבָּן אֹתָנָה בְּחָכְמָה טָווּ אֶת־הָעִזִּים, which might literally be rendered "and all the women who their heart lifted them in wisdom, they spun the goats [hair]."

Most readers of Exodus will likely be content to understand these verses, which speak of the "wise of heart" and the wisdom attributed to them, simply as linguistically complicated examples of the way the biblical words for wisdom or being wise sometimes refer to practical ability, skill, or know-how. As was said, certain expressions like חָכְמַת־לֵב by themselves or in isolated contexts may very well carry that sort of constrained sense.

However, the piling up of wisdom terms in these tabernacle-building passages in a convoluted syntax suggests more. Obviously, the text wants to highlight the divine origin of the tabernacle workers' abilities (or wisdom). Yet the rhetoric may also suggest that those who are חַכְמַת־לֵב, those who possess the know-how of spinning or working with silver, stone, and wood, and who are directing that work to a larger end in a community, exhibit a kind of "wisdom" that is more than merely a "wisdom of heart"—the basic abilities of a mason, woodworker, or textile producer. Put otherwise, in the Exodus tabernacle-building texts, the activities of the workers—who in other contexts merely, though perhaps skillfully, shape stone, cut wood, or spin yarn in order, say, to supply a product to someone in exchange for payment—are transformed into something else. That is, the laborers (whose wisdom is associated with the divine) are starting to engage in a practice in a more robust MacIntyrian sense. They are transported into the creative, community-building, responsible work of the construction of sacred space. Their activity is now directed more fully toward a larger "good" goal, and their work must be more fully submitted to the standards and evaluations of expert building practitioners, Bezalel and Oholiab. What is more, the reward they receive for all their service is no mere material wage; in fact, Exodus suggests that the work is voluntary and that the Israelites, including the tabernacle workers, donate their belongings for its completion (35:4–29). The laborers don't receive a salary but in a sense "pay" to work. Their work on the tabernacle results in a net loss for them, materially speaking.[4] Yet the "rewards" the workers receive can also be reckoned in terms of the practice of tabernacle building itself. What accrues to the artisans, from Bezalel and Oholiab on down, is an internal good: regular and reliable intercourse with the divine, which the tabernacle uniquely enables. This particular benefit also profits the entire Israelite community and could not have been attained in precisely the same fashion through some other activity. It enables a fuller flourishing of a host of others who surely would hold the tabernacle artisans in high(er) esteem (an external good) because of their efforts.

In the end, although sometimes the know-how and skillful work of a craftsperson in the Bible might not be best described as a practice in the MacIntyrian sense, what the "wise of heart" laborers in Exodus 31–38 carry out is not merely the "wise" skill of stone cutting, smithing, and spinning. It is a practice, a practice of wisdom.

The Practice of Political Shrewdness?

If the work of craftspeople on the tabernacle can be said to constitute a practice in a MacIntyrian sense, what of the wisdom in the Bible that takes the form of a ruthless, pragmatic political know-how? Recall that Pharaoh wanted to deal "wisely" (נִתְחַכְּמָה)—that is, oppressively—with the Hebrews in Exodus 1:10, and it was Solomon in 1 Kings 2 whom David knew would know how to eliminate potential rivals because he was "wise." Is the shrewdness of these two biblical characters a kind of practice like that of the temple-building artisans of Exodus? Probably not, though it is easy to imagine

---

4. This fact invites critical analysis of the texts from other perspectives not pursued here—through ideological or materialist lenses, for instance.

how wisdom as shrewdness *might* contribute to a broader practice, say, of statecraft—the skillful and just management of a nation's affairs—just as the practical virtues of Proverbs contribute to a full Practical Wisdom. But for statecraft to be regarded as a practice, we would have to fill out the concept further: it would have to be statecraft governed by clear standards and ways to evaluate the actions of those involved in governing; it would need to require its practitioners to apprentice themselves to good governors; it would have to involve the exercise of particular virtues to achieve clear good ends, such as the well-being of a people or the flourishing of a polity; and so forth.

The wise shrewdness of Pharaoh and Solomon, though perhaps brilliant in a reprehensible Machiavellian political sense, appears a far cry from the practice of good statecraft. The motivation for the rulers' acts in the Bible is less the good of achieving the well-being of a people or the flourishing of a polity and more obviously the individual monarch's securing of personal power, prestige, and control (and likely wealth) through unjust and unmerciful means. This seems clear in the case of Solomon's rise to power. By eliminating rivals to the throne, he secures his own advantage. This is so even if some traditions about Solomon ground his reign in the divine will (1 Kings 1:29–30; 1 Chron. 22:10) or, as in the Deuteronomistic strands of 1 Kings, present him as one who desires to be a morally wise and just ruler (e.g., 1 Kings 3).[5] The case of Pharaoh's wisdom is likewise somewhat complicated. This ruler's oppressive actions ostensibly are in the name of his kingdom's national security, although the Hebrews in Egypt are excluded from full membership in that society.

In Proverbs the legitimate place of the monarchy and the hierarchical social order it represents is not fundamentally questioned. However, on the moral terms of the book described in part 1 above, both Pharaoh and Solomon appear to misunderstand the worth and appropriate ends of the power they are able to exercise in the realm of political economy. They seek to shore up and consolidate their own stations and unduly restrain the domains of those for whom ancient statecraft—paternalistic and patriarchal as it was—ought to have been exercised. As we saw in Proverbs 8:15–16, political elites ought to rule and judge justly—by wisdom or the virtues that characterize wise and just people. Elsewhere in Proverbs the legitimacy of rulers is likewise bound up with the justice they might secure (e.g., 25:5; 29:4, 14; cf. 16:13; 17:7; 20:8, 26; 22:11; 28:2). As Proverbs 20:28 says, "Loyalty and faithfulness preserve the king, and his throne is upheld by righteousness." Though such a line might sound like the utterance of obsequious royal underlings, verses like it most fundamentally declare that a king's rule is legitimate only

---

5. On the Solomon traditions in the Hebrew Bible, see Dell, *Solomonic Corpus of "Wisdom."*

so far as the monarch conforms to certain ethical norms. This is so even if, by the standards of ancient West Asian and Egyptian realpolitik, the focus of Pharaoh's and Solomon's desires (for power, control, and so forth) and the actions they undertake to fulfill those aspirations are unsurprising or even exemplary. Indeed, Proverbs likewise knows—and warns its addressees about—the unpredictable and potentially dangerous sides of real world rulers (20:2; 24:21; 28:3, 15–16; cf. 17:7; 23:1; 25:15; 29:12, 26).

In contrast to Pharaoh and Solomon, the political wisdom or shrewdness of the wise women of Tekoa (2 Sam. 14) and Abel (2 Sam. 20) comes a bit closer to constituting a practice in the MacIntyrian sense. Interestingly, the "wise woman" of Tekoa is not said to have a חָכְמַת־לֵב, as do the tabernacle workers; instead, she is described as an אִשָּׁה חֲכָמָה (2 Sam. 14:2). Though some, as Kyle McCarter says, may regard the woman's wisdom as a mere "tool for accomplishing purposes and attaining goals," the locution may suggest her sagacity is something other than that of simple shrewd know-how or skill.[6] Recall that the woman employs deception, but not violence or injustice, in seeking a political end that is also ostensibly a morally laudable one—affecting the reconciliation of David with his son and thereby bringing an end to a certain political factionalism. The wise woman also courageously collaborates with a potentially dangerous male military figure, Joab, something that will require her to negotiate sagaciously a further unpredictable encounter with an even more powerful man, David. In doing so, she utters something like wise proverbial speech, noting that humans, who must die, are "like water spilled on the ground, which cannot be gathered up" (2 Sam. 14:14). The saying, coupled as it is with her claim that the deity will not "keep an outcast banished forever from his presence," serves the woman as a kind of warrant designed to allow David to justify his decision that Joab "bring back the young man Absalom" (v. 21).

Although the gender dynamics in the story are complex, the woman of Tekoa's encounter with Joab might be construed as her effort to apprentice herself to the general, who hatches the plan she carries out and whom she seems to regard as a master of politics. She confesses as much when David finally asks her if Joab is behind her ruse, saying that Joab "put all these words into the mouth of your servant" (v. 19). But he did so, she says (v. 20), "in order to change the course of affairs" (NRSV; or "to conceal the real purpose of the matter" in the NJPS), adding that "my lord has wisdom like the wisdom of the angel of God to know all things that are on the earth." These last words sound like the wise woman's acknowledgment of David's

---

6. McCarter, *II Samuel*, 345.

keen insight in uncovering the scheme. However, it may be a more sophisticated utterance that points to Joab's "wisdom" or political savvy, while also permitting David to hear it as her confession that it would be impossible to fully fool the king. The woman's words conceivably constitute her shrewd strategy to deflect the monarch's potential anger at being deceived by her and Joab. Indeed, throughout the passage the wise woman refers to David as "my lord the king" (vv. 9, 12, 15, 17 [2x], 19 [2x]; cf. Joab's words in v. 22). In verse 17 in particular, she notes to David that "my lord the king is like the angel of God, discerning good and evil [לִשְׁמֹעַ הַטּוֹב וְהָרָע]"; the king in other words is able to "hear" cases like the one she recounts in her ruse and judge them fairly. However, in the quite similar but *not quite identical* utterance of verse 20, she only speaks of "my lord" (not "the king") who "has wisdom like the wisdom of [חָכָם כְּחָכְמַת] the angel of God to know [לָדַעַת] all things that are on the earth," or to know "all that goes on in the land" (NJPS). The woman's words here certainly constitute an expression "fit for a king." It not only evokes ancient West Asian political ideologies that attribute special wisdom to monarchs, ensuring David would hear it as a complement; it also may discretely gesture toward the woman's recognition of Joab's ability to understand and manage the happenings of the realm even better than the king. Whatever the precise case with 2 Samuel 14:20, although some may associate the woman of Tekoa's shrewd deception with a "Machiavellian spirit," her words and her interaction with powerful men, designed to accomplish what can be conceived as a good end, suggest she exercises a political wisdom that begins to approximate a MacIntyrian practice.[7]

The case of the wise woman of the city of Abel, recounted in 2 Samuel 20, is even more complex than the tale of the woman of Tekoa since, similar to Pharaoh in Exodus 1 and Solomon in the initial chapters of 1 Kings, she achieves a political end by hatching and carrying out a violent plan:

> Then a wise woman [אִשָּׁה חֲכָמָה] called from the city, "Listen! Listen! Tell Joab, 'Come here, I want to speak to you.'" He came near her; and the woman said, "Are you Joab?" He answered, "I am." Then she said to him, "Listen to the words of your servant." He answered, "I am listening." Then she said, "They used to say in the old days, 'Let them inquire at Abel'; and so they would settle a matter. I am one of those who are peaceable and faithful in Israel; you seek to destroy a city that is a mother in Israel; why will you swallow up the heritage of the LORD?" Joab answered, "Far be it from me, far be it, that I should swallow up or destroy! That is not the case! But a man of the hill country of Ephraim, called Sheba son of Bichri, has lifted up his hand against King David; give him

---

7. McCarter, *II Samuel*, 352.

up alone, and I will withdraw from the city." The woman said to Joab, "His head shall be thrown over the wall to you." Then the woman went to all the people with her wise plan [בְּחָכְמָתָהּ]. And they cut off the head of Sheba son of Bichri, and threw it out to Joab. So he blew the trumpet, and they dispersed from the city, and all went to their homes, while Joab returned to Jerusalem to the king. (2 Sam. 20:16–22)

Initially, the wise woman's plan and actions—the beheading of Sheba to appease Joab—might sound like another bit of Machiavellian political shrewdness. Yet despite an obvious irony in the story that places the woman's wisdom in an ambiguous light (noted below), the broader passage suggests ways in which her wisdom can in part be understood as a practice. First, notice that as verse 21 recounts matters, the woman of Abel, like the woman of Tekoa, is not a woman "wise of heart" (חֲכְמַת־לֵב), one who possesses some practical skill or know-how. She is instead also a wise woman, an אִשָּׁה חֲכָמָה, who likewise negotiates a deal with the potentially dangerous man, Joab. To secure the general's withdrawal, the woman promises that Sheba's "head shall be thrown over the wall to you" (v. 21). Yet as the passage continues, we also learn that "the woman went to all the people with her wise plan" (v. 22). The woman's wise plan here is nothing other than her *chokmah*. She went to the people "with her wisdom" (בְּחָכְמָתָהּ), and we might surmise that she sought counsel on her plan from her fellow citizens (see below)—a practice that characterizes the wise in Proverbs too (see chap. 8 above). It appears the people found her wisdom compelling since "they cut off the head of Sheba son of Bichri, and threw it out to Joab. So, he [Joab] blew the trumpet, and they [Joab's troops] dispersed from the city" (v. 22).

But the woman of 2 Samuel 20 does not simply skillfully navigate a precarious political moment with a potentially dangerous adversary. In her interactions with Joab, the wise woman also characterizes her town, Abel. In verse 18 she explains to Joab that "they used to say in the old days, 'let them inquire at Abel'; and so they would settle a matter." Although this language of inquiry and settling matters might suggest the town was a site where people sought oracular advice, there is no explicit mention of this. Abel, rather, might be regarded as a "community of character," a place where outsiders could seek the advice or Practical Wisdom of at least certain residents of the town in order to reason together and settle disputes or figure out the best way forward in any particular matter. The wise woman calls the town "a mother in Israel" (v. 19), an image that suggests it is a venerable place whose inhabitants were concerned with the care and broader well-being of its "offspring," the people of Israel. As one from Abel, the wise woman believes she shares in the virtue of the town. She is of the "peaceable and faithful" in Israel, drawing a contrast—perhaps strategically in the face of the threat posed by Joab—between herself and her town on the one hand, and the political rebel Sheba who had "lifted up his hand against King David" (v. 21) on the other.[8] Because the wise woman is afraid that Joab would "swallow up" and "destroy" the town (vv. 19–20), she articulates all this about Abel and negotiates a deal with Joab against Sheba, thereby preserving the town and its function as a "mother in Israel."

Whether a reader thinks the woman and the town of Abel are justified in assassinating Sheba to save themselves or believes they should have harbored the revolutionary, the point is that the wise woman's shrewdness is not the sort of blatant effort to consolidate one's power, dominion, and wealth, as it is with Pharaoh in Exodus and Solomon in 1 Kings. It is no obvious play to secure personally beneficial external goods. Rather, it is a plan to preserve a community that emerges from and is consonant with the ancient character of the community itself. It is an integration of the practical virtue of shrewdness into a fuller set of virtues and values, something that constitutes what we earlier in Proverbs called Practical Wisdom. As such it has something in common with a MacIntyrian conception of a practice. There can, however, also be no doubt about the irony of "peaceable and faithful" persons executing and dismembering Sheba, who may not simply be hiding in Abel but seeking sanctuary there. As McCarter says, though Abel "opened its gates" to Sheba, "he found no deep sympathy there."[9]

This irony in the story of the wise woman of Abel means that the status of the woman's shrewdness—whether as part of a wise practice of something like statecraft or as Machiavellian politics as usual—must remain ambiguous. The tale itself thus functions as a kind of *mashal* ("proverb"), a provocative text whose meaning is to be puzzled out by readers in different times and places.[10]

The Practice of Knowledge and Intellectual Acumen?

When we ask whether the notion of wisdom as the acquisition of knowledge and the deployment of a mental acumen—as in the description of Solomon's knowledge in 1 Kings 5:9–14 [4:29–34]—might constitute a practice in something like MacIntyre's sense, we are again in the realm of ambiguity.

---

8. The Hebrew of vv. 18–19 is difficult; however, in light of the economy of images and themes in the passage, just alluded to, the NRSV's rendering (followed here) is quite defensible. For a discussion of the problems and an alternative rendering, see McCarter, *II Samuel*, 428, 430.

9. McCarter, *II Samuel*, 431.

10. Cf. Proverbs' prologue (1:2–7) and the discussion of it in chap. 2.

In principle, the pursuit of knowledge and the enhancement of intellectual ability could constitute a practice—or better, form an integral part of a more complex practice. Much again depends on other factors: how the intellectual work is undertaken, what virtues are needed to carry out the work, with whom it is undertaken, toward what (good) ends it is directed, and so forth. For example, many contemporary university professors (like me) are largely involved in the sorts of intellectual pursuits and the development of analytical abilities—our own and that of our students—that are broadly analogous to the biblical conception of wisdom as knowledge and intellectual acuity. We pursue the intellectual and academic life in ways similar to and distinct from others engaged in other professions. To do so we cultivate and strive to exercise appropriately particular virtues—things like diligence, discipline, fairness, truthfulness, and creativity—many of which are shared with others engaged in other practices.

Those in the professorate have also for years submitted ourselves to the norms and standards of our disciplines—following the direction of our PhD advisors, submitting our books and articles to peer review, and so forth. But most of us are also interested in making our own contributions to knowledge; we strive to enhance our intellectual and academic practice by contributing to and helping define our academic fields. Moreover, most of us (at least in the humanities) do so not out of any excessive desire for external goods; doctors, lawyers, and stockbrokers all tend to be better compensated and more socially valued than college professors! Most academics would like to believe we are motivated primarily by internal goods—the joy of figuring out a new response to an old problem perhaps or the pleasure of mentoring students and contributing to a shift in the shape of our disciplines. And all this is undertaken in relation to some broader good end. In the theological disciplines, where I am institutionally located, this might be formulated in theological terms—to serve God and God's people by helping prepare ministers and teachers to serve church and society. Others, in other disciplines, will prefer humanistic terms—to serve communities, small and large, by critically evaluating and transmitting human traditions or advancing human scientific knowledge and enhancing its application, for example.

Of course, professors don't always live up to the highest ideals of the practice of professorship. That's not the point. The point is that if we are to regard the biblical conception of wisdom as knowledge or rational capacity (like what Solomon is said to possess in 1 Kings 5 [4]) as a practice—or forming part of a more complex practice—we would have to understand that sort of wisdom in ways analogous to how the intellectual work of professors belongs to the practice of "professorship."

In the passage from 1 Kings, Solomon's "wisdom"—conceptualized as a form of knowledge or intellectual dexterity—doesn't seem to be obviously integrated into a broader, complex frame of reference that would warrant suggesting this sort of wisdom constitutes or contributes to a practice in MacIntyre's sense. The context of the Solomon story in the Kings text supports this claim. As already noted, the early chapters of 1 Kings characterize the king to a large extent as a kind of shrewd, at times ruthless, Machiavellian ruler concerned less with the good ends of statecraft—such as providing a just and secure realm for his subjects—and more with consolidating power and the trappings of empire. One can point to his eradication of political enemies (1 Kings 2), his use of forced labor (1 Kings 5, 9), and other details of his rule scattered throughout the first eleven chapters of the narrative. This is so even if the Deuteronomic passages in the account of Solomon's reign paint a more positive picture of the king (e.g., 1 Kings 3), at least until 1 Kings 11, when Solomon is censured by a Deuteronomistic voice for his idolatry, which the text associates with his "foreign wives."[11]

Most interesting, however, is the fact that in 1 Kings 5:9–14 [4:29–34] Solomon's wisdom is quantified as knowledge; it is something akin to the wealth and power that he accumulates, possesses, and controls. Subsequently, there emerges a parallel with other aspects of 1 Kings 5 [4] and with Solomon's rule more generally. First Kings 5:14 [4:34] says, "People came from all the nations to hear the wisdom of Solomon; they came from all the kings of the earth who had heard of his wisdom." The rhetorical affinities of these lines to descriptions of acts of political fealty directed toward Solomon, especially the offering of tribute to him by foreign rulers, is easy to discern. As 1 Kings 5:1 [4:21] reports, "Solomon was sovereign over all the kingdoms from the Euphrates to the land of the Philistines, even to the border of Egypt; they brought tribute and served Solomon all the days of his life." Solomon's interactions with those who come to hear his wisdom is structurally and conceptually parallel to his interactions with subject peoples and their rulers. This suggests that Solomon's acquisition and display of knowledge and intellectual acuity is not a piece of a larger practice like statecraft, where good ends are easily imagined; nor does it appear to be motivated by an internal good, say, the joy of teaching or the pleasure of increasing knowledge, the benefits of which might accrue to all wisdom seekers. Instead, when the text speaks of the nations coming to hear Solomon's wisdom, it exalts Solomon for his possession of intellectual acuity and facts. There is no master-apprentice relationship as one might expect in a MacIntyrian practice, or even an instance of peers taking

---

11. Cf. Sandoval, "Reconfiguring Solomon."

counsel with one another. Instead, Solomon's pursuit and display of "wisdom as knowledge" appears again as an effort to secure his own advantage, now via epistemological domination of others—an act that parallels his political domination of the nations.[12] Just as "all the kingdoms" (5:1 [4:21]) are compelled to offer their gifts and servitude to the more powerful king Solomon, so one can surmise "all the nations" submit their own knowledge and insight to Solomon's superior understanding only under compulsion (5:14 [4:34]), not truly to advance (their) wisdom and learning itself.

The Practice of Esoteric Wisdom?

When we turn to the question of whether the esoteric, divinely revealed wisdom of an Agur, Daniel, or Joseph can be regarded as a practice, we again have to answer with a clear and robust "perhaps." *Perhaps* the sort of wisdom represented by these figures, especially Daniel, does represent (or potentially belongs to) a kind of practice, but not overtly so.

In the tales of the first part of the book of Daniel, Daniel's primary activity of wisdom is to receive and communicate divine revelation about someone else's dream. (Later in the apocalyptic section of the book, he dreams his own dreams and an angelic being mediates interpretation.) The early portion of the narrative of Joseph in Egypt is likewise largely driven by the Hebrew man's ability to interpret dreams. In isolation, the esoteric wisdom of both Joseph and Daniel in dream interpretation likely would not constitute a practice in MacIntyre's sense. It is too restricted an activity.

Daniel, however, appears to belong to a circle of people who are wise in another sense. As noted above, we learn early on in the book that Daniel is learned in literature and writing (Dan. 1:17). He is also associated with the Chaldean magicians, whose expertise in mantic wisdom or a range of divinatory practices and rituals was surely gained through education at the hands of expert diviners; some such individuals would likely have also advised political elites, and in exercising their craft some perhaps would have striven to regulate elite conduct and management of society toward good ends. Furthermore, Daniel works closely with his Jewish and Babylonian colleagues, and when undertaking his dream-interpreting activities, he can be said to have a good end in mind—the well-being of the broader Jewish community. In Daniel 2, he also explicitly deploys his wisdom to save his Babylonian magician colleagues from execution. And certainly, behind the text of Daniel there may

---

12. Cf., too, 1 Kings 10 and the story of the queen of Sheba. On this tale see Camp, *Wise, Strange, and Holy*, 144–90; and Sandoval, "Reconfiguring Solomon," 26–30.

be a community of Jewish scribes whose own activities in collecting and composing the tales and traditions of the book, which can serve as a kind of symbolic resistance to imperial power, could be more robustly thought of as a practice than might the character of Daniel's dream interpretation alone.[13] Similarly, aspects of the Joseph story suggest he may have been involved in broader practices of wisdom beyond esoteric dream interpretation. Joseph's expertise in political economy is evident in his "wise" management of economic matters during seven years of abundance in Egypt. But during the subsequent seven years of famine, his Machiavellian shrewdness is on display in his ability to transfer large portions of wealth from the Egyptian population to Pharaoh—though by tale's end Joseph again acts on behalf of the broader community of his family.

For his part, Agur possesses a kind of wisdom as esoteric knowledge that on its own is likewise not well regarded as a practice, though it may be bound up with the broader activities and identities of an eschatologically oriented community whose complex way of life might be considered a kind of practice. In any case, Agur's "knowledge of the holy ones" (Prov. 30:3) is not the same sort of broad moral knowledge as Proverbs' vision of (Practical) Wisdom, and it was, as was noted, probably regarded by traditional scribal tradents as inferior to the rest of the book's virtue-oriented moral discourse.[14]

In the end, then, the sort of divinely received esoteric wisdom Agur, Joseph, and Daniel possess, even with the cultivation of the virtue of receptiveness to the divine that such an activity demands, seems too constrained to qualify on its own as a practice in MacIntyre's sense. However, the revelatory, esoteric wisdom that each of these individuals trades in can, much like the wisdom of the tabernacle artisans, be imagined as part of a complex human activity directed toward some broader good and thus constitute or contribute to a kind of wise practice.

The Practice of Moral Wisdom?

By contrast to Solomon's knowledge and intellectual acuity and Agur's, Joseph's, and Daniel's esoteric wisdom, various texts in the Bible speak of wisdom as a good or correct moral and religious orientation, as right living and a just ordering of society. This sort of wisdom should almost certainly be regarded as a kind of practice in MacIntyre's sense. Although the Pentateuch,

---

13. For apocalyptic literature's resistance to empire, see, e.g., Portier-Young, *Apocalypse against Empire*.

14. Sandoval, "Texts and Intertexts."

the Prophets, and to a lesser extent the Writings often present their messages as divine words, the wisdom in the texts we briefly discussed earlier is not merely practical know-how, political shrewdness, intellectual ability, or even esoteric knowledge. It entails being rightly guided by or emending one's way of life in light of Torah's instruction, a prophet's preaching, or a tradition's ethical-religious teachings. This sort of wisdom assumes a broad and complex context of relations involving instruction in literacy and in religious and moral virtue; it entails standards and traditions within which one is asked to locate oneself and to which one is expected to submit; the wisdom in these discourses is also directed toward a good end of enabling or reestablishing a well-ordered or just community—at least in the paternalistic and patriarchal manner by which the ancients understood and conceived of justice.

The wisdom of the book of Proverbs participates in the sort of religious-ethical discourse that these other biblical texts point toward when they speak of wisdom in terms of good moral action and justice. However, the wisdom of Proverbs also takes up the other conceptions of wisdom scattered throughout the Hebrew Bible—wisdom as a practical skill or know-how, shrewdness, or broad knowledge and mental acuity—which on their own may or may not contribute to or be conceived of as practices in MacIntyre's sense. Proverbs orders these under the moral-social virtues, which are particularly prized (cf. 1:2–7; see chap. 2). What Proverbs (and some analogous texts of "moral" wisdom) is uniquely able to do is hold these different inflections of "wisdom" together in a single concept, as a kind of practice. In other words, although Proverbs can distinguish between different sorts of wisdom, the book ultimately points to the centrality of a full, integrated conception of wisdom that entails the ability to exercise distinct virtues that enable right understanding of and appropriate yearning for the goods that contribute to people's happiness. We might say that the different intellectual, practical, and moral-social virtues or "excellencies" that Proverbs speaks of, many of which are designated as "wisdom" (or being wise) outside of the book, constitute a "wisdom" with a lowercase w; but the integrative exercise of these and the capacity to discern, desire, and do the good thing in any range of situations—this sort of practical moral reasoning—constitutes "Wisdom" with an uppercase W. It is the Practical Wisdom of which we spoke in chapter 8.[15]

That the "Wisdom" of Proverbs is well conceived as a kind of complex practice in the sense MacIntyre develops the term is evident in several ways. As we have seen, Proverbs can speak of wisdom or being wise in terms of

15. This (Practical) Wisdom, of course, can be analytically distinguished from the literary character "Woman Wisdom" in Prov. 1–9 who is, however, a personification of this Wisdom.

discrete virtues associated with knowledge, shrewdness, and skillful ability. Yet as MacIntyre says, a practice is "never just a set of technical skills"—a know-how, cleverness, intellectual acuity, and so forth—even if such skills are exercised for some "purpose" or might be "valued and enjoyed for their own sake." Although every genuine practice will require some practical skill, know-how, or rationality, what is more important in a given practice are the good ends toward which the practice is directed and the internal goods the practice generates. MacIntyre calls this the "good of a certain kind of life"; it is a good that in some sense enables or enhances the abilities of individuals and communities to flourish.[16] Enabling this "way" of life (cf. chap. 4) is largely what part 1 suggested is the concern of much of Proverbs' instruction.

Proverbs' wisdom project can be said to constitute a practice in MacIntyre's sense in other ways too. As with MacIntyre's sense of a practice, the novice addressees of Proverbs are called to submit their own desires and intelligence to the teaching of those who are expert in the moral-intellectual tradition the book represents—teachers and other wise and just exemplars. Students of a Proverbs scroll in an ancient educational context would have been subject to the reproof and discipline of these others as they honed their literary skills and internalized the values and virtues of the text (cf. chap. 10 above). This sort of apprenticeship demands that Proverbs' students initially prioritize and cultivate virtues—such as humility, openness to rebuke, and diligence in study—that will permit them to develop a fuller range of wise abilities and virtues. Eventually, as people become experts in this literary-moral tradition, they will take on the role of teaching and inspiring others in the "practice" of wisdom, a function that itself requires the exercise of many of Proverbs' most prized virtues—including the social virtues of cooperation, patience, and the practical insight of knowing when and how effectively to reprove and correct others.

When understanding Proverbs' wisdom as a kind of MacIntyrian practice, one should also recall how Proverbs' act-consequence rhetoric relates to pre-modern forms of causality (chap. 2) and the question of how virtuous living correlates to a flourishing life that entails some enjoyment of external goods. As we saw, the well-being that a life of wisdom or virtue enables, or with which a wise and just person might be "rewarded," should not be conceived narrowly in terms of the attainment of external goods. No isolated wise or just act ought to be thought of as a means to the end of some discrete external good. No single virtuous act reliably causes a particular external good,

---

16. MacIntyre, *After Virtue*, 193.

such as riches or status, and these goods can, of course, be attained in other nonvirtuous ways. Rather, the genuine happiness or flourishing associated with wise or virtuous living is the sort of good that is internally related to a life fully "practiced" (in the MacIntyrian sense) in just that way—as wise and virtuous. Just as only the baseball pitcher can fully enjoy the goods internal to baseball pitching, so too only those who most fully engage Proverbs' practice of wisdom can fully enjoy the well-being to which the book points. The "reward" of a full thriving life that Proverbs' wisdom enables (but of course can't guarantee)—which includes some enjoyment of external goods—is inextricably linked to the practice of living virtuously: you can't get the one without the other.

The "Craft" of Living Well

If exercising the wisdom of Proverbs approximates a MacIntyrian practice, it also resonates profoundly with the "wise" practice of the temple builders in Exodus as discussed above. The wisdom program Proverbs sets forth can itself be imagined as a kind of craft or skill. This is perhaps unsurprising since MacIntyre's reflection on practices is itself deeply indebted to Aristotle's consideration of virtuous living as *technē*, while the semantic range of the root חכם in the Bible often approximates that of the Greek term. Wisdom for Proverbs is the craft of living well. And just as one is not simply born with the ability to hew stone, weave textiles, or build a tabernacle but, through long effort, learns how to do them well, the skills necessary to live a good life are not innate, even if the potential to develop them is, along with certain desires that inchoately point to a yearning for such a life (cf. chaps. 3, 10–11). To flourish as humans, what "naturally" needs to be added to the natural capacities and desires—or wisdom—people are born with is training in the life of virtue, a capacity for which beings created "in Wisdom" are also born with (cf. chaps. 10–11): the "hearing" of instruction, the acceptance of rebuke, and the imitation of moral exemplars that results in the actual doing of virtuous acts and the development of Practical Wisdom.

Aristotle, too, reckoned the virtuous life as akin to the practice of a craft; and as we noted, MacIntyre's notion of a practice elaborates and develops Aristotle's thought in this regard. As Annas explains, for Aristotle "the virtuous person is not just the person who does in fact do the morally right thing, or even does it stably and reliably. She is the person who *understands* the principles on which she acts, and thus can explain and defend her actions."[17]

---

17. Annas, *Morality of Happiness*, 67 (emphasis original).

And that is the reason why the analogy with the skill exercised by artisans is "a good model for learning virtue." As Annas also says,

> The learner [of virtue], paradigmatically the young learner, begins by picking up what to do in particular cases; he copies his elders or follows their advice. But if he is intelligent he does not remain stuck at the state of depending on models for each new case or memorizing a list of cases and dealing with each new one by comparing it with past ones. Rather, he develops a sense of the *point* of doing these specific things, and when he grasps this he has a sense of the basis of these previous judgements, which will enable him to go on to fresh cases without mechanically referring back. Like the person who has acquired an expertise in a skill the learner has acquired understanding of what he is doing.[18]

Nonetheless, for Aristotle "virtue is not itself a skill." Though it may be possible to imagine the living of a virtuous life as "a special kind of skill," Aristotle seems ultimately to resist the identification because, as Annas says, "skills other than virtue can be practiced in comparative independence of the agent's moral character."[19] Even the best doctors, athletes, and musicians can be morally reprehensible persons.

Conclusions

Proverbs' moral discourse thus delineates for its readers/hearers how they might master the craft of living well; it offers a program for the flourishing of wise and just individuals in the context of wise and just communities in a fashion that is not unlike MacIntyre's notion of a practice. But it also represents the wisdom of socially stratified communities in ancient, small-scale urban centers and villages. The moral vision it (re)presents, if left unamended—or the practice of wisdom it holds forth, if left frozen in time—is one that most people today could not honestly claim would enhance or expand the possibilities for flourishing of all individuals in such communities, much less of those in other societies. The way of life in community that Proverbs imagines is riddled with hierarchies and expressions of domination in terms of sex and gender, class, and perhaps ethnic differences. The wisdom and flourishing that the book's moral vision imagines is one that is genuinely available only to economically secure adult male heads of households—those who are "full

---

18. Annas, *Morality of Happiness*, 67 (emphasis original).
19. Annas, *Morality of Happiness*, 68. Cf. Nussbaum's extended discussion of *technē* and related notions in *Fragility of Goodness*, 89–121. Nussbaum arrives at conclusions that are largely consonant with Annas's views.

members" of the community. Indeed, Proverbs' focus is on the moral-social education or enculturation of young males who are about to assume and enjoy full membership in their communities or older men who already have. Women and socially and economically marginalized males, though at points imagined as able to attain and exhibit wisdom and virtue in certain ways, are largely excluded from those the book addresses. Their ability to "flourish" with wisdom's help is constrained by their particular sex-gender and social-economic positions. It may be that with a bit of luck and by exercising wisdom's virtues, poor men—like the young males Proverbs' principally addresses—might come to rightly understand the worth of, and to appropriately pursue and possess, some of the goods necessary for significant human flourishing; but it is hardly a sure thing. It may be, too, that within Proverbs' moral vision, women are imagined as able to flourish "as women." (Wisdom, after all, is personified as a woman, and the final poem of the book, to which we will next turn, extols the virtues of a Woman of Valor). But if so, the female "nature" (and place in social life, goods requisite for well-being, and so forth) of these women cannot be regarded as fully commensurate with that of males. If Wisdom in Proverbs is a "tree of life" (3:18), access to its fruits is not uniform.

Yet must the wisdom tree be chopped down, burned off, and abandoned because of the shortcomings in Proverbs' moral vision—its particular, historically contingent moral conclusions and social exclusions? Some may certainly—and with good reason—conclude it must. Yet Proverbs' virtue-oriented discourse, its focus on the sort of being humans are, its emphasis on social virtue, and especially Practical Wisdom may point to ways the exclusions and hierarchies the book represents and perpetuates might be constructively critiqued and overcome. To borrow a phrase from another wisdom text, Proverbs' fundamental moral orientation, if not all of its particular and historically contingent ethical conclusions, may mean "there is hope for [this] tree" (Job 14:7). And so to torture the arboreal metaphor a bit more, we turn to the task of trimming a few branches of the wisdom tree that preclude full flourishing for many by considering how contemporary readers might critically engage Proverbs in their desire to find wisdom for themselves and their communities in this portion of Scripture.

Conclusion

Worthy Wisdom, Who Can Find?

One of the most common critiques of premodern virtue-oriented moral systems, like that of Aristotle, is that they are wed to an untenable ontology or natural philosophy. An ethics like Aristotle's presumes as "natural" for humans a series of hierarchies and exclusions—concerning gender, social status, or ethnicity—that are in reality historically contingent. Free, property-owning males of the Greek polis are considered superior by nature to slaves, women, and "barbarians." Similar hierarchies and exclusions are also at work in the moral discourse of Proverbs. The "mythical norm"—to borrow a phrase from Audre Lorde—of this wisdom work is also regularly assumed to be an able-bodied, heterosexual male, who as a full member of the community is a person of some means who makes himself available to the book's social-moral educative project.[1] The book as a whole is addressed primarily to male youths poised to become such wise *men*, and secondarily to those wise men themselves (Prov. 1:4–5). Brown, as we said (cf. chap. 9), even discerns a progression in the final design of the book, where the young male of the early chapters ends in Proverbs 31:10–31 as the prosperous male householder, civic leader, and husband of a "virtuous woman" (Eshet Chayil; אֵשֶׁת חַיִל).[2]

---

1. Lorde, "Age, Race, Class, and Sex," 116, cited in Anderson, *Ancient Laws and Contemporary Controversies*, 19. On ableness and disability in the Bible, see Avalos, Melcher, and Schipper, *This Abled Body*. On the relation of disability to virtue ethics (in a Christian key), see Clifton, *Crippled Grace*.

2. Brown, "Pedagogy of Proverbs"; cf. C. Yoder, "Forming 'Fearers of Yahweh.'"

Proverbial Problems

The model of wisdom or virtue that Proverbs puts forth is, in other words, profoundly tethered to ancient patriarchal maleness.[3] Subsequently, the book's efforts to sketch what virtues and values are necessary for *human* flourishing are formulated in terms of what it imagines as necessary for the flourishing of a particular kind of human—the male householder of some social and economic standing. Though much of the book's instruction is to different degrees appropriate to others too, the text hardly focuses on what might constitute the values, virtues, and social arrangements necessary for women, slaves, and the poor to fully thrive.[4] Though Proverbs does not categorically deny that women or slaves or the poor might attain wisdom, they are a *topic* of instruction and not the ones the book primarily addresses; their social position limits the nature and extent of the flourishing that is possible for them.

For example, although Proverbs does not much contemplate the possibility of women thriving, the book has positive representations of female figures. The book's teaching, though primarily directed to "sons" or young men, is sometimes associated not only with a father but a mother (1:8; 6:20; 23:22; 31:1; cf. 30:17), while good wives are often prized and lauded (18:22; 19:14; cf. 5:18). And, of course, wisdom itself is imagined as a woman (and probably a wife; see chap. 5). What is more, the book concludes with extensive praise of a virtuous female character, the Eshet Chayil (31:10–31; cf. 12:4), a passage to which we will soon turn. At the same time, however, women in the book are also negatively depicted. Certain women may lead men astray into adultery, with dire consequences (5:1–23; 6:20–35; 7:1–27), and some wives are presented as irksome and quarrelsome in relation to their husbands (19:13; 21:9, 19; 25:24; 27:15). In both positive and negative representations of women, however, Proverbs' focus is firmly on male well-being; interest in women is largely confined to how they might contribute to or detract from the happiness of the men who constitute Proverbs' mythical norm. The flourishing of women themselves is not truly considered.

The flourishing of other figures in Proverbs is likewise not the focus of the book's instruction. The book's male addressees who are or will become patriarchs—whether kings, scribes, or other householders—should, like a good father attending to the needs of his children, paternalistically care for these others in their charge. The legal rights of the poor ought to be respected, and the wise and just should deal generously with the destitute

---

3. Among commentators this is quite fully recognized by Bellis, *Proverbs*.
4. As, among others, Bellis, *Proverbs*, also recognizes.

and not ruthlessly oppress them (cf. chap. 7). Some economically marginalized persons may display virtue, as with the poor (דַּל) but "understanding" (מֵבִין) person of Proverbs 28:11, who sees through the pretensions of the rich (cf. 19:1; 28:6). But even if a poor person were in possession of a full range of wisdom's virtues, their status in the socially and economically stratified ancient context would ultimately make them unlikely candidates to experience the sort of full thriving Proverbs envisions for its primary addressees, a flourishing that includes a degree of economic prosperity and social recognition. A slave, too, might "act wisely" (מַשְׂכִּיל) and on occasion gain an "inheritance" in a master's household (17:2). But in Proverbs slaves or servants who transcend their social station are also suspect and so typically denied the full social recognition available to others (19:10; 29:21; 30:22). Like women and the poor, servants and slaves have their "natural" place in Proverbs, and this is not the same place as the book's primary addressees. Whatever "flourishing" the book imagines as available to any of these figures is surely tied to their inferior social status, just as the flourishing of the male householders—Proverbs' mythical norm—is bound up with their privileged social position.

Contemporary Aristotelian thinkers like Martha Nussbaum and Alasdair MacIntyre have sought to shed Aristotle's problematic natural philosophy and its hierarchical exclusions while retaining the central place of virtue and the good in ethics. Nussbaum grounds her Aristotelian program not in nature but in sociology. For her, the fact that always and everywhere humans live together grounds an Aristotelian project that prioritizes justice and practical wisdom. Practical reasoners can rationally work to construct communities characterized not by arbitrary hierarchies and exclusions but by a justice where a full human flourishing, which may take various forms in different communities, is reckoned as the telos for *all* humans living in relation with others.[5] MacIntyre, too, initially took a sociological route to ground his Aristotelian-Thomistic ethics. Indeed, his entire conception of "practices" in *After Virtue*, discussed above (chaps. 13–14), belongs to such an effort.[6] Ultimately, however, MacIntyre came to believe that his ethical project also needed a naturalistic grounding. Hence, in *Dependent Rational Animals*, he insists that we all depend profoundly on others of our kind not only for our physical survival (e.g., as infants, in times of significant illness or injury, and for many at the end of life). We also depend on other humans for our rational development—most fundamentally and often, parents and teachers. Consequently, certain

---

5. Nussbaum, "Aristotle on Human Nature"; Nussbaum, "Non-Relative Virtues."
6. MacIntyre, *After Virtue*.

human desires and needs (e.g., for food and sex), as well as our sociality and rationality, are grounded in natural relations, in nature.[7]

Despite a clear Aristotelian-Thomistic orientation, MacIntyre has sometimes been described and critiqued as a communitarian thinker, despite his explicit distancing of himself from that strain of thought.[8] For classical liberal thinkers, the individual, apart from social attachments, is regarded as primary; and these individuals form broader communities through voluntary acts. By contrast, for communitarians, the role of a community of shared interest and history is paramount in defining and shaping individuals. Feminist thinkers in particular have criticized communitarian thought for what is regularly viewed as its nostalgic valorization of communities in which inequalities and exclusions of different sorts—not least in terms of sex and gender—are constitutive. Penny Weiss aptly summarizes the shortcomings of communitarian thought (in words that could well describe Proverbs): "It seems that whatever the extent to which communitarian theorists might be said to be egalitarian, inegalitarian threads also connect—threads that, variously throughout history, define women out of certain communities, downplay the negative effects of women's domestication, exclude women in conceptions and calculations of the 'common' good, refuse to address sexual differentiation and inequality as obstacles to personal and political bonds and advocate patriarchal principles, values, and structures to guide their communities."[9] Like some communitarians, MacIntyre certainly places much emphasis on communities that are hierarchical and insular, as we saw in the above discussion of practices (chaps. 13–14). What is more, his preference for understanding the self as embedded in a community (rather than as what he regards to be the untenable autonomous subject of liberalism) might be criticized as insufficiently critical of the hierarchical and patriarchal character of the communities within which such selves have typically been constituted. At least to the extent that his leading examples of virtue-oriented communities are drawn from ancient Greece, such criticism is not unwarranted.

Because MacIntyre is perhaps ultimately not to be regarded as a communitarian thinker, his project may not be fully vulnerable to the sorts of concerns Weiss articulates. But neither is it completely immune to the force of such critique. What especially feminist analyses of communitarianism point out is that the self-contained, hierarchal communities that communitarians sometimes imagine enjoy a kind of immunity from critique.[10] This insular-

---

7. MacIntyre, *Dependent Rational Animals*.
8. As noted by Song, *Christianity and Liberal Society*, 128, as discussed by Knight, "Ethical Post-Marxism," 87–88.
9. Weiss, "Feminism and Communitarianism," 161.
10. Cf. Albrecht, *Character of Our Communities*.

ity not only may promote an internal authoritarianism; it also enables such communities to essentially say to outsiders, "This is the sort of community we are, and if you are not a member of the community, if you are not immersed in this community's story and discourse, your critiques are ultimately irrelevant." There is little mechanism for robust internal critique in the face of well-established communal norms and practices, and perhaps even less space for serious engagement with external criticisms in ways that might affect change in a community. MacIntyre's conception of practice, with its emphasis on expert practitioners as those who regulate the practice, can easily be regarded as sharing in this insularity.

Still, MacIntyre's notion of practice also mitigates against this communitarian immunity from critique, at least somewhat. Unlike Pope Stephen I's view of the Western church's tradition—"Nihil innovetur nisi quod tranditum est" (Nothing is to be introduced except that which has been received)—a practice or a tradition for MacIntyre, when it is healthy, will indeed be subject to change.[11] Those who have mastered a practice are the ones in a position to innovate it. They can find a new and effective strategy for chess, a better way to play quarterback, and a unique form of improvising jazz standards. When it comes to a moral discourse like that represented by the book of Proverbs, the wise and just practical reasoners of that tradition likewise might innovate, change, and advance that tradition. The questions, of course, are how regularly and how robustly such innovation might be carried out and *who* precisely might ever find themselves in a position to innovate. There is no question that American football is very different today than it was seventy-five years ago. Expert practitioners of the game have changed it. Yet, the game today is still quite recognizable as the game it was in 1950, suggesting that innovation to a practice by those in a position to provoke change may be inherently slow and rarely radical. What is more, the changes in football that *are* discernible are, at least to an extent, the result of the "tradition" of American football having to respond to primarily external critiques of its own hierarchies and exclusions, which of course have mirrored US society's prejudices. Once African Americans were permitted to participate more equally and fully in the practice with whites, new expert practitioners emerged who would leave their innovative stamp on the game.

It is, however, one thing to talk about changes to the practice of chess or baseball and another thing to talk about changes to the practice of a system of ethics. Whether there is more passing in football today than there was in 1950 is simply not as weighty a matter as whether women or people of African

---

11. Pope Stephen I, as quoted in Fogarty, "Scriptural Authority (Roman Catholicism)," 1024.

descent are believed to be as rational, morally capable, and responsible as males of European descent. The slow pace of change in chess strategies or baseball pitching is often acceptable for those engaging in those practices. The slow pace of change in social-ethical outlooks is regularly not so tolerable, and rarely so for those positioned low in its hierarchies and who most suffer its exclusions. What is more, when it comes to the development or "traditioning" of a social-moral tradition, one needs to reckon with the inherently interested nature of knowledge, including ethical knowledge, and its relationship to power. A chess master or a famous jazz musician or a star quarterback may each be very interested in innovation to their practices. Such developments will likely augment the internal (and perhaps the external) goods associated with the mastery of that practice, which they might enjoy. But can one say the same thing about masters of a social-ethical tradition that most basically envisions the flourishing of a privileged few? Would these sorts of expert practitioners be open to innovation of a practice that is already benefiting them so fully? A simple hermeneutic of suspicion or ideological critique quickly suggests they often would not. This is perhaps so especially if the practice of a system of ethics is grounded only sociologically, whereby only expert practitioners who already benefit socially (and otherwise) can legitimately innovate the practice. In a more contemporary idiom, one might think their "privilege" would function to discourage change and fund refusal to innovate.

However, MacIntyre's insistence that his Aristotelian ethics be grounded objectively in nature in part addresses this situation. A natural grounding of ethics, which is constructively tethered to an account of the sort of being humans naturally are, means that a master of a moral tradition has some potential resources for (self-)criticism; they potentially have access to new warrants and motivations for revision of their moral tradition. New and emerging accounts and data regarding the nature of humans—for instance, from science or other realms—ought to be rationally considered by expert practitioners of a tradition of ethics; and when they are, the revised view of the human that emerges can justify revised views of what constitutes flourishing for beings of this kind, as well as what sorts of virtues are requisite to procuring that happiness. Even as one must recognize and guard against the sorts of appeals to nature that have a long history of unjustly excluding and marginalizing some humans and nonhumans alike, the natural grounding of such a virtue ethics provides a means by which one might challenge what has (or might) come to be recognized not as natural facts but as merely conventional and contingent moral conclusions and positions.[12]

---

12. Cf. Annas's discussion of "Nature and Naturalism" in *Morality of Happiness*, 135–41.

The practically wise person, the expert of a virtue-oriented moral tradition that is objectively grounded in nature, may thus have good reason to innovate their traditions. They can, through rational engagement with other discourses on the nature of the human, recognize that the enhancement of their own flourishing is truly augmented (naturally and objectively) when appropriate innovations to their traditions are introduced.

There is no reason to be sanguine about all this, however. Yes, experts of a moral tradition should regularly be in a position to positively revise, expand, and advance that tradition. But surely they will not always do so; or at least those who should be, or appear to be, expert in the tradition won't always do so. In a way analogous to how institutions designed to support practices might come to focus on the attainment of external goods to maintain the institution itself rather than the practice (cf. chap. 13), expert practitioners of a tradition may sometimes fall prey to the deception that the advantages they already hold—say, their possession of economic and social goods—are alone, or most essentially, what constitute their well-being. At such times, other expert practical reasoners will likely need to step in to offer moral clarification, and to do so sometimes via the most urgent of rhetorics and actions. Not unlike Amos, whose book we discussed in chapter 10, the genuinely wise and just person is always potentially a prophet.

Worthy Proverbs?

What then shall we say about the book of Proverbs and its moral vision? Might one still today find something of theological-ethical worth in this text, which so obviously presumes as natural a range of exclusions and hierarchies? If so, how? There is surely no simple response to these questions, and any compelling answers will for many surely be tied up with understandings of how the Bible may be theologically and morally authoritative (or not). But leaving aside that particular matter for the moment, I suggest that initially two related matters must be attended to. First, one must acknowledge that Proverbs' own implicit natural philosophy and ontology, like Aristotle's, ultimately needs to be jettisoned or revised. Second and consequently, interpreters must acknowledge the historically conventional and contingent nature of much in Proverbs' instruction that is presented as part of a natural and so objectively grounded and universally valid moral outlook. This is so even if the transhistorical and transsocial worth of other features of the book's moral vison may be more defensible.

To properly discern the ongoing theological-ethical worth of Proverbs, the grounding of the book's moral discourse in nature—whether through a conception like the orders of creation or via a mythologically laden discourse such as Proverbs 8:22–31 (chaps. 11 and 12)—should be critically revised. Of course, for many contemporary theological readers of Proverbs, the Bible remains the Word of God; it is thus no insignificant step to leave aside the text's own claims as to how it grounds its ethics. Though some religious readers may wish to accept, for reasons established on other grounds, the theological conception of the orders of creation and deploy that as a lens for understanding Proverbs, that notion is neither without its own moral-theological shortcomings nor the way Proverbs itself founds its ethics naturally and objectively. It is, however, also the case that Proverbs' own mythologically laden account of the natural, objective grounding of its teachings can no longer be accepted as "true" by most people. If Proverbs is still to be seriously engaged, the natural, objective ground of the virtue-oriented moral project the book appears to be engaged in should be translated into something more defensible.

What may suffice for some, though surely not all, theological interpreters of Proverbs is a modest, general, and provisional reformulation of the book's symbolic-mythological claims: namely, that via its descriptions of Wisdom's intimate relation to Adonai's acts of creation (8:22–31), Proverbs regards the divine as somehow ultimately—or in the final instance (to borrow a phrase from Marxist discourse)—responsible for creating the sort of created-in-Wisdom being humans naturally are or might become.

Another way a serious contemporary critical engagement with, and appropriation of, Proverbs' teachings might be (re)grounded is to follow the lines that MacIntyre sketches when he naturally and objectively grounds his Aristotelian-Thomistic ethics via contemporary scientific, sociological, and philosophic discourse. These sorts of discourses, as MacIntyre shows, clarify how humans in diverse ways rely on others of our kind for physical survival and to advance in rationality; such discourses also reveal how our natural desires and needs might interface with our sociality and rationality. It is possible to connect these insights and conclusions from science, sociology, and philosophy about what is natural to humans with the sorts of moral-social values and virtues that a premodern virtue-oriented moral discourse like Proverbs insists are indispensable for human flourishing. This is so even as some of the particular, historically contingent formulations and instantiations of the values and virtues of those discourses—which limit or retard widespread human flourishing by (re)producing illegitimate exclusions and hierarchies—need to be dispensed with or reconstructed.

It would, of course, be disingenuous to suggest that the ancient sages who wrote Proverbs might have anticipated that the moral vision they articulated would need to be subjected to anything like the sort of rather full "traditioning" process that I am gesturing toward here. I suspect most of them were quite sure of the validity and necessity of the gender and social-economic hierarchies that were bound to their conceptions of wisdom. But the *text* they produced—or at least the one we have received—permits it, and the moral logic of the book warrants it. In terms of Proverbs' moral logic, the book's emphasis on Practical Wisdom (cf. chaps. 8–9) suggests that a continuation of the ancient sages' moral tradition must inevitably entail the ongoing exercise of human practical reasoning. As such, it would encompass an integrous effort to rationally engage new knowledge, novel and unpredictable facets of social life, and competing moral visions—all to the end of discovering ways forward to fuller realization of good and flourishing lives for more people.

A further way in which the text of Proverbs may warrant the possibility of a genuine "traditioning" process of its moral outlook, which acknowledges and begins to transcend the historical contingency of the book's wisdom, is in the way that the text itself starts to deconstruct a central binary opposition that it relies on in its presentation of wisdom—the male-female dichotomy. Proverbs' wisdom, as discussed, is primarily for well-placed, educated or educatable (future) household-heading males in an ancient, small-scale urban context. Such a context means that attainment of a full wisdom, and thus a full flourishing, is never really envisioned for women and others. Yet, somewhat ironically, women in Proverbs are not merely potential threats or contributors to male flourishing. Female figures are also set forth as parade examples of the actual embodiment of the wisdom and virtue after which men should strive. On the one hand, in Proverbs 1–9 wisdom itself is personified as a woman and presented as an object of desire for the male reader of the book (cf. chap. 5). On the other hand, at the end of the book the Eshet Chayil—the Woman of Valor of Proverbs 31:10–31—represents the kind of virtuous figure men who would be wise should emulate. When the logic of the male-female binary comes apart, as it most fully does in the book's final poem, a bit of interpretive space appears within which Proverbs' moral vision might be furthered in ways that both transcend its historically and socially contingent features and retain what is central to its status as a virtue-oriented moral discourse.

The Eshet Chayil

There has been nearly as much written on the Eshet Chayil (אֵשֶׁת חַיִל) of Proverbs 31 as there has been on Woman Wisdom and the strange or foreign woman of Proverbs 1–9. Often discussions of the book's final female figure center on whether she should be regarded as a real woman, a representation of the patriarchal imagination's "ideal" wife, or perhaps a symbolic representation of Woman Wisdom herself. Probably the literary depiction of the woman entails a bit of all three possibilities. Even as Proverbs 31:10–31 offers what is rather transparently an idealized description of a (potential) wife for the book's male addressee, the woman minimally represents *the sort of* real, good, and virtuous wife the text believes the male addresses of the book actually should look for. Her way of life to some extent likely corresponds to the activities of at least some real ancient woman, though perhaps of a well-to-do class.[13] Importantly, however, many interpreters of Proverbs also call attention to the ways the virtuous woman of the book's final lines evokes the figure of Woman Wisdom.[14] Roland Murphy, for example, avers in commenting on Proverbs 31:10–31 that "Woman Wisdom has cast a shadow here."[15] Though the Eshet Chayil is probably not to be identified *precisely* as the mythological, larger-than-life, personified, female Wisdom figure of Proverbs 1–9, the Woman of Valor calls to mind Woman Wisdom, and she also embodies many of the key virtues that in other parts of the book belong to a life of wisdom. Both Woman Wisdom and the Woman of Valor are described as more precious than jewels (cf. 3:15; 8:11; 31:10).[16] The Eshet Chayil is also depicted as trustworthy, industrious, discerning in her dealings, generous to the poor, and kind and wise in her speech. As Tikva Frymer-Kensky says, the woman of Proverbs 31:10–31 is "the very personification of earthly practical wisdom."[17] Because she exhibits many of wisdom's virtues, this wise woman—even if she is not precisely to be identified with Woman Wisdom—can thus be said to constitute another "literary" moral exemplar for the book's addressees, analogous to those noted above (cf. chaps. 8–9). The longings of male readers are directed toward the Eshet Chayil not merely because she is presented as the kind of real virtuous woman they should want to marry; the male addressees are also to desire for themselves the very virtues she (like desirable Woman Wisdom) embodies. To attain a life of wisdom, the book's male students should be like the woman for whom they ought to yearn.

13. On the Eshet Chayil as an image of real, ancient women, see most prominently C. Yoder, *Wisdom as a Woman of Substance*, and cf. Fox's interaction with Yoder's (and others') work in *Proverbs 10–31*, 890–917. Bellis (*Proverbs*, 268) has noted that although the Eshet Chayil may appear to some modern Western people as "an impossible superwoman," the level of work ascribed to her has been, and still is, regularly matched by nonelite women around the globe.

14. On this matter, the work of McCreesh ("Wisdom as Wife") in particular has generated significant response from commentators. Cf., e.g., Waltke's critical engagement with McCreesh in *Proverbs*, 517–19.

15. R. Murphy, *Proverbs*, 249; cf. Hausmann, "Beobachtungen zu Spr 31, 10–31"; and Camp, *Wisdom and the Feminine*, 263–64.

16. Many have noted this; see, e.g., Camp, *Wisdom and the Feminine*, 179–208.

17. Frymer-Kensky, "Sage in the Pentateuch," 282.

What is ironic in all this is that, although wisdom is personified as a woman and the Woman of Valor is likewise a female embodiment of virtue (and so a moral exemplar for men), wisdom in Proverbs and the well-being it makes possible remain primarily something males (of a certain social stratum especially) can and ought to acquire. It is precisely in the book's final poem, in praise of the Woman of Valor, where one can trace something of the unraveling of the tight connection the book constructs between men and a wisdom that is so frequently and robustly figured by the feminine.

A kind of deconstructive reading of the poem to the Eshet Chayil reveals that the passage not only eulogizes the virtuous woman because she contributes to her husband's well-being; it also indicates that Proverbs' wise men should, in a queer sort of way, be most like the wise women the book valorizes. The passage takes some clear rhetorical steps to masculinize the Eshet Chayil and thereby "undo" the feminization of men who like her are or strive to be embodiments of wisdom. The text's struggle to reassert the masculinity of the men whose characters are feminized by association with the book's wise female figures creates an aporia that, finally, undermines the text's otherwise predominant association of wisdom with patriarchal maleness. It opens up, in other words, a literary-interpretive space in the moral tradition that Proverbs represents so that an account of "human" flourishing and the virtues that enable well-being can be divorced from the way the book so intimately links thriving and wisdom to humans whose bodies are sexed and gendered as male.

Well-Being in Proverbs 31:10–31

Despite its eulogizing of a prominent female figure, the alphabetic acrostic poem to the Eshet Chayil is ambiguously appreciated by feminist readers. On the one hand, "some scholars argue that this image [of the Eshet Chayil] is positive, offering a picture of a woman who is flourishing, making a good life for herself and her family," as L. Juliana Claassens notes.[18] She is, as Carol Meyers contends, "portrayed as an efficient and successful household manager, exhibiting resourcefulness and acumen in economic success."[19] She breaks "some stereotypes of women in the Hebrew Bible as passive or not fulfilling a viable economic function."[20] On the other hand, as Christine Yoder

---

18. Claassens, "Woman of Substance," 16.
19. Meyers, "Was Ancient Israel a Patriarchal Society?" Also cited by Claassens, "Woman of Substance," 17.
20. Claassens, "Woman of Substance," 17.

notes, one might suspect that Proverbs' final female figure represents yet "another unrealistic and dehumanizing depiction of women created to entice and promote the values of men."[21] The poem itself reads as follows:

> A capable wife who can find?
>   She is far more precious than jewels.
> The heart of her husband trusts in her,
>   and he will have no lack of gain.
> She does him good, and not harm,
>   all the days of her life.
> She seeks wool and flax,
>   and works with willing hands.
> She is like the ships of the merchant,
>   she brings her food from far away.
> She rises while it is still night
>   and provides food for her household
>   and tasks for her servant-girls.
> She considers a field and buys it;
>   with the fruit of her hands she plants a vineyard.
> She girds herself with strength,
>   and makes her arms strong.
> She perceives that her merchandise is profitable.
>   Her lamp does not go out at night.
> She puts her hands to the distaff,
>   and her hands hold the spindle.
> She opens her hand to the poor,
>   and reaches out her hands to the needy.
> She is not afraid for her household when it snows,
>   for all her household are clothed in crimson.
> She makes herself coverings;
>   her clothing is fine linen and purple.
> Her husband is known in the city gates,
>   taking his seat among the elders of the land.
> She makes linen garments and sells them;
>   she supplies the merchant with sashes.
> Strength and dignity are her clothing,
>   and she laughs at the time to come.
> She opens her mouth with wisdom,
>   and the teaching of kindness is on her tongue.
> She looks well to the ways of her household,
>   and does not eat the bread of idleness.

---

21. C. Yoder, *Wisdom as a Woman of Substance*, 241.

> Her children rise up and call her happy;
> > her husband too, and he praises her:
> "Many women have done excellently,
> > but you surpass them all."
> Charm is deceitful, and beauty is vain,
> > but a woman who fears the LORD is to be praised.
> Give her a share in the fruit of her hands,
> > and let her works praise her in the city gates. (31:10–31)

In a helpful study of this "Woman of Substance," Claassens draws attention to Martha Nussbaum's catalog of "central human capabilities" that are "vital for an individual to live a good life—a life in which a person not only survives, but also thrives."[22] Claassens inquires as to whether, and to what extent, the woman of Proverbs 31:10–31 might be said to exhibit such capabilities and so might be fairly described as enjoying a flourishing human life on the terms Nussbaum identifies.[23] Nussbaum's list of central human capabilities, as helpfully summarized by Claassens, include the following:

1. *Life*. The ability to live a normal life, not dying before one's time.
2. *Bodily health and integrity*. The ability to have access to adequate food and shelter and health care.
3. *Bodily integrity*. The ability to be free from violent assault, including rape and domestic violence, and to have opportunities to enjoy one's sexuality.
4. *Senses, imagination, thought*. The ability "to imagine, to think, and to reason." This includes access to education, freedom of expression, and religious experience, in addition to the ability "to have pleasurable experiences."
5. *Emotions*. The ability to freely love and grieve significant others; the freedom to express human emotions, such as longing, gratitude, and anger without fear of recrimination.
6. *Practical reason*. The ability to form one's own conception of what is good and apply it to one's own life.
7. *Affiliation*. The ability to form meaningful relationships with others and engage freely in various forms of social interaction: "Being able to be treated as a dignified being whose worth is equal to that of others."

---

22. Nussbaum, "Women and Cultural Universals," 40.
23. Claassens, "Woman of Substance," 11.

8. *Other species.* The ability to show concern and be in relation to animals, plants, and nature.
9. *Play.* The ability to laugh, play, and have time for recreational activities.
10. *Control over one's environment*
    a. The ability to engage in politics, possessing "the rights of political participation, free speech, and the freedom of association."
    b. The ability to own property both individually and/or collectively.
    c. The right to seek employment on an equal basis with others.[24]

This list of central human capabilities represents not merely those capacities that are vital to flourishing. They are also interrelated capabilities: the presence of one enhances another; the absence of one affects a person's ability to experience another; and all must be present in some degree for any life to count fully as "a good human life."[25] In good Aristotelian fashion, for Nussbaum a person should be able to develop these capabilities by exercising some choice and agency as to how they are enjoyed.[26] The denial of basic goods necessary for life—whether "nutrition, health, shelter, education, and physical safety"—as well as the absence of "effective guarantees of the major liberties of expression, conscience and political participation" will unduly limit (as with the poor, slaves, and women of Proverbs noted above) a person's chances at flourishing.[27]

Although the "good life" Proverbs envisions as within the reach of its male addressees corresponds rather fully to Nussbaum's "capabilities" catalog, Claassens's verdict (which I share) as to whether the Woman of Valor in Proverbs 31 is portrayed as flourishing is mixed. On the one hand, the text does not indicate the woman's life or bodily health and integrity is threatened; she appears to have sufficient access to food and shelter (vv. 14–15). What is more, her activities suggest that she enjoys some "control over her environment and is able to work and apparently is able to own property" (vv. 13, 16, 19); she also plausibly can be imagined as enjoying multiple meaningful relationships, for example with her children (vv. 15, 28), her husband (vv. 12, 28), and perhaps with her servants (v. 15), who belong to the same household as she. The poem does not say much explicitly about the woman's "ability to show concern"

---

24. Claassens, "Woman of Substance," 8–9; Nussbaum, "Women and Cultural Universals," 41–42.
25. Nussbaum, "Women and Cultural Universals," 42; cf. Claassens, "Woman of Substance," 9.
26. Nussbaum, "Women and Cultural Universals," 44; cf. Claassens, "Woman of Substance," 9–10.
27. Nussbaum, "Women and Cultural Universals," 20; cf. Claassens, "Woman of Substance," 9.

for "animals, plants, and nature" (Nussbaum's eighth capacity), but it does gesture toward her relationship with these others. Indeed, she works with wool and flax, secures "food" (לֶחֶם; טֶרֶף) for herself and her household, and buys a field and plants a vineyard, all the while managing well winter's cold and snow. None of these relationships, of course, should be reckoned as ecologically reckless in a way analogous to modern exploitations of nature; they are better considered as part of the woman's wise negotiation of the human ecological niche, which overlaps with the niches of other species. Indeed, given her virtue one might think that her concern for the nonhumans she encounters could be aptly described by proverbs such as 12:10a ("The righteous know the needs of their animals") and 27:23–27.

> Know well the condition of your flocks,
>   and give attention to your herds;
> for riches do not last forever,
>   nor a crown for all generations.
> When the grass is gone, and new growth appears,
>   and the herbage of the mountains is gathered,
> the lambs will provide your clothing,
>   and the goats the price of a field;
> there will be enough goats' milk for your food,
>   for the food of your household
>   and nourishment for your servant girls. (27:23–27)[28]

The Eshet Chayil also is described as discerning and acting with wisdom (vv. 16, 26), thus exercising the "ability to imagine, think, and reason that is likewise considered by Nussbaum to be a capability necessary for a human to live a good life."[29] Though the text does not say much about the woman's interior emotional life, she is, as Claassens puts it, "neither anxious nor fearful for the well-being of her household" (v. 21); indeed, she is presented as one who enjoys "a sense of well-being and security that is likely not shared by most women."[30]

However, despite a "remarkable correspondence to Nussbaum's capabilities list" and the sense that the Eshet Chayil is the sort of woman whose "capabilities work together to ensure a better quality of life" for her, "which may also result in her being held in higher esteem within her family," Claassens rightly recognizes that the "woman's actions" appear less to benefit her than to promote her husband's flourishing. "Does this strong woman receive

---

28. On these passages and Proverbs' view of the relation of wise and just human lives to nonhuman others, see Sandoval, "Morality of Non-Human Animals."
29. Claassens, "Woman of Substance," 13.
30. Claassens, "Woman of Substance," 14.

anything more than praise from her husband and children?" she asks.[31] The woman, for instance, possesses little "right to political participation and free speech," which her husband instead enjoys in the city gate (v. 23). Missing, too, from the woman's life appears much enjoyment of rest and recreation. As Claassens says, "Even though contemporary understandings of leisure likely do not apply to this woman, one still could ask, based on the deeply human need to rest, whether she has the time to do so or to engage in leisure activities that were typical of her cultural context."[32] To what Claassens observes, one might add that, although the passage does not explicitly say the woman's bodily or emotional integrity is in peril, physical and psychological violence are perpetual threats to women and girls in androcentric, patriarchal contexts. In the end, Claassens concludes that "quite a few of the capabilities that Nussbaum lists are missing from [or, as I might suggest, are only ambiguously present in] Proverbs 31, which may indicate that women's lower status at that time may have hampered this woman's ability to flourish."[33]

Although Claassens does not underscore it, the poem is actually quite explicit that the women's activities and virtues serve not her own thriving but fundamentally the well-being of her husband (בַּעַל)—literally, her "lord" or "possessor." The woman's work in Proverbs 31:10–31 is praised not primarily because it enhances her own well-being (though it certainly seems to, to an extent) or even the thriving of her family (though again it seems to). The poem is only incidentally concerned with the flourishing of those who fall outside the mythical norm of the text's primary addressees. Instead, the Eshet Chayil's work is praised because it contributes to the thriving of her husband, the head or master of the household. As 31:11–12 says:

> The heart of her husband trusts in her,
>   and he will have no lack of gain.
> She does him good, and not harm,
>   all the days of her life.

Indeed, for the woman's husband, possessing her is not unrelated to his high social status, something that is integral to the "good" life he himself appears to enjoy.

> Her husband is known in the city gates,
>   taking his seat among the elders of the land. (31:23)

---

31. Claassens, "Woman of Substance," 14.
32. Claassens, "Woman of Substance," 15.
33. Claassens, "Woman of Substance," 14.

The chances that one of Proverbs' male addressees might flourish on the book's own terms are significantly augmented if he attains a wife like the Eshet Chayil.

It might be objected that the poem also has the woman's children call her happy (אַשְׁרֵי), suggesting some thriving on her part. This is undeniable. However, together with the poem's focus on the man's thriving, it surely simply underscores the fact that the text considers the Woman of Valor to flourish only according to the standards of what the work's author(s) regards as normatively and naturally possible for women; and this, as we have just seen, only approximately corresponds to Nussbaum's catalog of capabilities. On the book's own terms, Proverbs 31:10–31 imagines the Woman of Valor to in fact be thriving. Indeed, because she is a "wise" woman, a woman of virtue, she is doing so as much as any woman ever could.

Proverbs' final words thus suggest that for this ancient wisdom book the greatest flourishing possible for women (and one presumes for others who do not embody the book's mythical norm) is to be discovered in and through their "natural" but subservient roles in society. But the roles of women (and others) that Proverbs assumes and envisions are "natural" are obviously historically particular and contingent, as indeed is the place of the male household head that Proverbs imagines as most "human." In the end, whatever quality of life the Woman of Valor herself might enjoy is only discernible within the context of what she, via her virtuous life, contributes to the flourishing of her husband, the male head of the household; and for this she is eloquently eulogized by the acrostic poem (cf. vv. 28, 31).

Masculinizing Wisdom in Proverbs 31:10–31

However, as we have said, the Woman of Valor in Proverbs 31 is not merely presented to the book's addressees as the sort of wife they would do well to acquire. She is also described in terms reminiscent of that most prominent female figure in Proverbs—Woman Wisdom. Of course, the important role played by both the Woman of Valor and Woman Wisdom in the book is easily explained in terms of the text's androcentric and patriarchal logic. As we saw in chapter 5, for the book's young male addressees, who are assumed to desire women sexually, wisdom is or should be just as desirable as "woman." Wisdom is thus literally personified as a woman, and she is also (most likely) presented to the book's readers figuratively as a desirable wife. As such she is able to "save" the one who acquires her (one might say her בַּעַל, her "owner" or "husband") from the strange or foreign woman with whom one might commit adultery and thereby unambiguously travel down a wrong—foolish and wicked—life path. If men who are, or would be, wise should desire and acquire w/Wisdom as they might desire and take a good wife, the Eshet Chayil is precisely the sort of good wife they should long to marry. However, because the virtues the Woman of Valor embodies belong so fully to the way of wisdom, she also serves the male addressees as a literary-moral exemplar.[34] Readers and hearers of Proverbs ought not only to find wives like her, as the plain-sense level of the poem suggests. In terms of the larger literary-symbolic dynamics of Proverbs' instruction, the book's addressees should also strive to be (morally) like the Woman of Valor, who herself is a paragon of virtue. Consequently, through the book's efforts, via the erotic and androcentric rhetoric of patriarchal marriage, to convince males of the desirability of a "wise" life of virtue, the book, and its final poem in particular, inadvertently ends up encouraging men not only to yearn for but to be like a woman.

To counter this rhetorical feminizing of the book's male addressees, many of the activities of the Eshet Chayil are described not only as being ultimately beneficial to, and so desirable for, her husband or "possessor"; they are presented in terms that carry decidedly masculinist connotations. Together these depictions of the Woman of Valor masculinize the woman and the virtue she embodies and thus also symbolically preserve and augment the masculinity of the book's male addressees who should be like her.

Woman of Valor

Much of the poem's praise of the Eshet Chayil draws on a rhetoric of strength, but this fact alone is not conclusive evidence for the masculinizing of the female figure. Like men, women can well be characterized in terms of both a literal and figurative strength. But when one considers the particular discourse of strength that the poem primarily evokes, the masculinizing of the Woman of Valor by the male scribe(s) responsible for penning the poem is difficult to deny.

As has long been discussed, the term חַיִל in the Bible basically means "strength, whether in wealth, physical power, military might, practical competencies or character."[35] Yet the term belongs most prominently to a discourse of war and warriors (e.g., Exod. 14:4, 9, 17, 28; Pss. 33:16; 136:15). In

---

34. However, as we said earlier (chap. 9) in regard to the examples of wise and just figures in Proverbs, the book's lack of narrative shape means that even the most exemplary literary figures in the text can never serve readers as full and adequate moral exemplars that are necessary for persons to progress fully in (practical) wisdom. For that, readers of Proverbs need to look to their own real social environment for virtuous persons whom they can imitate and to whom they might apprentice themselves.

35. Fox, *Proverbs 10–31*, 891.

most societies, the vocation of the warrior is a decidedly male pursuit, and this was surely the case in ancient Israel. As Mark Smith explains, despite the "paradigmatic presence of goddesses in warfare" in ancient West Asia, in this milieu "the cultural expectation" remained "that human females are generally not part of combat."[36]

The coloring that a militaristic term like חַיִל leaves on the description of the woman of Proverbs 31:10–31 is thus a striking bit of cultural rhetoric; its interpretive import should not be minimized. In verse 29, for example, חַיִל is deployed in the phrase עָשׂוּ חָיִל, an idiom that Al Wolters notes "regularly means 'to do valiantly' in a military context."[37] Though Proverbs speaks of a woman (אִשָּׁה) who is valorous, in seventeen of the twenty-three times חַיִל occurs in the Bible with the "opposite" term "man" (אִישׁ), it is in a military context (e.g., Judg. 3:29; 20:44; 21:10; 1 Sam. 31:12; 2 Sam. 11:16; 23:20; 24:9).[38] It is also the case that forms of אִישׁ חַיִל are associated with the terminology of גִּבּוֹר ("mighty man") (e.g., Josh. 8:3; 1 Sam. 14:52; 16:18; 2 Kings 24:16; Isa. 5:22), while forms of the expression גִּבּוֹר חַיִל or גִּבּוֹרֵי חַיִל in military contexts are common (e.g., Josh. 6:2; 8:3; 10:7; Judg. 6:12; 11:1; 1 Sam. 16:18).[39] As a result, Wolters argues that the Eshet Chayil in Proverbs 31 should "probably be understood as the female counterpart of the *gibbôr ḥayil*, the title given to the 'mighty men of valour' which are often named in David's age."[40]

The poem to the Woman of Valor uses further terminology that either carries militaristic connotations or constitutes an explicit rhetoric of strength regularly associated with males. At the outset of the poem, for example, there is an allusion to the wealth the woman secures for her husband: "he will have no lack of gain" (31:11). The term used, however, is not הוֹן or עֹשֶׁר, words for "riches" that are relatively common in Proverbs. Instead, it is שָׁלָל, a word that is most at home in militaristic and violent contexts. It is the "booty" that victors in battle—the strong, the mighty, the proud—lay claim to and divide among themselves (e.g., Exod. 15:9; Josh. 22:8; Judg. 5:30; Prov. 16:19; Isa. 53:12).[41] In Proverbs itself, we saw in 1:13 that שָׁלָל is the literal "precious wealth" (הוֹן יָקָר) that constitutes the payoff the sinners promise the book's young addressee if he follows their "wrong" way of violent robbery (cf. chaps. 4–5). Similarly, in Proverbs 31:15, the Hebrew word טֶרֶף, which most basically

---

36. Smith, *Poetic Heroes*, 76.
37. Wolters, "Heroic Hymn," 453.
38. Eising, "חַיִל," 350.
39. Cf. Eising, "חַיִל," 350–51.
40. Wolters, "Heroic Hymn," 453.
41. Cf. Wolters, "Heroic Hymn," 454. Wolters does not cite particular texts, but cf. Judg. 20:18 and similar contexts.

means "prey," may simply serve as a poetic synonym for the bread or food (לֶחֶם) mentioned at the end of the previous verse. However, as Fox says, it can also be used figuratively to describe "robbed or plundered goods." Consequently, in the poem to the Woman of Valor the woman's acquiring of food might carry connotation of "aggression and pugnacity."[42] Finally, the phrase עָלִית עַל in verse 29 is also an idiom "often used elsewhere in the sense of going out to do battle against an enemy."[43]

Still other rhetoric in the poem to the Eshet Chayil carries connotations of male strength or military prowess. For example, because verse 19 includes reference to a distaff and spindle—"she puts her hand to the distaff, and her hands hold the spindle"—the rhetoric of יָדֶיהָ שִׁלְּחָה בַכִּישׁוֹר in the line's first clause obviously describes the woman's activities in producing textiles. However, as Wolters once more notes, the Hebrew expression reflects an idiom that "always has an aggressive connotation elsewhere, so that its use in this peaceful context is exceptional." Most intriguingly, the same expression (but with the preposition *lamed* instead of *bet*) is deployed to recount another woman's shrewd but violent exploits in a militaristic context. In the Song of Deborah, the phrase describes "Jael's grasping of the tent peg with which she kills Sisera" (Judg. 5:26).[44] Elsewhere in the poem to the Eshet Chayil, the woman is said to "gird her loins with strength" and to "strengthen her arms" (v. 17). Both phrases resonate with similar descriptions of male strength (e.g., Judg. 3:16; 18:11, 16; 1 Sam. 17:39) and military exploits (Isa. 51:9; Ezek. 17:9; 30:21–22) elsewhere in the Bible.[45] Finally, in verse 25 the Eshet Chayil is described as clothed in strength and honor (v. 25), language that can be applied to the Bible's powerful male deity (Ps. 96:6).

For Wolters, all this, along with the poem's affinities to the hymn form—best known from the Psalter (e.g., Pss. 146–50)—suggests that Proverbs 31:10–31 constitutes a "Heroic Hymn."[46] He says it likely reflects a "development of an earlier heroic tradition in Israel or its environment which is largely lost but still partially preserved, for example, in the Song of Deborah," an archaic

---

42. Fox, *Proverbs 10–31*, 894; cf. Claassens, "Woman of Substance," 11; Wolters, "Heroic Hymn," 454.

43. Wolters, "Heroic Hymn," 453.

44. Wolters, "Heroic Hymn," 453–54.

45. In Job 38:3 and 40:7, Job is exhorted by the deity to gird up his loins like a man (כְּגֶבֶר). The Job passage and rhetoric might be aptly compared to the rhetoric of the poem to the Eshet Chayil, but the terminology of the two passages is distinct.

46. Intriguingly, Wolters draws attention to וִיהַלְלוּהָ ("[let her works] praise her") in Prov. 31:31, which he believes would evoke the "hallelujah" typical of hymns (e.g., Pss. 146–50). Wolters recognizes that the hymn form regularly directs praise toward the deity rather than a human, but he reasonably contends that the literary form was not so fixed that tradents could not creatively innovate with it.

poem that Smith also connects with an Israelite heroic tradition.[47] Wolters concludes that the poem to the Eshet Chayil is thus well described as a species of "heroic poetry," which "typically describes the exploits of men belonging to an aristocratic class, a class in which honour and individual initiative rank high on the scale of values."[48]

The prevalence of militaristic images of strength in the "heroic hymn" to the Woman of Valor is good evidence that the poem in essence, even if subtly, masculinizes the woman of the poem. But to what end? What is the rhetorical effect or point of all the militaristic, masculinizing images of strength applied to the Woman of Valor? One might simply insist that such rhetoric only characterizes, colorfully and robustly, the woman's strength—her literal strength in her endeavors (e.g., in weaving or rising early), the strength of her abilities in managing a complex household, and the strength of her character revealed by the virtues she exhibits. The poem's "strength" language certainly does have this effect. There is no need to quarrel with such an interpretation of the rhetoric, except to suggest that it stops short in two ways. First, just as it is certain that the rhetoric of strength characterizes the abilities of the woman as formidable, her wealth as significant, and her moral fortitude as considerable, so it also serves to color her as a "masculine woman." The Septuagint of Proverbs recognizes this when it renders אֵשֶׁת חַיִל as γυναῖκα ἀνδρείαν—a "manly woman" or a "woman of (manly) courage." Second, the masculinizing images and rhetoric that describe the Eshet Chayil should also be integrated into an understanding of the larger dynamics of the book noted above—namely, the fact that the males to whom this poem and the entire book of Proverbs are primarily addressed are asked to acquire a wisdom that the book so thoroughly associates with exemplary female characters.

Wolters's conclusions regarding the significance of the images of strength and military ability in the heroic poem to the Eshet Chayil are important in regard to the matters just mentioned. For him, it reflects a "twofold polemic" against other discourses in Proverbs' ancient context. On the one hand, the heroic song "constitutes a critique of the literature in praise of women which was prevalent in the ancient Near East." Instead of praising the physical beauty of the woman or "the ideal of feminine perfection," which Wolters believes is reflected in much ancient erotic poetry, it "glorifies the active good works of a woman in the ordinary affairs of family, community, and business life" (cf. v. 30).[49] On the other hand, via the praise of the woman's this-worldly, active

---

47. Wolters, "Heroic Hymn," 456; Smith, *Poetic Heroes*, esp. 211–56.
48. Wolters, "Heroic Hymn," 455.
49. Wolters, "Heroic Hymn," 456–57. For a similar, more recent argument, see Vayntrub, "Beauty, Wisdom."

conduct of life, it more subtly polemicizes against "the abstract theoretical wisdom rooted in impartial rationality," which Wolters regards as "the intellectual ideal of Hellenism."[50]

Wolters may well be right on both counts. But for my purposes, what is more important than either of these possible polemic targets is Wolters's conclusion that the poem represents an "emerging revaluation of military prowess."[51] Here Wolters draws on Richard Marks's study of the reinterpretation of the ideal of "heroic prowess" in rabbinic literature. As Wolters explains, Marks suggests that "the rabbinic response to the *gibbôrîm* of Israel's Heroic Age" in part functioned to redefine "*gevurah* so that its associated glory applied to academic and moral victories." The poem to the Eshet Chayil "is an early variant" of this resignification process.[52]

Wolters more or less leaves his discussion of the revaluation of military prowess in Proverbs 31:10–31 at that. He does not elaborate on the function of the poem and its culturally masculine images applied to a woman within the broader context of the book of Proverbs itself. How, then, should the subordination of heroic virtue to intellectual and moral excellence, which the poem to the Eshet Chayil in part gestures toward, be reckoned with in the larger context of Proverbs? One answer is to suggest that the tensions and incongruities related to cultural expectations of gender and virtue, evident in the poem's form and content, are symptoms of what Fredric Jameson calls a text's "political unconscious."[53] On Jameson's terms, a poem like Proverbs 31:10–31 constitutes a socially symbolic act, a symbolic resolution of what was for the text's writers a real but intractable social contradiction.

The Date and Historical-Literary Context of the Eshet Chayil Poem

Before discussing the "political unconscious" of the poem in Proverbs 31:10–31 and fleshing out the intractable social contradiction that provoked the wisdom author(s) to compose a "heroic poem" to a Woman of Valor, it is important to note that it is hard to date the poem precisely to any particular epoch. This means it is difficult to locate its production in historical-social terms. The fact that it appears in final position in the book suggests it was perhaps added last to a Proverbs scroll, a text with a long history of literary development. As LXX Proverbs shows, the arrangement of Proverbs' sections

---

50. Wolters, "Heroic Hymn," 457.
51. Wolters, "Heroic Hymn," 456.
52. Wolters, "Heroic Hymn," 457; Marks, "Dangerous Hero," 181.
53. Jameson, *Political Unconscious*.

in different literary editions of the book was not fixed until well into the Hellenistic age. What is more, as Jacqueline Vayntrub notes, the moment that a distinct section of Proverbs was incorporated into a Proverbs scroll does not necessarily correspond to the time of its composition: "Any piece of the anthology could have been composed in any period in which such texts could reasonably have been composed. . . . The present form [of the book] does not necessitate any historical order to the book's arrangement; a frame can be composed before or after any other section."[54] Most scholars, however, would date the composition of the poem to sometime in the postexilic period. Yoder, for instance, suggests the language of the poem corresponds to Late Biblical Hebrew (LBH) and the woman's deeds are well related to the activities of at least certain privileged West Asian women of the Persian period.[55] Fox, however, though acknowledging that the language of the poem is "compatible" with LBH, thinks it also may be earlier.[56]

What is clear is that the poem to the Woman of Valor was composed after what Wolters and Smith would identify as Israel's heroic epoch, an age that probably came to an end by the early monarchy, even as some heroic poetry and accounts of the heroic age continued to be transmitted in Israel and Judah's prose historical literature.[57] The poem of Proverbs 31:10–31 certainly does not deploy the archaic language of a text like the Song of Deborah in Judges 5, a leading exemplar of what might be called heroic poetry. However, as Wolters's study shows, it does evoke such heroic literature, especially through its militaristic language of חַיִל. Such rhetoric can remind a reader of David's mighty men, their strength, and their militaristic virtues. Indeed, the rhetoric of חַיִל and of גִּבּוֹר חַיִל in particular continued long after Israel's heroic epoch concluded. On several occasions in the Hebrew Bible, the terminology of גִּבּוֹר חַיִל appears, as John Kampen says, with little "apparent military connection" (e.g., 1 Sam. 9:1; 2 Kings 15:20; and perhaps 1 Kings 11:28).[58] But in other contexts, the language may more or less obviously preserve traces of its earlier rhetorical home in militaristic contexts, even as it is accented in new ways.

The description of Boaz as an אִישׁ גִּבּוֹר חַיִל in Ruth 2:1 is an important example of this phenomenon, not least because later in the book of Ruth, Ruth herself will, like the woman of Proverbs 31:10–31, be called an Eshet Chayil (Ruth 3:11). Despite Boaz's designation as an אִישׁ גִּבּוֹר חַיִל, he is not

---

54. Vayntrub, "Beauty, Wisdom," 59n45; cf. Vayntrub, "Book of Proverbs."
55. C. Yoder, *Wisdom as a Woman of Substance*, chap. 3.
56. Fox, *Proverbs 10–31*, 899–900.
57. Smith, *Poetic Heroes*, 326–32.
58. Kampen, *Hasideans*, 98.

depicted as a military or warrior figure. Instead, he appears primarily as a typical wealthy, land-owning patriarch. As Kampen explains, together with the other texts just noted (1 Sam. 9:1; 2 Kings 15:20; and perhaps 1 Kings 11:28), the existence of the Boaz character makes clear that "a military meaning is not adequate to explain the range of uses of *gibbôr ḥayil* in the Hebrew scriptures." Yet Kampen is also quick to add, "We must remember that the military, and in particular an elite troop, . . . was frequently related to wealth and/or position." Consequently, he concludes that in many biblical texts (e.g., Judges, Samuel, Kings, Ruth), "strong warrior" terminology is "used to describe a class of noblemen who had either wealth or position (or both), which derived from or resulted in military service." Although Kampen does not much explore the fact, one can identify traces of these military connotations applied to Boaz in other aspects of his character. Boaz is presented as a quite powerful figure in Bethlehem and its environs, a kind of strong man or local chieftain who exercises control over significant resources (fields and servants; Ruth 2) and rather easily exerts his will over other males in local political proceedings (with perhaps an implicit threat of violence; Ruth 4). Indeed, "Boaz" ("in him is strength") is the great-grandfather of the paradigmatic warrior-hero David.[59] Whatever may be the precise case with Boaz, for Kampen those locutions in the Bible that are reminiscent of the rhetoric of גִּבּוֹר חַיִל, such as Ruth's depiction as an Eshet Chayil, are derivative of the rhetoric of "mighty men." That rhetoric points to "the character traits or the life of virtue"—industry, ability, and so forth—"which would be expected of a person having the status *gibbôr ḥayil*."[60]

Even late uses of the phrase גִּבּוֹר חַיִל (and related rhetoric) might exhibit a similar, though not identical, range of connotations or accentuations as those just discussed. In Chronicles, militaristic connotations associated with the expression are at points obvious. For example, 1 Chronicles 12 begins with an allusion to בַּגִּבּוֹרִים who "helped him [David] in the war" (v. 1). The same chapter (v. 21) speaks of גִּבּוֹרֵי חַיִל. However, these figures are not precisely the sort of elite military men associated with David in earlier texts. Instead, as Kampen says, they represent "persons from each tribe who came, as 12:24 says, 'to turn the kingdom of Saul over to him [David].'" Kampen concludes, "Clearly there is another definition operative here in addition to that one which designates the elite personal troops of David."[61]

---

59. On the warrior-like figure of the chief and the claim that early Israelite culture saw a transition from a loose tribal confederacy through a period of chieftainship to the monarchy, see MacDonald, *Not Bread Alone*, 134–65.

60. Kampen, *Hasideans*, 99.

61. Kampen, *Hasideans*, 101–2.

Kampen also considers 1 Chronicles 7 to elucidate who or what constitutes גִּבּוֹרֵי חַיִל in that book. Importantly, he notes that these figures are related to the רָאשֵׁי בֵית אָבוֹת, the heads of household mentioned in verses 7 and 40 of that chapter (cf. 1 Chron. 26:6).[62] These גִּבּוֹרֵי חַיִל are neither the sort of mighty warriors associated with David nor "noblemen" like Boaz, whom Kampen identifies in earlier biblical texts. Instead, they are "free men who are in a position to make decisions about their own and sometimes about other's lives"; they are "probably 'landed proprietors,' persons who own land, or craftsmen and artisans who are self-employed and perhaps have some slaves or hired workman."[63]

Such a description of the גִּבּוֹר חַיִל from the Persian-period books of Chronicles corresponds quite well with the picture of the Eshet Chayil of Proverbs 31, who owns property, engages in business, pursues independent artisanal work, and exercises authority over slaves or servants; it might thus support dating the composition of the Proverbs passage to the Persian epoch. What is most important for my purposes in all this, however, is that (1) the term חַיִל throughout the Bible is most fully associated with socially and economically powerful males and (2) even in late literary contexts the heroic, militaristic connotations of חַיִל, though transformed and accented differently, do not entirely disappear.

The Political Unconscious of the Eshet Chayil Poem

Although identifying a precise social-historical context for the Eshet Chayil poem is difficult, this ultimately is not prohibitive for an analysis of the text's political unconscious. As a Marxist literary critic, Jameson is deeply concerned with the relationship of texts to history but insists that such relations are more complex than many imagine. He is not so much interested in "the traditional notion of 'context' familiar in older social or historical criticism."[64] The work of uncovering this sort of background for texts, like that just offered in relation to the rhetoric of חַיִל, constitutes preliminary analysis at best. Instead, for Jameson, identifying the political unconscious of a text involves, as Barbara Foley explains, recognizing the way a "literary work symptomatically registers extra literary situations and conflicts."[65] Interpretation concerned with articulating a text's political unconscious should be understood, as

---

62. Kampen, *Hasideans*, 103.
63. Kampen, *Hasideans*, 104–5.
64. Jameson, *Political Unconscious*, 81.
65. Foley, *Marxist Literary Criticism*, 131.

Jameson says, as a kind of "rewriting of the literary text in such a way that the latter [i.e., the text] may itself be seen as the rewriting or restructuration of a prior historical or ideological subtext, it being always understood that that 'subtext' is not immediately present as such, not some common-sense external reality . . . but rather must itself always be (re)constructed after the fact." Put otherwise, a text will "draw the Real" of the context of its production "into its own texture"; it will "carry the Real within itself as its own intrinsic or immanent subtext."[66]

For Jameson a text takes shape as an ensemble of elements that each at once acknowledge and obscure their origins in the real, material contexts of class struggle and their accompanying modes of oppression and domination. In particular, it is via its anomalous formal maneuvers that a text, as Foley again explains, sutures over "unresolvable historical contradictions in the world beyond the text."[67] Indeed, for Jameson, "the notion of contradiction is central" for literary study, and the ability to articulate "a text's fundamental contradiction" is "a test of the completeness of the analysis."[68]

We have already identified contradictory and anomalous elements of the poem to the Eshet Chayil that might be regarded as symptomatic of this text's political unconscious. Most fundamentally, and in formal terms, one might expect a "heroic hymn" to celebrate the exploits of a strong, male warrior. But the poem in Proverbs 31:10–31 instead extols the domestic virtues of a woman. The text thereby masculinizes the virtuous woman it depicts, ascribing to her and her deeds the strength and praise that the literary form traditionally reserved for mighty military men.

A further contradiction we have already discerned in the form and content of Proverbs 31:10–31 involves the fact that wisdom in the book is typically a male prerogative. Like glory in battle, it is something that men (of a certain social position) normally are in the position to most fully pursue and embody. Yet in Proverbs' final lines, it is a woman, reminiscent of Woman Wisdom herself, who embodies a fully virtuous character like that to which men should aspire. Indeed, the alphabetic acrostic shape of the poem is the only instance of that literary technique in Proverbs and hence itself is a noteworthy formal feature of the book. It is intended, commentators sometimes suggest,

---

66. Jameson, *Political Unconscious*, 81. The conception of the Real in this quote, as well as in Jameson's materialist interpretive project more broadly, does a lot of rhetorical-philosophical work. Jameson's understanding of the Real owes much to the concept as developed in the poststructuralist, psychoanalytic work of Jacques Lacan. For an accessible account of Jameson's indebtedness to Lacan, see Roberts, *Fredric Jameson*, 62–72.

67. Foley, *Marxist Literary Criticism*, 134.

68. Jameson, *Political Unconscious*, 80.

to literarily underscore the fullness of the woman's character.[69] As Murphy says, in moving "from a to z" the poem bespeaks "totality and perfection" of the woman that men, who may (still) lack the sort of virtue she embodies, should be like.[70]

Finally, one might observe a kind of contradiction in one other aspect of the poem to the Eshet Chayil. Despite the poem's artistic praise of a woman for her virtue, the inscribed social status that this woman's femaleness carries means that she can never attain full social recognition, at least not the sort of social status that a man of virtue might reach and that her husband in fact seems to enjoy (v. 23). Indeed, as we said, her virtue is praised precisely because it primarily contributes to her husband's thriving.

But if the above sorts of contradictions and anomalies in the poem to the Eshet Chayil can be read as symptoms of the text's political unconscious, what precisely are they symptoms of? How might one begin to describe the intractable social contradiction that the text strives to resolve symbolically? Most likely, the real and unresolvable incongruities of social life that the text's authors experienced, and which the passage's tensions and contradictions regarding gender and virtue are symptomatic of, is the fact that the life experiences of a wise and just "man" are not what they "should" be. The wise man's embodiment of Proverbs' intellectual, practical, and especially cooperative moral-social virtues, which are requisite for genuine flourishing, does not invariably result in a full thriving that includes significant enjoyment of goods like status and wealth, as it ought to, or at least it does not entail a level of enjoyment of those goods that other men, including especially unvirtuous or vicious men, regularly experience—and this even though, so the sages insist, only the virtuous understand how best to pursue such things and how they might genuinely contribute to flourishing.

The literary masculinization of the Eshet Chayil and her virtuous way of life—and so of the (potentially) wise men who pursue that life—thus constitutes what was for the male authors of the poem a serious claim to social status and power at the level of symbolic discourse. What the poem symbolically accomplishes is the valorization of "wise men" whose prestige and authority in real social life are sometimes, perhaps even typically, subordinated to that of other males—men who themselves may regard the cooperative virtues the sages so fully valued as not properly "masculine" traits. That is, despite the strong association of virtue or wisdom with the feminine, the men who

---

69. Cf. Waltke, *Proverbs*, 514.
70. R. Murphy, *Proverbs*, 249, though Murphy himself does not believe "that perception of the meaning of an acrostic" (249) fits the poem to the Eshet Chayil.

embrace Proverbs' ethics ought not to be, as women customarily are, socially subordinated to other males—those who accumulate wealth and exercise social power in ways that are more obviously consonant with typical, culturally acknowledged, masculine virtues. Although some may, like "real men," be willing to deploy—even unjustly—physical, economic, and social strength (חַיִל) over others in their efforts to attain the goods they believe will secure their happiness, the wise and just "know better." In an effort to re-form a typical social-symbolic structure of value, Proverbs' final lines suggest that the virtuous, too, are strong, warrior-like, and manly, like those other males with whom they compete for social power and status. The strength of the wise and just, however, lies not in their literal warrior-like power but in their ways of life, their traveling moral-social paths that avoid undue striving for wealth or socially disruptive, agonistic pursuits of political and social advantage—those typical masculine modes of conduct that Proverbs elsewhere relegates to the way of the wicked and foolish.

On a surface-level reading of the text, then, the poem to the Woman of Valor insists that it is not beauty that should be praised in a woman but instead her virtue and ability to contribute to her husband's well-being.[71] On another level, however, the "rewriting" of the literary text in terms that point to its political unconscious—its "restructuration of a prior historical or ideological subtext"—contends that the typical manly attributes of powerful males are not what should be valued or result in social prestige.[72] Instead, what ought to be prized is a way of life characterized by a living out of wisdom's socially cooperative virtues and moral perspectives. Such ("feminine") wisdom, when pursued and cultivated, the sages believe, will make possible the sort of full individual and communal well-being for which humans long.[73]

---

71. Jameson, *Political Unconscious*, 81. Interestingly, in ancient West Asia and Egypt, the physical attractiveness of warrior heroes is sometimes alluded to; cf. Smith, *Poetic Heroes*, 273–75. In the Bible the description of David in 1 Sam. 16:12 perhaps reflects this motif. Vayntrub ("Beauty, Wisdom," 59–60) suggests that in ancient Israel beauty, like wisdom, may have been regarded as a sign of divine favor.

72. Jameson, *Political Unconscious*, 81.

73. The sort of initial uncovering of the intractable social contradiction that a text attempts to symbolically resolve, like that just described, is only the first of three steps or horizons in Jameson's critical hermeneutical program. The second step involves analysis of the text in terms of class conflict. In Jameson's first horizon of interpretation, the contradictions of a text are particular to that text and to the sociological context to which it forms a response; his second horizon of interpretation concerns the "irreconcilable demands and positions of antagonistic classes." To take this second step is "to perform a rather different operation" than that carried out in the first horizon of interpretation. Drawing an analogy with Sausurean linguistics, Jameson writes, "Now the individual text will be refocused as *parole*, or individual utterance of that larger system, or *langue*, of class discourse." At this level of analysis, a critic can "reread or rewrite" "hegemonic forms" so that they can be "grasped as a process of the reappropriation

Conclusions

The masculinization of the Eshet Chayil in Proverbs 31:10–31 has implications for the further "traditioning" of the virtue-oriented moral discourse of Proverbs. It confounds and destabilizes Proverbs' implicit understandings of the human being, virtue, and desire, in terms primarily related to patriarchal maleness. This destabilization or confounding of the book's gender-tethered moral discourse subsequently can be correlated not only to the necessarily responsive nature of Proverbs' Practical Wisdom to context and situation; it can also be linked to the way the wisdom of Proverbs might be considered a moral "practice" in a MacIntyrian sense, where those who are expert in the practice and devoted to the activities, values, and virtues integral to it are sometimes well justified in modifying the "traditions" of that practice. Considered together, these features of the wisdom of Proverbs mean that those today who wish to engage the book's ethical program (e.g., Jewish and Christian religious communities) ought not to reify the particular and exclusivist moral discourse of the ancient sages. Much in Proverbs' (implicit) moral logic and many of the social, practical, and intellectual virtues the book identifies as requisite to human flourishing will still have much to commend them, certainly. Yet many of the particular instantiations or specifications of the virtues that the sages in their time and place insisted on—the book's paternalistic view of justice, for instance—and much of the (implicit) "natural philosophy" that they presuppose cannot be universalized (e.g., assumptions about the inferiority of women or regarding the possibilities of flourishing for people with impairments or disabilities); they demand critical engagement and revision.

When this happens, when the terms upon which the virtue-oriented discourse of Proverbs are constructed are recognized as less than stable, and when the text's emphasis on Practical Wisdom is fully appreciated and the moral life it promotes recognized as a kind of MacIntyrian "practice," the book can inform the moral-theological reflections of those today who still study it. Indeed, it points to the ways in which a character-ethics approach to the moral life may be more adequate than other moral perspectives.

---

and neutralization of the cooption and class transformations, the cultural universalization of forms which originally expressed the situation of 'popular' subordinated, or dominated groups" (*Political Unconscious*, 85–86). Finally, the third horizon of Jameson's interpretive program concerns History itself, in particular the complex history of modes of production. At this level, "'form' is apprehended as content"; "formal processes" of a text can be viewed "as sedimented content in their own right, as carrying the ideological messages of their own, distinct from the ostensible or manifest content of the works" (*Political Unconscious*, 98–99). For the sake of space and simplicity, I reserve analysis of the poem to the Eshet Chayil in terms of Jameson's second and third horizons for another time.

Proverbs' virtue-oriented discourse most basically reminds us that deontological rule following or utilitarian pleasure seeking (or some other vision of the moral life) are not the only conceptualizations of ethics available to us. It also suggests that a basic rationality, which entails both the capacity to investigate and learn afresh what is necessary for our well-being as humans and to discern ways to promote and expand our flourishing, is natural to humans. As Annas explains for the Aristotelian tradition of virtue ethics, "The virtuous person may well, as a result of developing a virtue, revise or reject some of the initial judgment she accepted when learning to be virtuous."[74] Or as Nussbaum similarly says, "The person of practical wisdom must be prepared to meet the new with responsiveness and imagination, cultivating the sort of flexibility and perceptiveness that will permit" one "'to improvise what is required.'"[75]

The wisdom of Proverbs suggests, on the one hand, that practical moral reasoners in the tradition of the ancient wisdom book should be receptive to counsel and even rebuke—just as the wise people the sages spoke of were (e.g., 12:15; 13:10). We should thus not only respond generously, with openness and humility, to the critical and sometimes prophetic voices of others from within our traditions who, like the prophet Amos, insistently point out the unjust exclusions and hierarchies that too often characterize our lives together or who demand that we live out concretely the virtues and values we claim to possess. Proverbial practical reasoners should also be able to discern when it is necessary to utter prophetic critique themselves in some shape or fashion.

On the other hand, practical moral reasoners in the proverbial tradition should also be able to engage constructively new discourses of knowledge from outside their own communities and traditions—whether the insights of science, sociology, and philosophy or the moral discourses, demands, and epistemologies of different ethical and religious traditions. In doing so, practical reasoners in the sort of tradition Proverbs represents will recognize—perhaps more often than is comfortable—that they need to revise their own wisdom in response to any number of matters. For instance, some may need to acknowledge with a host of scientific, religious, and philosophical traditions (including Proverbs' itself) that humans are not first and foremost, or merely, the sort of free individual subjects imagined by liberal traditions, agents who may ultimately choose to pursue our happiness any way we see fit. We instead are fundamentally social beings whose own flourishing is bound up with the significant responsibility and care that we owe others, including nonhuman

74. Annas, *Morality of Happiness*, 114.
75. Nussbaum, *Fragility of Goodness*, 303 (citing Thucydides).

others, with whom our lives are embedded. Other practical reasoners in a tradition like Proverbs will have to honestly engage the insights of relevant discourses and the testimonies of wise individuals and communities regarding other matters—for example, how a remarkably diverse humanity might experience and legitimately express sex, gender, and sexuality in ways that our traditions have sometimes censured.

As a mere snapshot of an ongoing moral tradition, the book of Proverbs in the form we have it is a deeply conserving text. Yet the sort of moral life it promotes should not be reckoned as *only* traditional or as exclusively venerating the moral insights of past generations. Because these past generations regarded Practical Wisdom as central to the way of wisdom, Proverbs is also representative of a tradition that is fundamentally open to revision, whereby virtuous practical reasoners seek to find good and just ways to cope with and thrive in a complex world. Indeed, like Oholiab, whose wise practice of tabernacle building demanded that he employ his creativity to "devise artistic designs" appropriate to the sanctuary, so a text like Proverbs might be said to exhort individuals and communities to exercise a Practical Wisdom characterized by a moral imagination that strives to find ways for more humans (and other parts of the divine's creation) to flourish more.

For some, the status of Proverbs as Scripture—and so in some sense a theologically and morally authoritative discourse that should be seriously attended to—may sharply curtail any efforts *not* to "reify" the book's teaching. Should we not, after all, do what Scripture clearly says? This may be much less an issue for Jews than it is for some Christians, since, as Moshe Goshen-Gottstein writes, "the issue of biblical authority has never been a question which bothered Jews," who since at least the rabbinic era have fostered a robust culture of interpretation where multiple and diverse understandings of the Bible have been welcome and dialogically engaged.[76] Marc Zvi Brettler similarly notes, "Traditional rabbinic interpretation," which still lies at the heart of contemporary Judaism, "was extremely open to a wide variety of interpretations and interpretive methods—almost nothing was beyond the pale."[77]

Yet within Christianity, the religious tradition I know best and out of which I write, questions of biblical authority and the possibility of arriving at *the* correct interpretation of the Bible have long constituted lively topics of concern. For some Christians, especially in more conserving theological traditions with "high" views regarding the inspiration of Scripture, if the

76. Goshen-Gottstein, "Scriptural Authority (Judaism)."
77. Brettler, "Biblical Authority," 4.

Bible is God's Word, then what it says plainly is divine edict; and this Word is to be unquestionably and quite literally followed. However, to understand the particular and historically contingent aspects of the moral discourse of a book like Proverbs—its conceptions of social and gender hierarchies, for instance, or its paternalistic conceptions of justice—as instances of divine Word to be strictly adopted and followed is ultimately to transform the book's virtue-oriented moral discourse, with its emphasis on Practical Wisdom, into a deontological work, a set of divinely given rules to be obeyed. And to do this is to misconstrue the nature of this portion of Scripture, something that most who revere the biblical text will surely also be reluctant to do.

Although Christian accounts of the theological status and authority of the Bible are too many and diverse to describe in adequate fashion here at the end of an already long book, at least one thing can be said. Theological accounts of the Bible that reckon the texts as Word of God but that also view them in ways that can accommodate an understanding of Proverbs as, in large part, a virtue-oriented, theological-moral discourse are available.[78] Revising one's thinking about biblical authority and interpretation in light of the views of others—to take counsel with these others, as the sages might say—may often be difficult, even agonizing, especially for those who have long been committed to particular traditional perspectives. Still, for some Christians at least, arriving at a full appreciation of Proverbs' virtue-oriented moral discourse may inevitably entail expanding one's understanding of the theological status of the Bible.

---

78. See, e.g., McCormack's articulation of a Reformed, Barthian view of Scripture in "The Being of Holy Scripture Is in Becoming," and cf. the range of essays, including some by Jewish writers, in Brown, *Engaging Biblical Authority*.

Works Cited

Adams, Samuel L. *Wisdom in Transition: Act and Consequence in Second Temple Instructions*. Supplements to the Journal for the Study of Judaism 125. Leiden: Brill, 2008.

Akoto-Abutiate, Dorothy B. E. A. *Proverbs and the African Tree of Life: Grafting Biblical Proverbs on to Ghanaian Eve Folk Proverbs*. Studies in Systematic Theology 16. Leiden: Brill, 2014.

Albrecht, Gloria. *The Character of Our Communities: Toward an Ethic of Liberation for the Church*. Nashville: Abingdon, 1995.

Allen, James P. *Genesis in Egypt: The Philosophy of Ancient Egyptian Creation Accounts*. New Haven: Yale Egyptological Seminar, 1988.

Anderson, Cheryl B. *Ancient Laws and Contemporary Controversies: The Need for Inclusive Biblical Interpretation*. Oxford: Oxford University Press, 2009.

Annas, Julia. *The Morality of Happiness*. Oxford: Oxford University Press, 1993.

Ansberry, Christopher B. *Be Wise, My Son, and Make My Heart Glad: An Exploration of the Courtly Nature of the Book of Proverbs*. BZAW 422. Berlin: de Gruyter, 2011.

―――. "What Does Jerusalem Have to Do with Athens? The Moral Vision of the Book of Proverbs and Aristotle's *Nicomachean Ethics*." *HS* 51 (2010): 157–73.

Aristotle. *The Complete Works of Aristotle*. Edited by Jonathan Barnes. 2 vols. Princeton: Princeton University Press, 1984.

Assmann, Jan. *Ma'at: Gerechtigkeit und Unsterblichkeit im Alten Ägypten*. 2nd ed. Munich: Beck, 1995.

Avalos, Hector, Sarah J. Melcher, and Jeremy Schipper, eds. *This Abled Body: Rethinking Disabilities in Biblical Studies*. Semeia Studies 55. Atlanta: Society of Biblical Literature, 2007.

Ayad, Mariam F. *God's Wife, God's Servant: The God's Wife of Amun (c. 740–525 BC)*. London: Routledge, 2009.

Bakhtin, M. M. *The Dialogic Imagination: Four Essays*. Edited by Michael Holquist. Translated by Caryl Emerson and Michael Holquist. Austin: University of Texas Press, 1992.

———. *Problems of Dostoevsky's Poetics*. Edited and translated by Caryl Emerson. Theory and History of Literature 8. Manchester: Manchester University Press, 1984.

———. *Speech Genres and Other Late Essays*. Edited by Caryl Emerson and Michael Holquist. Translated by Vern McGee. Austin: University of Texas Press, 1986.

Banks, Mark. "MacIntyre, Bourdieu, and the Practice of Jazz." *Popular Music* 31, no. 4 (2012): 69–86.

Barr, James. *Biblical Faith and Natural Theology: The Gifford Lectures for 1991*. Oxford: Clarendon, 1993.

———. *The Concept of Biblical Theology*. Minneapolis: Fortress, 1999.

Barth, Karl. "Basic Problems of Christian Social Ethics: A Discussion with Paul Althaus." In *The Beginnings of Dialectic Theology*, vol. 2, edited by James Robinson, translated by Keith Crim, 46–57. Richmond: John Knox, 1968.

———. *Church Dogmatics*. 4 vols. in 13 parts. London: T&T Clark, 1936–77.

Barthes, Roland. "The Death of the Author." In *Image-Music-Text*, translated by Stephen Heath, 142–48. New York: Hill & Wang, 1977.

———. *S/Z*. Translated by Richard Miller. New York: Hill & Wang, 1974.

———. *Writing Degree Zero*. Translated by Annette Lavers and Colin Smith. New York: Hill & Wang, 1977.

Barton, John. "Ethics and Character Formation in Biblical Wisdom Texts." In *Seeking Wisdom's Depths and Torah's Heights: Essays in Honor of Samuel E. Balentine*, edited by Barry R. Huff and Patricia Vesely, 233–46. Macon, GA: Smyth & Helwys, 2020.

———. *Understanding Old Testament Ethics: Approaches and Explorations*. Louisville: Westminster John Knox, 2003.

Bauks, Michaela, and Gerlinde Baumann. "Im Anfang war . . . ? Gen 1,1 und Prov 8,22–31 im Vergleich." *Biblische Notizen* 71 (1994): 24–52.

Bayer, Oswald. "Nature and Institution: Luther's Doctrine of the Three Orders." *LQ* 12 (1998):125–59.

Beentjes, Pancratius C. *The Book of Ben Sira in Hebrew*. VTSup 68. Atlanta: Society of Biblical Literature, 2006.

Bellis, Alice Ogden. *Proverbs*. Collegeville, MN: Liturgical Press, 2018.

Bentham, Jeremy. *An Introduction to the Principles of Morals and Legislation*. Oxford: Clarendon, 1907.

Bergant, Dianne. *Israel's Wisdom Literature: A Liberation-Critical Reading*. Minneapolis: Fortress, 1997.

Birch, Bruce C., and Larry L. Rasmussen. *Bible and Ethics in the Christian Life*. Rev. ed. Minneapolis: Augsburg, 1989.

Boer, Roland. *The Sacred Economy of Ancient Israel*. Louisville: Westminster John Knox, 2015.

Bonnard, P. E. "De la Sagesse personifieé dans l'Ancien Testament à la Sagesse en personne dans le Nouveau." In *La Sagesse de l'Ancien Testament*, edited by M. Gilbert, 117–49. Louvain: Peeters, 1979.

Braaten, Carl E. "God in Public Life: Rehabilitating the 'Orders of Creation.'" *First Things* (December 1990). https://www.firstthings.com/article/1990/12/god-in-public-life-rehabilitating-the-orders-of-creation.

Brettler, Marc Zvi. "Biblical Authority: A Jewish Pluralistic View." In *Engaging Biblical Authority: Perspectives on the Bible as Scripture*, edited by William P. Brown, 1–9. Louisville: Westminster John Knox, 2007.

Brown, William P., ed. *Character and Scripture: Moral Formation, Community, and Biblical Interpretation*. Grand Rapids: Eerdmans, 2002.

———. *Character in Crisis: A Fresh Approach to the Wisdom Literature of the Old Testament*. Grand Rapids: Eerdmans, 1996.

———, ed. *Engaging Biblical Authority: Perspectives on the Bible as Scripture*. Louisville: Westminster John Knox, 2007.

———. "The Moral Cosmologies of Creation." In *Character Ethics and the Old Testament: Moral Dimensions of Scripture*, edited by M. Daniel Carroll R. and Jacqueline E. Lapsley, 11–26. Louisville: Westminster John Knox, 2007.

———. "The Pedagogy of Proverbs 10:1–31:9." In *Character and Scripture: Moral Formation, Community, and Biblical Interpretation*, edited by William P. Brown, 150–82. Grand Rapids: Eerdmans, 2002.

———. *Wisdom's Wonder: Character, Creation, and Crisis in the Bible's Wisdom Literature*. Grand Rapids: Eerdmans, 2014.

Brueggemann, Walter. Foreword to *Character Ethics and the Old Testament: Moral Dimensions of Scripture*, edited by M. Daniel Carroll R. and Jacqueline E. Lapsley, vii–xi. Louisville: Westminster John Knox, 2007.

Bryce, Glendon E. *A Legacy of Wisdom: The Egyptian Contribution to the Wisdom of Israel*. London: Associated University Presses, 1979.

Budge, E. W. *Facsimiles of Egyptian Hieratic Papyri in the British Museum*. Second Series. London: British Museum, 1923.

Camp, Claudia V. "Proverbs and the Problems of the Moral Self." *JSOT* 40, no. 1 (2015): 25–42.

———. "What's So Strange about the Strange Woman?" In *The Bible and the Politics of Exegesis: Essays in Honor of Norman K. Gottwald on His Sixty-Fifth Birthday*, edited by David Jobling, Peggy L. Day, and Gerald T. Sheppard, 17–31. Cleveland: Pilgrim, 1991.

———. *Wisdom and the Feminine in the Book of Proverbs*. BLS 11. Sheffield: Almond, 1985.

———. *Wise, Strange, and Holy: The Strange Woman and the Making of the Bible*. Sheffield: Sheffield Academic, 2000.

Carr, David M. *The Formation of the Hebrew Bible: A New Reconstruction*. Oxford: Oxford University Press, 2011.

———. *Writing on the Tablet of the Heart*. Oxford: Oxford University Press, 2005.

Carroll R., M. Daniel, and Jacqueline E. Lapsley, eds. *Character Ethics and the Old Testament: Moral Dimensions of Scripture*. Louisville: Westminster John Knox, 2007.

Casey, John. *Pagan Virtue: An Essay in Ethics*. Oxford: Oxford University Press, 1991.

Charry, Ellen T. *God and the Art of Happiness*. Grand Rapids: Eerdmans, 2010.

Cheung, Simon Chi-Chung. *Wisdom Intoned: A Reappraisal of the Genre "Wisdom Psalms."* LHBOTS 613. London: Bloomsbury T&T Clark, 2015.

Cho, Yong Hyun. "Wisdom's Wealthy: The Rich in Proverbs, LXX Proverbs, and the Wisdom of Ben Sira." PhD diss., Brite Divinity School, 2018.

Claassens, L. Juliana. "The Woman of Substance and Human Flourishing: Proverbs 31:10–31 and Martha Nussbaum's Capabilities Approach." *Journal of Feminist Studies in Religion* 32, no. 1 (2016): 5–19.

Clayton, Jay, and Eric Rothstein. "Figures in the Corpus: Theories of Influence and Intertextuality." In *Influence and Intertextuality in Literary History*, edited by Jay Clayton and Eric Rothstein, 3–36. Madison: University of Wisconsin Press, 1991.

Clayton, Ted. "Political Philosophy of Alasdair MacIntyre." *The Internet Encyclopedia of Philosophy: A Peer-Reviewed Academic Resource*. https://www.iep.utm.edu/p-macint/#H3.

Clifford, Richard J. *Creation Accounts in the Ancient Near East and the Bible*. CBQMS 26. Washington, DC: Catholic Biblical Association of America, 1994.

———. *Proverbs*. Old Testament Library. Louisville: Westminster John Knox, 1999.

Clifton, Shane. *Crippled Grace: Disability, Virtue Ethics, and the Good Life*. Waco: Baylor University Press, 2018.

Collins, John J. "The Biblical Precedent for Natural Theology." *Journal of the American Academy of Religion* 45, no. 1 Supplement (March 1977): B:35–67.

Crenshaw, James L. "The Influence of the Wise upon Amos: The 'Doxologies of Amos' and Job 5:9–16; 9:5–10." *ZAW* 79 (1967): 42–52.

———. "Method in Determining Wisdom Influence on 'Historical Literature.'" *JBL* 88, no. 2 (1969): 129–42.

———. *Old Testament Wisdom: An Introduction*. Rev. ed. Louisville: Westminster John Knox, 1998.

Cross, Frank Moore. *Canaanite Myth and Hebrew Epic*. Cambridge, MA: Harvard University Press, 1997.

Cuéllar, Gregory L. *Empire, the British Museum, and the Making of the Biblical Scholar in the Nineteenth Century: Archival Criticism*. London: Palgrave MacMillan, 2019.

Culler, Jonathan. *The Pursuit of Signs*. Ithaca, NY: Cornell University Press, 1981.

Curran, Charles E., and Richard A. McCormick, eds. *The Use of Scripture in Moral Theology*. Readings in Moral Theology 4. New York: Paulist, 1984.

Davies, G. I. "Were There Schools in Ancient Israel?" In *Wisdom in Ancient Israel: Essays in Honour of J. A. Emerton*, edited by John Day, Robert P. Gordon, and H. G. M. Williamson, 199–211. Cambridge: Cambridge University Press, 1995.

Davis, Ellen F. "Preserving Virtues: Renewing the Tradition of the Sages." In *Character and Scripture: Moral Formation, Community, and Biblical Interpretation*, edited by William P. Brown, 183–201. Grand Rapids: Eerdmans, 2002.

Delkurt, Holger. *Ethische Einsichten in der alttestamentlichen Spruchweisheit*. Neukirchen-Vluyn: Neukirchener Verlag, 1993.

Dell, Katharine J. *The Book of Proverbs in Social and Theological Context*. Cambridge: Cambridge University Press, 2006.

———. *The Solomonic Corpus of "Wisdom" and Its Influence*. Oxford: Oxford University Press, 2020.

Dentith, Simon. *Bakhtinian Thought: An Introductory Reader*. Critical Readers in Theory and Practice. London: Routledge, 1995.

Derrida, Jacques. *Of Grammatology*. Translated by Gayatri Chakravorty Spivak. Baltimore: Johns Hopkins University Press, 1976.

Driver, Julia. "The History of Utilitarianism." In *Stanford Encyclopedia of Philosophy*. Stanford University, 1997–. Article published March 27, 2009; last modified October 5, 2022. https://plato.stanford.edu/archives/win2022/entries/utilitarianism-history.

Eising, H. "חַיִל *chayil*." *TDOT* 4:348–55.

Emerton, John A. "'Spring and Torrent' in Psalm LXXIV 15." In Supplements to Vetus Testamentum 15 (1965): 122–33.

Erlandsson, Seth. "בָּגַד *bāghadh*." *TDOT* 1:470–73.

Erman, Adolf. "Eine ägyptische Quelle der 'Sprüche Salomos.'" *Sitzungsberichte der Preussischen Akademie der Wissenschaften, Philosophisch-Historische Klasse* 15 (1924): 86–93.

Falcon, Andrea. "Aristotle on Causality." In *Stanford Encyclopedia of Philosophy*. Stanford University, 1997–. Article published January 11, 2006; last modified March 7, 2023. https://plato.stanford.edu/archives/spr2023/entries/aristotle-causality.

Fichtner, J. "Isaiah among the Wise." In *Studies in Ancient Israelite Wisdom*, edited by James L. Crenshaw, 429–38. New York: Ktav, 1976.

———. "Jesaja unter den Weisen." *Theologische Literaturzeitung* 74 (1949): 75–80.

Fogarty, Gerald. "Scriptural Authority (Roman Catholicism)." *ABD* 5:1023–26.

Foley, Barbara. *Marxist Literary Criticism Today*. London: Pluto, 2019.

Fontaine, Carole R. *Traditional Sayings in the Old Testament*. BLS 5. Sheffield: Almond, 1982.

Fox, Michael V. *Proverbs 1–9: A New Translation with Introduction and Commentary*. AB 18a. New York: Doubleday, 2000.

———. *Proverbs 10–31: A New Translation with Introduction and Commentary*. AB 18b. New Haven: Yale University Press, 2009.

———. "The Social Location of the Book of Proverbs." In *Texts, Temples, and Traditions: A Tribute to Menahem Haran*, edited by Michael V. Fox, Victor Avigdor Hurowitz, Avi M. Hurvitz, Michael L. Klein, Baruch J. Schwartz, and Nili Shupak, 227–39. Winona Lake, IN: Eisenbrauns, 1996.

———. *A Time to Tear Down and a Time to Build Up: A Rereading of Ecclesiastes*. Grand Rapids: Eerdmans, 1999.

———. "What the Book of Proverbs Is About." In *Congress Volume Cambridge 1995*, edited by J. A. Emerton, 153–67. VTSup 66. Leiden: Brill, 1997.

———. "World Order and Maʿat: A Crooked Parallel." *JNES* 23 (1995): 37–48.

Frei, Hans W. *The Eclipse of Biblical Narrative: A Study in Eighteenth and Nineteenth Century Hermeneutics*. New Haven: Yale University Press, 1974.

Freuling, Georg. *"Wer eine Grube gräbt . . .": Der Tun-Ergehen-Zusammenhang und sein Wandel in der alttestamentlichen Weisheitsliteratur*. Neukirchen-Vluyn: Neukirchener Verlag, 2004.

Frymer-Kensky, Tikva. "The Sage in the Pentateuch: Soundings." In *The Sage in Israel and the Ancient Near East*, edited by John G. Gammie and Leo G. Perdue, 275–88. Winona Lake, IN: Eisenbrauns, 1990.

Fuhs, Hans F. *Das Buch der Sprichwörter: Ein Kommentar*. Forschung zur Bibel 95. Würtzburg: Echter Verlag, 2001.

Gafney, Wilda C. *Womanist Midrash: A Reintroduction to the Women of the Torah and the Throne*. Louisville: Westminster John Knox, 2017.

Garet, Ronald R. "Natural Law and Creation Stories." *Religion, Morality, and the Law* 30 (1988): 218–62.

Gese, Harmut. *Lehre und Wirklichkeit in der alten Weisheit: Studien zu den Sprüchen Salomos und zu dem Buche Hiob*. Tübingen: Mohr Siebeck, 1958.

Goering, Greg Schmidt. "Honey and Wormwood: Taste and the Embodiment of Wisdom in the Book of Proverbs." *Hebrew Bible and Ancient Israel* 5 (2016): 23–41.

Golka, Friedemann W. *The Leopard's Spots: Biblical and African Wisdom in Proverbs*. Edinburgh: T&T Clark, 1993.

Goshen-Gottstein, Moshe. "Scriptural Authority (Judaism)." *ABD* 5:1017.

Gottwald, Norman. "Sociology." *ABD* 6:79–89.

Green, Joel B., Jacqueline E. Lapsley, Rebekah Miles, and Allen Verhey, eds. *Dictionary of Scripture and Ethics*. Grand Rapids: Baker Academic, 2011.

Gressman, Hugo. "Die neugefundene Lehre des Amen-em-ope und die vorexilische Spruchdichtung Israels." *ZAW* 42 (1924): 272–94.

Grier, Nicholas F. *The Virtue of Non-Violence: From Gautama to Gandhi.* Albany: State University of New York Press, 2004.

Gyekye, Kwame. "African Ethics." In *Stanford Encyclopedia of Philosophy.* Stanford University, 1997–. Article published September 9, 2010; last modified September 20, 2011. https://plato.stanford.edu/archives/fall2011/entries/african-ethics.

Halliwell, Stephen. *Aristotle's Poetics.* Chicago: University of Chicago Press, 1998.

Harrison, Peter. *The Bible, Protestantism, and the Rise of Natural Science.* Cambridge: Cambridge University Press, 2001.

Hatton, Peter T. H. *Contradiction in the Book of Proverbs: The Deep Waters of Counsel.* Aldershot, UK: Ashgate, 2008.

Hauerwas, Stanley. "The Self as Story: A Reconsideration of the Relation of Religion and Morality for the Agent's Perspective." In *Vision and Virtue: Essays in Christian Ethical Reflection,* 68–89. Notre Dame: Fides, 1974.

Hausmann, Jutta. "Beobachtungen zu Spr 31, 10–31." In *Alttestamentlicher Glaube und Biblische Theologie: Festschrift für Horst Dietrich Preuss zum 65. Geburtstag,* edited by Jutta Hausmann and Hans-Jürgen Zobel, 261–67. Stuttgart: Kohlhammer, 1992.

Hayes, Christine. *What's Divine about Divine Law? Early Perspectives.* Princeton: Princeton University Press, 2015.

Hayes, John H. *Amos, the Eighth-Century Prophet: His Times and His Preaching.* Nashville: Abingdon, 1988.

Hays, Christopher B. "The Egyptian Goddess Mut in Iron Age Palestine: Further Data from Amulets and Onomastics." *JNES* 71, no. 2 (2012): 299–314.

Heim, Knut Martin. *Like Grapes of Gold Set in Silver: An Interpretation of Proverbial Clusters in Proverbs 10:1–22:16.* BZAW 273. Berlin: de Gruyter, 2001.

———. *Poetic Imagination in Proverbs: Variant Repetitions and the Nature of Poetry.* University Park, PA: Eisenbrauns, 2013.

Hermisson, Hans Jürgen. *Studien zur Israelitischen Spruchweisheit.* Wissenschaftliche Monographien zum Alten und Neuen Testament 28. Neukirchen-Vluyn: Neukirchener Verlag, 1968.

Hill, Thomas E., and Adam Cureton. "Kant on Virtue: Seeking the Ideal in Human Conditions." In *The Oxford Handbook of Virtue,* edited by Nancy Snow, 263–80. New York: Oxford University Press, 2018.

Houston, Walter J. *Contending for Justice: Ideologies and Theologies of Social Justice in the Old Testament.* London: T&T Clark, 2006.

Hrisztova-Gotthardt, Hrisztalina, and Melita Aleksa Varga, eds. *Introduction to Paremiology: A Comprehensive Guide to Proverbs Studies.* Berlin: de Gruyter, 2015.

Hurowitz, Victor A. "Two Terms for Wealth in Proverbs VIII in Light of Akkadian." *VT* 50 (2000): 252–57.

Hursthouse, Rosalind, and Glen Pettigrove. "Virtue Ethics." In *Stanford Encyclopedia of Philosophy*. Stanford University, 1997–. Article published July 18, 2003; last modified October 11, 2022. https://plato.stanford.edu/entries/ethics-virtue.

Jameson, Fredric. *The Political Unconscious: Narrative as Socially Symbolic Act*. Ithaca, NY: Cornell University Press, 1982.

Jamieson-Drake, David W. *Scribes and Schools in Monarchic Judah: A Socio-Archeological Approach*. Social World of Biblical Antiquity Series 9. Sheffield: JSOT Press/Almond, 1991.

Janowski, Bernd. "Die Tat kehrt zum Täter zurück: Offene Fragen im Umkreis des 'Tun-Ergehen-Zusammenhangs.'" *ZTK* 91, no. 3 (1994): 247–91.

Janzen, Waldemar. *Old Testament Ethics: A Paradigmatic Approach*. Louisville: Westminster John Knox, 1994.

Jastrow, Marcus. *A Dictionary of the Targumim, the Talmud Babli and Yerushalmi, and the Midrashic Literature, with an Index of Scriptural Quotations*. New York: Choreb, 1926.

Johnson, Robert, and Adam Cureton. "Kant's Moral Philosophy." In *Stanford Encyclopedia of Philosophy*. Stanford University, 1997–. Article published February 23, 2004; last modified July 14, 2022. https://plato.stanford.edu/entries/kant-moral.

Kamili, Isaac, ed. *Jewish Bible Theology: Perspectives and Case Studies*. Winona Lake, IN: Eisenbrauns, 2012.

Kampen, John. *The Hasideans and the Origin of Pharisaism: A Study in 1 and 2 Maccabees*. Atlanta: Scholars Press, 1988.

Kant, Immanuel. *Critique of Practical Reason*. Translated and edited by Mary J. Gregor. Cambridge: Cambridge University Press, 1997.

———. *Groundwork for the Metaphysics of Morals*. Translated and edited by Allen W. Wood. New Haven: Yale University Press, 2018.

———. *The Metaphysics of Morals*. Edited by Mary J. Gregor. Cambridge: Cambridge University Press, 1996.

Kayatz, Christa. *Studien zu Proverbien 1–9*. Neukirchen-Vluyn: Neukirchener Verlag, 1966.

Keefer, Arthur Jan. *The Book of Proverbs and Virtue Ethics: Integrating the Biblical and Philosophical Traditions*. Cambridge: Cambridge University Press, 2020.

———. *Proverbs 1–9 as an Introduction to the Book of Proverbs*. LHBOTS 701. London: T&T Clark, 2020.

———. "A Shift in Perspective: The Intended Audience and a Coherent Reading of Proverbs 1:1–7." *JBL* 136, no. 1 (2017): 103–16.

Keel, Othmar. *Die Weisheit spielt vor Gott: Ein ikonographischer Beitrag zur Deutung des mesahäqät in Spr. 8,30f*. Freiburg/Göttingen: Universitätsverlag/Vandenhoeck & Ruprecht, 1974.

Keel, Othmar, and Silvia Schroer. *Schöpfung: Biblische Theologien im Kontext altorientalischer Religionen*. Göttingen: Vandenhoeck & Ruprecht, 2002.

Keller, Catherine. *God and Power: Counter-Apocalyptic Journeys*. Minneapolis: Fortress, 2005.

Kelsey, David. "The Doctrine of Creation from Nothing." In *Evolution and Creation*, edited by Ernan McMullin, 176–96. Notre Dame: University of Notre Dame Press, 1985.

Kim, Jimyung. *Reanimating Qohelet's Contradictory Voices: Studies of Open-Ended Discourse on Wisdom in Ecclesiastes*. BIS 166. Leiden: Brill, 2018.

Klawans, Jonathan. *Purity, Sacrifice, and the Temple: Symbolism and Supersessionism in the Study of Ancient Judaism*. Oxford: Oxford University Press, 2005.

Kleingeld, Pauline. "Kant, History, and the Idea of Moral Development." *History of Philosophy Quarterly* 16, no. 1 (1999): 59–80.

Klotz, David. *Adoration of the Ram: Five Hymns to Amun-Re from Hibis Temple*. New Haven: Yale Egyptological Seminar, 2006.

Knight, Kelvin. *Aristotelian Philosophy: Ethics and Politics from Aristotle to MacIntyre*. Cambridge: Polity, 2007.

———. "The Ethical Post-Marxism of Alasdair MacIntyre." In *Marxism, the Millennium and Beyond*, edited by Mark Cowling and Paul Reynolds, 74–96. New York: Palgrave Macmillan, 2000.

Koch, Klaus. "Gibt es ein Vergeltungsdogma im Alten Testament?" *ZTK* 52 (1955): 1–42.

———. "Is There a Doctrine of Retribution in the Old Testament?" In *Theodicy in the Old Testament*, edited by James L. Crenshaw, translated by T. H. Trapp, 57–87. Issues in Religion and Theology 4. Philadelphia: Fortress, 1983.

Kraut, Richard. "Aristotle's Ethics." In *Stanford Encyclopedia of Philosophy*. Stanford University, 1997–. Article published May 1, 2001; last modified July 2, 2022. https://plato.stanford.edu/archives/fall2022/entries/aristotle-ethics.

Kristeva, Julia. "Word, Dialogue, and Novel." In *Desire in Language: A Semiotic Approach to Literature and Art*, edited by Leon S. Roudiez, translated by Thomas Gora, Alice Jardine, and Leon S. Roudiez, 64–91. New York: Columbia University Press, 1980.

Kselman, John S. "Ambiguity and Wordplay in Proverbs XI." *VT* 52 (2002): 545–48.

Kynes, Will. *An Obituary for "Wisdom Literature": The Birth, Death, and Intertextual Reintegration of a Biblical Corpus*. Oxford: Oxford University Press, 2019.

Lambert, W. G. *Babylonian Wisdom Literature*. Oxford: Clarendon, 1960.

Lapsley, Jacqueline E. *Can These Bones Live? The Problem of the Moral Self in the Book of Ezekiel*. BZAW 301. Berlin: de Gruyter, 2000.

Leibnez, Gottfried Wilhelm. *Theodicy: Essays on the Goodness of God, the Freedom of Man, and the Origin of Evil*. New Haven: Yale University Press, 1952. First published 1710.

Lenzi, Alan. "Proverbs 8:22–31: Three Perspectives on its Composition." *JBL* 125, no. 4 (2006): 687–714.

Levenson, Jon D. *Creation and the Persistence of Evil: The Jewish Drama of Divine Omnipotence*. San Francisco: Harper & Row, 1988.

———. *The Hebrew Bible, the Old Testament, and Historical Criticism: Jews and Christians in Biblical Studies*. Louisville: Westminster John Knox, 1993.

Levinson, Bernard M., Eckart Otto, with Walter Dietrich. *Recht und Ethik im Alten Testament, Beiträge des Symposiums "Das Alte Testament und die Kultur der Moderne" anlässlich des 100. Geburtstags Gerhard von Rads (1901–1971) Heidelberg, 18.–21. Oktober 2001*. Altes Testament und Moderne 13. Munster: Lit Verlag, 2004.

Lichtheim, Miriam. *Ancient Egyptian Literature*. 3 vols. Berkeley: University of California Press, 1973–1980.

Linafelt, Tod, and Timothy K. Beal. *Ruth and Esther*. Berit Olam: Studies in Hebrew Narrative and Poetry. Collegeville, MN: Liturgical Press, 1999.

Loader, James Alfred. *Proverbs 1–9*. Historical Commentary on the Old Testament. Leeuwen: Peeters, 2014.

Long, Thomas G. *What Shall We Say? Evil, Suffering, and the Crisis of Faith*. Grand Rapids: Eerdmans, 2011.

Longman, Tremper, III. *Proverbs*. Baker Commentary on the Old Testament: Wisdom and Psalms. Grand Rapids: Baker Academic, 2006.

Lorde, Audre. "Age, Race, Class, and Sex: Women Redefining Difference." In *Sister Outsider: Essays and Speeches*, 114–23. Freedom, CA: Crossing, 1984.

Luther, Martin. *Luther's Works*. Edited by Jaroslav Pelikan and Helmut T. Lehmann. Vol. 13. Saint Louis: Concordia; Philadelphia: Fortress, 1955–86; 2008–.

Lyu, Sun Myung. *Righteousness in the Book of Proverbs*. Forschungen zum Alten Testament 2. Reihe 55. Tübingen: Mohr Siebeck, 2011.

MacDonald, Nathan. *Not Bread Alone: The Uses of Food in the Old Testament*. Oxford: Oxford University Press, 2008.

MacIntyre, Alasdair. *After Virtue: A Study in Moral Theory*. 3rd ed. Notre Dame: Notre Dame University Press, 2007.

———. *Dependent Rational Animals: Why Human Beings Need the Virtues*. Chicago: Open Court, 2001.

———. "How Moral Agents Became Ghosts or Why the History of Ethics Diverged from That of the Philosophy of Mind." *Synthese* 53 (1982): 295–312.

———. "Moral Rationality, Tradition, and Aristotle: A Reply to Onora O'Neill, Raymond Gaita, and Stephen R. L. Clark." *Inquiry* 26, no. 4 (1983): 447–66.

Maier, Christl. *Die fremde Frau in Proverbien 1–9: Eine exegetische und sozialgeschichtliche Studie*. Orbis Biblicus et Orientalis 144. Göttingen: Vandenhoeck & Ruprecht, 1995.

———. "Wisdom and Women—Wisdom of Women." In *Gerhard von Rad and the Study of Wisdom Literature*, edited by Timothy J. Sandoval and Bernd U. Schipper, 211–34. AIL 46. Atlanta: SBL Press, 2022.

Marks, Richard G. "Dangerous Hero: Rabbinic Attitudes toward Legendary Warriors." *Hebrew Union College Annual* 54 (1983): 181–94.

McCann, J. Clinton, Jr. "The Book of Psalms: Introduction, Commentary, and Reflections." In *NIB* 4:639–1280. Nashville: Abingdon, 1996.

McCarter, P. Kyle, Jr. *II Samuel: A New Translation with Introduction, Notes and Commentary*. AB 9. New York: Doubleday, 1984.

McCormack, Bruce L. "The Being of Holy Scripture Is in Becoming: Karl Barth in Conversation with American Evangelical Criticism." In *Evangelicals and Scripture: Tradition, Authority and Hermeneutics*, edited by Vincent Bacote, Laura C. Miguélez, and Dennis L. Ockholm, 55–75. Downers Grove, IL: InterVarsity, 2004.

McCreesh, Thomas P. "Wisdom as Wife: Proverbs 31:10–31." *Revue biblique* 92 (1985): 25–46.

McKane, William. *Proverbs: A New Approach*. Philadelphia: Westminster, 1970.

McKenzie, Steven L., and John Kaltner, eds. *New Meanings for Ancient Texts: Recent Approaches to Biblical Criticisms and Their Applications*. Louisville: Westminster John Knox, 2013.

McLaughlin, John L. "Is Amos (Still) among the Wise?" *JBL* 133, no. 2 (2014): 281–303.

Medvedev, Pavel. *The Formal Method in Literary Scholarship: A Critical Introduction to Sociological Poetics*. Cambridge, MA: Harvard University Press, 1985.

Meilaender, Gilbert. "Dependent Rational Animals: Why Human Beings Need the Virtues and the MacIntyre Reader." *First Things* (October 1999). https://www.firstthings.com/article/1999/10/dependent-rational-animals-why-human-beings-need-the-virtues-and-the-macintyre-reader.

Meinhold, Arndt. *Die Sprüche*. 2 vols. Zurich: Theologischer Verlag, 1991.

Meyers, Carol. *Exodus*. Cambridge Bible Commentary. Cambridge: Cambridge University Press, 2005.

———. "Was Ancient Israel a Patriarchal Society?" *JBL* 133, no. 1 (2014): 8–27.

Mieder, Wolfgang. *Proverbs: A Handbook*. Westport, CT: Greenwood, 2004.

Mill, John Stuart. *Utilitarianism*. Edited by Roger Crisp. Oxford: Oxford University Press, 1998. First published 1861.

Mills, Mary E. *Biblical Morality: Moral Perspectives in Old Testament Narratives*. Aldershot, UK: Ashgate, 2001.

Morson, Gary Saul, and Caryl Emerson. *Mikhail Bakhtin: Creation of a Prosaics*. Stanford: Stanford University Press, 1990.

Murphy, Mark. "The Natural Law Tradition in Ethics." In *Stanford Encyclopedia of Philosophy*. Stanford University, 1997–. Article published September 23, 2002;

last modified May 26, 2019. https://plato.stanford.edu/archives/sum2019/entries/natural-law-ethics.

Murphy, Roland E. *Proverbs*. Word Biblical Commentary 22. Nashville: Nelson, 1998.

———. *The Tree of Life: An Exploration of Biblical Wisdom Literature*. 2nd ed. Grand Rapids: Eerdmans, 1996.

———. "Wisdom—Theses and Hypotheses." In *Israelite Wisdom: Theological and Literary Essays in Honor of Samuel Terrien*, edited by John G. Gammie, 35–42. Missoula, MT: Scholars Press, 1978.

Naré, Laurent. *Proverbes salomoniens et proverbes mossi: Étude comparive à partir d'une nouvelle analyse de Pr 25–29*. Publications Universitaires Europeennnes. Serie 23, Theologie v. 283. Frankfurt am Main: Peter Lang, 1986.

Newsom, Carol A. *The Book of Job: A Contest of Moral Imaginations*. Oxford: Oxford University Press, 2003.

———. "The Book of Job: Introduction, Commentary and Reflections." In *NIB* 4:317–637. Nashville: Abingdon, 1996.

———. "'If I Had Said . . .' (Ps 73:15): Retrospective Introspection in Didactic Psalmody of the Second Temple Period." In *Petitioners, Penitents, and Poets: On Prayer and Praying in Second Temple Judaism*, edited by Timothy J. Sandoval and Ariel Feldman, 69–82. BZAW 524. Berlin: de Gruyter, 2020.

———. "Models of the Moral Self: Hebrew Bible and Second Temple Judaism." *JBL* 131, no. 1 (2012): 5–25.

———. "Woman and the Discourse of Patriarchal Wisdom: A Study of Proverbs 1–9." In *Gender and Difference in Ancient Israel*, edited by Peggy L. Day, 142–60. Minneapolis: Fortress, 1989.

Niebuhr, Reinhold. *Faith and History: A Comparison of Christian and Modern Views of History*. London: Nisbet, 1949.

Nimmo, Paul T. "The Orders of Creation in the Theological Ethics of Karl Barth." *SJT* 60, no. 1 (2007): 24–35.

Nussbaum, Martha C. "Aristotle on Human Nature and the Foundations of Ethics." In *World, Mind, and Ethics: Essays on the Ethical Philosophy of Bernard Williams*, edited by J. E. J. Altham and Ross Harrison, 86–131. Cambridge: Cambridge University Press, 1995.

———. *The Fragility of Goodness: Luck and Ethics in Greek Tragedy and Philosophy*. Rev. ed. Cambridge: Cambridge University Press, 2001.

———. "Non-Relative Virtues: An Aristotelian Approach." In *The Quality of Life*, edited by Martha C. Nussbaum and Amartya Sen, 243–69. Oxford: Clarendon, 1993.

———. *Upheavals of Thought: The Intelligence of Emotions*. Cambridge: Cambridge University Press, 2001.

———. "Women and Cultural Universals." In *Sex and Social Justice*, 29–54. Oxford: Oxford University Press, 1999.

Oden, Robert A., Jr. "Cosmogony, Cosmology." *ABD* 1:1162–71.

Ogletree, Thomas W. *The Use of the Bible in Christian Ethics*. Philadelphia: Fortress, 1983.

Olbricht, T. H. "Toy, Crawford Howell," In *Dictionary of Biblical Interpretation (K–Z)*, edited by John H. Hayes, 583. Nashville: Abingdon, 1999.

Olojede, Funlola O. "Woman Wisdom and the Ethical Vision of the Book of Proverbs: An African Reflection." *HTS Teologiese Studies / Theological Studies* 71, no. 3 (2015), https://doi.org/10.4102/hts.v71i3.2846.

Perdue, Leo G. *Proverbs*. Interpretation: A Bible Commentary for Teaching and Preaching. Louisville: John Knox Press, 2000.

———. *Wisdom and Creation: The Theology of Wisdom Literature*. Nashville: Abingdon, 1994.

Perry, John, ed. *God, the Good, and Utilitarianism: Perspectives on Peter Singer*. Cambridge: Cambridge University Press, 2014.

Pinch, Geraldine. *Egyptian Mythology: A Guide to the Gods, Goddesses, and Traditions of Ancient Egypt*. Oxford: Oxford University Press, 2002.

Pleins, J. David. "Poor, Poverty." *ABD* 5:402–14.

———. "Poverty and the Social World of the Wise." *JSOT* 37 (1987): 61–78.

———. *The Social Visions of the Hebrew Bible: A Theological Introduction*. Louisville: Westminster John Knox, 2001.

———. "Wine, Women, and Song (of Songs): Gender Politics and Identity Construction in Postexilic Israel." In *Character Ethics and the Old Testament: Moral Dimensions of Scripture*, edited by M. Daniel Carroll R. and Jacqueline E. Lapsley, 153–68. Louisville: Westminster John Knox, 2007.

Plöger, Otto. *Sprüche Salomos (Proverbia)*. BKAT 17. Neukirchen-Vluyn: Neukirchener Verlag, 1984.

Portier-Young, Anathea E. *Apocalypse against Empire: Theologies of Resistance in Early Judaism*. Grand Rapids: Eerdmans, 2014.

Preuss, Hans Dietrich. "Erwägungen zum theologischen Ort alttestamentlicher Weisheitsliteratur." *Evangelische Theologie* 30 (1970): 393–417.

Propp, William H. C. *Exodus 19–40: A New Translation with Introduction and Commentary*. AB 2a. New York: Doubleday, 2006.

Quinn, Phillip L. "Theological Ethics." In *Encyclopedia of Ethics*, 2nd ed., edited by Lawrence C. Becker and Charlotte B. Becker, 1702–6. New York: Routledge, 2001.

Reeve, C. D. C. "Aristotle on the Virtues of Thought." In *The Blackwell Guide to Aristotle's "Nicomachean Ethics,"* edited by Richard Kraut, 198–217. Oxford: Blackwell, 2006.

Reventlow, Henning Graf. *The Authority of the Bible and the Rise of the Modern World*. Philadelphia: Fortress, 1985.

Ricoeur, Paul. *Interpretation Theory: Discourse and the Surplus of Meaning.* Fort Worth: Texas Christian University Press, 1976.

Ringgren, Helmer. "חָקַק *ḥāqaq.*" *TDOT* 5:139–48.

Roberts, Adam. *Fredric Jameson.* Routledge Critical Thinkers. London: Routledge, 2000.

Rogers, Cleon L., III. "The Meaning and Significance of the Hebrew Word אָמוֹן in Prov 8,30." *ZAW* 109 (1997): 208–21.

Rogerson, John. *Old Testament Criticism in the Nineteenth Century: England and Germany.* Minneapolis: Fortress, 1985.

———. *Theory and Practice in Old Testament Ethics.* Edited by M. Daniel Carroll R. JSOTSup 405. New York: T&T Clark, 2004.

Römheld, Diethard. *Wege der Weisheit: Die Lehren Amenemopes und Proverbien 22, 17–24, 22.* Berlin: de Gruyter, 1989.

Sandoval, Timothy J. *The Discourse of Wealth and Poverty in the Book of Proverbs.* BIS 77. Leiden: Brill, 2006.

———. "The Morality of Non-Human Animals in Proverbs." In *Exploring Animal Hermeneutics*, edited by Arthur Walker-Jones and Suzanna R. Millar. Semeia Studies. Atlanta: SBL Press, forthcoming.

———. "The Orality of Wisdom Literature." In *The Wiley Blackwell Companion to Wisdom Literature*, edited by Samuel L. Adams and Matthew J. Goff, 267–86. Hoboken, NJ: Wiley & Sons, 2020.

———. "Prophetic and Proverbial Justice: Amos, Proverbs, and Intertextuality." In *Second Wave Intertextuality and the Hebrew Bible*, edited by Marianne Grohman and Hyun Chul Paul Kim, 131–51. RBS 93. Atlanta: SBL Press, 2019.

———. "Reconfiguring Solomon in the Royal Fiction of Ecclesiastes." In *On Prophets, Warriors, and Kings: Former and Latter Prophets through the Eyes of Their Interpreters*, edited by Ariel Feldman and George Brook, 13–39. Berlin: de Gruyter, 2016.

———. "Revisiting the Prologue of Proverbs." *JBL* 126, no. 3 (2007): 455–73.

———. "Texts and Intertexts: A Proposal for Understanding Proverbs 30:1b." *JSOT* 45, no. 2 (2020): 158–77.

———. "Training Desire in Proverbs: A Response to 'Capitalism, the Crash, and Christianity' by Mark Douglas," @ *This Point: An Online Journal of Columbia Theological Seminary* 4, no. 1 (Spring 2009). https://web.archive.org/web/20200712105535/http://www.atthispoint.net/editor-notes/training-desire-in-proverbs/196.

Sandoval, Timothy J., and Bernd U. Schipper, eds. *Gerhard von Rad and the Study of Wisdom Literature.* AIL 46. Atlanta: SBL Press, 2022.

Sauneron, S., and J. Yoyette. "La naissance du monde selon l'Egypte ancienne." In *La naissance du monde*, 17–91. Sources Orientales 1. Paris: Seuil, 1959.

Schipper, Bernd U. "Egypt and Israel: The Ways of Cultural Contacts in the Late Bronze Age and Iron Age (20th–26th Dynasty)." *Journal of Ancient Egyptian Interconnections* 4, no. 3 (2012): 30–47.

———. *The Hermeneutics of Torah: Proverbs 2, Deuteronomy, and the Composition of Proverbs 1–9*. AIL 43. Atlanta: SBL Press, 2021.

———. *Proverbs 1–15*. Translated by Stephen Germany. Hermeneia. Minneapolis: Fortress, 2019.

———. *Sprüche (Proverbia) 1–15*. BKAT 17. Göttingen: Vandenhoeck & Ruprecht, 2017.

———. "'Teach Them Diligently to Your Son!' The Book of Proverbs and Deuteronomy." In *Reading Proverbs Intertextually*, edited by Katharine Dell and Will Kynes, 21–34. New York: T&T Clark, 2019.

Schipper, Bernd U., and D. Andrew Teeter, eds. *Wisdom and Torah: The Reception of "Torah" in the Wisdom Literature of the Second Temple Period*. Leiden: Brill, 2013.

Schroeder, Frederic M. "Friendship in Aristotle and Some Peripatetic Philosophers." In *Greco-Roman Perspectives on Friendship*, edited by John T. Fitzgerald, 35–57. Atlanta: Scholars Press, 1997.

Schwáb, Zoltán S. *Toward an Interpretation of the Book of Proverbs: Selfishness and Secularity Reconsidered*. Journal of Theological Interpretation Supplement 7. Winona Lake, IN: Eisenbrauns, 2013.

Seow, C. L. "Hosea 14:10 and the Foolish People Motif." *Catholic Biblical Quarterly* 44, no. 2 (1982): 212–24.

Sheppard, Gerald T. "'Enemies' and the Politics of Prayer in the Psalms." In *The Bible and the Politics of Exegesis: Essays in Honor of Norman K. Gottwald on His Sixty-Fifth Birthday*, edited by David Jobling, Peggy L. Day, and Gerald T. Sheppard, 61–82. Cleveland: Pilgrim, 1991.

———. *Wisdom as a Hermeneutical Construct: A Study in the Sapientializing of the Old Testament*. BZAW 151. Berlin: de Gruyter, 1980.

Sherwood, Yvonne. *Biblical Blaspheming: Trials of the Sacred for a Secular Age*. Cambridge: Cambridge University Press, 2012.

Sinnott-Armstrong, Walter. "Consequentialism." In *Stanford Encyclopedia of Philosophy*. Stanford University, 1997–. Article published May 20, 2003; last modified October 5, 2022. https://plato.stanford.edu/archives/win2022/entries/consequentialism.

Smith, Mark S. *The Early History of God: Yahweh and the Other Deities in Ancient Israel*. 2nd ed. Grand Rapids: Eerdmans, 2002.

———. *Poetic Heroes: Literary Commemorations of Warriors and Warrior Culture in the Early Biblical World*. Grand Rapids: Eerdmans, 2014.

Smith-Christopher, Daniel L. "The Quiet Words of the Wise: Biblical Developments toward Nonviolence as a Diaspora Ethic." In *Character Ethics and the Old Testament: Moral Dimensions of Scripture*, edited by M. Daniel Carroll R. and Jacqueline E. Lapsley, 129–52. Louisville: Westminster John Knox, 2007.

Sneed, Mark R., ed. *Was There a Wisdom Tradition? New Prospects in Israelite Wisdom Studies*. AIL 23. Atlanta: SBL Press, 2015.

Snell, Daniel C. *Twice-Told Proverbs and the Composition of the Book of Proverbs*. University Park, PA: Eisenbrauns, 1993.

Soggin, J. A. "Amos and Wisdom." In *Wisdom in Ancient Israel: Essays in Honour of J. A. Emerton*, edited by John Day, Robert P. Gordon, and H. G. M. Williamson, 119–23. Cambridge: Cambridge University Press, 1995.

Sommer, Benjamin D. "Conflicting Constructions of Divine Presence in the Priestly Tabernacle." *Biblical Illustrator* 9, no. 1 (2001): 41–63.

———. "Exegesis, Allusion and Intertextuality in the Hebrew Bible: A Response to Lyle Eslinger." *VT* 46 (1996): 479–89.

Song, Robert. *Christianity and Liberal Society*. Oxford: Oxford University Press, 1997.

Spohn, William C. *What Are They Saying about Scripture and Ethics?* Rev ed. New York: Paulist, 1995.

Steiert, Franz-Josef. *Die Weisheit Israels—Ein fremdkörper im Alten Testament? Eine Untersuchung zum Buch der Sprüche auf dem Hintergrund der ägyptischen Weisheitslehren*. Freiburg: Herder, 1990.

Steiner, Richard C. *Stockmen from Tekoa, Sycamores from Sheba: A Study of Amos' Occupations*. CBQMS 36. Washington, DC: Catholic Biblical Association of America, 2003.

Stewart, Anne Whitaker. *Poetic Ethics in Proverbs: Wisdom Literature and the Shaping of the Moral Self*. Cambridge: Cambridge University Press, 2016.

———. "Wisdom's Imagination: Moral Reasoning and the Book of Proverbs." *JSOT* 40, no. 3 (2016): 351–72.

Strawn, Brent, ed. *The Bible and the Pursuit of Happiness: What the Old and New Testaments Teach Us about the Good Life*. Oxford: Oxford University Press, 2012.

Strawson, Galen. "Against Narrativity." *Ratio* 17 (2004): 428–52.

Striker, Gisela. *Essays on Hellenistic Epistemology and Ethics*. Cambridge: Cambridge University Press, 1996.

Tafilowski, Ryan. "A Reappraisal of the Orders of Creation." *LQ* 31, no. 3 (2017): 288–309.

Taylor, Charles. *A Secular Age*. Cambridge, MA: Harvard University Press, 2007.

Terrien, Samuel. "Amos and Wisdom." In *Israel's Prophetic Heritage: Essays in Honor of James Muilenburg*, edited by Bernhard W. Anderson and Walter J. Harrelson, 108–15. New York: Harper & Brothers, 1962.

Tirosh-Samuelson, Hava. *Happiness in Premodern Judaism: Virtue, Knowledge, and Well-Being*. Monographs of the Hebrew Union College. Cincinnati: Hebrew Union College Press, 2003.

———. "Virtue and Happiness." In *The Cambridge History of Jewish Philosophy: From Antiquity through the Seventeenth Century*, edited by Steven Nadler and T. M. Rudavsky, 705–67. Cambridge: Cambridge University Press, 2008.

Toy, C. H. *Proverbs: A Critical and Exegetical Commentary on the Book of Proverbs*. International Critical Commentary. Edinburgh: T&T Clark, 1988. First published 1899.

VanDrunen, David. "Wisdom and the Natural Moral Order: The Contribution of Proverbs to a Christian Theology of Natural Law." *Journal of the Society of Christian Ethics* 33, no. 1 (2013): 153–68.

Van Leeuwen, Raymond C. "The Book of Proverbs: Introduction, Commentary, and Reflections." In *NIB* 5:17–264. Nashville: Abingdon, 1997.

———. *Context and Meaning in Proverbs 25–27*. Society of Biblical Literature Dissertation Series 96. Atlanta: Scholars Press, 1988.

———. "Proverbs XXV 27 Once Again." *VT* 36 (1986): 105–14.

———. "Wealth and Poverty: System and Contradiction in Proverbs." *HS* 33 (1992): 25–36.

———. "*Weisheit* in the Intellectual Context of Its Day." In *Gerhard von Rad and the Study of Wisdom Literature*, edited by Timothy J. Sandoval and Bernd U. Schipper, 9–45. AIL 46. Atlanta: SBL Press, 2022.

Vayntrub, Jacqueline. "Beauty, Wisdom, and Handiwork in Proverbs 31:10–31." *HS* 113, no. 1 (2020): 45–62.

———. "The Book of Proverbs and the Idea of Ancient Israelite Education." *ZAW* 128, no. 1 (2016): 96–114.

Vesely, Patricia. *Friendship and Virtue Ethics in the Book of Job*. Cambridge: Cambridge University Press, 2019.

von Rad, Gerhard. *Old Testament Theology*. Vol. 1. Translated by D. M. G. Stalker. New York: Harper & Row, 1962.

———. *Weisheit in Israel*. Neukirchen-Vluyn: Neukirchener Verlag, 1970.

———. *Wisdom in Israel*. Translated by James D. Martin. London: SCM, 1972.

Waltke, Bruce K. *The Book of Proverbs: Chapters 1–15*. New International Commentary on the Old Testament. Grand Rapids: Eerdmans, 2004.

Washington, Harold C. "The Strange Woman of Proverbs 1–9 and Post-Exilic Judean Society." In *Second Temple Studies*, vol. 2, *Temple and Community in the Persian Period*, edited by Tamara C. Eskenazi and Kent Harold Richards, 217–42. Sheffield: JSOT Press, 1994.

———. *Wealth and Poverty in the Instruction of Amenemope and the Hebrew Proverbs*. Atlanta: Scholars Press, 1994.

Weems, Renita J. *Battered Love: Marriage, Sex, and Violence in the Hebrew Prophets*. Minneapolis: Fortress, 1995.

Weinfeld, Moshe. *Deuteronomy and the Deuteronomic School*. Oxford: Oxford University Press, 1972.

Weiss, Penny. "Feminism and Communitarianism: Comparing Critiques of Liberalism." In *Feminism and Community*, edited by Penny Weiss and Marilyn Friedman, 161–86. Philadelphia: Temple University Press, 1995.

Westermann, Claus. *Roots of Wisdom: The Oldest Proverbs of Israel and Other Peoples*. Louisville: Westminster John Knox, 1995.

———. "Weisheit im Sprichwort." In *Schalom: Studien zu Glaube und Geschichte Israels. Alfred Jepsen zum 70. Geburtstag, dargebracht von Freunden, Schülern und Kollegen*, edited by Karl-Heinz Bernhardt, 73–85. Stuttgart: Calver, 1971.

———. *Wurzeln der Weisheit: Die ältesten Sprüche Israels und anderen Völker*. Göttingen: Vandenhoeck & Ruprecht, 1990.

Whiting, Jennifer. "The Nicomachean Account of Philia." In *The Blackwell Companion to Aristotle's "Nicomachean Ethics,"* edited by Richard Kraut, 276–304. Oxford: Blackwell, 2006.

Whybray, Roger Norman. *The Good Life in the Old Testament*. New York: T&T Clark, 2002.

———. *Proverbs*. New Century Bible Commentary. Grand Rapids: Eerdmans, 1994.

———. *Wealth and Poverty in the Book of Proverbs*. JSOTSup 99. Sheffield: JSOT Press, 1990.

———. *Wisdom in Proverbs*. Studies in Biblical Theology 41. London: SCM, 1965.

Wolff, Hans Walter. *Amos' geistige Heimat*. Wissenschaftliche Monographien zum Alten und Neuen Testament 18. Neukirchen-Vluyn: Neukirchener Verlag, 1964.

———. *Amos the Prophet: The Man and His Background*. Edited by John Reumann. Translated by Foster R. McCurley. Philadelphia: Fortress, 1977.

———. *Joel and Amos: A Commentary on the Books of the Prophets Joel and Amos*. Translated by Waldemar Janzen, S. Dean McBride Jr., and Charles A. Muenchow. Hermeneia. Philadelphia: Fortress, 1977.

Wolters, Al. "Proverbs XXXI 10–31 as Heroic Hymn: A Form-Critical Analysis." *VT* 38 (1988): 446–57.

Woodbridge, Frederick J. E. *An Essay on Nature*. New York: Columbia University Press, 1940.

Yee, Gale A. "'I Have Perfumed My Bed with Myrrh': The Foreign Woman (*'iššâ zārâ*) in Proverbs 1–9." *JSOT* 43 (1989): 53–68.

———. *Poor Banished Children of Eve: Woman as Evil in the Hebrew Bible*. Minneapolis: Fortress, 2003.

Yoder, Christine Roy. "Forming 'Fearers of Yahweh': Repetition and Contradiction as Pedagogy in Proverbs." In *Seeking Out the Wisdom of the Ancients: Essays Offered to Honor Michael V. Fox on the Occasion of His Sixty-Fifth Birthday*, edited by Ronald L. Troxel, Kelvin G. Friebel, and Dennis R. Magary, 167–83. Winona Lake, IN: Eisenbrauns, 2005.

———. "The Objects of Our Affections: Emotions and the Moral Life in Proverbs 1–9." In *Shaking Heaven and Earth: Essays in Honor of Walter Brueggemann and Charles Cousar*, edited by Christine Roy Yoder, Kathleen M. O'Connor, E. Elizabeth Johnson, and Stanley P. Saunders, 73–88. Louisville: Westminster John Knox, 2005.

———. "Path and Possession in Proverbs 1–9: A Feminist Biblical Theology of Flourishing." In *After Exegesis: Feminist Biblical Theology; Essays in Honor of Carol A. Newsom*, edited by Patricia K. Tull and Jacqueline E. Lapsley, 217–28. Waco: Baylor University Press, 2015.

———. *Proverbs*. Abingdon Old Testament Commentaries. Nashville: Abingdon, 2009.

———. *Wisdom as a Woman of Substance: A Socio-Economic Reading of Proverbs 1–9 and 31:10–31*. BZAW 104. Berlin: de Gruyter, 2001.

Yoder, Nathan Howard. *"Ordnung in Gemeinschaft": A Critical Appraisal of the Erlangen Contribution to the Orders of Creation*. New York: Peter Lang, 2016.

Zahavi, Dan. "Self and Other: The Limits of Narrative Understanding." In *Narrative and Understanding Persons*, edited by Daniel D. Hutto, 179–201. Royal Institute of Philosophy Supplement 60. Cambridge: Cambridge University Press, 2007.

Zimmerli, Walther. "Ort und Grenze der Weisheit im Rahmen der alttestamentlichen Theologie." In *Sagesses du Proce-oriente ancient*, 121–38. Paris: Presses Universitaires, 1963.

———. "The Place and Limit of the Wisdom in the Framework of the Old Testament Theology." *SJT* 17 (1964): 146–58.

Author Index

Adams, Samuel L., 27n18
Akoto-Abutiate, Dorothy B. E. A., 184nn26–27
Albrecht, Gloria, 352n10
Allen, James P., 288nn38–40
Anderson, Cheryl B., 349n1
Annas, Julia, 35nn41–42, 36n44, 37nn47–49, 41n58, 42n60, 57nn8–10, 68n1, 73n12, 75n16, 76nn18–19, 77n23, 148n6, 149n7, 161nn5–6, 176n5, 179n17, 210n9, 213n16, 214n17, 345n17, 346nn18–19, 354n12, 378n74
Ansberry, Christopher B., 4n17, 148n3
Aristotle, 49n86
Assmann, Jan, 253n28
Avalos, Hector, 349n1
Ayad, Mariam F., 303nn81–82

Bakhtin, M., 23, 90n10, 227n21, 227n23, 228n25
Banks, Mark, 322nn17–18, 323n20, 324n21, 326n23, 327n24
Barr, James, 24n4
Barth, Karl, 257n43
Barthes, Roland, 224n11
Barton, John, 1n1, 8nn31–33, 10nn41–43, 10nn45, 219n1
Bauks, Michaela, and Gerlinde Bauman, 284n27, 294n59
Bayer, Oswald, 256n36
Beal, Timothy K., 125n44
Beentjes, Pancratius C.
Bellis, Alice Ogden, 69n3, 350nn3–4, 358n13
Bentham, Jeremy, 33n36
Bergant, Dianne, 28n21, 44n72, 169n24
Birch, Bruce C., 1n1, 3n11

Boer, Roland, 186n34
Bonnard, P., 302n79
Braaten, Carl E., 256n37, 257n43
Brettler, Marc Zvi, 379n77
Brown, William P., 1n1, 2nn6–7, 3nn8–13, 4n15, 9n36, 53n1, 55n5, 99n22, 161n7, 163nn9–10, 183n23, 184n24, 212n11, 213nn14–15, 246nn1–2, 248nn7–9, 249n17, 250n19, 259n49, 262n54, 263nn60–61, 267n63, 349n2, 380n78
Brueggemann, Walter, 2n4
Bryce, Glendon E., 26n13, 133n55
Budge, E., 26n13, 133n55

Camp, Claudia V., 1n1, 6n29, 52n92, 93n14, 341n12, 358n16
Carr, David M., 29n24, 100n23, 101n24, 240nn53–57, 241n58, 242n62, 243n65, 275n13, 287n37, 317n7
Carroll R., 2n2
Casey, John, 177n12
Charry, Ellen T.
Cheung, Simon Chi-Chung, 318n13
Cho, Yong Hyun, 80n33, 171n29, 171n32
Claassens, L., 5n24, 71n6, 359nn18–20, 361n23, 362nn24–27, 363nn29–30, 364nn31–33
Clayton, Jay, 46n78, 223nn8–9, 225n14, 226nn16–17
Clayton, Ted
Clifford, Richard J., 123n38, 134n60, 286nn32–33, 287n34
Clifton, Shane
Collins, John J., 247n3, 271n3

Author Index

Crenshaw, James L., 41nn56–57, 42n60, 59, 220n3, 222n7, 248nn10–12, 310n1
Cross, Frank Moore, 305n90
Cuéllar, Gregory L., 51n89
Culler, Jonathan, 226n16
Curran, Charles E., 1n1

Davies, G., 240n53, 243n63
Davis, Ellen F., 5n19, 249n15
Delkurt, Holger, 1n1, 45nn74–75
Dell, Katharine J., 3n9, 312n2, 334n5
Dentith, Simon, 225nn12–13, 226nn17–19, 227n20, 227n22, 228n24, 231n34
Derrida, Jacques, 224n11
Dietrich, Walter, 1n1
Driver, Julia, 33n35

Eising, H., 367nn38–39
Emerson, Caryl, 15nn59–61
Emerton, John A., 297n65, 298n70
Erlandsson, Seth, 132n53
Erman, Adolf, 26n13, 133n55

Falcon, Andrea, 49n86
Fichtner, J., 220n3
Fogarty, Gerald, 353n11
Foley, Barbara, 373n65, 374n67
Fontaine, Carole R., 185n29
Fox, Michael V., 4n16, 9n35, 13n55, 26n13, 26n16, 29n25, 39, 49, 55n6, 58n12, 63, 72n7, 78n25, 86–87, 86n2, 94n16, 96n19, 98n21, 100n24, 104n32, 105n34, 105n35, 107n42, 112n8, 116nn17–18, 117n19, 118n21, 119n27, 120n28, 121nn29–30, 123nn36, 126n45, 129n46, 130n47, 131n51, 133n56, 134nn58–59, 139n65, 141n66, 142n68, 147n2, 150n8, 152n11, 153nn13–14, 154n15, 156n18, 157n19, 158nn20–21, 164nn12–14, 166n16, 168n20, 170nn25–26, 171n32, 178nn13–14, 180n18, 182n20, 184n26, 185n32, 187n36, 188n41, 188nn37–39, 192n45, 195nn47–48, 196n49, 197n51, 199n54, 200n56, 201n57, 204n2, 205n3, 206nn4–5, 208n8, 222n6, 233n40, 236n45, 240nn53–55, 252n26, 253n28, 262nn55–56, 263nn57–59, 270n1, 275nn12–13, 277nn15–16, 280n20, 282n23, 293n58, 296n61, 297n65, 299nn72–73, 300nn74–75, 301n75, 302n79, 304nn84, 306n92, 315n4, 358n13, 364n31–33, 366n35, 368n42, 371n56
Frei, Hans W., 50n88
Freuling, Georg, 27n18

Frymer-Kensky, Tikva, 358n17
Fuhs, Hans F., 53n2

Gafney, Wilda C., 331n3
Garet, Ronald R., 251n21
Gese, Harmut, 27n18
Goering, Greg Schmidt, 52n92
Golka, Friedemann W., 184n26
Goshen-Gottstein, Moshe, 379n76
Gottwald, Norman, 186n33
Green, Joel B., 1n1
Gressman, Hugo, 26n13, 133n55
Grier, Nicholas F., 177n11
Gyekye, Kwame, 12nn49–52

Halliwell, Stephen, 177n8
Harrison, Peter, 48n84
Hatton, Peter T., 24n3
Hauerwas, Stanley, 5, 6, 212, 213
Hausmann, Jutta, 358n15
Hayes, Christine, 242n60, 254nn30–33, 255n34
Hayes, John H., 239nn48–49
Hays, Christopher B., 287n36, 301n76
Heim, Knut Martin, 147n1, 169nn22–23
Hermisson, Hans Jürgen, 184n26
Hill, Thomas E., 35n43
Hill and Cureton, 35n43
Houston, Walter J., 171n30
Hrisztova-Gotthardt, Hrisztalina, 184n25
Hurowitz, Victor A., 116n18, 119n26
Hursthouse, Rosalind, and Glen Pettigrove, 250n20

Jameson, Fredric, 68, 370n53, 373n64, 374nn66, 376nn71–73, 377n73
Jamieson-Drake, David W., 243n63
Janowski, Bernd., 27n18
Janzen, Waldemar, 1n1
Jastrow, Marcus., 78n27
Johnson, Robert, and Adam Cureton, 249n16, 269n64
Johnson, Robert, and Adam Cureton., 34n39

Kaltner, John, 51n90
Kamili, Isaac, ed., 25n5
Kampen, John, 371n58, 372nn60–61, 373nn62–63
Kant, Immanuel, 249n17
Kant, Immanuel., 34n40
Kayatz, Christa, 282n23, 302n79
Keefer, Arthur Jan., 6n27, 16n62, 89n7, 147n1, 148n3

Keel, Othmar, 260n52, 278n17
Keller, Catherine, 285n28, 285n31
Kelsey, David, 247n6
Kim, Jimyung, 90n10
Klawans, Jonathan., 229n30
Kleingeld, Pauline., 42n61
Klotz, David, 288nn41–44, 289nn45–48, 290nn50–52, 303n80, 306n91
Knight, Kelvin, 61n18, 352n8
Koch, Klaus, 27n18, 51n91, 60n14, 259n50
Kraut, Richard., 148n5
Kristeva, Julia, 224n11
Kselman, John S., 188n41
Kynes, Will, 2n5, 32n33, 220n4, 318nn13–14

Lambert, W., 26n14
Lapsley, Jacqueline E., 2n2, 101n25
Leibnez, Gottfried Wilhelm., 82n37
Lenzi, Alan, 276n13
Levenson, Jon D., 82n39, 284n25, 285nn29–30, 290n55, 296n64
Levinson, Bernard M., 1n1
Lichtheim, Miriam, 26n14
Linafelt, Tod, 125n44
Loader, James Alfred, 67, 252n26, 253n27, 270n1, 275n12, 277n16, 280n20, 296n64, 297nn65, 300n74, 302n79
Long, Thomas G., 82n37
Longman, Tremper, III, 44n71, 74, 133n56, 144nn72, 198n53, 208n8
Lorde, Audre, 349n1
Luther, Martin, 256n36
Lyu, Sun Myung, 6n28, 147n1

MacDonald, Nathan, 134n61, 372n59
MacIntyre, Alasdair, 17n64, 19, 19n65, 46nn76–77, 60nn15–16, 61nn17, 62n20, 68n2, 69n4, 73n10, 76n20, 109n1, 143n70, 148n4, 160n1, 175nn1–2, 177n10, 179n15, 189n43, 319n15, 320n16, 324n22, 327n25, 344n16, 351n6, 352n7
Maier, Christl, 52n92, 93n14
Marks, Richard G., 370n52
McCann, J., 82n40
McCarter, P., 313n3, 335n6, 336n7, 338nn8–9
McCormack, Bruce L., 380n78
McCormick, Richard A., 1n1
McCreesh, Thomas P., 358n14
McKane, William, 26n11, 134n60
McKenzie, Steven L., 51n90
McLaughlin, John L., 220n2, 230n33
Medvedev, Pavel, 15n59

Meilaender, Gilbert, 73n11
Meinhold, Arndt, 105n34, 248n13
Melcher, Sarah J., 349n1
Meyers, Carol, 329n1, 330n2, 359n19
Mieder, Wolfgang, 184n25
Mill, John Stuart, 33n37
Mills, Mary E., 1n1
Morson, Gary Saul, 15nn59–61
Murphy, Mark, 251n22, 252nn23–24
Murphy, Roland E., 27n19, 42nn62–63, 43nn64–67, 53n2, 78n28, 144n75, 171n28, 248n15, 252n26, 253n27, 280n21, 358n15, 375n70

Naré, Laurent, 184n26
Newsom, Carol A., 1n1, 6n29, 9n37, 31n31, 52n92, 58n13, 77n24, 81n35, 82nn38–39, 95n18, 100n23, 101n27, 114n10, 147n2
Niebuhr, Reinhold, 257n42
Nimmo, Paul T., 257nn43–44, 258n45
Nussbaum, Martha C., 36nn45–46, 71n6, 72n8, 75n16, 76n17, 77n21, 81n36, 91n11, 160n3, 161n4, 163n10, 175n3, 176n4, 182nn21–22, 346n19, 351n5, 361n22, 362nn24–27, 378n75

Oden, Robert A., 284n24
Ogletree, Thomas W., 1n1
Olbricht, T., 39n52
Olojede, Funlola O., 11n47, 12n53
Otto, Eckart, 1n1

Perdue, Leo G., 45n73
Perry, John, 33n38
Pinch, Geraldine, 53–54, 290nn51
Pleins, J., 28n22, 169n24
Plöger, Otto, 25n6, 29n27, 47n80
Portier-Young, Anathea E., 342n13
Preuss, Hans Dietrich, 26n12
Propp, William H., 330n2

Quinn, Phillip L., 7n30

Rasmussen, Larry L., 1n1, 3n11
Reeve, C., 10, 177nn7
Reventlow, Henning Graf, 50n87
Ricoeur, Paul, 31n32, 91n12, 114n12, 121n34
Ringgren, Helmer, 248n15, 253n29
Roberts, Adam, 374n66
Rogers, Cleon L., 302n78
Rogerson, John, 1n1, 39, 50n87, 256nn35
Römheld, Diethard, 133n55
Rothstein, Eric, 223nn8–9, 225n14, 226nn16–17

Author Index

Sandoval, Timothy J., 7, 25n8, 30n29, 31n30, 40, 52n92, 53n3, 54n4, 55n6, 58n11, 62n21, 71n6, 87n4, 101n26, 101n27, 110nn3, 114n11, 115n16, 118n24, 120n28, 144n73, 145n76, 161n8, 165n15, 167n19, 184n27, 185n28, 233nn39, 235n43, 266n62, 289n49, 312n2, 314n4, 340n11, 341n12, 342n14, 363n28
Sauneron, S., 286n33
Schipper, Bernd U., 12–13, 25n8, 26n14, 27, 29n24, 78nn25, 79, 85n1, 90n8, 100n23, 100n24, 101n27, 104n32, 105nn33–34, 121nn30–32, 123n40, 130n48, 139n65, 156n18, 164n12, 185n30, 188nn37–38, 189nn40–41, 199n54, 208n8, 239n51, 241n58, 243n64, 248n15, 249n18, 253nn28–29, 258n47, 260n52, 270n1, 274n9, 275nn10, 276n13, 283n23, 287n35, 296n62, 300n74, 301n75, 302nn77, 304n85, 310n1
Schipper, Jeremy, 349n1
Schroeder, Frederic M., 172nn34–35
Schroer, Silvia, 260n52
Schwáb, Zoltán S., 5n20, 38n50
Seow, C., 317n11
Sheppard, Gerald T., 171n32
Sherwood, Yvonne, 29n26
Singer, Peter, 33n38
Sinnott-Armstrong, Walter, 33n34
Smith, Mark S., 204n1, 305n90, 367n36, 371n57, 376n71
Smith-Christopher, Daniel L., 4n15
Sneed, Mark R., 220n4
Snell, Daniel C., 169n23
Soggin, J., 224n10
Sommer, Benjamin D., 226n15, 329n1
Song, Robert, 352n8
Spohn, William C.
Steiert, Franz-Josef
Steiner, Richard C., 242n61
Stewart, Anne Whitaker, 1n1, 4–6, 6n25, 8n33, 9n40, 27n17, 51n90, 110nn2, 213nn12–14, 235n43
Strawn, Brent, ed., 2n2
Strawson, Galen, 6n26
Striker, Gisela, 81n34

Tafilowski, Ryan, 43, 256nn37–38, 257nn41
Taylor, Charles, 49n85, 247n5
Teeter, D. Andrew, 29n24, 100n23, 241n58, 317n9
Terrien, Samuel, 220n3, 222n5
Tirosh-Samuelson, Hava, 2n3, 5n18, 11n46, 16n63, 219n1
Toy, C., 10nn44, 39n51

VanDrunen, David, 247n4, 259n51, 261n53
Van Leeuwen, Raymond C., 27n19, 47n81, 78n26, 79n31, 112n8, 144n71, 169n22, 206nn5–6, 248n14, 258n46
Varga, Melita Aleksa, 184n25
Vayntrub, Jacqueline, 369n49, 371n54, 376n71
Vesely, Patricia, 172n35
von Rad, Gerhard, 25n7, 30n28, 39n53, 40n54, 47n79, 48nn82–83, 259n48, 279n19

Waltke, Bruce K., 41n55, 90n8, 193n46, 208n8, 358n14, 375n69
Washington, Harold C., 27n19, 93n15, 133n55, 186n35
Weems, Renita J., 317n12
Weinfeld, Moshe, 316n6
Weiss, Penny, 352n9
Westermann, Claus, 184n26, 252n26
Whiting, Jennifer, 172n35
Whybray, Roger Norman, 26n15, 43n68, 44n69, 79n30, 122n35, 131n52, 206nn4–5, 236n44, 272n5, 276n13, 297n66
Wolff, Hans Walter, 220n3, 222n5, 228n26, 229nn27–30, 230nn31–32, 231n35, 232n36, 234n41, 235n42, 237n46, 239n50
Wolters, Al, 40–41, 46, 367nn37, 368nn42–44, 369nn47–49, 370nn50–52
Woodbridge, Frederick J., 75nn14–15, 308n94

Yee, Gale A., 52n92, 186n34
Yoder, Christine Roy, 5nn21–23, 9n39, 58n12, 71n5, 72n9, 123n37, 125n42, 148n3, 237n47, 358n13, 360n21, 371n55
Yoder, Nathan Howard, 256n39, 257n40
Yoyette, J., 286n33

Zahavi, Dan, 6n26
Zimmerli, Walther, 25n6

Scripture and Ancient Sources Index

Old Testament

Genesis
1–3 29
1:2 285, 295n60, 296, 297n68
1:9 82, 285
1:11 285
1:20 285
1:20–21 285
1:24 285
1:24–25 285
7:11 297
8:2 297
8:13 285
12:13 125
20:12 125
25:14 26n16
26:7 125
35:14 278
39:21 130
41:15 315
41:16 316
41:39 315
42:23 57

Exodus
1:10 333
2:10 312
3:21 130
5:13 138n64
11:3 130
12:36 130
14:4 366
14:9 366
14:17 366
14:28 366
15:5 297n68, 298
15:8 297n68, 298
15:9 367
25:9 329
25:29 278
31 329
31–36 311
31:1–7 311
31:1–7 311
31:3 329
31:4 329
31:5 329
31:6 332
35 329
35:25 331, 332
35:25–26 311, 331
35:26 332
35:31 330
35:32 329
35:32–35 331
35:34 330
35:35 330
38:23 330
40:5 329
40:28–29 329

Numbers
25 94
28:7 278

Deuteronomy
4:6 101, 316
6:6–9 100
8:7 297, 297n68, 298
11:18–20 100
19:14 241n58
32:18 280

Joshua
6:2 367
8:3 367
10:7 367
15:9 297
22:8 367

Judges
3:16 368
3:29 367
5 371
5:26 368
5:30 367
6:12 367
8:2 185n29
8:21 185, 185n30
11:1 367
14:12–19 57
18:11 368
18:16 368
20:44 367
21:10 367
21:21 282
21:23 281

Ruth
2 372
2:1 371
3:6–13 125
3:11 125, 371
4 372
4:5 125

1 Samuel
9:1 371, 372
10:12 185n29
14:52 367
16:7 185n29
16:12 376n71

Scripture and Ancient Sources Index

16:18 367
17:39 368
19:24 185n29
24:13 185n31
24:14 185n29
31:12 367

2 Samuel

3:29 282
6:5 283
6:12 283
6:14 283
6:21 283
11:16 367
12:1–13 313
14 313, 335
14:2 335
14:6 313
14:9 336
14:12 336
14:14 335
14:15 336
14:17 336
14:19 335, 336
14:20 335
14:21 335
14:22 336
20 313, 335
20:16–22 337
20:19–20 338, 338n8
20:21 337, 338
20:22 337
23:16 278
23:20 367
24:9 367

1 Kings

1:29–30 334
1:40 281
2 333
2:5–9 312
2:6 312
2:9 312
3 334, 340
4–5 313
5 339, 340
5:1 340, 341
5:9–14 314, 338, 340
5:14 340, 341
9 340

9–10 313
10 341n12
11 340
11:28 371, 372
12:25 243
15:33 243
20:11 185n29

2 Kings

3:4 241
15:20 371, 372
24:16 367

1 Chronicles

1:7 373
1:30 26n16
12:1 372
12:24 372
13:8 283
15:29 283
22:10 334
26:6 373

2 Chronicles

32:4 297
32:31 57

Ezra

9–10 93

Nehemiah

13 93

Job

1:1 58, 208n8
6:30 189
11–6 310
15:7 280, 294
15:29 117
16:20 57
28:28 58
33:23 57
38–41 82
38:8–11 82
38:12–15 83
38:30 282, 368n45
40:7 368n45
40:23 282

Psalms

2:6 277
19 319
29 284
33:7 297n68
33:16 366
37:1 77, 137n63
37:30 318
49:5 58n11
51 319
68 284
73:15 77
74 284
78:2 58n11
78:15 297n68
84:12 130
87:7 281
89 284
90 319
90:2 280, 294
96:6 368
104 29
104:24 269
104:26 82
105 319
106:9 297n68, 298
111:10 318, 319
119 319
119:24 304
136:15 366
139:13 277
146–50 318, 368
148 29

Proverbs

1 118
1–9 13, 14, 15n59, 26, 59, 72, 84, 86, 87, 89–93, 94, 96, 97, 98–103, 106, 107, 111, 113–28, 179, 240, 240n56, 264, 287, 292, 356
1:1 54
1:1–7 14n56
1:2 54, 72, 139, 176
1:2–4 53, 55, 58
1:2–7 9, 14, 15n59, 53, 54, 59, 161, 266, 343

1:3 54, 55, 55n6, 56, 118, 118n22, 134, 161, 173, 180, 229, 312
1:4 9, 30, 54, 86, 156, 176, 179
1:4–5 56, 178, 349
1:5 9, 30, 86, 154
1:5–6 55
1:6 57, 58, 90, 115, 281
1:7 7, 9, 56, 58, 71, 100
1:8 86, 87, 317, 350
1:10 86, 90, 114, 127
1:10–19 89, 90, 94, 113, 114, 115, 126, 135, 137, 138, 202
1:11 90
1:11–12 114
1:11–14 90
1:12 95
1:13 115n14, 116, 367
1:14 181
1:15 86, 90
1:16 241n58
1:18–19 237
1:19 70, 103, 114
1:20–21 87, 102, 121
1:20–31 180
1:20–33 87, 96, 271, 276n13
1:22 96, 97, 152, 154, 157
1:22–23 152
1:25 96, 181
1:27 97
1:28 97
1:29 71
1:30 181
1:31 96
1:32 103, 157
1:33 236
2:1 86, 98
2:1–5 101n27
2:4–5 115
2:5 71
2:6 99, 100, 101
2:6–8 99, 99n22, 100, 101
2:6–16 233

2:7 99n22
2:8 88
2:9 88, 199, 229
2:11 72, 179
2:12 88, 92, 92n13
2:12–15 92
2:13 88, 89, 92, 97, 102
2:16 74
2:16–19 93, 94
2:17 123, 123n36
2:18 94
2:18–19 70
2:19 98, 103
2:20 101
2:22 131, 237
3:1 86, 317
3:1–5 100
3:2 70, 103, 165
3:3 25n10, 239
3:5 99, 171, 236
3:5–6 99, 100, 101
3:6 99
3:7 71, 102n28, 208n8
3:8 69, 112
3:9 88, 115n14
3:11 86, 158
3:13 72, 103, 199n55
3:13–20 271, 276n13
3:14–16 115
3:16 70, 73, 79, 103, 111, 116
3:17 102, 103, 165
3:18 70, 103, 347
3:18–19 100
3:19 270
3:19–20 7, 29, 233, 269, 270, 279
3:21 86, 98, 179
3:22 103
3:23 98, 236
3:27–31 84, 267
3:31 91
3:34 97, 130
3:35 97, 111
4 124
4–5 367
4:1 86
4:1–4 87
4:2 199
4:2–4 87
4:3 292

4:5 123, 275
4:5–7 115
4:5–9 96, 122, 124
4:6 123
4:7 123, 125
4:8 111, 123
4:9 123, 124
4:11 88, 102
4:12 98
4:13 70, 103, 158
4:14 91
4:16 93
4:18 102
4:19 91, 102
4:22 70, 103, 112
4:26–27 99
4:27 208n8
5:1–23 350
5:2 179
5:3–14 93
5:5 70, 95n18
5:5–6 94
5:6 88
5:8 74
5:8–10 74
5:11 69
5:12 158
5:15–20 94, 121
5:15–23 122
5:16 297
5:18 74, 94, 350
5:20 123
5:21 88n6, 89
5:22 232
6:1–5 113
6:6 88n6
6:6–8 260
6:9–11 260
6:12 92
6:12–15 93
6:13–15 92
6:20 87, 350
6:20–24 100
6:20–35 350
6:22 98
6:23 70, 88, 103
6:24 94
6:24–35 93
6:31 115n14
6:32 153
6:32–35 127
7:1–5 100

7:1–9 233
7:1–27 93, 350
7:3 239
7:4 125
7:4–27 74
7:5 121, 122
7:6–23 260
7:6–27 94
7:7 86, 98, 121, 153, 156, 157
7:7–23 121
7:7–27 96
7:10–13 121
7:11 94, 121
7:12 233
7:22 98
7:25–27 95
7:37 139n65
8 19, 83, 178, 247
8:1–3 121, 233
8:1–36 87, 180
8:2 88n6, 102
8:2–5 87
8:4–21 270
8:5 86, 97, 152, 157, 179
8:5 152
8:5–21 271
8:9 72, 154, 232
8:10–11 115, 157
8:12 179
8:12–14 117, 180, 181
8:12–16 87
8:13 58, 88, 181, 208n8
8:15 250
8:15–16 181, 182, 244, 312, 334
8:18 27n20, 73, 79, 111, 115n14, 116, 117, 118, 120n28
8:19 119
8:20 88, 103, 117, 119, 229
8:21 79, 119, 119n25
8:22 107, 270, 275, 277, 280, 281, 289, 291, 300, 301n75, 304
8:22 LXX 277n16
8:22 MT 276
8:22–23 99, 280

8:22–26 275, 283, 292, 297, 303
8:22–31 7, 19, 29, 59, 101n27, 121, 233, 246, 247, 248, 253, 258, 260, 265, 268–69, 270–309, 356
8:23 276, 277, 278, 280, 281, 291, 292, 296
8:23–26 291, 294
8:24 279, 281, 291, 292, 294, 296, 297, 298
8:24–25 283, 293
8:25 279, 281, 282, 291, 292, 293, 294, 295, 296, 297
8:25 LXX 292
8:26 294, 297
8:27 248, 274, 280, 297, 299
8:27–28 279
8:27–29 249, 278, 284, 290
8:27–31 275, 283, 292, 296
8:28 299
8:29 248, 249, 253, 280, 299
8:30 300, 301, 302, 303, 304, 305, 306
8:30–31 124, 274, 282, 292, 303, 304
8:31 304, 305
8:32 86, 103
8:32–36 270, 271
8:34 103, 199n55
8:35 70, 103
9:1–4 233
9:1–6 121
9:4 86, 157
9:4–6 96
9:6 86, 88, 157
9:7 97, 232
9:7–8 154
9:8 97
9:9 232
9:10 58
9:11 70
9:13 121
9:13–18 94, 121

Scripture and Ancient Sources Index 407

9:15 88n6
9:16 121, 153
9:16–17 97
10–15 14n56, 84, 85–87, 104–5
10–29 14, 15n59, 57, 72, 179, 183–202, 240n55, 264
10–31 59, 104–8, 128–46
10:1 86
10:1–22:16 13, 14, 14n56, 240
10:3 139, 140, 141, 142, 262
10:4 27, 30, 61, 62, 64
10:6 141, 232
10:8 192
10:9 104, 236
10:11 70, 141, 150, 232
10:12 164n11
10:13 154, 155
10:14 193, 194
10:15 79, 80, 108n43, 169, 170, 171
10:17 70
10:18 152
10:18–21 195n48
10:19 234
10:20 232
10:21 232
10:23 151, 155, 196n50
10:24 139, 140, 141, 142
10:27 70
10:28 137
10:29 107, 141
10:30 237
10:30–32 149
10:31 232
10:32 141, 150, 193, 194, 232
11:1 88, 163, 229
11:3 187
11:5 104
11:6 132, 139n65, 189, 189n41, 190, 191
11:8 190
11:9 190, 191

11:10 88
11:11 232
11:12 155, 195, 196
11:13 71
11:14 204
11:15 236
11:17 25n10
11:19 232
11:20 104, 107
11:21 238
11:23 139, 140, 142, 232
11:24–25 165
11:25 166
11:26 165n15
11:28 232, 236
11:29 192, 331
11:30 70, 81
11:31 238
12:1 158
12:2 179n16, 238
12:3 27n20
12:4 350
12:5 141, 179, 204, 232
12:5–7 150
12:6 141, 189, 190, 191, 232
12:7 238
12:10 71, 141, 163, 232, 363
12:11 61, 62, 153
12:12 128, 129, 130, 131, 135, 136, 139, 141, 152, 232
12:13 234
12:14 27n20, 131n50
12:15 102n28, 104, 197, 309, 378
12:16 156, 195
12:18 113, 193, 194
12:20 165, 187, 188
12:21 238, 262
12:23 152, 156
12:24 27n20
12:25 196, 199
12:26 104, 104n32, 141, 232
12:27 79
12:28 70, 88, 105n36
13:1 86, 154, 158
13:2 131

13:4 27n20, 142n67, 143n69
13:5 141, 232
13:6 104, 190
13:7 78, 79, 232
13:8 170n25
13:10 164n11, 197, 378
13:11 80, 117, 118
13:12 70
13:14 193, 194
13:15 105, 105n33, 130, 131
13:16 152, 155, 156, 194
13:17 113
13:18 158
13:19 151n10
13:20 102n28, 211
13:22 27
13:23 30, 60, 88
13:24 70, 158
13:25 27n20, 142, 143
14:4 88
14:6 154, 155
14:8 156, 188, 189n40
14:10 71
14:12 88n6, 205
14:13 71
14:14 27n20, 105
14:15 86, 156, 157
14:16 207, 208, 208n8, 210
14:17 179n16
14:18 155, 156, 157
14:19 27n20
14:20 167, 168, 169
14:21 168, 169, 173, 199n55
14:23 27n20, 61, 62
14:24 151n10
14:26 108n43
14:27 208n8
14:29 70, 196
14:30 70, 113
14:31 81, 162, 230
14:32 232, 238
14:33 154, 155
15:1 194, 195
15:4 70
15:5 9, 179
15:6 238

15:7 194
15:8 230
15:8–9 232
15:9 105, 107
15:10 88n6, 102n28, 105, 105n35, 238
15:12 154
15:13 71
15:14 72, 151n10, 155
15:18 164, 165, 187, 188
15:19 105
15:20 86
15:21 72, 153, 155
15:22 204
15:23 194, 195
15:24 70, 105n36, 154
15:25 162, 173
15:28 141, 193, 232
15:29 232
15:30 69
15:31 211
15:32 75
15:33 7, 111
16–29 105–6
16:1 204
16:1–22:16 85
16:2 70, 88n6
16:4 238
16:6 25n10, 208
16:7 88n6, 105, 107, 208n8, 262
16:8 30, 60, 229
16:9 88n6
16:11 88, 163, 229
16:12 162
16:13 334
16:19 367
16:20 155, 197, 198, 199, 199n55, 200, 201
16:21 154, 191, 192, 331
16:22 70, 204
16:23 72, 193
16:23–24 192
16:24 69, 73, 113, 192, 193
16:25 88n6, 205
16:28 164n11
16:29 81, 105

16:31 70
16:32 71
17:1 88, 164n11
17:2 351
17:5 162
17:7 334, 335
17:8 168
17:9 166
17:10 154, 155, 158
17:14 164n13, 195
17:17 166, 173
17:18 153
17:19 164n11
17:20 197, 198, 199, 200, 201
17:22 71, 113
17:23 88, 141, 232
17:24 154, 155
17:25 86
17:26 233n38
17:27 155, 195, 196
17:28 154, 155n17, 197
18:1 164n13
18:2 151, 151n10
18:5 229, 233n38
18:6 152, 164n11
18:7 194
18:8 69
18:9 27n20
18:10 107, 170, 171, 236
18:11 79, 80, 108n43, 169, 170, 171, 236
18:12 238
18:14 71
18:15 154
18:16 168
18:17 88
18:19 167, 167n17, 234
18:20 131n50
18:21 70
18:22 174, 198n52, 350
18:23 80, 172, 236
18:24 166, 173
19:1 79, 351
19:2 88n6, 138, 139
19:3 206
19:4 167, 168
19:6 167

19:6–7 168
19:7 167, 167n17, 168
19:8 197, 198, 199, 200, 201
19:10 151n10, 262n57, 351
19:11 196
19:12 237
19:13 174, 350
19:14 174, 350
19:15 27n20
19:16 88n6, 105, 105n36
19:16 MT 105n36
19:21 204
19:22 25n10, 130, 131, 132
19:23 70, 237
19:25 86, 154, 155, 157, 179
19:26 86
19:27 106
19:28 232
19:29 152, 154
20:2 237, 335
20:3 164, 165
20:5 155, 204
20:6 25n10
20:7 86, 106, 232
20:8 334
20:9 206
20:10 88, 163
20:13 34
20:18 204
20:20 262
20:22 262
20:23 163, 229
20:24 207
20:26 334
20:28 25n10, 334
21:3 163, 229, 230
21:4 141, 232
21:5 138, 204
21:6 30
21:7 232, 238
21:8 106, 106n38
21:9 350
21:10 128, 129, 131, 136, 137, 141, 232
21:10 LXX 129
21:11 72, 75, 154, 157
21:12 155, 199

21:12 LXX 129
21:13 162, 165
21:14 168
21:15 229, 232
21:16 88n6, 106
21:17 143, 144, 145, 145n76, 230, 236
21:18 131
21:19 174, 350
21:20 151, 151n10
21:21 25n10, 70, 111, 201, 202n58
21:24 154
21:25 MT 129
21:26 128, 130, 131, 134, 136, 137, 139, 141, 232
21:26 LXX 129
21:26 MT 129
21:27 230, 232
21:29 106, 187, 187n36
21:30 206
21:31 204
22:1 73
22:2 171, 172
22:3 156, 208, 209, 210
22:4 34, 70, 79, 111, 201, 202
22:5 106
22:6 86
22:7 80, 236
22:9 162, 232
22:10 154, 164n11
22:11 334
22:12 131
22:15 86, 158
22:17 13n54
22:17–23:11 13, 26, 133n56
22:17–24:22 13
22:17–24:34 86
22:22 58, 162, 230, 267
22:23 58, 86
22:24 267
22:24–25 106
22:28 241n58, 267
22:29 262
23:1 133, 335
23:1–5 133n56, 134

23:1–8 133, 136, 137, 172
23:2 134
23:3 134
23:4 75, 133n57, 134, 135
23:4–5 117
23:4–6 135n62
23:5 133n57, 134
23:6 133, 135
23:6–8 135
23:7 135
23:8 134, 136
23:10 173
23:10–11 162
23:12 72
23:13 158
23:15 86
23:17 136, 137
23:17–18 136
23:18 137
23:19 86, 88n6, 106, 107
23:20–21 144, 145, 145n76, 155n16, 230, 236
23:21 145
23:22 87, 350
23:26 86, 106, 107, 211
23:27–28 132
23:29 164n11
23:29–35 144, 230, 236
24–31 MT 14n57
24:1 77, 136, 137, 137n63
24:1–22 LXX 14n57
24:2 195
24:3 72
24:4 79
24:6 204
24:7 9
24:8 179n16
24:9 154
24:13 86, 106
24:14 136, 137, 138
24:15 81
24:21 86, 106, 335
24:21–22 237
24:23 13
24:23–34 LXX 14n57

Scripture and Ancient Sources Index   409

24:24–25 244
24:26 232
24:27 88
24:30 153
24:30–34 260
25–27 240
25–29 13, 14, 86
25:1 13
25:1–29:27 LXX
   14n57
25:4–5 162
25:8 88
25:15 335
25:16 75
25:19 132
25:23 261, 262, 264
25:24 174, 350
25:25 334
25:26 244
25:27 112, 156
26:1 111
26:3 152, 158
26:4 183
26:5 183
26:8 111, 151n10
26:11 261, 262, 264
26:21 164n11
26:22 69
26:24–25 195
27:10 166, 173
27:11 106
27:12 156
27:15 174, 350
27:17 197n51
27:22 9
27:23–27 363
28:2 155n17, 234, 334
28:3 335
28:6 30, 60, 80, 106, 106n39, 106n40, 351
28:7 86, 154, 155n16
28:8 80
28:10 106
28:11 78, 79, 80, 155n17, 236, 351
28:14 199n55
28:15 81
28:15–16 335
28:16 162
28:18 MT 106n40
28:18 106, 106n40

28:20 138, 236
28:22 134n58, 236
28:25 27n20, 164, 164n11, 166, 236
28:26 152, 236
28:27 162
29:1 238
29:2 81
29:3 86
29:4 162, 312, 334
29:7 162, 232
29:8 88, 102n28
29:11 71, 152
29:12 335
29:13 172
29:14 162, 312, 334
29:16 81, 234
29:18 156, 199n55
29:20 138n64
29:21 351
29:22 164n11
29:23 70, 111
29:25 236
29:26 335
29:27 232
30 14n56, 26, 101n27
30–31 86
30:1 13n55, 26n16, 233
30:1–4 101n27
30:1–14 LXX 14n57
30:2–3 101n27
30:3 314, 314n4, 315n4, 342
30:4 101n27, 315
30:5 315n5
30:5–9 315
30:14 230
30:15 146
30:15–16 145, 146
30:15–33 LXX 14n57
30:17 350
30:19 88n6
30:21–23 261, 262
30:22 351
30:24–28 260
30:33 164n11, 261, 262, 264
31 26
31:1 13n55, 26n16, 87, 350
31:1–9 LXX 14n57
31:1–31 5

31:3 88n6
31:4 230
31:8–9 162
31:9 229
31:10–31 14n56, 123, 125, 212, 349, 350, 356, 361, 364, 365, 367, 370, 371, 374, 377
31:10–31 LXX 14n57
31:11 367
31:11–12 364
31:12 362
31:13 362
31:14–15 362
31:15 362, 367
31:16 362, 363
31:17 368
31:19 362
31:21 363
31:21–23 262n57
31:23 123, 363, 364, 375
31:25 368
31:26 25n10, 363
31:27 88n6
31:28 106, 199n55, 362, 365
31:29 368
31:30 369
31:31 365, 368n46

Ecclesiastes

5:13 117
8:15 144
9:7–8 144
9:12 81
12:1 293n58
12:13 58

Song of Songs

3:11 123n38, 124
4 125
5 125

Isaiah

5:7 304
5:22 367
14:4 57
23:4 280

26:10 232
28 306
29:10 278
30:1 277
30:10 232
31 301
36 306
40–66 275
40:12 29
40:19 277
40:21–26 29
43:1–7 29
44:10 277
44:24–45:25 29
51:2 280
51:9 368
51:10 298
53:12 367
54:6–7 123n37
57:2 232
59:7 241n58
59:14 232
60:15 123n37
62 124
62:1–5 124
62:4 123n37, 124
62:5 124
63:13 297n68, 298
65:17–25 29

Jeremiah

3:1 123n36
3:4 123n36
3:20 132
7:18 277, 278
9:16 311
9:17 313
19:13 277
31:4 283
31:20 304
31:31–34 101
31:35–37 248
44:17–19 278
46:25 287, 302

Ezekiel

16:44 185, 185n30
17:2 57, 58n11
17:9 368
18:2 185n29

24:3 57
28:2 290
30:21–22 368
36:26–27 101

Daniel

1–6 315
1:4 315
1:17 315, 341
2 341
2:14 315
2:18 315
2:23 316

Hosea

7:2–3 318
7:13 318
10:13 318
10:15 318
11:6 281
12:1 318
14:9 317
14:10 317

Joel

3:1 278

Amos

1:1 241, 292
1:3 234
1:3–2:3 235
1:6 234
1:7–8 237
1:9 234
1:11 234
1:13 234
1:14–15 237
2:1 234
2:4 234
2:6 230, 233, 234
2:7 230, 235
2:8 230
2:12 235
2:13–16 237
3:8 236, 237
3:9–10 235
3:10 231
3:14 234
3:14–15 237
4:1 230, 235
4:4 234
4:4–5 235
5:4–6 235
5:7 229
5:10 235
5:11 230, 235
5:12 230, 233, 234
5:14–15 235
5:15 229
5:16–17 237
5:18–20 237
5:21–22 230
5:21–25 235
5:24 230
6:1 235, 236
6:3 235, 236
6:6 230
6:12 229
7:14 241n59

8:4 230, 235
8:5 235
8:6 230, 235
9:1–4 237

Jonah

2:5 298n70

Micah

1:12 281
11:6 139n65

Nahum

3:8 287, 302

Habakkuk

1:3 206
2:6 57, 58n11

Zechariah

8:5 282

Malachi

2:10–11 132

Apocrypha or Septuagint

Sirach

1:8 279
1:9 278, 281
11:18 78
11:19 232
11:21 232
24 101, 254, 269, 317
24:3 279
24:3–6 278, 279
24:5 279, 281
24:6 279
29:14 153n14
31 134
42:3 119, 120n28

Tobit

5:21 125
7:11 125
7:15 125

Old Testament Pseudepigrapha

1 Enoch

2:1–2 254
5:2–4 254
49:1 278

Dead Sea Scrolls and Related Texts

4QInstruction 101

Subject Index

Abel, wise woman of, 313, 336–38
Absalom, 313
act-consequence nexus, 27–28, 30, 40–41, 42, 60, 63–67, 259, 344
Adonai (YHWH), 26, 29, 58, 99, 100, 288, 289, 301
adultery, 121, 122, 127–28, 365
affiliation, 361
After Virtue (MacIntyre), 46, 319–20, 351
agency, 362
Agur, 314–15, 341–42
akratic types, 149–50, 151–54, 209
allegories, 57
Althaus, Paul, 257
Amenemope section, 240, 267
'āmôn, 300–307
Amos, Proverbs and, 220–21, 243–45
  chronologic priority and influence, 238–43
  dialogic relations, 235–38
  justice discourse in, 228–31
  McLaughlin on wisdom literature and, 222–23
  Terrien and Wolff on wisdom literature and, 221–23
  textuality and intertextuality, 224–28
  wisdom's influence on Amos, 223–24
"Amos and Wisdom" (Soggin), 220n3
Amos' geistige Heimat (Wolff), 220
Amun, 287–90, 292, 300–307
Amunet, 287
analogical thinking, 261–65
ancient ethics, 47
anthropology, Proverbs, 68–73
  goods of happiness, 73–74
  happiness, virtue, and vulnerability, 74–79

humans as physical and material, 69–70
human spirit, 70–71
intellectual rationality of human beings, 72–73, 378
natural law and, 251–52
rewards of virtue, 81–83
riches or wealth and, 79–81
sociality, 71
appetites, moderation in, 142–44
appropriate action, 186–91
archaeologic record, and dating of Proverbs, 242–43
aretē, 39
Aristotelianism, 36n44, 41, 48–50, 59–60
  authentic engagement in, 175–76
  causality, 49, 64–66
  critiques of, 349
  eudaemonism, 68–69
  friendship in, 173
  intellectual and moral virtues, 148
  metaphysical biology of, 160n2
  modern interpretations of, 351
  moral types, 148–51
  virtuous agents in, 210
  virtuous life, 345–46
as esoteric understanding, 314–16
audience, 86
authority, 324–27

Baal cycles, 284, 305
Bacon, Francis, 49
Bakhtin, Mikhail M., 221, 226–28, 231–35
Bezalel, 329–30
Bible, 219

411

biblical theology movement, 24–25
Boaz, 125, 371–73
bodily health and integrity, 361

categorical imperative, 34
causality, Aristotelian, 49, 64–66
causality in Proverbs, 63–67, 344
cause-and-effect rhetoric, 59–60, 344
central human capabilities, 361–65
change, and practices, 325–26, 353–54
chaos, 82–83
character, 44, 139–46
character development, 109–10
character ethic, 175–76
character ethics, natural law and, 265–68
character friendship, 173
Character in Crisis (Brown), 213
character types, 85, 89
child ("my child"), 86–87, 89, 90
choice, 362
chokmah, 310
clever person, 155–56, 208–9
communal ties, 166–68
communitarianism, 352–53
consequentialism, 33
control over one's environment, 362
corrigibility, 152–54
cosmology, of Proverbs 8:22–31, 268–69
counsel, 181
covetousness, 138
craftsmanship, 311, 328–33
creation, 270–72, 307–9
 'āmôn, 300–307
 Amun, 287–90, 300–307
 creation theology, 29
 exegesis of, 272–74
 mythological background of wisdom-infused deeps, 283–87
 natural law and, 249–52
 orders of, 255–59
 primordial mound, 290–95
 Wisdom's emergence, 274–83
 Wisdom's primordial priority to, 295–300
crookedness, 92–93, 104n30, 200
crown, 124–25
cunning, 54

dancing, 282–83
Daniel, 315–16, 341–42
darkness, 92, 102
David, 312, 313, 335–36, 372
deceit, 187–88, 189

deontological perspectives, 34–35, 36, 38, 39, 59–60, 249
Dependent Rational Animals (MacIntyre), 160, 175, 351
derivationism, 251–52
Descartes, Rene, 49
deservedness, 202
desire, 70
 moral and intellectual virtue and, 148–51
desires, training of, 109–10
 and akrasia, 151–54
 discipline and, 157–59
 and enkrasis, 149–51, 154–57
 honor and health as goods, 110–13
 of the rich and powerful, 133–36
 of the righteous, 139–46
 of sinners and the wicked, 136–39
 and symbol of wealth, 113–20
 and symbol of Woman Wisdom, 120–28
 of the wicked, 128–32
Deuteronomic literature, 100nn23–24, 241, 276n13, 316–17
dialogue, 227–28, 231–38
diligence, 75
discerning individual, 154–55, 156
discernment, 181
discipline, 157–59
discretion, 179
divine-command theories of ethics, 34, 99n22
divine grace, 98–103
divine obligation, 249–50
divine will, 205, 206
dolt, 111, 151–53, 189, 208–9
dread, 141

Ecclesiastes, 24
educational texts, 238–43
ego-driven virtue striving, 200–201
Egyptian mythological traditions, 284–86, 292, 295
El, 305
Elert, Werner, 257
emotions, 70–71, 361
empiricism in Proverbs, 259–65
Enki, 286, 289
enkratic types, 149–51, 154–57
Enlightenment rationalism, 49–50
enticement, 114. *See also* desires, training of
Enuma Elish, 284
envy, 136–37
Epicureanism, 41
equity, 54, 55

Subject Index

Eridu tradition, 286
erotic yearning, 110, 126. *See also* desires, training of
Eshet Chayil, 357–59, 377–80
  and Claassens's central human capabilities, 361–65
  dating and historical-literary context of, 370–73
  flourishing and, 359–61
  and male thriving, 364–65
  masculinizing of female figure, 365–70, 374–77
  political unconscious of, 373–76
esoteric understanding, wisdom as, 314–16, 341–42
ethics
  ancient ethics, 47
  deontological perspectives, 34–35, 36, 38, 39
  ethical-analytical language, 32
  historical-critical approach, 50–52
  modernist moral discourse, 46–48
  naive ethics, 27–28, 30
  Proverbs as textual guide to, 57
  utilitarian perspectives, 32–34, 37–38, 40, 45
  virtue-ethics perspectives, 35–38, 47–48, 50
eudaemonia, 31, 35, 37, 39, 41, 45, 62, 361–65
  Aristotelian, 68–69
  as result of life path, 103
  social virtues as central to, 160–74
  virtuous living and well-being, 323n19
exemplars, moral, in Proverbs, 209–15
external goods, 321–24
externality of means to end, 61
extravagant living, 230, 235–36

fairness, 75
faithfulness, 75
fear of the divine, 56, 58–59, 71–72, 75, 99n22, 137, 171, 181, 207, 208, 237–38
feelings, 35
figurative devices, 51n90
  language, 58
figures, 57
find (the) good, 197–200
flourishing. *See* eudaemonia
folk sayings, 183–86
food of lies, 134
fool, 164, 165, 183, 197
foreign woman, 93–96, 121–22, 128
fragility of goodness, 81–82
friendship and kinship, 166–68, 173
fruit of the mouth, 131

generosity, 129–30, 165–66
German-language scholarship, 255–59
God's wives of Amun, 303
goodness, fragility of, 81–82
good paths, 197–202
goods
  craftsmanship and internal, 333
  of happiness, 73–74, 202
  honor and health as, 110–13
  practices and acquisition of, 323–24
Great Pool of Hermopolis, 286–87
greedy persons, 164, 165

happiness, 35, 36–37, 44, 56, 103, 164
  Eshet Chayil and, 365
  goods of happiness, 73–74, 202
  internal and external states of, 74–79
  life of virtue and, 199n55
  rewards of virtue, 81–83
  See also eudaemonia
haste, 138
hatred, 195
healing, 112–13
health, as good, 110–13
heart, one who lacks, 153, 157
hedonism, 41
Hermopolis tradition, 286–87, 290
heroic literature, 371
heroic prowess, 370
heteroglossia, 227
Hezekiah, 240
hill, primordial, 290–95
historical-critical approach, 50–52, 59
ḥôlāltî, 280
honor, as good, 112–13, 123, 124
hope, 141–42
hot-tempered, 164, 165
human biology, 160n2
human nature. *See* anthropology, Proverbs
humility, 75, 111, 207
hurry, 138

iconic narratives, 31
immortality, 41
inclinationism, 252
"Influence on the Wise" (Crenshaw), 220n3
insatiability, 145–46
insight, 54
Instruction of Amenemope, 26, 133
intellectual acuity, wisdom as, 314, 338–41
intellectual rationality of human beings, 72–73

intellectual virtues, 54, 55, 72–73, 266
  and moral virtues, 147–48
internality of means to end, 61–63, 221
intertextuality, 224–28
invitation to Proverbs, 55
Isaiah, 241

Jameson, Frederic, 376–77n73
"Jesaja unter den Weisen" (Fichtner), 220n3
Joab, 313, 337
Job, 23, 82–83
Job, book of, 24, 42n60
Joel and Amos (Wolff), 220n3
Joseph, 315–16, 341–42
just, characteristics of the, 232
justice, 54, 55, 70, 117, 181, 190
  discourse in Amos and Proverbs, 228–31

kindness, 75
kindness to the poor, 162–63
kingship, 162, 181
kinship, 166–68
know-how, wisdom as, 310–11, 329–33
knowledge, 72–73, 75, 101n27
  and moral-social virtues, 147–59
  wisdom as, 314, 338–41

Lacan, Jacques, 374n66
laziness, 153
Leviathan, 82
life, 361
life, as symbol for flourishing, 70
light, 102
limiting strife, 163–65
living, extravagant, 230, 235–36
living well, 345–46
logos, 254
loyalty, 75
Luther, Martin, 256

MacIntyre, Alasdair, 351–53
marketplace, justice in, 162–63
marriage imagery, 124
masculinizing of Eshet Chayil, 365–70, 374–77
Massa, 26
materiality of humans, 266
ma'at, 253
means-end relations, 60–63, 66
mercilessness, 129, 130, 137
"Method in Determining Wisdom Influence" (Crenshaw), 220n3
military imagery, 367–70

Mishlei, 54
moderation, 70, 75, 142–43
modernism and historical-critical approach, 50–52
modernist moral discourse, 46–48, 59
modern science, 48–50
modesty, 156
"Morality of Nonhuman Animals" (Sandoval), 266n62
morals, 249
  deontological perspectives, 34–35, 36, 38, 39
  ethical-analytical language, 32
  historical-critical approach, 50–52
  modernist moral discourse, 46–48
  moral development, 42
  moral exemplars in Proverbs, 209–15
  moral terminology in Proverbs, 176–78
  natural moral order, 247–49
  utilitarian perspectives, 32–34, 37–38, 40, 45
  virtue-ethics perspectives, 35–38, 47–48, 50
  wisdom as morality, 316–19, 342–45
moral-social virtues, 54–55, 56, 266
  and akrasia, 151–54
  and enkrasis, 154–56
  and intellectual virtues, 147–48
  simpletons, 156–57
moral types and agents, 85–87, 91, 104–8
motto, 56
mound, primordial, 290–95
Mut, 287
my child, 86–87, 89, 90

narrative, 3, 6, 18, 31, 211, 212, 213, 214, 366n34
Nathan, 313
natural law, 247, 249–52, 265–68, 308, 353–55
Naunet, 286
Newton, Isaac, 49
Nineveh, 287
nissaktî, 276–77
nonhuman animals, 163, 266n62
Nubian pharaohs, 287
Nun, 286, 289

obedience of nature, 254
obligation, 249
observation of nature, 259–65
Ogdoad, 286
Oholiab, 330, 379
Old Testament Theology (von Rad), 25
one who acts wisely, 155
orality, 185
order in Proverbs, 252–55

Subject Index

orders of creation, 255–59
other species, 362

parental voice, 87, 98, 99, 102, 103
passions, 70, 127
path of wisdom and justice
    finding good paths, 197–202
    See also way of wisdom and justice
paths, moral, in Amos and Proverbs, 231–32
patriarchal vision of Proverbs, 3n13, 93, 95, 110, 114, 127–28, 163n10, 173–74, 198n52, 212n11, 350–51, 359, 364
perception, 263
person of understanding, 155
Pharaoh, 312, 313, 315, 333–35
phronēsis, 74, 75, 175–76, 177
play, 362
pleasure, 23, 41
polel, 281
political elites, 162
political shrewdness, wisdom as, 312–13, 333–38
polyphony, 227
poor, the
    justice and, 230
    kindness to, 162–63
    the rich and, 171–72
    virtue and, 351
poverty, 27, 30–31
practical reason, 361
practical skill, wisdom as, 310–11, 329–33
practical virtues, 54, 55, 178–79, 266
    limits and efficacy of, 203–5
Practical Wisdom, 56, 58–59, 65, 74, 75
    appropriate action, 186–91
    as central to way of wisdom, 379
    difficulties identifying in Proverbs, 176–80
    efficacy of, 205–9
    finding good paths, 197–202
    folk sayings, 183–86
    human sociality and, 175–76
    moral reasoning as, 343
    as *phronēsis*, 175–76
    in Proverbs, 1–9, 18–19, 180–83, 183–202
    silence, 195–97
    wise speech, 191–95
practice (MacIntyrian concept of), 160n2, 319–20, 353
    of esoteric understanding, 314–16, 341–42
    examples of, 320–21
    of intellectual acuity, 314, 338–41
    of know-how, 310–11, 329–33
    of knowledge, 314, 338–41

    of morality, 316–19, 342–45
    of practical skill, 310–11
    rules, standards, changes and, 324–27
    of shrewdness, 312–13, 333–38
    of tabernacle artisans, 329–33
    of understanding, 314–16
    virtue, goods and, 321–24
prevarication, 130
primordial mound, 290–95
primordial waters, 249, 253, 272, 278, 283–90, 296–300, 306
professors/professorship, 339
profligacy, 144
prologue of Proverbs, 53–54
    causality in Proverbs, 63–67
    and cause-and-effect rhetoric, 59–60
    social virtues and, 161
    two types of means-end relations, 60–63
    virtues, 54–59
prophetic oracles, 57
prosperity, 27, 30–31, 39, 44, 45, 63, 117, 164
proverb, 57
Proverbs
    ambiguous descriptions of, 38–46
    anthropology. *See* anthropology, Proverbs
    archaeologic record, and dating of, 242–43
    critiques of virtue-oriented moral system of, 349–55
    deontological perspectives, 34–35, 36, 38, 39
    as early education text, 238–43
    ethics and theology studies, 25n9
    historical-critical approach, 50–52
    history of modern scholarly interpretation, 24–31
    influences on, 26
    modernist moral discourse and, 46–48
    naive ethics of, 27–28, 30
    purpose of, 55
    in Revised Common Lectionary, 24
    as Scripture, 379–80
    secularity of, 26, 28, 29–30
    theological-ethical worth of, 355–57
    utilitarian perspectives, 32–34, 37–38, 40, 45
    virtue-ethics perspectives, 35–38, 47–48, 50
prudence, 54, 176, 179. See also *phronēsis*
punishment, 157–59
purpose of Proverbs, 55

rationality, 34, 251–52, 329, 378
Real, the, 374
rebuke, 157–59
rectitude, 55

Red Sea, 298
Reformation, 50, 256–57
restraint, 149–51
Revised Common Lectionary, 24
rewards of virtue, 81–83
rich, and virtue, the, 79–81, 170–72, 236
rich and powerful, desires of, 133–36
riddles, 57–58
righteousness, 54, 55, 70, 71, 117
  desires of the righteous, 139–46
  enkratic versus virtuous, 149
  in exercise of political shrewdness, 334–35
  and justice in Amos, 228–29
  moral and character types for, 85–86
  the rich and, 171
  of the upright, 189
robbers, 113–14
Roman Catholicism, 25n5
royal figures, 162
rulers, wisdom of, 181–82
rules, and practices, 324–25
rules and laws, 34–35, 36, 41–42, 44, 87
Ruth, 125, 371–72

sacrifice, 230
sapiential knowledge, 101n27
Schöpfungsordnungenslehre, 256–59
science, modern, 48–50
scoffers, 96, 97, 154
scribal moral vision, 186
secularity, 26, 28, 29–30
security, 236–37
self-control, 156
self-interest, 200–201
sense, one who lacks, 153
senses, imagination, thought, 361
servants, 351
sex, illicit and adulterous, 121, 122
sexual desire, 110, 126
sexual fulfillment, 73, 74
shame, 156
Sheba, 313, 337
Shimei, 312
shrewdness, 54, 179, 333–38
shrewdness, wisdom as, 312–13, 333–38
silence, 195–97
simpletons, 209
  moral-social virtues of, 156–57
  paths of, 96–98
simplicity thesis, 27
sinners, desires of, 136–39
skepticism, 23

skill, wisdom as, 310–11, 329–33
skillfulness, 331, 332
slaves, 351
snares of evildoers, 128–29
sociability, 160
social-ethical traditions, change in, 353–54
sociality of human beings, 71, 175, 266, 267
social justice, 228–31
social status, 111–12
social virtues, 118–19, 160–61, 166–68, 172–74
  friendship and kinship, 166–68
  generosity, 165–66
  justice and, 181
  kindness to the poor, 162–63
  limiting strife, 163–65
  other social virtues, 168–72
Socrates, 147, 148
Solomon, 124, 312, 314, 333–35, 340–41
Song of Deborah, 368–69, 371
sophia, 177
speech
  good and just, 113
  silence versus, 195–97
  wisdom manifested through, 190–95
spirit, human, 70–71
standards, and practices, 324–25
status, 39
stinginess, 133, 134, 135
stoicism, 36n44, 76
strange or foreign woman, 93–96, 121–22, 128
strength imagery, 366–70
strife, limiting, 163–65
success, 55, 56, 63, 117

tabernacle artisans, 329–33
taunts, 57
technē, 177
Tekoa, wise women of, 313, 335, 337
temperance, 142–43
textuality and intertextuality, 224–28
Thebes, 287
theodicy, 23
Torah, 253–54, 343
traditioning, 356–57
tranquility, 163–65
transgression, 233–34
treacherous, 85, 131–32, 189, 190
tree of life, 70
trust, 236
Tun-Ergehen Zusammenhang, 27, 60, 142
turning aside from evil, 208
Twenty-Fifth Dynasty, 287
two ways, 87–89

Subject Index

ummānu, 300
understanding, wisdom as, 314–16, 341–42
understanding person, 154–55, 156
universality, 91n11
unjust suffering, 23
uprightness, 92, 132, 187–90
utilitarian perspectives, 32–34, 37–38, 40, 45, 59–60

virgin-whore dichotomy, 95–96
virtue
  as its own reward, 42n60
  means-end relations and, 60–63
  practices and, 321–24
  in prologue, 54–59
  rewards of, 81–83
  the rich and, 79–81
  virtuous living and well-being, 323n19, 345–46
  Woman Wisdom as, 87
virtue-ethics approach to cosmogony, 246–49
  empiricism in Proverbs, 259–65
  natural law, 249–52
  natural law and character ethics in Proverbs, 265–68
  order in Proverbs, 252–55
  orders of creation, 255–59
virtue-ethics approach to cosmogony (test case of Proverbs 8:22–31), 307–9
  'āmôn, 300–307
  Amun, 287–90, 300–307
  exegesis of, 272–74
  mythological background of wisdom-infused deeps, 283–87
  primordial mound, 290–95
  Wisdom's emergence, 274–83
  Wisdom's primordial priority, 295–300
virtue-ethics perspectives, 35–38, 47–48, 50, 60
virtuous woman. *See* Woman of Valor
von Hoffman, J. C. K., 256
von Rad, Gerhard, 25

warriors, 366–70
way of folly and wickedness, 87–88, 89–93
way of the Lord, 107
way of wisdom and justice, 56–58, 87–89
  finding good paths, 197–202
  moral agents and their, 104–7
  role of divine in following, 98–103
waywardness, 103
weakness of will. *See* akratic types

wealth, 27, 30–31, 39, 70
  ephemeral nature of, 117
  generosity and, 167–68
  happiness and, 76–79
  training desire and symbol of, 113–20
  virtue and, 79–81
Weisheit in Israel (von Rad), 25, 26
well-being, 41–42, 361–65
West Asian educational texts, 238–43
West Asian mythological traditions, 284–86, 292, 295
whore-virgin dichotomy, 95–96
wicked, characteristics of the, 232–33, 237–38
wicked, desires of, 128–32, 195
wife, Wisdom as desirable, 123
wisdom, 54, 56, 70, 73–74
  delights of, 303–5
  emergence, 274–83
  enduring wealth of, 117–19
  as esoteric understanding, 314–16
  as knowledge and intellectual acuity, 314
  moral and character types for, 85–86
  as morality, 316–19
  mythological background of wisdom-infused deeps, 283–87
  as practical skill or know-how, 310–11
  primordial priority to creation, 295–300
  as (political) shrewdness, 312–13
  and Torah, 253–54
  way of wisdom and justice, 56–58
  worth of, 115–16
  See also Practical Wisdom; Woman of Valor; Woman Wisdom
Wisdom as Hermeneutical Construct (Sheppard), 220n3
Wisdom in Israel (von Rad), 25, 39–40, 47, 271
wisdom literature, 23
  Amos and, 220–31
  history of modern scholarly interpretation, 24–25
wisdom prosperity axiom, 31
wisdom psalms, 318
Wisdom's Wonder (Brown), 212, 213, 246
wise dealing, 55, 56
wise of heart, 332
wise speech, 191–95
wise women of Tekoa, 313, 335, 337
Woman Folly, 88n6, 93–96, 121–22
Woman of Valor, 212, 357–59, 377–80
  and Claassens's central human capabilities, 361–65
  dating and historical-literary context of, 370–73

flourishing and, 359–61
and male thriving, 364–65
masculinizing of female figure, 365–70, 374–77
political unconscious of, 373–76
Woman Wisdom, 87, 88n6, 97n20
contra Woman Folly, 93–96
and Eshet Chayil, 358, 365–66
as guide to path of life, 102–3
as personification of Practical Wisdom, 180–83
in Revised Common Lectionary, 24
and simpletons, 96–97
speech of, 271–72
training desire and symbol of, 120–28
women, in Proverbs, 350, 357. *See also* wise women of Tekoa; Woman Folly; Woman of Valor; Woman Wisdom

youth, 86

www.ingramcontent.com/pod-product-compliance
Lightning Source LLC
Chambersburg PA
CBHW021928290426
44108CB00012B/757